MY BEST GAMES
OF CHESS
1908-1937

ALEXANDER ALEKHIN

Alexander Alekhine

MY BEST GAMES OF CHESS
1908-1937

Two Volumes Bound as One

Dover Publications, Inc.
New York

This Dover edition, first published in 1985, is an unabridged and un-altered republication in one volume of *My Best Games of Chess 1908-1923*, first published by G. Bell & Sons, London, in 1927 and *My Best Games of Chess 1924-1937*, first published by G. Bell & Sons, London, in 1939. Readers should note that the original publishers spelled the author's name Alekhin at the time the first edition of Volume One was published and later switched to the current standard spelling, Alekhine.

Manufactured in the United States of America
Dover Publications, Inc., 31 East 2nd Street, Mineola, N.Y. 11501

Library of Congress Cataloging in Publication Data

Alekhine, Alexander, 1892-1946.
My best games of chess, 1908-1937.

Reprint. (1st work). Originally published under title: My best games of chess, 1908-1923. London : G. Bell, 1927.
Reprint (2nd work). Originally published under title: My best games of chess, 1924-1937. London : G. Bell, 1939.
1. Alekhine, Alexander, 1892-1946. 2. Chess players—France—Biog-raphy. 3. Chess—Collections of games. 4. Chess—Tournaments. I. Title.
GV1439.A4A35   1985   794.1'092'4 [B]   85-13046
ISBN 0-486-24941-7 (pbk.)

MY BEST GAMES
OF CHESS
1908-1923

Translated by
J. du Mont and M. E. Goldstein

BIOGRAPHICAL NOTE

Alexander Alexandrovitch Alekhin was born at Moscow on October 19th, 1892. When only sixteen he won the first prize in the Russian Amateur Chess Tournament held concurrently with the great St. Petersburg Tournament of 1909. Entering the Military School of St. Petersburg in 1909, his opportunities for tournament play were infrequent, but he succeeded in winning the first prize in three international events between 1909 and 1914.

Since the Revolution he has made Paris his permanent domicile and has recently obtained his Degree of Docteur en Droit at Paris.

His rapid rise to fame as a chess player since the war is well known, and he is now probably one of the three greatest living chess masters.

A short summary of his successes in tournament and match play is given overleaf.

SUMMARY OF RESULTS

The following tables summarise Alekhin's successes in tournament and match-play, the figures in the last four columns representing the number of games played, won, drawn, and lost respectively.

TOURNAMENTS

Date.		Prize.	Played.	Won.	Drawn.	Lost.
1909	St. Petersburg Amateur Tournament	1	16	12	2	2
1910	Hamburg	7 eq.	16	5	7	4
1911	Carlsbad	8 eq.	25	11	5	9
1912	Stockholm	1	10	8	1	1
1912	Vilna All-Russian Tournament	6 eq.	18	7	3	8
1913	St. Petersburg Quadrangular Tournament.	1 eq.	4	2	—	1
1913	Scheveningen	1	13	11	1	1
1913	St. Petersburg All-Russian Tournament	1 eq.	17	13	1	3
1914	St. Petersburg International Tournament	3	18	6	8	4
1914	Mannheim	1	11	9	1	1
1920	Moscow All-Russian Tournament	1	15	9	6	—
1921	Triberg	1	8	6	2	—
1921	Budapest	1	11	6	5	—
1921	The Hague	1	9	7	2	—
1922	Pistyan	2 eq.	18	12	5	1
1922	London	2	15	8	7	—
1922	Hastings	1	10	6	3	1

Year	Place		Played	Won	Drawn	Lost
1923	Carlsbad	1 eq.	17	9	5	3
1923	Portsmouth	1	12	11	1	—
1924	New York	3	20	6	12	2
1925	Paris	1	8	5	3	—
1925	Berne	1	6	3	2	1
1925	Baden-Baden	1	20	12	8	—
1926	Hastings	1 eq.	9	8	1	—
1926	Semmering	2	17	11	3	3
1926	Dresden	2	9	5	4	—
1926	Scarborough	1	8	7	1	—
1926	Birmingham	1	5	5	—	—
1927	New York	2	20	5	13	2
	TOTALS .		406	235	119	51

MATCHES

Date		Played.	Won.	Drawn.	Lost.
1908	v. Blumenfeld	8	7	1	—
1911	v. Levitski	10	7	—	3
1921	v. Teichmann	6	2	2	2
1921	v. Sämisch	2	2	—	—
1923	v. Muffang	2	2	—	—
1927	v. Euwe	10	3	5	2
	TOTALS	38	23	8	7

CONTENTS

PART II (1920-23)

CHAPTER XIX. INTERNATIONAL TOURNAMENT AT VIENNA, 1922

CHAPTER XX. TOURNAMENT AT MARGATE, 1923

CHAPTER XXI. INTERNATIONAL TOURNAMENT AT CARLSBAD, 1923

CHAPTER XXII. MAJOR OPEN TOURNAMENT AT PORTSMOUTH, 1923

CHAPTER XXIII. EXHIBITION GAMES AND SIMULTANEOUS GAMES

MY BEST GAMES OF CHESS

PART ONE

CHAPTER I

ALL-RUSSIAN AMATEUR TOURNAMENT AT ST. PETERSBURG, FEBRUARY, 1909

GAME 1

VIENNA GAME

White :	Black :
A. ALEKHIN.	B. GREGORY.

1. P—K 4	P—K 4
2. Kt—Q B 3	Kt—K B 3
3. B—B 4	Kt—B 3

The best move is 3. ....Kt × P !
(see game No. 41).

4. P—Q 3	B—Kt 5
5. B—K Kt 5	Kt—Q 5

This manœuvre is not to be recommended and, as the sequel shows, only results in the obstruction of the Q B. The best continuation is :
5. ......P—K R 3 ; 6. B×Kt, B×Kt ch ; 7. P×B, Q×B, etc., with equal chances.

6. P—Q R 3

The simplest, for now 6. ......
B—R 4; would be inferior because of 7. P—Q Kt 4, followed by 8. Kt—Q 5, etc. 6. P—B 4, P—Q 3 ; 7. Kt—B 3 was also worthy of consideration.

6.	B × Kt ch
7. P × B	Kt—K 3

Position after Black's 7th move.

8. P—K R 4 !

A strong move.

If instead 8. B—Q 2, P—Q 4 ; 9. P×P, Kt×P ; 10. Q—K 2, P—K B 3, whereas after 8. P—K R 4, P—K R 3 ; 9. B—Q 2, this manœuvre is not advantageous for Black, *e.g.* : 9. ....P—Q 4 ; 10. P×P, Kt×P ; 11. Q—K 2, Q—Q 3 ; (if 11. ....P—K B 3 ; 12. Q—R 5 ch ;) 12. Kt—B 3, P—K B 3 ; 13. Q—K 4, Kt—K 2 ; 14. P—Q 4, and White has the better game.

8. ......   P—K R 3

Clearly not 8. .....Kt×B ; 9. P×Kt, Kt—Kt 1 ; because of 10. P—Kt 6 !

9. B—Q 2	P—Q 3	13. R—Kt 1	B—B 3
10. Q—B 3		14. Kt—R 3	

The plan to advance the K Kt P, initiated by the last move, is somewhat perfunctory and devoid of real sting. The simple development by 10. Kt—K 2 followed by 11. Kt—Kt 3, would have given White the better game without any complications.

10.	B—Q 2
11. P—Kt 4	Q—K 2
12. P—Kt 5	

Position after White's 12th move.

12.	Kt—Kt 1

Here Black should have availed himself of the opportunity to exchange his inactive K R, after which he would have had a satisfactory game; *e.g.*:

12. ....P×P; 13. P×P, R×R; 14. Q×R (if instead 14. P×Kt, R×Kt ch; 15. K—K 2, R×R!; 16. P×Q, R—K Kt 8!; and Black has the advantage), 14. ...... Kt—Kt 1; 15. Q—R 7, Castles; etc. Black could have repelled his opponent's somewhat hazardous advance by a manœuvre both precise and energetic; but, on the contrary, he justifies it by the inferior tactics adopted here.

The unsatisfactory development of this Knight is the direct outcome of the risky moves preceding it.

14.	K—Q 2

There was indicated: 14. .... P×P; 15. P×P, Castles; 16. Q—K 3, K—Kt 1; 17. R—Kt 1, with a complicated position which held chances for Black. The Black King would be safer on the wing than in the centre, where he will soon be exposed to a successful attack.

15. Q—Kt 4!

The intention being to bring the Knight into the centre after an exchange of Pawns at K B 5.

15.	R—K B 1

Preparing the counter-attack 16. ....P—B 4; which White will however refute by a pretty sacrifice; in any case Black's game was already compromised in consequence of the mistake on his 14th move.

16. P—B 4	P—B 4

If 16. ....P—K R 4; 17. Q—Kt 3, P×P; 18. Kt×P, Kt×Kt; 19. B×Kt, B×P; 20. Castles! etc. with a winning attack.

Position after Black's 16th move.

17. P×B P !

The basic idea of this sacrifice, the consequences of which were not easy to determine, is to lure away the Black Q B. Furthermore White aims at the advance of his Q P (21st and 22nd moves) which is to make Black's Q Kt P indefensible.

17. ......   B×R
18. P×Kt ch   K—B 1

If 18. ....K—K 1 (K—Q 1 is evidently bad because of 19. Q—Kt 1, and 20. Q × P, threatening mate); 19. Q—Kt 1, P—Q 4; 20. B—Kt 5 ch, K—Q 1; (P—B 3; 21. B×P ch !) 21. B—Q 7 and White wins.

19. Q—Kt 1 !

The White Queen will, without loss of time, penetrate into the vitals of the hostile position.

19. ......   P—B 3 !

An ingenious resource. If now 20. Q×B, P—Q 4; 21. B—Kt 3, Q×KP; and Black assumes the initiative. It is clear that after 19. .... P—Q Kt 3 or K—Kt 1, White, having captured the B, would have retained the attack, in addition to material advantage.

20. Q×P !   P—B 4

The only way to prevent 21. R×P.

Position after Black's 20th move.

21. P—Q 4 !

Only this manœuvre can clearly demonstrate the soundness of the combination initiated by White's 17th move. Black cannot capture the Pawn, for after 21. ....K P ×Q P ; 22. P×P, P×P ; 23. B—R 5 ! and mate cannot be prevented.

21. ......   Q—Q B 2
22. P—Q 5

Now the threat 23. R ×P, is unanswerable. If 22. ....Q—Kt 1 ; 23. Q—R 4, R—Q 1 ; (or 23. .... Q—B 2 ; 24. R—Kt 5 ! followed by R—R 5, etc.) 24. R×P ! K×R ; (if Q×R ; 25. B—R 6 !) 25. Q—R 6 ch, K—B 2 ; 26. Q—B 6 mate.

22. ......   Kt—K 2
23. R ×P   Q ×R
24. B—R 6   B ×P
25. P—B 4 !

Winning another Pawn, the Black Bishop being held by the threat of 26. B—R 5 and mate next move.

25. ......   Q ×B
26. Q ×Q ch   B—Kt 2
27. Q ×P   Kt—B 3
28. Kt P ×P   Kt P ×P
29. P—B 5 !

The shortest way. Black is forced to capture the K B P, which involves the loss of a piece.

29. ......   R ×P
30. Q—Q 7 ch   K—Kt 1
31. P—K 7   Kt ×P
32. Q ×Kt   K R—K B 1
33. Q—Q 6 ch   K—R 1
34. B ×P   R (B 1)—B 3
35. Q—Q 8 ch   K—R 2
36. B—K 3   R—B 6
37. B ×P ch   K—R 3
38. Q—Q Kt 8   Resigns

GAME 2

RUY LOPEZ

White :	Black :
B. VERLINSKI.	A. ALEKHIN.

1. P—K 4	P—K 4
2. Kt—K B 3	Kt—Q B 3
3. B—Kt 5	P—Q R 3
4. B×Kt	Q P×B
5. P—Q 4	P×P
6. Q×P	Q×Q
7. Kt×Q	P—Q B 4
8. Kt—K 2	B—Q 2
9. P—Q Kt 3	

This move was played by Dr. Lasker in the first game of his match against Dr. Tarrasch (Düsseldorf, 1908). The latter continued : 9. ....B—B 3 ; 10. Kt—Q 2, B—K 2 ; 11. B—Kt 2, B—B 3 ; leading to an exchange of Bishops and the loss of his best chance—the combined action of the two Bishops.

Position after White's 9th move.

9.	P—B 5 !

If Black fails to regain the Pawn thus sacrificed, he will have sufficient compensation in the dislocation of the White Pawn-position on the Queen-side. But, as the sequel shows, White cannot long maintain his advantage in material, which tends to prove the insufficiency of his last move. I consider that the reply 9. ....P—B 5 demolishes White's 9th move.

10. P×P	B—R 5
11. P—Q B 3	Castles

Position after Black's 11th move.

12. Kt—Q 2

Other moves would be no better ; *e.g. :* 12. Kt—Q 4, P—Q B 4 ; 13. Kt—Kt 3, R—K 1 ; 14. P—B 3, P—B 4 ; 15. Kt—Q 2, Kt—B 3 ; and Black has the better game. Or 12. Castles, B—B 7 ; 13. Kt—Q 2, Kt—B 3 ; 14. Kt—K Kt 3 (if 14. P—B 3, B—B 4 ch ; followed by 15. ....B—Q 6), B—B 4 ; and Black wins back his Pawn with an excellent game.

12.	B—B 7
13. P—B 3	

13. Castles leads into the second variation shown above.

13.	B—B 4

Opposing 14. Kt—Q 4 (to which the reply is 14. ....R×Kt ! ; etc.) and forcing White to lose precious time to counteract the action of this Bishop.

14. P—Q R 4	Kt—B 3
15. B—R 3	

The blockade of Black's K B will be seen to be insufficient. The following variation offered better chances of a draw : 15. Kt—Q 4, B×Kt ; 16. P×B, R×P ; 17. B—Kt 2, R—Q 6, although in this case Black's pressure on the Q file would have been very harassing.

15.	B—K 6 !
16. Kt—K B 1	B—R 2
17. P—R 5	

If 17. P—B 5 at once, then 17. ....B×R P.

17.	R—Q 6
18. P—B 5	K R—Q 1
19. K—B 2	

White could have held out longer by : 19. B—Kt 4, R—Q 8 ch ; 20. R×R, R×R ch ; 21. K—B 2, Kt—Q 2 ; 22. Kt (B 1)—Kt 3, R×R ; 23. Kt×R, Kt×P ; 24. B×Kt (if 24. K—K 1, Kt—Kt 6 ; followed by 25.....P—Q B 4), B×B ch; 25. Kt—Q 4, P—Q Kt 3 ; 26. P×P, P×P ; but the issue would not have been in doubt, as Black remains with his two Bishops and a passed Pawn.

The text-move gives Black the chance of an elegant finish.

| 19. ...... | Kt—Q 2 |
| 20. Kt—K 3 | |

See Diagram.

| 20. ...... | Kt×P ! |

Threatening mate in 5 should White capture the B, *e.g.:* 21. Kt×B, Kt×P dbl. ch ; 22. K—K 1, R—Q 8 ch ! ; 23. R×R, B—B 7 ch ! ; 24. K—B 1, R×R ch ; 25. Kt—K 1, R×Kt mate.

Position after White's 20th move.

| 21. Kt—Q 4 | B—Kt 6 |

This wins the Q B P, for if 22. K R—Q B 1, or B—Kt 2, then 22. ....R (Q 6)×Kt (Q 5) ; followed by 23. ....Kt—Q 6 ch and Black wins.

| 22. K—K 2 | R×P |
| 23. B—Kt 2 | |

White could have avoided the loss of a piece by 23. Kt (Q 4)—B 5, which, however, would not have influenced the result.

23.	R×Kt ch !
24. K×R	Kt—K 3
25. R—R 3	

Or 25. K R—Q 1, B×R ; 26. R × B, Kt × Kt ; 27. B × Kt, B×B ch ; 28. R×B, R×R ; and the end-game is easily won for Black.

25.	Kt×Kt
26. K—B 4	B—B 4
27. K R—R 1	Kt—K 7 ch
28. K—Kt 4	B—K 3 ch
White resigns.	

CHAPTER II

INTERNATIONAL TOURNAMENT AT HAMBURG
JULY, 1910

GAME 3

FRENCH DEFENCE

White :   *Black :*
A. SPEYER.   A. ALEKHIN.

1. P—K 4   P—K 3
2. P—Q 4   P—Q 4
3. Kt—Q B 3   B—Kt 5

This move is far better than its reputation. Its object is to simplify the position, at any rate in the variation usually adopted by White, starting 4. P×P, a simplification which allows Black more easily to evolve a plan of development. It has been adopted with success at various times by Niemzovitch.

4. B—Q 2

This idea is interesting but does not produce any advantage if Black makes the correct reply. The most usual move is here 4. P×P, the consequences of 4. P—K 5, P—Q B 4 appearing to be rather in Black's favour (compare Dr. Lasker—Maróczy, New York, 1924).

See Diagram.

4. ......   Kt—K 2 !

Simplest, for the complications

Position after White's 4th move.

resulting from 4. ....P×P ; 5. Q—Kt 4 would give White attacking chances : *e.g. :*

I. 5. ....Kt—K B 3 ; 6. Q×Kt P, R—Kt 1 ; 7. Q—R 6, Q×P ; 8. Castles Q R, threatening 9. B—K Kt 5.

II. 5. ....Q×P ; 6. Kt—B 3, Q—B 3 ; 7. Q×K P, followed by Castles Q R with good attacking chances for White.

5. P×P

White was threatened with : 5. ....P×P and 6. ....Q×P.

6

5. ...... P×P
6. Q—B 3

This is not a normal developing move. As the sequel will show, most of the White pieces will find themselves on unfavourable squares. It might have been better to play 6. B—Q 3 followed by 7. K Kt— K 2 ; 8. Castles, etc.

6. ...... Q Kt—B 3
7. B—Q Kt 5

compulsory after the last move.

7. ...... Castles
8. K Kt—K 2 B—K B 4

....The Black pieces, on the other hand, are well placed for concerted action.

9. Castles Q R

White's object in playing 6. Q—B 3 was to Castle on the Queen's side; this is a strategic error, however, for on the King's side White has no prospect which might compensate for Black's attack on the Queen's side. 9. R—Q B 1, followed by 10. Castles, was certainly not so bad.

9. ...... P—Q R 3 !

White's K B must be eliminated in order to allow a Black Knight to occupy Q B 5.

10. B—Q 3 B×B
11. Q×B Kt—R 4 !
12. P—Q R 3

White takes advantage of the opportunity to force the exchange of one of Black's attacking pieces, for 12. ....B—Q 3 fails on account of 13. Kt×P, unmasking the White Bishop.

12. ...... B×Kt
13. B×B Kt—B 5
14. Q R—K 1

Position after White's 14th move.

14. ...... Kt—B 3

Strategically, the game is already won by Black, but the latter here makes a slight tactical error, which allows his opponent to exchange Queens. The simple plan of attack to lead to an easy win would be : P—Q R 4 followed by P—Q Kt 4—5, etc. *The decision of the game could and should have been brought about by a direct attack on the King.*

15. Kt—B 4 Q—Q 3

Against any other move, White's reply 16. Q—B 3 would have been still more awkward for Black.

16. Q—B 3 Q R—Q 1

The plausible K R—Q 1 would have been wrong, for then 17. Kt×P, and if Q×Kt; 18. R—K 8 ch, etc. However, White now succeeds in exchanging Queens.

17. Kt—Q 3 P—Q R 4 !

....Better late than never !

18. Q—B 4

Else Black's attack would become irresistible.

18. ...... Q×Q ch

If 18. ....Q—Q 2 ; White could already try a counter-demonstration with 19. P—K R 4 followed by R—R 3.

| 19. Kt×Q | P—Q Kt 4 |

This advance remains strong even after the exchange of Queens, for the White Bishop is very badly placed.

| 20. Kt—Q 3 | R—Kt 1 |
| 21. Kt—K 5 | |

There does not appear to be any other method of saving the Pawn. But after the exchange of Knights Black finds fresh resources for the attack, with the aid of his Q B P.

| 21. ...... | Kt (B 3)×Kt |
| 22. P×Kt | P—Q B 4 ! |

Less good would have been : 22. ....P—Kt 5 ; 23. P×P, P×P ; 24. B—Q 4, R—R 1 ; 26. P—Q Kt 3, etc.

23. P—Q Kt 3

again the only chance against the threat of P—Kt 5, etc.

Position after White's 23rd move.

| 23. ...... | P—Q 5 ! |

The winning move, for this Pawn will exert a decisive pressure in the ensuing Rook end-game. Should White avoid the exchange of pieces by 24. B—Kt 2, Black obtains a winning advantage by : 24. .... Kt—Kt 3 followed by P—R 5.

| 24. P×Kt | P×B |
| 25. R—K 3 | |

Compulsory, for after 25. P×P, R×P ; this move would not be feasible because of 26. ....K R—Kt 1.

| 25. ...... | P—Kt 5 |
| 26. P—Q R 4 | Q R—Q 1 |

Position after Black's 26th move.

For the better appreciation of this end-game, it may be pointed out that White cannot here offer the exchange of both Rooks ; e.g. :

27. R—Q 1, R×R ch ; 28. K×R, R—Q 1 ch ; 29. R—Q 3, R×R ch ; 30. P×R, P—Kt 4 ; 31. P—R 3, P—R 4 ! 32. P—Kt 3 (if 32. P—B 3, P—R 5 ;), P—Kt 5 ! followed by K—B 1, K 2, K 3 and K×P winning.

White's subsequent moves are therefore forced.

27. K R—K 1	R—Q 5
28. R—K 4	R×R
29. R×R	R—Q 1
30. P—K 6	

If 30. R—K 2 Black would win a
Pawn by 30. ....R—Q 5.

30.	P×P
31. R×P	R—Q 7

After this incursion by the Black
Rook the remainder of the game is
purely a matter of technique.

32. R—K 5	R×P
33. K—Kt 1	R—B 8 ch
34. K—R 2	R—B 8
35. R×P	R×P ch
36. K—Kt 1	R—Kt 7 ch
37. K—B 1	R×P
38. R—Q Kt 5	

to parry the threat of P—Kt 6.

38.	K—B 2
39. P—B 5	K—K 3
40. P—B 6	K—Q 3
41. P—B 7	K×P
42. R×R P	R×P
43. R—Q Kt 5	R—Q Kt 7
44 P—R 5	K—B 3
45. R—Kt 8	K—B 4
46. P—R 6	R—Q R 7
47. R—B 8 ch	K—Kt 4
48. R—Kt 8 ch	K—B 5

White resigns.

GAME 4

QUEEN'S GAMBIT DECLINED

White : A. ALEKHIN.	Black : F. D. YATES.
1. P—Q 4	P—Q 4
2. P—Q B 4	P—K 3
3. Kt—Q B 3	Kt—K B 3
4. B—Kt 5	B—K 2
5. Kt—B 3	Q Kt—Q 2
6. P—K 3	Castles
7. Q—B 2	

This move, followed by Castles
Q R, was very fashionable from 1903
to 1911 until Teichmann, in a well-
known game against Rotlevi (Carlsbad, 1911) proved its inferiority. In
itself the move 7. Q—B 2 is not bad,

but if Black should make the best
reply, 7. ....P—B 4, White, instead of castling, should play 8. R—
Q 1.
The position is then identical with
that of the fourth and tenth games
of the Capablanca–Lasker match
(with transposition of moves) and
offers chances to both White and
Black.

7.	P—Q Kt 3

After this reply Castles Q R affords
White very good chances of attack,
for the Pawn at Q Kt 3 hinders an
immediate counter-attack by Black,
obstructing Q R 4 and Q Kt 3 for the
Queen and Q Kt 3 for the Knight.

8. P×P	P×P
9. B—Q 3	B—Kt 2
10. P—K R 4 !	

An important move preventing
the liberating move 10. ....Kt—K 5,
which would be playable if White
at once Castled Q R.

10.	P—B 4
11. Castles Q R	P×P

If 11. ....P—B 5 White would
have seized the initiative by 12. B—
B 5, P—Q R 3 ; 13. P—K 4.

12. K Kt×P

By this move White wishes to secure possibilities of attack against
the isolated Q P, as shown for instance in the following variation :
12. ....Kt—K 4 ; 13. B×Kt,
Kt×B ch ; 14. Q×Kt, B×B ; 15.
K—Kt 1 followed by 16. R—Q B 1,
17. P—K Kt 3 and 18. K R—Q 1.
Instead of 12. K Kt×P White
could equally well have played 12.
P×P.

12.	R—K 1

Probably played so as to be able
to withdraw the Bishop to K B 1 if
White attacks it by Kt—B 5, but
this manœuvre loses time for Black.
He should have tried for a counter-

attack on the Queen-side by P—Q R 3 and P—Q Kt 4 without delay.

13. K—Kt 1

To stop Black from making the embarrassing reply 14. . . . . . Kt—K 4, threatening to take the K B with check, after the intended 14. P—K Kt 4.

| 13. . . . . . . | P—Q R 3 |
| 14. P—K Kt 4 | P—Kt 4 |

This move, played after mature consideration, nevertheless shows itself insufficient, because of a Rook sacrifice by White on his 22nd move, which Black could scarcely have foreseen at this stage of the game.

Nevertheless, if Black instead of the text-move had played 14. . . . . Kt—B 1 White would equally have secured a clear advantage by 15. K R—Kt 1, P—Kt 4 ; 16. Kt—B 5.

15. B × Kt	Kt × B
16. P—Kt 5	Kt—K 5
17. Kt × Kt	P × Kt
18. B × K P	B × B
19. Q × B	B × P

Now Black has obtained the position he played for with 14. . . . . P—Kt 4.

Position after Black's 19th move.

20. Kt—K 6 !

This combination will ultimately force Black to give up a Pawn, thus allowing White to gain the victory after an interesting end-game.

| 20. . . . . . . | Q—K 2 |
| 21. P × B | P—R 3 |

Forced, for after 21. . . . . P—Kt 3 ; White has an immediate win by 22. R × P ! Q × Kt ! ; 23. Q—K R 4, Q—K 5 ch ; 24. Q × Q, R × Q ; 25. Q R—R 1, etc. This is the crux of the attack inaugurated by 16. P—Kt 5.

| 22. P × P | Q × Kt |
| 23. Q—Q 4 ! | |

If White exchanges Queens at once the Black Rook recaptures at K 3, where it would be well posted. The object of the text-move is to force the Rook to recapture at K 5, a less favourable square.

23.	Q—K 5 ch
24. Q × Q	R × Q
25. P × P	K × P

With an extra Pawn and the better position White should certainly win. However, the Rook-ending which now follows presents certain technical difficulties.

26. Q R—Kt 1 ch	K—B 3
27. R—R 6 ch	K—K 2
28. R—Q B 1	R—R 2
29. R (B 1)—B 6 !	P—R 4

Black's last moves were compulsory. 29. . . . . R—K 3 would have been disastrous because of 30. Q R × R ch followed by R—R 7 ch, etc·

30. R—R 6	R × R
31. R × R	P—R 5
32. R—Q Kt 6	R—K 4
33. K—B 2	R—B 4 ch
34. K—Q 3	K—Q 2

If 34. . . . . R—Q 4 ch ; then 35. K—K 4, R—Q B 4 ; 36. P—R 3,

followed by 37. P—B 4 ; 38. K—
Q 4, etc.

35. P—R 3   R—B 4

....To play K—B 2

36. P—B 4   K—B 2
37. R—K R 6   R—Q 4 ch
38. K—B 3   P—B 4

By this move, which is his last
chance, Black prevents 39. P—K 4.

39. R—K 6 !   K—Q 2

Position after Black's 39th move.

This is the most interesting phase
of the ending. At first sight an exchange of Rooks seems of doubtful
value, for after 40. R—K 5, R×R ;
41. P×R, K—K 2 ! White cannot
play 42. K—Q 4, because of 42.....
K—K 3. On the other hand the
variation 42. K—Kt 4, K—K 3 ;
43. K×P, K×P ; etc., only leads to
a draw, the Black B P queening one
move later than the White Q P. The
end-game, however, is won by White,
thanks to a little artifice.

40. R—K 5 !   R×R
41. P×R   K—K 2
42. K—Q 3   K—Q 2
43. P—K 4   P—B 5
44. K—K 2 !

Forcing Black to attack the Pawn.

44. ......   K—K 3

If now 45. K—B 3 ?, K×P ; and
Black wins ! White's next move
settles the question.

45. K—B 2 !   Black resigns.

CHAPTER III

INTERNATIONAL TOURNAMENT AT CARLSBAD
JULY—AUGUST, 1911

GAME 5

FOUR KNIGHTS' GAME

White :	Black :
A. ALEKHIN.	DR. VIDMAR.

1. P—K 4	P—K 4
2. Kt—K B 3	Kt—Q B 3
3. Kt—B 3	Kt—B 3
4. B—Kt 5	B—Kt 5
5. Castles	Castles
6. B × Kt	Kt P × B

After the better move : 6. .... Q P × B ; White can either obtain an easy draw by 7. Kt × P, R—K 1 ; 8. Kt—Q 3, B × Kt ; 9. Q P × B, Kt × P ; 10. Q—B 3, or he can attempt a King-side attack by 7. P—Q 3 followed by Kt—K 2, Kt—Kt 3, P—K R 3, Kt—R 2, P—K B 4. But in my opinion Black can repel this attack, for he has two Bishops and good chances of a counter-attack on the Queen's file.

7. Kt × P	Q—K 1

After 7. ....R—K 1 ; 8. P—Q 4, B × Kt ; 9. P × B, Kt × P ; 10. Q—B 3, etc. White obtains a slight advantage.

8. Kt—Kt 4

Here the following line is considered stronger : 8. Kt—Q 3, with the continuation 8. ....B × Kt ; 9. Q P × B, Q × P ; 10. R—K 1, Q—K R 5 ; 11. Q—B 3, and 12. B—B 4. It is, however, uncertain whether this line of play is sufficient to prevail against a correct defence. The fault lies in the variation 6. B × Kt, which, in this opening, proves to be dull and lifeless.

8.	Kt × P

With 8. Kt × Kt ; 9. Q × Kt, P—Q 4 ; 10. Q—R 4, B × Kt ; 11. Kt P × B (threatening 12. B—R 3), Q × P ; 12. Q × Q, P × Q ; etc., Black could bring about a draw. The complications which he seeks with the text-move turn out to his discomfiture.

See Diagram.

9. Kt—R 6 ch !

With this unexpected sally, White completely assumes the initiative. It would have been relatively better for Black to remove the audacious Knight, though in that case also White's game would have remained superior after : 9. ....P × Kt ; 10. Q—Kt 4 ch, K—R 1 ; 11. Q × Kt, Q × Q ; (or 11. ....B × Kt ; 12. Q × Q, R × Q ; 13. Q P × B, etc.) 12. Kt × Q, B—K 2 ; 13. P—Q 3, P—K B 4 ; 14. Kt—B 3, P—B 5 ; 15. R—K 1 followed by R—K 4.

Position after Black's 8th move.

9. ......   K—R 1
10. R—K 1

This pin which, on the previous move, would not have been favourable because of the reply : 9. .... P—Q 4 ; (threatening 10. ....B × K Kt, etc.) now causes Black serious difficulties

10. ......   P—Q 4
11. P—Q 3   Q—K 4

The alternative was : 11. .... Kt × Kt ; 12. P × Kt, B—K 2 ; 13. Q—R 5, B—K 3 ; 14. P—K B 4, etc. with good prospects for White.

In giving preference to the text-move, Black probably did not sufficiently consider the consequences of 16. R—Kt 1.

12. P × Kt   P—Q 5
13. P—Q R 3   P × Kt
14. P × B   P × P
15. Kt × P ch

Here White had the choice between the variation in the text and the equally good continuation 15. R—Kt 1, with the sequel : 15. .... Q—K 3 ; (if P × B (Q) ; 16. Kt × P ch and Kt × Q) 16. R × P, P × Kt ; 17. R—Kt 3, and Black, forced to prevent B—Kt 2 ch followed by R—Kt 3 ch, will thus lose the K R P.

However, I gave the preference to the text-move both because I did not wish to give Black any chance of counter-action on an open K Kt file opposite the castled White King, and because the consequences of Kt × P ch seemed to be simpler and equally certain.

15. ......   K—Kt 1

Position after Black's 15th move.

16. R—Kt 1 !

With this move White secures an advantage in material. Indeed, Black has nothing better than to bring about an ending with Bishops of different colour, for the variation 16. ....P × B (Q) ; 17. Kt × Q, Q—K B 5 ; 18. Kt—Q 3, etc., leaves him not the slightest chance. On the contrary, White has chances of further gain, based not only on the possession of an extra Pawn, but also on the clear majority of Pawns on the King-side. On the Queen-side Black's extra Pawn is quite a negligible quantity, as two of his Pawns are doubled.

16. ......   R × Kt
17. B × P   Q—K Kt 4
18. Q—Q 3

Preventing 18. ....B—R 6.

18. ......   B—K 3
19. B—Q 4

Threatening 20. R—Q 1, etc.
Black's only choice lies between the
exchange of Queens or the loss of
another Pawn.

19. ......   R—Q 1
20. Q—K 3

Position after White's 20th move.

20. ......   Q—Kt 4

In the hope of creating complica-
tions with the Queens on the board.
After 20. ....Q×Q; 21. B×Q,
P—Q R 3; White would have an
easily won game, *e.g.*: 22. K R—
Q 1, K R—Q 2; 23. R×R, R×R;
24. P—K B 3, K—K 1; 25. R—
R 1, B—B 5; 26. K—B 2 followed
by K—K 1, R—R 3, R—B 3, R—
B 5, P—Q B 4, etc.

21. B×R P   Q—R 5
22. P—Q B 3   B—B 5
23. B—Q 4

He could have occupied the Q R
file now, but White is in no hurry,
his opponent having no means of
preventing this manœuvre.

23. ......   R—R 1
24. Q—Q 2   P—R 3
25. P—R 3   Q—Kt 4

Else White would play 26. Q—
Kt 2 followed by R—R 1.

26. R—R 1   R—R 5
27. Q—B 2   R×R
28. R×R   B—Q 6
29. R—R 8 ch   K—R 2
30. Q—R 2   Q—K R 4

If 30. ....B—B 5; 31. Q—R 7
followed by Q or R—Kt 8, etc.

31. Q—K 6

The Queen's irruption into the
adverse position decides the game
in a few moves.

Position after White's 31st move.

31. ......   B—B 8

Black has no satisfactory defence
and so he can without danger in-
dulge in this little pleasantry.

32. R—R 5   Q—Q 3
33. K—R 2   B×P

The last chance. If White takes
the Rook he loses his Queen by
Q—R 8 ch, Q×P ch, and Q—B 6
ch, etc.

34. K×B   Q—B 6 ch
35. K—Kt 1   R—B 5
36. R—R 8

Threatening mate in three, commencing with 37. Q—Kt 8 ch.

36. ......   R—B 2
37. Q—Kt 4   Q—Q 6
38. R—K B 8   Black resigns.

GAME 6

THREE KNIGHTS' GAME

White :	*Black :*
S. ALAPIN.	A. ALEKHIN.

1. P—K 4   P—K 4
2. Kt—K B 3   Kt—K B 3
3. Kt—B 3   B—Kt 5

This variation (an inverted Lopez) has often been played, with success, by Pillsbury. It seems sufficiently strong to equalize the position.

4. Kt×P   Q—K 2

The most normal continuation is 4. .... Castles ; 5. B—K 2, R—K 1 ; 6. Kt—Q 3, B×Kt ; 7. Q P×B, Kt×P ; 8. Castles, P—Q 3 ; with an equal game. However, 4. .... Q—K 2 is equally good.

5. Kt—Q 3   B×Kt
6. Q P×B   Kt×P
7. B—K 2   P—Q 4

This last move is not at all in the spirit of the opening, as it allows White to undouble his Pawns immediately. He should have played 7. .... Castles ; 8. Castles, P—Q 3.

8. Castles   Castles
9. Kt—B 4

See Diagram.

9. ......   P—Q B 3

Forced, as 9. .... R—Q 1 ; would be bad on account of 10. Kt×P !, Q—K 4 ; (or Q—Q 3 ; 11. P—

Position after White's 9th move.

Q B 4, etc.) 11. P—Q B 4, P—Q B 3 ; 12. B—B 4, Q—K 3 ; 13. B—Kt 4 !, P—K B 4 ; 14. B×P, and if then Q×B ; 15. Kt—K 7 ch and the Black Queen is lost. Now White assumes the initiative.

10. P—B 4   P×P
11. B×P   B—B 4
12. Q—K 2

Not 12. R—K 1 because of 12. .... Q—B 4.

12. ......   R—K 1
13. R—K 1

This pin on the King's file is very troublesome for Black.

13. ......   Q—Q 2

After 13. .... Q—B 1 ; White could by 14. Q—R 5 provoke the weakening 14. .... P—K Kt 3.

14. B—K 3   P—Q Kt 4

To be able at last to bring out the Q Kt (via R 3).

15. Q R—Q 1

White has played the opening well, but this is slightly weak, and he loses the positional advantage he has acquired. The text-move appears to be good, as it brings into play a non-developed piece without loss of time. But it allows Black to bring his Q Kt to a more favourable square than Q R 3. The logical sequence would have been : 15. B—Kt 3, Kt—R 3 ; 16. Q R—Q 1, Q—B 2 (or B 1) ; 17. Q—R 5 and White has the better game.

15. ......   Q—B 2
16. B—Q 3

More promising would have been B—Kt 3.

16. ......   Kt—Q 2

Position after Black's 16th move.

17. P—K B 3

Here White seems to pursue a will-of-the-wisp. The simplest and best plan would have been to try to equalize and to play for a draw, *e.g.* : 17. P—K Kt 4, B—Kt 3 ; 18. Kt×B, R P×Kt ; 19. B×Kt, R×B ; 20. B—Kt 6 !, R×Q ; 21. B×Q, R×R ch ; 22. R×R, etc.

17. ......   Kt—Q 3
18. P—K Kt 4

White thinks quite erroneously that Black cannot exchange Bishops without losing a piece.

18. ......   B×B
19. Q×B

Position after White's 19th move.

19. ......   Kt—K 4 !

The soundness of this move rests on the following main variation : 20. Q×Kt, Kt×P ch ; 21. K—B 2, Q×Q ; 22. R×Q, Kt×R ; 23. R—Q 2 !, P—Kt 3 ; 24. R—K 2, R×B ; 25. K×R, R—K 1 ch ; 26. K—Q 2, Kt—B 6 ch ; 27. K—B 3, R×R ; 28. Kt×R, P—Q B 4 ; etc. To avoid this losing line of play, White is reduced to a retreating manœuvre which will cost him a Pawn.

20. Q—B 1   Kt (Q 3)—B 5
21. B—B 1   Q—R 4

This threatens 22. ....Kt×P ch ; and so White must submit to the loss of the R P. Against that, however, the Black Queen, after capturing the R P, will momentarily be out of play, which will give White the necessary time to inaugurate a counter-attack.

22. R—K 2   Q×P
23. Q R—K 1

Now Black is under compulsion to provide against 24. P—Kt 3, winning a piece.

23. ......   P—B 3
24. Kt—Q 3   R—K B 1
25. P—Kt 3   Kt—Q 3
26. Kt×Kt   P×Kt
27. Q—Kt 2

Threatening R × P, as now White's Q B P is covered by the Queen.

27. ......   Q R—K 1

Position after Black's 27th move

28. P—K B 4 !

Conscious of his chances, White is wanting in neither energy nor astuteness. Indeed, he has prospects of a draw. Much less strong would have been : 28. R × P, R × R ; 29. R × R, Q—R 8 ; 30. R—K 1, Q—B 3 ; 31. R—B 1, P—Q R 4 ; giving Black a clear advantage.

28. ......   P—K 5

The only move. If 28. ....P × P; 29. R × R, Kt × R ; (or R × R ; 30. R × R ch, Kt × R ; 31. Q × P, etc.) 30. Q × P, Q—R 8 ; 31. Q—K 6 ch followed by 32. Q × Kt and White wins.

29. P—B 5   Q—R 8

The only way to bring the Queen back into play.

30. Q—Kt 3

The object of this move is clear ; it aims at keeping out the adverse Queen. However, it gives Black the chance of a counter-attack. Better

would have been : 30. B—B 4, Q—Q 5 ch ; 31. K—R 1 (not 31. Q—B 2 because of 31. ....P—K 6 ; followed by Kt—K 5 ; and Black has the better game.) Kt—Kt 2 ; 32. R × P, R × R ; 33. Q × R, Q × Q ; 34. R × Q, K—B 2, with good prospects of a draw for White in spite of Black's majority of Pawns on the Queen's side.

30. ......   Kt—B 2
31. P—B 3

Position after White's 31st move.

31. ......   P—Kt 5 !

The beginning of the final attack. By sacrificing his K P, Black easily brings his Queen into the centre of the Board, where, in co-ordination with the Knight, her action proves deadly, as the White King's position is dangerously exposed by reason of the advance of his Pawns.

32. B—Kt 2

Had White played 32. B—Q 2, the sequence would have been the same, with the difference that the Black Knight would have entered via K 4 instead of Kt 4.

32. ......   Q—R 4
33. R × P   R × R
34. R × R   Q—Q 4
35. R—K 2

A trap. If 35. ....Q×Kt P ; 36. P×P, Q×P ; 37. Q—Q B 3, Q×P ch ; (or if....Q×Q ; 38. B×Q, with an easy draw) 39. R—Kt 2, Q—Q 8 ch ; 40. K—B 2 and White wins.

35.	......	Q—Q 8 ch
36.	Q—K 1	Q×P
37.	P×P	Kt—Kt 4

The entry of the Knight should have decided the game in a few moves.

| 38. | Q—B 3 | Kt—R 6 ch |
| 39. | K—B 1 | |

The only move, for, if 39. K—R 1, Q—Q 4 ch ; and if 39. K—Kt 2, Kt—B 5 ch ; winning in either case.

| 39. | ...... | Q—Q 8 ch |
| 40. | Q—K 1 | Q—Q 4 |

Threatening Q—R 8 mate, which can only be prevented by R—K 4.

41. R—K 4.

Position after White's 41st move.

| 41. | ...... | Kt—Kt 4 |

This move wins ultimately, but the logical sequel to the attack initiated by 31. ....P—Kt 5 ; would have been 41. ....P—K R 4 ;

42. Q—B 3 (there evidently is nothing better), R×P ch ; 43. P×R, Q×P ch ; 44. K—Kt 2, Q×R ch ; 45. K×Kt, Q—Kt 5 mate. The text-move allows White to struggle on for some time.

42.	Q—B 3	R—B 3 !
43.	R—Q 4	Q—R 8 ch
44.	K—K 2	Q×P ch
45.	K—Q 1	P—K R 4 !
46.	R—Q 7	

Evidently threatening R×P ch, etc.

| 46. | ...... | Kt—B 2 |

Position after Black's 46th move.

47. P—K Kt 5

A desperate venture which only results in the loss of White's King-side Pawns. The trap is as follows : 47. ....Q—Kt 8 ch ; 48. Q—K 1, Q×Q ch ; (or Q×P ; 49. Q—K 8 ch, etc.) ; 49. K×Q, R×P ; 50. P—Kt 6, etc.

| 47. | ...... | Q—Kt 8 ch |
| 48. | Q—K 1 | R—Q 3 ch ! |

leading to an easily won end-game.

49.	R×R	Q×Q ch
50.	K×Q	Kt×R
51.	P—B 6	P×P
52.	B×P	

Evidently 52. P × P was no better, as the Pawn could not be defended.

52.	K—B 2
53. B—Q 4	P—R 3
54. K—K 2	K—Kt 3
55. K—Q 3	

or 55. B—B 6, Kt—K 5, etc.

55.	K × P
56. B—K 5	Kt—B 4
57. K—B 4	P—R 5
58. B—R 2	K—Kt 5
59. K—B 5	K—R 6
60. B—B 7	K—Kt 7
61. K × P	P—R 6
62. K—Kt 6	Kt—Kt 6
63. K × P	P—R 7
64. P—Kt 5	P—R 8＝(Q)
65. P—Kt 6	Kt—K 5
66. P—Kt 7	Kt—B 4 ch

White resigns.

GAME 7

ENGLISH OPENING

| *White :* | *Black :* |
| A. ALEKHIN. | O. CHAJES. |

| 1. P—Q B 4 | P—K 3 |
| 2. P—K 4 | P—Q B 4 |

Simpler and better would be 2. . . . .P—Q 4 ; 3. K P × P, P × P ; 4. P—Q 4, Kt—K B 3 ; leading to a good variation of the French Defence. After the text-move White can obtain a very good game by 3. Kt—K B 3, Kt—Q B 3 ; 4. P—Q 4, etc.

| 3. Kt—Q B 3 | Kt—Q B 3 |
| 4. Kt—B 3 | P—K Kt 3 |

The right move here is : 4. . . . . Kt—Q 5 (as played in a game Alekhin—Leonhardt in the same tournament), after which Black obtains at least an even game. The text-move weakens the Black

squares and White takes advantage of it in an energetic manner.

5. P—Q 4	P × P
6. Kt × P	B—Kt 2
7. K Kt—Kt 5 !	

This demonstrates the weakness of Black's fourth move. Now, in order to protect his Q 3, he must lose a *tempo* with his Bishop.

| 7. . . . . . . | B—K 4 |
| 8. P—B 4 | |

In order to reply to B—Kt 1 ; by 9. P—Q B 5, etc., thus permanently blocking the position.

Position after White's 8th move.

| 8. . . . . . . | P—Q R 3 |

Black attempts to bring about complications which would turn to his advantage upon the slightest mistake on White's part.

9. P × B	P × Kt
10. B—B 4	P × P
11. B × P	

White has now a splendid development and threatens 12. Kt—Kt 5 (after possibly 11. . . . . Q—Kt 3) or 12. Castles K R with an attack on the K B file.

11. ......   R—R 4

Directed against 12. Kt—Kt 5, which would now be countered by 12. ....R×Kt ; 13. B×R, Q—R 4 ch ; etc. It also threatens : 12. ....P—Q 4.

12. Castles !   P—Q Kt 4

12. ....Kt×P ; would be disastrous because of 13. B×Kt, R×B ; 14. Q—Q 6 ! followed by Kt—Kt 5, etc.

Position after Black's 12th move.

13. P—Q Kt 4 !

This combination, both elegant and sound, gives White a winning attack. The temporary sacrifice of two minor pieces for a Rook will allow the White Queen to enter decisively into the game. The point is the 17th move, R—Q Kt 1.

13.	Q—Kt 3 ch
14. K—R 1	Kt×Kt P
15. B×Kt P	R×B

It is clear that Black has no alternative.

| 16. Kt×R | Q×Kt |

Position after Black's 16th move.

17. R—Q Kt 1 !

This pin is decisive, as Black cannot relieve it, *e.g.* : 17. ....Q—B 4 ; 18. R—B 1, or 17. ....Q—B 5 ; 18. Q—R 4, or again 17....Q—R 4 ; 18. B—Q 2, winning in each case.

| 17. ...... | B—R 3 |
| 18. Q—Q 6 | |

Played not with a view to an immediate capture of the Q Kt, but in order to prevent 18. ....Kt—K 2 ; because of 19. Q×Kt, Q×Q ; 20. R×Q, B×R ; 21. R—Kt 8 ch, etc.

| 18. ...... | P—B 3 |
| 19. K R—B 1 | Q—Q 6 |

Now the Knight must be taken.

20. R×Kt	P—Kt 4
21. R—Q 4	Q—Kt 4
22. P—Q R 4	Q—Kt 2
23. R—B 7	Q—Kt 8 ch
24. R—Q 1	Black resigns.

GAME 8

ENGLISH OPENING

| *White :* | *Black :* |
| A. ALEKHIN. | F. DUS-CHOTIMIRSKI. |

1. P—Q B 4	P—K 4
2. Kt—Q B 3	Kt—K B 3
3. P—K Kt 3	

With this move White obtains a favourable variation of the Sicilian Defence with the additional advantage of having a move in hand.

3.	P—Q 4
4. P×P	Kt×P
5. B—Kt 2	B—K 3
6. Kt—B 3	P—K B 3

This move weakens the position of Black's Q B and will cause Black many difficulties. 6. .... Kt—Q B 3, the natural move, was far better.

7. Castles   Kt—B 3

In playing 6. ....P—K B 3; Black most probably intended continuing 7. ....P—Q B 4, but noticed in time that this advance would be downright bad because of the reply 8. Q—Kt 3 threatening 9. Kt×P. After the text-move 8. Q—Kt 3 would not have the same sting because of the defence : 8. ....B—Q Kt 5.

8. P—Q 4

After the exchange of Black's K P, which is now compulsory, the weakness of 6. ....P—K B 3 becomes manifest.

8.	P×P
9. Kt—Q Kt 5 !	B—Q B 4
10. Q Kt×Q P	Kt×Kt
11. Kt×Kt	B—B 2

The alternative was : 11. .... B×Kt ; 12. Q×B, Castles ; 13. R—Q 1 and the White Bishop exercises an overwhelming pressure on Black's game. The text-move is, however, hardly better, because it deprives Black of the chance of Castling.

See Diagram.

12. Q—R 4 ch !   K—B 1

Compulsory, for if 12. ....P—B 3 ; then 13. Kt×P, etc. ; and if

Position after Black's 11th move.

12. ....Q—Q 2 ; 13. Q×Q ch, K×Q ; 14. R—Q 1, threatening 15. P—K 4, and Black's position would be even more compromised than as actually played.

13. R—Q 1	Q—K 2
14. P—K 4	Kt—Kt 3
15. Q—B 2	B×Kt

Relatively best, for White threatened to win a piece by Kt—B 5.

16. R×B	P—Q B 4
17. R—Q 3	P—Kt 4

Black decides on this desperate advance in the hope of getting his K R into action. Naturally the weakness caused thereby will open new avenues of attack for White.

18. B—K 3

Here 18. P—Kt 3, was to be considered, as White can then retain his two Bishops, *e.g.:* 18. ....P—B 5 ; 19. P×P, Kt×P ; 20. R—Q B 3, R—B 1 ; with 21. ....K—Kt 2 to follow. But in this variation Black has more resources than in the actual game.

18.	Kt—B 5
19. Q R—Q 1	Kt×B
20. R×Kt	K—Kt 2
21. P—K 5 !	

The beginning of an attack which leads to a speedy win.

21. ...... Q R—Q 1

Disastrous would be 21....P × P; 22. Q R—K 1, etc. But 21. .... K R—K 1 ; leaving the Black King a refuge at R 1, would have given Black better chances of defence.

22. Q R—K 1 !

Insufficient to win would have been : 22. R × R, R × R ; 23. P × P ch, Q × P ; 24. B × P, R—Q Kt 1 ; etc. Now White threatens 23. P × P ch, Q × P ; 24. B × P, R—Q Kt 1 ; 25. R—K 7, etc.

22. ...... P—Kt 3
23. P—B 4

White's main threat is to establish a very strong passed Pawn by 24. P—K 6, followed by P—B 5.

23. ...... P × B P
24. P × P   P × P
25. R—Kt 3 ch !

The check was essential at this precise moment in order to prevent Black's B—Kt 3. He could not play it now because of 26. P—B 5 winning a piece. The Black King must therefore take flight to a square where he will be exposed to attack.

25. ...... K—B 1
26. P × P

Position after White's 26th move.

26. ...... Q—K 3

Black has no longer a sufficient defence, e.g. : 26. ....B—Kt 3 ; 27. R × B !, P × R ; 28. Q × Kt P, Q × P ; 29. R—B 1 ch, followed by R—B 7 ch and White wins. Or 26. ....B—K 3 ; 27. R—B 1 ch, K—K 1 ; 28. B—B 6 ch, B—Q 2 ; 29. Q—Kt 2 and White wins.

27. B—R 3   Q—B 5
28. Q—B 2   Q—Q 5

Or 28.....K—K 1 ; 29. P—K 6, B—Kt 3 ; 30. P—K 7, R—Q Kt 1 ; 31. R—K B 3, B—B 2 ; 32. R × B, followed by B—Q 7 ch and White wins.

29. P—K 6   Q × Q ch
30. K × Q   R—Q 7 ch
31. K—K 3   R × Kt P
32. R—K B 1   R × Q R P
33. R × B ch   K—K 1
34. R—Q Kt 7   R—R 6 ch
35. K—K 4   R × R
36. P × R   R—B 1
37. B—Kt 4   Black resigns.

CHAPTER IV

INTERNATIONAL TOURNAMENT AT STOCKHOLM
JUNE, 1912

GAME 9

PHILIDOR'S DEFENCE

White :	Black :
A. ALEKHIN.	G. MARCO.

1. P—K 4	P—K 4
2. Kt—K B 3	P—Q 3
3. P—Q 4	Kt—K B 3
4. Kt—B 3	Q Kt—Q 2

Marco's favourite defence, which I also have adopted on several occasions (compare game No. 47), but I have since come to the conclusion that against logical and sound play it is not altogether satisfactory.

| 5. B—Q B 4 | B—K 2 |
| 6. Castles | |

Sacrificial combinations commencing 6. Kt—Kt 5 or 6. B × P ch turn to Black's advantage.

6. ......   Castles

After Castling, Black's development becomes laborious and he has not the slightest chance of a counter-attack. It seems to be more in the spirit of the defence to play : 6. .... P—K R 3 followed by P—B 3, Q—B 2, Kt—B 1, P—K Kt 4 and Kt—Kt 3. This system was adopted successfully by my opponent in several recent tournaments (Yates—Marco, The Hague, 1921 ; Wolf—Marco, Pistyan, 1922). This line of play forces White to play with great care, for Black's manœuvre on the King-side may develop into a serious attack.

| 7. Q—K 2 | P—B 3 |
| 8. P—Q R 4 ! | |

In this variation it is essential once and for all to prevent Black's P—Q Kt 4.

8. ......   P—K R 3

The anxiety to provide against Kt—Kt 5 or B—Kt 5 is natural enough, but the resultant weakening of the King's position may have unfortunate consequences, as the bad development of the Black pieces does not warrant this move.

9. B—Kt 3

After 9. B—K 3 Black could have played 9. ....Kt × P, followed by P—Q 4. By preventing this manœuvre, the text-move maintains White's supremacy in the centre. However B—R 2 would have been still better (see Bogoljuboff v. Niemzovitch, Stockholm, 1920).

| 9. ...... | Q—B 2 |
| 10. P—K R 3 | |

To prevent Black from playing Kt—Kt 5 in reply to 11. B—K 3.

10. ......   K—R 2

Black adopts an unsound plan in an already difficult position. The development of the Queen-side by P—Q Kt 3, B—Kt 2 and Q R—Q 1, followed by an attempt to stabilize matters in the centre by P—Q B 4, would have been more to be recommended.

11. B—K 3   P—K Kt 3
12. Q R—Q 1   K—Kt 2

All this laborious manœuvring aims at getting the K R into play. But Black will not have even this meagre satisfaction, as White, now fully developed, will initiate a direct attack on the Black King.

13. Kt—K R 2 !   Kt—K Kt 1

If 13. ....Kt—R 4 ; then 14. Q—Q 2, followed by P—Kt 4 and P—B 4, etc.

14. P—B 4   P—B 3

Position after Black's 14th move.

15. Q—Kt 4 !

The strongest continuation of the attack. The plausible 15. P—B 5 would be less energetic, *e.g.* : 15. ....P×Q P ; 16. B×P, Kt—K 4 ; 17. B×Kt, B P×B ! ; 18. Q—Kt 4, B—Kt 4 ; and Black's position is defensible. After the move in the text Black has nothing better than to sacrifice the K Kt P, which will give him the necessary time to exchange the White K B. If on move 9 White had played B—R 2 Black would not have even this small resource.

15. ......   P×Q P
16. B×P   Kt—B 4
17. P—B 5 !   Kt×B

Or 17. ....P—Kt 4 ; 18. B×Kt followed by Q—R 5 and wins.

18. Q×P ch   K—R 1
19. P×Kt   B—Q 2

If now 20. Kt—Kt 4 ? the White Queen is lost by 20. ....B—K 1.

20. Q—Kt 3   R—B 2
21. Kt—Kt 4

threatening 22. P—K 5, etc.

21. ......   Q—Q 1
22. Kt—K 2 !

This Knight now journeys to Kt 6 and decides the game in a few moves.

22. ......   R—Kt 2
23. Kt—B 4   Q—K 1
24. Q—R 4   Q—B 2
25. R—Q 3

Here White could have won a second Pawn by Kt×R P, but he prefers to play for a mate.

25. ......   K—R 2
26. Kt—Kt 6

See Diagram.

26. ......   R×Kt

Frustrating White's intended combination, which would have terminated the game brilliantly. The threat was : 27. R—B 4 followed by 28. Kt×R P, Kt×Kt ; 29. Q×Kt ch ; K×Q ; 30. R—R 4 ch, K—Kt 4 !

Position after White's 26th move.

31. B—K 3 or R—Kt 3 mate. This threat could only be parried by giving up the Exchange, which anyhow leaves Black without hope.

27. P×R ch	Q×P
28. B×B P	B×Kt
29. B×B	R—K 1
30. R×P	Q—Kt 2
31. B—B 6	Kt×B
32. K R×Kt	Black resigns

GAME 10

SCOTCH GAME

White :	*Black :*
A. ALEKHIN.	E. COHN.

1. P—K 4	P—K 4
2. Kt—K B 3	Kt—Q B 3
3. P—Q 4	P×P
4. Kt×P	Kt—K B 3
5. P—K 5	

An innovation which has little to commend it. First of all Black can force a draw by 5. ....Kt×P ; 6. Q—K 2, Q—K 2 ; 7. Kt—B 5, Q—K 3 ; 8. Kt—Q 4, Q—K 2, etc. Furthermore he can attempt to play for a win by 7. ....Q—Kt 5 ch ; 8. Kt—B 3, P—Q 3 ; 9. Kt—K 3,

B—K 2 and it seems doubtful if White can work up an attack sufficient to compensate for the Pawn he has sacrificed. Black could and should have captured the Pawn.

5.	Q—K 2

On the contrary this move brings about a complicated game which finally will turn to White's advantage.

6. P—K B 4	P—Q 3
7. B—Kt 5	B—Q 2
8. B×Kt	P×B
9. Castles	P×P

9. ....Kt—Kt 5 at once would not be good because of 10. P—K 6, etc.

10. P×P	Kt—Kt 5
11. Kt—Q B 3	

Now 11. P—K 6 would be a mistake because of B×P ; 12. Kt×B, Q×Kt ; 13. R—K 1, B—B 4 ch, etc.

11.	Q—R 5

With this move Black expects to obtain the advantage, as 12. .... Kt—B 3 seems bad on account of 12. ....B—B 4 ch. After 11. .... Kt×K P ; White obtains a promising attack by 12. B—B 4, P—B 3 ; 13. Kt—K 4, etc.

Position after Black's 11th move.

12. Kt—B 3 ! !

This move spoils Black's attack.
If 12. ....B—B 4 ch ; 13. K—R 1,
Kt—B 7 ch ; 14. R×Kt, Q×R ;
15. Kt—K 4 and White wins the
Queen. This is the combination
which White had in mind when he
played 11. Kt—Q B 3.

12. ......   Q—R 4

After 12. ....B—B 4 ch ; 13.
K—R 1, White would gain an important *tempo* by Kt—K 4, etc.

13. Kt—K 4   B—K 2

Naturally not 13. ....Kt×K P ;
because of 14. Kt×Kt, followed by
15. Kt—B 6 ch, etc.

14. Q—Q 4 !

Defending the K P and preventing R—Q 1, which would leave the
Q R P unprotected.

14. ......   B—K 3
15. B—Kt 5 !

After this move, Black cannot
avoid the loss of a Pawn.

15. ......   B×B
16. Kt (K 4)×B

Position after White's 16th move.

16. ......   Castles K R

There is hardly anything better.
If 16. ....Kt×R P ; 17. Kt×B,
Kt×Kt ch ; 18. R×Kt, P×Kt ;
19. R—Q 1, and White wins.

17. P—K R 3   Kt—R 3
18. Q—K 4

winning the Q B P.

18. ......   B—B 4
19. Q×P   Q—Kt 3
20. Q×Q   B×Q

Black's game is not yet hopeless,
as his opponent is not likely to obtain a passed Pawn very speedily,
and he has an isolated Pawn. On
the other hand it is admittedly an
advantage for the end-game to have
a Bishop. For this reason White
attempts, and with success, to add
to his material advantage by complicated combinative play.

21. Kt—Q 4 !

The first aim of this move is to
stalemate Black's two minor pieces.
In addition the White Knight at
Q 4 protects the Q B P, for if now
21. ....P—Q B 4 ; 22. Kt—B 6,
B×P ; 23. K R—B 1 followed by
R×P, White would obtain a passed
Pawn on the Queen's side without
any difficulty.

21. ......   Q R—Kt 1
22. P—Q Kt 3   K R—K 1

This   ill-timed   demonstration
against the K P, which cannot be
taken because of Kt—B 6, suggests
a new plan for White. This consists
in luring the Rooks away from the
first rank and taking advantage of
the unfavourable position of the
minor pieces in order to create
mating threats.

23. Q R—Q 1   R—Kt 3

The logical sequence of the preceding move.

24. P—B 4   R×P

Position after Black's 24th move.

25. P—B 5 !!

Black probably expected 25.
Kt (Q 4)—K 6, upon which 25. .....R—
Kt 1 yielded a sufficient defence.
Now the Rook is forced to abandon
the Knight's file, for after 25. ....
R × B P ; White's reply would be :
26. Kt (Q 4)—K 6 and after 25. ....
R—Kt 2 ; the answer would be : 26.
Kt—B 6, R—K 1 ; 27. Kt—K 7 ch,
K—B 1 (if 27. ....K—R 1 ;
28. Kt × B ch, B P × Kt ; 29. R—
Q 7, etc.) ; 28. Kt × B ch, R P × Kt;
29. R—Q 7, R—K 2 ; 30. R—Q 8 ch,
R—K 1 ; 31. Kt—R 7 ch, K—K 2 ;
32. R (Q 7)—Q 1 ! and Black
cannot avoid the threatened mate
without serious loss in material.
The following moves are therefore
compulsory.

25. ......   R—R 3
26. Kt (Q 4)—K 6 K—R 1
27. R—Q 8 ch   Kt—Kt 1
28. Kt × Q B P

Not 28. K R—Q 1, R (R 3) × Kt ;
29. Kt × R, P × Kt ; etc.

28. ......   R × R P
29. K R—Q 1 !

This is clearer than the variation
29. Kt × P ch, B × Kt ; 30. R × B,
R—K 8 ch ; 31. K—R 2, R (K 8)—
K 7 ; 32. R (B 7)—B 8, R × P ch ;

33. K—R 1, P—R 3 ; 34. R × Kt ch,
K—R 2 ; in which Black has
chances of a draw.

29. ......   P—B 3

The only move.

30. R × Kt ch   K × R.
31. R—Q 8 ch   B—K 1
32. Kt × B

Threatening mate in two.

32. ......   K—B 1
33. Kt—Q 6 ch   K—K 2
34. R—K 8 ch   K—Q 2
35. R × R   P × R

After all these complications the
situation is now cleared up. With
two Knights for a Rook, White
should have no difficulty in winning
as he has a passed Pawn in addition.

36. Kt—B 4   K—B 3
37. Kt—K 4   R—R 8 ch

In order to advance the King without being exposed to Kt—B 3 ch,
winning a Rook.

38. K—B 2   K—Q 4
39. K—B 3

White, still under the spell of a
series of problem-moves, shows a
desire to continue in the same strain
by seeking extraordinary combinations for the end-game. A simple
way of winning was : 39. Kt (B 4)
—Q 2, followed by 40. K—K 3,
with the threat of 41. Kt—Kt 1,
and 42. Kt (Kt 1)—B 3 ch.

39. ......   P—Q R 4
40. K—K 2

Pretty, but scarcely logical. Here
also 40. Kt (B 4)—Q 2 was sufficient in order to win.

40. ......   P—R 5 !

Naturally, not 40. ....K × Kt ;
because of 41. P—B 6, after which

Black is compelled to give up the Rook for the passed Pawn. The text-move aims at simplification and a draw.

Position after Black's 40th move.

I had not provided against this advance as I thought that the following variation, which is not unlike an end-game study, would ensure the win: 41. P—Q Kt 4, K×Kt (B 5); 42. P—B 6, K×P; (or if R—R 7 ch; 43. K—Q 1!, K—Q 4; 44. Kt—B 3 ch, etc.); 43. Kt—B 3! and wins. I noticed in time, however, that on move 41 Black could capture the Kt at K 4, because after 42. P—B 6, R—Q B 8 the other Knight would not be supported by the Q Kt P. A draw was easily forced by: 41. Kt—B 3 ch, K×P; 42. Kt×P ch, K—Q 5; 43. Kt (R 4)—Kt 2, etc. But playing for a win at all cost I adopted another line, the consequences of which proved highly dangerous to my game.

41. Kt (B 4)—Q 2   P—R 6
42. P—Q Kt 4

White has obtained two passed Pawns, but the Black Q R P will cost him a piece.

42. ......   R—Q B 8
43. K—Q 3   P—R 7
44. Kt—Q Kt 3   R—Q 8 ch!

Gaining a most important *tempo* by which Black obtains prospects of an advantage. When playing my 41st move I had expected P—R 8 (Q); 45. Kt×Q, R×Kt; 46. Kt—B 3 ch, followed by K—B 4; with an ending similar to that which occurred in the game, but there only through a mistake on the part of my opponent.

45. K—B 2   P—R 8=Q
46. Kt×Q   R×Kt
47. Kt—B 3 ch

Position after White's 47th move.

47. ......   K—B 3

The decisive mistake. He should have played 47. ....K—B 5!; 48. P—B 6, R—R 6; 49. Kt—K 4, R—R 2; and the White Pawn being stopped, Black could have brought his material advantage to bear. Now White benefits from this lucky gift and forces a win.

48. K—Q 3   R—K B 8
49. P—Kt 3

Securing Q B 4 for the King.

49.	P—R 4
50. K—B 4	P—R 5
51. P—Kt 5 ch	K—Q 2
52. P×P	R—B 5 ch
53. K—Q 5	R×P
54. P—B 6 ch	K—B 2
55. K—B 5	R×P

There is nothing to be done.

56. P—Kt 6 ch	K—Kt 1
57. Kt—Kt 5	Black resigns

GAME 11

KING'S BISHOP OPENING

White :	Black :
R. SPIELMANN.	A. ALEKHIN.

1. P—K 4	P—K 4
2. B—B 4	Kt—K B 3
3. P—Q 4	P×P
4. Kt—K B 3	B—B 4

After 4. ....Kt×P ; 5. Q×P, etc. White obtains a very strong attack for the Pawn he has given up. On principle, in the opening, I never try to obtain such an advantage in material. It can only be had at the cost of time and of delay in development, which often proves fatal.

5. Castles

After 5. P—K 5 Black would naturally play 5. ....P—Q 4 ; etc.

5.	P—Q 3
6. P—B 3	

White insists on playing a gambit at all cost !

6.	P—Q 6

After 6. ....P×P ; 7. Kt×P, followed by 8. B—K Kt 5, White has a splendid development. The text-move, giving back the Pawn, hinders the rapid and efficacious development of the White forces.

It conforms to the general principle enunciated above regarding the danger of winning a Pawn in the opening.

7. Q×P	Kt—B 3
8. P—Q Kt 4	

This last move weakens the Queen's side. The reason why White plays it notwithstanding, is that in the quiet variation : 9. B—K Kt 5, P—K R 3 ; 10. B—R 4, B—K Kt 5 ; 11. Q Kt—Q 2, Kt—K 4 ; Black has an easy game.

8.	B—Kt 3
9. P—Kt 5	Kt—Q R 4
10. P—-K 5	

This advance forces Black to play with circumspection on account of the King's exposed position. It also frustrates the threat of 10. .... Kt×B, which, in conjunction with Castles, would give Black the better game.

10.	P×P
11. Q×Q ch	K×Q
12. B×P	P—K 5
13. Kt—K 5	B—Q B 4 !

Essential, for White threatened 14. B—R 3 with good prospects of attack. Failing this possibility, White must abandon the offensive and develop his backward pieces.

14. Kt—Q 2	R—B 1

Threatening to win a piece by 15. ....B—Q 3, etc.

15. Q Kt—B 4	Kt×Kt
16. B×Kt	K—K 2
17. B—Kt 5	B—Q 3 !

Forcing White to play 18. P—B 4, which eliminates the possibility of opening the King's file eventually by P—B 3.

18. P—B 4	B—K B 4 !
19. P—Kt 4	

The object of this move is to force the Bishop from the Diagonal Q Kt 1—K R 7. In fact, without this move Black, by playing P—K R 3, would secure a retreat for the Bishop at K R 2, rendering his passed Pawn invulnerable and very embarrassing for White. At the same time the text-move presents serious drawbacks, since it dangerously weakens the King-side.

19. ......   B—K 3
20. K R—K 1

White has the following variation in view: 20. ....B × Kt; 21. P × B, B × B; 22. R × P! etc., with advantage. That is why he does not play 20. Q R—K 1, for in this variation the K R would be *en prise* to the B at Q B 4.

Position after White's 20th move.

20. ......   P—K 6 !

Now the inferiority of White's position, weakened by the advance of Pawns on both wings, becomes obvious.

21. B—Q 3

It would have been somewhat better for White to get rid of Black's K P by playing 21. K—Kt 2. There

would have followed: 21. ....B × Kt; 22. P × B, B × B; 23. R × P, K—B 2; 24. P × Kt, P × P; etc., but the end-game would still have been in Black's favour.

21. ......   K—K 1 !

This move, relieving the Bishop's pin, allows not only the defence of the K P by Kt—Q 4, but also attacks White's K Kt P.

22. P—K R 3   Kt—Q 4

Now two more Pawns are attacked, demonstrating the inconvenience of having advanced them prematurely.

Position after Black's 22nd move.

23. P—B 5

By 23. B × P, White could momentarily have avoided material loss, but, after 23. ....Kt × K B P; 24. B × Kt, R × B; etc. his position remained precarious if not desperate. This is why he prefers to attempt a sacrificial combination in order to recover the initiative.

23. ......   B × Kt
24. P × B   B × P
25. B × P

Threatening the gain of the Exchange by 26. B—Kt 6 ch,

Position after White's 25th move.

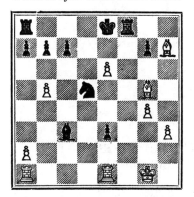

26. B—Kt 6 ch, followed by 27. R—K B 1; nor 25. ....Kt—K 2 (which move Spielmann probably anticipated); 26. Q R—Q 1, B × R; 27. R—Q 7, B—Kt 5; 28. B × Kt, followed by B—Kt 6 ch, would have been sufficient.

Now White is lost.

25. ......   Kt—B 5 !

The only way to ensure success definitely. Neither 25. .... R—B 6 ;

26. Q R—Q 1   B × R
27. R—Q 7

A last hope. If now 27. ....Kt— K 7 ch ; 28. K—Kt 2, R—B 7 ch ; 29. K—R 1, B—Kt 5 ; White would continue with 30. R × Kt P, threatening mate in three, and Black would have to be content with a draw by perpetual check.

27. ......   B—Kt 5 !
White resigns.

CHAPTER V

ALL-RUSSIAN MASTERS' TOURNAMENT AT VILNA, SEPTEMBER, 1912

GAME 12

QUEEN'S GAMBIT DECLINED

White :   *Black :*

DR. O. S. BERNSTEIN.   A. ALEKHIN.

1. P—Q 4   P—Q 4
2. Kt—K B 3   Kt—K B 3
3. P—B 4   P—B 3
4. P—K 3

In answer to 4. Kt—B 3, I have, on several occasions, successfully played 4. ....P×P ; and if 5. P—K 3, P—Q Kt 4, followed by P—Kt 5 ; or if 5. P—Q R 4, B—B 4 !, etc., as in the game against Rubinstein, London, 1922. After the text-move Black can play 4. .... B—B 4 ; 5. Q—Kt 3, Q—Kt 3 ; with a good game.

4. ......   P—K Kt 3

Played for the first time by Schlechter in a match-game against Lasker at Berlin, 1910. However, this system has little to commend it, as in this position the Bishop at K Kt 2 has for once not much scope, whilst the Q B, although not shut in by the K P, has no useful squares of development.

5. Kt—B 3   B—Kt 2
6. B—Q 3   Castles
7. Q—B 2   Kt—R 3
8. P—Q R 3

Up to now the position is identical with that in the game mentioned before. But on the next move Schlechter played 8. ....P×P ; followed by P—Q Kt 4 and P—Kt 5, after which his Queen's side naturally became very weak.

8. ......   Kt—B 2

After this move Black's position is constrained, but without any weak point. He can now hope to free his position by gradual stages.

9. Castles   B—K 3
10. P×P

If 10. P—Q Kt 3, R—B 1 ; 11. B—Kt 2, P—B 4 ; and if then 12. P×B P, P×B P, followed by ....Kt—R 3, and Black has a satisfactory game.

10. ......   K Kt×P !

The correct reply. After 10. .... P×P ; White would obtain the advantage by seizing the Q B file and by exploiting the lack of mobility of the Black pieces.

11. P—R 3

32

The object of this move is to prevent 13. ....B—Kt 5; after 12. P—K 4, Kt×Kt; 13. P×Kt. But Black takes advantage of this moment's respite to start operations in the centre on his own account.

11. ......   Kt×Kt
12. P×Kt   P—Q B 4 !

The position now recalls a variation of Grünfeld's defence : 1. P—Q 4, Kt—K B 3 ; 2. P—Q B 4, P—K Kt 3 ; 3. Kt—Q B 3, P—Q 4 ; etc., which was in fashion in recent Master Tournaments, with this difference in White's favour, however, that the Black Knight is at Q B 2 instead of Q B 3 or Q 2.

13. R—Kt 1   R—Kt 1
14. R—Q 1

If 14. P—K 4, then 14. ....P × P ; 15. P × P, Q—Q 3 ! , etc., with a good game, *e.g. :* 16. P—Q 5, B—Q 2 ; or 16. P—K 5, Q—Q 2 ; followed by K R—B 1.
It is clear that the capture of the Q B P either now or on the preceding move would not be to White's advantage, because of Q—Q 4.

14. ......   P—B 5

With this move Black allows his opponent to dominate the centre squares in order to gain an advantage on the Queen-side. More prudent and sufficient to equalize would have been 14. ....Q—Q 3 followed by K R—B 1.

15. B—K 2   P—Q Kt 4

Not 15. ....P—B 4 ; because of 16. Q—R 4 !

16. Kt—Q 2

After this unnecessary withdrawal Black takes the initiative. It was essential to have played 16. P—K 4, which would have been followed by 16. ....Q—Q 3 ; 17. B—K 3, P—Q R 3, with chances for both sides.

Position after White's 16th move.

16. ......   P—B 4 !

Permanently taking hold of the centre, as his Q 4 is definitely secured. From the strategic point of view this consideration is of paramount importance.

17. B—B 3   B—Q 4
18. P—K 4

Essential in order to develop the Q B at last, but too late to improve White's game.

18. ......   B—Q R 1 !

In order to bring his Knight to Q 4 and to prevent the White Knight from reaching Q B 5 via K 4.

19. Kt—B 1   P × P
20. B × P   Kt—Q 4

Now Black dominates the board and can, at will, undertake an attack on either wing.
If White play 21. Kt—Kt 3 (if 21. Kt—K 3, Kt×P ; etc., as in the game) Black would play 21. ....Q—Q 3, tying the Q B to the defence of the Q R P, and then P—Q R 3 ; following by the doubling of the Rooks on the K B file with an overwhelming advantage in position.

21. B—Kt 5

This move, plausible as it may seem strategically, is refuted by the combinative play which follows.

Position after White's 21st move.

21. ...... Kt×P !

If White replies B×B, then follows : 22. ....Kt×Q R ; 23. B—K 4, Kt×P ; followed by P—Kt 5 and Black has won the Exchange. White therefore choses the better alternative.

22. B×Kt P ! Q—Q 4 !

Not 22. ....Kt×Q R ; 23. B×P ch, K—R 1 ; 24. Q—Kt 6, Q—K 1 ; (otherwise Q—R 5, etc.) ; 25. Q×Kt, and White has a Pawn and prospects of an attack for the loss of the Exchange.

23. B×P ch K—R 1
24. P—B 4

Evidently compulsory.

24. ...... Kt×Q R
25. R×Kt Q×Q P ch
26. K—R 1

If 26. K—R 2, then 26.....R×P; 27. B×R, Q×B ch ; 28. K—R 1 (or 28. Kt—Kt 3, B—K 4 ; etc.) R—K B 1 ! (threatening Q×Kt ch ;

and mate in three), with a winning position for Black.

26. ...... Q—B 6 !

The simplest way of forcing the exchange of Queens, as Black now threatens Q×P ch.

27. K—R 2 Q×Q
28. B×Q P—K 4

At first sight this appears to be risky on account of White's three passed Pawns on the King's side, but Black had worked out that his Queen-side Pawns would queen first. The variation 28. ....B—K B 3 ; 29. B—R 6, followed by P—Kt 4, and Kt 5 promised no more than the text-move.

29. P—B 5 B—K B 3
30. B×B ch

If now 30. B—R 6, R—Kt 1 ; 31. P—Kt 4, P—R 4, and the White Pawns are stopped. White therefore decides to mobilize the Knight and to initiate a direct King-side attack with his remaining pieces.

30. ...... R×B
31. Kt—K 3 P—R 4
32. R—Q 1

If 32. Kt×P, Black wins easily by 32. ....R—B 3 ; 33. Kt—K 3, R—B 6 ; 34. R—K 1, R×P ; etc.

32. ...... R (B 3)—B 1

In order to seize the Queen's file at once, White's few checks being of no consequence.

33. R—Q 6 Q R—Q 1
34. R—R 6 ch K—Kt 2
35. R—Kt 6 ch K—B 2
36. Kt—Kt 4

My opponent, who was in the running with Rubinstein for the first prize in this tournament, offers a maximum of resistance and discovers unexpected resources in a desperate position. Now mate in two is threatened.

Position after White's 36th move.

36. ......   R—Q 7 !

This move, the climax of the manœuvre initiated by 32. .... K R—B 1, not only parries the mating threat but unexpectedly wins the Q B, which has no flight-square. It is the end.

37. Kt × P ch   K—K 2
38. B—Kt 1   R—Kt 7
39. R—K 6 ch   K—Q 1
40. R—Q 6 ch   K—B 1
41. P—K R 4   R × B
42. P—Kt 4   P—B 6
43. R—Q 3   P—Kt 5
44. P × P   P × P
White resigns.

GAME 13

QUEEN'S PAWN GAME

White :   *Black :*
A. NIEMZOVITCH.   A. ALEKHIN.

1. P—Q 4   P—Q 4
2. Kt—K B 3   P—Q B 4
3. B—B 4   Kt—Q B 3
4. P—K 3   Kt—B 3

Here 4. ....Q—Kt 3 would be premature on account of 5. Kt—B 3.

5. Kt—B 3

Now, however, this move is out of place. The usual line of play 5. P—B 3 followed by 6. B—Q 3 is certainly better.

5. ......   B—Kt 5

Equally satisfactory would be 5. ....P—Q R 3 followed by 6. .... B—Kt 5.

6. B—Q Kt 5   P—K 3
7. P—K R 3   B—R 4

This move will allow White to weaken the adverse position on both wings. Black had two ways of obtaining a good game :

I.—7. ....B × Kt ;   8. Q × B, P—Q R 3 ; 9. B × Kt ch, P × B etc.

or II.—7. ....P × Q P ;   8. P × P, B—R 4 ; 9. P—K Kt 4, B—Kt 3 ; 10. Kt—K 5, Q—Kt 3 ; 11. P—Q R 4, B—Kt 5.

8. P—K Kt 4   B—Kt 3
9. Kt—K 5   Q—Kt 3

Of course not 9. ....R—B 1, because of 10. Kt × Kt, followed by 11. B—Q R 6, etc.   However, 9. ....Q—B 1 would have been more prudent.

10. P—Q R 4 !

Very strong, as Black has no time to play P × P followed by B—Kt 5, because of 11. P—R 5, etc. Therefore he is compelled to yield the square at Q Kt 5 to his opponent.

10. ......   P—Q R 4
11. P—R 4   P—R 4

This move is relatively better than P—R 3, as it forces White to make an immediate decision on the King's wing.

12. Kt × B   P × Kt
13. Kt P × P

The variation 13. P—Kt 5, Kt—K Kt 1 ; 14. Q—Q 3, K—B 2 ;

15. R—K R 3, looks stronger than it really is, as Black can resist the attack by bringing his K Kt via K 2 to K B 4.

The text-move makes things easy for Black. His K Kt P, it is true, is weakened, but, on the other hand, he obtains excellent prospects in the centre.

13. ......   Kt P × P
14. Q—K 2   Castles

The King's position on the Queenside will be quite safe, as the White Bishop can easily be eliminated.

15. Castles Q R !

A very pretty trap.

Position after White's 15th move.

15. ......   B—Q 3

Black discovers in time the adversary's subtle plan : 15. ....P × P ; 16. P × P, Kt × P ; 17. R × Kt, Q × R ; 18. Q × K P ch, Kt—Q 2 ; 19. Q—B 6 ch !!, P × Q ; 20. B—R 6, mate. The text-move eliminates all danger.

16. B × B   R × B
17. B—Q 3

White has not sufficiently weighed the consequences of this move; in particular he has not realized that the Knight will have no time to settle down at Q Kt 5, and consequently Black will obtain an important advantage. Better would be : 17. B × Kt, P × B ; 18. K R—Kt 1, R—Q 2 ; etc., but in this case also Black's game is superior.

17. ......   P—B 5 !

Dislodging the Bishop and initiating a combined attack on both wings.

18. B—Kt 6

Naturally not 18. Kt—Kt 5, P × B ; 19. Kt × R ch, K—Q 2, followed by K × Kt, etc.

18. ......   Kt—K 2
19. K R—Kt 1   Q—Kt 5
20. K—Q 2

Position after White's 20th move.

20. ......   R—Kt 3 !

An amusing reply to White's trap on the 15th move. Black in his turn threatens mate by a Queen sacrifice, a Roland for an Oliver ! 21. .... Kt × B ; 22. R × Kt, Q × Kt P ; 23. R—Q Kt 1, Q × Kt ch ; 24. K × Q, Kt—K 5 mate. In addition the text-move allows the Queen to co-operate in a decisive action against the tracked White Bishop.

21. P—B 3

Evading the threat.

21. ......   R—K R 3
22. B—B 7

Hapless Bishop, with only one square on which to shelter !

22. ......   Kt—B 4
23. Q—R 2   Q—K 2 !
24. Kt—Kt 5

A desperate move. After 24. B—Kt 6 Black would win at once by 24. ....Kt × R P, threatening, if 25. Q × Kt, to win the Queen by 25. ....Kt—K 5 ch. In giving up the Bishop, White has a vague hope of complications resulting from the Queen reaching Q Kt 8.

24. ......   Q × B
25. Kt—R 7 ch   K—Q 2
26. Q—Kt 8   Kt—Q 3

Black could have continued with 26. ....Q—K 1. But his objective, which he indeed succeeds in achieving, is the capture of the White Queen.

27. R—Kt 5   Kt (B 3)—K 1
28. Q R—K Kt 1   R—K B 3

Not, of course, 28. ....Q × P ; because of 29. R × P ch.

29. P—B 4   P—Kt 3
30. K—B 1   Q—R 2
31. P—B 3   Q—B 2
32. K—Kt 1   Q—K 2

Taking advantage of the fact that White cannot capture the K Kt P because of the pin by 33. ....Q—R 2, etc.

33. K—R 2   R—B 1
34. Kt—Kt 5   Kt × Kt
35. P × Kt   Kt—B 2
36. Q—R 7   Q—Q 3

If now 37. R × Kt P, Kt × P ; 38. R—Kt 7 ch, K—B 3 ; 39. Q × P, R—R 3, and the Queen is lost.

White resigns.

GAME 14

SICILIAN DEFENCE

White :   *Black :*
A. Alekhin. Dr. O. S. Bernstein.

1. P—K 4   P—Q B 4
2. Kt—K B 3   P—K 3
3. Kt—B 3

I am now convinced that the best move here is 3. B—K 2, in order to be able to play P—Q B 4 if Black adopts the Paulsen variation (P—Q R 3 and Q—B 2 ; etc.).

3. ......   P—Q R 3
4. P—Q 4   P × P
5. Kt × P   Q—B 2

This defence, adopted frequently of late by Sämisch, forces White to play with circumspection.

6. B—K 2   Kt—K B 3
7. Castles   B—K 2
8. P—B 4   Kt—B 3

Threatening 9. ....Kt × Kt ; 10. Q × Kt, B—B 4, winning the Queen, and consequently preventing 9. P—K 5.

9. K—R 1

Was 9. B—K 3 more simple ? However, the King is better placed at R 1 and in a close game like the Sicilian the loss of time entailed is of no great consequence.

9. ......   P—Q 3
10. B—B 3   B—Q 2
11. B—K 3   Castles K R
12. Q—K 2

A position typical of Paulsen's system. At the moment the White pieces have the superior mobility, but subsequently the open Q B file may become an important factor in Black's favour.

12. ......   Q R—B 1

It would have been preferable to occupy this file with the K R as the King-side is not threatened at present. Probably Black's operations on the Queen-side would be more efficacious if supported by both Rooks.

13. Q—B 2

An important move which prevents 13. ....Kt—Q R 4, to which White's reply would be 14. Kt × P, and if P × Kt; 15. B—Kt 6 regaining the piece. Therefore Black is compelled to lose a *tempo* in order to make this manoeuvre with the Q Kt possible.

13. ......   P—Q Kt 4
14. Kt—Kt 3   Kt—K 1

After this last move, which shuts in the K R, White's advantage becomes manifest. Black had nothing better than to acknowledge the error of his 12th move by playing 14. ....R—Kt 1; followed by 15. ....K R—B 1. The move Kt—K 1 should only have been played in case of absolute necessity.

15. Q R—Q 1   R—Kt 1
16. R—Q 2

Played in anticipation of 16. .... Kt—R 4, as White foresees the coming attack. The text-move does not aim at doubling the Rooks on the Queen's file, but rather at defending the Q R P later on with the K R.

16. ......   Kt—R 4
17. Kt × Kt   Q × Kt

See Diagram.

18. P—K 5 !

With this unexpected move White assumes the initiative. It would be to Black's disadvantage to reply : 18. ....P—Q 4 ; because of :

I.—19. B × P !, P—Kt 5 ; 20. B—Kt 3, P × Kt ; 21. R × B, etc.

Position after Black's 17th move.

II.—19. B × P !, P × B ; 20. Kt × Q P, Q—Q 1 ; 21. B—B 5, B × B ; 22. Q × B and Black has no defence against the numerous threats.

III.—19. B × P !, P × B ; 20. Kt × Q P, B—Q 1 ; 21. B—B 5, B—K 3 ; 22. B × R, K × B ; 23. Q—B 5 ch, K—Kt 1 ; 24. P—B 5, B × Kt ; 25. Q × B, with an evident advantage in position.

IV.—19. B × P !, P × B ; 20. Kt × Q P, B—Q 1 ; 21. B—B 5, B—K 3 ; 22. B × R, K × B ; 23. Q—B 5 ch, K—Kt 1 ; 24. P—B 5, B × P : 25. P—Q Kt 4 and wins.

V.—19. B × P !, P × B ; 20. Kt × Q P, B—Q 1 ; 21. B—B 5, B—K 3 ; 22. B × R, K × B ; 23. Q—B 5 ch, K—Kt 1 ; 24. P—B 5, Q × R ; 25. P × B, and wins.

On the other hand the move actually chosen is merely a makeshift, offering the adverse Knight a particularly useful square.

18. ......   P—Kt 5
19. Kt—K 4   P—Q 4
20. Kt—B 5   B—Q Kt 4
21. R—R 1

See note to White's 16th move.

21. ......   Kt—B 2

By this move Black cuts off the retreat of his own Queen. White, by an energetic demonstration, takes immediate advantage of this injudicious manœuvre. Q—Q 1 or Q—B 2 would certainly have been better, although in any case Black's position would remain very precarious.

Position after Black's 21st move.

22. P—Q R 4 !

Threatening to win the Queen by 23. Kt—Kt 3. Black must submit to the loss of the Exchange, for after

I.—22. ....P×P e. p.; 23. R×R P, Q—Kt 5; 24. P—B 3, Q—B 5; 25. B—K 2, his Queen is lost, and after

II.—22. ....B×Kt; 23. B×B, K R—B 1; 24. P—B 3, B×P; 25. B—Q 1, P×P; 26. P—Q Kt 4, White wins equally.

22. ......   B—B 5

Black hopes to obtain some chances still by bringing his Knight to Q B 5 after pushing on the Pawn to Q Kt 6, but White does not leave him time to consummate this manœuvre.

23. Kt—Q 7

Not 23. P—Q Kt 3 because of 23. ....B—Q Kt 4 !, etc.

23.	P—Kt 6
24. Kt×Q R	R×Kt
25. P—B 3	Kt—R 1
26. B—K 2 !	

Preparing the coming attack on the Black King's position.

26.	R—Q B 1
27. P—B 5	B×B
28. R×B	B—B 4
29. R—K B 1	B×B
30. R×B	Q—Kt 3
31. P—R 5	Q—B 3
32. R—B 3	

Simpler would have been: 32. P—B 6, P—Kt 3; 33. Q—R 4, Q—K 1; 34. R—R 3, P—R 4; 35. Q—Kt 5, Q—B 1; 36. R×P, etc.

32.	P×P
33. R×P	Kt—B 2
34. R×P	Kt—K 3

Position after Black's 34th move.

35. Q—R 7 !

Threatening 36. R×P ch, Kt×R; 37. Q—B 7 ch, K—R 1; 38. Q—B 8 ch, R×Q; 39. R×R mate. If however White plays at once 35. R×P ch, then K×R and there is no more than a draw.

35.	P—R 3
36. R—K 7	Q—B 5

Black has no adequate defence against 37. R (B 1)—B 7.

37. R (B 1)—B 7   Q—K 5 !

Hindering 38. R × P ch and threatening P—Q 5 himself.

38. Q × P   R—B 3

The reply to 38. ....R—B 5 is 39. Q × Kt ! etc.

39. Q—B 1

again threatening R × P ch.

39. ......   K—R 2
40. R—B 6 !

The finishing stroke, for if 40. ....Kt—Q 1 ; 41. R—Q 6, and if 40. ....Q × P ; 41. Q—Q 3 ch and wins.

40. ......   P—Q 5
41. R (B 6) × Kt   R × R
42. R × R   P × P
43. P × P   P—Kt 7
44. R—Q Kt 6   Q—B 7
45. P—R 6   Q—B 8
46. Q—Kt 1   Black resigns.

GAME 15

RUY LOPEZ

White :   Black :
H. LÖVENFISCH.   A. ALEKHIN.

1. P—K 4   P—K 4
2. Kt—K B 3   Kt—Q B 3
3. B—Kt 5   P—Q R 3
4. B—R 4   Kt—B 3
5. Q—K 2

Alapin's move. Without being bad it leaves Black various ways of equalizing the game.

5. ......   B—K 2

Equally good is 5. ....P—Q Kt 4 followed by 6. ....B—B 4 (see game No. 16).

6. P—B 3   P—Q 3
7. P—K R 3

This move, which is apparently played in order to prevent the pin-

ning of the K Kt, by 7. ....B—Kt 5, would be understandable were it White's intention to play P—Q 4, which requires the free manœuvring of the Kt. As will be seen later on, however, White has only P—Q 3 in view and so this precautionary measure is superfluous. The move would be more logical after Black's B—Kt 5, so as to be clear from the first as to that Bishop's intentions.

7. ......   B—Q 2
8. P—Q 3   Castles
9. B—B 2

In order to avoid the possible threat of Kt—Q 5 ; etc.

9. ......   K—R 1 !

The timid manner in which White has played the opening allows Black at once to formulate a plan of attack.

10. Castles   Kt—Kt 1

Played, apparently, in order to continue with P—B 4. White prepares for this eventuality by placing the R on the King's file so as to obtain compensation in the centre by P—Q 4.

11. R—K 1   Q—K 1

Black pursues his concealed objective.

12. P—Q 4   P—B 3 !

In accordance with the principle that *an advance on the wings is only possible after the position in the centre is stabilized.*

13. Q Kt—Q 2

See Diagram.

13. ......   P—K Kt 4 !

The logical reaction against 7. P—K R 3 (see also game No. 18). The opening of the K Kt file after 14. ....P—Kt 5 ; 15. P × P, B × P ; would evidently be to Black's advantage. To avoid this threat

Position after White's 13th move.

White is compelled to weaken the position of his King still more.

14. P—Q 5

After 14. P—K Kt 4, P—K R 4 !, White would still be forced to block the centre.

14. ......   Kt—Q 1

The inactivity of this Knight and of the K B are the only drawbacks in Black's position.

15. P—K Kt 4   P—K R 4
16. Kt—R 2   Kt—R 3
17. Kt (Q 2)—B 1

Position after White's 17th move.

17. ......   P—B 3 !

Taking the initiative on the Queen's side also, Black still further improves his game, *e.g.* :

I.—18. P—Q B 4, P—Kt 4 ; 19. P—Kt 3, Kt—Kt 2 ; 20. B—K 3, P×Q P ; 21. B P×Q P, P—B 1 followed by Kt—Q B 4, etc.

II.—18. Kt—K 3, R P×P ; 19. R P×P, P×P ; 20. Kt×P, Kt—K 3 followed by Kt—B 5, etc.

18. Kt—Kt 3

An unsuccessful attempt to force the exchange or to compel the advance of Black's K R P.

18. ......   B P×P
19. K P×P   Q—B 2 !

Position after Black's 19th move.

Gaining an important *tempo*, which will allow Black, should White defend his Q P, to break up the centre by P—B 4, *e.g.* : 20. P—Q B 4, P×P ; 21. P×P, P—B 4 ; 22. P×P, Kt×P ; 23. Kt×Kt, B×Kt ; 24. B×B, Q×B ; etc., with advantage for Black. White prefers to avoid this threat by a manœuvre, whose drawback is a considerable weakening of his K B 5 and consequently of the Pawn which is to occupy that square.

20. Kt—B 5   Kt×Kt
21. B×Kt

Equally after 21. P×Kt the reply 21. ....Q—R 2 would be very strong.

21.	. . . . . .	B × B
22.	P × B	Q—R 2 !
23.	Q—K 4	Kt—B 2
24.	Kt—B 1	Kt—K 3
25.	Kt—K 3	R—K Kt 1
26.	K—Kt 2	

Anticipating the threat: 26. . . . .
P—Kt 5 and 27. . . . .P—Kt 6 ; etc.

| 26. | . . . . . . | B—Q 1 ! |

The entry of this Bishop into the
game marks the turning point.
Black now threatens 27. . . . .P—
Kt 4 followed by 28. . . . .B—Kt 3 ;
etc.

| 27. | P—Q R 4 | P—Q R 4 |

Securing the diagonal Q R 2—
K Kt 8 for the Bishop. By attempting to counteract the threat B—Kt 3
and B—B 4, White allows his
opponent to adopt a different line of
play which leads to a win just as
easily.

28.	P—Q Kt 4	P × P
29.	P × P	B—Kt 3
30.	Kt—B 4	

This move, which aims at giving
up two pieces for a Rook, is White's
best chance and can be refuted only
by energetic attacking play. If 30.
R—B 1, Black wins easily by 30.
. . . .P—Kt 5 ; 31. P—R 4, B × Kt ;
32. P × B, P—Kt 6 ; followed by
Kt—Kt 5.

| 30. | . . . . . . | B—Q 5 |
| 31. | B—Kt 2 | Q R—Q B 1 |

Black could also play 31. . . . .
B × B followed by Kt × P, but the
move in the text is more decisive.

32.	Q R—B 1	R × Kt
33.	R × R	B × B
34.	Q—B 2	

White had based his hopes upon
this position when giving up a piece.
Indeed, after 34. . . . .B—Q 5 ; 35.
R—B 7, R—Kt 2 ; 36. R × R, Q × R ;
37. Q—B 8 ch, K—R 2 ; 38.
R—Q B 1, etc., he had still some
chances.

Position after White's 34th move.

| 34. | . . . . . . | Kt × P ! |

The beginning of the end. Should
White capture the Bishop, Black
wins by 35. . . . .Kt—R 5 ch ; 36.
K—R 1, Q—Q 6 ; 37. R—B 3, Q ×
P ch ; 38. P—B 3, Kt × P.

| 35. | R—B 7 | Q—Kt 3 |

If now 36. Q × B, P—Kt 5 ; and
Black wins.

| 36. | R—B 8 | P—Kt 5 |

The commencement of the mating
combination.

| 37. | R × R ch | K × R |
| 38. | Q × B | |

Or 39. Q—B 8 ch, K—R 2 ; 40.
Q × P ch, K—R 3 and wins.

| 38. | . . . . . . | P × P ch |
| 39. | K × P | |

The flight of the King to B 1 would
have allowed the following pretty
ending : 39. K—B 1, Q—Kt 7 ch ;
40. K—K 2, Q—K 5 ch ; 41. K any,
Q × R ch followed by P—R 7.

After the text-move Black announced mate in five as follows :

39.	. . . . . .	Q—Kt 5 ch
40.	K—R 2	Kt—R 5
41.	P—B 4	Kt—B 6 ch
42.	K—R 1	Q—R 6 ch
43.	Q—R 2	Q × Q mate

CHAPTER VI

MASTERS' QUADRANGULAR TOURNAMENT AT ST. PETERSBURG, APRIL, 1913

GAME 16

RUY LOPEZ

White :	Black :
A. ALEKHIN.	O. DURAS.

1. P—K 4	P—K 4
2. Kt—K B 3	Kt—Q B 3
3. B—Kt 5	P—Q R 3
4. B—R 4	Kt—B 3
5. Q—K 2	P—Q Kt 4

This move, in conjunction with the next one, affords Black the simplest method of equalizing the game.

6. B—Kt 3	B—B 4
7. P—Q R 4 !	

The opening of the Q R file is of great moment in this variation. Black cannot prevent it, for if : 7. ....P—Kt 5 ; 8. B×P ch, K×B ; 9. Q—B 4 ch, P—Q 4 ; 10. Q×B, Q—Q 3 ; 11. Q×Kt !

7.	R—Q Kt 1
8. P×P	P×P
9. P—Q 3	

After 9. Kt—B 3, Black could simply Castle, for after 10. Kt × Kt P, P—Q 4 ! and he obtains an attack fully equivalent to the Pawn sacrificed. After the text-move White

can eventually play P—B 3 and bring his Knight to K 3 or K Kt 3 via Q 2 and K B 1.

9.	P—Q 3
10. B—K 3	B—Kt 5

Here Black could have obtained an even game by forcing the exchange of White's only well posted piece, the K B, by 10. ....B—K 3. It is clear that White would not have reaped any advantage by exchanging at K 6 and Q B 4, as Black would have had command of the centre, thanks to his Pawn position and the two open files.

11. P—R 3	B—R 4

Consequent but not best. 11. .... B—K 3 was even now preferable and would have brought about variations similar to those resulting from the immediate development of the B at K 3.

12. Q Kt—Q 2	Castles
13. Castles K R	Kt—Q 5

This offer to exchange is premature, and, as will be seen, gives White a marked positional advantage. Relatively better would have been 13. ....Q—K 2 followed by Kt—Q 1—K 3, although in either case Black has the inferior game.

43

14. B × Kt   B × Kt

Forced, for otherwise the Black Bishop would have been in jeopardy, *e.g.*: 14. ....B×B; 15. P—Kt 4, B—Kt 3; 16. Kt×B, P×Kt; 17. P—K B 4, etc., or 14. ....P×B; 15. P—Kt 4, B—Kt 3; 16. Kt—R 4, followed by P—K B 4, with advantage to White in either variation.

15. Kt × B   P × B

Position after Black's 15th move.

16. P—K 5 !

The beginning of a strong attack against Black's K B 2, weakened as it is by the premature exchange of Black's K B. Furthermore it is interesting to observe how important it is for White's attack to have the open Q R file.

16. ......   Q—K 2

Besides this move and the sequel it implies, Black had a further choice of two lines of play :

I.—16. ....P×P; 17. Q×P, Q—Q 3; 18. Q×Q, P×Q; 19. K R—K 1 with advantage to White ; or

II.—16. ....K R—K 1; 17. P—K 6 !, P×P; 18. B×P ch, K—B 1 (if K—R 1; 19. Kt—Kt 5); 19. P—Q Kt 4 !, B×P (if B—Kt 3; 20. K R—K 1, etc.); 20. Kt×P, R—Kt 3 !; 21. Q—B 3 !, B—B 6 ; 22. Kt—B 6 !, R×Kt; 23. Q×R, B×R ; 24. R×B, and White has the better game.

17. K R—K 1   Q R—K 1
18. Q—Q 2   P × P

Forced, as P—K 6 was threatened.

19. R × P   Q—Q 3
20. Q—Kt 5 !

Forcing a further exchange which brings the Knight into decisive action.

20. ......   R × R

It is clear that 20. ......P—R 3 would have achieved nothing after 21. Q—B 5.

21. Kt × R

Already threatening mate after Kt × P.

21. ......   Q—Kt 3

Relatively best. 21. Kt—Q 2 would not be sufficient, *e.g.* : 21. ....Kt—Q 2; 22. Kt×P !, R×Kt; 23. R—R 8 ch, Kt—B 1 ; 24. Q—B 5 !, Q—K 2; 25. B×R ch, Q×B; 26. Q×B and wins. The move in the text removes the immediate threat, for now 22. Q—B 5, would be insufficient as a preliminary to the Kt sacrifice, as Black could prepare a fresh defensive position by 22. ....P—Kt 3, followed by K—Kt 2, etc.

22. P—Kt 4 !

But this somewhat hidden preparation of the Kt sacrifice wins at once, as Black is compelled to make a reply which will render his position still more precarious.

| 22. ...... | B—Q 3 |

If 22. ....P—Kt 3, then 23. Q—R 6 threatening either Kt×B P or R—R 8 ; and if 22. ....B—K 2 ; 23. Kt—Q 7 !, Kt×Kt ; 24. Q×B, Q—Q 3 ; 25. Q×Q, P×Q ; 26. R—R 5, R—Kt 1 ; 27. R—R 7, R—Q 1 ; 28. R—Kt 7 and wins.

Position after Black's 22nd move.

| 23. Kt×P ! | R × Kt |
| 24. Q—B 5 ! | |

The point of the manœuvre started with 22. P—Kt 4 ! Against the double threat of 25. B×R ch, followed by 26. P—Kt 5, or else 25. Q—K 6 Black has no defence.

| 24. ...... | P—Kt 3 |

If 24. ....Q—B 3 ; 25. P—Kt 5, Q—Q 2 ; 26. B×R ch, K×B (if Q×B ; 27. P×Kt), 27. Q—B 3 ; and White wins.

25. Q—K 6	K—Kt 2
26. Q×R ch	K—R 3
27. B—K 6 !	Black resigns.

GAME 17

RUY LOPEZ

| *White :* | *Black :* |
| E. ZNOSKO-BOROVSKI. | A. ALEKHIN. |

1. P—K 4	P—K 4
2. Kt—K B 3	Kt—Q B 3
3. B—Kt 5	P—Q R 3
4. B—R 4	P—Q 3
5. P—Q 4	B—Kt 5

5. B—Q 2 is better. The variation in the text, favoured by Marshall, is not favourable to Black should White, as in the game Réti—Spielmann, Berlin, 1920, adopt the continuation 6. P—Q 5, P—Q Kt 4 ; 7. P×Kt, P×B ; 8. P—B 4 !

6. B×Kt ch

White also obtains a good game by this move, but allows Black some counter chances.

6.	P×B
7. P×P	P×P
8. Q—K 2	

It is clear that after exchange of Queens Black would protect his K P by 8. ....R×Q, threatening mate if White plays 9. Kt×P.

8.	B—Q 3
9. B—K 3	Kt—K 2
10. P—K R 3	B—R 4
11. Q Kt—Q 2	Castles

Black could equally play 11. .... P—B 3 in order to withdraw his Bishop to B 2 in case of need. But he considered that White would not find the time necessary to increase his pressure on the King's side on account of Black's counter-attack on the opposite wing, and in the centre.

| 12. P—K Kt 4 | B—Kt 3 |
| 13. P—K R 4 | |

If 13. Kt—R 4, Kt—Q 4 ! ; 14. Kt × B, Kt × B ; 15. Q × Kt, B P × Kt, with good prospects.

13.	......	P—B 3
14.	P—R 5	B—B 2
15.	Kt—R 4	Q—Kt 1 !

The Black Queen enters into the game very effectively through this outlet.

| 16. | P—Kt 3 | Q—Kt 5 ! |
| 17. | P—K B 3 | |

The opening of the K Kt file would here be without effect : 17. Kt—B 5, Kt × Kt ; 18. Kt P × Kt, Q—B 6 ! and White, to avoid the loss of his Q B P without any compensation, must decide to Castle on the Queen's side, whereupon his opponent would mate in two by 19. ....B—R 6 ch.

Position after White's 17th move.

| 17. | ...... | K R—Q 1 ! |

Stronger than 17. ....Q—B 6, whereupon White would obtain an equivalent in position sufficient for the Pawn sacrificed, by 18. K—B 2 !, Q × B P ; 19. K R—Q B 1, Q—Kt 7 ; 20. Kt—B 4 !, Q × Q ch ; 21. K × Q, etc.

18. K—B 2

After 18 Castles (K R) the ensuing reply, 18. ....B—B 4, would be still stronger.

18.	......	B—B 4
19.	Kt– B 1	R—Q 3
20.	B × B	Q × B ch
21.	Kt—K 3	Q R—Q 1
22.	K R—Q 1	Q—B 6 !

Undoubling the Q B P by force, and in this way removing the only weakness in his position.

23. R × R

If 23. Kt—B 1, Black would reply simply 23. ....P—R 4, and White could only defer the exchange of Rooks, which must be made sooner or later.

| 23. | ...... | P × R |
| 24. | R—Q 1 | P—Q 4 ! |

The most energetic. In exchange for the Q R P Black obtains a strong passed Pawn in the centre and besides, White's Q R P is a most noticeable object of attack.

| 25. | Q × P | P—Q 5 |
| 26. | Kt (K 3)—B 5 | |

As this Kt can no longer be assisted by the other pieces, its inroad on B 5 loses much of its efficacy.

26.	......	Kt × Kt
27.	Kt × Kt	Q × Q B P ch
28.	Q—K 2	Q—B 4
29.	Q—Q 3	

29. Q—Q 2 ! would be a little better, with the double threat 30. R—Q B 1 followed by R × P and Kt—K 7 ch, and 30. P—Kt 5. But in this case also Black would secure an advantage in position by 29. ....Q—B 1 !

| 29. | ...... | B—K 3 |

In order to be able to dislodge the Kt, at need, by P—Kt 3, but White prefers to withdraw it himself to maintain the defence of his seriously weakened left wing.

30. Kt—Kt 3	R—R 1
31. R—Q 2	Q—Kt 5 !
32. R—B 2	P—Q B 4
33. Kt—B 1	

Position after White's 33rd move.

33. ......   P—B 5 !

This temporary Pawn-sacrifice will allow the Black pieces to break through into the hostile camp, and to co-operate in a direct attack against White's King, an attack which will become irresistible thanks to the passed Pawn, which fixes the White pieces on the other wing.

34. P×P	R—R 6
35. Q—Q 2	Q—B 4
36. K—Kt 3	

After 36. K—Kt 2, B×B P Black would be threatening to capture the Knight with check.

36.	B×B P
37. Q—B 1	R—B 6 !
38. R×R	P×R
39. Kt—K 3	

Directed against the threatened Q—Kt 8 ch.

39.	B×P
40. Q—B 2 !	B—K 3
41. Kt—Q 1	

Else Black would win easily with his passed Pawn.

| 41. ...... | Q—Kt 8 ch |
| 42. K—R 4 | P—Kt 4 ch ! |

In conjunction with the following move this is the shortest road to victory.

43. P×P e. p.

Position after White's 43rd move.

43. ......   P—R 4 !

This Pawn now shares in the attack and settles the result outright. White is helpless against the threat : 44. ....Q—R 8 ch ; 45. K—Kt 3, P—R 5 ch ; 46. K—B 2, Q—R 7 ch. On the other hand 43. ....P×P would not have been so strong, for White could have still defended himself by 44. Q—K 2 !, K—Kt 2 ; 45. K—R 3 !

44. Kt—K 3	Q×Kt
45. Q—R 4	Q—B 7 ch
46. K—R 3	P—R 5
47. Q—K 8 ch	K—Kt 2
48. Q—K 7 ch	K×P

White resigns.

CHAPTER VII

INTERNATIONAL TOURNAMENT AT SCHEVENINGEN, AUGUST, 1913

GAME 18

RUY LOPEZ

White :	Black :
DR. A. G. OLLAND.	A. ALEKHIN.

1.	P—K 4	P—K 4
2.	Kt—K B 3	Kt—Q B 3
3.	B—Kt 5	Kt—Q 5

This old variation is not quite correct from a theoretical standpoint. The best line of play for White seems to be : 4. Kt × Kt, P × Kt ; 5. Castles, P—Q B 3 ; 6. B—B 4, Kt—K 2 (or P—K Kt 3) ; 7. P—Q 3 followed by 8. P—Q B 3 !

4. B—K 2

The fact that White yields the two Bishops to the opponent at the commencement of the game is certainly not calculated to refute Bird's variation, as he does not obtain the slightest compensation.

4.	......	Kt × B
5.	Q × Kt	P—Q 3
6.	P—Q B 3	

Even 6. P—Q 4 would not compel Black to surrender the centre, because after 6. ....P—Q B 3 ! ; 7. P × P, P × P, his K P would be defended by the threat Q—R 4 ch.

6.	......	P—Q B 3
7.	P—Q 4	Q—B 2
8.	B—K 3	Kt—B 3
9.	Q Kt—Q 2	

White has now developed all his minor pieces, but they have only a very limited range of action, whilst the white squares are weak on account of the premature exchange of the K B. On these grounds Black has already the better game.

9.	......	B—K 2
10.	P—K R 3	

In order to limit the action of Black's Q B. But, as experience has many a time shown, the advance of the K R P facilitates the formation of a direct attack on the King by the opponent.
10. Castles K R, and if 10. .... B—Kt 5 ; 11. Q—Q 3, etc., was comparatively better.

10.	......	P—Q Kt 3 !

With the double object of opening the diagonal Q R 3—K B 8 for the Q B and, in the event of the obstruction of this diagonal, blocking the centre before undertaking operations on the King-side.
The correctness of this plan is clearly shown in the course of the game.

48

11. Castles K R   P—Q R 4
12. P—B 4

If 12. K R—K 1, Black would be satisfied with B—R 3, followed by Q—Q, whereas he now avails himself of the opportunity to launch the attack which he intended.

12. ......   P—Q B 4 !
13. P—Q 5

The opening of the Q file would clearly be to Black's advantage.

13. ......   P—R 3 !
14. P—R 3

A counter-attack on the opposite wing. It is not difficult to foresee that it will not materialize as quickly as Black's direct attack against the adverse King.

14. ......   P—K Kt 4
15. P—Q Kt 4

If 15. Kt—R 2, then 15. ....P—R 4 ; 16. B×Kt P, Kt×Q P ; 17. B×B, Kt—B 5 !, etc. with good attacking chances.

15. ......   P—Kt 5
16. R P×P   B×P
17. P×B P   Kt P×P
18. Q—Q 3   Q—Q 2 !

White's ensuing combination could have been prevented by 18. ....Q—B 1, but Black, having assessed it at its proper value, seeks, on the contrary, to provoke it.

19. B×B P !

Ingenious and seemingly correct, for after 19. ....P×·B ; 20. Kt× P followed by P—B 4, White's Pawns would become formidable. Unfortunately for White, Black is by no means compelled to accept the sacrifice.

19. ......   B×Kt

Not at once 19. ....R—K Kt 1 because White could answer very energetically 20. Kt×P !, Black's Queen not having the resource of occupying the square K Kt 5. By the move in the text Black retains this option.

20. Kt×B

Position after White's 20th move.

20. ......   R—K Kt 1 !

The quiet refusal of the Greek Gift sets off in striking fashion Black's superiority in position.

If 21. B—K 3 (21. B—Kt 6, Q—R 6 !) Black would have continued his attack in the following manner : 21. ....R×P ch ; 22. K×R, Q—Kt 5 ch ; 23. K—R 2, Q×Kt ; 24. R—K Kt 1, Kt—Kt 5 ; 25. R×Kt, Q×R ; 26. R—K Kt 1, Q—R 4 ch ; 27. K—Kt 2, P—B 4 ! ; 28. P×P, K—B 2, after which White's position would rapidly become untenable.

This is the reason why White prefers by a fresh sacrifice to obtain two passed centre-Pawns whose advance will certainly threaten to become very dangerous.

21. Kt×P   P×Kt
22. B×B   Q—Kt 5 !

It was very important not to concede White time to play P—B 3, thus allowing his Rooks to defend the Kt P. This would have rendered the prosecution of the attack very difficult for Black.

23. P—Kt 3	K×B
24. P—Q 6 ch	K—B 1
25. K R—K 1	P—R 4 !

This advance of the R P comes just in time to thwart the intentions of the opponent.

26. Q R—Q 1

Threatening 27. P—Q 7 followed by Q—Q 6 ch and Q×P, etc.

26.	R—Q 1
27. P—B 5	P—K R 5
28. R—K 3	P×P
29. P×P	

Or 29. R×P, Q×P, and Black wins easily.

29. ......   Kt—R 4

Position after Black's 29th move.

30. P—Q 7

There is nothing else to be done. For example, if 30. R—Q 2, Q—R 6; 31. R—K Kt 2, Q×R ch, and if 30. K—B 2, then 30. ....R—Kt 3 !, etc. Nevertheless, the text-move loses still more rapidly.

30.	Kt×P
31. Q—Q 6 ch	K—Kt 2
32. Q×P ch	K—R 2
33. K—B 2	Q×R
34. R×Kt	Q—Q 7 ch
35. K—B 1	R×R
36. Q—B 5 ch	R—Kt 3
37. P—B 6	Q—B 8 ch
38. Resigns	

GAME 19

CENTRE GAME

| *White :* | *Black :* |
| J. MIESES. | A. ALEKHIN. |

1. P—K 4	P—K 4
2. P—Q 4	P×P
3. Q×P	

It is quite evident that such displacements of the Queen at an early stage in the opening are not likely to reap any advantage. However, Black is compelled to play with precision, so that his opponent may have no time to start an attack against the King-side or even in the centre. For, no doubt, the White Queen installed at K Kt 3 (via K 3) would exercise a pressure on Black's King-side if he eventually Castles on that side.

| 3. ...... | Kt—Q B 3 |
| 4. Q—K 3 | B—K 2 |

Black could also have played Kt —B 3, for the following variation is mere bluff and eventually turns to Black's advantage : 5. P—K 5, Kt—K Kt 5 ; 6. Q—K 4, P—Q 4 ! ; 7. P×P e. p. ch., B—K 3 ; 8. B— Q R 6 (or 8. P×P, Q—Q 8 ch !), Q×P ; 9. B×P, Q—Kt 5 ch ! 10. Q×Q, Kt×Q.

5. B—Q 2	Kt—B 3
6. Kt—Q B 3	Castles
7. Castles	P—Q 4 !

This advance, which at first sight appears somewhat risky, in view of the position of White's Q R, will on the contrary allow Black to extract the maximum return from his advanced development. 7. ....P—Q 3 ; would result in almost a close game and White would find time to complete his neglected development.

8. P × P   Kt × P
9. Q—Kt 3   B—R 5 !

Providing without loss of time against the threat 10. B—K R 6. Black's advantage is now evident.

10. Q—B 3   B—K 3

The sacrifice initiated by this move is full of promise and on the other hand devoid of risk, for Black will have an equivalent in material for his Queen. It would, however, have been more logical to adopt the following variation : 10. ....Kt × Kt ; 11. B × Kt, Q—Kt 4 ch ; 12. B—Q 2 (else 12. ....B—Kt 5), Q—Q B 4 !; 13. B—K 3, Q—Q R 4 ; which would have given Black a dominating position without such complications as defy exact calculation.

11. B—K 3 !

Calling for the subsequent combination, for 11. ....Q Kt—K 2 ; would be bad because of 12. Kt × Kt, followed by 13. Q—R 5, and 14. P—Q B 4, etc.

See Diagram.

11. ......   Kt × Kt !

Black obtains Rook, Knight, and Pawn for his Queen while maintaining the superior position. The sacrifice is therefore fully justified. Much less strong would be : 11. ....Q Kt—Kt 5; 12. P—Q R 3, Kt × Kt; 13. R × Q, Kt (Kt 5)—R 7 ch ; 14. K—Q 2, Kt—Kt 8 ch ; 15. K—K 1, and the two Black Knights would find themselves in a tragi-comical situation.

Position after White's 11th move.

12. R × Q   Kt × P ch
13. K—Kt 1   Q R × R
14. B—K 2   Kt (R 7)—Kt 5
15. Kt—R 3   K R—K 1

Essential as a basis for all the subsequent combinations.

16. Kt—B 4

16. R—Q 1, B—Q 4 ; 17. Q—R 5, B—B 3 was no better, as Black now threatens 18. ....B—K 5.

Position after White's 16th move.

16. ......   B—B 4
17. R—Q B 1   P—K Kt 3

Preparing the combination Kt × P followed by Kt (B 3)—Kt 5, etc. which at present would not be sufficient, *e.g.*: 17. ....Kt × P; 18. R × Kt, Kt—Kt 5; 19. Kt—Q 3!, R—K 5; 20. Kt × Kt!, etc.

18. P—Kt 4

In order to exchange the dangerous Black Bishop.

18. ......   B—K 5
19. Q—R 3   B—B 3
20. B—B 3

White seems to be able to disentangle his forces now; but nevertheless Black's position still remains very strong, even after the unavoidable exchange.

20. ......   B × B
21. Q × B   Kt—K 4
22. Q—K 2

It is clear that the capture of the Q Kt P would entail a rapid disintegration through the combined action of the K B and the Q R, the latter seizing the open Q Kt file.

Position after White's 22nd move.

22. ......   P—B 4!

A very important move which puts renewed vigour into Black's attack. White in particular threatened to force further simplifications by 23. P—B 3, Kt (Kt 5)—Q 6; 24. Kt × Kt, Kt × Kt; 25. R—Q 1, etc.

By his last move Black frustrates this plan, and, if necessary, aims at posting a Knight at Q 6 by P—B 5, etc. As White cannot reply 23. B × P, because of 23. ....Kt (K4)—Q 6; 24. Q × R ch, R × Q; 25. Kt × Kt, Kt—B 3, etc., weakening his right wing, he has to attempt a counter-attack which Black allows him no time to develop.

23. R—Kt 1   P—B 5
24. P—R 4   Kt—Q 4

The renewed complications resulting from this move required the most exact calculations.

25. Kt × Kt   R × Kt
26. P—B 4

If 26. P—Kt 5, B—Kt 2; 27. R—Q 1, then 27. ....R—Kt 4; 28. B—Q 4, R—K 3, etc., also to Black's advantage.

26. ......   Kt—Q 6!

Black takes immediate advantage of the weakening of the White Bishop resulting from 26. P—B 4.

27. Q—B 3

If White had taken the Knight the sequel would have been: 27. ....R × P; 28. R—Kt 3, B—Q 5!; 29. Q—Q B 2 (not 29. Q × R, P × Q; 30. B × B, R—K 8 ch; 31. K—R 2, P—Q 7! and wins), B × B; 30. Q × P, R (K 1)—Q 1; with the better game. However, this variation is more favourable than the one chosen by White, after which Black can force the win by a fresh sacrifice.

See Diagram.

27. ......   R—Q Kt 4!

Decisive! Now White has to take the Knight, for after 28. P—Kt 3, R—Q R 4; 29. P × Kt, Black could force the win by 29. ....P × Kt P;

Position after White's 27th move.

Position after Black's 30th move.

30. K—B 1, B—B 6 ; 31. K—Q 1,
R—R 8 ch, etc. A curious position,
for although Black has only a Rook
for the Queen, White is without
resource.

28. P×Kt	R×P ch
29. K—B 1	P×P
30. K—Q 1	

30. R—Kt 2, R—B 1 ch ; 31.
K—Q 1, etc., is merely an inversion of moves.

30.	R—Q B 1 !

See Diagram.

Against the threat 31. .... R (B 1)
—B 7, White's only defence was 31.
R—Kt 2. But it was in no way
sufficient for a draw, despite the
opinion of all the critics who anno-

tated the game at the time it was
played, and in this case Black would
have won as follows : 31. ....R—
Kt 8 ch ; 32. K—Q 2, R—Kt 6 ;
33. K—Q 1 (or A), B—B 6 ! ; 34.
B—B 1, B—Kt 5 ! and White is
helpless against the threats 35. ....
P—Q 7 ; and 35. ....R—Kt 8.
    A. 33. K—K 1, R—B 8 ch ; 34.
K—B 2 (or 34. B×R, P—Q 7 ch),
B×P ch and wins.

This analysis shows the correctness of the sacrifice initiated on
move 11, and the soundness of the
final combination.

31. P—Kt 5	R (B 1)—B 7 !
32. K—K 1	R—Kt 8 ch
33. Q—Q 1	B—B 6 ch

White resigns.

CHAPTER VIII

ALL-RUSSIAN MASTERS' TOURNAMENT AT ST. PETERSBURG, JANUARY, 1914

GAME 20

RUY LOPEZ

White :   *Black :*
A. ALEKHIN.   H. LÖVENFISCH.

1. P—K 4	P—K 4
2. Kt—K B 3	Kt—Q B 3
3. B—Kt 5	P—Q R 3
4. B—R 4	Kt—B 3
5. Q—K 2	B—K 2
6. P—B 3	P—Q Kt 4
7. B—Kt 3	Castles

An unusual move. The usual line of play commencing 7. ....P—Q 3 is Black's best.

8. P—Q R 4

But White does not answer with the strongest move, and thereby allows Black to equalize the game. He should play 8. P—Q 4 (but not 8. B—Q 5 because of 8. ....B—Q 3 !) 8. ....P—Q 3 (or 8. ....P×P ; 9. P—K 5, R—K 1 ; 10. Castles, etc.); 9. P—Q 5, Kt—Q R 4 ; 10. B—B 2 followed by Q Kt—Q 2 and P—Q R 4, thereby fully justifying 5. Q—K 2.

8. ......   P—Q 4 !

The right reply.

9. R P×P

The answer 9. K P×P would, of course, be unfavourable for White after 9. ....P—K 5 !

9. ......   Q P×P

This is very tempting and leads to very interesting complications, from which, however, White succeeds in emerging with advantage. By playing 9. ....B—K Kt 5 !; 10. P—Q 3 ! (if 10. P×Kt, P×P), Q P×P ; 11. Q P×P, P×P ; 12. R×R, Q×R ; 13. Castles. Black would have secured equality at least.

Position after Black's 9th move.

10. Kt—Kt 5 !

White in this manner wins a Pawn to the detriment of his development. He had, however, foreseen that Black's pressure would be only temporary, since he could not in the long run maintain his Pawn at K 5.

The whole variation is based on the fact that Black cannot now play 10. . . . . B—K Kt 5 on account of 11. Kt×B P ! (not 11. P—B 3, P×B P ; 12. P×B P, P×P ; 13. R×R, Q×R ; 14. P×B, Kt—R 4 ! with advantage to Black) ; 11. . . . . R × Kt ; 12. Q—B 4 ! and White wins at least the Exchange ; not, however, 12. B×R ch, K×B ; 13. Q—B 4 ch, B—K 3 ; 14. Q×Kt, B—Q 4 ! and Black wins.

10. . . . . . .   Kt—R 2 !

This is Black's best chance.

11. P×P

Of course 11. Kt×K P would be inadequate, because of 11. . . . . Kt×P !

11. . . . . . .   B—K B 4
12. B—B 2

The key of the adverse position, Black's Pawn on K 5, must be attacked as quickly as possible.

12. . . . . . .   Q—Q 4
13. P—B 4

Thus enabling his Q Kt to be developed ; but on the other hand the text-move renders the squares Q 5 and Q Kt 5 available to Black's Knight now occupying Q R 2.

13. . . . . . .   Q—Q 5

After the interesting continuation 13. . . . . Q—B 3 the danger White would run is more apparent than real, e.g.: 13. . . . . Q—B 3 ;

14. Kt—B 3, P—K 6 ; 15. B×B, Q×Kt P ; 16. R—B 1, Q×Kt (or 16. . . . . P×B P ch ; 17. R×P, Q×Kt ; 18. P—Q 4, etc.) ; 17. B P×P, Q—R 5 ch ; 18. K—Q 1 and White has the advantage.

14. Kt—B 3   B—K Kt 5
15. Q—K 3   Kt—B 3 !

Being unable to defend his K P any longer, Black attempts to rid himself of the dangerous White Q R P, a plan which he later on abandons, with very serious consequences.

16. Kt (Kt 5)×K P
                Kt—Q Kt 5 !
17. Kt×Kt ch   B×Kt

The variation 17. . . . . P×Kt ; 18. B—Kt 1 ! (but not 18. B—K 4 because of 18. . . . . P—K B 4) was no better.

18. B—K 4   Q×P

This continuation of the attack at all cost will be countered by a sacrifice on the 20th move, whereby White will secure a decisive advantage on the Queen-side. After 18. . . . . R×P ; 19. R×R, Kt×R ; 20. P—Q 3, Kt—Kt 5 ; 21. Castles, Black would have retained some drawing chances by reason of the weakness of White's Pawns on the Queen-side.

19. P—R 7 !

The despised Pawn now becomes formidable.

19. . . . . . .   K R—Q 1
20. P—Kt 3 !

By this sacrifice White is enabled to Castle, and he thereby puts an end to the hostile attack. Black cannot reply 20. . . . . Kt—Q 6 ch because of 21. K—B 1, etc.

| 20. ...... | Q × P |
| 21. Castles | Kt—B 7 |

A little better, but insufficient to save the game, was 21. ....P—B 3 etc.

Position after Black's 21st move.

22. Q—B 5 !

The decisive move. If 22. .... Kt × R ; 23. B × R, R × B ; 24. Q—B 6 ! and wins. Much less effective was 22. B × R, Kt × Q ; 25. B—Q 5, Kt × B ; 26. P—R 8 = Q, Kt × Kt ; 25. P × Kt, Q × P, and Black with his two Bishops has a very fine game, apart from the fact that he has two Pawns for the Exchange.

| 22. ...... | P—B 3 |

As hopeless as every other move.

23. R—Kt 1	Q—K 3
24. B × Kt	B—K 2
25. Q—Kt 6	Q—Q 2
26. R—R 1	P—K B 4
27. B—R 4	K R—Q B 1
28. B—R 3	B—Kt 4
29. B—B 5	B × P
30. Kt—Q 5 !	B—K 7
31. Kt—K 7 ch	K—R 1
32. Kt × R	R × Kt
33. B × P	Black resigns

GAME 21

RUY LOPEZ

White :   *Black :*
A. ALEKHIN.   A. NIEMZOVITCH

1. P—K 4	P—K 4
2. Kt—K B 3	Kt—Q B 3
3. B—Kt 5	P—Q R 3
4. B—R 4	Kt—B 3
5. Castles	Kt × P

The most analysed variation of the Ruy Lopez. In the latest practical tests the results are somewhat in White's favour, and it occurs less and less in master-play.

6. P—Q 4	P—Q Kt 4
7. B—Kt 3	P—Q 4
8. P × P	B—K 3
9. P—B 3	B—K 2
10. Q Kt—Q 2	

After 10. B—K 3, Castles ; 11. Q Kt—Q 2, Kt × Kt ; 12. Q × Kt, Kt—R 4 ; Black has a satisfactory game. Less recommendable, however, are : 11. ....P—B 4 ; 12. P × P e. p., Kt × P ; 13. Kt—Kt 5 ! etc. ; and 11. ....B—K Kt 5 ; because of 12. Kt × Kt, P × Kt ; 13. Q—Q 5 !, etc. (see game No. 91).

| 10. ...... | Kt—B 4 |

Better would have been 10. .... Castles ; 11. B—B 2, P—B 4 ; 12. P × P e. p., Kt × P (B 3) ; although in this case also White's game after 13. Kt—Kt 3 (not 13. Kt—Kt 5, because of 13. ....B—K Kt 5 ; 14. P—B 3, B—B 1 !, etc.) is somewhat preferable.

11. B—B 2

See Diagram

| 11. ...... | B—Kt 5 |

11. ....Castles, would be insufficient because of Bogoljuboff's ingenious innovation in his game against Réti (Stockholm Tournament, 1920):

Position after White's 11th move.

12. Kt—Q 4 !, Kt×P ; 13. P—
K B 4, B—Kt 5 ; 14. Q—K 1, B—
R 5 ; 15. Q×Kt, R—K 1; 16. Kt—
B 6, Q—Q 2 ; 17. P—B 5 !, and
White must win.

| 12. R—K 1 | Castles |
| 13. Kt—Kt 3 | Kt—K 5 |

If 13. ....Kt—K 3 (Janowski—
Lasker, Paris, 1913) White obtains
a fine attacking game after 14. Q—
Q 3. The text-move is an innovation which is refuted in the present
game.

14. B—B 4 !

Not 14. B×Kt, P×B ; 15. Q×Q,
R×Q ; 16. R×P, R—Q 8 ch ; 17.
Kt—K 1, B—K B 4 ; 18. R—K 2,
B—Q 6 ; 19. R—K 3, B—Kt 4 ;
whereas with the text-move White
threatens to win a Pawn.

14.	P—B 4
15. P×P e. p.	Kt×P (B 3)
16. Q—Q 3	Kt—K 5

This Pawn sacrifice will ultimately prove insufficient ; but
Black's position was already beset
with difficulties. If, for instance, 16.
....B—R 4 ; then 17. Kt—R 4 !
with a great positional superiority.

| 17. B×P | Q—Q 2 |

Obviously Black cannot afford 17.
....Q×B ; because of 18. Q×P ch,
etc.

| 18. Kt—K 5 ! | Kt×Kt |
| 19. B×Kt | B—R 5 |

It is clear that Black cannot capture the B P with the R because of
20. R×Kt.

| 20. B—Kt 3 | B×B |
| 21. R P×B | B—B 4 |

At first sight this move seems to
create difficulties for White, for
instance after 22. Q—K 2, the
manœuvre 22. ....B—Kt 5, would
force the White Queen back to Q 3.

Position after Black's 21st move.

22. Q—Q 4 !

This definitely ensures an advantage, since the threat of Kt×Kt P
by Black is illusory, *e.g.* : 22. ....
Kt×Kt P ; 23. Kt—B 5, Q—Q 3 ;
24. B—Kt 3 ! and wins. Consequently Black is now forced to look
after his weak point, Q 4.

22. ......   K R—Q 1

Q R—Q 1 would have been
slightly better, but the game was
lost in any event.

23. Q R—Q 1   Q—B 2

Renewing the threat of 23. ....
Kt × Kt P.

24. Kt—Q 2 !

To this move Black cannot reply
with 24. .... Kt × Kt P, because of
25. B—Kt 3 ; nor is 24. .... Kt × Kt
feasible, on account of the following variation : 25. B × B, Kt—
B 5 ; 26. B—K 6 ch, K—R 1 ; 27.
B × P !, Kt × P ; 28. R—Kt 1, Kt—
B 5 ; 29. B × R ! and wins.

24. ......   Kt × B P

A desperate sacrifice. But similarly after 24. .... B—Kt 3 ; 25.
B—Kt 3, Kt—B 3 ; 26. Kt—B 3,
the win was only a question of
technique.

25. B × B	Kt × R
26. R × Kt	Q × Kt P
27. B—K 6 ch	K—R 1
28. B × P	Q R—B 1
29. Kt—K 4	Q—R 5
30. P—Q Kt 3	R—B 3
31. Q—B 2	

More straightforward would have
been : 31. B × R !, R × Q ; 32. P × R,
and the passed Pawn would have
become irresistible. But once the
Queens are exchanged the ending
could not present any difficulties for
White.

31.	Q—R 4
32. Q—B 3	Q × Q

Evidently forced.

33. P × Q	P—Kt 3
34. R—Q 2	R—Kt 3
35. P—B 4	P × P
36. P × P	R—Kt 8 ch
37. K—B 2	P—Q R 4
38. P—B 5	R—B 8
39. P—B 6	K—Kt 2

See Diagram.

40. B—B 4 !

Position after Black's 39th move.

Winning the Exchange as well, for
after 40. .... R—Q B 1 ; 41. R—
Q 7 ch, K—R 3 ; 42. B—Q 5, or if

40. .... R × R ; 41. Kt × R, followed by 42. P—B 7 and Black
loses at once.

40.	R × B
41. R × R	R × P
42. R—Q 7 ch	K—R 3
43. K—Kt 3	R—B 5

Or if 43. .... R—B 7 ; 44. P—B 4,
R × P ; 45. Kt—Kt 5 and the
mate cannot be avoided.

44. Kt—B 2 !

Position after White's 44th move.

44. ...... K—Kt 4

If 44. ....R—Q R 5 ; 45. Kt—Kt 4 ch, K—R 4 ! ; 46. R—Q 5 ch, P—Kt 4 ; 47. R—Q 6 and mate to follow. Or 44. ....P—Kt 4 ; 45. Kt—Kt 4 ch, followed by 46. Kt—K 5 ch and White wins.

45. R—Q 5 ch K—B 3
46. R×P Black resigns.

GAME 22

QUEEN'S GAMBIT DECLINED

White : *Black :*
S. VON FREYMANN. A. ALEKHIN.

1. P—Q 4 P—Q 4
2. Kt—K B 3 Kt—K B 3
3. P—B 4 P—K 3
4. B—Kt 5

This move is of doubtful value, for it allows the following reply, hit upon by Duras. It is better to play 4. Kt—Q B 3 first.

4. ...... P—K R 3 !

After this move White has nothing better than to take the Knight, leaving his opponent with two Bishops, for if the Bishop retreats, the acceptance of the Gambit is in favour of Black.

5. B—R 4 P×P

More precise would have been 5. ....B—Kt 5 ch; followed by P×P; as then the Gambit Pawn could be held by P—Q Kt 4, etc.

6. Q—R 4 ch

The only way of regaining the Pawn. Black threatened 6. .... B—Kt 5 ch; followed by 7. ....P—Q Kt 4.

6. ...... Q Kt—Q 2
7. Q ×B P P—B 4
8. Kt—B 3 P—R 3

With the intention of developing the Q B on the long diagonal, a plan which White, as the sequel shows, will be unable to frustrate.

9. P—R 4

A scheme based on insufficient means. Evidently 9. P—K 3 would have been better, although in any case Black's position was preferable.

9. ...... P—Q Kt 4 !

Black still persists, for if 10. R P × P, R P × P ; the White Queen and Rook would both be *en prise*.

10. Q—Q 3 P—B 5
11. Q—Kt 1

Position after White's 11th move.

11. ...... B—Kt 2 !

A Pawn sacrifice, the object of which is to obstruct White's development through pressure on White's Q B 3.

12. P × P

It would have been preferable to decline the offer of a Pawn. But in any event, even after 12. P—K 3, Q—Kt 3 ; White's position would have remained distinctly inferior.

12.	P × P
13. Kt × P	B—Kt 5 ch
14. Kt—B 3	P—Kt 4
15. B—Kt 3	Kt—K 5
16. Q—B 1	

All White's last moves were obviously forced.

| 16. ...... | Kt—Kt 3 |

Threatening 17. ....Kt—R 5.

17. R × R	Q × R
18. Kt—Q 2	Kt × Kt (Q 7)
19. K × Kt	Q—R 7 !

Initiating the deciding manœuvre. Black again threatens 20. ....Kt—R 5 ; and does not allow his opponent the respite he needs to disentangle his position by 20. P—K 3.

| 20. K—Q 1 | Q—Kt 6 ch |
| 21. Q—B 2 | |

Now the Black Q B P will move straight on to Queen.

| 21. ...... | B × Kt |
| 22. P × B | |

Position after White's 22nd move.

| 22. ...... | B—K 5 ! |

Simple and immediately decisive.

| 23. Q × Q | P × Q |
| 24. P—K 3 | |

Or 24. K—B 1, Kt—B 5 ; and mates in a few moves.

| 24. ...... | P—Kt 7 |

White resigns.

GAME 23

FOUR KNIGHTS' GAME

| *White :* | *Black :* |
| A. NIEMZOVITCH. | A. ALEKHIN. |

1. P—K 4	P—K 4
2. Kt—K B 3	Kt—Q B 3
3. Kt—B 3	Kt—B 3
4. B—Kt 5	Kt—Q 5 !

Rubinstein has, in my opinion, made one of his finest contributions to the theory of the openings in the discovery and analysis of the variations springing from this move.

White, if he does not wish to run the risk of dangerous complications resulting from the capture of the proffered Pawn, has nothing better than 5. Kt × Kt, P × Kt ; 6. P—K 5, P × Kt ; 7. P × Kt, Q × P (not 7. ....P × P ch ; 8. B × P, Q × P ; 9. Castles with an irresistible attack) ; 8. Q P × P, B—K 2 ! ; 9. Castles, Castles with approximately an equal game.

The present game affords a typical example of the dangers to which White exposes himself when seeking the demolition of the Rubinstein variation.

5. B—B 4

Alternatives are :

I.—5. Castles, Kt × B ; 6. Kt × Kt, P—B 3 ; 7. Kt—B 3, P—Q 3 ; 8. P—Q 4, Q—B 2.

II.—5. Kt × P, Q—K 2 ; 6. Kt—B 3, Kt × B ; 7. Kt × Kt, Q × P ch ; 8. Q—K 2, Q × Q ch ; 9. K × Q, Kt—Q 4 ; 10. P—B 4, P—Q R 3 ; and in neither case does White have any advantage.

5.	B—B 4
6. Kt × P	Q—K 2 !
7. Kt—Q 3	

After 7. Kt—B 3 Black would also have obtained a strong attack by 7. ....P—Q 4 ! On the other hand, it is clear that White cannot capture the K B P with the Kt, because of 7. ....P—Q 4 ! nor with the B, because of 7. ....K—Q 1, followed by 8. ....P—Q 3.

| 7. ...... | P—Q 4 ! |

The point of this variation.

8. B × P

Or 8. Kt × P, Kt × Kt ; 9. B × Kt, P—Q B 3. If 8. Kt × B, P × B and Black has the advantage.

8.	Kt × B
9. Kt × Kt	Q × P ch
10. Kt—K 3	B—Q 3
11. Castles	B—K 3

Now the sacrifice of the Pawn is greatly compensated by the superiority in development secured by Black.

White finds himself confronted with great difficulties resulting from the fact that his Knights lack points of support in the centre.

| 12. Kt—K 1 | Castles (Q R) |

To profit as quickly as possible by the open files in the centre.

| 13. P—Q B 3 | Kt—B 4 |
| 14. Q—B 2 | |

14. P—Q 3 at once would be a little better, although in this case Black would also maintain a good attacking position by 14. ....Q—K R 5 ; 15. Kt—B 3, Q—R 4.

Now Black demolishes the hostile position by a series of moves, apparently quite simple and by that very fact difficult to discover.

Position after White's 14th move.

| 14. ...... | Q—K R 5 ! |

More plausible was 14. ....Q—K B 5, provoking 15. P—K Kt 3 and allowing Black to carry on the attack by the advance of the K R P. But the continuation 15. P—K Kt 3, Q—Kt 4 ; 16. P—Q 4, Q—B 3 ; 17. Kt (K 1)—Kt 2 or Kt—Q 3 seems to give White adequate defensive resources.

It is for this reason that Black sought to make the direct attack against the King coincide with a strong pressure on the centre.

To attain this latter end it was of paramount importance to compel White to weaken the K file by the advance of his K B P.

15. Kt—B 3

Now 15. P—K Kt 3 would be faulty, on account of 15. ....Q—R 6.

| 15. ...... | Q—K B 5 |

Threatening 16. ....Kt—R 5.

| 16. Kt × Kt | B × Kt |
| 17. P—Q 3 | Q—K Kt 5 |

Threatening 18. ....Q—R 4 ; followed by 19. ....B × P and 20. ....B × P ch.

18. Kt—Q 4   Q—R 4
19. P—K B 4

Black has thus attained the goal which he had in view on his 14th move.

19. ......   K R—K 1
20. P—Q Kt 4

If 20. B—Q 2, Black would maintain his advantage by 20. ....B—B 4 ; 21. Q R—K 1, R—K 7 !, etc.

20. ......   P—Q B 4 !

Thus forcing the exchange of White's only active piece.

21. Kt×B   Q×Kt

Threatening 22. ....P—B 5.

22. Q—Q 2   B—B 2
23. R—B 3

All this is compulsory.

23. ......   P×P
24. P×P

Position after White's 24th move.

24. ......   P—K Kt 4 !

After this move Black regains his Pawn at least, and maintains his superiority in position.

25. P×P

If 25. B—Kt 2, which was, however, better, the continuation would have been 25. ....P×P ; 26. Q—B 3, K—Kt 1, and Black would have won the weak Q P in the end. The text-move causes a speedy collapse.

25. ......   Q—K 4
26. B—Kt 2   Q×P ch
27. K—B 1

Position after White's 27th move.

27. ......   B—Kt 6 ?

This premature move allows White to secure a draw. The game was easily won by 27. ....Q—R 8 ch ; 28. K—B 2, Q—R 5 ch ; 29. K—B 1, B—Kt 6 !! ; after which White would have nothing else than 30. Q—B 3 ch, K—Kt 1 ; 31. Q—B 5, P—Kt 3! ; 32. Q—Kt 1, R×P! ; 33. R×R, Q—B 5 ch ; 34. R—B 3, Q—B 5 ch and mate next move.

28. B—Q 4 !

And now behold Black himself reduced to seeking a drawing variation ! The following sacrifice answers this purpose.

28. ′......	R × B !
29. Q—B 3 ch	K—Kt 1
30. Q × R	B—K 4
31. Q—Q 7	R—Q B 1
32. R × P !	

By this threat of mate White eliminates all danger. Unfortunately for him, he allows himself to be intoxicated by a mirage of victory ; but, by reason of the exposed position of his King, this conception bears great risks in its train.

| 32. ...... | Q—R 8 ch |
| 33. K—B 2 | Q—R 5 ch |

Naturally not 33. R—B 7 ch, because of 34. K—K 3 and wins.

| 34. K—K 2 | Q—R 4 ch |
| 35. P—Kt 4 | |

This move is altogether too venturesome, and merely gives Black fresh chances.

After 35. K—B 1 Black would have nothing better than the draw by 35. ....Q—R 8 ch, etc.

35	Q—R 7 ch
36. K—B 3	Q—Kt 6 ch
37. K—K 4	

Forced, for if 37. K—K 2, Q—Kt 7 ch, followed by 38. ....B × R or R—B 7 ch according to circumstances, and Black wins.

| 37. ...... | B—B 2 |

Threatening Q—K 4 ch followed by Q × R.

| 38. R—Q B 1 | Q—Kt 7 ch |
| 39. K—K 3 | B—Kt 3 ch |

Position áfter Black's 39th move.

40. P—Q 4

This loses at once. The only reply was 40. R—B 5, with the continuation 40. ....R—Q 1 ; 41. Q—B 5 ! (else 41. ....Q—Kt 6 ch), R—K 1 ch ; 42. K—Q 4, Q—Kt 7 ch ; 43. K—B 4, Q × R P ch ; 44. K—B 3, and Black, having to reckon with the threat R × P ch, could still not force the win.

| 40. ...... | R—Q 1 ! |

Decisive.

41. R—B 7

If the White Queen moves, Black would win by 41. ....B × P ch, followed by 42. ....Q—K B 7 ch, etc.

41.	Q—Kt 6 ch
42. R—B 3	Q—K 8 ch
43. K—Q 3	Q—Q 8 ch
44. K—K 3	B × R

White resigns.

CHAPTER IX

INTERNATIONAL TOURNAMENT AT
ST. PETERSBURG, MAY, 1914

GAME 24

PETROFF'S DEFENCE

White :   *Black :*
A. ALEKHIN.   F. J. MARSHALL.

1. P—K 4	P—K 4
2. Kt—K B 3	Kt—K B 3
3. Kt × P	P—Q 3
4. Kt—K B 3	Kt × P
5. P—Q 4	P—Q 4
6. B—Q 3	B—Q 3
7. P—B 4	

This variation of the Petroff does not cause Black any difficulty. White could secure better chances by 3. P—Q 4 (Steinitz), or 5. Q—K 2 (Lasker), or even 5. Kt—B 3.

7.	B—Kt 5 ch !
8. Q Kt—Q 2	Kt × Kt

This exchange, which allows White quite an appreciable advantage in development, appears hardly justified. The correct line of play was 8. ....Castles ; 9. Castles, B × Kt ! ; 10. B × B, B—Kt 5, with at least an equal game.

9. B × Kt	Q—K 2 ch
10. Q—K 2	Q × Q ch

It is interesting to notice that this plausible exchange is later on shown up as a decisive mistake. Black must first play 10. ....B × B ch ; 11. K × B, Q × Q ch ; 12. B × Q, P × P ; 13. B × P, Castles ; after which White would have maintained a slight superiority in position, but Black's game would still remain very defendable.

11. K × Q	B × B
12. K × B	B—K 3

If now 12. ....P × P, then 13. K R—K 1 ch ! with still greater effect than in the actual game, White having preserved his Bishop for the attack against his opponent's undeveloped game.

13. P × P	B × P
14. K R—K 1 ch	K—Q 1
15. B—K 4 !	B × B

Forced, for if 15. ....P—Q B 3 White would win a Pawn at once by exchange of Bishops, followed by 17. R—K 5.

16. R × B	R—K 1

This move was absolutely necessary to prevent the threatened doubling of White's Rooks on the K file.

| 17. | Q R—K 1 | R × R |
| 18. | R × R | Kt—B 3 |

Position after Black's 18th move.

19. R—Kt 4 !

The winning manœuvre. On the other hand, 19. Kt—Kt 5 was insufficient, on account of 19. .... K—Q 2 ! Now Black is going to lose a Pawn by force.

| 19. | ...... | P—K Kt 3 |
| 20. | R—R 4 ! | K—K 2 |

Best in the circumstances, for after 20. ....P—K R 4 ; 21. P— K Kt 4 followed by 22. P × P White would establish a passed Pawn.

21.	R × P	R—Q 1
22.	R—R 4	R—Q 4
23.	R—K 4 ch !	

Forcing the retreat of Black's King, for after 23. ....K—B 3 ; 24. K—B 3, the threat 25. R—K 8 would have been very dangerous for the opponent.

| 23. | ...... | K—B 1 |
| 24. | K—B 3 | R—K B 4 |

Contemplating ....Kt—Q 4 ; to cause White the maximum of technical difficulties.

| 25. | R—K 2 | P—R 3 |

If 25. ....Kt—K 2 White would have replied 26. R—K 5 and the continuation of the game would scarcely be modified.

| 26. | P—Q R 3 | Kt—K 2 |
| 27. | R—K 5 ! | R—B 3 |

After the exchange of Rooks, Black could no longer save the game.

28. K—Q 3

Preparing 29. R—Q B 5, which Black prevents by his reply, but at the cost of a new weakness at Q B 2 which White will proceed to exploit without delay.

| 28. | ...... | P—Kt 3 |
| 29. | R—K 2 ! | |

White, as we see from the sequel, proposes to sacrifice a Pawn in order to occupy the 7th rank with his Rook and thus to obtain a passed Pawn. This manœuvre is the shortest and surest means of securing the victory.

| 29. | ...... | Kt—Q 4 |
| 30. | K—K 4 | Kt—B 5 |

Or 30. ....R—K 3 ch ; 31. Kt—K 5, Kt—B 3 ch ; 32. K—B 3 and White dominates the board.

| 31. | R—B 2 | Kt × P |
| 32. | Kt—K 5 ! | |

Not at once R × P on account of 32. ....R—B 5 ch followed by 33. ....R × Kt, whereas now, since White threatens 33. Kt—Q 7 ch, Black cannot save his Q B P.

32.	......	K—K 1
33.	R × P	R × P
34.	Kt—B 4 !	

A very important move. The Knight is going to be posted on Q Kt 7, where it will guard the advance of the passed Q P.

34.	P—Q Kt 4
35. Kt—Q 6 ch	K—B 1
36. P—Q 5	P—B 3
37. Kt—Kt 7 !	Kt—B 5
38. P—Kt 4	P—Kt 4
39. P—Q 6	Kt—K 3

Position after Black's 39th move.

40. K—Q 5 !

The *coup de grâce*. White's Rook cannot be captured on account of 41. P×Kt, R—B 7; 42. Kt—B 5 ! Similarly, after 40. ....R—K 7 White would win easily by 41. K—B 6, Kt—Q 5 ch ; 42. K—Kt 6, etc., so, as a last resource, Black attempts to exploit his King-side Pawns after the sacrifice of the Rook for the passed Pawn. But this manœuvre is foredoomed to failure.

40.	Kt—B 5 ch
41. K—B 6	R×K R P
42. Kt—B 5	

Preventing the sacrifice of Black's Knight for the Pawn, and winning a whole Rook.

42.	R—Q 7
43. R—B 8 ch	K—B 2
44. P—Q 7	Kt—B 3
45. Kt×Kt	K×Kt
46. P—Q 8=Q	R×Q
47. R×R	P—Kt 5

48. R—K 8 ch	K—B 2
49. R—K 2	P—B 4
50. K—Q 5	K—B 3
51. K—Q 4	P—B 5
52. K—K 4	K—Kt 4
53. R—Q B 2	P—B 6
54. R—Q 2	K—R 5
55. K—B 4	Black resigns.

GAME 25

FALKBEER COUNTER-GAMBIT

| *White :* | *Black :* |
| A. ALEKHIN. | DR. S. TARRASCH. |

| 1. P—K B 4 | P—K 4 |
| 2. P—K 4 | |

From's Gambit accepted offers White at best only an equal game.

2.	P—Q 4
3. K P×P	P—K 5
4. P—Q 3	Kt—K B 3

At the time the present game was played the variations springing from this move were considered advantageous for White, thanks especially to analyses by the late Simon Alapin.

Recently, however, Dr. Tarrasch succeeded in invalidating this opinion, introducing in his game against Spielmann at Mährisch-Ostrau, 1924, an improvement of great importance (see note to Black's 6th move).

| 5. P×P | Kt×K P |
| 6. Kt—K B 3 | B—K B 4 |

An innovation which the sequel shows to be insufficient. The correct line of play, demonstrated by Dr. Tarrasch in the game mentioned, is 6. ....B—Q B 4 ; 7. Q—K 2, B—B 4 !, and if 8. P—K Kt 4? then 8. ....Castles !, with a winning sacrificial attack.

7. B—K 3

This move deprives Black of his best chance on the diagonal Q R 2 —K Kt 8, and leaves him without compensation for the Pawn he has given up.

7. ...... P—Q B 3
8. B—B 4 P—Q Kt 4

Trying to keep his opponent busy lest he secure his position definitely by Castling.

9. B—Kt 3

White could play equally well 9. B—K 2, P—Q R 3; 10. P—Q R 4 !, P—Kt 5; 11. P×P, Q×Q ch; 12. B×Q, Kt×P, etc., but the combination based on the text-move offered better prospects.

9. ...... P—B 4

Position after Black's 9th move.

10. P—Q 6 !

Bringing about an advantageous simplification in view of his extra Pawn. The Q P cannot be captured by the Black Queen on account of 11. Q×Q, followed by B—Q 5, etc.

10. ...... P—B 5
11. Q—Q 5 Kt—Q 2
12. Q×B Kt×P
13. Q—Q 5 B—K 2
14. Castles Castles
15. Kt—B 3 Kt—B 3
16. Q—Q 2 P×B

Just in time, for White threatened 17. Kt×P, etc.

17. R P×P

White's advantage in material is in no way diminished by his having a doubled Pawn, for he will always be in a position to obtain a passed Pawn by advancing his Q B P.

17. ...... P—Kt 5
18. Kt—Q 5 Kt—B 4
19. Kt×B ch Q×Kt

White has still a slight weakness in the centre, which he will subsequently eliminate by holding and strengthening his Q 4.

20. K R—K 1 K R—Q 1
21. B—Q 4 ! Kt×B
22. Kt×Kt Q—B 4
23. Q R—Q 1

Intending to play P—B 3 once the Black Rooks are doubled on the Queen's file.

23. ...... R—Q 4
24. P—R 3 Q R—Q 1

Position after Black's 24th move.

25. P—B 3

After this move White's position is invulnerable. Black is forced to adopt a waiting policy, which is all the more distressing as he is minus a Pawn.

White's next moves aim at un-pinning the Knight, which will take a decisive part in the final onslaught when the White Rooks are doubled on the King's file.

25.	P—K R 3
26. Q—Q 3	Q—Q 3
27. Q—B 3	Kt—R 4

An inoffensive demonstration which cannot hinder White's plans.

| 28. R—K 4 | Kt—B 3 |

Of course not 28. ....P—B 4, because of 29. R—K 6.

29. R—K 3	Kt—R 4
30. R—K B 1	Kt—B 3
31. R (B 1)—K 1	

To be able to play 32. R—K 5, in answer to 31. ....Kt—R 4.

31.	Q—B 4
32. K—R 2	R—Q B 1
33. R (K 1)—K 2	

A subtle preparation to the following attacking move.

| 33. ...... | K—B 1 |
| 34. R—K 5 ! | |

Now Black cannot play 34. .... P×P; 35. P×P, Q×P; because of 36. R—Q B 2.

| 34. ...... | R (B 1)—Q 1 |
| 35. Kt—B 5 | |

Threatening amongst other things 36. P—B 4, R×R; 37. P×R, followed by 38. P—K 6, etc.

35.	Q—Kt 3
36. Q—Kt 3	Kt—R 4
37. Q—R 4	

Threatening mate in three by 37· R—K 8 ch !, etc.

See Diagram.

| 37. ...... | R×R |

A desperate move in an untenable dosition. Against 37. Kt—B 3,

Position after White's 37th move.

recommended by Dr. Tarrasch in the Tournament book as providing a sufficient defence for the time being, White had prepared the following pretty winning combination: 38. Kt×R P !, P×Kt; 39. R—K 6 !, P×R (alternatives are:

I.—39. ....R (Q 4)—Q 3; 40. Q×Kt, R×R; 41. R×R.

II.—39. ....R (Q 1)—Q 3; Q×P ch and mate in two).

40. Q×Kt ch, K—K 1; 41. R×P, R (Q 4)—Q 3; 42. Q—Kt 6 ch, K—R 1 (or 42. ....K—B 1; 43. Q—B 5 ch, K any; 44. R—K 7, etc.); 43. Q×P ch, K—Kt 1; 44. Q—Kt 6 ch, K—R 1; 45. Q—R 5 ch !, K—Kt 1; 46. R—K 7 ! and mate is unavoidable. Such a finale would have given the game a good chance of a brilliancy prize.

| 38. P×R | R—Q 8 |
| 39. R—K 3 | |

White could also have captured the Kt and then brought his King to R 4. The text-move is still more simple and hinders 39. ....P—Kt 3, which would prove disastrous for Black after 40. Q—K 7 ch, K—Kt 1; 41. Q—K 8 ch, K—R 2; 42. Q×P ch, K—R 1; 43. Kt—K 7 ! and wins.

| 39. ...... | Q—Kt 3 |
| 40. Q×P ch | Black resigns |

GAME 26

FRENCH DEFENCE

White :   *Black :*
DR. S. TARRASCH. A. ALEKHIN.

1.	P—K 4	P—K 3
2.	P—Q 4	P—Q 4
3.	Kt—Q B 3	Kt—K B 3
4.	B—Kt 5	

The variation 4. P×P, P×P ; 5. B—Kt 5, recommended by Svenonius, brings White no advantage at all after 5. ....Kt—B 3, which is favoured by the author and was successfully tried by Bogoljuboff *v.* Mieses (Berlin, 1920).

4.	......	B—Kt 5
5.	P×P	

This variation has gradually fallen into desuetude of late years. Players prefer to aim at a rapid King's side attack by : 5. P—K 5, P—K R 3 ; 6. P—Q 2, B×Kt ; 7. P×B, Kt—K 5 ; 8. Q—Kt 4, K—B 1 ! ; 9. P—K R 4 !, etc. But the latest master-practice, and particularly some of Dr. Tarrasch's games, tend to show that here too Black disposes of sufficient resources from the defensive point of view. Interesting, too, is Tchigorin's continuation : 5. P—K 5, P—K R 3 ; 6. P×Kt, P×B ; 7. P×P, R—Kt 1 ; 8. P—K R 4, P×P ; with the improvement 9. Q—Kt 4 ! instead of 9. Q—R 5. A game played by the author in Moscow, 1915, continued as follows :

9.	......	B—K 2
10.	P—K Kt 3 !	P—Q B 4
(10 ....B—B 3 was better.)		
11.	Kt P×P	P×P

See Diagram.

12.	P—R 5 !	P×Kt
13.	P—R 6	P×P
14.	R—Kt 1	Q—R 4 ch
15.	K—K 2	Q×P
16.	P—R 7	Q×R
17.	P×R=Q ch	K—Q 2

Position after Black's 11th move in Sub-Variation

18.	Q×B P	Q×P ch
19.	K—B 3	Kt—B 3 !
20.	Q (Kt 4)×P ch	K—B 2
21.	Q—B 4 ch	K—Kt 3
22.	Q (K 6)—K 3 ch	B—B 4
23.	P—Kt 8=Q	P—Kt 8=Q

Position after Black's 23rd move in Sub-Variation.

In this extraordinary position White won by a *coup de repos :*

24. R—R 6 !!

Threatening 25. Q—Q 8 mate, for if now :

24.	......	Q×B
25.	Q—Kt 4 ch	Q—Kt 4
26.	Q—Q 8 ch	K—R 3
27.	Q (K 3)—R 3 ch	

and mates in two moves (*See Diagram.*

Final Position in Sub-Variation

This position is certainly unique of its kind !

5.	Q×P
6. B×Kt	B×Kt ch
7. P×B	P×B
8. Kt—B 3	P—Q Kt 3

Here the fianchetto is very strong, inasmuch as White, as has been demonstrated by a St. Petersburg amateur, cannot reply with a King's fianchetto without inconvenience.

9. P—Kt 3

To this Black could have replied : 9. . . . .Kt—Q 2 !, the idea being to wait for 10. B—Kt 2, and then to prevent White from castling on the King-side by 10. . . . .B—R 3 !, for 11. Kt—R 4 is not to be feared because of 11. . . . .Q—Q R 4 ! This important innovation casts doubt on the value of White's fifth move.

9. . . . . . .   B—Kt 2

But with this simple move he equally obtains a perfectly safe game.

| 10. B—Kt 2 | Q—K 5 ch |
| 11. K—Q 2 | |

White had nothing better than to propose the exchange of Queens by 11. Q—K 2, although in that case also Black had somewhat the better game on account of the possibility of an attack against the centre by P—Q B 4. The text-move, just as 11. K—B 1 (Réti—Bogoljuboff, Berlin, 1920) is insufficient, in view of the exposed position of his King. Black at once assumes the initiative and keeps it to the end.

11. . . . . . .   Q—Kt 3

The only move to parry the threat 12. Kt—R 4, but amply sufficient.

| 12. Kt—R 4 | Q—R 3 ch |
| 13. P—B 4 | Kt—B 3 ! |

Threatening 14. . . . .Castles Q R ; followed by 15. . . . .P—K 4, etc. and forcing the White King to retreat once more.

| 14. Q—K 2 | Castles Q R |
| 15. K—B 1 | K—Kt 1 |

Threatening 15. . . . .P—K 4, which at present would not be so good because of 16. P—Q 5, P×P ; 17. Q—Kt 4 ch, followed by Q×P.

16. K—Kt 2   Kt—R 4 !

The exchange of Bishops is essential in order to allow Black's Rook to participate in the attack via Q 4.

17. B×B	Kt×B
18. Q R—Q 1	R—Q 4
19. P—B 4	

In conjunction with R—Q 3 this provides comparatively the best means of defence, but White misses a fine point on the following move.

| 19. . . . . . . | R—Q R 4 |
| 20. Kt—Kt 2 | |

He should have played 20. R—Q 3 at once, so as to be able to defend himself with 22. R—Kt 3, etc., after 20. ....R—Q 1; 21. K R—Q 1, Q—B 1! Now Black's reply will no longer leave him time for this.

Position after White's 20th move.

20. ......   R—Q 1 !

For if now 21. R—Q 3, then 21. ....Q—B 1, with the very strong threat 22. ....R × P ! followed by 23.....Q—R 6 ch; 24.....Q × P ch; 25. ....Q —R 8 ch; and 26. ....Q × R. Confronted with these difficulties, White is compelled to weaken his position in the centre.

21. Kt—K 3   Q—B 1
22. P—B 5

Obstructing the Queen's diagonal, but not for long, unfortunately for White.

22. ......   P × P
23. P—Q 5   P—B 5 !

This Pawn can be taken only by the Knight, for if 24. Q × P, Q—R 6 ch would win a piece.

24. Kt × P   Q—Kt 5 ch
25. K—R 1   Q—B 6 ch
26. Kt—Kt 2   R—Q 3 !

Far stronger than the simple gain of a Pawn by Q R × P ; as now White has not sufficient defence against the doubling of Rooks on the Q R file, feasible as it is even should White play 27. R—Q 3.

27. Q—B 4

Position after White's 27th move.

27. ......   R (Q 3)—R 3 !

Forcing the exchange of both Rooks for Queen and two Pawns, which, in view of the exposed position of the White King, leads to an evidently favourable ending.

28. P × P

Clearly the Queen cannot be captured because of mate in two.

28. ......   P × P
29. K—Kt 1   R × P
30. Q × R (R 2)   R × Q
31. K × R   Q × B P
32. Q R—Q B 1   Q—Q 7
33. K—Kt 1   Kt—Q 3

The entry of the Knight into the game should have decided the game in a few moves.

34. R—B 2   Q—Kt 5
35. R—Q 1   Kt—Kt 4
36. R—Q 8 ch   K—Kt 2
37. R (B 2)—Q 2   P—K 4

Black, thinking the game won in any case, makes no effort to find the shortest way. More energetic is 37. ....P—Q R 4 !, White being without resource against this advance.

38. P × P	P × P
39. K—B 1	Kt—Q 5
40. R—Q 3	Q—K 8 ch
41. R—Q 1	Q—K 5
42. R—Q 3	Q—R 8 ch

Here again 42. ....P—Q B 4, followed by 43. ....P—B 5 ; led to a more speedy victory. It goes without saying that the capture of White's last Pawns was also sufficient.

43. R—Q 1	Q × P
44. K—Kt 1	Q × P
45. R—Q 3	Q—K 8 ch
46. K—R 2	P—K R 4
47. R—K 8	Q—K 5
48. R—Q B 3	Kt—Kt 4
49. R—B 5	Q—Kt 5 !

See Diagram.

With the last move, which threatens 50. ....Kt—B 6 ch ; 51. K—R 1, Q—R 6, mate, Black ensures the gain of the Exchange. Had White wished to play on, the

Final Position.

only alternative would have been 50. R (K 8) × P, Kt—B 6 ch ; 51. R × Kt, Q × R ; 52. R × P, after which Black wins in the following manner : 52. ....K—B 3 ; 53. R—R 4, K—Kt 4 ; 54. R—R 5 ch, P—B 4 ; 55. R—R 4, P—R 4 ; 56. R—K B 4, Q—B 7 ! ; 57. K—R 3, Q—Kt 7 ! and the White Rook must leave the fourth rank, after which Black wins easily by 58. ....Q—Kt 6 ch ; followed by 59. ....P—R 5 ; etc.

White resigns.

CHAPTER X

INTERNATIONAL TOURNAMENT AT MANNHEIM, JULY, 1914

GAME 27

RUY LOPEZ

White :	*Black :*
O. DURAS.	A. ALEKHIN.

1. P—K 4	P—K 4
2. Kt—K B 3	Kt—Q B 3
3. B—Kt 5	P—Q R 3
4. B × Kt	Kt P × B

Though unusual, this variation appears to me eminently practicable. In any case it has the advantage of not allowing White the majority of Pawns on the Queenside as happens after 4. ...Q P × P; 5. P—Q 4, P × P; 6. Q × P, Q × Q; 7. Kt × Q, etc.

5. P—Q 4

White would obtain no advantage from 5. Kt × P, Q—Kt 4; etc.

5.	P × P
6. Q × P	Q—B 3 !

A new move and probably the best. Black concludes that his somewhat cramped position will be more easily defendable after the exchange of Queens, and the sequel confirms the correctness of his judgment.

7. Castles

Conforming to the preceding note, White should have avoided the exchange of Queens. There was, for instance, to be considered 7. P—K 5, Q—Kt 3; 8. Castles, for after 8. ....Q × P ?; 9. Kt—B 3 he would have obtained an advantage in development compensating for the Pawn sacrificed.

7.	Q × Q
8. Kt × Q	R—Kt 1

To hinder the development of White's Q B.

9. Kt—Kt 3

After 9. P—Q Kt 3, Black could have given up a Pawn by P—Q B 4 and P—B 5 ! as in game No. 2, with good attacking chances.

9. ......   Kt—K 2 !

Far better than the plausible 9. ....Kt—B 3, after which White would have obtained a fine game by 10. B—B 4, P—Q 3 ; 11. R—K 1, with the threat of 12. P—K 5, etc.

10. B—Q 2

An attempt to oppose the development of Black's K B, but Black circumvents this plan by the manœuvre which follows.

| 10. ...... | Kt—Kt 3 |
| 11. B—B 3 | Kt—B 5 ! |

Threatening 12. ....Kt—K 7 ch followed by Kt × B, thus gaining the necessary time for the development of the K B.

| 12. R—K 1 | B—K 2 |
| 13. Q Kt—Q 2 | |

It can be seen that 13. B × P, R— Kt 1 ; followed by R × P ch would be to Black's advantage.

| 13. ...... | Castles |
| 14. Kt—B 4 | |

Position after White's 14th move.

| 14. ...... | R—K 1 |

Up to the present Black has played very carefully and obtained an entirely satisfactory game ; but his last move is perhaps too risky, for it allows White to prevent the advance of Black's Q P for a long time. It is true that after 14. .... P—Q 3 ; White could force a draw (but no more) by 15. Kt (B 4)—R 5, B—Q 2 ; 16. Kt—Q 4, R—Kt 3 ; 17. Kt—B 4, Q R—Kt 1 ; 18. Kt— R 5, etc. But from the theoretical point of view, this result was not to be disdained for Black in a Lopez.

15. Kt (B 4)—R 5	B—B 1
16. Q R—Q 1	P—Q B 4
17. P—K 5 !	

Again opposing 17. ....P—Q 3 (prepared by Black's last moves), to which White would now reply 18. P × P, R × R ch ; 19. R × R, P × P ; 20. R—K 8 with a winning position.

| 17. ...... | Kt—K 3 |
| 18. Kt—B 4 | |

White has achieved his object, which was to prevent definitely the advance of Black's Q P. Black's position, though very restricted, is easy to defend, as it has no weaknesses. White's only threat would consist eventually in an advance of the King-side Pawns. By his next move Black seeks to obviate this danger.

| 18. ...... | P—R 3 ! |

Preparing P—Kt 4 which would secure the square K Kt 3 for the King.

| 19. P—K R 4 | |

After 19. P—Kt 3, Black would have obtained the advantage by 19. ....Kt—Kt 4 ; 20. R—K 3, B— Kt 2 ! ; 21. R × P, Kt—B 6 ch ; 22. K—B 1, Kt × P ch ; 23. K—K 2, Kt—Kt 5 ; 24. K R—Q 3, Q R—B 1, etc. The text-move was played in the hope—shown to be illusory by the sequel—of developing an attack by doubling the Rooks on the K R file.

19.	B—K 2
20. P—Kt 3	P—Kt 4 !
21. P × P	P × P
22. Kt (Kt 3)—R 5	

The two adversaries pursue their respective plans with consequence. However White, through not taking into account a very hidden resource of his opponent's, initiated by a Pawn sacrifice on the 24th move, will see his chances diminish.

22.	......	K—R 2 !
23.	K—Kt 2	K—Kt 3
24.	R—K R 1	

As will soon be seen, 24. P—R 3 ! was necessary, after which, however, Black could have occupied the K R file and eased his defence by exchanging one Rook. The text-move gives him the long awaited opportunity to take the initiative.

Position after White's 24th move.

| 24. | ...... | Kt—Q 5 ! |

An unexpected sacrifice which White is compelled to accept, for after 25. R—Q 2, Kt—Kt 4 ; 26. R—Q 3, Kt×B ; 27. R×Kt, P—Q 4 !, or 25. Kt—K 3, P—Q 3 !, Black would have obtained the superior game without difficulty.

| 25. | B×Kt | P×B |
| 26. | R×P | B—Kt 5 |

Indirectly threatening the K P and the Q Kt P. That is why White should have played 24. P—Q R 3.

27. Kt—Kt 3

The only move to preserve the extra Pawn temporarily.

| 27. | ...... | P—Q 4 ! |

The point of the sacrifice is only apparent now. White cannot play 28. P×P e. p., B—Kt 2 ch ; 29. P—B 3, R—K 7 ch ; 30. K—B 1, Q R—K 1, with a winning position for Black.

| 28. | Kt—K 3 | P—Q B 4 ! |

Stronger than 28. ....R×P ; 29. P—R 3, B—Q 3 ; 30. Kt×P, B—Kt 2 ; 31. K R—Q 1, with uncertain result.

29. R×P !

His best chance. If 29. R (Q 4)—Q 1, P—Q 5 ; 30. Kt—B 4, B—Kt 2 ch; 31. P—B 3, B—Q 4, followed by R×P, would secure a decisive advantage for Black.

| 29. | ...... | B—Kt 2 |
| 30. | P—Q B 4 ! | |

Not 30. P—K B 4 because of 30. ....P—B 5 ; and Black wins.

| 30. | ...... | R×P |

Position after Black's 30th move.

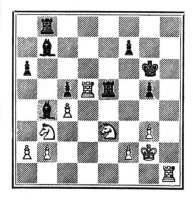

31. P—R 3 !

An ingenious resource which allows White to save the Exchange, at first sight irretrievably lost.

31.	B × P !
32. Kt—R 5	B × R ch
33. P × B	

Position after White's 33rd move.

After the excitement of the last moves the situation is clear at last. Black, although forced to give back the Exchange because of the threats Kt—B 6, Kt—B 4 or P × B, secures the gain of a Pawn and retains excellent chances for the ensuing ending.

33.	R × Kt !
34. P × R	R × P ch
35. K—B 3	P—B 4 !

The only move to preserve the advantage, for now White can neither play 36. Kt—B 4, because of 36. ....P—Kt 5 ch followed by 37. ....R—Kt 5 ; nor 36. P—Q 6, because of 36. ....P—Kt 5 ch ; 37. K—B 4, P—B 5 ! ; threatening B—Q 3 mate.

36. P—Kt 4

In order to bring his King into the centre and to obtain some chance with the two passed Pawns.

| 36. ...... | P × P ch |
| 37. K—K 4 ! | |

Not 37. K × P, on account of 37. ....P—B 5.

| 37. ...... | R—Kt 5 ch |
| 38. K—Q 3 | |

The alternative 38. K—K 5 would only occasion loss of time, Black continuing 38. ....P—B 5 ; 39. K—Q 4, B—Kt 7 ch, etc.

38. ......   B—Kt 7

Black has just time to bring back the Bishop to stop the dangerous White Queen's Pawn.

| 39. P—Q 6 | B—B 3 |
| 40. R—K B 1 | |

Position after White's 40th move.

40. ......   P—Kt 6 !

The deciding move, based on the following variation : 41. P—Q 7, R—Kt 1 ; 42. Kt—B 6, P—Kt 7 ; 43. R × B ch (or 43. R—any, R—Kt 2 !), K × R ; 44. Kt × R, K—K 2 ; 45. Kt—B 6 ch, K × P ; 46. Kt—K 5 ch, K—K 3 ; 47. Kt—B 3, P—Kt 5 ; 48. Kt—Kt 1, K—K 4 ; and Black evidently wins.

| 41. P—Q 7 | R—Kt 1 |
| 42. R—Q 1 | |

This offers no better chances for White than the preceding variation.

42.	P—Kt 7
43. K—K 2	R—Kt 7 ch
44. K—B 3	R—Q 7
45. R—K Kt 1	R×P
46. R×P	

The remainder is only a question of technique.

46.	R—Q 6
47. R—Q B 2	R—B 6
48. R×R	B×R
49. Kt—B 4	P—R 4
50. Kt—Kt 6	B—Kt 5

Now the Black King will move to the Queen's side and escort his passed Pawns to Queen.

White resigns.

GAME 28

RUY LOPEZ

| *White :* | *Black :* |
| A. FLAMBERG. | A. ALEKHIN. |

1. P—K 4	P—K 4
2. Kt—K B 3	Kt—Q B 3
3. B—Kt 5	P—Q R 3
4. B—R 4	Kt—B 3
5. Castles	Kt×P
6. P—Q 4	P—Q Kt 4
7. B—Kt 3	P—Q 4
8. P×P	B—K 3
9. P—B 3	B—K 2
10. R—K 1	

The best line of play for White is, in my opinion : 10. Q Kt—Q 2, Castles ; 11. B—B 2 or 11. Kt—Q 4.

| 10. ...... | Castles. |
| 11. Q Kt—Q 2 | Kt—B 4 |

In order to reply to 12. B—B 2 with Tarrasch's move, 12. ....P—Q 5 !

12. Kt—Q 4

But this is hardly better than 12. B—B 2. Speaking generally, in this variation 10. R—K 1 appears to be loss of time.

12.	Kt×Kt
13. P×Kt	Kt—Q 6
14. R—K 3	Kt—B 5 !

Much better than 14. ....Kt× B ; after which White is able to exercise a pressure on the open Q B file, which would justify the line of play he has adopted.

15. B—B 2

With the intention of preventing 15. ....P—Q B 4 by the threat : 16. P×P, followed by 17. B×P ch, and 18. Q—B 2 ch.

Position after White's 15th move.

| 15. ...... | P—Q B 4 ! |

Yet as the following variation shows, the move is quite playable : 16. P×P, B×P ; 17. B×P ch, K×B ; 18. Q—B 2 ch, K—Kt 1 ; 19. Q×B, P—Q 5 ; 20. R—K 4, R— B 1 ; 21. Q—R 3, Q—Kt 4 ! ; 22. P—K Kt 3 (or 22. Q—K Kt 3, Q×Q ; followed by 23. ....Kt—Q 6 ; and wins) ; 22. ....Kt—R 6 ch ; followed by 23. ....R×B, and Black wins.

16. Kt—Kt 3

In order to block up the position in the centre (for 16. ....P×P ; 17. Kt×P would not be to Black's advantage) and then to attempt a King-side attack. But the majority of Pawns on the Queen-side which Black secures with his next move constitutes, as will be seen later, a far more potent weapon than his opponent's problematic chances on the King-side.

16. ......   P—B 5
17. Kt—Q 2   P—B 4

This and the following move are dictated by motives of a purely defensive character. Black wishes to consolidate his King's position before attempting a decisive action on the Queen-side.

18. Kt—B 1

18. P×P e. p., B×P ; 19. Kt—B 3, B—Kt 5 would be insufficient.

18. ......   R—B 2 !

An excellent defensive move which, in case of need, reserves the square K B 1 for the Black Knight and which, at the same time, protects his K Kt 2. 18. ....Kt—Kt 3 would be less good, for after 19. R—K R 3, Black could not have played 19. ....P—B 5 because of 20. R×P !

19. R—K Kt 3   Kt—Kt 3
20. P—B 4   P—Q R 4
21. B—K 3   P—Kt 5
22. Kt—Q 2   Q—Kt 3

Opposing for the moment 23. Q—R 5, because of the reply : 23. ....Kt×B P ; 24. B×Kt, Q×P ch ; 25. B—K 3, Q×Kt P, with the better game.

23. Kt—B 3

Of course not 23. Kt×P, P×Kt ; 24. P—Q 5, B—B 4 ; and Black wins.

23. ......   B—Q 2

Preparing 24. ....P—R 5, and aiming eventually at posting the Knight at K 3.

24. Kt—Kt 5

After 24. B—R 4, B×B ; 25. Q×B, Kt—B 1, followed by 26. ....Kt—K 3, Black's game remains preferable.

24. ......   B×Kt
25. R×B

This exchange implies further loss of time and brings the Rook still farther away from the threatened sector.

25. ......   P—R 5
26. K—R 1

In order to play 27. Q—R 5, impossible hitherto because of 26. ....Kt×B P, etc. It would have been better, however, for White to retire the Rook to Kt 3 and to resign himself to the defensive.

26. ......   Kt—K 2

Providing once and for all against White's 27. P—Kt 4, which, if played on the previous move, would have been disastrous for White, e.g. : 26. P—Kt 4, P×P ; 27. P—B 5, Kt×P.

27. Q—R 5

A last attempt which will be refuted by an energetic counter-demonstration by Black on the other wing.

27. ......   P—Kt 6
28. P×P   B P×P
29. B—Q 3
          See Diagram.

29. ......   P—R 6 !

The passed Pawn which Black obtains by this temporary sacrifice wins the game in a few moves.

30. R×P   R×R
31. P×R   P—Kt 7
32. Q—Q 1

White begins a general retreat, but it is far too late !

Position after White's 29th move.

32.	......	R—B 1 !
33.	R—Kt 3	R—R 1
34.	B—Q Kt 1	R × P
35.	B—Kt 1	R—R 8
36.	R—Q B 3	B—R 5 !

The final manœuvre. This Bishop is to be posted at Q Kt 4 *without loss of time.*

37. Q—Q 3

Or 37. Q—K 1, B—Kt 4.

37.	......	B—Kt 4
38.	Q—Q 1	Q—R 3 !

Final Position.

White has no resource against the threat : 39. ....R × B !; 40. Q × R, Q—R 8. If 39. R—Q Kt 3, Q—R 5 !; if 39. R—B 2, B—R 5 ; and if 39. R—K 3, B—R 5 followed by 40. ....B—B 7 and wins.

White resigns.

GAME 29

GIUOCO PIANO

White :	*Black :*
A. ALEKHIN.	DR. S. TARRASCH.

1. P—K 4	P—K 4
2. Kt—K B 3	Kt—Q B 3
3. B—B 4	B—B 4
4. P—B 3	Q—K 2

This ancient defence is better than its reputation, but it demands particularly accurate opening play on the part of Black.

5. P—Q 4	B—Kt 3

5. ....P × P would be quite illogical, for after 6. Castles, White would obtain a very strong attacking game.

6. Castles	P—Q 3

The most usual move, but not the best. With 6. ....Kt—B 3 attacking the K P, Black could gain valuable time by compelling White to make a defensive move.

7. P—Q R 4	P—Q R 3
8. B—K 3	

In a game Gunsberg—Alekhin, in the St. Petersburg Tournament, 1914, White continued here : 8. P—R 5, but after 8. ....Kt × R P ; 9. R × Kt, B × R ; 10. Q—R 4 ch, P—Kt 4 ; 11. Q × B, P × B ; he did not secure sufficient compensation for the sacrifice of the Exchange.

8.	B—Kt 5

As the sequel will show, this Bishop was needed for the defence of the Q Kt P. Therefore it would have been better to play first 8. ....Kt—B 3.

9. P—Q 5   Kt—Kt 1

The intention is to protect later on the Pawn at Q Kt 3 by Q Kt—Q 2, in the event of White playing Q—Kt 3 after exchanging the Bishops.

10. P—R 5 !

Less good would have been 10. B×B, P×B, as the open Q B file would give Black sufficient prospects to compensate for the weakness of his Queen-side Pawns.

The text-move forces Black either to retire his Bishop to R 2, which would leave his Q R badly placed after 11. B×B, R×B ; or to open White's K B file, thus giving the latter the initiative on both wings.

10. ......   B×B
11. P×B   Kt—K B 3
12. Q Kt—Q 2

If 12. Q—Kt 3, then 12. .... B—B 1.

12. ......   Q Kt—Q 2
13. Q—K 1

More simple would have been 13. P—Kt 4, followed by 14. Q—K 1, etc. The text-move, however, can hardly be said to be inferior and, in fact, results in luring his opponent to retire his B to B 1, a somewhat peculiar manœuvre which will give White further possibilities of attack.

13. ......   Kt—B 4
14. Q—Kt 1 !

Not 14. Q—Kt 3, because of 14. ....P—K R 4 !, etc.

14. ......   B—B 1

Better was 14. ....Castles K R ; after which White would have con-

tinued his advance on the Queen-side, e.g. : 15. P—Kt 4, Q Kt—Q 2 ; 16. B—Q 3 and by 17. P—B 4. After the text-move Black's game becomes very precarious.

15. P—Q Kt 4   Q Kt—Q 2
16. Kt—R 4 !

In order to open a file on the Queen-side by 17. P—Kt 5, should Black play 16. ....Kt—B 1. But Black, with his next move, prefers to create a first weak point on the King-side.

16. ......   P—K Kt 3
17. Q—K 1   P—B 3

This counter-attack in the centre complicates the game. After 18. ....P×P ; 19. P×P, P—K 5 ; Black secures the square at K 4. Against that White will be able to exercise pressure on the opposing K P, and will, sooner or later, post his Knight at Q 4. In the end the insecure position of Black's King will be the deciding factor in White's favour.

18. K Kt—B 3   P×P
19. P×P   P—K 5

Position after Black's 19th move.

20. Kt—Kt 5 !

An unexpected move. Instead of playing this Knight at once to Q 4, White takes five moves, but the Knight arrives there with decisive results ! The idea is to provoke a further weakening of Black's position by the attack on the K P. Had White played 20. Kt—Q 4, at once, Black would have obtained a satisfactory position after 20. ....Kt—K 4 ; 21. R—B 4, Castles !, and White could not capture the K P because of 22. ....Kt×Kt ; 23. R×Kt, P—B 4 ; etc., or 21. Q—R 4, Kt×P !

20. ......   P—R 3

If now 20. ....Kt—K 4 ; 21. B—Kt 3 !, B—B 4 ; 22. B—R 4 ch, K—B 1 ; 23. B—B 2 !, and White has the advantage.

21. Kt—R 3

21. Q—R 4 was not feasible because of 21. ....Kt—R 2.

21. ......   Q—K 4

Black over-estimates the efficacy of this counter-attack. He should, after all, have played 21. ....Kt—K 4 ; and the continuation would have been : 22. Kt—B 4, B—B 4 ; 23. P—R 3, P—R 4 ; 24. B—Kt 3, R—Q B 1 ; 25. P—B 4, followed by Kt—K 2 and Kt—Q 4 with the better prospects for White.

22. R—B 1 !

Only the B P had to be defended, for Black would gain no advantage from capturing the Q P, e.g. : 22. ....Kt×P ; 23. B×Kt, Q×B ; 24. Kt—K B 4, Q—B 3 ; 25. P—B 4 ! followed by 26. P—Kt 5, and White regains the Pawn with a dominating position.

22. ......   Kt—Kt 5

Only leading to a further weakening of the position, for Black will not be able to play P—B 4. Somewhat better would be 22. .... Castles.

23. Kt—B 4 !   P—K Kt 4
24. P—R 3   K Kt—B 3

Forced, for if 24. ....P×Kt ; 25. P×P, followed by 26. P×Kt, would spell immediate disaster for Black.

25. Kt—K 2   Kt×P

Seeking some sort of compensation for his precarious position, which, it is clear, could not be held for long in any way.

26. B×Kt   Q×B
27. Kt—Q 4 !

Position after White's 27th move.

27. ......   Q—K 4

After 27. ....Castles, there were many threats for Black, as for instance 28. R—B 5, Kt—K 4 ; 29. P—B 4 ! or 28. ....Q—R 7 ; 29. R—R 1, Q—Kt 7 ; 30. Kt—B 4 !, winning the Queen in either case. If 27. ....Kt—B 1, the sequel would have been 28. Q—K 2 ! (threatening Kt—B 4 and Q 6), B—K 3 ; 29. P—B 4, Q—K 4 ; 30. P—B 5, P—Q 4 ; 31. P—B 6 !, P×P ; 32. Q R×P, followed by 33. R×Q R P, and the passed Pawns on the Queen-side would win easily.

After the text-move White wins
easily by a direct attack on the
Black King's position.

28. Kt—B 4	Q—Q 4
29. Kt—B 5 !	K—B 1
30. Kt (B 5) × Q P	R—K R 2
31. R—Q 1	Q—B 3
32. R—Q 4 !	

More simple and direct than combinations starting with Kt × B P.
Now Black has no move.

32.	P—Kt 4
33. P × P e. p.	B—Kt 2
34. Kt—R 5	Black resigns

GAME 30

GIUOCO PIANO

White :	Black :
J. MIESES.	A. ALEKHIN.
1. P—K 4	P—K 4
2. Kt—K B 3	Kt—Q B 3
3. B—B 4	B—B 4
4. Kt—B 3	P—Q 3
5. P—Q 3	B—K 3

A good way of avoiding the symmetrical variations springing from
5. ....Kt—B 3.

6. Kt—Q 5

This plausible move, however,
allows Black a series of favourable
exchanges. The best continuation at
this stage is 6. B—K 3 !

| 6. ...... | Kt—R 4 ! |
| 7. B—K 3 | |

If 7. B—Kt 3 there would likewise
follow 7. ....Kt × B, and 8.....
P—Q B 3, dislodging White's advanced Knight with advantage.

| 7. ...... | Kt × B |
| 8. P × Kt | |

If 8. B × B, then 8. ....Kt × P.

| 8. ...... | B × B |

Taking advantage of the fact that
White cannot recapture with the
Pawn, because of 9. ....P—Q B 3.

| 9. Kt × B | Kt—B 3 |
| 10. Q—Q 3 | |

10. Kt—Q 2 would be a little
better. After the text-move Black
provokes a weakening of the hostile
Queen-side.

| 10. ...... | Kt—Q 2 ! |
| 11. P—Q Kt 4 | |

If now 11. Kt—Q 2, then 11.....
Kt—B 4 ; 12. Q—K 2, Q—R 5 !
also to Black's advantage.

11.	P—Q R 4 !
12. P—B 3	Castles
13. Castles K R	

Position after White's 13th move.

| 13. ...... | P—K Kt 3 ! |

Having assumed the initiative on
the Queen-side, Black by this move
prepares an advance on the other
flank. This advance aims at either
the formation of a strong centre
after 14. ....P—B 4 ; 15. P × P,
P × P ; or at the decisive attack
resulting from the opening of the
K Kt file after the blockade by 14.
....P—B 5, which sooner or later
forces White's reply P—K B 3.

14. Kt—Q 2	P—B 4
15. P—B 3	P—B 5
16. Kt—Q 1	

Not 16. Kt—Q 5 on account of 16. ....P—B 3. After the text-move White's Knights have an extremely limited range of action.

16.	P—K Kt 4
17. Kt—B 2	P—R 4
18. P—R 3	Kt—B 3
19. K R—Q 1	Q—K 2

Black could definitely have pre-vented White's next move by 19. ....P—Kt 3, but this precaution seemed needless to him, since the variation resulting from 20. P—B 5 leaves him with a Pawn to the good in the end-game.

20. P—B 5

Compelling the opponent to modify his plan of attack—but at what a cost ! It is true that without this diversion Black would ulti-mately have shattered the enemy position by P—Kt 5, after the pre-paratory moves K—R 1, R—K Kt 1, R—Kt 3, Q—Kt 2 and R—K Kt 1.

20. ......   R P×P

There was equally to be con-sidered the line of play 20. .... Q P×P ; 21. Kt—B 4, B—B 2 ! ; 22. Kt×R P (or 22. P×R P, Q—K 3), P×P. But in the variation adopted in the text Black's material advan-tage will be still more readily ex-ploited in the end-game.

21. P×Q P   Q×P !

At first sight Black does not seem to have gained very much, for after 22. P×P, Q×P White would ob-tain good counter-chances by 23. K R—Kt 1. The finesse of the vari-ation selected does not become apparent until Black's 24th move.

22. P×P	R×P
23. R×R	Q×Q !
24. Kt×Q	B×R

Position after Black's 24th move.

And now White cannot take the K P on account of 24. R—Q 1 !, threatening B—Kt 6, and forcing the gain of the Exchange. The en-suing end-game still offers Black some technical difficulties, because of the weakness of his K P, but he makes certain of victory by a far-sighted pinning combination.

25. R—R 1	R—Q 1
26. R×B	R×Kt
27. Kt—B 4	R—Q 5
28. R—Q B 2 !	

Position after White's 28th move.

28. ......   Kt—K 1 !

The most difficult move in the whole game, for other defences of his Q B P would be inadequate, *e.g.* :

I.—28. ...P—B 3 ; 29. P—Kt 5 !, P×P ; 30. Kt×P, and Black's material advantage would be illusory.

II.—28. ....Kt—Q 2 ; 29. Kt—R 5, P—Kt 3 ; 30. Kt—B 6, and the strong position of this Knight would give White good drawing chances.

After the text-move Black threatens P—Kt 4.

29. P—Kt 5

Threatening 30. P—Kt 6 and 31. Kt×K P.

29. ......   P—Kt 3
30. Kt×K P

Forced, for if 30. K—B 2, then 30. ....P—Kt 5 ! White now expects to find sufficient compensation for his lost Pawn in the entry of his Rook at Q B 6.

30.	R—Kt 5
31. R—B 6	R×Kt P
32. R—Kt 6 ch	Kt—Kt 2
33. R×K Kt P	P—R 5 !

The point of the whole combination ! White's pieces are paralysed and 34. Kt—B 7, the sole way to free White, is temporarily impossible because of 34. ....R—Kt 8 ch. White therefore selects the continuation :

34. K—B 2   R—B 4
35. K—K 2

See Diagram.

35. ......   K—R 2 !

White would reply to the plausible move 35. ....P—Kt 4 by 36. Kt—B 7 ! and would then be out of all his difficulties. The text-move, on the contrary, removes this last resource. In fact, if now 36. Kt—B 7, R×R ; 37. Kt×R ch, K—Kt 3,

Position after White's 35th move.

winning the Knight. And against any other reply by White the Q Kt P would go straight on to Queen.

White resigns.

GAME 31

FRENCH DEFENCE

| *White :* | *Black :* |
| A. ALEKHIN. | H. FAHRNI. |

1. P—K 4	P—K 3
2. P—Q 4	P—Q 4
3. Kt—Q B 3	Kt—K B 3
4. B—Kt 5	B—K 2
5. P—K 5	K Kt—Q 2
6. P—K R 4 !	

This energetic move has been especially played in off-hand games by the ingenious Paris amateur, M. Eugène Chatard, and previously by the Viennese master, A. Albin.

It was during the present game that it was introduced for the first time in a Master Tournament.

6. ......   B×B

6. ....Castles, adopted on several occasions in international

tournaments in recent years, was refuted by Bogoljuboff in his game against Spielmann at Vienna, 1922, which continued 7. B—Q 3, P—Q B 4; 8. Kt—R 3!, R—K 1; 9. Kt—Q Kt 5, P—B 4; 10. Kt—Q 6, P×P; 11. Kt×R, Q×Kt; 12. B—Kt 5! and White should win.

6. ....P—Q B 4, and if 7. Kt—Kt 5 then 7. ....P—B 3, seems somewhat better.

7. P×B   Q×P
8. Kt—R 3   Q—K 2

After 8. ....Q—R 3 Black's Queen would be in a precarious position, and in this case White could gradually have strengthened his position by 9. P—K Kt 3 and 10. B—Kt 2.

9. Kt—B 4   Kt—B 1

White refutes this plausible move by an enterprising attack, but against any other reply he would have obtained ample compensation for the Pawn sacrificed.

A particularly interesting continuation has been suggested here by Bogoljuboff: 9. ....P—Q R 3; 10. Q—Kt 4, P—K Kt 3; 11. Castles, P—Q B 4; 12. Q—Kt 3!, Kt—Kt 3; 13. P×P, Q×P; 14. B—Q 3, Q—B 1.

Position after Black's 14th move in sub-variation.

15. B—K 4!! and White's Knight will force its way into the hostile camp via K 4 or Q 5, with decisive effect.

10. Q—Kt 4!

Threatening both 11. Q×Kt P and 11. Kt×Q P! Black's reply is therefore compulsory.

10. ......   P—K B 4
11. P×P e. p. P×P
12. Castles

White is again threatening 13. Kt×Q P, his King having removed from the King's file.

12. ......   P—B 3
13. R—K 1   K—Q 1

There is no other way to develop the Queen-side. If 13. ....B—Q 2 the sacrifice of the Knight at Q 5 would once more be decisive.

14. R—R 6!

In order to tie up Black's pieces still more, on account of the pressure on his K B P. From now onwards all Black's moves are forced.

14. ......   P—K 4
15. Q—R 4   Q Kt—Q 2
16. B—Q 3

Threatening among other moves 17. B—B 5.

16. ......   P—K 5
17. Q—Kt 3!

An essential preliminary for the ensuing sacrifice. White now threatens to win off-hand by 18. Kt×Q P. Black cannot play 17. ....Q—Q 3, for after 18. B×P!, P×B; 19. R×P! he would be defenceless against the threat 20. Q—Kt 7!

17. ......   Q—B 2

The only resource!

Position after Black's 17th move.

18. B×P !

This sacrifice, which must be accepted by the opponent, wins the game in a few moves.

| 18. ...... | P×B |
| 19. Kt×P | R—K Kt 1 |

If 19. ....Q×P ; 20. Kt×P !, Kt×Kt ; 21. Q—Kt 7 ! and wins.

20. Q—Q R 3 !

If 20. Kt—Q 6 Black could still have defended himself by 20. .... Q×P, seeing that White's discovered checks do not lead to mate.

But after the text-move he has no longer an adequate defence.

| 20. ...... | Q—Kt 2 |

If 20. . . .Q—K 2 ; 21. Q—R 5 ch, P—Kt 3 ; 22. Q—B 3 and wins.

21. Kt—Q 6 !   **Kt—Kt 3**

Position after Black's 21st move.

22. Kt—K 8 !

Forcing the win of the Queen, or else mate, *e.g.* : 22. ....Q—Q 2 ; 23. Kt×P ; or 22. ....Kt—B 5 ; 23. Q—B 5, Q—B 2 ; 24. R×P.

| 22. ...... | Q—K B 2 |
| 23. Q—Q 6 ch | |

and mates in two moves.

CHAPTER XI

LOCAL TOURNAMENTS, EXHIBITION AND MATCH GAMES, SIMULTANEOUS AND CORRESPONDENCE GAMES, ETC.

GAME 32

KIESERITSKI GAMBIT
(RICE GAMBIT)

Played by correspondence in Russia, 1908–1909.

White :   *Black :*
A. ALEKHIN.   W. DE JONKOVSKI.

1. P—K 4	P—K 4
2. P—K B 4	P × P
3. Kt—K B 3	P—K Kt 4
4. P—K R 4	P—Kt 5
5. Kt—K 5	Kt—K B 3
6. B—B 4	P—Q 4
7. P × P	B—Q 3
8. Castles	

This move, suggested by Professor I. L. Rice, has not, truth to tell, any theoretical value, since Black can revert to a variation of the Kieseritski Gambit, not unfavourable for him, by 8. .... Castles. Moreover, he runs no risks in accepting the temporary sacrifice of the Knight, since White, as Master practice has shown, cannot hope for more than a draw after a long and difficult struggle.

However, as the position arising from the sacrifice offers the two adversaries a multitude of very complicated tactical possibilities, it lends itself to the wish of players eager for combinations, and still more particularly to those who desire to devote themselves to the detailed analyses required by correspondence play.

8.	B × Kt
9. R—K 1	Q—K 2
10. P—B 3	

Not 10. P—Q 4 on account of B × P ch.

10.	P—Kt 6

With this move Black attempts the refutation of the Knight-sacrifice by a violent counter-attack. He had also the choice between 10. ....P—B 6 (tried in the match Lasker—Tchigorin at Brighton, 1904) and Jasnogrodski's move, 10. ....Kt—R 4 !, which is in my opinion the strongest move.

11. P—Q 4	Kt—Kt 5
12. Kt—Q 2	Q × P
13. Kt—B 3	

See Diagram.

13.	Q—R 3

Threatening to win the Queen by Kt—B 7. After 14. R × B ch, Kt × R ; 15. P × Kt, B—Kt 5 White has not sufficient compensation for the lost Exchange, and 14. Q—K 2 (if 14. Q—Q 2, Kt—K 6 !) would be demolished by 14. ....Castles ; 15.

87

Position after White's 13th move.

Position after Black's 15th move.

P × B, Kt—B 7 ; 16. K—B 1, Q—R 8 ch ; 17. Kt—Kt 1, Kt—R 6 !

There consequently remains nothing better than to attempt the following diversion :

14. Q—R 4 ch   B—Q 2
15. Q—R 3

This move was also played by Professor Rice, in a consultation game at New York, which resulted in a draw. In a game between Lipschutz and Napier played about the same period, the continuation was : 15. Q—Kt 4, Kt—Q B 3 ! ; 16. P × Kt, B × B P ; 17. B—Kt 5, Castles Q R ; 18. B × B, P × B ; 19. P × B, Kt—B 7 ; 20. K—B 1, Q—R 8 ch ; 21. Kt—Kt 1, Kt—R 6 ! ; 22. Q—B 5 (if 22. P × Kt, P—B 6), P—B 6 ! ; 23. P × P, Kt × Kt, and wins.

But at Q R 3 also White's Queen remains out of play for a very long time.

15. ......   Kt—B 3 !

See Diagram.

16. P × Kt

White has no choice. After 16. P × B, Q Kt × P, followed by Castles Q R, Black's attack would become irresistible.

16. ......   B × B P
17. P—Q 5

Clearly forced.

17. ......   B × Q P

Very ingenious. It is probable, however, that the simple variation, 17. ....B—Q 2 ; 18. Q—B 5 !, P—K B 3 ! ; 19. P—Q 6, P—B 3 ; leaving Black two Pawns ahead in a defendable position, was preferable.

The text-move leads to extremely interesting complications most difficult to fathom.

18. B × B   Q—Kt 3 ch
19. Kt—Q 4   Castles Q R

Having brought his King into safety, Black has a splendid attacking position and White, to avoid immediate disaster, must decide to sacrifice some of his material.

20. R × B

Reckoning on the variation 20. ....Kt × R ; 21. Q—Kt 3, Q × Q ; 22. B × Q, Kt—Kt 3 ; 23. B—Q 2, which would give White excellent drawing chances. But Black replies by another surprise-move.

Position after White's 20th move.

Position after Black's 25th move.

20. ...... R×B !

A very long-headed combination by means of which Black attempts to force a win when a Rook and Bishop to the bad.

21. R×R   Q—K R 3
22. Kt—B 3

After 22. Q×P, Q—R 7 ch ; 23. K—B 1, Q—B 8 ch ; 24. K—K 2, Q×P ch ; 25. K—Q 3, Q×R ; 26. Q—R 8 ch, K—Q 2 ; 27. Q×R, Black would have at least a draw by perpetual check : 27. ....Kt—K 4 ch ; 28. K—B 2, Q—K 5 ch ; 29. K—Kt 3, Q—Q 4 ch, but he could also have attempted to utilise his dangerous passed Pawns on the King-side by playing 27. ....P—B 6.

22. ......   Kt—B 7
23. K—B 1   R—K 1 !

Threatening 24. ....Q—R 8 ch ; 25. Kt—Kt 1, Q×Kt ch ; 26. K×Q, R—K 8, mate.

24. B×P !

The only resource to escape the deadly coils which are enveloping him more and more.

24. ......   Q—R 8 ch !
25. Kt—Kt 1   Kt—Kt 5

26. R—K R 5 !

This sacrifice is the simplest and surest way of saving the game. By playing 26. R—K 5 White would expose himself to fresh dangers without the slightest chance of a win, as the following very interesting variations show :

26. R—K 5, Kt—R 7 ch ; 27. K—K 2, R—Q 1 ! (preventing the flight of White's King to the Queen-side) ; 28. B×P !, Q×P ch ; 29. B—B 2, Q—Kt 5 ch ; 30. K—K 3 (if 30. K—K 1, Q—Kt 7 ! ; 31. K—K 2, Q—Kt 5 ch, and Black has already a draw), 30. ....P—K B 4.

See Diagram.

And against the threat 31. .... Q—Kt 4 ch ; 32. K—K 2, Q—Q 7 mate, White has only the two following defences :

I.—31. Q—K 7, P—B 5 ch ; 32. K—K 4, Q—Kt 7 ch ; 33. K×P, Q×B ch, and Black has at least perpetual check, for the White King cannot go to Kt 5 because of mate in three by Q—Kt 6 ch, Q—Kt 5 ch and Q—Kt 3.

II.—31. Q—Kt 4, Q—Kt 4 ch ; 32. Q—B 4, Kt—Kt 5 ch ! (stronger than 32. ....R—Q 6 ch) ; 33. K—B 3, Kt×R ch ; 34. Q×Kt, Q—Kt 5 ch ; 35. K—K 3, P—B 5 ch ;

Position after Black's 30th move in sub-variation arising on White's 26th move.

Position after Black's 27th move.

28. K—Kt 1 !

36. K—K 4, Q—Kt 7 ch ; 37. Kt—B 3, Q × B, etc., with good winning chances, as White cannot protect both his King and his Queen-side Pawns.

These variations demonstrate the extraordinary vitality of the attack initiated by Black on his 20th move.

26. ......   Q × R
27. Kt—R 3   Q—Kt 4 ch

Equally the tempting manœuvre 27. ....Kt—R 7 ch ; 28. K—Kt 1, Kt—B 6 ch ; 29. K—R 1, R—Kt 1 !, threatening 30. ....Q × Kt ch and 31. ....P—Kt 7 mate, would lead only to a draw against a correct defence, *e.g.* : 30. B × Kt P, R × B ; 31. Q—B 8 ch, K—Q 2 ; 32. R—Q 1 ch, K—B 3 ; 33. Q—K 8 ch, K—Kt 3 ; 34. Q—K 3 ch, K—R 3 ; 35. Q—Q 3 ch ! (if 35. Q—K 2 ch, P—Kt 4 ! ; 36. Q—B 1, Kt—R 5 and Black must win), K—Kt 3 ! (not 35. ....P—Kt 4, because of 36. Q—Q 7 !, threatening mate in three moves) ; 36. Q—K 3 ch, K—R 3 ! (if 36. ....P—B 4 ; 37. R—Q 6 ch, K—R 4 ; 38. R—K R 6, Q—B 4 ; 39. Kt—Kt 1 and wins) ; 37. Q—Q 3 ch and the game is a draw.

28. P—B 4 would allow White to preserve his material, but would leave Black winning chances, *e.g.* : 28. P—B 4, Q × P ch ; 29. K—Kt 1, Q—Q 5 ch ; 30. K—R 1, Kt—B 7 ch ; 31. Kt × Kt, P × Kt ; 32. B—Kt 3 (or A), Q—B 3 ; 33. R—K B 1, Q—R 3 ch ; 34. B—R 2, R—K 8 ; 35. Q—Q 3, Q—B 8 and wins.

(A) Or 32. Q—K Kt 3, Q × P (if 32. ....R—K 8 ch ; 33. R × R, P × R = Q ch ; 34. Q × Q, Q × B ; 35. Q—K 8 mate) ; 33. R—K B 1, Q × P and Black should win.

28. ......   Q—Kt 3 ch
29. K—R 1   Kt—B 7 ch
30. Kt × Kt   Q × Kt

Not 30. ....P × Kt ; 31. R—K B 1, Q—K B 3 ; 32. P—K Kt 3 and wins.

31. B × Kt P   Q × B
32. Q × P

The fluctuating struggle has ended in a peaceful finish with equal forces. Black rightly contents himself with perpetual check, for the only possible attempt to win, 32. ....R—K 5, is easily refuted by 33. K—Kt 1 !

32.	......	R—K 8 ch
33.	R × R	Q × R ch
34.	K—R 2	Q—R 5 ch
35.	K—Kt 1	Q—K 8 ch

Drawn game.

GAME 33

VIENNA GAME

Played by correspondence in Russia, 1908.

| White : | Black : |
| A. WJAKHIREFF. | A. ALEKHIN. |

1.	P—K 4	P—K 4
2.	Kt—Q B 3	Kt—K B 3
3.	B—B 4	Kt—B 3
4.	P—Q 3	B—Kt 5
5.	K Kt—K 2	

This game was played before the stronger move 5. B—Kt 5 was introduced into master practice by Mieses.

5.	......	P—Q 4
6.	P × P	Kt × P
7.	B × Kt	Q × B
8.	Castles	Q—Q 1

This retreat is preferable to 8. ....B × Kt, as played by Dr. Bernstein against myself in Paris (February, 1922). The continuation was 9. Kt × B, Q—Q 1; 10. P—B 4, P × P; 11. B × P, Castles; 12. Kt—Kt 5 ! by which White obtained the advantage and ultimately won.

9. Kt—Kt 3

In a game Mieses—Tchigorin (Monte Carlo, 1902) White continued 9. P—B 4, Castles; (better is 9. ....P × P; 10. B × P, Castles; 11. Kt—K 4, B—K 2); 10. P—B 5, with advantage for White.

| 9. | ...... | Castles |
| 10. | P—B 4 | |

Now this move is not so good, for Black by his reply will assume the initiative on the King-side.

10.	......	P—B 4
11.	Q Kt—K 2	Q—R 5
12.	K—R 1	B—Q 3

Opposing the manœuvre Kt—Kt 1—B 3, etc.

13. P—Q 4

White, with the inferior game, tempts Black to play for a passed Pawn, which would give White chances of counter-attack in the centre.

13. ...... P—K 5

Nowadays, I should have adopted the simple variation : 13. ....P × Q P; 14. Kt × Q P, Kt × Kt; 15. Q × Kt, B—K 3; or 15. ....B—Q 2, followed by B—B 3. But my lack of experience was a poor shield against the temptation of an attack with brilliant sacrifices; and though my anticipations were realized, it was solely due to the defective strategy adopted by my opponent.

14.	P—B 4	R—B 3
15.	P—B 5	R—R 3
16.	P—K R 3	B—B 1
17.	Q—Kt 3 ch	K—R 1

Position after Black's 17th move.

18. Q—B 3

A grave error of position judgment, which gives up the very important square at Q 5. 18. P—Q 5 was absolutely necessary, *e.g.* : 18. ....Kt—K 2 or Q 1 ; 19. B—K 3, with a good position in the centre. The move in the text leaves Black with a marked advantage.

18. ......   Kt—K 2 !

Of course not 18. ....B—K 3 because of 19. P—Q 5 !, etc.

19. B—K 3   B—K 3
20. B—B 2   Q—B 3
21. P—R 3

The Pawn advance on the Queenside (see also White's 23rd and 26th moves) leads to nothing, as there is no threat. But White's game is so much compromised by his 18th move that it is hardly possible to suggest a valid plan of defence.

21. ......   B—Q 4

Threatening 22. ....P—K 6, followed by R × P ch, etc. The square Q 4 has to be occupied precisely by the B, as the Knight has another and a very important rôle to play.

22. B—K 3   Kt—Kt 3
23. P—Kt 4   Kt—R 5
24. K—Kt 1

To any other move Black would reply, as in the game, with 24. .... Kt—B 6, blocking up the King in the corner square, exposed to most violent attacks, such as Q—R 5, threatening Q × P ch !, etc.

24. ......   Kt—B 6 ch !
25. K—B 2

For the capture of the Knight spelt disaster, *e.g.* : 25. P × Kt, P × P ; 26. Kt—B 1, R × P ; 27. K—B 2 (or B—B 2), Q—R 5 ; and Black wins.

Position after White's 25th move.

25. ......   Q—R 5 !

A rather peculiar position ; Black's intention is to play R—Kt 3 and B—K 2, followed by R × Kt ! ; Kt × R ; Q × Kt ch ! ; K × Q, B—R 5 mate, and White has no satisfactory defence against this threat !

26. P—Kt 5   R—Kt 3
27. K R—B 1   B—K 2 !
28. K—B 1

As White sees it is impossible to oppose the threat shown above, he seeks compensation in the capture of the Black Knight. But Black's attack still remains strong and will lead to a new mating position.

28. ......   R × Kt
29. Kt × R

If 29. B—B 2, Kt—Q 7 ch ; 30. K—Kt 1 (or if K—K 1, R × Q), R × P ch ; 31. K × R, P—K 6 ch ; 32. K—Kt 1 (or R 2), Q × B mate.

29. ......   Q × Kt
30. B—B 2   Q—R 7
31. P × Kt   P × P
32. R—B 2   R—K 1 !

The initial move in the combination which is to prevent the White King from taking refuge on the Queen-side.

33. B—K 3

If 33. B—Kt 1, Q—Kt 6 ; followed by B—R 5, etc.

33.	Q—R 8 ch
34. B—Kt 1	B—R 5 !
35. R—K R 2	

Now Black's Queen is lost, but the loss allows the Black Pawn to administer the *coup de grâce*.

Position after White's 35th move.

35.	Q—Kt 7 ch !
36. R × Q	P × R mate

GAME 34

RUY LOPEZ

Played by correspondence in Russia, 1908–1909.

White :	Black :
K. WYGODCHIKOFF.	A. ALEKHIN.

1. P—K 4	P—K 4
2. Kt—K B 3	Kt—Q B 3
3. B—Kt 5	P—Q R 3
4. B—R 4	Kt—B 3
5. Castles	B—B 4

This move, suggested in 1908 by the Danish master Möller, is in my opinion much better than its reputation as, up to the present, it has in no way been refuted and the few games in which it has been adopted rather tend to militate in its favour.

6. Kt × P

White could also play 6. P—B 3, to which the best reply is 6. .... B—R 2 ; as in a game Yates—Alekhin (Hastings, 1922), which continued as follows : 7. P—Q 4, (interesting would be 7. R—K 1, Kt—K Kt 5 ! ; 8. P—Q 4, P × P ; 9. P × P, Kt × Q P ! ; 10. Kt × Kt, Q—R 5 ! ; with a winning attack), Kt × K P ; 8. Q—K 2, P—B 4 ; 9. P × P, Castles ; 10. Q Kt—Q 2, P—Q 4 ; 11. P × P e. p., Kt × Q P ; 12. B—Kt 3 ch, K—R 1 ; 13. Kt—B 4, P—B 5 ; 14. Kt (B 4)—K 5, Kt × Kt ; 15. Kt × Kt, Q—Kt 4 ; 16. B—Q 2, B—R 6 ; 17. B—Q 5, Q R—K 1 ; 18. K R—K 1, R—K 3 ! ; 19. Q—Q 3, and now Black, who played the surprise move 19. ....B—K 6 !?, finally obtained only a draw, whereas he could have won a Pawn simply by 19. ....B × P ; followed by 20. ....R × Kt.

6.	Kt × Kt
7. P—Q 4	Kt × P !

Position after Black's 7th move.

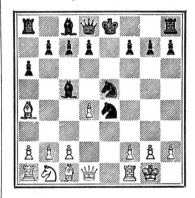

8. R—K 1

After 8. P × B, Kt × Q B P ; 9. Q—Q 4 or Q 5, Q—K 2 ! ; 10. B—

B 4, P—K B 3 ; (Dr. Groen—
Alekhin, Portsmouth, 1923) White
has not sufficient compensation for
his Pawn.

If 8. Q—K 2 (Takacs—Alekhin,
Vienna, 1922), then 8. . . . .B—K 2 ;
9. Q×Kt, Kt—Kt 3 ; 10. P—
Q B 4, Castles ; 11. Kt—B 3, P—
K B 4 ; with good attacking chances.
The continuation of this interesting
game was 12. Q—B 3, Kt—R 5 ;
13. Q—Q 3, P—Q Kt 4 ; 14. B—
Kt 3, K—R 1 ; 15. B—B 4, Kt—
Kt 3 ; 16. B—Q 2, B—Kt 2 ; 17.
K R—K 1, P×P ; 18. B×P, P—
Q 4 ; 19. B—Kt 3, P—B 4 ! ; 20.
P×P, P—Q 5 ; 21. Kt—R 4, B—
K 5 ; 22. Q—B 4, B—Kt 4 ; 23.
Q—Q B 1, B×B ; 24. Q×B, Kt—
R 5 ; 25. P—B 3, B×P ; 26. P—
Kt 3, and Black could have won at
once by the sacrificial combination :
26. . . . .P—B 5 ; 27. P×Kt, Q×P ;
for after 28. B—B 2, P—Q 6 ! ;
29. B×P, Q R—Q 1, is decisive.

8.	B—K 2
9. R×Kt	Kt—Kt 3
10. Kt—B 3	Castles
11. Kt—Q 5	B—Q 3 !

It was most important to preserve this Bishop. Now that Black
has overcome most of the opening
difficulties, he must in the sequel
obtain at least an equal game.

12. Q—B 3

To 12. P—Q B 4, Black had the
powerful reply 12. . . . .P—K B 4 ;
13. R—K 1, P—B 4 !, etc.

12.	P—K B 4

But in this position this advance
is premature. White gains an important *tempo* by playing his K B to
Kt 3 and Black loses the chance of
playing P—Q B 4. The correct play
was 12. . . . .P—Kt 4 ; 13. B—Kt 3,
B—Kt 2, etc., with very good
chances for Black.

13. B—Kt 3 !	K—R 1

Evidently the Rook could not be
captured because of mate in four :
14. Kt—K 7 dbl disc ch, K—R 1 ;
15. Kt×Kt ch, P×Kt ; 16. Q—
R 3 ch, Q—R 5 ; 17. Q×Q mate.

14. R—K 2	P—B 5

In preparation for 15. . . .P—B 3.
If 14. . . . .Q—R 5 ; 15. P—K R 3,
Q×Q P ; 16. P—B 3, Q—B 4 ;
17. B—K 3, Q—B 3 ; 18. B—Q 4,
etc., with a strong attack.

15. P—B 4	P—B 3

Aiming at the Rook sacrifice on
move 17. Insufficient would be 15.
. . . .Q—Kt 4 ; 16. P—B 5, Kt—
R 5 ; because of 17. Q—Kt 3 ! or
15. . . . .P—Q B 4, because of 16.
B—B 2, a move which is threatened
in any event.

16. P—B 5	B—Kt 1
17. Kt—Kt 6	

Position after White's 17th move.

17.	P—Q 4 ! !

This Rook sacrifice is absolutely
sound, and White would have been
better advised not to accept it and
to play 18. Kt×B ! (not 18. B—B 2
at once because of 18. . . . .Q—
Kt 4 ! ; etc.), Q×Kt ; 19. B—B 2 !
with a slight advantage.

It is easy to understand that White was tempted to capture the Rook, considering that Black's strong attack which follows was not obvious.

18. Kt×R   Kt—R 5

Position after Black's 18th move.

19. Q—B 3

Naturally not 19. Q—R 5, because of 19. ....P—K Kt 3 ; 20. Q—R 6, Kt—B 4 ; followed by 21. Kt×P ; etc.

If 19. Q—Q 3 ! there would have been interesting complications. The probable line of play would have been : 19. ....B—B 4 ; 20. Q—Q B 3 (if 20. Q—Q 1, Q—Kt 4!), P—B 6 ; 21. R—K 3 ! (if 21. P×P, Q—B 3 ; 22. P—B 4, B—Kt 5), P×P ; 22. P—B 3 !, Q—Kt 4 ! (threatening B×P ch), 23. R—K 5, B×R ! ; 24. B×Q, B×Q P ch ; 25. Q×B, Kt×P ch ; 26. K×P, Kt×Q ; 27. Kt—Kt 6, B—K 5 ch ; 28. K—Kt 3, R—B 6 ch ; 29. K—R 4, B—B 4 ! and mate in a few moves.

The text-move in some ways facilitates Black's attack, as he now has a serious threat comprising a Queen sacrifice.

19. ......   P—B 6
20. R—K 5

Compulsory. After the plausible reply 20. R—K 3, the continuation would be 20. ....Q—Kt 4 ! ; 21. P—Kt 3, B×P ! ; 22. R P×B, Q×P ch ; 23. P×Q, P—B 7 ch ; 24. K—B 1, B—R 6 ch and Black wins.

20. ......   B×R
21. P×B   Kt×P !

Threatening Q—R 5—R 6.

22. Q—Q 4   Q—Q 2

Black could also win by 22. .... Kt—B 5 ! ; 23. B×Kt, Q—R 5 ! ; etc., but the variation adopted is equally decisive.

23. P—K 6

A desperate move. But after 23. K—R 1, Q—R 6, White had no defence against 24. ....Kt—K 8 !, etc.

23. ......   Q×P
24. B—Q 2

Position after White's 24th move.

24. ......   Q—Kt 3 !

Stronger than 24. ....Q—R 6 ; 25. B—B 3, R—Kt 1 ; 26. Q—K 5, Kt—B 5 ; 27. Q—Kt 5, and

Black cannot play 27. ...B—Kt 5; because of 28. B×P ch! with perpetual check.

25. B—B 2

If instead 25. K—R 1, then 25. ....Kt—K 8; or if 25. K—B 1, B—R 6; and Black wins.

25.	Q×B
26. K—R 1	Q—Kt 3
27. R—K Kt 1	

The only resource.

| 27. ...... | B—R 6 |
| 28. Kt—Kt 6 | |

Position after White's 28th move.

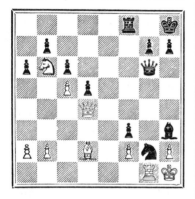

| 28. ...... | Kt—B 5! |

This manœuvre, prepared by Black's last few moves, is immediately decisive, for after the exchange of Queens and the loss of the Exchange White's game remains absolutely without resource.

29. R×Q	B—Kt 7 ch
30. R×B	P×R ch
31. K—Kt 1	Kt—K 7 ch
32. K×P	Kt×Q

White resigns.

GAME 35

QUEEN'S FIANCHETTO DEFENCE

Local Tournament in Moscow,* September, 1908.

| *White :* | *Black :* |
| A. ALEKHIN. | W. ROSANOFF. |

1. P—K 4	P—Q Kt 3
2. P—Q 4	B—Kt 2
3. Kt—Q B 3	P—K 3
4. Kt—B 3	P—Q 4

A move which is not in the spirit of the opening selected by Black, for it restrains the action of the Q B. More logical would have been : 4. ....B—Kt 5; 5. B—Q 3, P—Q 3; followed by Kt—Q 2 and Kt—K 2.

| 5. B—Kt 5 ch | P—B 3 |
| 6. B—Q 3 | Kt—B 3 |

Relatively better would have been 6. ....P×P; 7. Kt×P, Kt—B 3; leading into a variation—in truth not very favourable for Black—of the French Defence. White takes advantage of this move by commencing an immediate attack on the Black King's position.

| 7. P—K 5 | K Kt—Q 2 |
| 8. Kt—K Kt 5! | |

Threatening 9. Kt×K P, P×Kt; 10. Q—R 5 ch, followed by B—Kt 5 ch, etc.

| 8. ...... | B—K 2 |

If 8. ....P—K R 3; 9. Kt×K P, P×Kt; 10. Q—R 5 ch, K—K 2; 11. Q—R 4 ch, and White wins.

9. Q—Kt 4

Much better than 9. Q—R 5, after which Black would have had a sufficient defence by 9. ....P—Kt 3; 10. Q—Kt 4, Kt—B 1; etc. After the text-move Black has nothing better than : 9. .....B×Kt;

* First prize.

10. B×B, Q—B 2 ; 11. B—R 4 !, P—Kt 3 ; 12. Kt—K 2, P—Q B 4 ; 13. P—Q B 3, and White has a fine attacking position.

| 9. ...... | Kt—B 1 |

This allows of a sacrificial combination.

| 10. Kt×R P ! | R×Kt |

If 10. ....Kt×Kt ; 11. Q×Kt P, etc.

| 11. B×R | Kt×B |
| 12. Q×Kt P | Kt—B 1 |

At first sight it would appear that White has a simple win by advancing his K R P after P—K Kt 3, after which it would cost Black at least a piece by the time it reached K R 7. But Black in that case could, by a counter-attack in the centre, hinder that plan or else obtain compensation elsewhere.

E.g.: 13. P—K Kt 3, P—Q B 4 ; 14. P—K R 4 (or 14. Kt—K 2, Kt —B 3 ; 15. P—Q B 3, P×P ; 16. P×P, B—R 3 ! followed by Kt— Kt 5), P×P ; 15. Kt—K 2, P— Q 6 !; 16. P×P, P—Q 5 ; 17. R any, B—R 3, etc.

There is only one way for White to obtain an immediate win from his advantage in position.

Position after Black's 12th move.

13. P—K R 4 !

A surprise move, the first link in the chain of the ensuing combination, in the course of which Black will have to give up his Queen.

13.	B×P
14. R×B !	Q×R
15. B—Kt 5	

Black, being unable to keep the White Queen from K B 6, with a double threat of mate at K 7 and Q 8, is compelled to give up his Queen for the Bishop.

15.	Q—R 8 ch
16. K—Q 2	Q×P
17. Q—B 6	Q×B ch
18. Q×Q	

The rest is only a matter of routine.

18.	Kt—Kt 3
19. P—B 4	Kt—K 2
20. R—R 1	Kt—Q 2
21. Kt—Q 1	Kt—K B 1
22. Kt—K 3	B—B 1
23. Kt—Kt 4	B—Q 2
24. R—R 8	Kt—Kt 3
25. Kt—B 6 ch	K—Q 1
26. Q×Kt !	

The simplest, White remaining with an extra Rook.

Black resigns.

GAME 36

PHILIDOR'S DEFENCE

Second game of the match played at Moscow, October, 1908.
(*Result* +7, =1, —0)

| White : | Black : |
| B. BLUMENFELD. | A. ALEKHIN. |

1. P—K 4	P—K 4
2. Kt—K B 3	P—Q 3
3. P—Q 4	Kt—Q 2

More correct is Niemzovitch's
move : 3. ....Kt—K B 3, as the
variation 4. P×P, Kt×P ; 5. B—
Q B 4, P—Q B 3 presents no difficulties at all for Black. But after
the text-move White can adopt the
Schlechter variation : 4. B—Q B 4,
P—Q B 3 ; 5. Kt—B 3, B—K 2 ;
6. P×P, P×P ; 7. Kt—K Kt 5,
B×Kt ; 8. Q—R 5 !, which gives
him a slight advantage for the end-
game.

4. P—Q Kt 3

After this move Black has no
surprises to fear and can quietly
attend to his development.

4.	P—Q B 3
5. B—Kt 2	Q—B 2
6. Q Kt—Q 2	

Intending to attack the K P a
third time with Kt—B 4 and so to
force his opponent to modify the
arrangement of his Pawns. Black
frustrates this plan in a very
simple manner.

| 6. ...... | Kt—K 2 |

This Knight is to be posted at
K Kt 3, and, whilst assuring from
that square the defence of the K P,
is to await an opportune moment to
establish itself at K B 5, a square
which has been left weak by White's
development of his Q B at Kt 2.

7. B—K 2

It would certainly have been better to forestall Black's threat by 7.
P—Kt 3, followed by B—Kt 2,
especially as the Bishop's action
from K 2 is practically nil.

7.	Kt—K Kt 3
8. Castles	B—K 2
9. P—Q R 4	

Loss of time. In this position 9.
....P—Kt 4 was not to be feared.

| 9. ...... | Castles |
| 10. Kt—B 4 | R—Q 1 |

In the Hanham variation of
Philidor's Defence the Queen's file
is of as paramount importance as
the King's file in the exchange variation of the French Defence.

11. Q—B 1

The White Queen very reason-
ably evades the uncomfortable
opposition of the adverse Rook. It
would, however, have been more
urgent to prevent the exchange of
the K B, which might subsequently
have proved most useful, by first
playing 11. R—K 1, followed by
B—K B 1. Black immediately exploits this slight strategical error.

11.	Kt—B 5
12. R—K 1	Kt×B ch
13. R×Kt	P—B 3

In the absence of a White K B,
the weakening of the White squares,
resulting from the advance of
Black's K B P, is no longer dangerous.

14. Kt—R 4   Kt—B 1

Black's Q Kt now aims at K B 5.

15. Kt—K 3   Kt—K 3
16. P×P

White realizes that he can no
longer hinder the opening of the
Queen's file and this is tantamount
to a condemnation of his opening
strategy. Certainly the continuation : 16. K Kt—B 5, B—B 1 ;
17. P—Q B 3, P—K Kt 3 ; 18. Kt
—Kt 3, Kt—B 5 ; 19. R—Q 2, B—
K 3 ; 20. Q—B 2, Q—B 2 ; etc.,
was even less attractive than the
variation actually adopted.

| 16. ...... | Q P×P |
| 17. Kt (R 4)—B 5 | |

See Diagram.

| 17. ...... | B—Kt 5 ! |

A well thought-out manœuvre
which aims at the permanent command of the Queen's file. It at once

Position after White's 17th move.

threatens : 18. ....Kt—B 5 ; and hence provokes the reply 18. P—Q B 3, and, in consequence, the weakening of White's Q 3.

18. P—Q B 3

The alternatives were :

I.—18. P—Kt 3, Kt—Kt 4.

II.—18. P—K B 3, Kt—B 5 ; 19. R—B 2, B×Kt ; 20. P×B (if 20. Kt×B, B—B 4 ; 21. Kt—K 3, Q—Kt 3 ; 22. P—R 5 !, B×Kt ; 23. P×Q, B×Q ; 24. R×B, P×P ; with an extra Pawn), B—B 4 ; and Black, threatening as he does 21. ....Kt—Q 4 and Q—Kt 3, must win.

18. ...... Kt—B 5

Gaining a precious *tempo* which will allow Black to bring his Q R rapidly into play after 19. ....B×Kt. Had Black played 18. ....B—B 1, White had an easy defence by 19. R—Q 2, Kt—B 5 ; 20. R×R, Q×R ; 21. Q—Q 1, etc.

19. R—Q 2 B×Kt
20. Kt×B B—B 4
21. P—Q Kt 4

Without this precaution, Black, after 21. ....P—Q R 4, would have secured his B in a dominating position on the diagonal Q R 2—K Kt 8.

21. ...... B—B 1
22. R×R

White has no choice, and control of the Queen's file is definitely lost.

22. ...... R×R
23. Q—B 2 Q—Q 2
24. R—K B 1

To free the White Queen, at present immobilized by the threat of mate at Q 1.

24. ...... Q—Q 6 !
25. Q—Kt 3 ch

After 25. Q×Q, R×Q ; 26. Kt—Kt 3, P—Q B 4 ; 27. P×P, B×P ; followed by R—Q 7, etc., White's position would be hopeless.

25. ...... K—R 1
26. Kt—Kt 3

Evidently compulsory. Black now dominates the board.

26. ...... P—K R 4

But this is not the shortest way to win. More direct would have been 26. ....Kt—K 7 ch ; 27. Kt×Kt, Q×Kt ; 28. B—B 1, Q×P ; 29. Q—B 7, P—Q B 4 ! ; 30. P×P, B×P ; 31. Q—B 7, B—Kt 3 ; and Black, with a fine position and an extra Pawn, must win easily.

Position after Black's 26th move.

27. B—B 1

White, in his turn, does not adopt the best continuation and thus lets slip his last chance : 27. P—R 4 ! after which Black cannot play 27. ....P—K Kt 4 ; which would considerably weaken his King's position, *e.g.* : 27. P—R 4 !, P—K Kt 4 ; 28. Q—B 7 !, B—Kt 2 ; 29. P×P, P×P ; 30. B—B 1, etc. In this case Black would have contented himself with 27. ....Kt—K 7 ch ; 28. Kt×Kt, Q×Kt ; 29. B—B 1, Q×P ; 30. Q—B 7, P—Q B 4 ! ; 31. Q×R P ch, K—Kt 1 ; with a advantage sufficient to win, but at the cost of some technical difficulties.

27. ......   P—R 5 !

The end, so to speak, plays itself.

28. B×Kt   P×B
29. Kt—B 5

If now 29. ....Q×K P ; then 30. Kt×R P with some defensive possibilities. But Black's reply destroys his opponent's last illusions.

Position after White's 29th move.

29. ......   P—R 6 !

Decisive, as the following variations show.

I.—30. P—B 3, Q—K 7 ! ; 31. P×P, R—Q 7 ; and wins.

II.—30. P×P, Q×K P ; 31. Kt —Q 4, R—Q 4 ! and wins, for if 32. P—B 3, Q—K 6 ch ! followed by R×Kt.

III.—30. R—K 1, Q—Q 7 ! ; 31. R—K B 1, Q—K 7 and wins.

30. Q—K 6   P×P
31. K×P

A desperate move. If 31. R—K 1, Q×B P ; 32. R—Kt 1, Q—B 7 ; 33. R—K 1, R—Q 8 (the simplest) ; 34. R×R, Q×R ch ; 35. K×P, Q—Kt 5 ch ; 36. K—B 1, B×P ; 37. Q—B 8 ch, K—R 2 ; 38. Q× Kt P, P—R 4 ; 39. Q×P, P—B 6 ! and wins.

31. ......   P—B 6 ch
32. K—Kt 1   Q×R ch !

and mates next move.

GAME 37

RUY LOPEZ

Exhibition game played during the Cologne Tournament, June, 1911.

	White : A. ALEKHIN.	Black : S. VON FREYMANN.
1.	P—K 4	P—K 4
2.	Kt—K B 3	Kt—Q B 3
3.	B—Kt 5	Kt—B 3
4.	Castles	P—Q 3
5.	Kt—B 3	B—Q 2
6.	P—Q 4	P×P

This capture is premature and should be preceded by 6. ....B—K 2 ; 7. R—K 1 !, etc. The inversion of moves affords White advantageous possibilities of development.

| 7. | Kt×P | B—K 2 |
| 8 | Kt×Kt | |

Also very strong would be 8.
B × Kt, P × B ; 9. Q—B 3 ! But
the system adopted by White brings
about a most promising position.

8. ......   B × Kt

After 8. ....P × Kt the best reply
would be 9. B—R 4, as adopted
successfully by Marco against
Breyer in the Budapest Tournament
of 1913.

9. Q—K 2 !

White delays the exchange of
Bishops at B 6 until he has ensured
the means of weakening Black's
strong Pawn-position at B 2, B 3
and Q 3 entailed by this exchange.
This is strategically a correct
point of view.

9. ......   Castles
10. B—Kt 5   R—K 1
11. K R—K 1

To parry the threatened 11. ....
Kt × P.

11. ......   P—K R 3

Apparently Black's object in
playing this move is to follow it up
with 12. ....Kt—R 2 in the event
of 12. B—K R 4, so as to force an
exchange of Bishops, which would
ease his position. White consequently selects another flight-
square for his Bishop, to avoid this
line of play.

12. B—K B 4   Kt—Q 2

If now 12. ....Kt—R 2, then
13. B—B 4, and Black can no
longer exchange his K B (13. ....
B—Kt 4 ; 14. B—K Kt 3, B—R 5 ;
15. Q—R 5).
After the text-move White can
realize the plan he had in mind
when playing 9. Q—K 2, namely,
the weakening of the adverse
Queen's wing after the exchange of
Black's Q B.

13. B × B !   P × B
14. Q—B 4   B—Kt 4

An ingenious defence which does
not, however, bring about the
desired result. But White cannot
play 15. B × B, Q × B ; 16. Q × P ?
on account of 16. ....Kt—K 4 and
17. ....Kt—B 6 ch.

15. B—Kt 3   P—Q B 4
16. Q R—Q 1

Threatening P—K 5.

16. ......   B—B 3
17. P—Kt 3   Kt—K 4
18. Q—K 2   P—Kt 3

In order to retain the Bishop,
which will act effectively on the
opponent's Black squares. White
must now manœuvre with the utmost precision in order to maintain
his advantage.

19. Kt—Q 5   B—Kt 2

Position after Black's 19th move.

20. Q—R 6 !

The most effective means of exploiting the weakness of Black's
Queen-side. White now threatens to
win a Pawn by 21. B × Kt and 22.
Q—Kt 7. Black is consequently
constrained to play P—Q B 3. It is

interesting to note how this weakening move will impel Black to compromise his position more and more,
until it finally becomes untenable.

20.	Q—B 1
21. Q—R 5	P—Q B 3
22. Kt—K 3	R—Q 1
23. B—R 4 !	

Forcing Black to play either 23.
....P—Kt 4 or 23. ....P—B 3,
which is not much better ; for 23.
....R—Q 2 is impossible because
of 24. P—K B 4.

23.	P—Kt 4
24. B—Kt 3	Q—K 3
25. Kt—B 5	B—B 1
26. Q—B 3	

Now the threat of 27. P—B 4,
Kt—Kt 3 ; 28. P×P, followed by
29. B×P, etc., forces Black to
weaken his King-side still more.

| 26. ...... | P—B 3 |
| 27. P—B 4 | Kt—Kt 3 |

In answer to 27. ....Kt—B 2
White would bring his Queen to
K R 5 via K B 3, with decisive
effect. After the text-move he wins
at least a Pawn.

28. Kt×P ch !	B×Kt
29. P—B 5	Q—K 2
30. P×Kt	B—B 1
31. Q—B 4 ch	K—Kt 2

If 31. ....K—R 1 ; 32. R—K B 1
followed by 33. Q—K 2 wins
easily for White.

| 32. B×Q P ! | Black resigns |

GAME 38

SICILIAN DEFENCE

Winter-Tournament of the St.
Petersburg Chess Society, March,
1912.

| *White :* | *Black :* |
| POTEMKIN. | A. ALEKHIN. |

| 1. P—K 4 | P—Q B 4 |
| 2. P—K Kt 3 | |

A good system of development
against the Sicilian Defence, which
was much favoured by Tchigorin.
It has been adopted with success by
Dr. Tarrasch in several Tournaments of recent years.

2.	P—K Kt 3
3. B—Kt 2	B—Kt 2
4. Kt—K 2	Kt—Q B 3
5. P—Q B 3	

But the advance of P—Q 4, prepared by this move, is not in the
spirit of this system. White should
simply have developed his pieces by
5. Q Kt—B 3 ; 6. P—Q 3 ; 7.
Castles, etc.

| 5. ...... | Kt—B 3 |
| 6. Kt—R 3 | |

This illogical move allows Black
to obtain at once the superior game.
It would certainly have been better
to play 6. P—Q 4, P×P ; 7. P×P,
P—Q 3 ; although in this case also
the White centre Pawns would have
become weak.

| 6. ...... | P—Q 4 |

Of course !

7. P×P	Kt×P
8. Kt—B 2	Castles
9. P—Q 4	

After this move the White Q P at
once becomes weak. But 9. P—Q 3
was not much better.

9.	P×P
10. P×P	B—Kt 5
11. P—B 3	

The alternative 11. B—K 3 followed by Q—Q 2 and R—Q 1 was
also unsatisfactory.

| 11. ...... | B—B 4 |

Threatening to win the Q P by
B × Kt, etc.

| 12. Kt—K 3 | Q—R 4 ch |

This last move prevents Castling, for after 13. Q—Q 2 or 13. B—Q 2 the answer 13. ....Kt×Kt wins a piece.

13. K—B 2   Kt (Q 4)—Kt 5

Threatening amongst other things to win the Q P after B—Q 6.

14. Kt×B   Q×Kt
15. P—Kt 4   Kt—Q 6 ch
16. K—Kt 3

Position after White's 16th move.

16. ......   Kt×Q P !

Decisive.

17. P×Q

For if 17. Kt×Kt, Q—K 4 ch, etc., would give Black an easy win.

17. ......   Kt×P ch

and mates in two. If 18. K—Kt 4, P—R 4 ch and mate next move by the B or the Kt. If 18. K—R 3, Kt—B 7, a " pure mate."

GAME 39

QUEEN'S PAWN GAME

Winter Tournament of the St. Petersburg Chess Society, March, 1912.

White :	Black :
A. ALEKHIN.	H. LÖVENFISCH.

1. P—Q 4   P—Q B 4

The advance of this Pawn is rightly considered inferior even when prepared by 1.....Kt—K B 3; 2. Kt—K B 3. On the first move it constitutes in my opinion a grave positional error, for White at once obtains a great advantage in position by simply advancing the centre Pawns.

2. P—Q 5   Kt—K B 3
3. Kt—Q B 3   P—Q 3
4. P—K 4   P—K Kt 3

If instead of the text-move Black replies with 4. ....P—K 3 White's answer would be 5. B—Q B 4, etc., and the sequel would not be satisfactory for Black because of the weakness at his Q 3.

5. P—B 4

Already threatening P—K 5.

5. ......   Q Kt—Q 2
6. Kt—B 3

Position after White's 6th move.

If now 6. ....B—Kt 2 ; then 7. P—K 5, P×P ; 8. P×P, Kt—Kt 5 ; 9. P—K 6, Q Kt—K 4 ; 10. B—

Kt 5 ch, etc. This is why Black
plays :

6.	P—Q R 3
7. P—K 5	P × P
8. P × P	Kt—Kt 5
9. P—K 6 !	

This demolishes Black's variation.

| 9. ...... | Kt (Q 2)—K 4 |
| 10. B—K B 4 | |

Position after White's 10th move.

| 10. ...... | Kt × Kt ch |

Or 10. ....B—Kt 2 ; 11. Q—
K 2, Kt × Kt ch ; 12. P × Kt, Kt—
B 3 ; 13. P × P ch, K × P ; 14.
Castles Q R, etc., with overwhelming advantage for White. After the
text-move Black probably hopes for
the reply 11. Q × Kt upon which he
would obtain a playable game by
11. ....P × P !

| 11. P × Kt ! | Kt—B 3 |
| 12. B—B 4 ! | |

This is preferable to the immediate capture of the K B P, a capture
which the text-move renders much
more threatening.

| 12. ...... | P × P |
| 13. P × P | Q—Kt 3 |

The alternative was : 13. ....
Q × Q ch ; 14. R × Q, B—Kt 2 ;

15. B—B 7, Castles ; 16. B—Kt 6,
and White wins a Pawn, at the
same time maintaining the pressure. The move 13. ....Q—Kt 3,
threatening two Pawns at the same
time, is shown to be insufficient by
an unexpected combination comprising a sacrifice by White.

14. Q—K 2 !

The initial move.

| 14. ...... | Q × Kt P |

At first sight there appears to be
little danger in this capture, for K—
Q 2 would be frustrated by 15. ....
Kt—R 4 ; 16. B—K 5, B—R 3 ch ;
17. K—Q 3, B × K P ; 18. B × B,
R—Q 1 ch, etc. But White had a
different scheme in mind.

Position after Black's 14th move.

15. Kt—Kt 5 !

This attack by the Knight (which
cannot be captured because of 15.
....P × Kt ; 16. B × P ch, K—Q 1 ;
17. Q R—Q 1 ch) decides the issue
in a few moves. Black has therefore
nothing better than to accept the
sacrifice and to capture both Rooks.

15.	Q × R ch
16. K—B 2	Q × R
17. Kt—B 7 ch	K—Q 1
18. Q—Q 2 ch	B—Q 2
19. P × B	

Threatening Kt—K 6 mate.

Black resigns.

For if 19. ....Kt×P; 20. B—
K 6; or if 19. ....P—K 4 then
20. Kt—K 6 ch, K—K 2; 21. P—
Q 8 (Q) ch, R×Q; 22. Q×R ch,
K—B 2; 23. Kt×B dis. ch, K—
Kt 2; 24. Q—K 7 mate.

GAME 40.

BISHOP'S GAMBIT

Second game of the match played
at St. Petersburg, March, 1913.
(Result +7, =0, —3)

White :	Black :
A. ALEKHIN.	S. LEVITSKI.

1. P—K 4	P—K 4
2. P—K B 4	P×P
3. B—B 4	Kt—K B 3

This defence is now considered to
be the best. The old line of play :
3. ....Q—R 5 ch ; 4. K—B 1, P—
Q 4 ; 5. B×P, P—K Kt 4 is played
less and less on account of Tchigorin's attack, 6. P—K Kt 3, P×P ;
7. Q—B 3 !, etc.

4. Kt—Q B 3   B—Kt 5

Black has now a "Ruy Lopez" with
Schliemann's defence (P—K B 4)
but with a move behind, evidently
an important consideration. Very
interesting, and probably better, is
Bogoljuboff's move 4. ....P—B 3,
as played by him successfully
against Spielmann (Carlsbad, 1923).

5. K Kt—K 2

A new move which this game
fails to refute. After 5. Kt—B 3,
Castles ; 6. Castles, Kt×P ; White
loses the initiative by 7. Kt×Kt,
P—Q 4, etc., and therefore would
have to sacrifice a Pawn permanently by playing 7. Kt—Q 5, with
some attacking chances.

5. ......   P—Q 4

If 5. ....Kt×P White Castles
and obtains a good attack for the
sacrificed Pawn. With the text-
move, Black in his turn intends a
very audacious Pawn sacrifice, the
soundness of which is, however, open
to question.

6. P×P   P—B 6

Intending to compromise the
White King's position ; but, as
the sequel will show, the opening
of the K Kt file is not without
danger for Black and on the other
hand White will momentarily have
an extra Pawn.

7. P×P   Castles
8. P—Q 4

This move is inconsequent. After
8. Castles !, P—B 3 ; 9. P×P, Kt
×P ; 10. P—Q 4, B—K R 6 ; 11.
R—B 2, R—B 1 ; etc., and Black's
development is favourable, but the
attack is insufficient to make up for
the loss of a Pawn.

But after the text-move Black
could and should have regained his
Pawn by 8. ....Kt×P ; 9. Castles,
B—K 3, etc., with a good game.

8. ......   B—K R 6

Position after Black's 8th move.

9. B—Kt 5 !

The plausible move was 9. Kt—B 4, protecting both Pawns and attacking the Bishop, but upon this Black had the following win in view: 9. ....R—K 1 ch; 10. K—B 2, Kt—Kt 5 ch! (seemingly inoffensive because of White's reply); 11. K—Kt 3, Kt—B 7 !!, etc. With the text-move White definitely assumes the initiative.

9. ......   B—Kt 7
10. R—K Kt 1   B × P
11. Q—Q 2   B—K 2

11. ....Kt—K 5 would be bad because of 12. B × Q, Kt × Q; 13. B—B 6, etc. On the other hand Black was threatened with 12. Q—B 4, and the variation 11. ....B × K Kt; 12. B × B, B × Kt; 13. Q × B, R—K 1 would be refuted by 14. Castles, R × B; 15. Q—B 3, etc.

12. Castles

Position after White's 12th move.

12. ......   B—R 4

Here again 12. ....Kt—K 5 would lose for Black, *e.g.:* 13. B × B, Kt × Q (if 13. ....Q × B; 14. Q—R 6 !); 14. B × Q, Kt × B; 15. R × P ch !, K × R; 16. R—Kt 1 ch, K—R 3; 17. B—Kt 5 ch, K—Kt 3 (if K—R 4; 18. Kt—B 4 mate); 18. B—K 7 ch, followed by B × R, etc.

Now White has a comfortable attacking game.

13. Q R—K 1   Q Kt—Q 2
14. Kt—B 4   B—Kt 3
15. P—R 4 !

Obviously threatening 16. P—R 5, etc.

15. ......   R—K 1
16. Q—Kt 2

Now the threat is still more acute.

16. ......   B—B 1
17. P—R 5   B—K B 4

17. ....R × R ch first offered Black a more prolonged defence; but it is evident that in any event White's attack would have succeeded ultimately.

Position after Black's 17th move.

18. Kt—K 6 !

This irruption opens new lines of attack of a decisive nature for White. Black is forced to capture the Knight, as after 18. ....Q—B 1 White wins by 19. Q—B 3 !

18. ......   P × Kt
19. P × P   K—R 1
20. P × Kt   R × R ch
21. R × R   B × Q P
22. P—R 6

The winning move. Black must at the very least lose a piece at K B 3.

22.	......	B—B 3
23.	P—Q 5	B—Q 2
24.	R—B 1	P—Kt 4
25.	B—Kt 3	Q—K 1
26.	P—Q 6	

26. R × Kt was also sufficient.

26. ...... Kt—R 4

Or 26. .... B—B 3 ; 27. P—Q 7 !, giving two variations :

I.—27. .... B × Q ; 28. P × Q (Q), R × Q ; 29. R × Kt !, etc.

II.—27. .... Q × P ; 28. Q—B 2 !, Kt—Kt 1 ; 29. Q × B ! and wins.

It is with a view to the latter variation that White played 26. P— Q 6.

27. B—B 7   Black resigns

GAME 41

VIENNA GAME

Eighth game of the match at St. Petersburg, March, 1913.

White :	*Black :*
A. ALEKHIN.	S. LEVITSKI.
1. P—K 4	P—K 4
2. Kt—Q B 3	Kt—K B 3
3. B—B 4	Kt × P !

It is solely on account of this reply, which gives Black easily an equal game, that I have at the moment given up the Vienna opening.

4. Q—R 5

It is clear that after 4. Kt × Kt, P—Q 4 ! ; or else 4. B × P ch, K × B ; 5. Kt × Kt, P—Q 4 ; Black emerges unscathed from the tribulations of the opening stages.

| 4. | ...... | Kt—Q 3 |
| 5. | B—Kt 3 | |

Here White could have equalized by 5. Q × K P ch, Q—K 2 ; 6. Q × Q ch, B × Q, etc. But the sacrifice of a Pawn, which the text-move implies, is of doubtful value.

5. ...... Kt—B 3 !

The intention is to sacrifice the Exchange in the following variation : 6. Kt—Kt 5, P—K Kt 3 ; 7. Q— B 3, P—B 4 ; 8. Q—Q 5, Q—B 3 ; 9. Kt × P ch, K—Q 1 ; 10. Kt × R, P—Kt 3 ! ; which ensures for Black a very strong and probably irresistible attack. The simple move 5. ....B—K 2 is also amply sufficient and would result, by a transposition of moves, in a position of the actual game.

6. P—Q 3   B—K 2

6. ....P—K Kt 3 followed by 7. ....B—Kt 2 was also to be considered. As can be seen Black, in this variation, has a wide choice of moves.

7. Kt—B 3   P—K Kt 3

This move, which was already played in the Paris Tournament of 1900 (Mieses—Marco) does not look natural, especially after B—K 2, and, indeed, is not the best. Black should simply have Castled, as the variation 8. Kt—K Kt 5, P—K R 3 ; 9. P—K R 4, Kt—Q 5 ! is not sufficient : after the move in the text Black will be unable to Castle.

| 8. | Q—R 3 | Kt—B 4 |
| 9. | P—Kt 4 | |

This move has also been tried before, on several occasions, with varying continuations.

| 9. | ...... | Kt (B 4)—Q 5 |
| 10. | B—R 6 | Kt × B |

An interesting idea aiming at a counter-attack, but at the same time premature, as Black is not yet sufficiently developed. The right move is 10. ....B—B 1 !, for after 11. B×B, R×B White is not in a position to regain the Pawn by 12. Kt×Kt, Kt×Kt ; 13. Q×P, because of the very strong reply 13. ....Q—Kt 4 !, preventing him from Castling on the Queen-side and leaving him with very doubtful prospects of attack.

11. R P×Kt   P—B 4

This move gives the clue to the preceding exchange, which would otherwise seem inexplicable. If now White were to play 12. P×P, Black would obtain a fine development by 12. ....P—Q 3, and 13. B×P.

12. B—Kt 7 !   P×P
13. Q—R 6 !

This sacrifice of a second Pawn promises White an attack both lasting and vigorous.

13. ......   B—B 1

Obviously forced.

14. B×B   R×B
15. Kt—K Kt 5   Kt—Q 5 !

This counter-attack offers on the whole the best chances. Quite insufficient would be 15. ....Q—B 3 ; because of 16. Castles K R !, etc.

16. Kt×P   R—K Kt 1

See Diagram.

17. Kt—Q 5 !

The only correct continuation of the attack, whose point will become evident on White's 23rd move. After the plausible move 17. Castles Q R, Black can disentangle himself by 17. ....Kt—B 4 ; 18. Q—Q 2, Q—R 5 ; etc., and White's attack can be repelled successfully.

17. ......   Kt×P ch

Position after Black's 16th move.

As the threatened 18. Kt—B 6 ch cannot be avoided, Black is compelled to seek compensation in the capture of the adverse Rook.

18. K—Q 2   Kt×R
19. R×Kt   P—B 3

Or if 19. ....P—Q 3 ; 20. Kt (R 7)—B 6 ch, K—B 2 ; 21. Kt× R, Q×Kt ; 22. Kt×P, followed by 23. Kt—Kt 5, etc., with a decisive attack.

20. Kt (R 7)—B 6 ch !
        K—B 2
21. Kt×R   Q×Kt

If 21. ....P×Kt ; 22. Q—R 7 ch, K—B 1 ; 23. Q×Kt P, Q—K 1 ; 24. Q—Kt 5 !, Q—B 2 ; 25. Kt—B 6 !, P—Q 3 ; 26. P—R 3 !, P×P ; 27. R—K Kt 1, etc., with a winning attack.

22. Kt—Kt 6   R—Kt 1

See Diagram.

23. Kt—B 4 !

The winning move, for Black cannot prevent the opening of the King's file, which will prove decisive.

23. ......   P—Q 3

Position after Black's 22nd move.

If 23. ....K—K 3 ; 24. Kt×P, K×Kt ; 25. Q—Kt 5 ch and White will win the Black Rook by a check at K 5 or K B 4

24. Kt×Q P ch	K—K 2
25. Kt—B 4	B—B 4
26. R—K 1	Q—R 1
27. Q—K 3 !	R—Q 1

After 27. ....K—Q 2 White wins by Q×R P, etc. The text-move allows of a still quicker termination.

28. Kt×P	K—B 3
29. Kt×P ch !	B×Kt
30. Q—K 5 ch	Black resigns

GAME 42

KING'S KNIGHT'S OPENING

Played in Paris, August, 1913.

White :	*Black :*
J. DE RODZYNSKI.	A. ALEKHIN.

1. P—K 4	P—K 4
2. Kt—K B 3	Kt—Q B 3
3. B—B 4	P—Q 3

Although seldom played this move is not inferior to 3. ...B—K 2, which constitutes the Hungarian Defence. The present game affords a typical example of the dangers

to which White is exposed if he attempts to refute this move forthwith.

4. P—B 3	B—Kt 5
5. Q—Kt 3	Q—Q 2

Position after Black's 5th move.

6. Kt—Kt 5

Anticipating the gain of two Pawns. If at once : 6. B×P ch, Q×B ; 7. Q×P, K—Q 2 ! ; 8. Q×R, B× Kt ; 9. P×B, Q×B P ; 10. R— Kt 1, Q×K P ch ; 11. K—Q 1, Q— B 6 ch ; and Black has at least a draw, as White cannot move his K to Q B 2, on account of Kt—Kt 5 ch, etc.

6.	Kt—R 3
7. B×P ch	

After 7. Q×P, R—Q Kt 1 ; 8. Q—R 6, R—Kt 3 ; 9. Q—R 4, B— K 2 ; followed by Castles, Black would obtain a sufficient compensation in development in exchange for the Pawn sacrificed.

7.	Kt×B
8. Kt×Kt	Q×Kt
9. Q×P	K—Q 2 !

The sacrifice of the Exchange is entirely sound and yields Black a strong counter-attack.

10. Q×R   Q—Q B 5 !
11. P—B 3

Evidently forced.

Position after White's 11th move.

11. ......   B×P !

By this unexpected combination Black secures the advantage in any event. Incorrect would be, however, 10. ....Kt—Q 5; because of 11. P—Q 3, Q×Q P; 12. P×Kt, B×P; 13. Kt—B 3 !, etc.

12. P×B   Kt—Q 5 !
13. P—Q 3

This move loses at once. The only chance was perhaps: 13. P×Kt, with the following variation: 12. ....Q×B ch; 13. K—K 2, Q×R; 14. P—Q 5, Q×R P ch; 15. K—Q 3, Q—Kt 8 !; 16. Q—B 6 ch, K—Q 1, etc., but Black's position is manifestly superior.

13. ......   Q×Q P
14. P×Kt   B—K 2 !

On this move White has the choice between the loss of the Queen or mate. He prefers the latter.

15. Q×R   B—R 5 mate.

GAME 43

QUEEN'S GAMBIT DECLINED

One of twenty simultaneous games played at Paris, September, 1913.

White :	Black :
A. ALEKHIN.	M. PRAT.

1. P—Q 4	P—Q 4
2. Kt—K B 3	Kt—Q B 3
3. P—B 4	P—K 3

Tchigorin's Defence is only playable if the Q B is developed at K Kt 5. The text-move which, on the contrary, obstructs this Bishop, can only create difficulties for Black.

4. Kt—B 3	P×P

A further renunciation. Black now abandons the centre, and it is not surprising that White, in a few moves, obtains an overpowering position.

5. P—K 3	Kt—B 3
6. B×P	B—Kt 5
7. Castles	B×Kt
8. P×B	Castles
9. Q—B 2	Kt—K 2
10. B—R 3	P—B 3
11. P—K 4	P—K R 3

Opposing the threat 12. P—K 5 followed by 13. Kt—Kt 5, but at the cost of a considerable weakening of the Castled position.

12. Q R—Q 1	B—Q 2
13. Kt—K 5	R—K 1

In order to liberate the Queen. A catastrophe at K B 7 is already in the air.

14. P—B 4	Q—B 2
15. P—B 5	Q R—Q 1

See Diagram.

16. Kt×B P !

This can hardly be termed a sacrifice, as White is in a position to

Position after Black's 15th move.

Position after Black's 21st move.

regain the piece with the superior position, but it is rather the initial move of the elegant final combination.

16.	......	K × Kt
17.	P—K 5	Kt (K 2)—Kt 1
18.	B—Q 6	

Here White could have regained his piece by 18. P × Kt, P × P ! (if instead 18. ....Kt × P ; 19. P × P ch, B × P ; 20. R × Kt ch, etc.) ; 19. P × P ch, K—Kt 2 ! He quite rightly prefers to aim at the mate.

18.	......	Q—B 1
19.	Q—K 2	P—Q Kt 4
20.	B—Kt 3	P—Q R 4
21.	Q R—K 1 !	

The sequel clearly shows the object of this move.

21.	......	P—R 5

See Diagram.

Here White announced mate in 10 moves as follows : 22. Q—R 5 ch ! !, Kt × Q ; 23. P × P dbl ch, K—Kt 3 ; 24. B—B 2 ch, K—Kt 4 ; 25. R—B 5 ch, K—Kt 3 ! ; 26. R—B 6 dbl ch, K—Kt 4 ; 27. R—Kt 6 ch, K—R 5 ; 28. R—K 4 ch, Kt—B 5 ; 29. R × Kt ch, K—R 4 ; 30. P—Kt 3 !, any ; 31. R—R 4 mate.

GAME 44

VIENNA GAME

Exhibition game played at Paris, September, 1913.

White :	*Black :*
A. ALEKHIN.	ED. LASKER.

1.	P—K 4	P—K 4
2.	Kt—Q B 3	Kt—K B 3
3.	B—B 4	Kt—B 3
4.	P—Q 3	B—B 4
5.	B—K Kt 5	

At the present time I should prefer 5. P—B 4, P—Q 3 ; 6. Kt—B 3, bringing about a position in the King's Gambit Declined favourable for White. The text-move, on the contrary, allows Black to equalize the game easily.

5.	......	P—Q 3
6.	Kt—R 4	

The continuation 6. Kt—Q 5 ; B—K 3 ; 7. Kt × Kt ch, P × Kt , 8. B × B, P × K B ; 9. Q—R 5 ch, K—Q 2, etc., leaves White with no advantage at all.

6.	......	B—Kt 3

In similar positions it is far more advantageous to play 6. ...B—K 3, with the intention of opening the centre files. However, the retreat of the B to Q Kt 3 is not wrong.

7.	Kt×B	R P×Kt
8.	Kt—K 2	B—K 3
9.	Kt—B 3	

It is most important to maintain the command of the square at Q 5.

| 9. | ...... | P—R 3 |
| 10. | B—R 4 | Q—K 2 |

Position after Black's 10th move.

11. P—B 3 !

By this positional move, the result of exhaustive analysis, White, whilst reserving for himself full liberty of action on either wing, forces his opponent to decide on which side to Castle, in order to be able to elaborate his plan of attack accordingly.

Besides, the advance of the K B P is justified by the following considerations : the K B has a safe retreat should Black play P—K Kt 4, and there is an immediate attack by White's P—K Kt 4 should Black Castle on the King-side.

In the following variations Black would have had the advantage :

I.—11. Q—Q 2, B×B ; 12. P×B, Kt×P !

II.—11. Castles K R, P—K Kt 4; 12. B—K Kt 3, P—R 4.

| 11. | ...... | Castles Q R |

As the sequel shows, White's attack, favoured by the imminent opening of the Q R file, will mature more quickly than Black's counter-attack on the King-side. Better therefore is 11. ....R—Q 1, although in this case White would secure an excellent game by 12. Kt —Q 5 !

12. Kt—Q 5

Forcing the exchange of several pieces, after which White will have a clear field and will be able to launch an attack against Black's Castled position by a general advance of his Pawns.

12.	......	B×Kt
13.	B×B	P—K Kt 4
14.	B—B 2	Kt×B
15.	P×Kt	Kt—Kt 5

16. ....Kt—Kt 1 is somewhat better, though equally insufficient.

16. P—Q B 4

It is interesting to note that from this point until a decisive advantage is secured, White's plan of action comprises almost exclusively Pawn-moves.

In the handling of this game White is inspired by the example of the Grand-master of the eighteenth century, the immortal Philidor.

| 16. | ...... | P—K B 4 |
| 17. | Castles | P—R 4 |

17. ....Q R—Kt 1 would have saved a *tempo*. But Black's position was so compromised that the gain of one *tempo* would not have been sufficient to restore it.

18.	P—Q R 4	Q R—Kt 1
19.	P—R 5	P×P
20.	R×P	

Threatening 21. R—R 8 ch and 22. Q—R 4 ch.

20.	Kt—R 3
21. P—Q Kt 4 !	K—Q 1
22. P—B 5	

Equally satisfactory was 22. P—Kt 5, Kt—B 4 (if 22. ....Kt—Kt 1; 23. R—R 7); 23. P—Q 4, but White intends to win a piece and consequently adopts the text-move.

| 22. ...... | K—K 1 |
| 23. P—Q 4 | K—B 2 |

This forced flight of the King shows clearly Black's mistake in Castling Q R.

24. P—Kt 5

Position after White's 24th move.

| 24. ...... | Q P × P |

Obviously the only chance, for 24. ....Kt—Kt 1; 25. Q P × P, P × K P; 26. R—R 7 would have led to immediate disaster.

| 25. P × Kt | P—Kt 3 |
| 26. P—Q 6 | |

Interesting, and quite sufficient for victory. But 26. R—R 2, B P × P (or 26. ....K P × P; 27. R—K 1, Q—Q 3; 28. Q R—K 2); 27. Q—Kt 3, K—Kt 2; 28. R—B 1 and 29. Q R—B 2 was still simpler.

| 26. ...... | Q × P |

If 26. .... P × P (Q 3), then 27. Q—Kt 3 ch and 28. Q × Kt P.

27. Q—Kt 3 ch	Q—K 3
28. P—Q 5	Q—Q 3
29. R—R 2	R—R 1
30. R—K 1	

The commencement of the decisive action against the weak Pawns on the adverse left wing.

| 30. ...... | K R—Q 1 |
| 31. Q—Q 3 | Q—K B 3 |

The only defence, for if 31. .... K—B 3; 32. P—B 4! and if 31. ....K—Kt 3; 32. P—Kt 4! and in both cases White wins easily.

Position after Black's 31st move.

32. P—Kt 4 !

In order to utilize the Q B against the Pawns on Black's K 4 and K Kt 4, after which Black's position will speedily become untenable.

| 32. ...... | P—B 3 |
| 33. P × K B P | R × P |

If 33. ....P × P; 34. B—Kt 3, P—B 5; 35. Q—Q 1 and wins.

| 34. Q—K 4 | P—R 5 |

Preventing 35. B—Kt 3.

35. Q—K Kt 4   Q—R 3
36. B—K 3   K—B 3
37. R—K Kt 2   R—K Kt 1
38. P—B 4 !

The *coup de grâce.*

38. ......   K P × P
39. B × K B P !

Much stronger than 39. B—Q 4 ch, to which Black could still have replied by 39. ....K—B 2.

Black resigns.

GAME 45

SCOTCH GAME

Exhibition Game played at Moscow, March, 1914.

White :   *Black :*
A. ALEKHIN.   DR. EM. LASKER.

1. P—K 4   P—K 4
2. Kt—K B 3   Kt—Q B 3
3. P—Q 4

In adopting in this my first encounter with the World's Champion, this comparatively little-played opening, my object was simply to avoid the well-trodden paths of the Ruy Lopez and the Queen's Gambit, both positional openings for which at the time I did not deem myself ripe enough.

3. ......   P × P
4. Kt × P   Kt—B 3
5. Kt—Q B 3   B—Kt 5
6. Kt × Kt   Kt P × Kt
7. B—Q 3   P—Q 4

These last moves constitute the best defence to the Scotch Game.

8. P × P   P × P
9. Castles   Castles
10. B—K Kt 5   B—K 3

The usual move, which offers Black the best chances, is here 10. ....P—B 3. After the text-move

White could already play for a draw with 11. B × Kt, Q × B ; 12. Kt × P (not Q—R 5, P—K Kt 3 ; 13. Kt × P, Q—Q 1 ! and Black wins), B × Kt ; 13. Q—R 5, P—Kt 3 ; 14. Q × B, Q × P ; 15. Q R—Kt 1.

11. Q—B 3   B—K 2
12. K R—K 1

Preparing the combination which is to follow.

12. ......   P—K R 3

Position after Black's 12th move.

13. B × P !

With these little fireworks White forces the draw.

The fact that this combination, so closely connected with this opening, should never have occurred in master play nor have been pointed out in any analysis, is both curious and surprising.

This note was written before the game Romanovski—Capablanca, Moscow, 1925, was played, in which an analogous combination led to a draw.

13. ......   P × B
14. R × B !   P × R
15. Q—Kt 3 ch   K—R 1

Not 15. ....K—B 2, because of 16. Q—Kt 6 mate.

16. Q—Kt 6 !

The point. Black cannot prevent the perpetual check by 17. Q × P ch and 18. Q—Kt 5 ch, etc. He can force it by playing *e.g.* : 16. ....
Q—K 1. Therefore :
Drawn game.

GAME 46

QUEEN'S PAWN GAME

Moscow Championship Tournament,* 1916.

Brilliancy Prize

White :	Black :
A. ALEKHIN.	N. ZUBAREFF.
1. P—Q 4	Kt—K B 3
2. P—Q B 4	P—K 3
3. Kt—Q B 3	B—Kt 5
4. Q—B 2	P—Q Kt 3

In this position the fianchetto is hardly indicated, as White can obtain a very strong position in the centre. The right move was 4. ....
P—B 4, hindering 5. P—K 4.

| 5. P—K 4 ! | B—Kt 2 |
| 6. B—Q 3 | B × Kt ch |

In order to secure at least some chances on account of White's doubled Pawn. After 6. . . . P—Q 4 ; 7. B P × P, P × P ; 8. P—K 5, Kt—K 5 ; 9. Kt—K 2, etc. White's game would remain superior.

7. P × B	P—Q 3
8. Kt—K 2	Q Kt—Q 2
9. Castles	Castles
10. P—B 4	

Already threatening to win a Pawn by 11. P—K 5.

10.	P—K R 3
11. Kt—Kt 3	Q—K 2
12. Q—K 2 !	

Preparing 13. B—R 3, which, if played at once, would cause un-

* First prize without loss.

necessary complications after 12. ....Kt—Kt 5, threatening 13. ....
Kt × P !.

| 12. ...... | Q R—K 1 |

Black has completed his development very rapidly, but none of his pieces have any scope. It is easy to foresee that he will be unable to withstand the attack which his opponent is preparing in the centre.

13. B—R 3

With the strong threat 14. P—K 5, which compels Black to weaken his position still further.

| 13. ...... | P—B 4 |
| 14. Q R—K 1 | K—R 1 |

To make room for the Knight.

15. P—Q 5 !

Taking advantage of the fact that Black cannot play 15. ....P × P, because of 16. Kt—B 5.

| 15. ...... | Kt—K Kt 1 |
| 16. P—K 5 | P—Kt 3 |

Preparing the capture of the Q P, still impossible at present for the above-mentioned reason.

17. Q—Q 2

Position after White's 17th move.

17. ......   K P×P

If here 17. ....Q P×P; 18.
B P×P, P×P; 19. P—K 6!,
B P×P; 20. B×Kt P, R×R ch;
21. Kt×R, R—K B 1; 22. P×P,
and White's advantage is sufficient
to win.

18. B P×P   P×P
19. P—B 4!

The opening of the long diagonal
for the Q B decides the game in a
few moves.

19. ......   K—R 2
20. B—Kt 2! Kt (Kt 1)—B 3

If 20. ....P—B 3; 21. B×P ch,
K×B; 22. Q—Q 3 ch, P—B 4;
23. Kt×P, R×Kt; 24. P×P,
and White wins.

21. P×P   Kt—Kt 5
22. P—K 6   Q—R 5

The last hope. Evidently if 22.
....P×P; 23. B×P ch.

Position after Black's 22nd move.

23. R×P ch.

This combination forces the mate
in a dozen moves.

23. ......   R×R
24. B×P ch! K×B
25. Q—Q 3 ch K—Kt 4
26. B—B 1 ch Black resigns

For if 26. ....R—B 5; 27. Q—
B 5 mate; or if 26. ....K—B 3;
27. Q—B 5 ch and mates in a few
moves.

GAME 47

PHILIDOR'S DEFENCE

Exhibition Game at Kieff, May,
1916.

White :	Black :
A. EVENSSOHN.	A. ALEKHIN.

1.	P—K 4	P—K 4
2.	Kt—K B 3	P—Q 3
3.	P—Q 4	Kt—K B 3

This move, introduced by Niemzovitch into Master play, is now
thought stronger than 3. ....Kt—
Q 2 (the Hanham variation, see
Game No. 36).

4.	Kt—B 3	Q Kt—Q 2
5.	B—Q B 4	B—K 2

The usual move. In my opinion
5. ....P—K R 3 is more prudent.

Position after Black's 5th move.

6. Castles

For now White could have
secured a slight advantage for the
end-game by playing 6. P×P!,
Q Kt×P! (not P×P, because of 7.

B × P ch, K × B ; 8. Kt—Kt 5 ch, K—Kt 1 ; 9. Kt—K 6, Q—K 1 ; 10. Kt × B P, followed by 11. Kt × R, and White has the advantage) ; 7. Kt × Kt, P × Kt ; 8. Q × Q ch, B × Q ; 9. B—Kt 5 followed by Castles Q R, and White, besides having the better development, has prospects of seizing the only open file.

The immediate sacrifice, however, would be unsound, e.g. : 6. B × P ch, K × B ; 7. Kt—Kt 5 ch, K—Kt 1 ; 8. Kt—K 6, Q—K 1 ; 9. Kt × B P, Q—Kt 3 ; 10. Kt × R, Q × P ! ; 11. R—B 1, P × P ! ; 12. Q × P, Kt—K 4, and Black has a winning attack.

| 6. ...... | Castles |
| 7. P × P | |

This exchange of Pawn only disengages Black's game. Better would be 7. Q—K 2, P—B 3 ; 8. P—Q R 4 ! and White has the advantage. (See game No. 9.)

7.	P × P
8. B—K Kt 5	P—B 3
9. P—Q R 4	

This move is essential in this variation to prevent the possibility of a counter-attack eventually by ....P—Q Kt 4.

| 9. ...... | Q—B 2 |
| 10. Q—K 2 | Kt—B 4 |

Now Black's game is preferable, for he has the prospect of occupying the squares Q 5 and K B 5, without giving his opponent counter-chances on the King-side or in the centre.

11. Kt—K 1

Without any necessity White assumes the defensive. 11. Q R—Q 1, followed by the doubling of Rooks on the Q file, was more likely to equalize the game.

Broadly speaking, the retreat of a Knight to the first rank, where it cuts the line of communication of the Rooks, is only admissible in very exceptional cases.

11.	Kt—K 3
12. B—K 3	Kt—Q 5 !
13. Q—Q 1	

Or 13. B × Kt, P × B ; 14. Kt—Q 1, B—Q 3 ; 15. P—K Kt 3, B—K R 6 ; 16. Kt—Kt 2, Q R—K 1 ; with a marked advantage for Black.

13.	R—Q 1
14. Kt—Q 3	B—K 3
15. B × B	

After the compulsory exchange of this Bishop, the development of which is the most serious difficulty of this variation, Black's game becomes far superior.

| 15. ...... | Kt × B |
| 16. Q—K 1 | |

In view of the threat 16. ....P—B 4 ; and also to prepare the eventual advance of White's P—K B 4. But Black, quite rightly, ignores this counter-attack and simply increases the pressure in the centre.

| 16. ...... | R—Q 2 ! |
| 17. P—B 3 | |

For if now 17. P—B 4, then Kt—Kt 5 !, and White cannot play 18. P—B 5, because of R × Kt, followed by 19. ...Kt × B and 20. ...B—B 4.

17.	Q R—Q 1
18. B—B 2	Kt—R 4
19. Kt—K 2	P—Q B 4 !

This move prepares the following exchanges, the object of which is to weaken the Black squares in the adverse position.

20. P—Q Kt 3

If 20. Kt—B 3, P—B 5 ; 21. Kt—Q 5, Q—Q 3 ; 22. Kt—B 1, Kt (R 4)—B 5 ; and this last move will be even more powerful than in the actual game.

Position after White's 20th move.

20. ......   Kt (R 4)—B 5 !

Simple and decisive strategy. Black brings about the exchange of the two adverse minor pieces which might counteract his pressure on the Q file, leaving White with a Bishop only, the action of which is manifestly nil. The second phase of the game is a typical example of a regular blockade leading to the complete smothering of White's position.

21. Kt (K 2)×Kt Kt×Kt
22. Kt×Kt   P×Kt
23. P—B 3

White was threatened with 23. ....P—B 5 ; 24. P—Q Kt 4, P—B 6 ; followed by R—Q 5.

23. ......   Q—K 4
24. R—R 2   R—Q 6
25. R—B 2   P—Q Kt 3
26. Q—B 1   Q—K 3

Freeing the square at K 4 with the intention of posting his Bishop there.

27. Q—Kt 1   B—B 3
28. P—Q Kt 4

A desperate bid for freedom. If Black takes the Pawn the White Rooks can occupy the Q B file.

28. ......   P—B 5

But Black opposes this plan.

29. Q—B 1   P—K Kt 4

Before assaulting the enemy's entrenchments it is essential to block the King-side completely and to secure the command of the diagonal Q R 2—K Kt 8.

30. P—R 3   B—K 4
31. Q—R 1

Another attempt to free himself, this time by opening the Q R file. Like the preceding one it is doomed to failure.

31. ......   P—K R 4
32. P—R 5   P—Kt 5
33. P×Q Kt P   P×Kt P

Position after Black's 33rd move.

34. B—R 4

If 34. R P×P, R P×P ; 35. P×P, Q×P ; 36. B×P, R—Q 7 ; 37. R×R, R×R ; 38. B—B 2, P—B 6 ; and Black wins.

34. ......   P—B 3
35. B—K 1

Otherwise Black plays 35. .... P—Kt 6 and the White B would remain locked out for the rest of the game.

35. ......   P—Kt 6
36. Q—R 7

This skirmish momentarily retards the Pawn's advance to Q Kt 4, followed by the entry of the Queen at K 6 via Q Kt 3.

36. ......   Q—B 3 !

Threatening 37. ....R—R 1.

37. Q—R 3   P—Kt 4
38. Q—Kt 2   Q—Kt 3 ch
39. K—R 1   R—Q 8
40. R—B 1

Position after White's 40th move.

40. ......   Q—K 6 !

Definitely maintaining one Rook at Q 8 after the exchange of the other, which settles the fate of White's Bishop and of the game.

41. R—R 1   R × R
42. Q × R   Q—K 7
43. R—Kt 1   R—Q 8 !

Winning at once, for there is no perpetual check.

44. Q—R 8 ch   K—Kt 2
45. Q—R 7 ch   K—Kt 3
46. Q—K 7   Q × B !
47. Q—K 8 ch   K—Kt 4
48. Q—Kt 8 ch   K—R 5

White resigns.

GAME 48

FRENCH DEFENCE

Played in a blindfold exhibition at the military hospital in Tarnopol, September, 1916.

White :	*Black :*
A. ALEKHIN.	M. FELDT.

1. P—K 4   P—K 3
2. P—Q 4   P—Q 4
3. Kt—Q B 3   Kt—K B 3
4. P × P   Kt × P
5. Kt—K 4

More usual is 5. Kt—B 3, but the text-move, which aims at preventing 5. ....P—Q B 4, is equally to be recommended.

5. ......   P—K B 4

A weakening of the centre which will ultimately prove fatal. The best move was 5. ....Kt—Q 2, with P—Q B 4 to follow eventually.

6. Kt—Kt 5 !

A good move. White intends to play his Knight to K 5, thereby taking immediate advantage of the weakness created by his opponent's previous move.

6. ......   B—K 2

7. Kt (Kt 5)—B 3
     P—B 3

A lost *tempo*. Better is 7. .... Castles.

8. Kt—K 5   Castles
9. K Kt—B 3   P—Q Kt 3
10. B—Q 3   B—Kt 2
11. Castles   R—K 1

If here 11. ....Kt—Q 2, then 12. P—B 4, Kt (Q 4)—B 3 ; 13. Kt —Kt 5, etc.

12. P—B 4   Kt—B 3
13. B—B 4   Q Kt—Q 2
14. Q—K 2   P—B 4

Here 14. ....Kt—B 1 was essential. The text-move allows of a brilliant finish.

Position after Black's 14th move.

15. Kt—B 7 !

This threatens 16. Q×P, followed by the smothered mate, if the Black Queen moves.

15. ......   K×Kt
16. Q×P ch !

The point of the combination.

16. ......   K—Kt 3

Or if 16. ....K×Q ; 17. Kt—Kt 5, mate. Or if 16. ....K—B 1 ; 17. Kt—Kt 5, and White wins.

White announced mate in two by 17. P—K Kt 4 !, B—K 5 ; 19. Kt—R 4, mate.

GAME 49

Conclusion of an Odds Game, played at Petrograd, December, 1917.

White :   *Black :*
A. ALEKHIN.   M. GOFMEISTER.
See Diagram.

Black in this position threatens on the one hand 1. ....Kt—K 5 and 2. ....B—B 2 ch ; and on the

Initial Position.

other hand perpetual check by 1. ....Kt—B 8 ch ; 2. K—R 1, Kt—Kt 6 ch.

Despite these two threats White succeeds in forcing the win as follows :

1. P—B 5 !

Threatening to open the Q B file with decisive effect, as the following variations prove :

I.—1. ....Kt—B 8 ch ; 2. K—R 1, Kt—Kt 6 ch ; 3. R×Kt, Q×R ; 4. P×P, Q×Q (or 4. ....R×R ; 5. Q×B ch, Q—Kt 1 ; 6. Q×R, P×P ; 7. Q×P and wins) ; 5. R×R ch, Q—Kt 1 ; 6. P—Kt 7 ch, R×P ; 7. P×R ch, K×P ; 8. R×Q ch, K×R ; 9. B—B 2, P—B 4 ; 10. P—Kt 3 and White has a won endgame with his extra Pawn.

II.—1. ....Kt—K 5 (B 4) ; 2. P×P, Kt×Q ; 3. P—Kt 7 ch, R×P ; 4. P×R ch, Kt×P ; 5. R×R mate.

To avoid these dangers Black is therefore compelled to play :

1. ......   P—Kt 4.

Black by this move keeps up his threats, which indeed appear still more formidable.

Position after Black's 1st move.

Position after White's 4th move.

2. P×P !

A fresh surprise. As on the preceding move, the attempt at perpetual check proves abortive, *e.g.* :
2. ....Kt—B 8 ch ; 3. K—R 1,
Kt—Kt 6 ch ; 4. R×Kt, Q×R ;
5. P—Kt 6, Q×Q (or 5. ....P×P,
6. P×P !) ; 6. P×Q !, R×R ; 7.
P×R, B×K P ; 8. P—Kt 7 ch, K—
Kt 1 ; 9. B—R 2 ch, R—B 2 ; 10.
B—B 4 !, B—B 4 ; 11. P—Kt 3,
P×P ; 12. P—R 4, B—Q 5 ; 13.
B×R ch, K×B ; 14. P—Q 6 ch,
K—Kt 1 ; 15. P—Q 7, B—Kt 3 ;
16. P—R 5 and wins.

Black is therefore compelled to try out his counter-chances with his next move.

2. ......   Kt—K 5
3. P—Kt 6 !   Kt×Q

Already there is no longer any choice, for if 3. ....P×P ; 4. P×
P ! and wins.

4. P×Kt

A truly extraordinary position ! Black, with a whole Queen to the good, can no longer save the game !
See Diagram.

4. ......   R (K 2)—Q B 2

All other moves of Black would irretrievably have resulted in his defeat, *e.g.* :

I.—4. ....R×R; 5. P—Kt 7 ch,
R×P ; 6. P×R ch, K—Kt 1 ;
7. B×P ch, and mates in two.

II.—4. ....R—Kt 1 ; 5. P—
Kt 7 ch and mates in three.

III.—4. ....P×P ; 5. R×R
ch, K—R 2 ; 6. P×R, B×P (6.
....Q—K 4 ch or Q—B 5 ch would
only modify the inevitable result,
seeing that the Queen, situated on
a black square, would still be *en
prise* after the discovered check) ;
7. B×P ch, K×P ; 8. R—R 8 ch
and wins with the discovered check
from 9. B—K 3.

IV.—4. ....B—B 2 ! ; 5. P—
Kt 7 ch, K—Kt 1 ; 6. P×B ch, R
(K 2)×P [if 6. ....R (B 1)×P ? ;
7. B×P ch !] ; 7. R×R !, Q—B 5 ch
(White's Rook cannot be captured by the Rook, on account of
B×P ch, nor by the King, on
account of R—B 3 ch ; if instead 7.
....R—Kt 1, then 8. R—B 2,
threatening 9. K—R 1 ; 10. B—R 2
and wins) ; 8. K—R 1, Q×R ; 9.
B—R 2, Q×B ch ; 10. K×Q and
White easily wins the end-game.

5. P—Kt 7 ch   K—Kt 1
6. P—Q 7 !

The *coup de grâce.*

| 6. ...... | Q—Kt 6 ch |
| 7. K—R 1 ! | Black resigns |

Final Position.

GAME 50

PETROFF'S DEFENCE

Masters' Triangular Tournament at Moscow, May, 1918.*

White :	*Black :*
A. ALEKHIN.	A. RABINOVITCH.
	(Vilna)

1. P—K 4	P—K 4
2. Kt—K B 3	Kt—K B 3
3. Kt × P	P—Q 3
4. Kt—K B 3	Kt × P
5. Kt—B 3	P—Q 4

This ingenious sacrifice of a Pawn is not quite sound, but not for the reasons adduced in the eighth edition of the *Handbuch* and other works. The variation adopted by White in the present game seems to be the only one which secures the advantage.

6. Q—K 2	B—K 2
7. Kt × Kt	P × Kt
8. Q × P	Castles
9. B—B 4	

* First prize, without loss.

Not 9. P—Q 4, to which Black can reply 9. ....R—K 1 ; which would now be useless because of 10. Kt—K 5.

| 9. ...... | B—Q 3 |

Position after Black's 9th move.

10. Castles

An innovation.

In the game Leonhardt—Schlechter (Barmen, 1905)—which according to the *Handbuch* refutes Black's fifth move—White continued 10. P—Q 4, R—K 1 ; 11. Kt—K 5, B × Kt ; 12. P × B, Q—K 2 ? ; 13. P—B 4, B—B 4 ; 14. Q × B, Q—Kt 5 ch ; 15. B—Q 2, Q × B ; 16. Q—Q 3, maintaining the Pawn with an excellent game. But by simply playing 12. .... Kt—B 3 (instead of 12. .... Q—K 2) Black could have obtained an even game, as the following main variation shows : 12. .... Kt—B 3 ; 13. B—B 4 (if 13. P—B 4, Q—R 5 ch ; 14. P—Kt 3, Q—R 6 ; 15. B—B 1, Q—R 4, with a strong attack for Black), Q—R 5 ; 14. Castles Q R, R × P ; 15. R—Q 8 ch, Q × R ; 16. B × R, Q—K 2 ; 17. R—K 1, Kt × B ; 18. Q × Kt, Q × Q ; 19. R × Q, K—B 1.

| 10. ...... | R—K 1 |
| 11. Q—Q 3 | Kt—B 3 |

At first sight Black's prospects seem very promising, for his opponent has to contend with serious difficulties of development. But thanks to the manœuvre which follows, and which alone explains the tactics adopted hitherto, White not only surmounts all obstacles, but secures in addition a lasting initiative.

| 12. P—Q Kt 3 ! | Q—B 3 |

Position after Black's 12th move.

13. B—Kt 2 !

An unexpected sacrifice which Black is compelled to accept, for after 13. ....Q—R 3 ; 14. K R—K 1, B—K Kt 5 ; 15. P—K R 3, he has no sort of compensation for the lost Pawn, *e.g.* : 15. ....B×P ; 16. P×B, Q×R P ; 17. B×P ch, etc.

| 13. ...... | Q×B |
| 14. Kt—Kt 5 | B—K 3 |

The following alternative is hardly better : 14. ....P—K Kt 3 ; 15. B×P ch, K—Kt 2 (or 15. ....K—B 1 ; 16. B×R, K×B ; 17. Q R—K 1 ch, followed by 18. P—Q B 3 ! with a decisive attack for White) ; 16. B×R, Q—K 4 ;

17. Q—Q B 3, Kt—Kt 5 ; 18. P—B 4 !! and White maintains the gain of the Exchange.

| 15. B×B | P×B |
| 16. Q×P ch | K—B 1 |

Position after Black's 16th move.

17. Q R—K 1

Immediately decisive would be 17. P—Q B 3 !, *e.g.* :

I.—17. P—Q B 3 !, Q×Q P ; 18. Q—R 8 ch, K—K 2 ; 19. Q×P ch, K—Q 1 ; 20. Q R—Q 1, Q—B 5 ; 21. P—K Kt 3 ! and Black's Queen is trapped, for if 21. ....Q—B 1 ; 22. Kt×P ch and wins ; or if 21. ....Q—B 4 ; 22. Kt—B 7 ch, K—B 1 ; 23. R×B ! and wins.

II.—17. P—Q B 3 !, B—K 4 ; 18. Q—R 5 !, K—Kt 1 ; 19. Q—B 7 ch, K—R 1 ; 20. P—K B 4, B—B 3 ; 21. R—B 3 !, Q×R ch ; 22. K—B 2, B×Kt ; 23. P×B and White wins.

The move in the text also leads to a win, but with somewhat greater difficulty.

| 17. ...... | Q—B 3 ! |
| 18. Q—R 5 | |

Insufficient would be here 18. Q—R 8 ch, K—K 2 ; 19. R×P ch, K—Q 2 !

18. ......   K—Kt 1
19. R—K 3 !

The strongest continuation of the
attack, and at the same time setting
a trap which takes Black unawares.

19. ......   B—B 5

Relatively better would be 19.
....Kt—Q 5 ; 20. R—R 3, P—
K Kt 3 ; 21. Q—R 7 ch, K—B 1 ; 22.
Q—Q 7 !, R—K 2 (the only move,
for if 22. ....K—Kt 1 ; 23. R—
R 8 ch ! and White wins) ; 23. Kt—
R 7 ch, K—Kt 2 ; 24. Kt × Q, R × Q ;
25. Kt × R, R—Q 1 ; 26. R—Q 3,
Kt—K 7 ch ; 27. K—R 1, R × Kt.
(or 27. ....Kt—B 5 ; 28. Kt—
K 5, etc.) ; 28. P—Kt 3, P—K 4 ;
29. P—Q B 3 and White has the
advantage.

20. Q—R 7 ch   K—B 1
21. Q—R 8 ch   K—K 2
22. R × P ch   Q × R

Now compulsory, for if 22. ....
K—Q 2 ; 23. R × Q, followed by
24. R × B. etc.

23. Q × P ch   K—Q 3
24. Kt × Q   R × Kt

Black's three pieces for the Queen
are not a sufficient compensation,
for in addition to White's extra
Pawns, he has prospects of a direct
attack on the adverse King.

25. P—Q 4   Q R—K 1
26. P—B 4   R (K 1)—K 2
27. Q—B 8   R—K 5

See Diagram.

28. Q—B 5 !

Winning at least another piece.
The only possible defence is 28. ....
R (K 2)—K 3 ; after which there
follows 29. Q—B 5 ch, and 30.
P—Q 5. But Black selects the
shortest way.

28. ......   R × P
29. P—B 5 mate.

Position after Black's 27th move.

GAME 51

BISHOP'S OPENING

(Berlin Defence)

Played in a blindfold performance
of six games at Odessa, December,
1918.

White :	*Black :*
W. GONSSIOROVSKI.	A. ALEKHIN.

1. P—K 4   P—K 4
2. B—B 4   Kt—K B 3
3. P—Q 3   P—B 3 !

The most energetic line of play
against the opening selected by
White.

4. Q—K 2   B—K 2
5. P—B 4   P—Q 4 !
6. K P × P

If 6. B P × P, then 6. ....Kt × P.

6. ......   K P × P
7. B × P   Castles
8. Q Kt—Q 2

White, being already behind in
his development, cannot afford to
further that of his opponent by
playing 8. P × P, Kt × P ; etc.

8. ......   P × P
9. B—Kt 3

Position after White's 9th move.

9. ......   P—Q R 4 !

In order to induce the weakening of White's Queen-side by compelling the reply 10. P—Q R 4.

Less strong is 9. ....R—K 1, because of 10. Castles.

10. P—B 3

This move leads to the loss of an important Pawn. Comparatively better is 10. P—Q R 4.

10. ......   P—R 5
11. B—B 2   P—R 6 !
12. P—Q Kt 3   R—K 1
13. Castles Q R

There is nothing better.

13. ......   B—Q Kt 5
14. Q—B 2   B × P
15. B—Kt 5   Kt—B 3
16. Kt—B 3   P—Q 5 !
17. K R—K 1

This plausible move causes an immediate catastrophe. But in any case the game was virtually lost.

17. ......   B—Kt 7 ch
18. K—Kt 1   Kt—Q 4 !

A disagreeable surprise. The threat of an immediate mate can only be parried with the loss of a piece.

19. R × R ch   Q × R
20. Kt—K 4   Q × Kt !
21. B—Q 2

Position after White's 21st move.

21. ......   Q—K 6 !
22. R—K 1 !

White returns the compliment by leaving his Queen *en prise*, as mate is threatened by R—K 8. But the danger is short-lived.

22. ......   B—B 4 !
23. R × Q   P × R
24. Q—B 1

Black announced mate in three by 24. ....P × B ; 25. B—Q 1, Kt (B 3)—Kt 5 !; 26. any, Kt—B 6 mate.

GAME 52

DANISH GAMBIT

Moscow Championship,* October, 1919.

White :	Black :
A. ALEKHIN.	K. ISSAKOFF.

1. P—K 4   P—K 4
2. P—Q 4   P × P
3. P—Q B 3   P × P

First prize, without loss.

Declining the Gambit by 3. . . . .
P—Q 4. or 3. . . . . Q—K 2 is, in my
opinion, preferable.

4. Kt × P !

White, by giving up only one
Pawn, secures as vigorous an attack
as in the Danish Gambit, which has
been completely neglected since
Schlechter's discovery : 4. B—Q B 4,
P × P ; 5. B × P, P—Q 4 ! ; 6.
B × Q P, Kt—K B 3 !

4. . . . . . .   B—Kt 5

In a game Alekhin—Verlinski,
played at Odessa in 1918, Black
played 4. . . . . Kt—Q B 3. There
followed : 5. B—Q B 4, P—Q 3 ;
6. Kt—B 3, Kt—B 3 ; 7. Q—Kt 3,
Q—Q 2 ; 8. Kt—K Kt 5, Kt—K 4
(Kt—Q 1 is better) ; 9. B—Kt 5,
P—B 3 ; 10. P—B 4 !, P × B ; 11.
P × Kt, P × P ; 12. B—K 3 !, B—
Q 3 ; 13. Kt × Kt P, Castles ; 14.
R—Q 1, Kt—K 1 ; 15. Castles, Q—
K 2 ; 16. Kt × B, Kt × Kt ; 17.
Q—R 3 ! (not 17. Q—Kt 4, because
of Kt—B 4), R—Q 1 ; 18. Kt × B P,
B—Kt 5 ; 19. R × Kt, R—K 1 ; 20.
B—Kt 5, Q—B 2 ; 21. Q—Q Kt 3,
B—K 7 ; 22. Kt × P ch, K—
R 1 ; 23. R—B 1, R—K B 1 !, an
ingenious resource which very
nearly saves the game.

See Diagram.

24. Q—Q 1 ! ! (the only move),
Q—R 4 ; 25. Q × B, Q × Kt ; 26.
R—Q 5, and Black resigns.

5. B—Q B 4   P—Q 3

Black need not fear 6. B × P ch,
K × B ; 7. Q—Kt 3 ch, B—K 3 ;
8. Q × K B, Kt—Q B 3 ! ; 9. Q × P,
Kt—Q 5 ; which, on the contrary,
would give him a very strong
attack.

6. Kt—B 3   B × Kt ch
7. P × B   Kt—Q B 3
8. Castles   Kt—B 3
9. B—R 3

*Position after Black's 23rd move,
in sub-variation on Black's 4th
move.*

More in the spirit of the opening
is at once 9. P—K 5, and if 9. . . . .
P × P ; 10. Q—Kt 3, with prospects of a strong attack for White.
After the text-move Black could
have secured a satisfactory game by
9. . . . . B—Kt 5 ; 10. Q—Kt 3,
Kt—Q R 4 ! ; 11. B × P ch, K—B 1 ;
12. Q—R 4, B × Kt ; 13. P × B,
K × B ; 14. Q × Kt, R—K 1, etc.

9. . . . . . .   Castles
10. P—K 5   Kt—K Kt 5

After 10. . . . . Kt—K 1 ; 11. P—
K R 3 !, B—B 4 ; 12. R—K 1, etc.
Black would have a very precarious
game, the K R and K Kt being
immobilized. He therefore prefers
to give back the Pawn in order to
complete his development.

11. P × P   P × P
12. B × P   R—K 1
13. R—K 1 !

Preparing to sacrifice the K B
eventually. It is clear that Black
cannot play 13. . . . . R × R ch ; 14.
Q × R, Q × B ; 15. Q—K 8 ch, Q—
B 1 ; 16. B × P ch, K—R 1 ; 17.
Q × Q mate.

13. . . . . . .   B—B 4

Preferable, however, would be 13.
....R × R ch ; 14. Q × R, B—B 4 ;
15. R—Q 1, Q—K 1 ; 16. Kt—Q 4 !,
and Black, although having slightly
the inferior game, is safe from
immediate disaster.

Position after Black's 13th move.

14. B × P ch !

A pretty combination. Its object
is to keep the K Kt from K B 3 by
forcing the Black King to occupy
that square.

14. ......   K × B
15. Q—Q 5 ch   K—B 3

Evidently compulsory. If 15.
....B—K 3 ; 16. Kt—Kt 5 ch, etc.,
and if 15. ....K—Kt 3 ; 16. R × R,
followed by 17. Kt—R 4 ch and
White wins.

16. P—K R 3   B—K 3

Or if 16. ....Kt—R 3 ; 17. P—
Kt 4, etc.

17. Q—Q 2 !   Kt—R 3
18. P—Kt 4

Regaining by force the piece he
has sacrificed.

See Diagram.

18. ......   P—K Kt 3 !

The only resource.

Position after White's 18th move.

If 18. ....Kt—B 2 or K Kt 1,
White wins with the following problem-like variation : 19. Q—B 4 ch,
K—Kt 3 ; 20. B—K 7 ! !, Q × B ;
21. R × B ch and mates.

19. P—Kt 5 ch

Also very strong would be 19. Q ×
Kt, Q × B ; 20. P—Kt 5 ch, K—
B 2 ! ; 21. Q × R P ch, K—B 1 ;
22. Q × K Kt P, with a winning
attack.

After the text-move, which wins
back the piece, the Black King con-
trives to escape danger temporarily.

19. ......   K—B 2
20. P × Kt   Q—B 3
21. Kt—Kt 5 ch   K—Kt 1
22. P—K B 4   Q R—Q 1
23. Q R—Q 1   B—B 5

Black hopes to take advantage of
the fact that White's Q B is pinned,
in order to seize the open King's file,
but White's reply destroys this last
hope.

See Diagram.

24. B—K 7 !

The same move as in the variation referred to after Black's 18th
move, but with an entirely different
aim.

24. ......   R × Q

Position after   Black's 23rd move.

Compulsory, for if 24. .... Kt × B ;
25. Q × R ; and if 24. .... Q × B ;
25. R × Q and White wins.

25.	B × Q	R × R ch
26.	R × R	B—B 2
27.	Kt—K 4 !	

Winning at least the K R P and
at the same time creating a mating
position.

27.	......	R × P
28.	B—Kt 7	B—Kt 6
29.	Kt—B 6 ch	K—B 2
30.	Kt × P	Black resigns.

PART TWO

CHAPTER XII

ALL-RUSSIAN MASTERS' TOURNAMENT AT MOSCOW, OCTOBER, 1920

GAME 53

QUEEN'S PAWN GAME

White :	*Black :*
E. RABINOVITCH. (St. Petersburg)	A. ALEKHIN.

1. P—Q 4	Kt—K B 3
2. Kt—K B 3	P—Q Kt 3
3. P—B 4	P—K 3
4. Kt—B 3	

Rubinstein's system, 4. P—K Kt 3 and 5. B—Kt 2 here, or on the next move, is considered better.

4.	B—Kt 2
5. P—K 3	

This allows Black to occupy the square K 5 with effect, and thus to secure at least an equal game.

5.	B—Kt 5
6. Q—B 2	Kt—K 5
7. B—Q 3	P—K B 4

In this manner Black has brought about a position, favourable to himself, of the Dutch Defence.

8. Castles

White could here have selected another line of play : 8. B—Q 2,

B × Kt ; 9. B × B, Castles ; 10. Castles Q R, after which Black seizes the initiative by 10. . . . . P— Q R 4 ! and 11. . . . . Kt—R 3 (Sämisch—Alekhin, Pistyan, 1922).

8.	B × Kt
9. P × B	Castles
10. Kt—Q 2	

The only way to enforce the advance of the K P.

10.	Q—R 5 !

An important developing move to which White cannot reply by 11. P—Kt 3 without disadvantage, because of 11. . . . . Kt—Kt 4 ! and if 12. P—K 4 then 12. . . . . P × P ! and Black wins.

11. P—B 3	Kt × Kt
12. B × Kt	Kt—B 3

12. . . . . P—B 4 would not be so good, because of 13. P—Q 5 !

13. P—K 4	P × P
14. B × P	

White appears to over-rate the strength of his position.
More correct was 14. P × P, P—K 4 ! ; 15. P—Q 5 ; Kt—K 2 ; 16. P—B 5 !, Kt—Kt 3 (not 16. . . . . P × P, because of 17. P—Q 6 and

129

18. Q—Kt 3 ch); 17. P×P,
R P×P, with about an equal game.

14. ......   Kt—R 4

Securing a slight advantage,
should White choose the best variation, 15. B×B, Kt×B ; 16. K R—
K 1, by reason of White's doubled
Pawns on the Q B file.

15. Q R—K 1

This plausible move leads to the
loss of a Pawn.

15. ......   B×B !
16. R×B   Q—R 4
17. Q—R 4

There was no satisfactory defence
to the Q B P, *e.g. :* 17. R—K 5,
R←B 4 ! ; 18. R×R, Q×R ; 19.
Q×Q, P×Q, and Black has virtually a won end-game.

17. ......   Kt×P !

Now Black has every justification
for anticipating victory, yet in
spite of his advantage in material it
is not easy to achieve it, for the
adverse position shows no weak
point.

18. R—K 2

Clearly, if 18. Q×Kt, P—Q 4 ;
19. Q—Kt 5, P—Q R 3 and Black
wins.

18. ......   P—Q Kt 4
19. Q—Kt 3   Q—K B 4
20. K R—K 1   Q R—Kt 1
21. B—B 1   P—Q R 4
22. R—K 4   P—R 5
23. Q—Q 1   Q R—K 1

Having consolidated the dominating position of his Knight, Black
now prepares an action in the
centre which will enable him to
shatter the hostile position, although
allowing his opponent apparent
compensations.

24. Q—K 2   P—B 4 !

Although this temporarily increases the range of action of White's
Q B, yet by this reason the Bishop
later on becomes an object of
attack.

This plan demanded an exhaustive examination of the tactical
possibilities of the position, and was
not undertaken until Black was perfectly convinced that it would ultimately result in his favour.

25. B—K 3   P×P
26. B×P

Position after White's 26th move.

26. ......   P—K 4 !

The beginning of a series of
extremely interesting complications.
The Pawn cannot be captured by
the Bishop, because of 27. ....P—
Q 4 !, and the variation 27. B—B 5,
P—Q 4 ; 28. R×Kt, Kt P×R ;
29. B×R, Q×B, would also be to
Black's advantage.

27. P—B 4 !

Undoubtedly the best chance.
White intends to answer 27. ....
P—Q 4 with 28. R×P, Kt×R ; 29.
B×Kt, which would give him quite
a defendable game.

27. ......   P—Q 3

Sufficing for the protection of the Pawn, because of the mate in two moves after 28. P×P, P×P ; 29. B×P ?, Kt×B ; 30. R×Kt, R×R ; 31. Q×R, etc.

28. P—R 3

Again threatening Black's K P, which he will at once defend in an indirect manner.

28.	R—K 3 !
29. P×P	P×P
30. B—B 5 !	

Not 30. B×P on account of 30. ....R (B 1)—K 1 ; 31. R—K B 1, Q—Kt 3 ; 32. R×Kt, R×B and wins.
The text-move appears full of promise, seeing that the Black Rook cannot leave the K B file, e.g. : 30. ....R—Q 1 ; 31. R—K B 1, Q—Kt 3 ; 32. R—Kt 4, Q—R 3 ; 33. Q—B 3 ! and wins.

30. ......   R—B 2 !

The initial move of a sacrificial combination intended to yield a decisive attack. As a mere defensive move, 30. ....K R—B 3 would be adequate, as White could not answer 31. R—Kt 1 because of 31. ....Kt—Q 7 !

31. R—Kt 1

Seemingly recovering his Pawn with a good game, for 31. .... Kt—Q 7 is now impossible on account of 32. Q×Kt, threatening Q—Q 8 ch, etc.

31. ......   P—R 3

This parries the threat of mate and compels the opponent to persevere on the perilous path on which he is proceeding.

| 32. R×Kt P | Kt—Q 7 ! |
| 33. R×R P | |

White has no longer any defence, for if 33. R—K Kt 4, Black would

win in an analogous manner to that in the text.
If 33. R—K 3, then 33. ....R—K Kt 3 (this diversion was the special point of playing the K R to B 2 instead of B 3 on the 30th move) ; 34. R—Kt 8 ch, K—R 2 ; 35. R—Kt 2 (or 35. Q×Kt, Q—B 8 ch ; 36. K—R 2, R—B 7 and wins), Kt—B 6 ch ; 36. K—R 1, Q×P ch ! and mates next move.

Position after White's 33rd move.

33. ......   Q—B 7 !

After this move, which explains the foregoing sacrifice of two Pawns, White is lost, owing to inability to withdraw his Rooks to secure the defence of his first rank.

34. R—R 8 ch	K—R 2
35. K—R 1	R—B 8 ch
36. B—Kt 1	R×B ch !

A pretty final combination.

37. K×R	Q—B 8 ch
38. K—B 2	R—B 3 ch
39. K—K 3	

If 39. K—Kt 3, Kt—B 8 ch. Now Black's next move wins the Queen or mates.

39. ......   Kt—Kt 8 ch !
White resigns.

CHAPTER XIII

INTERNATIONAL TOURNAMENT AT TRIBERG
JULY, 1921

GAME 54

QUEEN'S PAWN GAME

White :   *Black :*

A. A. SELESNIEFF.   A. ALEKHIN.

1. P—Q 4   Kt—K B 3
2. Kt—K B 3   P—Q Kt 3

This move is possible before P—K 3, because White has played 2. Kt—K B 3, but after 2. P—Q B 4 it is not good on account of 3. Kt—Q B 3, B—Kt 2 ; 4. Q—B 2 ! (see Game No. 77)

3. P—K Kt 3

In my opinion best, as White's Bishop on K Kt 2 is at least as strong as Black's on Q Kt 2.

3. ......   B—Kt 2
4. B—Kt 2   P—Q 3

This system of development was introduced by the author in one of his match-games against Teichmann at Berlin, 1921. Its only defect is that Black's Q B 3 may eventually become weak, a weakness, however, which does not present very great drawbacks.

5. Castles

In the course of the same tournament, a game Brinckmann—Alekhin was continued as follows : 5. P—Kt 3, Q Kt—Q 2 ; 6. B—Kt 2, P — K 4 ; 7. P × P, P × P ; 8. Castles, P—K 5 ! ; 9. Kt—K 5, B—Q 3 ; 10. Kt × Kt, Q × Kt ; 11. Kt—Q 2, Q—K 3 ; 12. P—K 3, P—K R 4 ! ; 13. Q—K 2, P—R 5 ; 14. Kt—B 4, B—B 4 ; 15. K R—Q 1, B—Q 4 ; 16. Kt—R 3, P × P ; 17. R P × P, P—R 3 ; 18. P—Q B 4, B—Kt 2 ; 19. Kt—B 2, Q—B 4 ; 20. B—R 3, B × B ; 21. Kt × B, Kt—Kt 5 ; 22. Kt—B 2, R—R 7 ; 23. Q—Q 2, K—K 2 ! ; 24. Kt—Kt 4, Q R—R 1 ; 25. Q—K 2, Q—B 6 ! ! ; 26. Resigns.

5. ......   Q Kt—Q 2
6. B—B 4

To prevent 6. ....P—K 4.

6. ......   P—K R 3

Threatening P—K Kt 4 in some combinative variations ; but the real intention is to make this advance only when Black is assured of an immediate and definite advantage.

7. Kt—B 3

Allowing the following demonstration aimed at the Q P.

| 7. ...... | P—B 4 |
| 8. P—Q 5 | |

After 8. P×P, Kt×P, Black would also have secured a very promising position.

| 8. ...... | P—Q Kt 4 ! |

Otherwise White by playing 9. P—Q R 4 ! would prevent Black from seizing the initiative on the Queen-side.

9. Kt—K 1

White's Q P is certainly more valuable than Black's Q Kt P.

9.	P—Q R 3
10. P—Q R 4	P—Kt 5
11. Kt—K 4	Kt×Kt
12. B×Kt	P—Kt 3

So as to develop the Bishop at K Kt 2, the object of the manœuvre commencing 7. ....P—B 4.

| 13. P—B 4 | P×P e. p. |

Absolutely essential to prevent White from blocking the Queen-side, which would have enabled him to undertake a strong attack by the advance of his centre Pawns, without fear of molestation.

14. P×P	B—Kt 2
15. R—Kt 1	R—Q Kt 1
16. P—B 4	Castles
17. Q—B 2	P—Q R 4

Preparing the following sacrifice of the Exchange.

18. Kt—B 3	Q—B 2
19. B—Q 2	B—R 3
20. B—Q 3	

See Diagram.

| 20. ...... | R—Kt 5 ! ! |

Absolutely correct. The strong passed Pawn thus resulting, supported by the Bishop on K Kt 2, and the possibilities of attack on White's Q B P are, on the whole, worth more than the Exchange.

Position after White's 20th move.

| 21. B×R | B P×B |
| 22. Kt—Q 2 | Kt—B 4 |

But this move is illogical. Black could have demonstrated the correctness of his sacrifice more clearly by 22. ....R—Q B 1, followed by 23. ....Kt—Kt 3 or also 23. .... Kt—K 4, and if necessary 23. .... B—B 6.

23. Kt—Kt 3 !

Position after White's 23rd move.

A strong move, the value of which was not appreciated in good time. If Black replies to it by 23. .....Kt×P, White could advantageously continue 24. R—R 1 !, Kt—B 4 ; 25.

Kt×P, B×R ; 26. R×B, K—R 2
(else 27. B×P !) ; 27. Kt—B 6. Or
if 23. ....R—B 1 ; 24. Kt×Kt,
Q×Kt ; 25. K R—B 1, B—B 6 ;
26. Q—Kt 3 (not 26. R—Kt 3,
B×P ; 27. R×B, P×R ; 28. B×P,
on account of 28. ....K—Kt 2 !),
Q—Q 5 ; 27. R×B, P×R ; 28.
R—Q B 1 and White cannot lose.

23. ......   Kt—Q 2

So Black must submit to this
temporary retreat, while threatening 24. ....R—Q B 1. But White
seizes the opportunity to eliminate
his weak Q B P by a counter-sacri-
fice which opens new lines and
affords at the same time excellent
chances.

Position after Black's 23rd move.

24. P—B 5 !   B×B
25. P×B !

After 25. Q×B, P×P, Black's
passed Pawns would soon decide the
game. The text-move parries this
danger, whilst opening the King's file
for White. On the other hand there
is the drawback, very slight though
it may be, of weakening the King's
position, and particularly K B 3, a
weakness which Black will exploit
later on.

25. ......   P×P
26. K R—K 1

Against the plausible move 26.
Q—B 4, which was equally to be
considered, Black would have re-
torted 26. ....Q—Q 3 ! ; 27. Kt×
R P, Kt—K 4 ; 28. Q—Kt 3, R—
R 1, with excellent chances.

26. ......   Kt—K 4
27. R—K 3

The attempt to give back the
Exchange, in his turn, would have
been insufficient : 27. Q×P, Kt—
B 6 ch ; 28. K—B 1, Q×Q ; 29.
Kt×Q, Kt—Q 7 ch ! ; 30. K—K 2,
Kt×R ; 31. R×Kt, R—Q 1 ! and
Black wins a Pawn.

27. ......   R—B 1
28. R—Q B 1   Q—Q 2 !
29. P—Q 4   Kt—Kt 5
30. R—K 4

If 30. P×P, Kt×R ; 31. P×Kt,
Q×R P !, but not 31. ....Q×Q P.

30. ......   P—B 5 !

Now Black's Queen-side Pawns
become very threatening. The question is, how to maintain them ! The
game now enters upon its most
critical phase.

31. Kt—B 5

If 31. Kt×P, obviously 31. ....
Q×Q P and Black wins easily.

31. ......   Q—B 4 !
32. Q—K 2 !

White has defended himself excel-
lently, and hopes to obtain a
decisive advantage by the text-
move, which threatens the Knight
and the B P at the same time ; but
Black's reply gives him a disagreeable surprise.

See Diagram.

32. ......   P—Kt 6 ! !

Before deciding on this surprising
move, Black had to visualize the
following variations, apart from the
continuation in the text.

Position after White's 32nd move.

I.—33. R—B 4, Q—R 4 ; 34. R×Kt, P—Kt 7 ; 35. R—Kt 1, Q 1 or K 1 (if 35. Q×Kt P, Q×R as in the game), B×P and Black's Pawns become overwhelming.

II.—33. Q×Kt, P—Kt 7 ; 34. R—Kt 1, Q×Q ; 35. R×Q, P—B 6 ; 36. Kt—Q 3, R—B 5 ; 37. Kt×P !, R—Kt 5 ! ; 38. R—K 4, K—B 1 with advantage to Black, for if 39. R—Q B 1, P—B 4 ! ; 40. Kt—Q 3, P×R ; 41. Kt×R, P×Kt ; 42. P—R 5, B×P ; 43. P—R 6, K—B 2 ! and wins.

33. R×Kt	P—Kt 7
34. Q×Kt P	Q×R
35. R×P	

Apparently White has chosen the simplest method of extricating himself from his difficulties, for he has eliminated the passed Pawns and remains a Pawn to the good. However, Black's next move creates new difficulties for him.

35. ......   P—K R 4 !

Profiting by the immobility of the hostile pieces to threaten a mating attack by P—R 5—R 6, followed by Q—B 6.

36. Q—B 2

The only resource for the defence, in fact, consists in playing the White Queen to Q 3.

36. ......   P—R 5

Naturally not B×P, on account of 37. K—Kt 2 !

37. Q—Q 3   R—Q 1 !

37. P—R 6 would be insufficient, as after 38. P—B 3, Q—R 4 (38. ....Q—Kt 4 ? ; 39. Kt—K 4 !) ; 39. Q—K 4, Q—R 3 ; 40. R—B 2, White could defend himself satisfactorily.

38. P—B 3   Q—R 4

Not 38. ....Q—R 6 on account of 39. P—Kt 4, R—Kt 1 ; 40. Kt—K 4, R—Kt 7 ; 41. R—B 8 ch !, B—B 1 ; 42. Kt—B 2 and White would win the Exchange.

39. Q—K 4	P×P
40. P×P	Q—Kt 4 !
41. K—Kt 2	Q—Q 7 ch

After 41. R×P White would have forced the exchange of Queens by 42. P—B 4, Q—R 4 ; 43. Q—B 3, and Black would have difficulty in securing the win.

42. K—R 3   B—B 3 !

In order to occupy the K R file with the Rook : the only means of securing the win.

43. R—B 2	Q—R 3 ch
44. K—Kt 2	K—Kt 2
45. P—Kt 4	

Otherwise this Pawn would be lost, without any compensation.

45.	R—K R 1
46. K—B 2 !	

It will be admitted that White defends himself with remarkable coolness.

Position after White's 46th move.

46. ......   R—Q Kt 1 ! !

The point of the manœuvre initiated by 42. ....B—K B 3. Black's Rook was brought to the K R file solely in order to force the entry of the Queen into the hostile game by that means. Its mission accomplished, the Rook returns to the Queen-side and contributes to an attack against the key of the hostile positions (White's Pawn on Q 4), a manœuvre against which White is absolutely defenceless.

47. K—K 2   R—Kt 5
48. R—Q 2   Q—R 7 ch
49. K—K 3

Or 49. K—Q 3, Q—Kt 8 !

49. ......   Q—Kt 8 ch
50. K—K 2   B × P

Now White could well have resigned, but, on the contrary, he tries a desperate move and by his tenacity he achieves a partial success.

51. Kt—Q 3   R—Kt 8

51. ....B—B 6 ! ; 52. Kt × R, Q—Kt 7 ch was immediately decisive.

52. Kt—B 1 !   B—B 6 !

With 52. ....R—Q Kt 5 ; 53. Kt—Q 3 (there is nothing better) Black could have brought about the same position as after White's 51st move ; but he prefers to accept the *fait accompli*, as the variation on the text appears to him to be sufficiently clear and satisfactory.

53. Q × R   Q—Kt 7 ch
54. K—Q 3   Q × R ch
55. K—B 4   Q—Q 5 ch
56. K—Kt 3

Position after White's 56th move.

56. ......   B—R 8 !

The continuation which Black had in view when playing 52. .... B—B 6. Now White will find it impossible to defend his Pawns.

For example, if 57. Kt—Q 3, Q × Q P ch ; 58. K—R 3, B—B 3 ; 59. Q—Q 1, P—Kt 4 ! ; 60. Q—K 2, Q—Q B 5 ! ; 61. Q—Q 1, Q—B 6 ch ; 62. K—R 2, P—K 3 ! and Black wins.

57. K—R 3   Q—B 4 ch
58. K—R 2   B—B 3
59. P—Kt 5

Another desperate attempt. As the sequel will show, White follows a plan which promises him an illusory salvation.

59.	......	Q × P ch
60.	Kt—Kt 3	Q × Kt P
61.	Q—K 1	

Staking his last hope on the Q R P, but his opponent will soon destroy this last illusion, by sacrificing his B for the Q R P, after which the Black passed Pawns on the Kingside win very easily.

61.	......	Q—Kt 7 ch
62.	Q—Q 2	Q × P !
63.	Q × P	P—Kt 4
64.	Q—K 1	Q—B 6
65.	Q × Q	B × Q
66.	P—R 5	B × P
67.	Kt × B	P—Kt 5
68.	Kt—B 4	P—Kt 6
69.	Kt—Q 2	K—Kt 3
70.	K—Kt 2	K—B 4
71.	Kt—B 3	K—B 5
72.	Kt—Kt 1	K—K 6
73.	K—B 2	K—B 7
74.	Kt—R 3 ch	K—B 8

White resigns.

A very difficult and interesting game in all its phases.

GAME 55

QUEEN'S PAWN OPENING

Brilliancy Prize

| White : | Black : |
| A. ALEKHIN. | E. D. BOGOLJUBOFF. |

1.	P—Q 4	Kt—K B 3
2.	Kt—K B 3	P—K 3
3.	P—B 4	P—Q Kt 3

This variation, abandoned by Bogoljuboff in consequence of this game, has been played with success in recent tournaments by the masters Sämisch and Niemzovitch. Black's defeat in this game cannot therefore be attributed to this variation, but solely to his fifth move. (See note thereto.)

| 4. | P—K Kt 3 | B—Kt 2 |
| 5. | B—Kt 2 | P—B 4 |

This move gives White the choice of two replies. Besides 6. P × P as in the present game, White can also continue with 6. P—Q 5, P × P ; 7. Kt—R 4 (proposed by Rubinstein in the latest edition of Collijn's *Lärobok*), and it is difficult to see how Black is to free his game. (Compare, however, the game Alekhin—Capablanca from the New York Tournament, 1927.)

The correct move for Black is : 5. ....B—K 2 ; followed by 6. Castles, Castles ; 7. Kt—B 3, P—Q 4 ; 8. Kt—K 5 !, Q—B 1 ! (suggested by Sämisch), with a satisfactory game.

Less good, however, would be :

I.—8. ....Q Kt—Q 2 ; 9. P × P, Kt × Kt (P × P is better) ; 10. P—Q 6 ! (Bogoljuboff—Niemzovitch, Carlsbad, 1923), or

II.—8. ....P—B 3 ; 9. P—K 4, Q Kt—Q 2 ; 10. Kt × Q B P !, B × Kt ; 11. K P × P, B—Kt 2 ; 12. P—Q 6 and White wins a Pawn (a variation suggested by the author).

6. P × P

As the sequel shows, White secures an advantage by this simple move, thanks to the pressure he will exert on the open Q file.

6. ...... B × P

The position of the Black Bishops is stronger in appearance than in fact, as White's castled position is perfectly secure.

| 7. | Castles | Castles |
| 8. | Kt—B 3 | P—Q 4 |

Giving White the opportunity of unmasking the K B with advantage. Relatively better is : 8. ....Kt—R 3, although in this case also the weakness of his Q P would have been a source of difficulty for Black.

9. Kt—Q 4 !

Not 9. Kt—K 5, because of the reply 9. ....Q—B 2 ; 10. B—B 4, Kt—R 4, etc.

9. ......   B×Kt

Perceiving the possibility of ridding himself of the troublesome Q P, Black allows his opponent the advantage of having two Bishops, which, in this position, implies a very marked superiority. On the other hand, it is true that the alternative : 9. ....Kt—B 3 ; 10. Kt ×Kt, B×Kt ; 11. B—Kt 5, B—K 2 ; 12. R—B 1, is hardly more attractive.

10. Q×B   Kt—B 3
11. Q—R 4   P×P

Hoping to obtain an approximately equal game by Kt—K 4 or Kt—Q R 4, once White has recaptured the Q B P with the Queen. But White is careful to refrain from that course, and prefers to launch a direct attack on the King's position, which, despite appearances, is insufficiently defended.

12. R—Q 1 !   Q—B 1

Forced. If 12. ....Q—K 2 ; 13. B—Kt 5, P—K R 3 ; 14. B×Kt, Q×B ; 15. Q×Q, P×Q ; 16. R—Q 7, winning Kt and B for the Rook.

13. B—Kt 5 !   Kt—Q 4

Or 13. ....Kt—Q 2 ; 14. Kt—K 4, with a strong attack for White. With the text-move Black hopes to exchange one of the White Bishops by discovering his Q B on the 15th move.

14. Kt×Kt   P×Kt
15. R×P !

This unexpected capture which, at first sight, seems to expose the Rook to an attack by Black's Q B, is fully justified by the sacrificial variations following upon White's next move.

15. ......   Kt—Kt 5

It is clear that other replies would be no better.

Position after Black's 15th move.

16. B—K 4 ! !

Decisive, as is shown in the variations given farther on. The reader will clearly perceive a similarity with other games (which also gained brilliancy prizes) namely : *v.* Sterk at Budapest (Game No. 56), Rubinstein at Carlsbad (Game No. 80) and Selesnieff at Pistyan (Game No. 63).

The leading characteristic in these games is an unforeseen but immediately decisive attack.

The chief point in these attacks lies in the fact that none of them was prepared in the immediate vicinity of its objective. On the contrary, all the preliminary manœuvres which tended to divert the adverse pieces from the defence of their King took place in the centre or on the opposite wing. Furthermore, it is interesting to note that the deciding move, a real hammer-blow, is played by a Bishop and always involves sacrificial variations.

These repeated attacks in the same manner, in the course of games of widely different character, seem to me to constitute a very precise criterion of a player's style, or at least, of the evolution of his style.

16. ......   P—B 4

Other variations would be no better, *e.g. :*

I.—16. ....P—K R 3 ; 17. B×P, P—B 4 ; 18. Q—Kt 5, Q—B 2 ; 19. B×Kt P, Q×B ; 20. Q×Q ch, K×Q ; 21. R—Q 7 ch, followed by B×B and White wins.

II.—16. ....P—Kt 3 ; 17. B—B 6, Kt×R ; 18. B×Kt and White wins. After the text-move Black loses the Queen against Rook and Bishop, and White's victory is only a question of time.

17. B×P !	R×B
18. R—Q 8 ch	Q×R
19. B×Q	R—Q B 1
20. R—Q 1	R—K B 2
21. Q—Kt 4	Kt—Q 6

An inoffensive manœuvre. Black is quite helpless, and can only hope for a miracle !

22. P×Kt	R×B
23. P×P	Q R—K B 1
24. P—B 4	R—K 2
25. K—B 2	P—K R 3
26. R—K 1	B—B 1
27. Q—B 3	R (K 2)—K B 2
28. Q—Q 5	P—K Kt 4
29. R—K 7	P×P
30. P×P	Black resigns

CHAPTER XIV

INTERNATIONAL TOURNAMENT AT BUDAPEST
SEPTEMBER, 1921

GAME 56

QUEEN'S GAMBIT DECLINED

Brilliancy Prize

White :	*Black :*
A. ALEKHIN.	K. STERK.

1. P—Q 4	P—Q 4
2. Kt—K B 3	Kt—K B 3
3. P—B 4	P—K 3
4. Kt—B 3	Q Kt—Q 2
5. P—K 3	

After Black's last move, which is probably inferior to 4. ....B—K 2, White has the choice of several good continuations :

I.—5. B—Kt 5 (if 5. B—B 4 ?, P×P ; 6. P—K 3, Kt—Kt 3 !).

II.—5. P×P, P×P ; 6. B—B 4 ! (suggested by Sämisch). On the other hand, Soldetenkoff's ingenious move, 6. Q—Kt 3, proves insufficient, as the following variation shows : 6. ....P—B 3 ; 7. P—K 4, Kt×P ! ; 8. Kt×Kt, Q—K 2 !

III.—5. P—K 3, the text-move, less energetic perhaps, but affording White a slight advantage in development, if correctly followed up.

5. ......   B—Q 3

A risky move which White does not exploit in the most energetic manner. Black obtains a satisfac-

tory game by the more solid variation 5. ....B—K 2 ; 6. B—Q 3, P×P ; 7. B×B P, P—B 4.

6. Kt—Q Kt 5.

With this reply, original but of doubtful value, White lets slip his chances. The retort 6. P—B 5, B—K 2 ; 7. P—Q Kt 4 followed by 8. B—Kt 2 was indicated, and would have enabled White to exercise pressure on the Queen's side before Black, by reason of his loss of time, could undertake a counter-demonstration in the centre. The text-move is intended to prevent 8...P—K 4, after 6. B—Q 3, P×P ; 7. B×B P, Castles ; 8. Castles, but the loss of time occasioned allows Black to equalize the game without difficulty.

6.	B—K 2
7. Q—B 2	P—B 3
8. Kt—B 3	Castles
9. B—Q 3	P×P
10. B×P	P—B 4 !

Black, as can easily be seen, has been fortunate enough to surmount all the difficulties of the opening.

11. P×P

After 11. Castles, Kt—Kt 3 ; 12. B—Q 3, P×P ; 13. P×P, B—Q 2 White would not have sufficient compensation for his isolated Q P.

11.	. . . . . .	B × P
12.	Castles	P—Q Kt 3
13.	P—K 4	

White, after his careless treatment of the opening, seeks complications which are not without danger to himself.

13. P—Q Kt 3, B—Kt 2 ; 14. B—Kt 2, R—B 1 ; 15. Q—K 2 would suffice to equalize the game.

13.	. . . . . .	B—Kt 2
14.	B—K Kt 5	

Not 14. P—K 5, Kt—Kt 5 ! ; 15. Kt—K Kt 5, P—Kt 3 ; 16. Kt × R P, Q—R 5 ; 17. P—K R 3, Q—Kt 6, followed by mate.

14.	. . . . . .	Q—B 1 !

A very good move which puts an end to all the opponent's fond hopes. Not only is Black out of danger, but it is actually he who is going to undertake a counter-attack.

15. Q—K 2

Preventing the threatened 15. ....B × P ch. However, 15. B—Q 3 was preferable.

15.	. . . . . .	B—Kt 5 !

Position after Black's 15th move.

This move marks the critical phase. White, whose game is compromised, will make a serious effort to maintain equality. What is he to do ? Neither 16. P—K 5, Kt—Kt 5 ; nor 16. Q R—B 1, B × Kt ; 17. B—Q 3, Kt—B 4 ! ; 18. R × B, B × P ! ; 19. B × Kt, B × B, threatening B × R, etc., would be sufficient. After a quarter of an hour's perplexity, White succeeded in resolving the difficulty.

16.	B—Q 3	B × Kt

Position after Black's 16th move.

17. K R—Q B 1 !

The saving move, because if Black now plays 17. ....Kt—B 4, which is his best, the continuation would be 18. R × B, B × P ; 19. B × Kt, B × B ; 20. Q—K 3 ! Here is the difference from the preceding variation : Black's Q B no longer attacks White's Rook on K B 1. 20. ....P × B ; 21. P—Q Kt 4, B—Kt 3 ; 22. P × Kt, P × P ; 23. R × P, Q moves anywhere ; 24. P— K R 4 and White will find his attacking possibilities adequate compensation for the Pawn thus sacrificed.

17.	. . . . . .	Kt × P

Black attempts to win a Pawn without compromising the position of his King, but does not sufficiently count the danger to which he exposes his Kt on B 4.

18. B × Kt   B × B
19. Q × B   Kt—B 4
20. Q—K 2 !

More energetic than 20. Q—Kt 1, suggested by some annotators, which would have yielded the win of only two minor pieces for a Rook, after 20. ....B—Kt 5; 21. P—Q R 3, Q—Kt 2, while allowing Black numerous defensive possibilities.

20. ......   B—R 4
21. Q R—Kt 1   Q—R 3
22. R—B 4   Kt—R 5

An ingenious resource, but inadequate. If 23. P—Q Kt 4, then 23. ....Kt—B 6 !

However, Black has no longer any saving move. If, for example, 22. ....P—B 3, then 23. B—R 4 !, etc.

Position after Black's 22nd move.

23. B—B 6 ! !

The initial move of a mating attack as elegant as it is unexpected, which leads to this end in a few moves. Black is threatened

with 24. R—K Kt 4, Q × Q; 25. R × P ch and mate next move. If 23. ....P—R 4; 24. R—K Kt 4 !, Q × Q; 25. R × P ch, K—R 1; 26, Kt—Kt 5 ! and Black has no defence against 27. R—R 7 ch, followed by 28. R—R 8 mate. If 23. ....P—R 3; 24. Kt—K 5 ! with the threat Q—Kt 4, and White wins.

23. ......   K R—Q B 1 !

The only move ! White replies to it by a new surprise.

24. Q—K 5 !

The necessary corollary to the preceding move.

Position after White's 24th move.

24. ......   R—B 4

The following variations are also insufficient :

I.—24. ...Q × R; 25. Q—K Kt 5, K—B 1; 26. Q × P ch, K—K 1; 27. Q—Kt 8 ch, K—Q 2; 28. Kt—K 5 ch, K—B 2; 29. Q × P ch, followed by 30. Kt × Q.

II.—24....R × R; 25. Q—K Kt 5, R—K Kt 5; 26. Q × R, P—Kt 3; 27. Q × Kt.

III.—24. ....P×B ; 25. R—
Kt 4 ch and mate in two moves.

The text-move avoids the variation 25. R×R, P×B, etc., but
White answers with a still stronger
reply.

25. Q—Kt 3 !

Simple and decisive.

25.	P—Kt 3
26. R×Kt	Q—Q 6
27. R—K B 1	Q—B 4
28. Q—B 4	Q—B 7
29. Q—R 6	Black resigns.

GAME 57

QUEEN'S PAWN GAME

White :   *Black :*
A. ALEKHIN.   E. D. BOGOLJUBOFF.

1. P—Q 4	Kt—K B 3
2. P—Q B 4	P—K 3
3. Kt—K B 3	B—Kt 5 ch

3. ....P—Q 4 or 3. ....P—
Q Kt 3 would be preferable.

4. B—Q 2   B×B ch

This exchange assists White's
development. Black's K B in the
Queen's Gambit is far too valuable
a defensive piece to be exchanged
at the commencement with loss of
time.

5. Q×B	Castles
6. Kt—B 3	P—Q 4
7. P—K 3	Q Kt—Q 2
8. B—Q 3	P—B 3
9. Castles K R	

Allowing Black to free himself by
an ingenious manœuvre. White
could have frustrated this plan by
9. R—Q 1 !, and Black's position
would have remained very cramped.

| 9. ...... | P×P |
| 10. B×P | P—K 4 ! |

Taking advantage of the exposed
position of White's Queen, for if now
11. P×P, then 11. ....Kt×P !,
and Black equalizes with ease.

Position after Black's 10th move.

11. B—Kt 3 !

By this move, which prevents
Black from gaining time later on
with Kt—Kt 3, White indirectly
meets 11. ....P—K 5, which would
now result merely in the loss of a
Pawn after 12. Kt—Kt 5, and thus
White still maintains a slight superiority.
The sacrifice 11. B×P ch would
only lead to a draw, e.g. :—

I.—11. B×P ch, R×B ; 12. P×
P, Kt—Kt 5 ; 13. P—K 6, R×Kt ! ;
14. P×Kt, B×P ; 15. P×R, Kt×
R P ! (not 15. ....Q—R 5, because
of 16. Q—Q 6) ; 16. K×Kt, Q—
R 5 ch and draws by perpetual check.

II.—11. B×P ch, K×B ? ; 12.
P×P, Kt—Kt 5 ; 13. Q R—Q 1 !,
Q—K 2 ; 14. P—K 6 ch !, K×P ;
15. Q—Q 4, Kt (Kt 5)—K 4 ; 16.
Kt×Kt, Kt×Kt ; 17. P—B 4 !,
and White obtains a strong attack.

11. ......   Q—K 2

In his game against Johner
(Pistyan, 1922), Grünfeld tried
11. ....P×P ; 12. Q×P (12.

P × P also deserves consideration),
Q—Kt 3 and finally secured the
draw. After the text-move the
superiority of White's game is clear.

12. P—K 4 !	P × P
13. Kt × P	Kt—B 4

13. ....Kt × P is impossible,
both now and on the next move, on
account of Q—K 3, winning a piece.

14. B—B 2	R—Q 1
15. Q R—Q 1	

Threatening 16. Kt × P, etc.

15.	B—Kt 5
16. P—B 3	Kt—K 3
17. Q—B 2	Kt × Kt
18. R × Kt	B—K 3
19. K R—Q 1	

Black was compelled to abandon
the only open file in order to develop
his Q B. Furthermore, the White
centre Pawns, thanks to their
mobility, will be able to attack
Black's Knight and Bishop successfully.

As against this, the notorious
" majority of Pawns on the Queen-
side " is not, at the moment, of any
value, for their advance, as is
shown in the present game, will
give rise to new weaknesses, which
the opponent will turn to advantage.
The game is already virtually
decided.

19.	P—Q Kt 3

Defending his Q R P, which is
indirectly attacked.

20. P—K R 3 !

Preparing the advance of the B P.

20.	P—B 4

This move leads to nothing, seeing that it does not compel the
exchange of Rooks. It would have
been rather better (now or on the
22nd move) to take measures
against the advance of White's K P
and K B P, by playing, for example,
....Kt—K 1 followed by ....P—
B 3.

21. R (Q 4)—Q 2	R × R
22. Q × R	P—B 5
23. P—B 4	P—Kt 3

If 23. ....Q—B 4 ch, simply 24.
Q—Q 4 ! and Black's position after
the exchange of Queens would be
untenable, despite his majority on
the Queen's side.

24. Q—Q 4

Threatening to win a Pawn by
25. P—B 5.

24.	R—Q B 1

Position after Black's 24th move.

25. P—K Kt 4 !

Decisive ! Black has no longer
any adequate defence against the
threats 26. P—B 5, or 26. P—K 5,
followed by 27. P—B 5.

25.	B × P

A desperate sacrifice which cannot defer the imminent catastrophe
any more than other attempts.

26. P × B	Kt × Kt P
27. K—Kt 2 !	P—K R 4
28. Kt—Q 5	Q—R 5
29. R—K R 1	Q—Q 1
30. B—Q 1 !	Black resigns.

An instructive game from the
strategic point of view.

GAME 58

ALEKHIN'S DEFENCE

White :   *Black :*
A. STEINER.   A. ALEKHIN.

1. P—K 4   Kt—K B 3

This new defence was played for the first time by myself in a consultation game at Zurich (August, 1921), and was introduced into master practice shortly afterwards at the Budapest Tournament in September of the same year. Its correctness now seems perfectly established. One of the most searching proofs of its vitality lies in the fact that Dr. Emmanuel Lasker, ex-champion of the world, although openly opposed to this defence, successfully adopted it against Maróczy at the New York Tournament (March–April, 1924), after having tried in vain to demolish it.

In the course of an encounter between Dr. Lasker and Dr. Tarrasch, Black obtained a clearly superior, if not a winning, game in the following way : 1. P—K 4, Kt —K B 3 ; 2. P—K 5, Kt—Q 4 ; 3. P—Q 4, P—Q 3 ; 4. P—Q B 4, Kt—Kt 3 ; 5. P—B 4, P×P ; 6. B P×P, Kt—B 3 ; 7. B—K 3, B— K B 4 ; 8. Kt—Q B 3, P—K 3 ; 9. Kt—B 3, B—Q Kt 5 ; 10. B—Q 3, B—Kt 5 ! ; 11. B—K 2, B×Kt ; 12. P×B, Q—R 5 ch ; 13. B—B 2, Q—B 5 !

2. P—K 5

In a game Bogoljuboff—Alekhin (Carlsbad, 1923), White tried 2. Kt —Q B 3, upon which Black replied by 2. ....P—Q 4 (2. ....P—K 4, transposing into the Vienna Game, is also to be considered), leading to the continuation 3. P—K 5, K Kt— Q 2 ! ; 4. P—Q 4, P—Q B 4 ! ; 5. B—-Q Kt 5, Kt—Q B 3 ; 6. Kt—B 3,

and Black could have led into a very advantageous variation of the French Defence by 6. ....P—K 3, in place of the risky line 6. .... P—Q R 3 ; 7. B×Kt ch, P×B ; 8. P—K 6 !

2. ......   Kt—Q 4
3. P—Q 4

In a game Sämisch—Alekhin from the same tournament, White continued by 3. Kt—Q B 3, P—K 3 ! ; 4. Kt×Kt, P×Kt ; 5. P—Q 4, P—Q 3 ; 6. Kt—B 3, Kt—B 3 ; 7. B—K 2, B—K 2 ; 8. B—K B 4, Castles ; 9. Castles, P—B 3 ; 10. P×B P, B×P and Black has a slightly superior game.

3. ......   P—Q 3
4. B—Kt 5

After this move, whose object is to hinder the advance of the hostile K P, White loses his advantage, because of the difficulties he will experience in defending his K P. The most dangerous line of play for Black is undoubtedly 4. P—Q B 4 followed by 5. P—B 4.

4. ......   P×P
5. P×P   Kt—Q B 3
6. B—Kt 5   B—K B 4 !

Black is not concerned about the possibility of doubled Pawns. If 7. B×Kt ch, the possession of his two Bishops, the open Q Kt file and his better development would constitute a great compensation for the slight weakness on Q B 3.

7. Kt—K B 3   K Kt—Kt 5 !

The win of a Pawn by this last move required a minute examination of all its consequences.

8. Kt—R 3   Q×Q ch
9. R×Q !

The best reply, for if 9. K × Q, Castles ch ; 10. K—B 1, P—B 3, Black's game would be distinctly superior.

9.	Kt × P ch
10. Kt × Kt	B × Kt
11. R—Q B 1	B—K 5
12. Kt—Q 4	

If 12. P—K 6, Black would have answered simply 12. ....P—B 3 ! followed by 13. ....Castles.

12.	B × P
13. R—K Kt 1	

Position after White's 13th move.

13.	Castles

The point of the manœuvre initiated on the 7th move. Nevertheless, the material advantage of a Pawn which Black has succeeded in securing seems very difficult to utilize, because of his backward development.

14. Kt × Kt	B × Kt
15. B × B	P × B
16. R × P	R—Q 4
17. B—B 4	P—K 3
18. K—K 2	

See Diagram.

How ought Black to strengthen his position now ? For example,

Position after White's 18th move.

here are two plausible suggestions which give no satisfactory result against a correct defence :

I.—18. ....P—Kt 3 ; 19. R (Kt 1) —Q B 1, R—Q 2 ; 20. B—K 3, K — Kt 2 ; 21. R (B 6)—B 3, B—Kt 2 ; 22. R—Kt 3 ch, K—R 1 ; 23. B × P !, B × P ; 24. R—B 4 with the better game for White.

II.—18. ....P—K Kt 4 ; 19. R × Kt P !, B—R 3 ; 20. R—Kt 4, B × B ; 21. R × B, R × P ch ; 22. K—B 1, K—Kt 2 ; 23. R—Q B 3, and Black has no chance of winning.

18.	B—B 4 !

....whereas this move, which at first sight does not seem better than the preceding moves, is the only one enabling Black to maintain his advantage.

19. P—Q Kt 4 !

The right reply, permitting White to force a favourable exchange. It is clear that Black's Kt P cannot be taken at once, owing to 19. ...K— Kt 2.

19.	B × Kt P
20. R × Kt P	R—Q 2
21. B—K 3	

Position after White's 21st move.

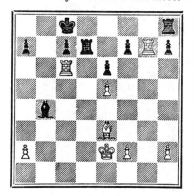

Black is once again faced with a very difficult problem. How is he to secure the defence of his weak Pawns on both wings ? His lone Bishop is insufficient for this task, since if it be brought to Q Kt 3 via Q R 4, thereby adequately protecting his right wing, White would transfer his attack to the opposite wing and would eventually win at least a Pawn by R—B 4 followed by R—K R 4.

On the other hand, if Black withdraws his Bishop to K B 1, in order to secure the protection of his left wing, White would take the Queenside as his objective and would obtain a strong attack by R—Kt 4 followed by R—Q R 4.

Black must therefore provisionally avoid the displacement of his Bishop, in order to be able to utilize it for the defence of whichever wing is threatened.

His following moves are dictated by the above considerations.

21.	......	P—Q R 4 !
22.	R—B 4	P—R 4
23.	R—R 4	B—B 6 !
24.	R—Kt 5	R—Q 4
25.	P—B 4	P—K B 3 !

Definitely maintaining his material advantage, which he is enabled to exploit by the following exchanges.

26.	R (Kt 5) × P	R × R
27.	R × R	P × P
28.	P × P	B × P
29.	R—R 7	

29. P—K R 4 would leave White some hope of a draw, but after the text-move Black forces the exchange of this dangerous Pawn.

29.	......	R—Kt 4 !
30.	K—B 3	R—Kt 7
31.	R—R 5	

Forced, since after 31. P—K R 4, R × P, Black's passed Q R P would be at least as dangerous as White's passed K R P.

| 31. | ...... | B × P |
| 32. | R × P | B—Q 3 |

The ensuing end-game, although won for Black, nevertheless offers several technical difficulties, and is not devoid of interest.

| 33. | K—K 4 | K—Q 2 |
| 34. | B—Q 4 | |

Temporarily preventing 34.'.... P—K 4, which Black now prepares by the following Rook-manœuvre.

| 34. | ...... | R—Q 7 ! |

Hindering K—Q 3—B 4, etc.

35.	B—K 3	R—K 7
36.	K—Q 3	R—K 8 !
37.	B—Q 4	R—Q B 8

37. ....P—K 4 would still be premature, on account of 38. B—B 3.

38.	B—K 3	R—Q 8 ch
39.	K—K 4	R—K 8
40.	K—Q 3	P—K 4

At last it is playable !

41. B—B 2	R—K B 8
42. B—K 3	K—K 3
43. K—K 4	R—K R 8
44. B—B 2	R—R 7
45. B—K 3	R—R 5 ch
46. K—Q 3	B—Kt 5 !

Thereby securing for his King access to the square Q 4, which is clearly of great importance.

47. R—R 7

Or 47. R—R 4, K—Q 4 ; 48. P—Q R 3, P—K 5 ch ; 49. K—B 2, B—Q 3.

47.	P—B 4
48. P—R 3	P—B 5 ch
49. K—K 2	B—Q 3
50. R—R 8	

In order to pin the adverse Bishop by R—Q 8, after .... K—Q 4.

50.	R—R 7 ch
51. K—Q 1	R—R 6 !
52. K—Q 2	K—Q 4
53. R—Q 8	

Position after White's 53rd move.

| 53. ...... | P—B 6 ch ! |

The *coup-de-grâce*.

54. K—K 2

If 54. K—Q 3, Black had foreseen the following pretty finish : 54. ....P—B 7 ; 55. R—Q B 8, B—

K2 ! ; 56. R×P, B—Kt 4 ; 57. R—K 2, P—K 5 ch ; 58. K—Q 2, R×B ; 59. R×R, K—Q 5, and wins.

54.	K—K 5 !
55. R×B	R×B ch
56. K—B 2	R—Q 6
57. R—Q B 6	R—Q 7 ch
58. K—K 1	K—Q 6
59. R—Q 6 ch	K—B 7
60. R—K 6	R—Q 4
61. K—K 2	K—Kt 6
62. R—Q B 6	P—B 7

White resigns.

GAME 59

QUEEN'S PAWN GAME

| *White :* | *Black :* |
| A. ALEKHIN. | Z. v. BALLA. |

1. P—Q 4	P—Q 4
2. Kt—K B 3	P—K 3
3. B—B 4	P—Q B 4
4. P—K 3	Kt—Q B 3
5. P—B 4	

5. P—B 3 would be more in accordance with the system springing from B—B 4. The main object of the text-move is to avoid the beaten track.

| 5. ...... | Kt—B 3 |

If 5. ....Q—Kt 3 White could have answered 6. Kt—B 3 !, and if Q×Kt P ; 7. Kt—Q Kt 5, etc.

| 6. Kt—B 3 | B P×P |
| 7. K P×P | Kt—K 5 |

This demonstration is clearly premature, White being better developed. 7. ....Q—Kt 3 was also unfavourable for Black, on account of 8. P—B 5 !, Q×Kt P ; 9. Kt—Q Kt 5, etc. On the other hand, he could have obtained a fairly satisfactory game by 7. .... B—Kt 5 ; 8. B—Q 3, P×P ; 9. B×B P, Castles.

8. B—Q 3	B—Kt 5
9. R—Q B 1	Q—R 4
10. Q—Kt 3	P×P
11. B×P	P—K Kt 4

Having embarked on a dangerous voyage, Black is compelled to persevere at all costs. This advance makes it unsafe to Castle King-side, without inconveniencing White in any way.
Better was 11. ....Castles ; 12. Castles, Kt×Kt ; 13. P×Kt, B—K 2 ; 14. K R—K 1 !, and if 14. ....P—Q Kt 3 ; 15. P—Q 5, etc., although in this case also White's superiority in position is manifest.

| 12. B—K 3 | P—Kt 5 |
| 13. Kt—K 5 ! | |

If this Knight had been compelled to retire, perhaps to Kt 1 or Q 2, Black's preceding manœuvre would have had some measure of justification.

13.	Kt×K Kt
14. P×Kt	B×Kt ch
15. P×B	P—Kt 3

If 15. ....Q×K P ; 16. B—Q 4, Q—B 5 ; 17. B—Kt 5 ch, followed by 18. Castles, with a winning attack.

16. Castles

Intending the following sacrifice. But owing to the complications to which it gives rise, I would prefer now-a-days the simpler variation, 16. B—Kt 5 ch, B—Q 2 ; 17. B× B ch, K×B ; 18. Castles, as now the Black King is left in the centre, and White obtains a strong attack (18. ....K—B 2 ; 19. Q—Kt 4 !). But White hoped for a still better result with the text-move, and his opponent lends himself to it by accepting the sacrifice.

| 16. ...... | B—Q 2 ! |

16. Castles (K R) would clearly be equivalent to suicide.

Position after Black's 16th move.

17. K R—Q 1 !

The most energetic way of taking advantage of Black's compromised position ; in reply to this move Black should decide upon : 17. ....Castles (Q R) ! ; 18. Q—Kt 4 !, Q×Q ; 19. P×Q, K—Kt 2 ; 20. B—K 2 !, threatening P—B 3, after which Black would have lost a Pawn, with a long end-game in view. But he cannot resist the bait of the Rook, and this indiscretion costs him the game.

| 17. ...... | B—R 5 |
| 18. Q—Kt 1 | Kt×Q B P |

If 18. ....B×R ; 19. B—Kt 5 ch ! [not 19. Q×Kt, Castles (Q R)!], K—K 2 ; 20. Q×Kt, with a winning attack.

| 19. R×Kt | Q×R |

19. ....B×R would evidently be equally disastrous.

20. B—Kt 5 ch	B×B
21. Q×B ch	K—B 1
22. B—R 6 ch	K—Kt 1
23. Q—Q 7 !	

If now 23. ....Q—B 1, then 24. Q—K 7 followed by mate in two moves.

Black resigns.

CHAPTER XV

INTERNATIONAL TOURNAMENT AT THE HAGUE, NOVEMBER, 1921

GAME 60

SICILIAN DEFENCE

White :   Black :
F. D. YATES.   A. ALEKHIN.

1. P—K 4   P—Q B 4
2. Kt—K B 3   P—K 3
3. P—Q 4

This move has the disadvantage of allowing Black to choose the following equalizing variation. On this account it is preferable to play first 3. B—K 2 (see game No. 97).

3. ......   P×P
4. Kt×P   Kt—K B 3
5. Kt—Q B 3

Concerning 5. B—Q 3 see Game No. 93.

5. ......   B—Kt 5
6. B—Q 3   P—K 4 !

6. ....P—Q 4 would be inferior, on account of 7. P—K 5, K Kt—Q 2; 8. Q—Kt 4 ! The text-move was introduced into master practice by Jaffe at the Carlsbad Tournament of 1911.

7. Kt—K 2

If 7. Kt—B 5, Castles ; 8. B—K Kt 5, P—Q 4! and Black has the better game, since if 9. P×P, P—K 5 !; 10. B×P, R—K 1; 11. Kt—Kt 3, Kt×B, winning a piece.

7. ......   P—Q 4
8. P×P   Kt×P
9. Castles   Kt—Q B 3

Black has achieved a satisfactory development. There is room for improvement in one respect, the impossibility of Castling immediately, on account of Kt×Kt, followed by B×P ch winning the Queen.

10. Kt×Kt   Q×Kt
11. P—Q R 3 !

Preparing the advance of the Queen-side Pawns, which can be utilized for the end-game, and also seeking to keep the Black King in the centre as long as possible by the tactical threats which are made possible by the momentarily exposed position of Black's pieces.

11. ......   B—R 4

Not 11. ...B—K 2 ; 12. Kt—B 3, Q—K 3 (or 12. ....Q—Q 1 ; 13. Q—R 5) ; 13. Kt—Kt 5, with the better game.

12. P—Q Kt 4   B—B 2
13. R—K 1

Now 13. Kt—B 3 would be
ineffectual after 13. ....Q—K 3 ;
14. Kt—Kt 5, B—Kt 1, or 14. Q—
R 5, Q—Kt 5 !

Position after White's 13th move.

13. ......   P—B 4

A risky move whose chief object
is to reserve a good square of
retreat for the Black Queen on K B 2.
13. ....B—K 3 was more prudent and sufficient for equality.
A game Euwe—Alekhin (Pistyan,
1922), continued as follows : 14.
Kt—B 3, Q—Q 2 ; 15. Kt—K 4,
B—K Kt 5 ; 16. Kt—B 5, Q—B 1 ;
17. Q—Q 2, Castles ; 18. B—K 4 !,
B—Kt 3 ; 19. Q—B 3, B × Kt ; 20.
Q × B, B—B 4 ; 21. B × Kt, Q × B ;
22. Q × Q, P × Q. Drawn game.

14. P—Q B 4

This colourless line of play allows
Black at last to bring his King into
safety and thus obtain the better
game.
   More energetic was 14. Kt—B 4,
Q—B 2 ; 15. P—Kt 5 !, Kt—K 2 ;
16. P—Kt 6 !, P × P ; 17. B—Kt 5 ch,
Kt—B 3 ; 18. Q—Q 3 !, definitely
fixing the hostile King, with excellent chances of attack.

14. ......   Q—B 2
15. Kt—B 3   Castles
16. Kt—Q 5

This Knight, as will be seen in the
sequel, cannot be maintained in this
position and will soon be exchanged
against a Black piece inactive until
now.
   This simple fact sufficiently
demonstrates White's faulty
strategy initiated by 14. P—Q B 4.

16. ......   B—K 3

Position after Black's 16th move.

17. B—Kt 2

A little trap. If now 17. ....B × Kt ;
18. P × B, Q × P ; then 19. B × B P,
Q × Q ; 20. B—K 6 ch, regaining
his Pawn with a very good game.

17. ......   P—K 5
18. Kt × B

If at once 18. B—K B 1, then 18.
....B—K 4, with a manifest
superiority of position.

18. ......   Q × Kt
19. B—K B 1   Kt—K 4 !
20. B × Kt

Relatively best, for if 20. P—B 5,
then 20. ....Kt—Kt 5, provoking
the weakening of White's King's

position, the consequences of which might have been disastrous for him very quickly.

20. ......   Q×B
21. Q—B 2   Q R—Q 1
22. Q R—Q 1   R×R !

By this unexpected exchange (unexpected, because it temporarily yields to the adversary the only open file) Black forces either (1) the advance of his P to B 5, whereby, sooner or later, in addition to good prospects of direct attack, he can secure a strong passed Pawn on the King's file, or (2) as in the actual game, the exchange of Queens, which secures for him a superior end-game.

23. Q×R

If 23. R×R, then 23. ....P—B 5!

Position after White's 23rd move.

23. ......   Q—B 6 !

Against this move White has nothing better than to offer an exchange of Queens, because after 24. R—K 3 Black would gain the necessary time by 24. ....Q—B 3, to occupy the Queen-file, which would be decisive.

The ensuing end-game, which offers some analogy with that which

I played against Teichmann (see Game No. 91), admits of a majority of Pawns on the Queen-side for White, but this advantage is here somewhat illusory. On this subject I am anxious to state that one of the most notorious prejudices of modern theory lies in the fact that this majority is *in itself* considered an advantage, without any reference to whatever Pawns or, more especially, pieces are concerned.

In the present game Black has very evident compensations : (1) the greater mobility of the Black King, the adverse King being hampered by his own Pawns. (2) the dominating position of the Black Rook on the only open file. With correct play, these points should ensure a win.

24. Q—B 1   Q×Q
25. R×Q   R—Q 1
26. P—K Kt 3

This and the next two moves aim at the exchange of Bishops, since the Rook ending would yield White an almost certain draw.

26. ......   K—B 2
27. P—B 5   K—B 3

Avoiding exchanges, on the above grounds.

28. B—B 4   B—B 1 !
29. P—Q R 4   P—K Kt 4
30. P—Kt 5   P—B 5
31. K—B 1

With the object of opposing his Rook to that of Black, after 32. K—K 1, but the latter voluntarily abandons the command of the Queen-file in order to occupy the seventh rank with his Rook, thus facilitating the decisive advance of his Pawns.

31. ......   R—Q 7 !
32. K—K 1   R—Kt 7
33. P×P   P×P
34. B—K 2

White was threatened, if 34.
R—Q 1, with 34. .... B—Kt 5 ; 35.
R—Q 6 ch, K—K 2 ; 36. R—Q 4,
B—B 6, followed by P—K 6,
winning.

34. ......   K—K 4 !
35. P—B 6   P×P

Position after Black's 35th move.

36. R×P

If 36. P×P, P—B 6 ; 37. B—Q 1,
P—K 6 ; 38. B×P, P×P ch ;
39. K—B 1, B—R 3 ch ; or 37.
B—B 1, P—K 6 ; 38. P×P,
P—B 7 ch ; 39. K—Q 1, B—
Kt 5 ch and mates next move.

36. ......   B—K 3
37. B—Q 1   R—Kt 8

With the double threat 38. ....
B—Kt 6 and 38. .... B—Kt 5,
against which White cannot defend
himself by 38. K—Q 2 on account
of 38. .... P—K 6 ch ; 39. P×P,
P×P ch ; 40. K—B 2, B—B 4 ch.

38. R—B 5 ch   K—Q 5
39. R—B 2   P—K 6
40. P×P ch   P×P
41. R—B 6   B—Kt 5
42. R—Q 6 ch   K—B 4
43. P—R 3   B—R 4

Now the threat of 44. .... P—K 7
wins both the Rook and the Bishop.

White resigns.

GAME 61

QUEEN'S GAMBIT DECLINED

White :   *Black :*
A. ALEKHIN.   A. RUBINSTEIN.

1. P—Q 4   P—Q 4
2. Kt—K B 3   P—K 3
3. P—B 4   P—Q R 3

A move of Janowski's, quite frequently played by Rubinstein in
recent tournaments, but without
appreciable success. Necessary in
the greater number of the variations
of the Queen's Gambit Accepted.
3. .... P—Q R 3 is here merely a
loss of time, and in addition creates
weaknesses on the Queen-side when
White continues by 4. P×P, or
even 4. P—B 5, as in the present
game.

4. P—B 5

4. P×P is quite sufficient to
secure a slight superiority of posi-
tion, as was shown by the games
Johner—Rubinstein and Kostich—
Rubinstein in the Teplitz-Schönau
Tournament of 1922 among others.
The former game continued 4.
P×P, P×P ; 5. Kt—B 3, Kt—K
B 3 ; 6. B—Kt 5, B—K 2 ; 7. P—
K 3, Castles ; 8. B—Q 3, P—Q Kt 3
(a little better, but also insuffi-
cient to equalize the game, was 8.
.... Q Kt—Q 2 ; 9. Q—B 2 !) ; 9.
B×Kt !, B×B ; 10. Q—B 2, P—
K R 3, and Johner could have
obtained a very strong attack
against Black's weakened Castled
position by 11. P—K R 3, followed
by 12. Castles Q R and P—K Kt 4.
In his game against Kostich
Rubinstein tried 5. .... B—K 2 in
place of 5. .... Kt—K B 3, and the
continuation was 6. B—B 4, Kt—
K B 3 ; 7. P—K 3, Castles ; 8.
B—Q 3, Q Kt—Q 2 ; 9. Castles,
R—K 1 ; 10. R—B 1, P—Q Kt 3,
after which White could have obtained a distinctly superior game by

11. P—K R 3 (in order to conserve his Q B against the threat of exchange by Kt—R 4).

In the present game, the first which I played against Rubinstein after a seven-year interval, I voluntarily adopted a new line of play in order to avoid the variations resulting from 4. P×P (because I rightly thought them very familiar to Rubinstein), resolved that I would do or die !

4. ......　　　　Kt—Q B 3

Wishing to play 5. ....P—K 4, which White must oppose by every means at his disposal.

5. B—B 4　　　K Kt—K 2
6. Kt—B 3　　　Kt—Kt 3

Position after Black's 6th move.

7. B—K 3 !

A move rather out of the common ! White, while preventing 7. .... P—K 4, avoids the exchange of his Q B.

I learnt, some time after the game ended, that Rubinstein in Collijn's *Lärobok* only examined 7. P—K 3, a variation leading to equality.

7. ......　　　　P—Kt 3

Black, giving up hope of breaking through in the centre, at least eliminates the cramping adverse Q B P, and reckons to secure an advantage in development, by reason of the unusual position of White's Q B at K 3.

8. P×P　　　　　P×P
9. P—K R 4 !

The only means of weakening the black squares of the enemy's position, and thus obtaining a future for his Q B.

9. ......　　　　B—Q 3

If 9. ....P—K R 4, then 10. B—K Kt 5, P—B 3 ; 11. Q—Q 2 followed by 12. B—Q 2, P—K 3, P—Q R 3 and B—Q 3, with the better game for White.

10. P—R 5　　　K Kt—K 2

Not 10. ....Kt—B 5 ? ; 11. P—K Kt 3.

11. P—R 6 !

The point ! If Black captures the R P, he weakens his own R P without the slightest compensation. In the other case White's Q B will occupy the diagonal K R 4—Q 8, where it exercises a very embarrassing pressure.

11. ......　　　　P—Kt 3
12. B—Kt 5　　　Castles

More prudent was 12. ....P—B 4 first, after which Black would not have had to fear the threat of mate at K Kt 2, although in any case White's game would have already been preferable.

13. B—B 6 !

See Diagram.

An extraordinary position after the 13th move of a Queen's Gambit ! During the first thirteen moves White has played his Q B P thrice, his K R P thrice and his Q B four

Position after White's 13th move.

times, after which he has obtained a position in sight of a win, if not actually a winning one.

It is especially with respect to the original opening of this game that people often speak of a " hypermodern technique," a " neo-romantic school," etc.

The question is in reality much simpler. Black has given himself over to several eccentricities in the opening (3. ....P—Q R 3 ; 5. .... K Kt—K 2 ; 6. ....Kt—Kt 3) which, without the reaction of his opponent (for example, 7. P—K 3 instead of 7. B—K 3 or 9. P— K Kt 3 instead of 9. P—K R 4) would in the end give him a good game.

It is, therefore, as a necessity, and not with a preconceived idea, that I decided upon the advance of the K R P, preventing Black from securing an advantage in the centre. But, as a rule, in the opening stages of a game such eccentricities are in accordance neither with my temperament nor my style, as the reader can see from the perusal of this book.

13.	P—Q Kt 4
14. P—K 3	B—Q 2
15. B—Q 3	R—B 1

Black dreams only of the possibility of an immediate attack by

White (commencing by Kt—K Kt 5, or Kt—K 5 followed by Q—B 3), which he hopes to thwart by a demonstration on the Queen-side (Q—R 4, B—Kt 5).

With this idea, the preparatory move 15. ....R—B 1 would have been very useful. But as White is not compelled to bestir himself as long as the opponent does not trouble him seriously, it would have been better for Black to play at once 15. ....Kt—R 4, followed by 16. ....B—Kt 5, and thus compel White, by this semblance of a counter-attack, to take some defensive measures.

16. P—R 4 !

Whereas it is now White who seizes the initiative on the left flank, forcing Black to block this side, which allows him to post his Q Kt in a dominating position, without loss of time.

16.	P—Kt 5
17. Kt—K 2	Q—Kt 3
18. Kt—B 1 !	

Preventing 18. ....P—Kt 6.

| 18. ...... | R—B 2 |
| 19. Kt—Kt 3 | Kt—R 4 |

Too late !

Position after Black's 19th move.

20. Kt—B 5 !

By this manœuvre White transforms his positional advantage into a gain of material, Black being unable to capture the Knight, *e.g.* : 20. ....B×Kt ; 21. P×B, Q×P ; 22. B—Q 4, Q—B 3 ; 23. Kt—K 5, Q—Kt 2 ; 24. Kt—K Kt 4, etc., winning the Exchange. If 20. .... B—B 1, then 21. Kt—K 5, with similar variations.

20. ......   Kt—B 5

This move is not a whit better than those which precede it. It allows White the choice between two very good variations, but it happens that White chose the less decisive one.

21. B×Kt   P×B
22. Kt—K 5

22. Kt—K 4 would force the win of the Exchange, and also maintain the attack, in view of the double threat 23. Kt×B followed by 24. B—K 5 ; and 23. B—Kt 7, followed by 24. Kt—B 6 mate.

22. ......   B×Kt (K 4)
23. B×Kt !

Position after White's 23rd move.

23. ......   B—Q 3 !

With his clear judgment of position, Rubinstein at once recognizes that the sacrifice of the Exchange still offers him the best chance.

Indeed, after 23. ....R—K 1 ; 24. P×B, R×B ; 25. Kt—K 4 ! (not 25. Q—B 3, P—B 4 ; 26. P× P e. p., R—B 2 with defensive chances), Black would have lost more speedily than in the actual game, *e.g.:*

I.—25. ....P—B 4 ; 26. Q—Q 6, B—B 3 ; 27. Kt—B 6 ch, K—B 2 ; 28. Q—Q 8 !, B—K 1 ; 29. Kt×P and wins.

II.—25. ....B—K 1 ; 26. Kt— B 6 ch, K—R 1 ; 27. Q—Q 8, R— Kt 2 ; 28. R—Q 1, Q—B 3 ; 29. Castles, and White wins.

24. B×R   B×B
25. Kt×B   R×Kt
26. P—R 5 !

Preventing the consolidation of Black's Pawn-position by 26. .... P—R 4.

26. ......   Q—B 3
27. Q—B 3   R—Q 4
28. R—Q B 1 !

This move, which forces the advance of the Q B P, is intended to clear up the position on the Queen's side, in order to place his pieces in the most favourable way.

28. ......   Q—B 2
29. Q—K 2   P—B 6
30. P×P   P×P
31. Q×P   R×R P
32. Q—Q 3   B—R 6

If 32. ....R—R 6, White would have continued 33. K—K 2, followed by 34. R—R 1.

33. R—B 2   B—Kt 7
34. K—K 2 !

Not 34. Castles, on account of 34. ....R—R 4, winning the K R P, with good drawing chances.

34.	......	Q—B 3
35.	P—B 3	P—B 4
36.	R—Q Kt 1	Q—Q 3

If 36. ....Q—Q 4, then 37. K—B 2, threatening 38. R×P, B×R ; 39. Q×B, R—R 1 ; 40. Q—B 7 and wins.

| 37. | Q—B 4 | K—B 2 |
| 38. | Q—B 8 | Q—R 3 ch |

The exchange of Queens is forced, as White threatens 39. Q—K R 8.

39.	Q×Q	R×Q
40.	P—K 4	P—Kt 4
41.	K—Q 3	K—Kt 3

Position after Black's 41st move.

42. P—Q 5 !

Thus obtaining a passed Pawn, which decides the game in a few moves. Black's desperate attempts to obtain a last chance on the King's side merely succeed in leading his King into a *cul-de-sac*.

42.	......	P×P ch
43.	P×P	P×P
44.	P×P	R—R 5
45.	R—Q 1 !	

Indirectly securing the advance of the Q P.

45.	......	K×P
46.	P—Q 6	K—R 4
47.	P—Q 7	R—R 1
48.	K—K 4	R—Q 1
49.	K—B 5	K—R 5
50.	R—R 1 ch	K—Kt 6
51.	R—R 3 mate.	

CHAPTER XVI

INTERNATIONAL TOURNAMENT AT PISTYAN
APRIL, 1922

GAME 62

QUEEN'S PAWN GAME

Brilliancy Prize

White :	Black :
DR. S. TARRASCH.	A. ALEKHIN.

1. P—Q 4	Kt—K B 3
2. Kt—K B 3	P—K 3
3. P—B 4	P—B 4

With the intention of investigating, on the next move, the gambit discovered by the Moscow amateur, Blumenfeld. Since then it has been shown that this Gambit is not favourable for Black if White should decline it.

4. P—Q 5	P—Q Kt 4
5. P×K P	

The acceptance of the gambit yields Black a formidable position in the centre. The right move was 5. B—Kt 5 ! Equally possible, although less strong, is 5. P—K 4, played by Rubinstein against Tartakover at Teplitz—Schönau, 1922.

An instructive game, Grünfeld—Bogoljuboff, from the Vienna Tournament of 1922, was continued as follows : 5. B—Kt 5, P—K R 3 ; 6. B×Kt, Q×B ; 7. Kt—B 3, P—Kt 5 ; 8. Kt—Q Kt 5, Kt—R 3 ; 9. P—K 4 !, Q×P ; 10. B—Q 3 !, Q—B 3 ; 11. P—K 5, Q—Q 1 ; 12.

P×P, Q P×P ; 13. B—K 4 !, Q× Q ch ; 14. R×Q, R—Q Kt 1 ; 15. B—B 6 ch, K—K 2 ; 16. Kt×P, P—Kt 4 ; 17. B—Kt 5, B—K Kt 2 ; 18. Kt—B 6 ch and mates next move.

5.	B P×P
6. P×P	P—Q 4
7. P—K 3	

Black threatened to regain his Pawn with the better game by 7. ....Q—R 4 ch. However, 7. Q Kt —Q 2 followed by P—Q Kt 3 and B—Kt 2 offered White better defensive chances.

7.	B—Q 3
8. Kt—B 3	Castles
9. B—K 2	B—Kt 2
10. P—Q Kt 3	Q Kt—Q 2
11. B—Kt 2	Q—K 2

Black has completed his development, and prepares in perfect safety the advance of his K P, which, encompassing still more the adverse game, secures him a very strong attack against White's King.

12. Castles	Q R—Q 1

Black has no need to hasten the advance of his K P, his opponent at present being able to attempt absolutely nothing.

13. Q—B 2   P—K 4
14. K R—K 1

In order to defend the square
K R 2, by bringing his K Kt via
Q 2 to K B 1.

From now on White defends himself in the most skilful way, but his
game is already too far compromised
by the strategic error of the opening,
ceding the centre to his opponent
in exchange for a Pawn of little
value.

14. ......   P—K 5
15. Kt—Q 2   Kt—K 4
16. Kt—Q 1   Kt (B 3)—Kt 5
17. B × Kt (Kt 4)

This exchange is forced, for if 17.
Kt—B 1, then 17. ....Kt—B 6 ch !

17. ......   Kt × B
18. Kt—B 1

Position after White's 18th move.

18. ......   Q—Kt 4 !

The correct continuation of the
attack.   White has adequately
defended the squares K B 2 and
K R 2, but the point K Kt 2 is still
vulnerable.   So it is against this
point that Black intends to undertake a double attack, bringing the
Knight to K R 5 via K R 3 and
K B 4.

To parry this threat White will
be compelled to weaken his position
afresh by playing P—K R 3 which,
as we shall see by the sequel, will
allow the decisive advance of
Black's Q P.

19. P—K R 3   Kt—R 3
20. K—R 1   Kt—B 4
21. Kt—R 2

It is clear that White's three last
moves were the only ones possible
to secure the defence of the threatened point by R—K Kt 1.

21. ......   P—Q 5 !

This Pawn becomes a new and
formidable means of continuing the
attack. White cannot capture it,
e.g.: 22. P × P, P—K 6 !; 23. Kt × P
(or 23. R—K Kt 1, Q—Kt 6 !
and wins), Kt × Kt ; 24. P × Kt,
Q—Kt 6 ! and wins.

22. B—B 1   P—Q 6
23. Q—B 4 ch   K—R 1
24. B—Kt 2

Position after White's 24th move.

24. ......   Kt—Kt 6 ch

The beginning of the final
manœuvre. It is clear that the
Knight cannot be taken, on account
of 25. ....Q × Kt P, forcing mate.
After the following move Black

could have won the exchange by 25. ....P—Q 7, but he preferred to wind up the game by a forced combination.

25. K—Kt 1   B—Q 4
26. Q—R 4

If 26. Q—B 3 or 26. Q—B 1; Kt—K 7 ch, winning easily.

26. ......   Kt—K 7 ch
27. K—R 1   R—B 2 !

There was no reason to complicate the game by the sacrifice of the Q R P.

28. Q—R 6   P—R 4 !

As we shall see by the continuation, this was necessary to prepare the sacrifice of the Bishop on the 34th move.

29. P—Kt 6   Kt—Kt 6 ch

Not 29. ....P×P on account of 30. R×Kt, P×R ; 31. Q×K P, giving White possibilities of defence.

30. K—Kt 1   P×P
31. Q×Kt P   P—Q 7 !

Now this advance of the Q P is absolutely decisive.

32. R—K B 1   Kt×R
33. Kt×Kt

Position after White's 33rd move.

33. ......   B—K 3 ! !

After this move White can no longer defend himself against the ensuing mating attack. For example, if he had attempted to protect the square K Kt 2 by 34. Q—B 6 followed by 35. Q×K P, the game would have terminated as follows: 34. Q—B 6, R—B 6 !; 35. Q×K P, B—Q 4 ; 36. Q—Q R 4, Q×P ch ! !; 37. K×Q, R—Kt 6 ch ; 38. K—R 2, R—Kt 7 ch ; 39. K—R 1, R—R 7 ch ; 40. K—Kt 1, R—R 8 mate. Against the plausible move 34. K—R 1 the sacrifice of the Q B wins at once.

34. K—R 1   B×P !
35. P×B   R—B 6
36. Kt—Kt 3   P—R 5 !

The object of 28. ....P—K R 4 ! is now shown.

37. B—B 6

Ingenious but doomed to failure, like all other attempts.

37. ......   Q×R
38. Kt×P   R×P ch

If now 39. K—Kt 1, B—R 7 ch and Black wins the Queen ; and if 39. K—Kt 2, Q—B 6 ch and mates next move.

White resigns.

GAME 63

QUEEN'S GAMBIT DECLINED

White :	*Black :*
A. ALEKHIN.	A. SELESNIEFF.

1.	P—Q 4	P—Q 4
2.	Kt—K B 3	Kt—K B 3
3.	P—B 4	P—K 3
4.	Kt—B 3	B—K 2
5.	B—Kt 5	Q Kt—Q 2
6.	P—K 3	Castles
7.	R—B 1	P—B 3
8.	B—Q 3	

I consider this old move at least as good as the modern move 8. Q—B 2, because the White Queen must lose a *tempo* in order to occupy K 2, *its natural square in the Queen's Gambit Declined.*

8. ......   P×P

The best reply, beyond doubt. It is essential for Black to capture the B P, and to play 9. .... Kt—Q 4, *before White has Castled,* because otherwise the latter can prevent the exchange of his Knight on Q B 3 by playing Kt—K 4 ! with a far superior game (see Game No. 88); whereas before Castling the move is not without danger and leads to variations of great complexity.

9. B×P   Kt—Q 4
10. B—B 4

In order to avoid the dull equalizing variation, 10. B×B, Q×B ; 11. Castles, Kt×Kt ; 12. R×Kt, P—K 4.

But this move is venturesome, as Black's energetic play in the present game shows.

It is more playable in the variation arising from 8. Q—B 2, which, against Black's Kt—Kt 3, allows of the withdrawal of the K B to Q 3 without loss of time, owing to the threat on the hostile K R P.

10. ......   Kt×B
11. P×Kt   Kt—Kt 3
12. B—Kt 3   Kt—Q 4
13. Q—Q 2

Again best. If 13. P—K Kt 3, Kt×Kt ; 14. P×Kt, P—Q B 4, followed by 15. .... P—Q Kt 3 and 16. .... B—Kt 2, and the security of White's King will be compromised in view of the weakness of the white squares.

13. ......   Q—Q 3
14. Kt—K 5

Avoiding P—K Kt 3 for the above reason.

14. ......   Kt×Kt !

Simple and strong ! Black, in addition to his two Bishops, has chances of undertaking a counter-attack on the Queen's side.

15. P×Kt   P—Q B 4
16. Castles P—Q Kt 4 !

Black's game seems at present preferable, and White must manœuvre with circumspection to preserve equality.

17. B—B 2 !

An important move with the double threat 18. Q—Q 3, followed by Q×Kt P ; and 18. B—K 4, followed by Kt—B 6, and on this account preventing Black from completing his development by 17. .... B—Kt 2.

17. ......   B—R 3
18. K R—K 1 Q R—Q 1
19. Q R—Q 1 P×P

By playing 19. .... P—Kt 3 immediately, Black would have maintained an excellent position, with good chances on the Queen's side. On the contrary, the text-move, which frees the position in the centre, is distinctly advantageous to White, and the latter succeeds in taking advantage of it by undertaking an attack as lively as it is interesting.

20. P×P   P—Kt 3

Inevitable, sooner or later.

See Diagram.

21. B—Kt 3 !

This move first threatens 22. Kt × B P ! and secondly prevents the manœuvre 21. .... B—Kt 2 and 22. .... B—Q 4, on account of the following variation : 21. .... B—Kt 2 ;

Position after Black's 20th move.

Position after Black's 25th move.

22. Q—Q 3, P—Q R 3 (or P—Kt 5); 23. Kt×Kt P ! !, R P×Kt ; 24. R×P !, P×R (if 24. .... Q moves anywhere ; 25. R×P ch); 25. Q×P ch, K—R 1 ; 26. B—B 2 and mates in a few moves.

21. ......   B—B 1

Preventing the threatened sacrifice.

22. Q—K 2 !   P—Q R 3
23. P—Q 5   Q—Kt 3

If 23. ....P×P ; 24. B×P followed by 25. Kt×B P.

24. Kt—B 6   Q R—K 1
25. Kt×B ch   R×Kt

See Diagram.

26. P—B 5 !

If Black accepts the sacrifice, White wins as follows : 26. Kt P×P ; 27. P—Q 6 !, R—Kt 2 (or A); 28. Q—K 5, P—R 3 ; 29. Q—B 6, K—R 2 ; 30. B×P.

(A).—27. ....R—Q 2 ; 28. Q—Q 2 !, K R—Q 1 ; 29. Q—Kt 5 ch, K—B 1 ; 30. Q—R 6 ch, K—K 1 (if 30. ....K—Kt 1 ; 31. R—Q 3 !); 31. R×P ch and mates in three moves.

26. ......   R—Kt 2

In this way Black loses a **Pawn** without weakening White's attack. Black's game rapidly becomes hopeless.

27. B P×K P   P×P
28. P×P   R—K 2
29. R—Q 7 !   K R—K 1

The Rook cannot be taken, for if 29. ....B×R ; 30. P×B (dis. ch), K—R 1, White would not continue 31. Q×R ?, but would first play 31. P—Q 8=Q !

30. Q—B 3   Q—B 4
31. Q—B 7 ch !   K—R 1
32. Q—B 6 ch   K—Kt 1
33. P—K R 4 !

If now 33. ....R—K B 1, then clearly 34. Q×R (K 7), Q×P ch ; 35. K—R 2, Q—B 5 ch ; 36. K—R 1 and wins.

Black resigns.

GAME 64

QUEEN'S PAWN GAME

White :   *Black :*
P. JOHNER.   A. ALEKHIN.

1. P—Q 4   Kt—K B 3
2. Kt—K B 3   P—K 3
3. P—B 4   P—B 4

It has been shown subsequently that this move is not quite correct (see Game No. 62). The right move here was 3. ....P—Q 4, or 3. .... P—Q Kt 3.

4. Kt—B 3

This answer is insufficient to secure White an advantage. He must play 4. P—Q 5, and if 4. .... P—Q Kt 4 ; 5. B—Kt 5 !, with the better game.

But my opponent had still fresh in his memory my game against Dr. Tarrasch, played in the first round of the same tournament (see Game No. 62), in which White, having adopted the continuation 4. P—Q 5, sustained a classic defeat ; and he therefore preferred the move in the text, apparently more conservative, but also duller.

4. ......   P × P
5. Kt × P   P—Q 4

This move allows White, should he so desire, to simplify the position, with an almost certain draw in view. 5. ....B—Kt 5 was more energetic, leading to a complicated game not without chances for Black.

6. P × P   Kt × P
7. Kt (Q 4)—Kt 5 !

Threatening 8. Kt × Kt, P × Kt ; 9. Q × P !

7. ......   B—Q 2

In order to answer 8. Kt × Kt with 8. ....B × Kt.

8. P—K 4   Kt × Kt
9. P × Kt !

Much better than 9. Kt × Kt, after which Black could have obtained a slight advantage in position by 9. ....B—B 4.

9. ......   Q—R 4
10. R—Q Kt 1 !

More energetic than the defensive move 10. Q—Kt 3. For the sacrificed Q R P White, thanks to his two Bishops, obtains a position full of promise, and Black in the sequel will be compelled to return the Pawn, in order to complete his development.

10. ......   P—Q R 3

If any other move, White would defend his Pawn by R—Kt 3 ; or he could play 11. Kt—Q 6 ch in spite of it.

11. Kt—Q 6 ch   B × Kt
12. Q × B   Q × P ch
13. B—Q 2   Q—Q B 3
14. Q—B 4

White over-estimates his prospects of attack, forgetting that his own King is not in safety. He ought to have been content to regain his Pawn, with a good game, by 14. Q—Kt 4, P—Q R 4 ! ; 15. Q × Kt P, Castles ! The text-move, on the contrary, speedily allows Black to seize the initiative.

14. ......   Castles
15. B—Q 3

Position after White's 15th move.

15. ......   P—K 4 !

By this sacrifice Black opens up new lines for his pieces, and taking advantage of the fact that White has still not Castled, undertakes a direct attack against the position of the hostile King.

Against any other move White would himself have obtained a powerful attack by 16. P—K 5 !

16. Q × K P   R—K 1
17. Q—Q 4

If 17. Q—Kt 3, R × P ch ; and if 17. Q—B 4, B—K 3 followed by 18. ....Kt—Q 2 and 19. ....Kt—B 4, both with advantage to Black.

17. ......   Q—K Kt 3 !

Position after Black's 17th move.

18. P—B 3

White already finds himself in a very difficult position, since he cannot Castle on account of 18. .... B—R 6, winning the Exchange. On the other hand, if 18. P—B 4 Black would have avoided the dangerous variation resulting from 18. ....Q × Kt P ; 19. R—Kt 1, Kt—B 3 ; 20. Q—K 3, Q × R P ; 21. B—B 3, and would have made certain of an advantage by 18. .... Kt—B 3 ! ; 19. Q—B 2 (or 19. Q × B, Q × P ; 20. R—K B 1, Q R— Q 1), B—B 4 !

18. ......   Q × P !

This move, at first sight hazardous, was the result of a long and minute calculation.

19. R—K Kt 1   Kt—B 3
20. Q—K 3   Q × R P
21. B—B 3   P—K Kt 3 !

Not 21. ....Kt—K 4 on account of 22. R × P ch !, K × R ; 23. Q— Kt 5 ch, K—R 1 (if 23. ....K—B 1 ? ; 24. B—Kt 4 ch !) ; 24. P—B 4 ! and Black would have been compelled to satisfy himself with a draw.

22. R × P   Q R—Q 1 !

The preparation for the final action.

23. B—B 6

It is manifest that with a Pawn less and in view of the exposed position of his King, other moves would not save White. That chosen allows Black to conclude energetically and rapidly.

23. ......   Kt—K 4 !

Threatening 24. ....Kt × P ch.

24. B—K 2

Position after White's 24th move.

24. ......   B—Kt 4 !

Practically ending the game, for if 25. B×R, then 25. ....B×B wins at once, on account of the threat 26. ....Kt×P ch. White is therefore forced into a general liquidation, after which his position remains absolutely without the slightest hope.

25. B×Kt	R×B
26. B×B	R×B
27. R×R	P×R

Threatening to lead into a winning Pawn-ending by 28. R—Q 7 !, etc. If 28. R—B 1, then 28. .... Q—Q B 7 and wins.

White resigns.

GAME 65

QUEEN'S GAMBIT DECLINED

Brilliancy Prize

| White : | Black : |
| A. ALEKHIN. | H. WOLF. |

1. P—Q 4	P—Q 4
2. Kt—K B 3	P—Q B 4
3. P—B 4	B P×P

The usual move is 3. ....P—K 3, transposing into the Tarrasch Defence. After the exchange of Pawns in the centre we reach a symmetrical position in which the advantage of the move always secures for White a slight advantage in position.

If in this game he obtains a better result, that is solely due to the fact that his opponent allows himself to go in for an innovation especially risky when his development is already behindhand.

| 4. P×P | Kt—K B 3 |
| 5. Kt×P | P—Q R 3 |

Black wished to avoid the variation 5. ....Kt×P ; 6. P—K 4, Kt—K B 3 ; 7. B—Kt 5 ch, B—Q 2; 8. P—K 5 !, B×B ; 9. Kt×B,

Q×Q ch ; 10. K×Q, Kt—Q 4 ; 11. Kt (Kt 1)—B 3, to the advantage of White, mentioned in the latest edition of Collijn's *Lärobok*. But this variation, like many others indicated in that work, which are indeed interesting but scarcely accurate, can be improved by 6. .... Kt—Kt 5 ! in place of 6. ....Kt—K B 3, after which White's advantage would be difficult to demonstrate.

The text-move does not seem risky, Black intending to capture the Q P on the next move. Its refutation is therefore only the more instructive.

Position after Black's 5th move.

6. P—K 4 ! !

Sacrificing the K P to retain the Q P which, as will be seen in the sequel, exercises a very strong pressure on the opponent's game.

| 6. ...... | Kt×K P |
| 7. Q—R 4 ch ! | |

In order to provoke the obstruction of the Queen's file by a Black piece, which cuts off the attack of Black's Queen on his Q P.

| 7. ...... | B—Q 2 |

Not 7. ....Q—Q 2 on account of 8. B—Q Kt 5.

8. Q—Kt 3   Kt—B 4

This square is hardly indicated for the Knight, but on the other hand he must secure the defence of his Q Kt P ; and 8. ....Q—B 2 or 8. ....B—B 1 is scarcely any better, seeing that Black's Queen would soon be dislodged from this file by White's Rook.

9. Q—K 3 !

Much stronger than the plausible move 9. Q—K B 3, on which Black could have freed himself by 9. .... P—K 4, for if 10. P × P e. p., Kt × P; 11. Kt × Kt, B × Kt ! ; 12. Q × P ?, B—Q 4 ! and Black must win. Whereas, after the text-move, the advance of Black's K P would give White the opportunity of exercising strong pressure on the King-file.

Black therefore resigns himself to the development of his K B in fianchetto, but equally without success.

9. ......   P—K Kt 3

Position after Black's 9th move.

10. Kt—K B 3 !

This gain of time allows White to prevent 10. ....B—Kt 2, followed by 11. ....Castles. Black's King being kept in the centre, White's attack will be facilitated, thanks to his superior development.

The opening of this game offers some analogies with that of Game No. 61, played at The Hague against Rubinstein.

In the one, as in the other, the advantage won results from repeated movements of the same pieces (here the first eleven moves contain four displacements of the Queen and three of the King's Knight).

But the possibility of like manœuvres in the opening phase is *solely* attributable, I must reiterate, to the fact that the opponent has adopted faulty tactics, which must from the first be refuted by an energetic demonstration. It is clear, on the contrary, that in face of correct development, similar anomalous treatment would be disastrous.

It cannot therefore be any question of a "Modern System," but just simply of exploiting in a rational manner the opponent's mistakes.

I cannot conceive why there is such an ardent desire to discover in a game of chess anything more subtle than it has to offer, for I am of opinion that the real beauty which it possesses should be more than sufficient for all possible demands.

10.	Q—B 2
11. Q—B 3	R—K Kt 1
12. B—K 3	P—Kt 3
13. Q Kt—Q 2	

13. P—Q Kt 4 would be an error of judgment, because Black would have saved his piece by 13. .... B—Kt 2 ; 14. Kt—Q 4, Q—R 2 ! White therefore prefers to complete his development before undertaking decisive action.

13.	B—Kt 2
14. B—Q 4	B × B
15. Q × B	

White, having rid himself of Black's K B, the only piece which could inconvenience him, the position of the opponent will very soon become desperate.

15. ......   B—Kt 4

It would be difficult to suggest another means of developing his Queen-side. After 15. ....B—B 4 ; 16. B—K 2, Q Kt—Q 2 would be impossible, on account of 17. P—K Kt 4, B—B 7 ; 18. R—Q B 1.

16. B × B ch   P × B
17. Castles (K R) R—R 5

This skirmish comes to nothing. To tell the truth, it is difficult to point out here a rational move.

18. P—Q Kt 4   Q—Q 1
19. P—Q R 3 !

White has no reason to hurry himself, considering the lack of resource of the adverse position.

19. ......   Q Kt—Q 2
20. K R—K 1   K—B 1
21. P—Q 6 !

A preparation for the following sacrifice. If Black reply to this move with 21. ....P—K 3, the continuation would be 22. Q—K 3, Kt—Kt 2 ; 23. Q—Q 3, R—R 1 ; 24. Kt—K 4, winning the Q Kt P to start with.

21. ......   Kt—K 3

Position after Black's 21st move.

22. R × Kt !

By this combination, based on a precise calculation of all its possibilities, White demolishes the last defences of the enemy. He regains the Exchange sacrificed in a few moves, with a mating-attack.

22. ......   P × R
23. Kt—Kt 5   Q—Kt 1

Or 23. ....P—K 4 ; 24. Q—Q 5, Q—K 1 ; 25. Kt—K 6 ch, K—B 2 ; 26. Kt—B 7 ch, P—K 3 ; 27. Q—B 3 ch and wins.

24. Kt × K P ch   K—B 2

If 24. ....K—K 1 ; 25. Kt—K 4 !

25. Kt—Kt 5 ch   K—B 1

If now 25. ....K—K 1 ; 26. R—K 1 !

26. Q—Q 5 !   R—Kt 2

Clearly forced.

27. Kt—K 6 ch   K—Kt 1
28. Kt × R ch   K × Kt
29. P × P   Kt—B 3
30. Q × P   R—R 2
31. R—K 1   Q—Q 3
32. P—K 8 (Kt) ch

The simplest method of securing the win.

32. ......   Kt × Kt
33. Q × Kt   Q × Kt
34. Q—K 5 ch   K—B 2
35. P—K R 4   R × P

This desperate capture conceals a last trap.

36. Q—K 8 ch   K—Kt 2
37. R—K 7 ch   K—R 3
38. Q—B 8 ch   K—R 4
39. R—K 5 ch   K—Kt 5
40. R—Kt 5 ch !

Avoiding the trap. If now 40. P—B 3 ch, K—Kt 6 ; 41. R—Kt 5 ch, Q × R ! ; 42. P × Q, R—R 8 mate !

Black resigns.

GAME 66

RUY LOPEZ

White :   *Black :*
DR. K. TREYBAL.   A. ALEKHIN.

1.	P—K 4	P—K 4
2.	Kt—K B 3	Kt—Q B 3
3.	B—Kt 5	P—Q R 3
4.	B—R 4	Kt—B 3
5.	Kt—B 3	B—K 2
6.	Castles	P—Q Kt 4
7.	B—Kt 3	P—Q 3
8.	P—Q R 4	R—Q Kt 1

This move, although recommended by Collijn's *Lärobok*, is distinctly inferior to 8. ....P—Kt 5, for it abandons the Q R file to White without any compensation.

9.	P×P	P×P
10.	P—K R 3	Castles
11.	Q—K 2	B—Q 2

Indirectly defending the Pawn attacked, for if 12. Kt×Kt P, Kt×P; 13. Kt×B P, Kt×Q P (or Kt—B 4); 14. B×Kt, Q×Kt and Black has an excellent game.

12. P—Q 3

Position after White's 12th move.

12. ......   Q—B 1

Insufficient would be 12. .... Kt—Q 5; 13. Kt×Kt, P×Kt; 14. Kt—Q 5, Kt×Kt; 15. B×Kt, P—Q B 3; 16. B—Kt 3, B—K 3; 17. B×B, P×B; 18. R—R 7, R—R 1; 19. R×R, Q×R; 20. Q—Kt 4, Q—B 1; 21. B—R 6, R—B 2; 22. R—R 1 with advantage to White.

The text-move prepares the following series of exchanges, and allows Black to adopt a more complicated line of play, commencing 13. ....Kt—Q 1, and 14. ....P—Q B 4 should White choose to prevent 13. ....Kt—Q 5 by 13. B—K 3.

13. K—R 2

Preventing a subsequent sacrifice of Black's Q B at K R 3. But as the danger was not imminent White would have done better to continue his development by 13. B—K 3.

After the text-move Black has at least an equal game.

13.	......	Kt—Q 5
14.	Kt×Kt	P×Kt
15.	Kt—Q 5	Kt×Kt
16.	B×Kt	P—B 3
17.	B—Kt 3	B—K 3 !
18.	P—K B 4	

The variation 18. B×B, Q×B; 19. P—K B 4, P—K B 4 would not yield White any advantage.

The text-move is the prelude to a hazardous King-side attack, since Black will get in first with an energetic counter-attack in the centre.

18.	......	B×B
19.	P×B	R—R 1 !

Not 19. ....Q—K 3 because of 20. P—B 5, Q×Kt P; 21. R—R 3, Q—Kt 5; 22. P—B 6 !, B×P; 23. R×B, P×R; 24. B—R 6, K—R 1; 25. Q—B 3, P—K B 4; 26. Q×P, P—B 3; 27. R—R 7 and wins.

20. R × R

If 20. R—Kt 1, then 20. ....
Q—K 3, etc.

20. ......   Q × R
21. P—B 5   P—B 3 !

Much better than 21. .... B—B 3,
upon which White would have
obtained a very fine game by 22.
B—B 4, R—Q 1 ; 23. Q—K 1 !
followed by Q—Q R 1 or Q—Kt 3.

The move chosen prepares the
advance of the centre Pawns.

22. P—K Kt 4

Having embarked on a perilous
journey, White has no option but
to persevere, for, were he to adopt
a purely defensive plan, Black
would have a still more easy game
than in the text, *e.g.:* 22. P—Q Kt 4,
P—B 4 ; 23. Q—Q B 2, Q—B 3
followed by 24. .... R—R 1.

22. ......   P—B 4
23. P—R 4   P—Q 4 !

Position after Black's 23rd move.

24. P—Kt 5

White has nothing better, *e.g. :*

I.—24. P × P, B—Q 3 ch ; 25.
B—B 4, R—K 1 ; 26. Q—Kt 2,
B × B ch ; 27. R × B, Q—Kt 1 ;

28. Q—K B 2, Q—K 4 ! and Black
has the better game.

II.—24. P—K 5, Q—Kt 1 ! (not
however 24. .... P × P ; 25. Q × P,
B × P because of 26. P—Kt 5 !, R—
K 1 ; 27. Q—B 4, B—K 8 ; 28.
P—B 6 with a strong attack for
White) ; 25. B—B 4, P × P ; 26.
B × P, B—Q 3 with advantage to
Black.

24. ......   Q P × P
25. Q P × P   Q—B 3
26. K—R 3

Preparing 27. P—K 5. If 26. P—
Kt 6, P—R 3 ; 27. Q—R 5, Q × P ;
28. B × P, P × B ; 29. Q × P, Q—
K 7 ch, followed by 30. . . Q—K 6 ch,
wins for Black.

26. ......   P—B 5
27. P—K 5

White attempts the impossible to
obtain the semblance of an attack,
but in vain, for Black gets there first.

27. ......   P—Q 6
28. Q—K 1 !

The only move. If 28. Q—K 3,
P × K Kt P ! ; 29. R P × P, R × P ! ;
30. R × R, Q—K 3 ; 31. Q—K 4,
P—Kt 3 ; 32. K—Kt 4 (or 32. Q—
R 8 ch, K—Kt 2), P × R ch ; 33.
Q × P, Q × Q ch ; 34. K × Q, B—R 6 !!
and wins.

28. ......   P × K P

If now 28. .... P × K Kt P White
would have replied 29. B × P.

29. Q × P   B—Kt 5 !
30. P × P   P × P
31. Q—Q 4 !

Threatening to break up the
hostile Pawn formation by 32. P—
Kt 3.

See Diagram.

31. ......   Q—Kt 4 !

The only move to win. It
threatens both 32. .... R × P and

Position after White's 31st move.

32. ....P—Q 7 ! followed by 33.
....P—B 6. If White plays 32. K—
Kt 2, then 32. ....B—R 4 ! and
33. ....R—Q 1 would also win
without difficulty.

  32. P—B 6   P—Q 7 !
  33. Q—B 4 !

Position after White's 33rd move.

Anticipating the continuation 33.
....P×B=Q; 34. R×Q, R—B 1;
35. Q—Kt 4 ! with drawing chances,
since Black's K R 8 is not of the
same colour as his Bishop.

By the ensuing combination, *the
longest which I have ever undertaken,* Black avoids this doubtful
variation and secures a winning
Pawn-ending.

33.	......	Q—Q 2 ch !
34.	K—Kt 2	P—Q 8=Q !
35.	R×Q	Q×R
36.	Q×P ch	R—B 2
37.	Q×B	Q×B
38.	Q—Kt 8 ch	R—B 1
39.	P—B 7 ch !	

The key-move of a variation
enabling White to recover his Rook.
As we shall see shortly, Black's
winning manœuvre initiated by 33.
....Q—Q 2 ch ! comprises no less
than 20 moves !

  39. ......   K×P

Position after Black's 39th move.

  40. Q—Kt 3 ch?

It is astonishing that a master of
the strength of Dr. Treybal, so con-
spicuously endowed with the imagi-
native sense, should not have per-
ceived 40. P—Kt 6 ch !, the only
logical continuation.

Black could not have answered it
by 40. ....K—Kt 1, on account of
41. P×P ch ; nor by 40. ....P×P
for in that case White would have
forced a draw by perpetual check,
e.g. : 41. Q—Kt 3 ch, K—B 3 ; 42.
Q—K B 3 ch, K—K 2 ; 43. Q—
R 3 ch, K—K 1 ; 44. Q—R 4 ch !,
K—Q 1 ; 45. Q—R 8 ch, K—K 2 ;
46. Q—R 3 ch, K—B 2 ; 47. Q—
Kt 3 ch, etc.

The only move to win was consequently 40. ....K×P !, leading to the forced continuation:

41. Q×R, Q×P ch ; 42. K—B 3, Q—B 6 ch ; 43. K—Kt 2, Q—Q 7 ch ; 44. K—Kt 3, Q—K 6 ch ; 45. K—Kt 2, Q—K 5 ch ; 46. K—Kt 3, Q—K 4 ch ; 47. K—Kt 2, K—R 4 ! ; 48. Q—B 3 ch, K×P ; 49. Q—R 3 ch, K—Kt 4 ; 50. Q×P, Q—K 7 ch ; 51. K—Kt 3 or K—Kt 1, Q—Kt 5 ch ; 52. any, Q—B 4 ch or Q—R 4 ch, and Black wins by forcing exchange of Queens next move.

40. ...... K—Kt 3 !

And White can only give a few harmless checks, e.g.: 41. Q—K 6 ch, K—R 4 ; 42. Q—K 2 ch, K×P ! and wins.

White resigns.

GAME 67

QUEEN'S GAMBIT DECLINED

White :   *Black :*
A. ALEKHIN.   K. HROMADKA.

1. P—Q 4   P—Q 4
2. Kt—K B 3   Kt—K B 3
3. P—B 4   P—B 3
4. Kt—B 3   Q—Kt 3

Played for the first time by Süchting against Schlechter at the Carlsbad Tournament, 1911. The best reply to this move seems to be 5. P—B 5, Q—B 2 ; 6. P—K Kt 3 !, followed by 7. B—B 4. The line of play which still gives Black the most chances is in my opinion 4. ....P×P, followed by 5. .... P—Q Kt 4 and, if needed, P—Kt 5 etc. (See Game No. 71).

5. P—K 3

Solid, but without vigour. As we shall see later, Black could have equalised the game at a certain stage.

5. ...... B—Kt 5
6. P×P B×P
7. Q—R 4 ch B—Q 2

Best. If 7. ....Kt—B 3 ; 8. Kt—K 5, B—Q 2 ; 9. B—Kt 5, P—K 3 ; 10. Kt×B, Kt×Kt ; 11. P—K 4 ! with an attack similar to that in the present game, after White's 13th move.

8. B—Kt 5 P—Q R 3
9. B×B ch Q Kt×B
10. Castles P—K 3
11. Kt—K 5

White has not secured an advantage of development sufficient to be able to exploit the pinning of Black's Q Kt, especially against a correct defence.

11. ...... Q—R 2

It is solely owing to this loss of time that White succeeds in getting up an attack. The right move was 11. ....Q—Kt 5 ! provoking the exchange of Queens and unpinning the Knight, after which Black would have had nothing to fear. Whereas now, for want of being able to Castle, his position in the centre will be completely demolished.

12. Kt×Kt ! Kt×Kt

Position after Black's 12th move.

13. P—K 4 !

The commencement of a danger-ous offensive whose result will be the formation of a strong passed Pawn in the centre.

The following moves of Black are practically forced, because he must necessarily and at all costs prevent the opening of the King's file.

13.	......	P—Q Kt 4
14.	Q—B 2	P × P
15.	P—Q 5 !	P—K 4
16.	P—Q R 4 !	

Before recapturing the Pawn, it is not unnecessary to provoke a new weakness in the adverse Queen-side.

| 16. | ...... | P—Kt 5 |
| 17. | Kt × P | Q—Kt 2 |

If 17. ....B—B 4 ; 18. B—K 3 !, B × B ; 19. Kt—Q 6 ch, K—K 2 ; 20. Kt—B 5 ch followed by 21. P × B, with a very strong attack.

| 18. | R—Q 1 | R—B 1 |
| 19. | Q—K 2 | B—K 2 |

Black vainly hopes to bring his King under cover.

| 20. | Q—Kt 4 | P—Kt 3 |

Forced, for if 20. ....Castles ; 21. B—R 6.

Position after Black's 20th move.

21. B—Kt 5 !

Definitely fixing the Black King in the centre, which, in conjunction with the numerous weaknesses in his position, ends in a rapid col-lapse by Black. Indeed, he can play without disadvantage neither 21. ....P—B 3, on account of 22. Q—K 6, nor 21. ....P—B 4, on ac-count of 22. Q—R 4 !, and has nothing better than the exchange of Bishops, which deprives him of Castling.

21.	......	P—R 3
22.	B × B	K × B
23.	Q—R 4 ch	

In order to provoke a new weak-ness in the position of the adverse Pawns.

| 23. | ...... | P—Kt 4 |

If 23. ....P—B 3 ; 24. P—B 4 ! with a very strong attack.

| 24. | Q—Kt 4 | R—B 5 |
| 25. | Q—B 5 | |

Among other things, threatening 26. Q × P ch followed by 27. Kt—Q 6 ch.

| 25. | ...... | R—K B 1 |
| 26. | P—Kt 3 ! | |

26. Kt—B 6 would be premature, on account of 26. ....R—B 5.

| 26. | ...... | R (B 5)—B 1 |
| 27. | Kt—B 6 ! | |

The decisive move. If 27. .... Kt × Kt ; 28. P—Q 6 ch !

| 27. | ...... | R—B 4 |
| 28. | Kt × Kt | Q—B 1 |

If 28. ....Q × Kt ; 29. Q × K P ch, K—Q 1 ; 30. Q R—B 1, R × R ; 31. R × R and White wins.

| 29. | P—Q 6 ch | |

Winning a Rook after 29. .... K—Q 1 ; 30. Q—B 6 ch, K × Kt ; 31. Q—K 7 ch, K—B 3 ; 32. P—Q 7 !

Black resigns.

CHAPTER XVII

INTERNATIONAL TOURNAMENT AT LONDON
AUGUST, 1922

GAME 68

QUEEN'S PAWN GAME

White : *Black :*
A. ALEKHIN. M. EUWE.

1. P—Q 4 Kt—K B 3
2. Kt—K B 3 P—K Kt 3

This variation, introduced into master-practice by Grünfeld, rests upon the following ideas :—The development of the K B in fianchetto, and the withholding of P—Q 4 until White has developed his Kt at Q B 3. By this means Black, after 3 P—B 4, B—Kt 2 ; 4. Kt—Q B 3, P—Q 4 ; 5. P×P, Kt×P ; 6. P—K 4, Kt×Kt ; 7. P×Kt reserves the possibility of attacking the hostile centre by P—Q B 4, opening up good prospects for his Bishop on K Kt 2.

Consequently, the best line of play for White consists in moving the Q Kt only after having augmented the pressure on the square Q 5 by P—K Kt 3 and B—Kt 2, which seems to secure him a slight advantage, as shown among others by the games Alekhin—Muller (Margate, 1923), Sämisch—Grünfeld (Carlsbad, 1923) and Alekhin—Réti (New York, 1924).

3. B—B 4

Trying a new system which occasions Black less difficulty than the line of play quoted above. Compare also the games Capablanca—Réti and Rubinstein—Euwe from the same Tournament.

3. ...... B—Kt 2
4. Q Kt—Q 2 P—B 4 !

A good move.

5. P—K 3

If 5. P×P, Black regains the Pawn with advantage by 5. ....Kt—R 3 !

5. ...... P—Q 3
6. P—B 3 Kt—B 3
7. P—K R 3

This move is essential to reserve a square of retreat for the Q B in case of Kt—K R 4.

7. ...... Castles
8. B—B 4 !

The best square for this Bishop. The reply 8. ....P—Q 4 is clearly not to be feared, as it would merely enhance the prospects of the opposing Q B.

8. ...... R—K 1

Preparing P—K 4, which will, however, have the disadvantage of weakening the square Q 3.

| 9. Castles | P—K 4 |
| 10. P × K P | Q Kt × P |

The capture with the Knight yields White at once a very perceptible, if not decisive, advantage in position. Black would do better by 10. ... P × P; 11. B—R 2, B—K 3; 12. B × B, R × B; 13. Kt—B 4, after which White's advantage, undeniable as it is, would be very difficult to take advantage of.

| 11. B × Kt ! | P × B |

Position after Black's 11th move.

12. Kt—K Kt 5 !

This simple move, as seen later on, assures White the possession of the only open file.

| 12. ...... | B—K 3 |

An heroic resolution, because after the doubling of the Pawns, Black's K B is left quite without action. Somewhat better was 12. ... R—B 1; 13. Kt (Q 2)—K 4 !, Q × Q (if 13. ... Kt × Kt ?; 14. B × P ch !); 14. K R × Q, Kt × Kt; 15. Kt × Kt, P—Kt 3, although, in this case also, White would have secured excellent winning chances.

13. B × B	P × B
14. Kt (Q 2)—K 4	Kt × Kt
15. Q × Q	K R × Q
16. Kt × Kt	P—Kt 3
17. K R—Q 1	K—B 1
18. K—B 1 !	

White could have won a Pawn by 18. Kt—Kt 5, but that would have allowed Black to force exchange of Bishop against Knight, by 18. ... K—K 2; 19. Kt × R P, B—R 3; 20. P—K R 4, R—R 1, with good drawing chances.

| 18. ...... | K—K 2 |

If 18. P—B 5, then 19. Kt—Q 6 ! But now Black threatens, by means of 19. ... P—B 5, to occupy Q 4 and later Q 6 with his Rook.

19. P—Q B 4 !

Preventing the above threat, and at the same time making the third rank free for the Rook, which is very important, as shown later.

19.	P—K R 3
20. K—K 2	R × R
21. R × R	R—Q Kt 1

Black is compelled to avoid the exchange of Rooks, which would enable White to force the win in the following way: 21. ... R—Q 1; 22. R × R, K × R.

Position after Black's 22nd move in sub-variation.

1st phase.—23. P—K R 4 ! followed by P—K Kt 4 and P—Kt 5 on which Black will have nothing better than P—K R 4, seeing that the exchange of Pawns abandons the square K R 4 to White's Knight.

2nd phase.—P—Q Kt 3, followed by K—Q 3, Kt—B 3 and K—K 4.

3rd phase.—The manœuvring of the White Knight to Q 3, after which Black must immobilize his King on Q 3 in order to be able to defend the doubly attacked K P.

4th phase.—And lastly P—B 4 ! forcing the win of the K P or the K Kt P, after which the advantage secured will be decisive.

By avoiding the exchange of Rooks, Black will make the task of his opponent more difficult.

22. R—Q 3   B—R 1

Position after Black's 22nd move.

23. P—Q R 4 !

The only means of forcing the decisive entry of the White Rook into the enemy's game. White takes advantage of the fact that Black cannot reply by 23. ....P—Q R 4, on account of 24. R—Kt 3 ! winning the Q B P or the Q Kt P.

23. ......   R—Q B 1
24. R—Kt 3   K—Q 2
25. P—R 5 !   K—B 3

It is obvious that it is better to abstain from capturing White's Q R P, because of 26. R—Kt 5.

26. P × P   P × P
27. R—R 3   B—Kt 2
28. R—R 7   R—B 2

Black reconciles himself to the exchange of Rooks, but White now considers that by avoiding it he will attain the victory still more speedily.

29. R—R 8 !   R—K 2
30. R—B 8 ch   K—Q 2
31. R—K Kt 8 !   K—B 3
32. P—R 4

In order to block in the Bishop completely before undertaking the decisive manœuvre with his Knight.

32. ......   K—B 2
33. P—K Kt 4   K—B 3
34. K—Q 3

This was not quite necessary, seeing that White's King will be compelled to return to its starting point. By 34. P—Kt 3 White could have shortened the game by several moves.

34. ......   R—Q 2 ch
35. K—B 3   R—K B 2
36. P—Kt 3   K—B 2
37. K—Q 3   R—Q 2 ch
38. K—K 2   R—B 2
39. Kt—B 3 !

In order to post this Knight on Q Kt 5, where its action will be still more powerful than on K 4.

39. ......   R—K 2
40. P—Kt 5   P × P
41. P × P   K—B 3
42. K—Q 3

White has at his command another winning line also, based upon the manœuvre Kt—K 4—Q 2— B 3—R 4 winning the K Kt P, but he prefers to follow the path which he has traced out for himself.

42.	R—Q 2 ch
43. K—K 4	R—Kt 2
44. Kt—Kt 5	R—K 2

If 44. ....R—K B 2, then 45. R—B 8 ch followed by Kt—Q 6 ch, winning the Rook.

| 45. P—B 3 | K—Q 2 |

The only move. If 45. ....K—Kt 2, then 46. Kt—Q 6 ch followed by Kt—K 8, winning the Bishop.

| 46. R—Q Kt 8 | K—B 3 |
| 47. R—B 8 ch | K—Q 2 |

Or 47. ....K—Kt 2 ; 48. Kt—Q 6 ch, K—R 2 ; 49. R—K Kt 8 and wins.

| 48. R—B 7 ch | K—Q 1 |
| 49. R—B 6 ! | |

Forcing the first gain of material, but also immediately decisive.

| 49. ...... | R—Kt 2 |
| 50. R × K P | Black resigns. |

GAME 69

QUEEN'S GAMBIT DECLINED

| White : | Black : |
| A. ALEKHIN. | F. D. YATES. |

1. P—Q 4	Kt—K B 3
2. P—Q B 4	P—K 3
3. Kt—K B 3	P—Q 4
4. Kt—B 3	B—K 2
5. B—Kt 5 ;	Castles
6. P—K 3	Q Kt—Q 2
7. R—B 1	P—B 3
8. Q—B 2	R—K 1

This move is inferior to 8. ....P—Q R 3, because after 9. B—Q 3 ! Black can no longer transpose into the system of defence which still offers him the best chances.

| 9. B—Q 3 | P × P |

Reverting to Capablanca's defence (see Game No. 79) with the sole difference that his K R is at K 1 instead of K B 1, which is not of much importance. If 9. ....P—Q R 3 White could now advantageously reply 10. P × P !, taking advantage of the fact that Black cannot at this point recapture the Pawn with his Knight.

On the other hand, after 9. ....P—K R 3 ; 10. B—B 4 ! (see Game No. 80, note to Black's 8th move), P—R 3, the exchange at Q 5 would be entirely to White's advantage, e.g. :

11. P × P ! (but not 11. P—B 5, B × P ! ; 12. P × B, P—K 4, threatening 13. ....P—K 5, thus regaining the piece with a very fine game—compare the game Euwe—Spielmann, Mährisch-Ostrau, 1923), Kt × P ; 12. Kt × Kt, K P × Kt ; 13. Castles, Kt—B 3 ; 14. P—K R 3, etc., and White will be able to undertake an attack on the Queenside by R—Kt 1, P—Q Kt 4, P—Q R 4 and P—Kt 5, leaving his opponent without appreciable counter-chances.

| 10. B × P | Kt—Q 4 |
| 11. Kt—K 4 | |

The right move here was 11. B × B. Regarding the inadequacy of 11. Kt—K 4, compare Game No. 79.

It should be noticed that in the variation 11. ....Q—R 4 ch, etc., the position of the Rook at K 1 is rather an advantage for Black.

| 11. ...... | P—K B 4 |

Among the various replies to be considered by Black this is undoubtedly the least worthy of commendation. Apart from the fact that it in no wise incommodes White's Castling, it yields the splendid square at K 5 to the adverse Knight without the slightest compensation.

From this point Black's game may be considered strategically lost, which is not to say that the realization of victory will be an easy matter.

12. B × B   Q × B
13. Q Kt—Q 2   P—Q Kt 4

This move, which aims at the liberation of the useless Q B, is worse than the disadvantage which it seeks to mitigate, for White will now seize control of the Q B file and especially the square Q B 5, which Black has just given up by the text-move.

Black would have done better to occupy the opponent with the following diversion : 13. .... Kt (Q 4) —Kt 3 ; 14. B—Q 3, P—K Kt 3, preparing P—K 4 ; or 14. B—Kt 3, P—Q R 4 ; 15. P—Q R 4, Kt—Q 4 and Kt—Kt 5, although in these cases also his prospects were doubtful.

14. B × Kt   B P × B

Position after Black's 14th move.

15. Castles

White's next moves are based upon simple but indisputable logic. By the occupation of the square Q B 5 by one of his Knights, he will force its exchange against the opposing Q Kt, after which he will be able to settle his second Knight on the same square without fear of molestation.

15. ......   P—Q R 4

16. Kt—Kt 3   P—R 5
17. Kt—B 5   Kt × Kt
18. Q × Kt !   Q × Q

The exchange of Queens would ultimately have become inevitable.

And now Black is entirely at the mercy of his opponent, who will be free to choose the best road to victory.

19. R × Q   P—Kt 5
20. K R—B 1   B—R 3
21. Kt—K 5 !

The Knight arrives at the right moment to prevent Black opposing his Rooks on the Q B file, *e.g.* : 21. .... K R—Q B 1 ; 22. R × R ch, R × R ; 23. R × R ch, B × R ; 24. Kt—B 6, with the double threat 25. Kt—K 7 ch and 25. Kt × Kt P, which would make the win certain for White.

21. ......   K R—Kt 1
22. P—B 3 !

Preparing the decisive advance of the White King.

22. ......   P—Kt 6
23. P—Q R 3   P—R 3

Position after Black's 23rd move.

24. K—B 2 !

The starting-point of a mating-manœuvre based on the following considerations : as Black must avoid the exchange of Rooks and as his pieces are kept on the Queen-side, to secure the defence of his Pawns, the Black King must sooner or later succumb to the combined assault of the four White pieces, including the King.

```
24. ......        K—R 2
25. P—R 4 !
```

Hindering ....P—Kt 4, after ....K—Kt 3 and ....K—R 4.

```
25. ......        R—K B 1
26. K—Kt 3        R (B 1)—
                        Q Kt 1
```

Black has to resign himself to complete inactivity.

```
27. R—B 7
```

Threatening among other things 28. Kt—Q 7 and 29. Kt—B 5 or 29. Kt—Kt 6.

```
27. ......        B—Kt 4
28. R (B 1)—B 5 !
```

In order to double Rooks on the 7th rank by 29. R—K 7 !, R—K 1 ; 30. R (K 7)—K B 7 and 31. R (B 5) —B 7.

```
28. ......        B—R 3
29. R (B 5)—B 6   R—K 1
30. K—B 4
```

The doubling of the Rooks on the 7th rank by R—K B 7 being now assured, White brings his King to the centre.

```
30. ......        K—Kt 1
31. P—R 5 !
```

Foreseeing the final manœuvre, for whose success it is essential to prevent Black's King from emerging at K Kt 3 after 35. Kt—Q 7 !

```
31. ......        B—B 8
```

It is curious to observe that the Q B, although having full liberty of action, cannot take any part in the defence.

```
32. P—Kt 3
```

A waiting-move. 32. R—B 7 would now be premature, because of 32. ....Q R—B 1.

```
32. ......        B—R 3
```

If 32. ....B—K 7 White would have continued his attack by 33. Kt—Kt 6 followed by 34. Kt—R 4 and 35. K—K 5.

```
33. R—B 7         K—R 2
```

Black is quite unable to forestall the mating attack by 33. ....R—K B 1, since White would have very speedily concluded the game after capturing the K P.

```
34. R (B 6)—B 7   R—K Kt 1
35. Kt—Q 7 !
```

This threat to win the Exchange forces the following reply.

```
35. ......        K—R 1
36. Kt—B 6 !      R (Kt 1)—
                        K B 1
```

In the hope of bringing about the exchange of one Rook at least.

```
37. R × P !
```

This sacrificial combination forces mate in at most seven moves.

```
37. ......        R × Kt
```

See Diagram.

```
38. K—K 5 !
```

The point of the combination ! The Black Rook can neither retire, nor can it be defended by the other Rook, without allowing a mate in two moves. But even after its capture by the White King, mate can only be delayed by problem moves.

Black resigns.

Position after Black's 37th move.

GAME 70

QUEEN'S GAMBIT DECLINED

White :	*Black :*
A. RUBINSTEIN.	A. ALEKHIN.

1. Kt—K B 3	P—Q 4
2. P—Q 4	Kt—K B 3
3. P—B 4	P—B 3
4. Kt—B 3	P × P

The acceptance of the Gambit at this stage of the game was made the object of an analysis by Alapin about fifteen years ago, but his attempts to popularize it did not fructify.

His analysis mentioned, after 5. P—K 3, P—Q Kt 4 ; 6. P—Q R 4, the moves Kt—Q 4 and Q—Kt 3. Not until the London Tournament of 1922, where my innovation 6. ....P—Kt 5 ! was disclosed, did the variation receive a new lease of life.

5. P—Q R 4

Rubinstein, who was already familiar with my analysis, followed religiously the line of play adopted against me by Bogoljuboff some rounds previously in the same tournament, but Black gets out of all his difficulties by the development of his Q B.

5.	B—B 4 !
6. P—K 3	P—K 3
7. B × P	B—Q Kt 5 !

This is played not to exchange the K B against the Q Kt, but solely to post the Bishop in the most effective manner in this position.

8. Castles	Castles
9. Kt—K 2	

This manœuvre, which aims at the exchange of Black's Q B, requires too much time and is the chief cause of all White's subsequent difficulties. The simple developing move B—Q 2, here or on the next move, would have most easily secured equality, for he could not hope for more in the present circumstances.

9.	Q Kt—Q 2
10. Kt—Kt 3	B—Kt 3
11. Kt—R 4	P—B 4 !

Black takes advantage of the time given him by his opponent to complete his development by undertaking an action in the centre.

12. Kt × B

Bogoljuboff in the above-mentioned game here continued with the hazardous move 12. P—B 4, Kt—Kt 3 ; 13. B—R 2, P × P ; 14. P × P, Kt (B 3)—Q 4 ; 15. Kt—B 3, Q R—B 1 ; 16. Kt—K 5, B—B 7 ! ; 17. Q—B 3, P—B 4 !, with a great superiority in position for Black.

The exchange in the text, although more prudent, also leaves White struggling to develop his inactive Q B.

12.	R P × Kt
13. P × P	Kt × P
14. Q—K 2	

Threatening the advance of the K P, which Black will at once prevent.

14.	Kt (B 3)—K 5 !
15. Kt × Kt	Kt × Kt
16. Q—Kt 4	

The combination 16. B × P, P × B; 17. Q—B 4, Q—Q 4 !; 18. Q × B, Kt × B P ! turns to Black's advantage. The text-move is preferable to 16. Q—B 3, against which Black could have replied 16. ....Kt—Q 3, a move at present impossible because of 17. B × P, etc.

| 16. ...... | Kt—B 3 |
| 17. Q—B 3 | |

A fresh attempt to enforce P—K 4.

| 17. ...... | Q—B 2 |

Gaining the necessary time to prevent once and for all the advance of the K P.

18. P—Q Kt 3	Q—K 4
19. R—R 2	Kt—K 5
20. P—R 5	

Simpler was 20. B—Kt 2. The continuation of the game shows that the text-move offers Black a chance of victory, by allowing him to support his Kt at Q B 6 by P—Kt 5 on his 29th move.

20.	K R—Q 1
21. B—Kt 2	B—B 6
22. B × B	

It is obvious that White cannot keep his two Bishops.

22.	Kt × B
23. R—B 2	P—Q Kt 4 !
24. P × P e. p.	P × P

The opening of the Q R, due to White's incautious 20th move, is an evident advantage for Black.

| 25. K R—B 1 | Kt—R 7 |

To gain the time to advance his Q Kt P.

26. R—K 1	P—Q Kt 4
27. B—B 1	Kt—B 6
28. Q—B 4 !	

The exchange of Queens still affords White the best chance of escaping, seeing that it leads to the opening of the King's file for his Rooks, the other files being in his opponent's possession.

But the ensuing end-game is not a little in Black's favour.

28.	Q × Q
29. P × Q	P—Kt 5
30. P—Kt 3	

Position after White's 30th move.

| 30. ...... | R—R 6 |

However, this thoughtless move, which involves an important loss of time, deprives Black of most of his chances, for there was no reason to persuade White to post his Bishop at B 4, where it would have to go in any event.

It would have been far wiser to bring his King quickly to the centre by K—B 1, K—K 2, R—Q 5 and K—Q 3, after which Black could have contemplated the exchange of one Rook and the investment of the Q Kt P by the three remaining pieces.

After the text-move he lacks precisely one *tempo* to execute this manœuvre.

31. B—B 4	K—B 1
32. K—Kt 2	K—K 2
33. R—K 5 !	

It is just this reply which Black did not sufficiently appreciate when playing his 30th move. Now he has no time to play 33. ....R—Q 5, for White is threatening to enter into the hostile game via Q B 5 and Q B 8. Being compelled to defend himself, Black must temporarily forego the victory.

33. ......   R—Q B 1
34. P—R 4

This demonstration, which has no real point, would have been without effect had Black simply answered it by 34. ....R—B 3, whereas his actual reply allows White to introduce fresh complications.

34. ......   Kt—Q 4
35. R (B 2)—K 2 !

A good move which meets the threat 35. ....Kt—Kt 3 on account of 36. B × P !, and thus gains an important *tempo*.

35. ......   Kt—B 6
36. R—Q 2   R—B 3

Position after Black's 36th move.

37. P—R 5 !

This ingenious Pawn-sacrifice, which would have had no object if

White's Rook were still on Q B 2, requires the greatest circumspection on Black's part, without impairing White's game.

The present game, more than any other, marks the evolution of Rubinstein's style : the deep strategist has become transformed into a clever tactician, whose every move conceals a hidden bolt, or prepares a fresh combination.

This opinion is confirmed, moreover, by the number of Brilliancy Prizes which he has carried off in recent tournaments, alongside such specialists in that art as Mieses and Spielmann.

37. ......   P—B 3
38. R—K 3   P × P
39. P—B 5   P—K 4
40. R (K 3)—Q 3

Threatening mate in three. Now we perceive the strong attacking position secured by White with his sacrifice.

40. ......   R—R 2
41. R—Q 8

This continuation of the attack, although deeply conceived, is finally shown to be inadequate because of a hidden defensive manœuvre, which, however, is the sole means of saving Black's game.

Whereas by 41. P—B 3, preventing 41. ....Kt—K 5, White could have forced the draw at once : 41. ....Kt—Kt 8 ; 42. R—Q 1, Kt—B 6 ; 43. R (Q 1)—Q 2, Kt—Kt 8, etc.

41. ......   Kt—K 5

The only way to prevent the threatened 42. R—K Kt 8.

42. R (Q 2)—Q 5 !

Black cannot answer this by the plausible move 42. ....Kt—Q 3, because of 43. R—K Kt 8, Kt × P (or 43. ....Kt × B ; 44. R × Kt P ch,

etc.); **44.** R (Q 5)—Q 8, Kt—Q 3;
45. R—Q Kt 8 ! and White wins.

   42. ......   R—Q 3 !
   43. R—K Kt 8 !

This appears at first sight decisive, as Black cannot continue 43. ....R×R without losing the Exchange by force after 44. B×R, but Black in his turn prepares a surprise for his opponent.

Position after White's 43rd move.

   43. ......   R—R 7 !

The saving move ! Black is now protected from the threatened mate in a few moves commencing with **44.** R—Kt 5, for he himself is menacing a mate in three moves by **44.** ....R×P ch. White's next moves are therefore forced.

   44. R×P ch   K—B 1
   45. R—Kt 8 ch   K×R
   46. R—Q 2 dis ch K—Kt 2
   47. R×R (R 2)   R—Q 7 !

The point of the whole combination—Black forces the exchange of the second Rook and leads into an ending which is clearly favourable for him, by reason of the weakness of White's Q Kt P and the limited range of action of White's King.

   48. R×R   Kt×R
   49. B—Q 5   P—K 5

Opposing 50. P—B 3 and by that fact hindering the approach of the White King to the Knight.

   50. P—B 4 ?

This makes White's game indefensible, owing to his inability after to dislodge the 50. ....P—K 6, Knight, and thus oppose the march of Black's King to the Queen's wing.

Rather better was 50. P—Kt 4 !, P—R 5 ; 51. K—R 3, Kt—B 6 ; 52. P—Kt 5 !, and the sacrifice of the Pawn would afford White some drawing chances owing to the reduced material left on the board.

The last phase of the game is instructive.

   50. ......   P—K 6 !

Now Black's King can proceed without hindrance to annex White's Q Kt P.

   51. K—Kt 1   K—B 1
   52. K—Kt 2   K—K 2
   53. B—Kt 8   K—Q 3
   54. B—B 7   K—B 4
   55. B×P   Kt×P
   56. K—B 3

White could have prolonged his resistance by 56. P—Kt 4, in which case the continuation would have been 56. ....Kt—Q 5 ; 57. P—Kt 5 !, P×P (if 57. ....P—Kt 6 ? ; 58. P×P !) ; 58. P×P, Kt×P ; 59. B—B 7, K—Q 5 ; 60. K—B 1, K—Q 6 ; 61. K—K 1, Kt—R 5 ; 62. B—Q 5, P—Kt 6 ! and wins.

   56. ......   K—Q 5
   57. B—B 7

Now 57. P—K Kt 4 would yield White no chance after 57. ....K—Q 6, etc.

   57. ......   K—Q 6 !

The simplest.

   58. B×Kt   K—Q 7 !
   59. B—B 4   P—Kt 6
   60. B×P   P—K 7
White resigns.

CHAPTER XVIII

INTERNATIONAL TOURNAMENT AT HASTINGS
SEPTEMBER, 1922

GAME 71

QUEEN'S GAMBIT DECLINED

White :   *Black :*
A. ALEKHIN.   DR. S. TARRASCH.

1. P—Q 4	P—Q 4
2. P—Q B 4	P—Q B 3
3. Kt—K B 3	

The system of play introduced by Rubinstein against Bogoljuboff in this same tournament, namely 3. Kt—Q B 3, Kt—B 3 ; 4. P—K 3, B—B 4 ; 5. P×P, Kt×P ; 6. B—B 4 followed by 7. K Kt—K 2 ! is very interesting.

3.	Kt—B 3
4. Kt—B 3	

During the London Tournament a few weeks previously I had introduced against this line of play a system of defence which I consider perfectly correct : 4. ....P×P, followed by 5. ....P—Q Kt 4 and 6. ....P—Kt 5.

Desiring to test its value when playing against it myself, I wished to give my opponent the opportunity here, presuming that Dr. Tarrasch, always on the watch for theoretical novelties, would be tempted to employ it in the present game.

Although the struggle turned in my favour, the result does not impair the value of the variation in question.

Indeed, there is reason to think that my opponent was not sufficiently versed in the particularly delicate subtleties of this defence.

The system has been subsequently adopted by masters of unquestionable authority, such as Dr. Em. Lasker against Réti at Mährisch-Ostrau, 1923 ; and Grünfeld against Bogoljuboff at Carlsbad, 1923.

4.	P×P
5. P—K 3	

5. P—Q R 4 does not occasion Black any difficulties (See Game No. 70).

5.	P—Q Kt 4
6. P—Q R 4	P—Kt 5 !

6. ....Kt—Q 4, suggested by Alapin, has fallen into disuse as a result of his game against Rubinstein in the Pistyan Tournament of 1912.

7. Kt—R 2

If 7. Kt—Q Kt 1, Black can temporarily maintain his Pawn, free to give it back at a more propitious moment, *e.g.* : 7. Kt—Q Kt 1, B—R 3 ; 8. Kt—K 5, Q—Q 4 ! ; 9. P—B 3, P—B 4 !

| 7. ...... | P—K 3 |
| 8. B×P | |

White has thus regained his Pawn, but his Q Kt is very badly placed. On the other hand, Black is slightly behind in his development and his Q B P, if he does not advance it in good time, runs the risk of becoming weak.

| 8. ...... | B—K 2 |

Grünfeld played here 8. ....B—Kt 2 followed by 9. ....Q Kt—Q 2 and 10. ....P—B 4, which, in my opinion, is the only logical continuation. By delaying this manœuvre Black enables his opponent to forestall it.

| 9. Castles | Castles |
| 10. Q—K 2 | B—Kt 2 |

10. ....P—B 4 would now be dangerous, *e.g.* : 10. ....P—B 4 ; 11. P×P. B×P ; 12. P—K 4, B—Kt 2 ; 13. B—K Kt 5 and 14. K R—Q 1 with advantage to White.

| 11. R—Q 1 | Q Kt—Q 2 |
| 12. P—K 4 | |

Now White's game is clearly preferable, owing to his strong position in the centre.

It is astonishing that in an identical position, Réti continued here against Lasker with 12. P—Q Kt 3 and 13. B—Kt 2, which dangerously weakens the square Q B 3.

But in this variation the square Q Kt 3 should be reserved for the Q Kt.

| 12. ...... | P—Q R 4 |

The Q R P may become very weak, but if Black does not make this move White, after the manœuvre Kt—B 1 and Kt—Kt 3, threatens the advance of his own Q R P to Q R 6.

| 13. B—Kt 5 | R—K 1 |

Black assures the subsequent protection of his K B by this Rook, thus freeing the Queen, which can escape from the uncomfortable opposition of White's Rook.

| 14. Kt—B 1 | Q—Kt 3 |

Position after Black's 14th move.

15. Kt—Kt 3 !

This posting of the Q Kt is particularly strong in similar positions, as I have already found in my two games against Maróczy and Rubinstein in the Hague Tournament of 1921.

Now White plays for the effective blockade of the adverse Q B P.

| 15. ...... | P—R 3 |
| 16. B—K 3 | B—R 3 |

Hindering 17. P—Q 5, to which he would now reply 17. ....B×B. 18. Q×B, K P×P ; 19. P×P, freeing his game.

17. K Kt—Q 2 !	B×B
18. Kt×B	Q—B 2
19. Q—B 3	

Defending his K P, and preparing P—Q 5 should Black later play P—B 4.

19.	P—B 4
20. B—B 4	

20. P—Q 5 at once would give Black some chances after 20. .... P × P ; 21. P × P, B—Q 3.

20.	Q—Kt 2
21. P—Q 5	P × P
22. P × P	Q—R 3 !

An ingenious defence of the threatened Pawn, but of merely temporary efficacy.

Position after Black's 22nd move.

23. Q R—B 1

Black's Q R P could not be captured by the Kt on Kt 3, because of 23. ....B—Q 1 !, nor by the Kt on B 4, because of 23. ....P—B 5 !

But after the text-move this Pawn is defenceless. Upon 23. .... B—Q 1 there were several winning lines open to White, the simplest being probably 24. B—K 3 !, Kt—K 5 ; 25. P—Q 6 ! threatening 26. B × R P, etc.

23.	B—B 1
24. Kt (Kt 3) × P	Kt—K 5
25. Kt—B 6 !	

Simplest, for if now 25. ....Q × P ; 26. B × P !, P × B ; 27. Q—Kt 4 ch and 28. Q × Kt (Q 7).

25.	P—K Kt 4

A despairing move !

26. B—K 5 !	Kt × B
27. Kt (B 6) × Kt	P—B 3

Obviously the only possible reply.

28. Q × Kt	P × Kt
29. P—Q 6 !	B—Kt 2
30. Q—Q 5 ch	K—R 1
31. Q × B P	Black resigns.

GAME 72

QUEEN'S GAMBIT DECLINED

White :	*Black :*
A. ALEKHIN.	E. D. BOGOLJUBOFF.

1.	P—Q 4	Kt—K B 3
2.	Kt—K B 3	P—K 3
3.	P—B 4	P—Q 4
4.	Kt—B 3	Q Kt—Q 2
5.	B—Kt 5	B—K 2
6.	P—K 3	Castles
7.	R—B 1	P—Q R 3

This move is rightly held to be inferior, as White retains the option of blocking the opponent's game.
Somewhat better was 7. .... P—B 3.

8.	P—B 5 !	P—B 3
9.	P—Q Kt 4	Kt—K 5
10.	B—K B 4	

Best, for each exchange of pieces would merely free Black's position.

10.	P—Kt 4

Energetic, but hazardous, quite in Bogoljuboff's style. Black wishes at all costs to free himself of White's dangerous Q B.

11.	B—Kt 3	Kt × B
12.	R P × Kt	P—B 4

Now it is Black in his turn who threatens to block White's position and thus repel the latter's attack, *e.g.*: 13. Kt—K 5, Kt × Kt; 14. Q—R 5, R—B 2; 15. P × Kt, P—Kt 5, and Black's position is still defendable. White's next move is intended to foil this plan.

Position after Black's 12th move.

13. P—Kt 4 !

The only way to keep the initiative. White must already have foreseen the possibilities afforded him by the position arising from the exchange of Queens on the 18th move, despite his material inferiority.

13.	P × P
14. Kt—K 5	Kt × Kt
15. P × Kt	Q—B 2
16. Q—Q 4	R—B 4

The only logical answer; against any other developing or waiting move White would have secured a marked advantage by B—K 2 followed by B × P and P—B 4.

| 17. B—Q 3 ! | Q × P |
| 18. Q × Q ! | |

Black, of course, hoped for 18. B × R, Q × B, with two Pawns for the Exchange and splendid attacking chances, but the text-move is a great disillusion for him.

| 18. ...... | R × Q |
| 19. R × P | |

Black is temporarily a Pawn ahead, but his pieces are all so badly developed or situated that he will be compelled to submit to substantial loss of material.

| 19. ...... | B—B 3 |

The only move. If 19. .... B—B 1 ?; 20. R—Q B 7, with 21. Kt—R 4 and 22. Kt—Kt 6 to follow.

It is interesting to observe that were it not for the unfortunate advance of the Q R P (6. ....P—Q R 3), which now allows of this Knight manœuvre, Black would have nothing to fear.

| 20. K—Q 2 ! | B—Kt 2 |
| 21. Q R—K R 1 | |

Preventing the development of Black's Q B, for if 21. ....B—Q 2 it is evident that White would win by 22. R × B ch and 23. R—R 7 ch.

| 21. ...... | R—Kt 1 |
| 22. Kt—R 4 ! | |

Position after White's 22nd move.

| 22. ...... | R—B 4 |

The only means of developing the Queen-side. In spite of the gain of the Exchange White will experience some difficulty in improving upon his advantage.

23. B×R   P×B
24. R (R 7)—R 5!   B—K 3

Black is compelled to abandon the K Kt P, for if, *e.g.* : 24. ....B—B 3 ; 25. R—R 6, B—Kt 2 (or 25. ....K—Kt 2 ; 26. R×B, K×R ; 27. R—R 8 and 28. Kt—Kt 6 wins for White) ; 26. R—Kt 6, etc.

25. R×P   P—Q 5 !

Once again Black's best chance ; he thereby opens important diagonals for his Bishops and seizes the initiative for a time.

26. P×P   R—Q 1
27. K—B 3 !

Not 27. K—K 3 because of 27. ....P—B 5 ch, etc.

27. ......   K—B 1

If 27. ....K—B 2 at once, then 28. R—R 7.

28. R—Q 1   K—B 2
29. Kt—Kt 6 !

White plans to give back the Exchange on his next move, remaining a Pawn ahead in an evidently superior end-game.

29. ......   R—K R 1

Threatening 30. ....B—B 3.

30. R×B ch !   K×R
31. P—R 4   R—R 7
32. R—K Kt 1   P—B 5

See Diagram.

33. P—Q 5 !

White by this move, which could not be prevented by his opponent, secures a passed Pawn on the left wing, which will shortly cost Black

Position after Black's 32nd move.

a piece. The remainder is merely a question of technique.

33. ......   P×P
34. K—Q 4   P—Kt 6
35. P—B 3   K—B 3
36. P—Kt 5   P×P
37. P×P   R—R 4
38. P—B 6   P×P
39. P×P   K—K 2
40. P—B 7   K—Q 3

There is nothing to be done, *e.g.* : 40. ....R—R 1 ; 41. R—Q B 1, B—B 1 ; 42. Kt×B ch, R×Kt ; 43. K×P and wins.

41. P—B 8=Q   B×Q
42. Kt×B ch   K—Q 2
43. R—B 1   R—R 7
44. R—B 2   Black resigns.

GAME 73

DUTCH DEFENCE

White :   *Black :*
E. D. Bogoljuboff. A. Alekhin.

1. P—Q 4   P—K B 4

A risky defence which up to the present I have adopted only very infrequently in serious games.

But in the present game I had positively to play for a win in order to make sure of first prize, whereas a draw was sufficient for my opponent to secure third prize, and hence I found myself forced to run some risks which were, after all, justified by the result.

2. P—Q B 4   Kt—K B 3
3. P—K Kt 3

It is better to prepare the flank development of the K B in the Dutch Defence before playing P—Q B 4, because now Black can advantageously exchange his K B, which has only a very limited range of action in this opening.

3. ......   P—K 3
4. B—Kt 2   B—Kt 5 ch
5. B—Q 2   B × B ch
6. Kt × B

The recapture with the Queen, followed by 7. Kt—Q B 3, is a little better.

6. ......   Kt—B 3
7. K Kt—B 3   Castles
8. Castles   P—Q 3
9. Q—Kt 3

This manœuvre does not prevent Black from realizing his plan, but it is already difficult to suggest a satisfactory line of play for White.

9. ......   K—R 1
10. Q—B 3   P—K 4 !
11. P—K 3

If 11. P × P, P × P ; 12. Kt × P ?, Kt × Kt ; 13. Q × Kt, White's Q Kt would be *en prise* to Black's Queen.

11. ......   P—Q R 4 !

It was very important to prevent P—Q Kt 4 temporarily, as will be seen later.

12. P—Kt 3

Not 12. P—Q R 3 on account of 12. ....P—R 5.

12. ......   Q—K 1 !
13. P—Q R 3

Position after White's 13th move.

13. ......   Q—R 4 !

Now Black has secured an attacking position, for White cannot answer 14. P × P, P × P ; 15. Kt × P, Kt × Kt ; 16. Q × Kt on account of 16. ....Kt—Kt 5, winning outright ; nor can he play 14. P—Q Kt 4 ?, P—K 5 ; 15. Kt—K 1, P × P.

14. P—K R 4

A good defensive move, which secures new squares for his K Kt and revives the threat 15. P × P.

14. ......   Kt—K Kt 5
15. Kt—Kt 5

White seeks to dislodge Black's Knight at once by 16. P—B 3, which, however, weakens his Pawn position still further. Possibly 15. P—Q Kt 4 would now be preferable.

15. ......   B—Q 2
16. P—B 3

If 16. B × Kt, B × B ; 17. P—B 3, P × P ! ; 18. P × Kt, P × Q ; 19. P × Q, P × Kt, with the better endgame for Black.

16. ......   Kt—B 3
17. P—B 4

Already compulsory, in view of the threatened 16. ....P—B 5 !

17. ......   P—K 5
18. K R—Q 1

In order to protect the K Kt P (which was threatened by 18. .... Q—Kt 5 and 19. ....Kt—R 4) by Kt—B 1. However, the preliminary advance 18. P—Q 5 !, preventing Black from forming a centre, would have yielded White more chances of a successful defence.

18. ......   P—R 3
19. Kt—R 3

Position after White's 19th move.

19. ......   P—Q 4 !

By this move Black completely wrecks his opponent's hopes in the centre, and shortly seizes the initiative on the Queen-side in quite unexpected fashion.

20. Kt—B 1   Kt—K 2

Preparing 21. ....P—R 5 !

21. P—R 4   Kt—B 3 !

Now this Knight can penetrate into the hostile camp via Q Kt 5 and Q 6.

22. R—Q 2   Kt—Q Kt 5
23. B—R 1

The fact that White had to conjure up this complicated manœuvre in order to create faint chances on the King-side shows clearly the inferiority of his position.

Position after White's 23rd move.

23. ......   Q—K 1 !

This very strong move yields Black a new advantage in every case : either control of the square Q 4 after 24. P × P, or the opening of a file on the Queen-side after 24. P—B 5, P—Q Kt 4 !, or lastly, as in the actual game, the win of a Pawn.

24. R—K Kt 2

White is still trying for 25. P—K Kt 4, but even this weak counter-chance will not be vouchsafed him.

24. ......   P × P
25. P × P   B × P
26. Kt—B 2   B—Q 2
27. Kt—Q 2   P—Q Kt 4 !

The renewal of the struggle for the centre squares, a struggle whose vicissitudes will culminate in a stirring and original finish.

28. Kt—Q 1   Kt—Q 6 !

Preparing the ensuing combination. 28. ....P × P would have been weak, for White's Knight would later have secured a good square at K 5.

29. R × P

If 29. P × P, B × P ; 30. R × P, Kt—Q 4 ; 31. Q—R 3, R × R ; 32. Q × R, Q—B 3 and Black has a winning attack.

29. ......   P—Kt 5 !
30. R × R

If 30. Q—R 1, R × R ; 31. Q × R, Q—R 1 ! ; 32. Q × Q, R × Q, and Black's Rook makes an inroad into White's game with decisive effect.

30. ......   P × Q !

As will be seen, this continuation is much stronger than 30. .... Q × R ; 31. Q—Kt 3, B—R 5 ; 32. Q—Kt 1, after which White could still defend himself.

31. R × Q

Position after White's 31st move.

31. ......   P—B 7 ! !

The point ! White cannot prevent this Pawn from Queening.

32. R × R ch   K—R 2
33. Kt—B 2

It is clear that this is the only possible move.

33. ......   P—B 8=Q ch
34. Kt—B 1

Position after White's 34th move.

34. ......   Kt—K 8 !

Threatening an unexpected and original " Smothered Mate."

35. R—R 2   Q × B P

A new threat of mate in a few moves, commencing with 36. .... B—Kt 4, which compels White to sacrifice the Exchange.

36. R—Q Kt 8   B—Kt 4
37. R × B   Q × R
38. P—Kt 4

The only chance for White to prolong his resistance ; but Black retorts with a fresh surprise-move.

38. ......   Kt—B 6 ch !
39. B × Kt   P × B
40. P × P

Forced, for if 40. P—Kt 5 Black would have obtained two united passed Pawns after 40. ....Kt—Kt 5.

Position after White's 40th move.

40.	Q—K 7 !!

This move leads to a problem-like position, wherein White cannot move any piece without exposing himself to immediate loss, for example 41. Kt—R 3 or Kt 4, Kt—Kt 5 ! or Kt×Kt ; or 41. R—R 3 or R 1, Kt—Kt 5 and wins.

Hence, after two unimportant moves, he must play P—K 4, which leads to an immediate liquidation, with a won end-game for Black.

41. P—Q 5	K—Kt 1 !

Not, however, the plausible 41. ....P—R 4, upon which White could have saved himself by 42. Kt—R 3, followed by 43. Kt—Kt 5 ch.

42. P—R 5	K—R 2
43. P—K 4	Kt×K P
44. Kt×Kt	Q×Kt
45. P—Q 6	

Being unable to defend his Pawns White endeavours to dislocate those of his opponent, but his game is hopelessly lost.

45.	P×P
46. P—B 6	P×P
47. R—Q 2	

Position after White's 47th move.

47.	Q—K 7 !

A pretty finish, worthy of this fine game. Black forces a winning Pawn end-game.

48. R×Q	P×R
49. K—B 2	P×Kt=Q ch
50. K×Q	K—Kt 2
51. K—B 2	K—B 2
52. K—K 3	K—K 3
53. K—K 4	P—Q 4 ch

White resigns.

CHAPTER XIX

INTERNATIONAL TOURNAMENT AT VIENNA
NOVEMBER, 1922

GAME 74

RUY LOPEZ

White :	Black :
A. ALEKHIN.	R. RÉTI.

1.	P—K 4	P—K 4
2.	Kt—K B 3	Kt—Q B 3
3.	B—Kt 5	P—Q R 3
4.	B—R 4	Kt—B 3
5.	Kt—B 3	P—Q Kt 4
6.	B—Kt 3	B—B 4

If it was Black's intention to develop his B at Q B 4, he should have done so before playing P—Q Kt 4, for after 5. ....P—Q Kt 4 he has nothing better than 6. ....B—K 2, which, however, gives him a satisfactory game.

The text-move, on the contrary, needlessly exposes him to grave perils.

7. Kt × P !

The correct reply, yielding White in every variation an extremely dangerous attack.

7.	......	Kt × Kt
8.	P—Q 4	B—Q 3
9.	P × Kt	B × P
10.	P—B 4 !	

This move, which would be bad if Black's Q Kt P were still at Kt 2 and White's K B at Q R 4, because of 10. ....B × Kt ch and 11. .... Kt × P, shows the error of Black's 6th move.

10.	......	B × Kt ch
11.	P × B	Castles

Forced now, for if 11. ....Kt × P ; 12. B—Q 5.

12. P—K 5

If now 12. ....Kt—K 1 ; 13. Castles, P—Q 3 ; 14. P—B 5 with an irresistible attack for White.

White appears to have secured a decisive positional advantage, for the withdrawal of the Knight to K 1 is compulsory (12. ....Kt—K 5 ; 13. Q—Q 5 ! and wins): but my ingenious opponent succeeds in finding the only move to give him defensive chances, and in the sequel he shows in exemplary manner how to make the most of them.

12.	......	P—B 4 !

See Diagram.

The text-move threatens, should White capture the Knight, to shut off the hostile K B by 13. ....P—B 5, thereby leading into an end-game with Bishops of opposite colours.

Position after Black's 12th move.

What is White to play to keep his advantage? The following variations, considered during the actual game, seemed to him quite inadequate :

I.—13. P×Kt, R—K 1 ch ; 14. K—B 1, P—B 5.

II.—13. P—B 4, P—Q 4 ! ; 14. P×Kt, R—K 1 ch ; 15. K—B 1, Q×P ! and 16. ....Q P×P.

III.—13. Castles, P—B 5 ; 14. P×Kt, Q×P ; 15. Q—Q 5, Q—Kt 3 ch and 16. ....B—Kt 2.

IV.—13. B—Q 5, Kt×B ; 14. Q×Kt, Q—Kt 3 ! ; 15. B—K 3, B—Kt 2 ; 16. Q×B P, Q—Kt 3 !, or :

V.—13. B—Q 5, Kt×B ; 14. Q×Kt, Q—Kt 3 ! ; 15. B—K 3, B—Kt 2 ; 16. B×P, B×Q ; 17. B×Q, B×Kt P ; 18. R—K Kt 1, B—K 5.

Black has the better game in the first four variations and has equality in the fifth.

13. B—R 3 ! !

The key-move of a deep combination whose principal variation consists of some ten moves and which results in the gain of a Pawn in a superior position.

It was evidently quite impossible to foresee, at this stage of the game, that this material advantage, in conjunction with the position, would prove insufficient for victory against the impeccable defence set up by Black.

13. ......   Q—R 4 !

The best reply. Black indirectly defends his Q B P whilst attacking the hostile Q B, but White's manœuvre initiated by 13. B—R 3 ! is based upon the temporary removal of the Black Queen from the centre.

14. Castles   Q×B
15. P×Kt   P—B 5

Black is not excessively uneasy concerning the reply 16. Q—Q 5 (with the double threat 17. Q—Kt 5 and 17. Q×R), being convinced that he will save the situation by 16. ....Q—R 4 followed by the capture of the K B, which is cut off.

But, as the sequel shows, this calculation is only partly correct.

16. Q—Q 5 !   Q—R 4 !

Position after Black's 16th move.

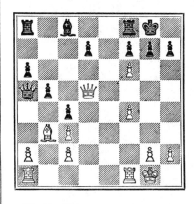

17. P×P

Not 17. Q × R because of 17. . . . .
Q—Kt 3 ch and 18. . . . .B—Kt 2,
winning for Black.

| 17. ...... | Q—Kt 3 ch |
| 18. K—R 1 | K × P ! |

Once again the only move. If 18.
. . . .R—Q 1 ; 19. B × P !, P × B
(forced) ; 20. Q × R, B—Kt 2 ; 21.
Q R—Kt 1 and White wins the
Exchange.

Position after Black's 18th move.

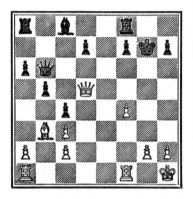

19. B × P !

The point of the whole combination ! This Bishop, which appeared
hopelessly doomed, gains a fresh
lease of life, for if 19. . . . .P × B,
then 20. Q × R and 21. Q R—Kt 1,
as in the preceding note.

White, with his Pawn plus and
considering the exposed position of
Black's King, seems to have a comparatively easy win, but this is only
a will-o'-the-wisp.

| 19. ...... | B—Kt 2 ! |
| 20. Q—K 5 ch | |

Equally after 20. Q—Kt 5 ch,
Q—Kt 3 ; 21. B—Q 3, P—B 4 !
Black would have sufficient re-
sources available.

| 20. ...... | Q—B 3 |
| 21. B—Q 3 | |

Position after White's 21st move.

21. ......   K R—K 1 !

An excellent defensive move by
which Black sacrifices a second
Pawn in order to occupy the central
files with his Rooks.

After 21. . . . .Q × Q ; 22. P × Q,
Q R—B 1 ; 23. R—B 4, R × P ; 24.
R—Kt 4 ch, K—R 1 ; 25. R—R 4,
etc. Black probably could not save
the game.

22. Q—R 5	P—R 3
23. Q—Kt 4 ch	K—R 1
24. Q × P	R—K 2
25. Q—Q 4	Q × Q !
26. P × Q	Q R—Q 1

Taking advantage of the fact that
White's Q P cannot readily be
defended, *e.g.:* 27. P—B 3, P—
Kt 5 ! ; 28. P × P, R × P, followed by
29. . . . .R × Kt P, etc.

27. P—B 5 !

In order to secure an outpost by
28. P—B 6 after 27. . . . .R × P,
with good attacking chances against
the position of the hostile King, but
Black prefers to temporize and to
postpone the capture of the Q P
until later, first taking a precautionary measure.

27. ......   P—B 3 !

Position after Black's 27th move.

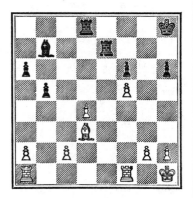

28. Q R—K 1

Reconciling himself to giving back one Pawn in order to exchange the formidable Black Bishop.

28. R—B 4, although temporarily preserving the advantage of two Pawns, would be insufficient for success, *e.g.* : 28. ....R—Kt 2 ; 29. B—B 1, R—Q B 1 ! ; 30. R—B 2 or R—B 1, R—B 6 followed by 31. ....B—Q 4 or R—R 6, and White cannot possibly defend all his Pawns.

28. ......   R—Kt 2 !

Of course not 28. ....R×R ; 29. R×R, R×P because of 30. R—K 8 ch, K moves ; 31. R—K 7 ch and White wins.

29. B—K 4   R×Q P
30. B×B   R×B
31. R—K 6

Winning a Pawn once again, but only momentarily.

31. ......   K—Kt 2 !
32. R×R P   R—Q B 5

Still more exact was 32. ....R—Q R 5 !, although the text-move is also adequate.

33. R—B 3

Obviously if 33. R—B 2, then 33. ....R (Kt 2)—B 2, and the Q B P could not be defended.

33. ......   R×P
34. P—R 3   K—B 2 !

Forestalling the threatened 35. R—Kt 3 ch and 36. R—Kt 6.

35. R—K Kt 3   R—B 7
36. R—K Kt 6   R×P
37. R×P   K—Kt 2
38. R—K R 4   P—Kt 5 !

After this move, which creates a permanent threat to dissolve the Queen-side Pawns, White's winning chances are reduced to vanishing point.

39. R—Kt 4 ch   K—B 2
40. R—Kt 3   R (B 4)—
                         Q Kt 4
41. R—Kt 3   K—Kt 3
42. K—R 2   R—Q B 4
43. R—R 4   R (B 4)—
                         Q Kt 4
44. P—R 4   R (Kt 4)—Kt 3
45. K—R 3   R (Kt 2)—Kt 1
46. P—Kt 3   P—B 4 !
47. R—R 5   R—Q B 1
48. R—K B 3   R—K B 3
49. K—Kt 2   R—B 6 !
50. R—R 8   R×R
51. K×R   R—B 3
52. R—Kt 8   R—B 5
53. R—Kt 6 ch   K—Kt 2
54. P—R 5   R—Q 5
55. R—Q B 6 !   R—K 5
56. R—Kt 6 ch   K—B 2
57. P—Kt 4

The supreme effort !

See Diagram.

57. ......   R×P !

At once forcing the draw.

58. R×R   P×R ch
59. K×P   K—Kt 2 !

Drawn game.

Black's King arrives just in time to stop White's Q R P, *e.g.* :

Position after White's 57th move

60. K—B 4, K—R 3; 61. K—K 4, K×P; 62. K—Q 4, K—Kt 4; 63. K—B 4, K—B 4; 64. K×P, K—K 3; 65. K—Kt 5, K—Q 2; 66. K—Kt 6, K—B 1, etc.

A splendid example of Réti's careful defence.

GAME 75

QUEEN'S GAMBIT DECLINED

White :	Black :
H. KMOCH.	A. ALEKHIN.

1. P—Q 4   Kt—K B 3
2. Kt—K B 3   P—Q 4
3. P—B 4   P—B 3
4. P—K 3

If 4. Kt—B 3, the reply would be 4. ....P×P (see Games Nos. 70 and 71).

4. ......   B—B 4
5. Q Kt—Q 2

This system of development, involving the advance of the Queen-side Pawns, was successfully adopted by Réti against Spielmann in the Tournament at Teplitz-Schönau, which took place a few weeks before the Vienna Tournament, where the present game was played.

Doubtless this is the reason why my opponent, hypnotized solely by the result, adopted this system in preference to the usual moves 6. Q—Kt 3 or 6. P×P, without sufficiently fathoming the depths of this novelty.

5. ......   P—K 3
6. B—K 2   Q Kt—Q 2
7. Castles   B—Q 3
8. P—B 5   B—B 2
9. P—Q Kt 4   Kt—K 5
10. Kt × Kt   P × Kt !

Far better than the recapture with the Bishop, which Spielmann played in an analogous position in his game with Réti, for in this case Black, after 10. Kt—Q 2, P—B 4 ; 11. Kt × B, etc., cannot obtain sufficient attack to compensate for White's advantage on the Queen-side.

11. Kt—Q 2   P—K R 4 !

The signal for the attack. As White will in any case be compelled to play P—B 4, there is no reason for Black to provoke it by Q—R 5. He therefore utilizes the time thus saved to strengthen his attacking position by a move which will enhance his prospects.

12. P—B 4

Black was threatening the sacrifice B × P ch, followed by Q—R 5 ch and Kt—B 3, yielding him a very powerful attack.

12. ......   P—K Kt 4
13. P—Kt 3

After this timid defensive move, which anticipates the desire of White's opponent, Black's attack becomes irresistible.

It would have been better to continue 13. Kt—B 4, Kt—B 3 ; 14. Kt—K 5, P×P; 15. P×P, P—R 3, although in this case also Black would remain with the better position on account of the weakness of the adverse Q P.

13. ...... Kt—B 3 !

Preparing the advance of the K R P, which would at this juncture be insufficient, because of 14. P—K Kt 4.
Obviously, if 14. P×P, Black would reply 14. ....Kt—Kt 5.

14. B—Kt 2   P×P
15. K P×P

Or 15. Kt P×P, Kt—Kt 5, etc.

15. ......   P—R 5
16. Q—Kt 3

If 16. P—Kt 4, R—K Kt 1 ; 17. P—K R 3, Kt—Q 4 and White's K B P could not be saved.

16. ......   P×P
17. P×P   Kt—Q 4
18. Kt—B 4

White is already defenceless against the threatened sacrifice at his K B 4.

Position after White's 18th move.

18. ......   Kt×B P !

Decisive, for if 19. P×Kt, Q—R 5 ! winning ; and if 19. R×Kt, B×R ; 20. P×B, Q—R 5 ! and Black wins.

19. Q R—K 1   Q—Kt 4
20. P—Q 5   Kt—Q 6

....forcing mate in a few moves.

White resigns.

This short game shows once again the risks run by young players when blindly adopting certain innovations of the masters, without having carefully calculated all their consequences.

GAME 76

SICILIAN DEFENCE

White :	*Black :*
A. ALEKHIN.	F. SÄMISCH.

1. P—K 4   P—Q B 4
2. Kt—K B 3

With this move White secures the option sooner or later of advancing his Pawn to Q 4.
2. Kt—Q B 3, followed by P—K Kt 3, B—Kt 2, P—Q 3, K Kt —K 2, etc., has been successfully adopted on several occasions by Dr. Tarrasch.

2. ......   Kt—Q B 3

Giving up the idea of playing the Paulsen variation (P—K 3 followed by P—Q R 3 and Q—B 2, etc.), in which Black's Q Kt has no place at Q B 3.
If 2. ....P—K 3, White would still have delayed P—Q 4, and would have played 3. B—K 2, in order to answer 3. ....Q—B 2 with 4. P—Q 4, P×P ; 5. Kt×P, P—Q R 3 ; 6. P—Q B 4 !, thus obtaining a very fine game.

3. P—Q 4   P×P
4. Kt×P   P—K Kt 3
5. P—Q B 4

This system, which is aimed at contesting Black's fianchetto in the

Sicilian, was introduced about fifteen years ago by Maróczy, with the continuation :

5. ....B—Kt 2 ; 6. B—K 3, Kt—B 3 ; 7. Kt—Q B 3, P—Q 3 ; 8. B—K 2, upon which Black can secure a satisfactory game by 8. ....Kt—K Kt 5 !, as was shown by Breyer.

5.	B—Kt 2
6. Kt—Kt 3	

An innovation which seems to yield White a very good game; its main object is to suppress at once the pressure exerted by Black on the square Q 4.

With the same idea 6. Kt—B 2, followed by Kt—K 3, was also worthy of consideration.

6.	Kt—B 3
7. Kt—B 3	P—Q 3
8. B—K 2	B—K 3

The Q B is very badly posted on K 3, as White can discount the attack on his Q B P by the advance of this Pawn.

However, even after 8. .... Castles ; 9. Castles, B—Q 2 ; 10. B—K 3 followed by 11. P—B 3 and 12. Kt—Q 5 White's game would also have been superior.

9. Castles	P—K R 4

Position after Black's 9th move.

Ingenious, but hardly sound. Black intends to answer 10. P—B 4 with 10. ....Q—Kt 3 ch followed by 11. ....Kt—K Kt 5 ; and if 10. P—B 3 then 10. ....P—R 5 followed by 11. ....Kt—K R 4 (another of Breyer's manœuvres). But White, by playing simply 10. B—Kt 5 !, threatening 11. P—B 5, could have maintained the superiority in position which he had gained in the opening.

10. P—B 5

But this move is premature, for Black could obtain a satisfactory game by 10. ....P—Q 4 !, *e.g. :* 11. Kt—Q 4, Kt × Kt ; 12. Q × Kt, P × P ; 13. Q—Kt 4 !, Q—B 1 ; 14. Kt × P, Kt × Kt ; 15. Q × Kt, Castles, after which White's majority of Pawns on the Queen-side would have been largely compensated by the dominating position of the Black Bishops.

10.	P × P

A decisive strategic error. Despite the exchange of Queens Black will be unable to ward off the direct attack against his King, which is fixed in the centre.

11. Kt × P   B—Q B 1

If Black avoids the exchange of Queens by 11. ....Q—B 1, White would secure a positional advantage sufficient for victory by 12. Kt—Q 5, Castles ; 13. Kt × B, P × Kt (not 13. ....Q × Kt ; 14. Kt—B 7) ; 14. Kt—B 4, etc.

12. Q × Q ch   K × Q

Black would equally lose by 12. ....Kt × Q ; 13. Kt—Kt 5, Castles ; 14. Kt—B 7, R—Kt 1 ; 15. B—K B 4.

13. R—Q 1 ch   Kt—Q 2

He relies on being able to repulse the attack by 14. ....B × Kt followed by 15. ....K—B 2, or also

by 14. ....Kt—Q 5, but White's
next move shatters this hope.

14. B—Q B 4 !

Decisive, for Black cannot defend
his K B P, *e.g. :* 14. ....R—B 1 ;
15. Kt—Q Kt 5 !, P—Q R 3 (or
15. ....P—Q Kt 3 ; 16. B—Q 5 !,
P×Kt ; 17. B×Kt, R—Q Kt 1 ;
18. B—Q 2 ! and wins) ; 16. B×P !,
R×B ; 17. Kt—K 6 ch, K—K 1 ;
18. Kt (Kt 5)—B 7, mate.

14. ...... B×Kt

All other moves would likewise
be inadequate.

Position after Black's 14th move.

15. B×P !

Not only winning a Pawn, but
also completely demolishing the
hostile position.

15. ...... K—B 2

If 15. ....Kt—Q 5 White would
continue 16. R×Kt and 17. Kt—
K 6 mate.

16. Kt—K 6 ch K—Kt 1
17. P×B Kt (Q 2)—K 4
18. B—B 4 B×Kt
19. B×B R—K B 1
20. B—Kt 3

Threatening 21. R—Q 5. Black
therefore loses another Pawn after
20. ....P—R 5 ; or else the
Exchange by 20. ....R—B 3 ; 21.
B×Kt ch and 22. R—Q 8 ch.

Black resigns.

GAME 77

QUEEN'S PAWN GAME

White :	Black :
A. ALEKHIN.	E. KÖNIG.

1. P—Q 4 Kt—K B 3
2. P—Q B 4 P—Q Kt 3

This move is not good after 2. P—
Q B 4, as the present game shows.
2. ....P—K 3 is more correct, in
order to reply to 3. Kt—Q B 3 by
3. ....B—Kt 5 !, and 3. Kt—K B 3
by 3. ....P—Q Kt 3 !

3. Kt—Q B 3 B—Kt 2
4. Q—B 2 !

The right move. It was played
for the first time by Teichmann
against myself in our match at
Berlin, 1921.
Now Black can no longer prevent
his opponent from securing a strong
position in the centre by P—K 4.

4. ...... P—Q 4

Adopting the continuation of the
game Euwe—Alekhin, Budapest,
1921, which ran 5. P×P, Kt×P ;
6. P—K 4 (the correct move, introduced in the present game, is 6. Kt—
B 3 !), Kt×Kt ; 7. P×Kt, P—K 4 ! ;
8. P×P, Q—R 5 ! ; 9. B—Kt 5 ch,
Kt—Q 2 ; 10. Kt—B 3, Q×P ch ;
11. Q×Q, B×Q, and ultimately
resulted in a draw.
4. ....Kt—B 3, played in the
above - mentioned match - game
Teichmann—Alekhin, is equally
inadequate, because of 5. Kt—B 3,
P—K 3 ; 6. P—K 4, P—K 4 ;

7. P×P, Kt—K Kt 5; 8. B—B 4,
B—B 4; 9. B—Kt 3, Q—K 2; 16.
Castles.

| 5. | P×P | Kt×P |
| 6. | Kt—B 3 | |

Preventing the counter-attack 6.
....P—K 4, which alone could give
Black equalizing chances.

6.	......	P—K 3
7.	P—K 4	Kt×Kt
8.	P×Kt	B—K 2
9.	B—Kt 5 ch	P—B 3
10.	B—Q 3	Castles

It was more prudent to delay
this move, by playing first 10. ....
Kt—Q 2, for now White will utilise
his great advantage in development
to undertake a strong attack against
the inadequately defended position
of the Black King.

| 11. | P—K 5 | P—K R 3 |

Comparatively best.

Position after Black's 11th move.

12. P—K R 4 !

The initial move of the decisive
attack. Apart from the manœuvre
of the Rook via R 3, White
threatens 13. Kt—Kt 5, followed by
14. B—R 7 ch and 15. B—Kt 8 !

| 12. | ...... | P—Q B 4 |

To meet the latter threat, 13. Kt
—Kt 5, by 13. ....P×P !; 14.
B—R 7 ch, K—R 1; 15. B—Kt 8,
P—Q 6 !, but the entry of White's
Rook decides the game in a few
moves.

| 13. | R—R 3 ! | K—R 1 |

This is not an adequate defence
against the threatened 14. B×P.
But equally after 13. ....P—B 4;
14. P×P e. p., B×P; 15. Kt—Kt 5,
White wins easily.

| 14. | B×P ! | P—B 4 |

If 14. ....P×B, then of course
15. Q—Q 2 wins off-hand.

15.	P×P e. p.	B×P
16.	B—K Kt 5 !	P×P
17.	Kt—K 5 !	Kt—B 3
18.	Q—K 2 !	P—Kt 3

If 18. ....Kt×Kt, White mates
in four moves.

| 19. | B×P | K—Kt 2 |
| 20. | B—R 6 ch | K—Kt 1 |

Or 20. ....K×B; 21. Q—R 5
ch and mates next move.

21. Kt×Kt

Since mate cannot be forced,
White proceeds to a general liquidation which will leave him a Rook
ahead.

21.	......	B×Kt
22.	Q×P ch	K—R 1
23.	B×R	Q×B
24.	Q×B	Black resigns.

GAME 78

FRENCH DEFENCE

White : 　　　　　*Black :*
A. ALEKHIN. 　DR. S. TARTAKOVER.

1.	P—K 4	P—K 3
2.	P—Q 4	P—Q 4
3.	Kt—Q B 3	Kt—K B 3
4.	B—Kt 5	P×P

A good move which seems to yield a perfectly satisfactory defence, especially in the variation adopted here by White.

5. B × Kt

Slightly preferable, although equally insufficient to yield White an advantage, is 5. Kt × P, B—K 2 ; 6. B × Kt, B × B ; 7. Kt—K B 3.

5.	P × B
6. Kt × P	P—K B 4
7. Kt—Q B 3	

The withdrawal of this Knight to K Kt 3 offered still less prospect, because of the reply 7. ....P—B 4 !

7.	B—Kt 2
8. Kt—B 3	Castles
9. Q—Q 2	

If 9. B—B 4, P—B 4 ! ; 10. P—Q 5, P—Kt 4 ; 11. B × P, Q—R 4 ; 12. B—K 2, B × Kt ch ; 13. P × B, Q × P ch, followed by 14. ....P × P with advantage to Black.

9. ......   P—B 4 !

This move increases the action of Black's K B, and compels White to play very prudently to maintain equality.

| 10. P × P | Q—R 4 |
| 11. Kt—Q Kt 5 ! | |

The exchange of Queens resulting from this move avoids all danger of an attack directed against the White King. This attack might have become very dangerous with the aid of the two Black Bishops.

| 11. ...... | Q × Q ch |
| 12. Kt × Q | Kt—R 3 |

Not 12. ....B × P on account of 13. R—Q Kt 1, B—K 4 ; 14. Kt—B 4, with the better game for White.

| 13. P—Q B 3 | Kt × P |
| 14. Kt—Kt 3 ! | Kt × Kt |

Black's Knight had no good square ; however, the resulting

opening of the Q R file will allow White to exert pressure on his opponent's weakened Queen-side.

15. P × Kt	P—Q R 3
16. Kt—Q 6	R—Kt 1
17. P—Q Kt 4	

Preparing to undouble his Pawns by P—Kt 5.

| 17. ...... | R—Q 1 |
| 18. Castles | |

It would have been more prudent to capture the Q B at once with the Knight (with an end-game analogous to that in the game), for after the text-move Black could have provoked complications by 18. .... B—Q 2 and if 19. P—Kt 5, B—K 4 !, the outcome of which would have been difficult to foresee.

18.	B—K 4
19. Kt × B	R × R ch
20. K × R	R × Kt

Position after Black's 20th move.

The ensuing end-game is clearly in White's favour :

(1) He has the majority of Pawns on the Queen-side.

(2) The position of his King, which is already in the centre of the board, is very promising for utilizing this advantage.

(3) All Black's Pawns are temporarily situated on squares of the same colour as the adverse Bishop, and those on the Queen-side can only be moved with difficulty.

(4) Black's K R P is isolated and therefore weak.

(5) Lastly, White will have a base for operations in the Q R file, possession of which cannot be disputed.

But the neutralizing force of the Bishops of opposite colour is such that, despite all these advantages, it is not certain that White could have succeeded in winning, if his opponent had not allowed him to occupy the fifth rank with his Rook (see Black's 24th move).

21. B—K 2	K—B 1
22. K—B 2	R—B 2
23. R—R 1	K—K 2
24. P—R 3	P—B 5

This attempt at counter-attack, which aims principally at playing B—Q 3 followed by P—K 4 and P—B 4, is premature and must be considered the decisive mistake.

The correct move was 24. . . . . B—Q 5, followed by 25. . . . .B—Kt 3, with drawing chances for Black.

The continuation of this game, whose conclusion resembles a composed study, compensates in some degree for the monotony of its first phase.

25. K—Kt 3

Definitely depriving Black of the possibility of B—Q 5.

| 25. . . . . . . | R—Q 2 |
| 26. R—R 5 ! | B—B 2 |

Again best, for if 26. . . . .R—Q 4 ; 27. B—B 3 !, R×R ; 28. P×R and White wins the Queen-side Pawns. And if 26. . . . .P—B 3 ; 27. B—B 3, K—Q 1 ; 28. P—Kt 5, P×P ; 29. R×P, K—B 1 ; 30.

R—Kt 6, R—K 2 ; 31. K—B 4 and 32. K—Q 3, followed by the victorious advance of White's Queen-side Pawns.

| 27. R—R 5 | R—Q 7 |
| 28. B—B 3 | P—Kt 3 |

Clearly Black must at all costs maintain his Pawn.

| 29. R×P | R×P |

Position after Black's 29th move.

30. B—R 5 !

The consequences of this move, which allows Black two very dangerous passed Pawns, had to be examined very accurately by the two opponents, for it held out, in appearance at least, as much danger for the one as for the other.

Finally White had the good fortune to foresee, in the critical position, the possibility of a problem-move, the only move to win.

| 30. . . . . . . | R×P |
| 31. R×P ch | K—Q 1 ! |

After 31. . . . .K—Q 3 ; 32. R×P, Black, a Pawn down and with a bad position, would have lost slowly but surely.

32. B—Kt 4 !   P—K 4 !

Forced, for the same reason as the previous move.

33. R—Q 7 ch   K—B 1
34. R—Q 2 dis ch R × B
35. P × R   P—B 6 !

Position after Black's 35th move.

The hidden point of the combination commenced by 26. .... B—B 2. If 35. ....P—K 5 ; 36. R—Q 4 !, P—B 6 ; 37. R × P, P—B 7 ; 38. R—K 8 ch and 39. R—K B 8 wins easily.

What must White play now to avoid a draw or even the loss of the game in some contingencies?

Here are the leading variations to be considered :

I.—36. K—B 4, P—K 5 ; 37. K—Q 4, B—B 5 ; 38. R—K B 2, P—K 6 ; 39. R × P, P—K 7 and Black wins.

II.—36. K—B 2, P—K 5 ; 37. R—Q 4 !, P—K 6 ; 38. K—Q 1, B—Kt 6 ; 39. R—K 4, P—K 7 ch ; 40. K—Q 2, B—R 5 ; 41. R—K 5, B—Kt 6 and draws.

III.—36. P—K Kt 5, P—K 5 ; 37. R—Q 5 (if 37. P—Kt 6, B—K 4

followed by 38. ....P—K 6 and Black wins), P—B 7 ; 38. R—K B 5, P—K 6 ; 39. P—Kt 6, P—K 7 ; 40. P—Kt 7, P—B 8 = Q ; 41. P—Kt 8 = Q ch, K—Kt 2 ; 42. Q—Q 5 ch, K—R 2 and White cannot win, on account of the threats 43. .... P—K 8 = Q, and 43. ....Q—Q 8 ch.

IV.—36. R—R 2, P—K 5 ; 37. R—R 8 ch, K—Q 2 ; 38. R—K B 8, B—Kt 6 ! ; 39. R—B—Q 3 ! ; 40. R—B 6, B—K 4 ! ; 41. R—B 7 ch or R—B 5, K—K 3, and Black draws by chasing the White Rook along the K B file, which it dare not leave.

And yet the win is there !

36. R—Q 5 !

The variations springing from this rather unlikely move (it attacks one solidly defended Pawn and allows the immediate advance of the other) are quite simple when we have descried the basic idea : *The Black Pawns are inoffensive :*

(1) *When they occupy squares of the same colour as their Bishop,* for in that case White's King can hold them back without difficulty, by occupying the appropriate White squares.

(2) *When the Rook can be posted behind them,* as in the variation IV above, but *without loss of time,* and as the two main variations from the text-moves :

I.—36. ....P—B 7 ; 37. R—Q 1, P—K 5 ; 38. K—B 2, B—B 5 ; 39. R—K B 1 and 40. K—Q 1.

II.—36. ....P—K 5 ; 37. R—K B 5, B—Kt 6 ; 38. P—Kt 5, P—K 6 ; 39. R × P, P—K 7 ; 40. R—K 3,
answer the above aim, the victory is assured to White.

36. ......   P—K 5
37. R—K B 5   B—Kt 6
38. P—Kt 5   K—Q 2

This is the only possibility, for 38. ....P—K 6 has been shown to be inadequate in variation II above.

39. P—Kt 6	K—K 3
40. P—Kt 7	K × R
41. P—Kt 8 = Q	B—B 5
42. Q—B 7 ch	K—Kt 5

If 42. ....K—K 4 White wins just as quickly by 43. P—B 4.

43. Q—Kt 6 ch	B—Kt 4
44. Q × P ch	K—Kt 6
45. Q—Kt 6	K—Kt 5
46. Q × P	Black resigns.

CHAPTER XX

TOURNAMENT AT MARGATE
APRIL, 1923

GAME 79

QUEEN'S GAMBIT DECLINED

White :	*Black :*
A. ALEKHIN.	A. MUFFANG.

1. P—Q 4	P—Q 4
2. P—Q B 4	P—K 3
3. Kt—K B 3	Kt—K B 3
4. Kt—B 3	B—K 2
5. B—Kt 5	Q Kt—Q 2
6. P—K 3	Castles
7. R—B 1	P—B 3
8. Q—B 2	P×P

This move has been adopted by Capablanca on several occasions, amongst others against myself in the London Tournament of 1922.

Without considering it bad we can affirm that it is certainly not the best, for there are numerous defensive resources available to Black which can later on yield him chances of a win.

Here is the continuation of my game against Capablanca : 9. B×P, Kt—Q 4 ; 10. B×B, Q×B ; 11. Castles, Kt×Kt ; 12. Q×Kt, P—Q Kt 3 ; 13. Q—Q 3. In this position White has the choice between several continuations which give him an excellent game, and the most Black can hope for is a draw. The game continued 13. ....P—Q B 4 ;

14. B—R 6, B×B ; 15. Q×B, P×P ; 16. Kt×P, Kt—B 4 ; 17. Q—Kt 5 and White has still a slight advantage owing to the weakness of the square at his Q B 6. This superiority is, however, not sufficient to force the win.

9. B×P	Kt—Q 4
10. Kt—K 4	

This move, of doubtful value in the variation 8. B—Q 3 (see Game No. 87), is still less commendable in the present position, because of the presence of the White Queen at Q B 2.

The only correct move is 10. B×B followed by 11. Castles.

10.	Q—R 4 ch !
11. K—K 2	

The position of White's King is not safe, but 11. K—B 1 has the disadvantage of shutting in the K R.

11.	R—K 1

A serious loss of time which allows the opponent to maintain his advantage in position.

The line of play indicated was 11. ....P—B 3 ! ; 12. B—R 4, Kt (Q 2)—Kt 3, forcing the exchange of the adverse K B, for 13. B—Kt 3

would evidently be bad because of
13. ....Kt—Kt 5, threatening Q—
R 3 ch or Q—Kt 4 ch.

Black by this manœuvre could
have secured at least an equal game,
which shows the inadequacy of 10.
Kt—K 4.

| 12. K R—Q 1 ! | Kt (Q 2)—Kt 3 |
| 13. B—Kt 3 | Q—Kt 4 ch |

Now 13. ....Kt—Kt 5 would
not cause White any inconvenience,
e.g. : 14. Q—Kt 1, Q—Kt 4 ch ;
15. K—K 1, etc.

14. Q—Q 3

The exchange of Queens is forced,
but it is entirely to the advantage
of White, who had continually to
reckon with the threats of the
dangerous Black Queen.

| 14. ...... | Q × Q ch |
| 15. R × Q | B × B |

The withdrawal of Black's K B
to K B 1 would have prevented
White's Knight from occupying Q
6, but in any case Black's game
would have remained very cramped.

16. Kt (B 3) × B   Kt—B 3

Grünfeld in the Teplitz-Schönau
Tournament-Book recommends here
first 16. ....P—K R 3. Nevertheless, it seems doubtful whether
this transposition of moves can be
of great importance for the general
valuation of a position in which
Black has no compensation for his
shut-in Q B.

17. Kt—Q 6	R—K 2
18. P—K 4	P—K R 3
19. Kt—B 3	R—Kt 1

In order to develop his Q B and
subsequently dislodge the Knight
on Q 6 by ....Kt—Q B 1.
White must therefore cast about
for a very energetic line of play if he
wishes to maintain his advantage.

Position after Black's 19th move.

20. P—Kt 4 !

This Pawn-sacrifice compels
Black to modify his plan, for if now
20. ....B—Q 2 ; 21. P—Kt 5,
P × P ; 22. Kt × K Kt P, Kt—B 1 ;
23. Kt—B 4 with an overwhelming
position for White.

It would be comparatively best
for Black to resolve to maintain his
Bishop in its blocked position and
to continue 20. ....R—Q 2 ; 21.
P—K 5, Kt (B 3)—Q 4 ; 22. K
—Q 2 !, with 23. P—K R 4 and
24. P—Kt 5 to follow for White.

20. ......   Kt × P

On the contrary, the capture of
the Pawn is rash, for the open lines
of attack now available to White
are heavy ransom for such sorry
booty.

| 21. R—K Kt 1 | Kt—B 3 |
| 22. Kt—K 5 ! | |

Threatening, if 22. ....B—Q 2,
to win by 23. R—K B 3, K—B 1 ;
24. Kt (K 5) × K B P !, R × Kt ;
25. Kt × R, K × Kt ; 26. P—K 5.

22. ......   Kt (Kt 3)—Q 2

This move is not really an actual
mistake. But in this laborious position all other moves would equally

give the impression of being mistakes.

23. Kt (K 5) × K B P !

Regaining the Pawn sacrificed with a strong attack.

23. ......   **Kt—R 4**

If 23. ....R × Kt White wins by 24. B × P.

24. R—K B 3   **K—R 2**
25. P—K 5 !

Threatening 26. B—B 2 ch followed by 27. Kt × P ch.

25. ......   **Kt—B 1**
26. Kt × R P !   **P—Q Kt 3**

Indirectly defending the Knight by the threat of the Bishop's check at Q R 3.

27. Kt (R 6)—B 7 K—Kt 1
28. K—K 3

Threatening 29. R—R 3.

28. ......   **P—Kt 3**
29. B—B 2   **K—Kt 2**
30. R—Kt 5

After this move Black has no defence against the threatened 31. R × Kt ! and 32. R—Kt 3 ch.

Final Position.

Black resigns.

CHAPTER XXI

INTERNATIONAL TOURNAMENT AT CARLSBAD
MAY, 1923

GAME 80

QUEEN'S GAMBIT DECLINED

Brilliancy Prize

White :   Black :
A. ALEKHIN.   A. RUBINSTEIN.

1.	P—Q 4	P—Q 4
2.	P—Q B 4	P—K 3
3.	Kt—K B 3	Kt—K B 3
4.	Kt—B 3	B—K 2
5.	B—Kt 5	Q Kt—Q 2
6.	P—K 3	Castles
7.	R—B 1	P—B 3
8.	Q—B 2	

This move, which was very fashionable since the Ostend Tournaments of 1905-7 and which had almost completely superseded the old move, 8. B—Q 3, will soon become quite obsolete, for every International Tournament brings a fresh and sufficient line of play for Black.

In the Mährisch-Ostrau Tournament of 1923 Wolf played against the great theorist Grünfeld the simple continuation: 8. ....Kt—K 5; 9. B×B, Q×B; 10. B—Q 3 (10. Kt×Kt obviously leads to nothing, for if White captures the Pawn on K 4 he loses his Q Kt P). 10. ....Kt×Kt, with a very defendable game which resulted in a draw.

But apart from 8. ....Kt—K 5 there are available to Black at least four replies whose inadequacy has not yet been demonstrated: (a) 8. ....P×P ; (b) 8. ....P—B 4 ; (c) 8. ....R—K 1 ; and (d) last but not least, 8. ....P—Q R 3 !

8. ....   P—Q R 3 !

In my opinion better than 8. ....P—K R 3, upon which White could have replied advantageously 9. B—B 4, *e.g.* : 9. ....R—K 1 (if 9. ....Kt—K 5, then 10. B—Q 3 !, P—K B 4 ; 11. P—K R 4 followed at need by P—K Kt 3 and Kt—K 5, with advantage to White ; but not 10. Kt×Kt, P×Kt ; 11. Q×P, B—Kt 5 ch ; 12. Kt—Q 2, Q—R 4 ; 13. Q—B 2, P—K 4 ! ; 14. P×P, Kt—B 4 and Black has a strong attack) ; 10. B—Q 3, P×P ; 11. B×P, P—Q Kt 4 ; 12. B—Q 3, P—R 3 ; 13. P—Q R 4 !, etc.

The game Alekhin—Teichmann (Carlsbad, 1923) unfolded itself in the following way : 13. ....B—Kt 2 ; 14. Castles, R—B 1 ; 15. Q—Kt 3, Q—Kt 3 ; 16. Kt—K 5, K R—Q 1 ; 17. Kt—Kt 6 ! ; B—B 1 ; 18. Kt×B, Kt×Kt ; 19. Kt—K 4, Kt×Kt ; 20. B×Kt, Kt—Q 2 ; 21. B—Q 6 !, Kt—B 3 ; 22. B—Q B 5, Q—B 2 ; 23. B—B 3, P—Q R 4, and White by playing for example 24. K R—K 1 or 24.

R—B 2, instead of accepting the Pawn sacrificed, which only led to a draw, would have retained a winning position.

8. ....P—B 4 usually results in the isolation of White's Q P, but on the other hand it allows White to undertake a rather dangerous attack on the King-side. This variation admits of a complicated and very difficult game, with nearly equal chances.

Concerning 8. ....R—K 1 and 8. ....P×P, see Games No. 79 (Alekhin-Muffang) and 69 (Alekhin-Yates) respectively.

9. P—Q R 4

As this identical variation had yielded me a win the previous evening against Grünfeld, who played here 9. P—Q R 3 (see Game No. 81), I wished to avoid fighting against the defence which I considered then, and still consider now, the best.

This is the reason which decided me in favour of 9. P—Q R 4, a move which Rubinstein, my present adversary, had adopted against me, without conspicuous success, in a similar position in the Hastings Tournament of 1922.

The game continued as follows :
8. ....P—K R 3 ; 9. B—R 4, P—R 3 ; 10. P—Q R 4, P—B 4 ; 11. B—Q 3, B P×P ; 12. K P×P, P×P ; 13. B×P, Kt—Kt 3 ; 14. B—R 2, Q Kt—Q 4 ; 15. B—Kt 1, Kt—Q Kt 5 ; 16. Q—K 2, B—Q 2 ; 17. Castles, B—B 3 ; 18. K R— Q 1, R—B 1 ; 19. Kt—K 5, K R— Q 4 ; 20. B—Kt 3, B—K Kt 4 ; 21. P—B 4 !, B—R 5 ; 22. Kt×B, R×Kt ; 23. Kt×Kt, R×R ; 24. R×R, Kt×Kt ; 25. Q—K 4, P— K Kt 3 ; 26. B×B, Q×B ; 27. P— B 5 ?, Q—Kt 4 ! and Black wins easily.

It is manifest that the move 9. P—Q R 4 cannot pretend to yield

any advantage, since Black can answer it by 9. ....Kt—K 5 ! with greater force than on the preceding move, White's Queen-side being now slightly weak.

Rubinstein, however, seeks to take advantage of the weakness by a different method.

9. ......   R—K 1

If 9. ....P—R 3 White replies 10. B—B 4 with advantage.

10. B—Q 3   P×P
11. B×P   Kt—Q 4

We now realize the idea conceived by Black—a fusion of the new defensive system (....P—Q R 3) with the old system (....P×P and ....Kt—Q 4), in the hope of thus profiting by the weakening of the square Q Kt 5 created by the advance of White's Q R P.

Position after Black's 11th move.

12. B—B 4 !

White in his turn deviates from the beaten track. The text-move is here much stronger than in the analogous position where I played it against Selesnieff at Pistyan, 1922 (see Game No. 54) for the following reasons :

(1) After 12. ....Kt×B; 13. P×Kt the position of the Black Rook at K 1 is less favourable than on K B 1, where it hinders a subsequent attack on the point K B 2.

(2) The manœuvre Kt—Kt 3—Q 4 which, in the game cited, allowed Black to undertake a counter-attack, loses its sting because White's Queen is at Q B 2 and he can therefore gain a *tempo* by B—Q 3, threatening the K R P.

In addition the move P—Q R 4, unfavourable in other cases, here affords him the possibility of B—R 2 and B—Kt 1, a manœuvre analogous to the Grünfeld variation (9. P—Q R 3), but still more effective here because of the opening of the King's file.

We can therefore anticipate a slight advantage in position for White, after the ensuing exchange.

| 12. ...... | Kt×B |
| 13. P×Kt | P—Q B 4 |

This move, which goes against *the general principle of not opening up fresh lines to a better-developed opponent*, is dictated by the wish to eliminate White's troublesome Pawn on K B 5.

White, who has not yet Castled, can scarcely oppose this plan, and the game speedily assumes a most animated appearance.

14. P×P

Forced, for if 14. Castles, then 14. ....P×P and 15. ....Kt—Kt 3.

| 14. ...... | Q—B 2! |

The usual complement to the previous move. If now 15. P—K Kt 3, Q—B 3; 16. B—K 2, P—K 4! and Black would have freed himself once and for all.

| 15. Castles! | Q×K B P |

The capture of the Q B P would also be insufficient to maintain equality, *e.g.* : 15. ....B×P; 16. B—Q 3, Kt—B 3; 17. Kt—K 4!; or 15. ....Kt×P; 16. Kt—K 5.

Position after Black's 15th move.

16. Kt—K 4!

This Pawn sacrifice is the only way to keep the initiative.

The attempt to defend the Q B P by P—Q Kt 4 would be inadequate, for the Q Kt P could not be supported by the Q R P, *e.g.* : 16. Kt—K 2, Q—R 3; 17. P—Q Kt 4, P—R 4!

| 16. ...... | Kt×P |

If 16. ....B×P; 17. Q Kt—Kt 5, P—K Kt 3 (forced, since if 17. ....Kt—B 1 White wins by 18. B—Q 3); 18. K R—K 1!, Kt—B 3; 19. P—K Kt 3, Q—Q 3; 20. K R Q 1, Q—K 2; 21. Kt—K 5 with an overwhelming attack for White.

The text-move simplifies the game and allows Black some chances of salvation.

| 17. Kt×Kt | B×Kt |
| 18. B—Q 3 | P—Q Kt 3 |

If 18... B—Q 3, then 19. B×P ch and 20. K R—Q 1, threatening R—Q 4.

19. B×P ch   K—R 1

This seemingly plausible move (and not the next move, as the majority of annotators have thought) is the decisive mistake !

After 19. ....K—B 1 ! Black's King would be less endangered than after the text-move, and it would have been very difficult for White to show how he could win, despite his positional superiority.

20. B—K 4

Position after White's 20th move.

20. ......   R—R 2

Better was 20. ....R—Kt 1, although in this case White would have obtained a decisive superiority by the following lines of play :—

I.—21. P—K Kt 3, Q—B 3 ; 22. P—Q Kt 4, B—Q 3 (else 23. Q—B 7 ! follows) ; 23. K R—Q 1, Q—K 2 ; 24. B—B 6, R—Q 1 ; 25. R—Q 4, P—Kt 3 ; 26. Q—Q 2 !, K—Kt 2 ; 27. R—Q 1 and White wins.

II.—21. P—K Kt 3, Q—Q 3 ; 22. K R—Q 1, Q—K 2 ; 23. Kt—K 5, Q—B 2 ; 24. Q—B 3 !, P—Q R 4 ; 25. Kt—B 6, and 26. Q—B 3, winning for White.

21. P—Q Kt 4 !

From this point up to the end of the game Black has not a moment's respite.

Obviously he cannot capture the Q Kt P, because of 22. Q×B ! and wins.

21. ......   B—B 1

Therefore this retreat is absolutely forced.

22. Q—B 6

Attacking both the Rook and the Q Kt P. Black's reply is the only way to parry temporarily this double threat.

22. ......   R—Q 2
23. P—Kt 3 !

Position after White's 23rd move.

23. ......   Q—Kt 1

The alternative was 23. ....Q—Q 3, after which White had the choice between two winning lines :

I.—24. K R—Q 1, Q×R ch (or 24. ...Q×Q ; 25. B×Q, R×R ch ; 26. R×R, R—K 2 ; 27. R—Q 8 and wins) ; 25. R×Q, R×R ch ; 26. K—Kt 2, B—Q 2 ; 27. Q×Kt P, B×R P ; 28. Q×R P, B—Q 2 ; 29. Kt—Kt 5, K—Kt 1 ; 30. Q—K 2 and White wins.

II.—24. Q—B 4, K—Kt 1 (or 24. ....Q—K 2 ; 25. Kt—K 5 !, R—Q 3 ; 26. B—B 6 ! and wins) ; 25. B—B 6, R—B 2 ; 26. K R—Q 1, Q—K 2 ; 27. Q—Q 3 ! and White wins.

24. Kt—Kt 5 !

Threatening 25. Kt × P ch !

24. ...... R (K 1)—Q 1

Position after Black's 24th move.

25. B—Kt 6 ! !

The *coup de grâce*. Should Black capture this Bishop, the following mating variation would ensue :

26. Q—K 4 !, B × P ; 27. Q—R 4 ch, K—Kt 1 ; 28. Q—R 7 ch, K—B 1 ; 29. Q—R 8 ch, K—K 2 ; 30. Q × P ch, K—K 1 (or 30. ....K—Q 3 ; 31. K R—Q 1 ch and mates next move) ; 31. Q—Kt 8 ch, B—B 1 ; 32. Q × Kt P ch, K—K 2 ; 33. Q × P mate.

On the other hand 25. ....B—Kt 2 ; 26. Q—B 4 ! would transpose into identical variations.

Black is consequently forced to sacrifice the Exchange, after which his game is hopeless.

25.	Q—K 4
26. Kt × P ch	R × Kt
27. B × R	Q—K B 4
28. K R—Q 1 !	

Simple and decisive.

28.	R × R ch
29. R × R	Q × B
30. Q × B	K—R 2
31. Q × R P	Q—B 6
32. Q—Q 3 ch !	Black resigns.

GAME 81

QUEEN'S GAMBIT DECLINED

Brilliancy Prize

White :	Black :
E. GRÜNFELD.	A. ALEKHIN.

1. P—Q 4	Kt—K B 3
2. P—Q B 4	P—K 3
3. Kt—K B 3	P—Q 4
4. Kt—B 3	B—K 2
5. B—Kt 5	Q Kt—Q 2
6. P—K 3	Castles
7. R—B 1	P—B 3
8. Q—B 2	P—Q R 3 !
9. P—Q R 3	

Grünfeld is probably correct in affirming that this move is the best here, but this assertion simply demonstrates that White's whole system, or rather 8. Q—B 2, yields no more than equality.

9. ...... P—R 3

This advance should not be made until Black has definitely made up his mind between the two systems of defence : ....P × P, followed by P—Q Kt 4 and P—Q B 4 ; or .... P × P, followed by Kt—Q 4.

But although this move has the advantage of weakening the attack on the point K R 2, when White succeeds in posting his K B on Q Kt 1 (Grünfeld's variation), it is, on the other hand, insufficient after ....P×P and ....Kt—Q 4, since it affords White the opportunity to retain his Q B by B—K Kt 3, which thereby leaves Black's pieces in their confined positions.

10. B—R 4   R—K 1 !

An important improvement on the line of play adopted by Maróczy against Grünfeld in the Vienna Tournament of 1922.

This game continued 10. .... P×P; 11. B×P, P—Q Kt 4; 12. B—R 2, B—Kt 2 ; 13. B—Kt 1, R—K 1 ; 14. Kt—K 5 !, Kt—B 1 ; 15. Castles, and White has far the better game.

The text-move gains an extremely important move by eliminating the subsequent mating threat at K R 2 and thereby enables Black to free his game speedily by ....P—Q B 4 !

11. B—Q 3

White could have played 11. P—R 3 without loss of time, seeing that Black has nothing better than the following capture of the Q B P.

The question is whether this move would in the end prove useful or detrimental to him.

In my game against Chajes (see Game No. 85) I wished to try this experiment, but my opponent, who adopted an altogether abnormal system of defence, did not give me the chance.

11. ......   P×P
12. B×P   P—Q Kt 4
13. B—R 2   P—B 4

The liberating move !

See Diagram.

14. R—Q 1

Upon 14. P×P, Black would have replied 14. ....Kt×P, and if 15. B—Kt 1, B—Kt 2 !, for the variation 16. B×Kt, B×B ; 17. Q—

Position after Black's 13th move.

R 7 ch, K—B 1 ; 18. Kt×P, P×Kt ; 19. R×Kt, B×P would be completely in his favour.

After the text-move Black gradually succeeds in seizing the initiative. 14. Castles, P×P (14. ....Q—Kt 3 is also worthy of consideration) ; 15. P×P was a little better, as played by Réti and Grünfeld against Teichmann in the same tournament.

Here is the continuation of the game Grünfeld—Teichmann : 15. ....B—Kt 2 ; 16. K R—Q 1, Q—Kt 3 ; 17. Kt—K 5, and instead of the passive move 17. ....Kt—B 1 Black could have obtained a slight advantage in position by a pretty combination discovered by Victor Kahn : 17. ....Kt×Kt ! ; 18. P×Kt, Q—B 3 ! ; 19. P—B 3, Kt—Kt 5 ! ; 20. Kt—Q 5 ! (White has nothing better, for 20. B×B is refuted by 20. ....Q—Kt 3 ch), 20. ....P×Kt ; 21. Q×Q, B×Q ; 22. P×Kt (not 22. B×B, Kt×K P ; 23. B—Q 6, Kt—B 5), 22. ...B×B ; 23. R×B, R×P ; 24. P—K Kt 3 ! (not 24. B×P, Q R—Q 1), 24. ....B—B 3 or B—Kt 4 ; 25. R×P, R—K 8 ch followed by Q R—K 1, with advantage to Black.

This variation shows once again the frailty of the variation 8. Q—B 2 and 9. P—Q R 3.

14. ......   P × P

Simplest, for after the removal of the Rook from the Q B file Black could not with certainty visualize a counter-attack on the Queen-side.

15. Kt × Q P

Hoping to break through with his attack by a subsequent sacrifice of the Exchange on Q 7.

15. ......   Q—Kt 3
16. B—Kt 1

This move appears to prevent the reply 15. ....B—Kt 2 owing to the possibility of 16. Kt (Q 4) × Kt P, P × Kt; 17. R × Kt!, with a winning attack for White.

But . . . . . .

Position after White's 16th move.

16. ......   B—Kt 2 !

Black plays this move all the same, for 17. Kt (Q 4) × Kt P would be refuted by 17. ....Q—B 3!!; 18. Kt—Q 4 (forced), Q × P, with a strong counter-attack.

In this way Black has successfully completed his development. There consequently remains nothing else for White than Castling, after the failure of his premature attack.

17. Castles   Q R—B 1
18. Q—Q 2

Hindering the double threat B—K 5 or Kt—K 5. 18. Q—K 2 would be insufficient on account of 18. ....B × R P; 19. Kt (B 3 or Q 4) × Kt P, B—Kt 5! and Black wins a Pawn.

18. ......   Kt—K 4 !

This Knight will occupy the square Q B 5, thereby fixing the weakness of the Queen-side, induced by 9. P—Q R 3.

19. B × Kt

In order to exchange Black's dangerous Q B, White's next manœuvre is finely conceived, but insufficient to equalize.

19. ......   B × B
20. Q—B 2   P—Kt 3

Not at all to prevent a harmless check at K R 2 but rather to secure a retreat subsequently for his K B, whose action on the long diagonal will be very powerful.

21. Q—K 2   Kt—B 5
22. B—K 4 !

Feeling himself in a strategic inferiority, Grünfeld attempts to save himself by tactical skirmishing.
Having provoked 20. ....P—Kt 3 he now hopes for the variation : 22. ....Kt × R P; 23. Q—B 3 !, B × B; 24. Kt × B, B × Kt; 25. P × B, etc., which would ensure him the gain of the Exchange.

22. ......   B—Kt 2 !

But by this simple move, which is part of his plan, Black retains his advantage.

23. B × B   Q × B
24. R—B 1

The threat 24. .... Kt × R P compels White to retrace his 14th move.

24. ......   P—K 4 !

This advance of the K P will give Black's Knight a new out-post on Q 6, still more irksome for the opponent than its present position.

25. Kt—Kt 3   P—K 5

Renewing the threat 26. .... Kt × R P.

26. Kt—Q 4   K R—Q 1 !

To make the following Knight-manœuvre still more effective, for now when it reaches Q 6 it will intercept the defence of the White Knight by the Rook.

27. K R—Q 1   Kt—K 4
28. Kt—R 2

After this move, which removes the Knight from the field of action, White is definitely lost.

Comparatively better was 28. P—B 3, upon which Black would have continued 28. .... P × P ; 29. P × P, Kt—B 5 with attacking chances on both flanks, and a probable win after a long and difficult struggle.

28. ......   Kt—Q 6
29. R × R   Q × R
30. P—B 3

Too late ! But already there was no satisfactory reply, e.g. : after 30. Kt—B 3, P—B 4 ; 31. P—B 3, Black would have gained the victory by the same sacrifice which occurred in the actual game : 31. ... R × Kt ! ; 32. P × R, B × P ch ; 33. K—B 1, Kt—B 5 ; 34. Q—Q 2, Q—B 5 ch ; 35. Kt—K 2, P—K 6 ! ; 36. Q—K 1, B × P ; 37. R—Q 8 ch, K—B 2 ; 38. Q—Q 1, B × P ! ; 39. Q—Q 7 ch, B—K 2 ; 40. Q—K 8 ch, K—B 3 ; 41. Q—R 8 ch, K—Kt 4 ; 42. P—R 4 ch, K—R 4 ; 43. P—Kt 4 ch, P × P ; 44. Q—K 5 ch, P—Kt 4 ! ! and Black wins.

Position after White's 30th move.

30. ......   R × Kt !
31. P × P

If 31. P × R, B × P ch ; 32. K—B 1, Kt—B 5 ; 33. Q × P (or 33. Q—Q 2, Q—B 5 ch ; 34. K—K 1, P—K 6 ! and wins), Q—B 5 ch ; 34. K—K 1, Kt × P ch ; 35. K—Q 2, B—K 6 ch and Black wins.

White, who does not perceive the hidden point of the sacrifice, hopes to save himself by the text-move.

31. ......   Kt—B 5 !
32. P × Kt

Evidently forced.

32. ......   Q—B 5 ! !

Winning at least a piece ; but White chooses the speediest death.

33. Q × Q   R × R ch
34. Q—B 1   B—Q 5 ch

and mates next move.

GAME 82

RUY LOPEZ

White :	*Black :*
Dr. S. Tarrasch.	A. Alekhin.

1. P—K 4   P—K 4
2. Kt—K B 3   Kt—Q B 3
3. B—Kt 5   P—K Kt 3

Pillsbury's favourite defence, with which he opened at the Hastings Tournament and gained several fine wins ; but modern theory not unreasonably considers it inferior.

If I adopted it in the present game, doubtless for the last time, it was solely to verify in practice a variation indicated by Rubinstein in Collijn's *Lärobok*, and then, should White play 4. Kt—B 3 to try out the new move 4. .... Kt—Q 5 !, which seems to give Black complete equality : 5. Kt×P ?, Q—Kt 4 ; or 5. Kt×Kt, P×Kt ; 6. Kt—K 2 ?, Q—Kt 4 ! ; 7. Kt×P, B—Kt 2 ; 8. P—Q 3, Q—Q B 4 ! and Black wins a piece.

4. P—Q 4 !   Kt×P

If 4. ....P×P ; 5. B—Kt 5, P—B 3 ; 6. B—K R 4 and White will recover his Pawn in a few moves, with a strong attacking position.

5. Kt×Kt   P×Kt
6. Q×P   Q—B 3

Position after Black's 6th move.

7. Q—Q 3

Without the slightest doubt the correct move here is 7. P—K 5, after which 7. ....   Q—Kt 3 (recommended in the *Lärobok*)

would be quite bad, because of 8. Q×Q !, R P×Q ; 9. Kt—B 3, B—Kt 2 ; 10. B—K B 4 !, and Black would experience great difficulty in developing his Queen-side.

Likewise after 7. ....Q—K 2 White can lead into very interesting complications, which appear to result in his favour, *e.g.*: 8. Kt—B 3, P—Q B 3 (or 8. ....B—Kt 2 ; 9. Kt—Q 5 !, Q×P ch ; 10. Q×Q, B×Q ; 11. Castles, threatening 12. R—K 1, with a good attack for the Pawn) ; 9. Kt—K 4 !, B—Kt 2 ! (if 9. ...P×B, then 10. Kt—Q 6 ch, K—Q 1 ; 11. B—K 3 [threatening mate in two by Q—Kt 6 ch !], 11. ....Q—K 3 ; 12. Castles K R and White has a winning attack) ; 10. Kt—Q 6 ch, K—B 1 ; 11. B—K B 4, P×B (or 11. ....P—B 3 ; 12. Kt×B, R×Kt ; 13. P—K 6 !, Q×P ch ; 14. B—K 2, and White recovers the Pawn sacrificed with an obvious advantage in position) ; 12. Castles K R, Kt—R 3 ; 13. B×Kt !, B×B ; 14. P—B 4, B—Kt 2 ; 15. Q R—K 1, with an overwhelming attack for White.

On the contrary, the move actually chosen by White does not occasion his opponent any difficulty, and even allows him shortly to seize the initiative.

7. ......   B—Kt 2
8. Kt—B 3   P—B 3
9. B—Q B 4   Kt—K 2
10. B—K 3

10. Castles was preferable, for after the text-move White will be compelled to protect his Q Kt P by withdrawing his Knight to Q 1, where it remains immobile.

10. ......   P—Q Kt 4 !
11. B—Kt 3   P—Q R 4

See Diagram.

12. P—Q R 4

12. P—Q R 3 was a little better, although in this case also the reply

Position after Black's 11th move.

12. ....B—Q R 3 would have forced the disadvantageous retreat of White's Knight, *e.g.* :

12. ....B—Q R 3; 13. Kt—Q 1, Castles K R ! ; 14. Castles K R (if 14. Q×P, K R—Q 1 ; 15. Q—Kt 4, P—R 5 ; 16. B—R 2, P—Kt 5 ; 17. P×P, P—R 6 ; 18. P—B 3, P×P ; 19. R—Q Kt 1, Q×P ch ! ; 20. Kt×Q, B×Kt ch ; 21. B—Q 2, R×B and wins), 14. ....P—Q 4 ! with by far the superior game for Black.

The text-move results in the complete blockade of White's Queenside, which is strategically equivalent to the loss of the game.

Nevertheless, the tactical realization of victory is fraught with very serious difficulties, owing to the consummate skill with which Dr. Tarrasch defends himself.

12. ......   P—Kt 5
13. Kt—Q 1

Compulsory in order to protect the Q Kt P. However, the immobility of this Knight on a square on which it prevents communication between the White Rooks will soon have fatal consequences for White.

13. ......   Castles
14. Castles   P—Q 4 !

Much stronger than 14. ....B—Q R 3 ; 15. B—Q B 4, B×B ; 16. Q×B, P—Q 4, after which White could still have avoided the decisive opening of the Q B file, by playing 17. Q—Q 3.

15. P×P   B—Q R 3
16. B—Q B 4   B×B
17. Q×B   P×P
18. Q—Q 3   P—Q 5 !

Opposing 19. P—Q B 3 and initiating an attack difficult to meet against the weak Q B P.

19. B—Q 2   Q R—B 1
20. K R—K 1

Temporarily preventing 20. .... Q—B 4.

20. ......   R—B 2
21. P—Q Kt 3

White hopes to free his unfortunate Knight and afterwards post it on Q B 4, but, as will be seen later on, Black will not leave him time for this.

21. ......   K R—B 1
22. R—Q B 1

Position after White's 22nd move.

22. ......   Q—B 4 !

This move, which White could not escape, at once settles the fate of the backward Pawn. Obviously White cannot exchange Queens without losing the Pawn subsequently.

On the other hand, the interposition of the White Rook at K 4 will favour the successful entry of Black's Knight at Q B 6, thereby forcing the exchange of White's Q B, his best defensive piece.

23. R—K 4	Kt—Q 4
24. Kt—Kt 2	Kt—B 6
25. B × Kt	

Forced, for if 25. R—K 1, Q × Q ; 26. Kt × Q, Kt—R 7, winning the Pawn ; or 26. P × Q, Kt—K 7 ch.

25.	R × B
26. Q—K 2	B—R 3 !

The final point of the attack against White's Q B P, initiated by 14. ....P—Q 4 !

27. P—Kt 4

A desperate counter-attack, the refutation of which leads to very interesting positions.

27.	Q—B 3
28. R—K 8 ch	R × R
29. Q × R ch	K—Kt 2
30. R—B 1	R × B P

At last !

31. Kt—Q 3

See Diagram.

31. ......   Q—B 6 !

This move, which is no doubt the most difficult in the whole game, is based on the following considerations :

White threatens to consolidate his position by 32. Q—K 4 and 33.

Position after White's 31st move.

P—B 4, after which the win would be very difficult for Black, because of the unfavourable position of his K B.

On the other hand, the possible end-game resulting from 31. .... Q—K 3 ; 32. Q × Q, P × Q ; 33. R—Q 1 ! is not without resources for White, e.g. : 33. ....K—B 3 ; 34. P—B 4, P—Kt 4 ; 35. P—R 4 !

Therefore 32. Q—K 4 or 32. P—B 4 must be prevented.

The text-move alone answers this end.

32. Kt—K 5

The capture of the Q P by 32. Q—K 5 ch, K—Kt 1 ; 33. Q × Q P would have facilitated Black's victory, e.g. : 33. ....R—Q 7 ; 34. Kt—K 5 (or 34. Q—Q 8 ch, B—B 1 ; 35. Kt—K 5, Q—B 5 ! ; 36. Q—Kt 8, K—Kt 2, followed by 37. ....B—Q 3 and Black wins), 34. ....Q × P ; 35. Q—R 7, Q—Q 4, followed by 37. ....P—Kt 6, and wins.

32.	Q—Q 4
33. Kt—Q 7	

Now White threatens mate on the move !

33. ......   Q—Q 3
34. R—Q 1

Preventing the advance of the Q P, and threatening 35. R × P ! But Black's next move puts things in their proper place.

Position after White's 34th move.

34. ......   B—K 6 !

White is compelled to bring his Rook back again to its starting point, for if 35. P × B, Q × P ch and mates next move ; or if 35. Q × B, P × Q ; 36. R × Q, P—K 7 and wins.

35. R—K B 1   B—Kt 4

Threatening now 36. .... B—K 2 followed by 37. .... P—Q 6, which threat forces the exchange of Queens.

36. Q—K 5 ch   Q × Q
37. Kt × Q   B—B 5

The ensuing end-game is undoubtedly won for Black, but it still requires very precise tactics.

38. Kt—B 4   P—Q 6
39. R—Q 1   R—B 6 !

Not 39. .... P—Q 7, which would appreciably diminish the strength of the passed Q P, after 40. K—B 1.

40. Kt × P   K—B 3 !

It is much more interesting to bring the King to the centre of the board without delay, rather than to recover the lost Pawn by 40. .... B—B 2. Moreover, White cannot protect his Q Kt P for ever.

41. P—R 4   K—K 4
42. K—Kt 2   K—Q 5
43. K—B 3   B—B 2
44. Kt—B 4   R × P
45. Kt—K 3   R—B 6
46. R—Q Kt 1   B—R 4
47. Kt—Q 1   R—R 6
48. Kt—K 3   R × P
49. P—Kt 5   R—R 6
50. R—Kt 1   P—Kt 6
51. R—Kt 4 ch   K—B 4
52. R—B 4 ch   K—Kt 4
53. R—B 8   R—R 8 !

Avoiding White's last trap, 53. .... P—Kt 7 ; 54. R—Kt 8 ch, B—Kt 3 ; 55. R × B ch, followed by 56. Kt—B 4 ch and 57. Kt × R.

54. R—Kt 8 ch   B—Kt 3 !

If now 55. Kt—Q 5, then simply 55. .... P—Q 7 !, etc.

White resigns.

GAME 83

QUEEN'S GAMBIT DECLINED

White :	Black :
A. ALEKHIN.	G. MARÓCZY.

1. P—Q 4   Kt—K B 3
2. P—Q B 4   P—K 3
3. Kt—K B 3   P—Q 4
4. Kt—B 3   B—K 2
5. B—Kt 5   Castles
6. P—K 3   Kt—K 5

A defence practised on several occasions by Dr. Em. Lasker, and subsequently by Capablanca, in their respective matches with Marshall.

It is doubtless no worse than other defences, and has the advantage of simplifying the game, without creating weaknesses in Black's camp.

In the London Tournament of 1922 Maróczy tried against me 6. ....P—B 4, recommended by Rubinstein in Collijn's *Lärobok*, and obtained a very inferior game. Here is the instructive continuation of the game.

6. ....P—B 4; 7. B P×P, K P×P; 8. P×P, B—K 3; 9. B—Kt 5 !, B×P; 10. Castles, Kt—B 3; 11. R—B 1, B—K 2; 12. B×Q Kt !, P×B; 13. Kt—Q R 4, R—B 1; 14. Kt—Q 4, B—Q 2; 15. B×Kt !, B×B; 16. Kt—Q B 5, B—K 1; 17. Q—Kt 4, R—Kt 1; 18. P—Q Kt 3, P—Kt 3; 19. R—B 2, Q—Q 3; 20. K R—B 1, B—K 4; 21. Kt—B 3 !, B—Kt 2; 22. Q—Q R 4, Q—K 2; 23. Kt—Q 4, R—Kt 3; 24. P—K R 3, B—K 4; 25. Kt—Q 3 !, B×Kt; 26. P×B, R—Kt 2; 27. R—K 1, Q—Kt 4 and by 28. R—K 5 White could have easily maintained a winning advantage in position.

7. B×B   Q×B
8. Q—Kt 3

In order to avoid the variation 8. P×P, Kt×Kt; 9. P×Kt, P×P; 10. Q—Kt 3, R—Q 1; 11. P—B 4, Kt—B 3 !, which seems to yield Black equality.

But with this idea 8. Q—B 2 is certainly preferable, for after the text-move Black need not have captured the Knight, and could first have played 7. ....P—Q B 3, and continued by 8. ....P—K B 4, etc.

8. ......   Kt×Kt
9. Q×Kt   P—Q B 3

At New York, 1924, in an identical position, Maróczy played against me 9. ....P—Q B 4, but after 10. B P×P, B P×P; 11. Kt×P, White has an evident advantage owing to the weakness of Black's Q P and control of the open Q B file.

10. B—Q 3   Kt—Q 2
11. Castles K R   P—K B 4

The "Stonewall" formation is here quite without value, for even supposing that Black's Q Kt were to occupy the square K 5, it could be dislodged by P—K B 3, or else exchanged against White's K B.

On the other hand, the square K 5 will furnish White with an impregnable position for his K Kt, Black's Q B being of a different colour from that of the square mentioned.

12. Q R—B 1 !

Anticipating the manœuvre 12. ....Kt—B 3 followed by 13. .... Kt—K 5, to which he would have replied 13. Kt—K 5, White seizes his moment's respite to complete his development.

12. ......   P—K Kt 4

But this attack, quite astonishing from a master of Maróczy's reputation, hopelessly compromises the already insecure position of the Black King.

13. Kt—Q 2 !   R—B 2

As inexplicable as the previous move. Comparatively better was 13. ....Kt—B 3 followed by 14. ....B—Q 2, etc.

14. P—B 3   P—K 4

In the hope of forcing exchange of Queens on the 18th move, but without sufficiently appreciating the reply 19. Q—B 7 !, although in any case the game was lost for Black.

15. B P × P   B P × P
16. P—K 4 !   B P × P
17. B P × P   R × R ch
18. R × R   K P × P

Still reckoning on 19. Q × P, Q—B 4, etc. But White's next move shatters this last illusion.

Position after Black's 18th move.

19. Q—B 7 !

Paralysing in a single move all the Black pieces, after which Black's position becomes hopeless.

19. ......   K—Kt 2
20. R—B 5 !   P × P
21. Kt × P   Q—Kt 5

Surrendering to the inevitable. If 21. ....P—K R 3 White wins easily by 22. P—R 3, followed by 23. K—R 2 and 24. Kt—Q 6.

22. R × P ch   Black resigns.

GAME 84

FOUR KNIGHTS' GAME

White :   *Black :*
H. Wolf.   A. Alekhin.

1. P—K 4   P—K 4
2. Kt—K B 3   Kt—Q B 3
3. Kt—B 3   Kt—B 3

4. B—Kt 5   Kt—Q 5
5. Kt × Kt   P × Kt
6. Kt—Q 5

This move, introduced by Selesnieff in his game against Spielmann in the Pistyan Tournament of 1922, does not achieve its object, namely, an easy draw, as the present game shows.

Best here is 6. P—K 5, P × Kt ; 7. P × Kt, Q × P ; 8. Q P × P, B—K 2 ; 9. Castles, Castles ; 10. Q—Q 4 with a satisfactory game for White.

6. ......   Kt × Kt
7. P × Kt   Q—B 3 !

Avoiding the exchange of Queens, which White could have forced after 7. ....B—K 2 ; 8. Q—Kt 4, B—B 3 ; 9. Q—K 4 ch.

8. Castles   B—K 2
9. P—K B 4

White is not sufficiently developed to be able to anticipate a lasting initiative which could alone justify this advance.

He would have been better advised to recognize the inadequacy of his 6th move, namely to play 9. B—K 2, followed by 10. P—Q B 4 and 11. P—Q 3, with approximate equality.

9. ......   Castles
10. Q—B 3   P—B 4 !

Definitely securing the position of his Q P, which would have been troublesome had he at once played 10. ....P—Q 3.

11. P—Q Kt 3

Preparing the fianchetto development of the Q B, so as not to restrict the action of his K B attendant upon 11. P—Q 3 or 11. P—B 4.

11.	P—Q 3
12. B—Kt 2	B—B 4
13. Q R—K 1	

Upon 13. B—Q 3 Black would have retained his slight advantage in position by 13. ....Q—Kt 3 !

| 13. ...... | B—Q 1 ! |

In order to post this Bishop on Q R 4, an especially favourable position as White cannot screen his Q P from its attack, because of the unfavourable position of his K B.

14. B—Q 3	B—R 4
15. R—K 2	Q R—K 1
16. P—Kt 3	

White could still have avoided immediate material loss by playing 16. B—B 1, but in any event his game remained obviously inferior.

Position after White's 16th move.

| 16. ...... | B × B ! |

This exchange secures Black a decisive advantage in position, White being unable to recapture with the Queen on account of 17. ....R × R ; 18. Q × R, P—Q 6 ! and Black wins a piece; nor 17. R × R, B × R ; 18. R × R ch, K × R ; 19. K × B, B × P with an easy win.

17. P × B	R × R
18. Q × R	Q—B 4
19. R—B 2	

The end-game a Pawn to the bad resulting from 19. Q—K 4, Q × Q ; 20. P × Q, B × P would not afford White any drawing chances.

| 19. ...... | Q × P (Q 4) |
| 20. Q—K 4 | Q—K 3 ! |

Preventing undoubling of the adverse Pawns, which would have allowed White's Q B sooner or later to join in the defence.

21. P—B 5

If 21. Q × P, then 21. ....B × P ! and wins.

| 21. ...... | Q—K 4 ! |
| 22. Q × Q ! | |

The best alternative. After the exchange, the absence of open lines for Black's Rook and the advantageous position of White's King will occasion Black not a few technical difficulties, even though White's Q B remains imprisoned.

22.	P × Q
23. K—Kt 2	P—B 3
24. K—B 3	B—Q 1 !

The Bishop has played its part at Q R 4, and it is important to barricade the Queen-side with Pawns promptly, in order to deprive White's Q B of all hopes of escape.

| 25. K—K 4 | B—K 2 |
| 26. R—B 1 | |

After 26. K—Q 5, R—Q 1 ch ; 27. K—B 4 (if 27. K—K 6, K—B 1 ! and mates next move), P—Q R 3 ; 28. P—Q R 4, K—B 2, Black would have penetrated the hostile position on the King-side still more easily than in the actual game, White's King being doomed to inactivity.

| 26. | ...... | R—Q 1 |
| 27. | R—B 1 | P—Q R 4 ! |

Not 27. P—Kt 3 because of 28. Q Kt 4 !

| 28. | B—R 3 | P—Q Kt 3 |
| 29. | P—K Kt 4 | |

In his turn hoping to block the King-side, after which the draw would be forced ; but Black at once prevents this.

29.	......	K—B 2
30.	P—R 4	P—Kt 3
31.	R—B 1	

Or 31. P—R 5, P × R P ; 32. P × P, R—K Kt 1 ! ; 33. K—Q 5, R—Kt 6 ; 34. K—B 6, R × P ; 35. K × P, R × Q P ; 36. B × P, P—K 5, and Black's passed Pawns win easily.

Position after White's 31st move.

| 31. | ...... | P—R 4 ! |

Compelling the White King to relinquish its dominating position, and consequently to abandon the passive resistance upon which White had built his hopes.

32. P × P ch

Or 32. P—Kt 5, P × P ; 33. P × P, B × P ; 34. P × P ch, K × P ; 35. K × P, P—K R 5 and wins.

| 32. | ...... | K × P |
| 33. | P × P ch | K—B 2 ! |

The point ! After 33. ....K × P ; 34. K—B 5, a win for Black would be very difficult, if not impossible.

34. P—R 6

Or 34. K—B 5, R—K R 1 ; 35. K—Kt 4, K—K 3.

34.	......	K—K 3 !
35.	R—K Kt 1	R—K R 1
36.	R—Kt 6	B—B 1

White resigns.

GAME 85

QUEEN'S GAMBIT DECLINED

| *White :* | *Black :* |
| A. ALEKHIN. | O. CHAJES. |

1.	P—Q 4	Kt—K B 3
2.	P—Q B 4	P—K 3
3.	Kt—K B 3	P—Q 4
4.	Kt—B 3	Q Kt—Q 2

After this move White, apart from the text-move (5. B—Kt 5), could very well have replied 5. P × P, P × P ; 6. B—B 4 !, etc., with an excellent position. This is the reason why 4. ....B—K 2 is considered better.

5. B—Kt 5   B—K 2

After 5. ....P—B 3 ; 6. P—K 3, Q—R 4 ; 7. Kt—Q 2, B—Kt 5 ; 8. Q—B 2, Castles, White, should he wish to avoid the variation played in the game Grünfeld — Bogoljuboff (Mährisch-Ostrau, 1923), namely, 9. B—K 2, P—K 4 ! ; 10. P × P, Kt—K 5 !, could continue simply 9. B × Kt, Kt × B ; 10. B—Q 3, R—Q 1 ; 11. Castles K R, with a slight advantage in position, as played by Johner against Dr. Tarrasch at Trieste, 1923.

6. P—K 3	Castles
7. R—B 1	P—B 3
8. Q—B 2	P—Q R 3 !
9. P—Q R 3	R—K 1
10. P—R 3	

In order to avoid the loss of a
move by 10. B—Q 3, which would
have transposed into a position in
the game Grünfeld—Alekhin which
is perfectly safe for Black (see Game
No. 81) after 10. ....P—R 3 ; 11.
B—R 4.

Position after White's 10th move.

| 10. ...... | P—Kt 4 |

A very interesting idea which may
actually have some future for it.
But its tactical realization here
lacks precision. It is on the 9th
move before 10. P—K R 3, if such
was his intention, that Black
should have played 9. ....P—Kt 4,
for in that case he could have
answered 10. P—B 5 by 10. ....
P—K 4 ; 11. P×P, Kt—Kt 5,
with a very promising game.
On the other hand, should White,
instead of 11. P×K P, open the
Q B P file by 11. P×Q P or 11. P×
Kt P, this would ultimately turn in
Black's favour, White having to
lose two moves to bring his King
into safety.

This example emphasizes once
again the numerous resources
afforded by the defence 8. ....P—
Q R 3 ! in this variation.

11. P—B 5 !

Whereas now Black will not succeed in breaking through in the
centre, and the weakness of his
Q B P will make itself felt sooner or
later. It is, however, without immediate consequences, on account of
the blocked position of the two
adversaries and the difficulties
experienced by White in penetrating
the hostile lines.

| 11. ...... | Kt—R 4 |
| 12. B—K B 4 ! | |

The only logical reply. White
must at all cost retain control of the
square K 5.

12.	Kt × B
13. P × Kt	P—Q R 4
14. B—Q 3	P—Kt 3 !

The best line of defence. Black
guards against the possibility of P—
B 5 and prepares a solid defensive
position.

15. P—K R 4 !

Not with the illusion of a mating
attack, but simply to secure at the
right moment, the opening of the
K R file which will later on become a winning factor for White.

15.	B—B 3
16. P—R 5	Kt—B 1
17. P—K Kt 3	

Quietly strengthening a position
which Black can scarcely modify
appreciably.

| 17. ...... | R—R 2 |
| 18. Kt—Q 1 ! | |

Threatening to post this Knight on K Kt 4. Black's next move is intended to prepare the double advance of the K B P and thus to shut out White's Knight from the coveted square.

18. ......   B—K Kt 2
19. Kt—K 3   P—B 4

If this move has the advantage of further strengthening the Castled position, it does on the other hand leave Black with indifferent chances for the end-game.

20. Q—K 2 !

Preparing to occupy the square K 5 with a White piece.

Position after White's 20th move.

20. ......   P—R 5

This is the only move of Black's in the game which can be criticized, seeing that without apparent reason it abandons the square Q Kt 4 to the adverse Knights.

If Black had not modified the Pawn-position, White's right plan would have been Kt—B 2, K—B 1, Q Kt—K 1, B—Kt 1, Kt—Q 3 and Kt (Q 3)—K 5.

21. Kt—B 2

Now this Knight can at need be brought to K 5 via Q Kt 4 and Q 3, saving time.

21. ......   R (R 2)—K 2
22. K—B 1

In order to render innocuous the threat ....B—Q 2 followed by ....B × P ! and ....P — K 4, should White play, *e.g. :* 22. Kt—Kt 4, Q—B 2.

22. ......   B—B 3
23. Kt—K 5

This move to be sure compromises nothing, but the logical continuation was 23. Kt — Kt 4, followed by B—Kt 1, Kt—Q 3 and Kt (Q 3)—K 5.

Had Black made the correct reply White would have been forced to return to this plan.

23. ......   B × Kt

Better was 23. ....Q—B 2 ! followed by 24. ....B × Kt, forcing White either to recapture the Bishop with the Queen, which would have led to an exchange of Queens, or else to recapture it with one of the Pawns ; in both cases his chances of winning would have been reduced to vanishing point.

In these circumstances White would have withdrawn his Knight to K B 3, intending to carry out in perfect safety the manœuvre sketched above.

24. Q × B

This exchange, provoking the weakening of the Black squares in the hostile position, yields White new winning chances.

24. ......   Q—B 2
25. Q—B 6 !

An excellent manœuvre intended to create a new weakness at the adversary's K R 2.

25. ......   R—B 2
26. Q—R 4   Q—K 2

Position after Black's 26th move.

27. P×P !

The right moment for this exchange has come at last, for Black cannot recapture with the Pawn, which would allow him to oppose his Rooks on the K R file.

Now White has a strategic advantage sufficient for victory, but its tactical realization is far from easy.

27. ......   Kt×P
28. Q—R 5 !

White must avoid every exchange which would simplify Black's defence.

28. ......   Q—B 3
29. B—K 2

White's following moves are intended to reduce to a minimum the mobility of the Black pieces, in order to undertake a long range manœuvre with his King.

29. ......   R—K Kt 2
30. Q—B 3   Kt—B 1
31. Q—K 3   R (K 1)—K 2
32. Kt—Kt 4   B—Q 2

Position after Black's 32nd move.

33. B—R 5 !

This move leads to a curious position in which Black's Queen, both Rooks and the Bishop are immobilized.

The problem still requires to be solved, for at present the doubling and even the trebling of the White pieces on the K R file would lead to nothing.

The rather complicated plan which White will strive to pursue, which must, of course, be modified in accordance with his adversary's manœuvres, can be summarized as follows :

1st phase.—Bringing the King to the centre where, after the subsequent exchange of Queens and Rooks on the K R file, it will threaten a rapid penetration of the hostile camp via Q R 5.

These tactics will logically induce a corresponding displacement of the Black King, the more plausible since its presence in the centre will consolidate the weak points Q B 3 and K 3.

2nd phase.—Compelling the Black pieces to remove themselves in succession from the King-side, by the tactical threats aimed either at the King himself or at the adverse Pawns (39th and 41st moves).

The prospect of the occupation of the square K 5 by a White Knight, thereby immobilizing the Black Knight at Q 2, increases still more the difficulty of concerted action by the Black pieces, which is already difficult enough on account of the limited space available to them.

3rd phase.—Finally, at an opportune moment, namely, when the Black pieces are at their greatest distance from the King-side, doubling the Rooks on the K R file. The Rooks, after the forced exchange of Queens and Bishops, will penetrate into the heart of the hostile position.

As we shall see by the sequel, the execution of this strategic plan requires not less than twenty-eight moves !

| 33. ...... | Kt—Kt 3 |
| 34. Kt—Q 3 | |

Not at once 34. K—K 2, on account of 34. ....P—K 4 !

34.	B—K 1
35. K—K 2	K—B 1
36. K—Q 2	R—Kt 2

Making way for the King.

37. B—B 3	K—K 2
38. K R—K 1	Kt—B 1
39. Kt—Kt 4	

Threatening 40. B × P, etc.

39.	K—Q 1
40. K—Q 3	R (K Kt 2)— K 2
41. Q—Q 2 !	

Threatening, after 42. Kt—R 6 !, the entry of the Queen at Q R 5.

| 41. ...... | R—R 2 |
| 42. R—K R 1 | R (K 2)—Q B 2 |

In order to utilize the Bishop for the defence of the K R P when the Knight abandons it to guard the square K 4.

| 43. R—R 2 | B—Kt 3 |
| 44. Q—K 3 | K—B 1 |

Black, in order to make his Rooks available for the defence of the King-side, proposes to defend his Q B P with his King, but this manœuvre demands far too much time, and White is now ready for the assault.

45. Q R—K R 1	K—Kt 2
46. K—Q 2	R—K 2
47. Kt—Q 3	Kt—Q 2
48. B—R 5 !	

By this exchange of Black's best piece for the defence of his weak points, White takes an important step forward.

| 48. ...... | R—R 1 |
| 49. B × B | P × B |

After 49. ....Q × B his K R P would later on prove difficult to defend.

| 50. R—R 7 | R (R 1)—K 1 |

For the moment Black's defence is still adequate, but White's next move discloses the difficulties of the hostile position.

Position after Black's 50th move.

51. Kt—K 5 !

The point of this move rests in the fact that for the first time in this game White can profitably consider the *recapture at K 5 with a Pawn*.

In fact, if 51. ....Kt×Kt ; 52. B P×Kt, Q—B 1 ; 53. Q—Kt 5 ! and White wins the K Kt P to start with.

Black's reply is therefore forced.

| 51. ...... | Kt—B 1 |
| 52. R—R 8 ! | |

Now the position demands exchange of Queens and not of Rooks.

| 52. ...... | R—Kt 2 |
| 53. Kt—B 3 ! | R—Q Kt 1 |

To secure freedom of movement for the Knight, in case of need.

| 54. Kt—Kt 5 | R—K 2 |

Black is defenceless against White's next move.

| 55. Q—K 5 ! | |

After the compulsory exchange of Queens, the doubling of the Rooks on the eighth rank will be decisive.

55.	Q×Q
56. B P×Q	K—R 1
57. R—Kt 8	P—Kt 5

In the hope of obtaining some last chance after R P×P, R (K 2)—Kt 2.

58. R (R 1)—R 8 !	R (K 2)—K 1
59. P×P	K—R 2
60. K—B 3	K—R 3
61. Kt—B 7 !	

More energetic than the plausible move 60. Kt×P. White now goes straight for mate.

61.	R—R 1
62. Kt—Q 6	R (K 1)—Kt 1
63. R—R 1 !	Kt—Q 2
64. R—R 1 ! !	Black resigns.

Final Position.

GAME 86

QUEEN'S PAWN GAME

| *White :* | *Black :* |
| A. ALEKHIN. | SIR G. A. THOMAS. |

1. P—Q 4	Kt—K B 3
2. P—Q B 4	P—Q 3
3. Kt—K B 3	P—K Kt 3

This old defence is at present very fashionable in England. The two English champions, F. D. Yates and Sir George Thomas, have shown a predilection for it, justified by numerous successes.

4. P—K Kt 3	B—Kt 2
5. B—Kt 2	Castles
6. Castles	Kt—B 3

This move, suggested by Burn in place of 6. ....Q Kt—Q 2, adopted up till then, is aimed at forcing White to disclose his intentions in the centre as soon as possible.

Nevertheless, it does not seem sufficient to equalize.

| 7. P—Q 5 | |

The most energetic and also the best continuation.

The defeat inflicted on me by Yates, in particularly sparkling style, during a previous round of the same tournament, did not in the least shake my opinion as to the value of this move, seeing that I lost an advantage in position which had been already acquired, solely on account of several tactical errors.

7.	Kt—Kt 1
8. Kt—B 3	P—K 4

This apparently plausible move is certainly not best, for it allows White to open up the game by an exchange in the centre, and thus to profit by his superior development. More in accordance with the spirit of the opening was 8. .... P—Q R 4, followed by 9. .... Q Kt—Q 2 or Kt—R 3 and 10. .... Kt—B 4, as played by Yates in an analogous position in the game cited.

9. P×P e. p. !

This frees Black's game only in appearance, for if he retakes with the Bishop, White replies 10. Kt—Q 4 ! with marked advantage ; and if he retakes with the Pawn he will sooner or later be forced to play P—K 4, to free his Q B, which will weaken the square Q 4 and will give White distinct chances in the centre and on the Queen's wing.

9.	P × P
10. B—Kt 5	

In order to exchange Bishops by 11. Q—Q 2 and B—R 6, or else to provoke the reply 10. ....P—K R 3. In both cases the position of Black's King is weakened.

10.	Kt—B 3
11. Q—Q 2	Q—K 1
12. Q R—Q 1	

In order to meet 12. ....B—Q 2 with 13. P—B 5 !

12.	R—Kt 1
13. B—R 6	Q—B 2
14. B × B	Q × B

Position after Black's 14th move.

15. Kt—K Kt 5 !

A very strong position for this Knight, which cannot be dislodged without compromising the position of Black's King.

In addition, this move will be the prelude to an offensive in the centre, commencing with P—K B 4, which will bring about a contact of the Pawns, Black's reply P—K 4 being practically forced.

15.	P—K 4
16. Kt—Q 5	Kt—Q 5

In order to provoke P—K 3 and thus to develop his Q B with the gain of a move.

17. P—K 3   Kt—B 3

After 17. ....Kt—K 3 the reply 18. P—B 4 ! would have been still stronger, e.g. : 17. ....Kt—K 3 ; 18. P—B 4 !, Kt×Kt (Kt 4) ; 19. P×Kt, Kt×Kt ; 20. B×Kt ch, K—R 1 ; 21. R×R ch, Q×R ; 22. R—K B 1 and White has a winning position.

18. P—B 4 !	B—Kt 5
19. Q R—K 1	Q R—K 1
20. P—Q Kt 4 !	

With the object of dislodging the adverse Q Kt, in order to give White's K B its maximum efficiency.

20. ......   P—K R 3

To defend his Queen-side successfully Black has nothing better than
to expel the White pieces from their
threatening positions.

21. Kt×Kt ch   R×Kt
22. Kt—K 4   R (B 3)—B 1
23. P—Kt 5   Kt—Q 1
24. P—B 5 !

Much better than attempting to
win a Pawn by 25. Q—R 5, which
would have yielded Black sufficient
counter-chances, *e.g.*: 24. ....P×P;
25. Kt P×P, B—B 4; 26. Kt
—B 2, B—K 3 !

24. ......   Q P×P
25. Kt×P   B—B 1
26. P—Q R 4

White now exercises strong pressure on the Queen-side, for which
Black has no compensation.
Nevertheless, had he on the next
move played 26. ....K—R 2 he
would have propounded a problem
of great difficulty for his opponent,
whereas against his actual reply
White can undertake a forcible
offensive.

26. ......   P—B 3
27. Q—Q 6 !

This entry of White's Queen
is very dangerous. White now
threatens 28. Q—Kt 8 !

27. ......   P—Kt 3
28. Kt—K 4 !   K P×P

There is no longer any good move.
28. ....B P×P or 28. ....P—
B 4, indicated by many annotators
with surprising unanimity, would
lead to an immeditae catastrophe
after 29. P×K P ! threatening 30.
Kt—B 6 ch.

29. P×Q B P !

This Pawn, defended by the K B,
will decide the game in White's
favour.

29. ......   R—K 3
30. Q—Q 5

Threatening 31. B—R 3.

30. ......   K—R 2

Position after Black's 30th move.

31. Kt—Q 6 !

The winning move, of which the
consequences, in the leading variation, had to be analysed twelve and
fifteen moves ahead.

31. ......   B—R 3 !

The reply creating most difficulty
for White.
If 31. ....Q—Q B 2, then simply
32. R—Q 1 ! retaining the passed
Pawn, with a winning position.

32. R×P   R×R
33. Kt P×R

See Diagram.

33. ......   Q—K 2

As in Game No. 66, my opponent
facilitated my task, and rendered
superfluous my detailed analysis,
which had taken more than half-an-
hour.
The principal variation considered by me was the following :
33. ....Q—B 6 !; 34. R—Q 1 !,
R×P ! (if 34. ....Q×P ch ; 35.

Position after White's 33rd move.

K—R 1 and wins) ; 35. Q—Q 2 !, Q × Q (if 35. ....Q—B 4 ; 36. Q— K B 2) ; 36. R × Q, R—Q B 6 ; 37.

Kt—K 4 !, R—B 8 ch ; 38. K—B 2, Kt × P ; 39. R—Q 7 ch, K—Kt 1 ! ; 40. Kt—B 6 ch, K—B 1 ; 41. B—Q 5, Kt—K 2 ; 42. R—Q 8 ch, K—Kt 2 ; 43. Kt—K 8 ch, K—R 2 ; 44. R—Q 7, R—B 7 ch ; 45. K—B 3, R—K 7 ; 46. B—K 4 and White wins a piece and the game.

34. R—Q 1	R × P
35. Kt—K 4 !	Kt—K 3
36. Q—K 5 !	

Winning at least the Exchange.

36.	R—Q 6
37. R × R	B × R
38. Kt—B 6 ch	K—R 1
39. Kt—Q 5 ch	Q—Kt 2
40. Q × Kt	Black resigns.

CHAPTER XXII

MAJOR OPEN TOURNAMENT AT PORTSMOUTH
AUGUST, 1923

GAME 87

QUEEN'S GAMBIT DECLINED

White :	Black :
A. ALEKHIN.	DR. A. VAJDA.

1.	P—Q 4		Kt—K B 3
2.	P—Q B 4		P—K 3
3.	Kt—K B 3		P—Q 4
4.	Kt—B 3		B—K 2
5.	B—Kt 5		Q Kt—Q 2
6.	P—K 3		Castles
7.	R—B 1		P—B 3
8.	B—Q 3		P × P
9.	B × P		Kt—Q 4
10.	Kt—K 4		

10. B × B, Q × B ; 11. Castles does not yield White any advantage and also 10. B—B 4, tried by me against Selesnieff in the Pistyan Tournament of 1922 (see Game No. 54) is scarcely any better ; I therefore hoped to secure an advantage with the text-move.

But although in the present game the result was favourable to me, because of the tame reply of my opponent, later analysis has convinced me that 10. Kt—K 4 allows Black sufficient chances.

10. ......   P—K R 3

After this move White, without running any risks, attains his object,

which is to conserve at least temporarily three minor pieces, an important consideration on account of his opponent's cramped position.

The correct continuation was : 10. ....Q—R 4 ch ; 11. K—B 1 ! (if 11. K—K 2 the ensuing variation is even stronger), 11. ....P—B 3 ! ; 12. B—R 4, Kt (Q 2)—Kt 3 ; 13. B—Kt 3, Kt—Kt 5 ! and Black has the initiative.

This is the reason why 10. Kt—K 4 is hardly commendable. It is, however, playable after 10. B × B, Q × B (not 10. ....Kt × Kt ; 11. B × Q, Kt × Q ; 12. B—K 7, R—K 1 ; 13. B—R 3 and wins). 11. Kt—K 4, Q—Kt 5 ch ; 12. Q—Q 2, Q × Q ch ; 13. K × Q, and White's game is, of course, preferable. (Compare Alekhin—Treybal, Baden-Baden, 1925).

It cannot be denied, however, that the exchange of Queens in this variation increases Black's chances of drawing.

11.	B × B	Q × B
12.	Castles	P—Q Kt 3
13.	Kt—Kt 3	

Preparing P—K 4 later on.

13. ......   R—Q 1

Position after Black's 13th move.

14. B × Kt

Yielding to the influence of certain critics who have maintained that I seek complications " at all costs," to the detriment of clear and simple solutions, I was here the victim of deliberate simplification. But the exaggeration of this quality is not always favourable, for the advantage secured by White after the text-move, thanks to the control of the Q B file, would have been insufficient for victory against an absolutely correct defence.

On the contrary, the continuation 14. P—K 4, Kt (Q 4)—B 3 (or 14. ....Kt—B 5 ; 15. Q—Q 2) ; 15. R—K 1 threatening later P—Q 5, or also 15. P—K 5 followed by Kt—K 4—Q 6, would have afforded more favourable although less definite prospects than those in the actual game.

The choice between the two variations is above all a question of style and I ought to have dropped a half-point through not following my natural inclination on this occasion.

14. ...... B P × B
15. Q—R 4 !

Preventing 15. ....B—R 3, and threatening 16. R—B 7, which would not have been effective on the 15th move because of 15. .... Q—Q 3.

15. ...... Kt—B 1
16. Kt—K 5 B—Kt 2
17. R—B 3 P—B 3

This slight weakening of the Castled position was inevitable, as the White Knight was in a dominating position on K 5 ; but Black's position is solid enough to stand this weakness.

18. Kt—Q 3 Q—Q 2

In order to oppose his Rooks on the open Q B file, which would enable him to equalize if accomplished without inconvenience.

19. Q—R 3 B—B 3
20. K R—B 1 K R—B 1
21. P—R 3 !

Absolutely essential, as will be seen later.

21. ...... B—Kt 4
22. Kt—B 4

Threatening to win the Q R P after all the Rooks are exchanged.

22. ...... P—Q R 4

It is curious that this plausible move leads to the inevitable loss of the game. 22. P—K 4 would also be bad, because of 23. Kt × P !, etc.

On the other hand, 22. ....R × R ; 23. Q × R, B—R 3 !, or 23. R × R, P—K 4, would have yielded Black a satisfactory defence, temporarily at least.

23. R × R ! R × R
24. R × R Q × R
25. Q—Q 6 !

The White Queen enters the adverse game with decisive effect.

Black is unable to dislodge it, his mobility being restricted by the necessity of defending his weak K P and Q Kt P.

25. ......   B—B 3

Or 25. ....Q—B 3; 26. Q—Q 8, etc.

Position after Black's 25th move.

26. Kt (Kt 3)—R 5 !

An unexpected mating-attack commencing 27. Kt × Kt P !, K × Kt; 28. Q—K 7 ch, K moves; 29. Kt—R 5 and wins.

As a direct result of this move the White Queen will occupy the square Q Kt 8, which his opponent will be compelled to yield to him; and as an indirect result Black must advance his Q Kt P, which abandons the square Q B 5 to the White Knights.

26. ......   Q—Q 2
27. Q—Kt 8   P—Q Kt 4

If 27. ....Q—Kt 2, then 28. Q—Q 8, K—B 2; 29. P—K Kt 4 threatening 30. P—K R 4 and 31. P—Kt 5, with a strong attack.

28. P—Kt 4 !

Not at once 28. Kt—Q 3 because of the possible reply 28. ....Q—K 1.

28. ......   K—B 2
29. Kt—Q 3

Threatening to win a Pawn by 29. Kt—B 5, Q—K 2; 30. Q—Kt 6, etc.

29. ......   P—R 5
30. Kt—B 5   Q—K 2
31. Q—Kt 6   B—K 1

Black's pieces are clustered round his King like a flock of sheep round the ram before the tempest !

32. Kt—B 4 !

The second White Knight takes the same road as the first in order to enter the adverse position by the open breach on the Queen-side (Q B 5).

32. ......   P—Kt 4

A despairing manœuvre.

33. Kt (B 4)—Q 3   P—R 4
34. Kt—Kt 7   P × P
35. P × P   K—Kt 2
36. Kt (Q 3)—B 5 !

White reserves the option of winning a Pawn by Kt—Q 6, a threat which Black cannot evade and which is made still more definite by the text-move.

36. ......   P—K 4
37. Kt—Q 6   B—Kt 3
38. Kt × Kt P   Kt—Q 2
39. Q—B 7   B—K 1
40. Kt—Q 6   K—B 1
41. Kt—B 5   Q—R 2

Or 41. ....Q—B 2; 42. Q—Q 6 ch and 43. Kt—R 6 ch wins the Queen.

42. Kt—K 6 ch   K—B 2
43. Q—Q 8 !   Black resigns.

Final Position.

GAME 88

QUEEN'S GAMBIT DECLINED

White :	Black :
A. ALEKHIN.	A. WEST.

1.	P—Q 4	Kt—K B 3
2.	P—Q B 4	P—K 3
3.	Kt—K B 3	P—Q 4
4.	Kt—B 3	B—K 2
5.	B—Kt 5	Q Kt—Q 2
6.	P—K 3	Castles
7.	R—B 1	P—B 3
8.	B—Q 3	R—K 1

Black lets slip the opportunity of playing 8. ....P×P followed by 9. ....Kt—Q 4 before White has Castled, for after the text-move he will not succeed in freeing himself by ....P—K 4.

The move R—K 1 is only to be considered before White's K B has moved, *e.g.* if White should play 8. Q—B 2.

9.	Castles	P×P
10.	B×P	Kt—Q 4
11.	Kt—K 4 !	

A very natural move. As he has already Castled, White need not fear the variation ....Q—R 4 ch ; K—K 2 or B 1.

11.	......	B×B
12.	Kt (B 3)×B	Kt (Q 2)—B 3

If 12. ....P—K B 4 ; 13. Q—R 5 !, P—K R 3 ; 14. Q—B 7 ch, K—R 1 ; 15. Kt—Q 6, R—K 2 ; 16. Kt×B P !

13. Kt—Kt 3 !

When possessing greater freedom of movement than the opponent—and this is the case for White here—*it is good strategy to retain the greatest possible number of pieces on the board, in order to reap the greatest profit from this freedom.*

13.	......	P—K R 3
14.	Kt—B 3	Kt—Kt 3
15.	B—Kt 3	Kt (Kt 3)—Q 2

Black wishes to enforce the move ....P—K 4 all the same, but, as we shall see, it is much too late !

In an exhibition game played at Paris in February, 1922, Znosko-Borovski adopted 15. ....B—Q 2 against me, but also without satisfactory results.

Here is the continuation of that game :—

16. Kt—K 5, Q—K 2 ; 17. P—B 4, Q R—B 1 ; 18. Q—B 3, R—B 2 ; 19. Kt—K 2 !, B—B 1 ; 20. Kt—Q 3, Kt (Kt 3)—Q 2 ; 21. Kt—B 3, and White threatens a strong King-side attack commencing P—K Kt 4, etc.

16. P—K 4

White not only does not attempt to prevent the following reply by 17. P—K R 3, but on the contrary, having recognized its futility, he seeks to provoke it.

16.	......	P—K 4

Facilitating his opponent's task, although in any case White's game was won strategically.

17. P×P   Kt—Kt 5
18. P—K 6 !

Simplest. The Black Pawn at K 3 is a fresh stumbling-block in the way of Black's already laborious development.

18. ......   P×P
19. Kt—Q 4   Kt (Q 2)—K 4
20. P—K R 3   Kt—B 3
21. P—B 4   Kt—B 2

Position after Black's 21st move.

K—R 1

This and the next move, incomprehensible at first sight, form the necessary preparation for the decisive attack. They arise from the following reasoning :

(1) White must win the game if he can attain the formation: Kt at K R 5 and Q at K Kt 4. But this plan is at present impracticable, for the opponent, after 22. P—K 5, Kt—Q 4, threatens Kt—K 6.

(2) On the other hand the White Queen when played would no longer defend the Knight on Q 4, which Black would threaten to capture with a check.

Therefore the text-move avoids this latter contingency, and the next move prevents the threat of the Black Knight (Kt—K 6).

After this explanation the final manœuvre reveals itself without difficulty.

22. ......   P—Q R 4

Hopeless, like every other move.

23. R—Q B 3 !   Q—Kt 3
24. P—K 5   Kt—Q 4
25. Kt—R 5 !

The point of the decisive manœuvre. If 25. ....Kt×R ; 26. Q—Kt 4, P—Kt 4 ; 27. Kt—B 6 ch, K—B 1 ; 28. P×Kt and White wins.

25. ......   R—K 2
26. R—Kt 3   Kt—R 1
27. Q—Q 3

Threatening 28. B—B 2 or B×Kt, against which Black is defenceless.

27. ......   Q—B 2

Position after Black's 27th move.

28. B×Kt !

Falling under the spell of a beautiful variation in mind, I was tempted to continue here by 28. B—Q 1, Kt—Kt 5 ; 29. Q—R 7 ch ! !, K×Q ; 30. R×P ch !, R×R ; 31. Kt—B 6 ch, K—Kt 3 ; 32. B—R 5 mate.

But as, first, the move 28. ....
Kt—Kt 5 is not at all forced, and
moreover, the text-move equally
leads to mate, I decided in favour
of a forced and logical continuation.

28. ......   K P×B
29. Kt—B 6 ch

If now 29. ....K—B 1 ; 30. Q—
R 7, or if 29. ..K—B 2; 30. R × P ch,
and mates in two moves.

Black resigns.

GAME 89

IRREGULAR OPENING

White :   *Black :*
A. ALEKHIN.   J. A. J. DREWITT.

1. Kt—K B 3   P—Q 4
2. P—Q Kt 4

An innovation of the Hyper-
modern School (Réti, Bogoljuboff,
Grünfeld, Sämisch), which has a
predilection (at times carried to
excess) for the development of the
Bishops on the long diagonals.
The move 2. P—Q Kt 4 is intended to establish a fianchetto in
an enlarged form. Should Black, as
in the present game, reply with
P—Q B 4, White can secure the
majority of Pawns in the centre by
3. P × P. This is of far greater
moment than the majority of
Pawns on the Queen-side, of which
so much is made, although it only
offers very problematical chances
for the end-game.

2. ......   P—K 3
3. B—Kt 2   Kt—K B 3
4. P—Q R 3   P—B 4
5. P × P   B × P
6. P—K 3   Castles
7. P—B 4   Kt—B 3
8. P—Q 4   B—Kt 3

8. ....B—Q 3 seems more plausible, although in this case also
White obtains a very good game by
9. Q Kt—Q 2, R—K 1 ; 10. P—
B 5, B—B 2 ; 11. B—Kt 5 !

9. Q Kt—Q 2   Q—K 2
10. B—Q 3   R—Q 1

If 10. ....B—B 2, preparing
....P—K 4, White has the choice
between the complications resulting
from 11. Kt—K 5 and the simpler
move 11. P—K 4.

11. Castles   B—Q 2
12. Kt—K 5 !

Taking advantage of the fact that
the best square of retreat for Black's
K Kt will be occupied by his Q B
(after 12. .....Kt × Kt ; 13. P × Kt).

12. ......   B—K 1
13. P—B 4   Q R—B 1
14. Q R—B 1   Kt—Q 2

This move will allow White to
obtain a decisive advantage. Black,
threatened on every side, has
already no adequate plan of defence.

Position after Black's 14th move.

15. Kt × Kt (B 6) !

By this unexpected exchange of
his best placed piece White takes
immediate advantage of the
cramped position of Black's piece.

15. ......   R × Kt

If 15. ....P × Kt, then 16. P—
B 5, B—R 4 (or 16. ....B—B 2 ;
17. Q—R 4) ; 17. Kt—Kt 3, B—
B 2 ; 18. B—B 3, R—Kt 1 ; 19.
Kt—R 5, Kt—B. 1 ; 20. Q—R 4,
and the exploitation of White's
strategic advantage on the Queen-
side is merely a question of technique.

Black by the text-move prepares
a sacrifice of the Knight which at
first sight seems not devoid of
chances.

16. P—B 5   Kt × P

Practically forced, for if 16. ....
B—R 4 then 17. Kt—Kt 3, B—B 2 ;
18. B—Kt 5 winning the Exchange.

17. P × Kt   B × P

Black has secured two Pawns for
the piece and appears certain to
capture yet another Pawn, but
White speedily concludes the game
by the following sacrifice, which is
the point of the 15th move, Kt ×
Kt (B 6).

18. R—K B 3 !   B × P
19. R × R   B × R

See Diagram.

20. B × P ch !

This sacrifice of both Bishops has
its precedents in the games Lasker—
Bauer, Amsterdam, 1889, and

Position after Black's 19th move.

Niemzovitch—Tarrasch, St. Petersburg, 1914.

In the present game its interest
rests solely in the way in which
White has masked his plan of attack
up to the last moment, by occupying his opponent with a demonstration on the opposite wing.

20. ......   K × B
21. R—R 3 ch   K—Kt 1
22. B × P !

If now 22. ....P—B 3 White
would not be satisfied to win the
Queen for Rook and Bishop, but
would play :

23. B—R 6 !, Q—R 2 ; 24. Q—
R 5, B—B 1 ; 25. Q—Kt 4 ch, B—
Kt 2 ; 26. B × B and White wins.

Black resigns.

CHAPTER XXIII

EXHIBITION GAMES AND SIMULTANEOUS GAMES

GAME 90

KING'S GAMBIT DECLINED
(by transposition of moves)

The second of a series of match-games* played at Berlin, June, 1921.

White :	Black :
A. ALEKHIN.	R. TEICHMANN.

1. P—K 4	P—K 4
2. Kt—Q B 3	Kt—Q B 3

As we have already mentioned, the best move is 2. ....Kt—K B 3 followed, if 3. B—B 4, by 3. .... Kt × P !

3. B—B 4	Kt—B 3
4. P—Q 3	B—B 4
5. P—B 4	P—Q 3
6. Kt—B 3	

By transposition of moves White has led into a safe and very promising position in the King's Gambit Declined.

6. ...... B—Kt 5

Stronger was 6. ....B—K 3 and if 7. B—Kt 5, then 7. ....P—Q R 3; 8. B × Kt ch, P × B; 9. Q—K 2, P × P!, with approximate equality

* Result : 2 wins, 2 draws, 2 losses.

(Spielmann—Dr. Tarrasch, Pistyan, 1922).
After the text-move White obtains a slight advantage in position.

7. Kt—Q R 4

The only correct move.
On the other hand, the old move 7. P—K R 3 is inadequate, on account of 7. ....B × Kt; 8. Q × B, P × P ! (but not 8. ....Kt—Q 5; 9. Q—Kt 3 !, Q—K 2 !; 10. P × P, P × P ; 11. K—Q 1 with the better game); 9. Q × P (if 9. B × P, Kt—Q 5 !; 10. Q—Kt 3, Kt—R 4), Kt—K 4, and White, in view of the threat 10. ....Kt—R 4, has no way to avoid the exchange of his K B, after which Black has emerged from all the difficulties of the opening.

7. ...... P—Q R 3

Hardly customary, and certainly not best. His opponent's previous move clearly showed his intention to eliminate the Q B, and it was therefore futile to force him to do that.

An interesting variation, which is, however, advantageous for White, was 7. ....B × Kt; 8. Q × B, Kt—Q 5 ; 9. Q—Q 1, P—Q Kt 4; 10. B × P ch, K × B ; 11. Kt × B,

239

P × Kt ; 12. P × P followed by 13.
Castles ch, and White would have
formidable attacking chances, apart
from the two Pawns for the sacrificed piece.

In a game Alekhin—O. Tenner
(a Berlin amateur), played at
Cologne in 1907, the latter con-
tinued 7. ....P × P ; 8. Kt × B,
P × Kt ; 9. B × P, Kt—K R 4 ; 10.
B—K 3, Kt—K 4 ? ; 11. Kt × Kt,
B × Q ; 12. B × P ch, K—K 2 ; 13.
B × P ch, K—B 3 ; 14. Castles ch,
K × Kt ; 15. R—B 5 mate.

Comparatively best was 7. ....
B—Kt 3 or 7. ....Castles.

8. Kt × B	P × Kt
9. Castles	Q—K 2
10. P—K R 3	

Securing the advantage of two
Bishops against two Knights.

10.	B × Kt
11. Q × B	Castles K R
12. B—K 3	P × P
13. Q × P	Kt—K 4
14. B—Kt 3	Q R—K 1

Further loss of time, which
seriously compromises Black's game.
The following was equally disadvantageous : 14. ....P—B 5 ; 15. P × P,
Kt—Kt 3 ; 16. Q—Kt 5 !, Q × P ;
17. Q R—K 1 with the better
game.

On the other hand 14. ....Q R—
Q 1 would clearly have been better,
as it would make the advance of
White's centre Pawns more difficult.

15. Q—B 2 !

With the double threat 16. B × P
and 16. B—Kt 5.

15.	Kt (B 3)—Q 2
16. Q R—Q 1	P—Q Kt 3
17. P—B 3	

Preparing 18. P—Q 4, against
which there is no defence. The loss
of the present game by Black can
be attributed to the fact that his
Knights lack bases in the centre,

and that in positions of this
character the possession of the
two Bishops constitutes a decisive
advantage for the opponent.

17. ......   Kt—Kt 3

Position after Black's 17th move.

18. Q—B 5 !

The first move of a new regroup-
ing, the completion of which will
give White a won-game. White's
Q B is to be posted on K Kt 3,
whence it will exercise pressure on
Black's Pawn at his Q B 2, which
will be weakened still more by the
imminent opening of the Q B file
after White's P—Q 4.

Throughout the execution of this
plan Black will find himself reduced
to absolute passivity.

18.	K—R 1
19. B—K B 2 !	R—Q 1
20. B—Kt 3	Kt (Q 2)—K 4
21. P—Q 4	P × P
22. P × P	Kt—B 3
23. P—Q 5	Kt (B 3)—K 4
24. P—K R 4 !	

This threat to win a piece compels Black to weaken his position
still more, thus enabling White's
Rook to break through into his
game.

24. ...... Q—B 4 ch
25. K—R 2

Not 25. B—B 2 on account of 25. ....Q—Q 3.

25. ...... P—B 3

Evidently forced.

26. R—B 1 Q—Q 3
27. R—B 6 Q—K 2

If 27. ....Q—Q 2 ; 28. Q×Q, R×Q ; 29. P—R 5, Kt—Kt 5 ch ; 30. K—R 3, Kt (Kt 3)—K 4 ; 31. K R—B 1 ! and wins.

28. R—K 6 ! Q—Q 2
29. P—R 5 Kt—K 2
30. Q—R 3 Kt—B 2

Again forced, because of the double threat 31. B×Kt and 31. P—R 6.

31. B—K B 4 P—R 3
32. Q—Q B 3 ! Kt—Q 3

Allowing a decisive sacrifice. 32. ....R—B 1 was a little better, upon which White would have continued his winning attack by 33. Q—Kt 4 and 34. B—R 4.

Position after Black's 32nd move.

33. B×P !

Putting an end to all resistance, for if 33. ....P×B ; 34. R (B 1) ×P, K—Kt 1 ; 35. Q—Kt 3 ch and mates in a few moves.

33. ...... Kt×K P

A desperate move.

34. R×Kt Kt×P
35. Q—B 1 !

If now 35. ....P×B ; 36. B×Kt, Q×B ; 37. Q×P ch, K—Kt 1 ; 38. R—Kt 4 ch, K—B 2 ; 39. Q×P ch and wins.

Black resigns.

GAME 91

RUY LOPEZ

Fourth of a series of match-games played at Berlin, June, 1921.

White :	*Black :*
A. ALEKHIN.	R. TEICHMANN.
1. P—K 4	P—K 4
2. Kt—K B 3	Kt—Q B 3
3. B—Kt 5	P—Q R 3
4. B—R 4	Kt—B 3
5. Castles	Kt×P
6. P—Q 4	P—Q Kt 4
7. B—Kt 3	P—Q 4
8. P×P	B—K 3
9. P—B 3	B—K 2
10. B—K 3 !	Castles
11. Q Kt—Q 2	B—K Kt 5

This line of defence is inadequate, on account of White's following manœuvre, invented by the Dutch amateur, Van Gelder.

11. ....Kt×Kt and 12. .... Kt—R 4 is preferable. On the other hand, 11. ....P—K B 4 is not advisable, by reason of 12. P×P e. p., Kt×P (B 3) ; 13. Kt—Kt 5 !, B—K B 4 ; 14. Kt (Q 2)—K 4 !, with advantage to White.

| 12. Kt×Kt | P×Kt |
| 13. Q—Q 5 ! | Q×Q |

If 13. ....P×Kt ; 14. Q×Kt, P×P ; 15. Q×K Kt P, Q—Q 2 ; 16. Q—Kt 3 and White has excellent prospects of attack on the open K Kt file.

After the present exchange of Queens, White's game remains a little superior, thanks to the weakness of the hostile Queen-side.

14. B×Q   P×Kt
15. B×Kt   P×P
16. K×P   Q R—Q 1
17. P—Q R 4 !

As soon as White succeeds in playing this move without immediate inconvenience in this variation of the Lopez, he obtains the advantage.

17. ......   P—B 3 !

Black rightly prefers to attempt a counter-attack, based on the somewhat exposed situation of White's King, rather than a laborious and unpromising defence by 17. ....B—Q 2.

18. R P×P

Naturally not 18. P×B P, R×P ; 19. P×P, P×P ; 20. B×P, R—K Kt 3 !

18. ......   R P×P
19. B×P   P×P
20. B—B 4 ch

With the double aim of :

(1) Removing Black's King from the centre, with a view to the end-game.

(2) Preventing Black's Q B from withdrawing to K 3.

20. ......   K—R 1
21. P—B 3   B—R 4
22. R—R 5

By this move, which incidentally attacks Black's K P, White in reality intends to consolidate the position of his King by B—Q 5 and B—K 4, and later on to make use of his majority of Pawns on the Queen-side.

To thwart this scheme Black discovers an ingenious resource which is nevertheless insufficient to equalize the game.

22. ......   R—Q 8 !

Apparently as discreet as it is elegant, since it is difficult to foresee how White, with the little material left to him, can secure the victory in the end-game, against equal forces.

Position after Black's 22nd move.

23. B—Q 5 !

The only way to maintain the advantage, because the capture of the K P would lead only to a draw : 23. R×P, R×R ; 24. K×R, R× P ch ; 25. B—B 2, B—R 5 ; 26. R×B, R×B ch ; 27. K—Kt 1, R—B 5.

23. ......   R×R
24. K×R   B×P
25. B×B   R×B ch
26. K—K 2   R—B 1
27. K—Q 3 !

The first move of a strategic winning plan—White, instead of capturing the hostile K P, prefers to immobilize it and to make use of it to limit the range of action of Black's K B, after which the advance of his Queen-side Pawns will decide the game in White's favour.

27. ...... K—Kt 1

If Black had recognized in time his opponent's intentions, and the dangers to which he is exposed, it is probable that he would immediately have rid himself of the embarrassing Pawn by 27. ....P—K 5 ch !, which would have afforded him some drawing chances.

28. K—K 4 ! R—Kt 1

After this useless move Black's game becomes hopeless. But even the best move would in the end be shown up as inadequate, for example : 28. ....R—B 8 ; 29. K—Q 5 (not 29. R—R 7, R—K 8, threatening 30. ....R × B ch), K—B 2 ; 30. R—R 7.

29. P—Kt 4 K—B 2
30. P—Kt 5

The advance of the Pawns now becomes irresistible.

30. ...... K—K 3
31. P—B 4 K—Q 2
32. R—R 7 B—Q 3

In the vain hope of sacrificing the Bishop for two Pawns, after 33. P—B 5.

33. K—Q 5 !

Preparing the next move which, if played at once, would not be so strong on account of the reply : 33. ....K—B 3.

33. ...... P—K 5

Too late !

Position after Black's 33rd move.

34. P—Kt 6 !

Decisive, for if 34. ....B × P ; 35. P—B 5, K—B 1 ; 36. K—B 6, P × P ; 37. R × P ! and wins.

34. ...... R—K B 1
35. P—B 5 R—B 4 ch
36. K—B 4 Black resigns

GAME 92

ENGLISH OPENING

Exhibition Game played at Berlin, July, 1921.

White :	*Black :*
A. ALEKHIN.	F. SÄMISCH.

1. P—Q B 4 P—K 4

By answering 1. P—Q B 4 with 1. ....P—K 4 Black accommodates White in his desire to play a Sicilian with a move ahead. As a reply to White's first move Black has the choice between several good continuations : 1. ....Kt—K B 3, 1. ....P—K 3, 1. ....P—Q B 4 and 1. ....P—K B 4, the Dutch Defence being more playable for him by the fact that White has already advanced his Pawn to Q B 4.

2. Kt—Q B 3   Kt—K B 3

2. ....Kt—Q B 3, with the
intention of developing his K Kt at
K 2 after the fianchetto of Black's
K B, was also to be considered.

It is true that against this move
White is not compelled to answer
3. P—K Kt 3, seeing that 3. Kt—
B 3, followed by 4. P—Q 4, seems
preferable.

3. P—K Kt 3   P—K Kt 3

Regarding 3. ....P—Q 4 see
Game No. 8.

4. B—Kt 2   B—Kt 2
5. Kt—B 3   P—Q 3
6. P—Q 4   P × P

It was preferable to keep the
Pawn-position intact by playing
6. ....Q Kt—Q 2, free to disturb
it at a more opportune moment.

7. Kt × P   Castles
8. Castles   Q Kt—Q 2
9. P—Kt 3 !

In an analogous position, save
that the exchange of centre-Pawns
had not occurred, I played the
weaker move 8. Q—B 2 against
Réti at Pistyan, 1922, after which
Black equalized the game by 8. ....
P × P ; 9. Kt × P, Kt—Kt 3 ; 10.
Q—Q 3, P—Q 4 !
9. P—Kt 3 is probably the only
move to maintain an appreciable
advantage.

9. ......   Kt—B 4
10. B—Kt 2   R—K 1
11. Q—B 2   Kt—K 3
12. Q R—Q 1

12. Kt—B 3 was better. Black's
position is so hemmed-in that White
should seek to avoid every exchange capable of alleviating this
constraint.

12. ......   Q—K 2

For the above reason, 12. ....
Kt × Kt was the best alternative.

13. K R—K 1   R—Kt 1
14. Kt—B 3 !   Q—B 1

Black's position, although free
from weaknesses, is almost without
resource, on account of the lack of
range of his pieces, which obstruct
each other. Under such conditions
it is generally impossible to establish an adequate plan of defence,
and the loss of the game is only a
question of time.

15. P—K 4   Kt—Q 2

Position after Black's 15th move.

16. B—Q R 3 !

The commencement of the decisive manœuvre, which finally ends
in the win of a Pawn, with a
dominating position.

White now threatens on the one
hand 17. P—K 5, and on the other
hand 17. Kt—Q 5 or Q Kt 5, followed by 18. Kt × Q B P and 19.
B × P. Black's next moves are
therefore forced.

16. ......   Kt—K 4
17. Kt × Kt   B × Kt
18. P—B 4   B—Q 5 ch
19. K—R 1   Q—Kt 2

Black was threatened with 20.
P—K B 5.

20. Kt—Q 5 !   B—B 3

Or 20. ....P—Q B 4 ; 21. P—
B 5, Kt—B 1 ; 22. P×P, R P×P ;
23. R×B, P×R (if 23. ....Q×R ;
24. B—Kt 2) ; 24. B×P and
White recovers the Exchange with
a Pawn ahead.

21. Kt×B ch	Q×Kt
22. B—Kt 2	Q—K 2
23. Q—B 3	

The simplest. White leads into an
end-game with two Bishops and a
Pawn against Bishop and Knight.

23.	P—B 3
24. Q×P	Q×Q
25. B×Q	P—Q Kt 4

A desperate attempt to free his
pieces, but in reality merely easing
White's task.

26. P×P	R×P
27. P—K 5	P×P
28. B×P	

Not 28. B—B 6, B—Kt 2.

28.	B—Kt 2
29. B×B	R×B
30. R—Q 7	P—K R 4
31. K R—Q 1 !	

Instead of playing 31. R—K B 1
White temporizes, reserving this
possibility until after Black's plausible move, K—B 1, when he no
longer has the defence ....R—
K B 1 at his disposal.

| 31. ...... | K—B 1 |
| 32. R—K B 1 | R—K 2 |

See Diagram.

33. P—B 5 !

Winning a second Pawn and
therefore the game.

| 33. ...... | P×P |

Clearly forced, since if 33. ....
R×R ; 34. P×Kt ch would win a
piece.

Position after Black's 32nd move.

34. R×P ch	K—K 1
35. R×R ch	K×R
36. R×P	Black resigns

GAME 93

SICILIAN DEFENCE

Consultation Game played at
Berlin, December, 1921.

White :   *Black :*
MESSRS. WEGEMUND. A. ALEKHIN.
    BRENNERT.
    FRIEDRICH.
    DEISSNER.

1. P—K 4	P—Q B 4
2. Kt—K B 3	P—K 3
3. P—Q 4	P×P
4. Kt×P	Kt—K B 3
5. B—Q 3	

This allows Black to obtain at
least an equal game by the advance
of the centre Pawns. The correct
move is 5. Kt—Q B 3 (see Game
No. 60).

5.	Kt—B 3
6. B—K 3	P—Q 4
7. Kt—Q 2	P—K 4
8. Kt (Q 4)—B 3	P—K R 3 !

A good move. The threat 8.....
P—Q 5 compels White to weaken
his position by the advance of his
Q B P, unless he cares to abandon
his centre immediately by 9. P×P.

9.	P—B 3	B—K 2
10.	Castles	Castles
11.	Q—K 2	B—K 3
12.	K R—Q 1	Q—B 2
13.	P×P	

Practically forced, as Black
threatens 13.....P×P; 14. Q Kt×
P, Kt×Kt; 15. B×Kt, P—B 4
with formidable attacking prospects.

13.	......	Kt×P
14.	Kt—K 4	Kt—R 4 !

14. ....P—K B 4 was premature,
since after 15. Kt—B 5, B×Kt;
16. B×B, Kt—B 5 ; 17. Q—B 1,
Black would have no appreciable
advantage, whereas after the text-
move the threat P—B 4 becomes
still more objectionable.

15. B—Q 2 !

If 15. P—Q Kt 4 Black's Knight
would simply withdraw to Q B 3,
and White would merely have
weakened his Queen-side. The text-
move conceals a trap. If, for
example, 15. ....P—B 4, then 16.
Kt—Kt 3, P—K 5 ; 17. Kt×K P !,
P×Kt ; 18. Q×P and wins.

15. ......   Q R—K 1 !

This move strengthens the position in the centre, and its purpose
will soon become clear.

16.	Kt—Kt 3	B—Q 3
17.	Kt—B 5	

White, engrossed by the latent
threat P—B 4, does not perceive
another danger. The best move here
was 17. Kt—R 4, Kt—K B 5 ; 18.
B×Kt, P×B ; 19. Kt—K 4, B—
K 2 ; 20. Kt—B 3, B—K Kt 5 !,

after which Black would obtain the
better game on account of his two
Bishops.

17.	......	B×Kt
18.	B×B	P—K 5 !
19.	Kt—Q 4	

If 19. B×K P, then 19. ....
Kt—K B 3 wins a piece.

19.	......	B×P ch
20.	K—R 1	B—B 5

Black has won a Pawn, but the
win is not without difficulties.
White by his next move introduces
fresh complications, and seeks to
fish in troubled waters.

Position after Black's 20th move.

21. P—B 4 !

After 21. B×P victory would
have been quite easy for Black :
21. B×P, B×B ; 22. R×B, Kt—
Q B 5 ; 23. R—B 2, Kt (Q 4)—K 6 ;
24. P×Kt, R×B ; 25. Kt—B 5,
Q—K 4 ; 26. Q—B 3, Kt×K P ;
27. R—K 2, Kt—B 8 ! and wins.

Whereas, after the text-move,
Black is compelled to make lengthy
and elaborate calculations before
deciding upon the ensuing sacrificial
variation.

21.	......	Kt×P !
22.	Q R—B 1	P—Q Kt 4 !

The necessary preliminary to the following counter-attack. If now 23. Kt × P, then 23. .... Q—K 4 ! and Black is out of all his difficulties, with a Pawn ahead.

23. P—Q Kt 3

Position after White's 23rd move.

23. ......   P—K 6 !

Saving the threatened piece, and at the same time imperilling the position of White's King, which allows him to undertake a mating-attack.

24. P × P	Kt (Q 4) × P
25. B × Kt	B × B
26. Kt × P	Q—Kt 6 !

The point of the combination. On the contrary, 26. .... Q — K 4 would be insufficient, on account of 27. R × Kt, Q × Kt ; 28. B—Q 7, winning the Exchange ; or 27. .... Q × B ; 28. Kt—Q 6.

27. Q × Kt

It is manifest that if 27. R or P × Kt, Black's next move would win at once.

27.	B—B 5
28. K—Kt 1	

Now White is a piece ahead and Black seems to have only perpetual check by 28. .... B—K 6 ch ; 29. K—R 1, B—B 5 ; 30. K—Kt 1, since 28. .... Q—R 7 ch ; 29. K—B 2, B—Kt 6 ch ; 30. K—B 3 is indecisive.

By his next two moves Black, however, demonstrates the whole import of his sacrifice of the Knight.

28. ......   R—K 4 !

In order to occupy K R 4 with this Rook. White cannot prevent this plan without submitting to a decisive loss of material.

29. Kt—Q 6

If 29. Q—Q 3, Q—R 7 ch ; 30. K—B 2, B × R followed by 31. .... Q—B 5 ch and wins.

Position after White's 29th move.

29. ......   P—Kt 3 !

This quiet move wins at once. White is compelled either to leave the Bishop *en prise* (which would weaken Black's attack only momentarily) or to allow Black to continue the plan which he has mapped out for himself.

30. B—R 3	B—K 6 ch
31. K—R 1	R—R 4

And White is defenceless against the threatened 32. ....R×B ch. If 32. Q—K 2 or Q—B 1, then 32. ....B—B 5 ; 33. K—Kt 1, R×B and mates in a few moves.

White resigns.

GAME 94

SCOTCH GAME

Played in a *séance* of four consultation games at Basle, March, 1922.

White :	*Black :*
Dr. Fleissig	
Messrs. Ad. &	A. Alekhin,
H. Staehelin.	

1. P—K 4	P—K 4
2. Kt—K B 3	Kt—Q B 3
3. P—Q 4	P×P
4. Kt×P	B—B 4

This move is more ancient and on the whole less certain than 4. .... Kt—B 3, which leads to equality, but on the other hand it has the advantage of engendering more lively variations.

5. B—K 3	B—Kt 3

Introduced by Lasker against Mieses at St. Petersburg, 1909, in place of the usual continuation up till then, 5. ....Q—B 3 ; 6. P—Q B 3, K Kt—K 2. It should be remarked that Blumenfeld's move 6. Kt—Kt 5 (instead of 6. P—Q B 3) is inadequate, on account of the following variation : 6. ....B×B ; 7. P×B, Q—R 5 ch ; 8. P—Kt 3, Q×K P ; 9. Kt×P ch, K—Q 1 ; 10. Kt×R, Q×R ; 11. Q—Q 6, Kt—B 3 ! ; 12. Kt—Q 2, Kt—K 1 ; 13. Q—R 3, Q×P ; 14. Castles, Q×P, with advantage to Black.

6. P—Q B 3	

But in the present position this move is no longer necessary, and merely obstructs the best square of development for the Q Kt. He should play 6. Kt—Q B 3, K Kt—K 2 ; 7. B—K 2 followed by 8. Q—Q 2 and later Castles Q R with a very fine game (Spielmann—Dr. Tarrasch, Breslau, 1912).

6.	K Kt—K 2
7. B—K 2	Castles
8. Castles	P—Q 3
9. Kt—Q 2	P—B 4 !

The opening of the K B file yields Black an initiative of long duration, without any ill results.

10. P×P	B×P
11. R—K 1	

The command of the King-file, however, is only of little value for White, as we shall recognize later on. But even after 11. Kt×B, Kt×Kt ; 12. B×B, R P×B, White would remain with the inferior game.

11.	Kt×Kt
12. B×Kt	B×B

Not 12. ....P—B 4 ; 13. B—K 3, P—Q 4 on account of 14. B—K Kt 5.

13. P×B	K—R 1

Black was threatened with 14. Q—Kt 3 ch followed by 15. Q×P.

14. Kt—B 3	P—B 3 !

Preventing 15. P—Q 5, followed by the manœuvre of White's Knight with the square K 6 as an objective.

15. R—Q B 1	Kt—Kt 3
16. R—B 3	Q—B 3

Black mobilizes all his available forces before unleashing an attack against the weak points of the hostile position (K B 2 and K Kt 2).

17. B—Q 3	

In order to exchange the dangerous Knight should Black play 17.
....B—Kt 5 immediately.

17. ......   Kt—B 5 !
18. B—B 2

This allows Black to force the
win in a few moves. 18. B×B was
somewhat better, although in this
case also Black's attack must inevitably end in victory.

18. ......   B—Kt 5

18. ....Q—Kt 3 would be inadequate against 19. Kt—R 4 !

19. R (B 3)—K 3

Now White finds himself defenceless against the next manœuvre.

19. ......   Kt—R 6 ch !
20. K—B 1

Position after White's 20th move.

20. ......   Q—R 5 !

The only move which forces an
immediate win. 20. ....Kt—Kt 4
would be insufficient, on account of
21. Q—Q 3 !, P—K Kt 3 ; 22. B—
Q 1.

21. Q—K 2

Or 21. Q—Q 2, B×Kt ; 22. R×B,
R×R ; 23. P×R, Kt—B 5 and
wins. If 21. P—K Kt 3, Q—R 4
followed by 22. ....Kt—Kt 4.

21. ......   Q—R 4

Threatening 22. ....Kt—Kt 4
and 22. ....Kt—B 5, against which
White is defenceless.

22. Q—Q 3   Kt—B 5
23. Q—K 4   Kt×P !

If now 24. K×Kt, Q—R 6 ch ;
25. K—Kt 1, B×Kt ; 26. R×B,
R×R ; 27. Q—K 8 ch, R—B 1 and
wins.

White resigns.

GAME 95

QUEEN'S PAWN GAME

Exhibition Game played at
Madrid, May, 1922.

| *White :* | *Black :* |
| A. ALEKHIN. | M. GOLMAYO. |

1. P—Q 4   Kt—K B 3
2. P—Q B 4   P—Q 3
3. Kt—K B 3   Q Kt—Q 2

The usual continuation in practice is 3. ....P—K Kt 3 followed
by 4. ....B—Kt 2, 5. ....Castles
and 6. ....Kt—B 3.

4. Kt—B 3   P—K 4
5. P—K Kt 3 !

The best system of development
in this variation.

5. ......   B—K 2
6. B—Kt 2   Castles
7. Castles   R—K 1
8. P—Kt 3   P—B 3

Threatening 9. ....P—K 5 followed by 10. ....P—Q 4, which
White at once prevents.

9. Q—B 2   B—B 1
10. P—K 4 !   P×P

Black is already obliged to surrender the centre, in order to disentangle his pieces and develop his Queen-side.

| 11. Kt×P | Q—B 2 |
| 12. B—Kt 2 | P—Q R 4 |

Clearly with the object of securing the square Q B 4 for his Knight, without allowing it to be dislodged by P—Q Kt 4.

13. P—K R 3	Kt—B 4
14. Q R—K 1	B—Q 2
15. P—B 4	Kt—K 3
16. Kt—B 5 !	

Having the greater freedom of action, White should avoid any exchange capable of relieving the enemy's game.

| 16. ...... | Kt—B 4 |
| 17. Kt—K 3 | |

But here 17. P—K Kt 4, instead of the withdrawal of the Knight, would have been simpler and would ultimately have led to a winning attack, without great complications.

Whereas after the text-move Black succeeds in evolving a very interesting counter-attack.

| 17. ...... | R—K 2 ! |
| 18. P—K Kt 4 | |

There is, nevertheless, nothing better than this move.

| 18. ...... | Q R—K 1 |
| 19. Kt—B 5 | |

As we can see, White has lost two moves. The second phase of the game will be only the more lively by reason of this.

| 19. ...... | B×Kt |
| 20. Kt P×B | P—Q Kt 4 ! |

Bold, but very accurately calculated. White is compelled to play very cautiously to maintain his advantage.

| 21. P×P | P×P |

If now 22. Kt×P, Q—Kt 3 with advantage to Black.

Position after Black's 21st move.

22. P—K 5 !

The correct reply to the manœuvre commenced by 20. ....P—Q Kt 4. If now 22. ....P×P; 23. P×P, R×P then 24. Kt×P, Q—Kt 3 ; 25. R×R, R×R ; 26. R×R and Black's discovered check would be perfectly harmless, on account of the answer 27. B—Q 4. Black's next move is therefore again best.

| 22. ...... | Kt (B 4)—Q 2! |
| 23. Q—B 2 | |

With the double threat 24. Kt×P and 24. P×Kt ; Black has accordingly no choice of reply.

| 23. ...... | P×P |
| 24. Kt×P | Q—Kt 1 |

If 24. ....Q—Q 1 or Q—B 1, then clearly 25. Kt—Q 6.

See Diagram.

25. Kt—R 7 !

The point of the manœuvre initiated by 22. P—K 5! Black must lose at least the Exchange, but

Position after Black's 24th move.

Position after Black's 31st move.

he rightly prefers to sacrifice the Queen for Rook and Bishop, which would indeed have yielded him some defensive resources had occasion offered.

25.	......	P×P
26.	Kt—B 6	R×R !
27.	Kt×Q	R (K 8)—K 7
28.	Kt×Kt !	Kt×Kt

If 28. ....R×Q, then 29. Kt×Kt ch, P×Kt ; 30. R×R (but not 30. K×R, B—B 4 ch ; 31. K—B 3, R—K 6 ch ; 32. K×P, R—K 7), B—B 4 ; 31. K—B 1 and White wins without difficulty.

| 29. | Q×P | R×B |
| 30. | B—B 6 ! | |

The only move to win.

| 30. | ...... | B—B 4 ch |
| 31. | K—R 1 | R—K 2 |

31. ....R—K 6 would have been a little better, although in this case also White would have won as follows :

32. Q—R 4 !, R (K 6)—K 7 ! ; 33. Q—Q 8 ch, Kt—B 1 ; 34. Q—B 7 !, R—K 6 ; 35. B—B 3, R—Q B 7 ; 36. Q×P.

32. P—B 6 !

White wins another piece by this pretty move.

32.	......	P×P
33.	B×Kt	R×B
34.	Q—Kt 4 ch	Black resigns

GAME 96

RUY LOPEZ

Exhibition Game played at Seville, June, 1922.

| *White :* | *Black :* |
| DR. TORRES. | A. ALEKHIN. |

1.	P—K 4	P—K 4
2.	Kt—K B 3	Kt—Q B 3
3.	B—Kt 5	P—Q R 3
4.	B—R 4	Kt—B 3
5.	Castles	P—Q 3

This move, commended by Rubinstein, seems to me less sound than 5. ....B—K 2, as White has at his disposal several good continuations and as he can obtain a draw by a forced variation (compare the next note).

6. B×Kt ch

This exchange, however, is not to be commended. White would do better to adopt one of the following continuations :

(1) 6. P—B 3 and if 6. ...Kt×P ; 7. P—Q 4, with a fine attack.

(2) 6. Q—K 2.

(3) 6. P—Q 4 and if 6. ....P— Q Kt 4 ; 7. B—Kt 3, P×P ; 8. P— B 3 !, sacrificing a Pawn for the attack. This line of play was successfully played by Yates against Rubinstein on two occasions (London, 1922, and Carlsbad, 1923).

(4) 6. R—K 1, P—Q Kt 4 ; 7. B—Kt 3, Kt—Q R 4. A game Aurbach—Alekhin, played in Paris in October, 1922, continued thus : 8. P—Q 4, Kt×B ; 9. R P×B, B—Kt 2 ; 10. P×P, Kt×P ; 11. P×P, B×P ; 12. Q—Q 4 !, Q—K 2 ; 13. Kt—B 3 ! (not 13. Q×P ?, Castles ; 14. B—Kt 5, Kt×B ! and wins), P—K B 4 ; 14. B—Kt 5, Q—Q 2 (if 14. ....Q—B 2, given in Collijn's *Lärobok*, 15. Kt×Kt, P×Kt ; 16. R×P ch !, B×R ; 17. Q×B ch, K—Q 2 ; 18. R—Q 1 and wins) ; 15. Kt×Kt, P×Kt.

Position after Black's 15th move in sub-variation.

16. R×P ch !, B×R ; 17. Q×B ch, K—B 2 ; 18. R—K 1 !, Q R— K 1 ! ; 19. Q—Q 5 ch, K—B 1 ;

20. R—K 5 !, R×R ; 21. Kt×R, Q—K 1 ; 22. Q—B 3 ch, K—Kt 1 ; 23. Q—Q 5 ch and White draws by perpetual check.

6.	......	P×B
7.	P—Q 4	Kt×P !
8.	R—K 1	P—B 4
9.	P×P	P—Q 4

Now Black has undoubtedly the better game, with his two Bishops and his strongly-posted Knight in the centre.

| 10. | Kt—Q 4 | B—B 4 |
| 11. | P—Q B 3 | |

Sooner or later necessary in order to develop the Q Kt at Q 2, without leaving the K Kt *en prise* to Black's K B.

| 11. | ...... | Castles |
| 12. | P—K B 4 | |

It would have been rather better to dislodge the Black Knight by 12. P—B 3 and then to play 13. P— K B 4. Nevertheless, in this blocked position the gain of a *tempo* is hardly capable of improving his game sufficiently.

12.	......	Q—K 1
13.	B—K 3	B—Kt 3
14.	Kt—Q 2	B—Kt 2

In perfect safety Black prepares the advance of his centre Pawns, thus enabling his Bishops to exercise pressure on the hostile King.

15.	Kt (Q 2)—B 3	Q R—Q 1
16.	Q—B 2	P—B 4
17.	Kt—Kt 3	

17. Kt—K 2 at once was preferable, upon which Black would probably have continued 17. .... P—R 3, followed by 18. ....K—R 1 and 19. ....R—K Kt 1, preparing to open the K Kt file by ....P—Kt 4. The text-move allows him to increase his pressure on the centre to a still greater extent.

| 17. | ...... | P—B 5 ! |

Profiting by the fact that White cannot play 18. B × B on account of 18. ....P × Kt.

18. Kt (Kt 3)–Q 4   P—B 4
19. Kt—K 2   Q—B 3
20. Q R—Q 1   P—R 3 !

In continuation of the above-mentioned plan.

21. R—K B 1   K—R 1 !

In order that the Q B P shall not be captured by the hostile Queen with a check, in the event of ....
P—Q 5, a precaution whose purpose will appear later on.

22. K—R 1   Q—Kt 3

Black intends to occupy K R 4 with his Queen, which would make the advance of the Kt P still more effective.

23. Kt (K 2)—Kt 1

By attempting to prevent this strategically decisive advance White allows his opponent to conclude the game with a pretty combination, based upon the hidden action of his Q B on the long diagonal.

23. ......   Q—R 4
24. Kt—R 3

Position after White's 24th move.

24. ......   P—Q 5 !

Allowing the sacrifice of the Queen on the 28th move, thanks to which Black wins a piece or forces mate.

25. P × P   P × P
26. B × P   B × B
27. R × B   R × R
28. Kt × R   Q × Kt !
29. P × Q   Kt—B 7 ch
30. K—Kt 1   Kt × P mate

GAME 97

SICILIAN DEFENCE

Exhibition Game played at Berlin, February, 1923.

White :	*Black :*
A. ALEKHIN.	F. SÄMISCH.

1. P—K 4   P—Q B 4
2. Kt—K B 3   Kt—Q B 3
3. B—K 2

In the Vienna Tournament of 1922, playing against the same opponent, I had played 3. P—Q 4 (see Game No. 76).

The text-move indicates White's intention to Castle, before undertaking any action in the centre.

3. ......   P—K 3
4. Castles   P—Q 3

After 4. ....P—Q 4 ; 5. P × P, P × P ; 6. P—Q 4, Black's Q P would be isolated and therefore weak.

5. P—Q 4   P × P
6. Kt × P   Kt—B 3
7. B—B 3 !

White delays the plausible move 7. Kt—Q 3 in order to play first P—Q B 4 thus preventing all counter-attack on the Q B file.

7. ......   Kt—K 4

To secure the advantage of the two Bishops, which is rather illusory in this position. But this manœuvre loses valuable time which would be better utilized in playing B—K 2, Castles and B—Q 2, etc.

8.	P—B 4 !	Kt × B ch
9.	Q × Kt	B—K 2
10.	Kt—B 3	Castles
11.	P—Q Kt 3	

The occupation of the long diagonal being threatening, Black prepares to oppose his K B, a manœuvre which, however, implies a further loss of time.

11.	......	Kt—Q 2
12.	B—Kt 2	B—B 3
13.	Q R—Q 1	P—Q R 3

Preventing the threatened Kt (Q 4) —Kt 5, but in any case his Q P remains permanently weak.

14.	Q—Kt 3	Q—B 2
15.	K—R 1 !	

An essential preliminary to the decisive manœuvre commencing by the advance of the K B P.

15.	......	R—Q 1
16.	P—B 4	P—Q Kt 3
17.	P—B 5 !	

White's advantage in position and attacking chances are already so great that the abandoning of the square K 5 to the opponent cannot present any strategic inconvenience.

Moreover the text-move, if Black answers it in the most plausible manner, is shown to be the prelude to a beautiful final combination.

17.	......	B—K 4

Black's game is untenable, for White's attack is already too strong, e.g.: 17. ....B × Kt ; 18. R × B, Kt—K 4 ; 19. P—B 6, Kt—Kt 3 ; 20. B—R 3 ! with decisive advantage for White.

Position after Black's 17th move.

18. P × K P ! !

The Queen-sacrifice, which Black is compelled to accept, decides the game in a few moves.

18. ......   B × Q

If 18. ....P × P ; 19. Kt × P.

19. P × P ch   K—R 1

Also forced.

20. Kt—Q 5 ! !

Position after White's 20th move

The whole point of the sacrifice ! 20. Kt—K 6 would not be so good, because of 20. ....Q—Kt 1 ; 21. Kt—Q 5, B—K 4, and Black could still defend himself, whereas after the text-move he remains defenceless, as the following variations show :

I.—20. ....Q—Kt 1 ; 21. Kt—Q B 6, B—K 4 (if 21. ....Q—Kt 2 ; 22. Kt×R, etc.) ; 22. B×B, P×B ; 23. Kt×Q, R×Kt ; 24. Kt—B 7 !, R—B 1 ; 25. Kt—K 6 followed by 26. Kt×R and 27. R—Q 8, and White wins.

II.—20. ....Q—R 2 ; 21. Kt—Q B 6, B—K 4 ; 22. B×B, P×B ; 23. Kt×Q, R×Kt ; 24. Kt×P, R—B 1 ; 25. Kt×B, R×Kt ; 26. R×Kt and White wins.

III.—20. ......Q—Kt 2 ; 21. Kt—K 6 !, B—K 4 ; 22. Kt×R and White wins.

IV.—20. ....Q—B 4 ; 21. Kt—K 6, B—K 4 ; 22. B×B, P×B ; 23. Kt×Q, P×Kt ; 24. Kt—B 7, R—Q Kt 1 ; 25. Kt—K 8 ! and White wins.

As can be seen, in all these variations White's K B P is stronger than Black's Queen !

Black resigns.

GAME 98

RUY LOPEZ

Played in a *séance* of six consultation games at Antwerp, February, 1923.

White :	*Black :*
A. ALEKHIN.	MESSRS. PRILS & BLAUT.

1. P—K 4	P—K 4
2. Kt—K B 3	Kt—Q B 3
3. B—Kt 5	P—Q R 3
4. B—R 4	Kt—B 3
5. Kt—B 3	

This move, especially recommended by Dr. Tarrasch, gives White a safe and solid game, but Black, truth to tell, has nothing much to fear in this variation.

5. ......   B—K 2

He has also the choice between this move, which is in practice the most usual, and 5. ....B—B 4, which is equally playable (see Game No. 74).

6. Castles	P—Q Kt 4
7. B—Kt 3	P—Q 3
8. P—Q R 4	

The main object of this move is to avoid the exchange of White's K B against Black's Q Kt, an exchange which would be inevitable after 8. P—Q 3, Kt—Q R 4 ; but the loss of time which it entails creates new troubles for White. It is therefore admissible that Svenonius' manœuvre, 8. Kt—K 2, B—Kt 5 ; 9. P—B 3, is preferable to the text-move.

8. ......   P—Kt 5 !

Much better than 8. ....R—Q Kt 1, which surrenders the Q R file to White (see Game No. 66).

9. Kt—Q 5

Position after White's 9th move.

9. ......   Castles

Simplest, and perhaps also best. Apart from Castles, Black could also have adopted one of the following three variations :

I.—9. ....Kt×P ; 10. P—Q 4, Castles ; 11. R—K 1, Kt—B 3 ; 12. Kt×B ch, Kt×Kt (if 12. .... Q×Kt ; 13. B—Kt 5 with the better game) ; 13. P×P, P×P ; 14. Q×Q, R×Q ; 15. Kt×P with advantage to White.

II.—9. ....R—Q Kt 1 ; 10. P—Q 4, B—Kt 5 ; 11. P—B 3, Castles ; 12. B—Q B 4 ! (but not 12. R—K 1, Kt P×P ; 13. Kt P×P, P×P ; 14. P×P, B×Kt ; 15. P×B, Kt×P, winning a Pawn for Black, but giving White a slight advantage in position : Marco—Alekhin, Pistyan, 1922).

III.—9. ....Kt—Q R 4 ; 10. Kt×B ! (not 10. B—R 2, Kt×Kt ; 11. B×Kt, P—Q B 3 ; 12. B—R 2, P—Q B 4 ! ; 13. P—B 3, R—Q Kt 1 ; 14. B—Q 5, Castles ; 15. P—Q 4, K P×P ; 16. P×Q P, P—B 5, with marked advantage to Black, Alekhin — Bogoljuboff, Pistyan, 1922), Q×Kt ; 11. P—Q 4 !, Kt×B ; 12. P×Kt, Kt×P ! ; 13. P×P, B—Kt 2 ; 14. P×P, Q×P, with an equal game.

10. P—Q 4

This move is premature in the present position. White will soon find himself under the necessity of sacrificing a Pawn for a problematical initiative.

Collijn's *Lärobok* here rightly recommends 10. R—K 1, and if 10. ....B—Kt 5 then 11. P—B 3 (preparing 12. P—Q 4), with a satisfactory game.

10. ......   B—Kt 5
11. P—B 3

11. P×P, Q Kt×P would avoid the loss of the Pawn, but would transfer the attack to Black. By the text-move White, while maintaining his pressure on the centre, hopes later to profit by a certain weakness in the adverse Queen-side.

11. ......   Kt P×P
12. Kt P×P   Kt×K P
13. R—K 1

If 13. Kt×B ch Black could have answered 13. ....Q×Kt, for if then 14. B—Q 5 ?, Kt×Q B P.

13. ......   Kt—B 3
14. P—R 3

Compelling the opponent, should he wish to maintain the Pawn which he has won, to abandon the idea of utilizing his Q B later on to secure the defence of the weak squares on his Queen's wing.

14. ......   B—R 4
15. Kt×Kt ch

The attempt to regain the Pawn by 15. P—Kt 4, B—Kt 3 ; 16. Kt×B ch, Q×Kt ; 17. P×P, Kt× K P ; 18. Kt×Kt, P×Kt ; 19. B—R 3, P—B 4 ; 20. P—K B 4, K R—Q 1 ; 21. Q—B 1, Q—Kt 2 ! would ultimately end in White's discomfiture.
By the move chosen he definitely abandons this, but has prospects of a positional advantage resulting from the following :

15. ......   B×Kt
16. B—Q 5   Q—Q 2
17. P—R 5

Threatening to win a piece by 18. Q—R 4.

17. ......   Q R—Q 1
18. Q—Q 3   Kt—Kt 1

The remoteness of this Knight, which remains on this useless square until the conclusion of the game, is a substantial compensation for White's material inferiority.

19. B—R 3   K R—K 1
20. B—K 4

Having already in mind the following sacrifice of a second Pawn.

20. ......   B—Kt 3

Not 20. ....P—R 3 on account of 21. P—Kt 4.

21. B × B   R P × B
22. P—Q 5 !

Position after White's 22nd move.

22. ......   P—K 5

The critical moment of the game. Black who, up to the present, has played in irreproachable style, allows himself to be led astray by a fresh capture which in the end will prove fatal for him.

He would do better to attempt to free his Queen-side by 22. .... P—B 3, after which the game would probably have resulted in a draw; for example : 22. ....P—B 3 ; 23. Q R—Q 1, P × P (if 23. ....P—B 4 ; 24. R—K 4 !, followed by 25. R—Kt 1) ; 24. Q × Q P, Q—Q 3 ; 25. Q × Q, Kt × Q ; 26. R—Q 5 ! (better than 26. R × P) and even if Black could maintain his material advantage he would have only the slightest chances of winning, in view of the position of White's pieces.

23. R × P   R × R
24. Q × R   B × P

Now White's Q R P is untenable, for if 25. R—R 2, B × P ; 26. B × P, B—Kt 3 ! and Black in the end would win the Q P.

But its capture will remove from the King-side the only piece which could secure him an adequate defence, and White will profit by this *tempo* to undertake a very strong attack against the weakened position of the Black King.

25. R—B 1 !   B × P

After 25. ....B—B 3 the Pawns on Q R 3 and Q B 2 would obviously be very weak.

26. B—Kt 2 !

Threatening 27. Kt—Kt 5, as Black's reply 27. ....B—Q 7, previously feasible, would no longer be so, on account of 28. Q—Q 4 !

26. ......   R—K 1

In order to play 27. ....P—K B 3.

27. Q—K R 4   P—K B 3
28. Kt—Q 4 !

White does not fear an exchange of Rooks, since after 29. ....R—K 8 ch ; 30. R × R, B × R ; 31. Q—K 4 ! he would regain one of the sacrificed Pawns, while maintaining his powerful pressure upon the adverse position.

28. ......   K—B 2

Recognizing the danger threatened by the inroad of White's Knight at K 6, Black merely prepares to sacrifice the Exchange. Indeed, after 29. Kt—K 6, R × Kt ; 30. P × R ch, Q × P, White would no longer have any satisfactory continuation of the attack, and Black's two centre Pawns would win ultimately.

Position after Black's 28th move.

35. Q—B 8 with a winning attack for White.

33. R—K 4	Q—Q 2
34. P—Kt 4 !	R—R 1
35. R—K B 4 !	

This move leaves Black defenceless against the threats 36. B×P, 36. Kt×Kt P and 36. P—Kt 5.

35. ......   R—K 1

Position after Black's 35th move.

36. B×P !   P×B

This capture leads to mate. Black could have escaped immediate danger by 36. ....R×Kt, but after 37. P×R ch, Q×P ; 38. B—Q 4 ch, K—Kt 1 ; 39. B×B, P×B ; 40. R—Q 4 ! his game would be hopeless.

37. R×P ch !   K×R

If 37. ....K—K 2 ; 38. Q×Kt P ! and mates in two moves. Or if 37. ....K—Kt 1 ; 38. Q×P ch, K—R 1 ; 39. Q—R 5 ch, K—Kt 1 ; 40. R—Kt 6 ch and mates.

After the text-move White mates in three moves by 38. Q—Q B 3 ch, B—Q 5 ; 39. Q×B ch, K moves ; 40. Q—Kt 7 mate.

---

29. R—B 4 ! !

This move, which is the result of a close examination, is the only one which offers prospects of a winning attack, because it prevents the sacrifice of the Exchange. For example, 30. Kt—K 6, R×Kt ; 31. P×R ch, Q×P ; 32. R—K 4 !, Q—B 4 (or anywhere else) ; 33. B×P ! and wins.

Black therefore can no longer prevent White's Knight from occupying K 6, and from this moment White's attack becomes irresistible.

29.	R—K 4
30. Kt—K 6 !	R—R 4

If 30. ....R×P, White wins by 31. Kt×Kt P !

31. Q—K 4   Q—K 2

And if now, or on the next move, R×P, then 32. Kt—Q 8 ch ! wins a Rook.

32. Q—Q 3 !

Preparing the decisive action of the Rook on the fourth rank.

32. ......   B—Kt 3

Or 32. ....Kt—Q 2 ; 33. R—K 4, Kt—K 4 ; 34. Q×P, B—Kt 3 ;

GAME 99

QUEEN'S GAMBIT DECLINED

First game of a match at Paris, February, 1923.

White :   *Black :*

A. ALEKHIN.   A. MUFFANG.

1. P—Q 4	P—Q 4
2. P—Q B 4	P—K 3
3. Kt—K B 3	P—Q B 4

This variation, favoured by Tarrasch, is disadvantageous for Black should White adopt Rubinstein's system (P—K Kt 3 and B—Kt 2), as in the present game.

4. B P×P	K P×P
5. P—K Kt 3	Kt—Q B 3
6. B—Kt 2	Kt—B 3
7. Castles	B—K 3

After 7. ....B—K 2 White has the choice between the line of play adopted in this game, and the continuation 8. P×P, B×P; 9. Q Kt —Q 2 followed by 10. Kt—Kt 3, successfully put into practice by Sämisch against Dr. Tarrasch (Carlsbad Tournament, 1923).

8. Kt—B 3	B—K 2
9. P×P	B×P
10. Kt—Q R 4 !	

This new continuation, introduced by Réti against Dr. Tarrasch in the Pistyan Tournament of 1922, aims at occupying, once and for all, the square Q 4, of vital importance in the Tarrasch variation.

This innovation, in my opinion, constitutes a notable strengthening of the Rubinstein variation.

10.	B—K 2
11. B—K 3	Castles

Dr. Tarrasch continued 11. .... P—Q Kt 3 in his game against Réti, without, however, obtaining a satisfactory game. Here is the continuation of the game : 12. Kt—

Q 4, Kt×Kt ; 13. B×Kt, Q—Q 2 ; 14. Kt—B 3, R—Q 1 ; 15. Q— Kt 3, Castles ; 16. K R—Q 1 and White's advantage is obvious.

12. Kt—B 5

This move is sufficient to yield White a slight advantage. It is, however, probable that 12. Kt—Q 4 first would have given a more marked advantage.

12. ......   Kt—K 5 !

Comparatively best. White evidently cannot capture the Q Kt P, because of 13. Q—B 2.

The ensuing liquidation reduces White's winning chances, which will consist solely in the weakness of the adverse centre Pawns and the slight advantage of a Bishop against a Knight in this type of position, where it is not blocked by Pawns.

13. Kt×B	P×Kt
14. Kt—Q 4	Kt×Kt
15. Q B×Kt	

On the other hand, the advantage of the two Bishops is illusory, for it is clear that after ....B—B 3 White cannot avoid the exchange of his Q B.

15.	Kt—Q 3
16. Q—Kt 3 !	

Already threatening 17. P—K 4.

16.	B—B 3
17. Q R—Q 1	B×B
18. R×B	Q—B 3
19. P—K 3 !	

Preparing 20. R—K B 4 ! which would not be so strong if played at once, because of 19. ....Q—K 4.

19.	Q R—B 1
20. R—K B 4 !	Q—K 2

The weakness of the grouping of Black's Pawns on K 3 and Q 4 is felt the more as the hostile K B dominates the White squares.

The plausible move 20. ....Q—
K 4 would be quite bad because
of the subtle reply 21. Q—R 4 !
attacking the Q R P and threatening to enter at Q 7 with decisive
effect.

21. R×R ch   K×R

Again best. If 21. ....Q×R ;
then 22. P—K 4 ! or if 21. ....
R×R ; 22. R—Q B 1, R—B 1 ; 23.
R×R ch, Kt×R ; 24. P—K 4 !
and White's K B enters into action
with very great effect.

22. R—Q 1   K—Kt 1

This retreat of the Black King
to the square it originally occupied
is intended to hinder the threatened
23. Q—Q 3 followed by 24. P—K 4,
etc.

It will, however, enable White to
force the gain of a Pawn by a
hidden manœuvre.

Better was 22. ....P—Q R 3,
prolonging the resistance.

23. Q—R 3 !

After this move Black has no
defence against the double threat,
24. Q×P and 24. P—K 4 !

23. ......   R—B 7

Position after Black's 23rd move.

24. P—K 4 !

Attacking the centre and thereby
enabling his Queen to join in the
defence of the King-side, since it
will protect the K B P after capturing the Q R P.

24. ......   Q—B 1
25. Q×P   Kt—Kt 4

Reckoning to secure a passed
Pawn on Q 5, but the realization of
this plan necessitates an immobility
of the Black pieces of which White
will take advantage to conclude the
game by a direct attack.

On the other hand, it was scarcely
possible for Black to entertain other
continuations, *e.g.* :

I.—25. ....Kt×P ; 26. B×Kt,
P×B ; 27. Q—Kt 6 !

II.—25. ....P×P ; 26. Q—Kt 6,
R—B 3 ; 27. Q—Kt 4.

With an easy win for White in
both variations.

26. Q—Kt 6   P—Q 5

Threatening mate in two.

27. R—K B 1 !   Q—Q B 4
28. Q×P ch   K—B 1
29. P—K 5 !

Enabling White's K B to enter
into the adverse game with decisive
effect.

29. ......   Q—B 1
30. Q—Q Kt 6   R×Kt P
See Diagram.

31. B—Q 5 !

Not 31. P—Q R 4 because of 31.
....Q—B 2, whereas now White
threatens inevitably 32. P—Q R 4,
Q—B 2 ; 33. Q—K 6.

31. ......   Q—Q 2
32. B—B 4   R—Kt 5
33. Q—B 5 ch   Q—K 2
34. Q—B 8 ch   Q—K 1
35. Q—K B 5 ch   K—K 2
36. Q—K 6 ch   K—B 1

Position after Black's 30th move.

If 36. ....K—Q 1, then 37. Q—Kt 6 ch, K—B 1; 38. Q—B 5 ch, winning the Rook.

37. Q—Kt 8 ch	K—K 2
38. Q×P ch	K—Q 1
39. Q×Kt P !	Q×P
40. R—B 1	Black resigns

GAME 100

FRENCH DEFENCE

Second game of a match at Paris, February, 1923.

White :	*Black :*
A. MUFFANG.	A. ALEKHIN.
1. P—K 4	P—K 3
2. P—Q 4	P—Q 4
3. P—K 5	

Steinitz's move, reintroduced by Niemzovitch a few years ago. It leads to a very complicated game, not disadvantageous for Black.

3.	P—Q B 4
4. P—Q B 3	Kt—Q B 3
5. Kt—B 3	P—B 3

In an analogous position at St. Petersburg, 1914, Dr. Lasker played 5. ....P—B 4 against Dr. Tarrasch.

The text-move, although perhaps less solid, aims at creating a tension in the centre which necessitates perfectly correct play on the part of his opponent.

| 6. B—Q 3 | B—Q 2 |

More prudent was here 6. .... Q—B 2 ; 7. B—K B 4, Q—Kt 3 !, for after the text-move White could have introduced complications equally dangerous for both players by 7. Kt—Kt 5 !?, *e.g. :* 7. Kt—Kt 5 !?, P—B 4 ; 8. P—K Kt 4 !, P×Q P ; 9. P×B P, Kt×P ; 10. P×K P, B—B 3 ; 11. P×P, Kt×B ch ; 12. Q×Kt, Q—B 3 ; 13. Castles, Kt—R 3, followed by Castles Q R, and in spite of White's Pawn plus the chances can be considered approximately equal, since the position of White's King is compromised by the opening of the K Kt file.

| 7. Q—B 2 | |

As White's Queen cannot be maintained on this file, it was useless to lose a move to provoke a reply which would sooner or later be forced on account of the dangers arising from Kt—Kt 5.

It was therefore better to play 7. Q—K 2 at once.

| 7. ...... | P—B 4 |
| 8. P—K Kt 4 | |

Very energetic . . . . . but as will be seen subsequently, the opening of the K Kt file is rather to the advantage of his opponent.

8.	P—K Kt 3
9. Kt P×P	Kt P×P
10. P×P	

Once again best. He must prevent the threatened exchange of Knight against the Pawns, leading to the opening of the Q B file and the weakening of White's square at Q 4.

10. ......   B×P
11. Q—K 2

Threatening a demonstration on the right wing, commencing 12. Kt—Kt 5, but Black opposes it by the following move.

11. ......   Q—B 2 !
12. Q Kt—Q 2   K Kt—K 2
13. Kt—Kt 3   B—Kt 3
14. Kt (Kt 3)—Q 4

This move should not have been played until his Q B had been developed, which would have enabled White to occupy the Q B file in the event of an exchange.

Better was 14. B—K Kt 5, with the probable continuation 14. .... Castles Q R ; 15. B—B 6, K R—Kt 1 ; 16. Kt (Kt 3)—Q 4, B×Kt ; 17. P×B, Q R—K 1 ; 18. R—Q B 1, K—Kt 1, with a slight advantage to Black, whereas after the text-move he secures a practically won position after a few moves.

14. ......   B×Kt !
15. P×B   Q—Kt 3
16. Q—K 3

If 16. B—K 3, the reply 16. .... Kt—Kt 5 would be still more disagreeable.

16. ......   Kt—Kt 5
17. B—Kt 1   R—Q B 1
18. B—Q 2

While the position of Black's King is sufficiently protected, that of White's King appears seriously compromised.

White should have taken the chance to Castle, thereby securing some prospects of a satisfactory defence.

18. ......   Kt—B 7 ch
19. B×Kt   Q×Kt P !

The entry of the Black Queen into the enemy's game should speedily terminate the game.

20. R—Q Kt 1   Q×B
21. R×P

Position after White's 21st move.

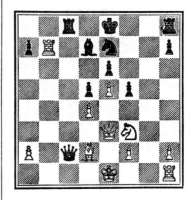

21. ......   Q×P

This useless capture makes the win difficult again, as White can temporarily bring his King into safety.

The right move was 21. .... R—K Kt 1, definitely preventing Castling by White, after which the victory would have been' fairly easy, e.g. :

22. Q—Kt 3, Q—K 5 ch ; 23. Q—K 3, P—B 5 ; 24. Q—K 2, P—Q R 3 ! and White has not sufficient defence against 25. ....B—Kt 4, which will have fatal consequences.

22. Castles !   R—Kt 1 ch
23. K—R 1

See Diagram.

23. ......   Q—B 7 !

Black, in order to retain his slight advantage in position, has no other resource than to provoke an exchange of Queens on K 5, for all other manœuvres, tending to maintain his material advantage, would have turned in the adversary's favour, e.g. :

I.—23. ....Q—R 3 ; 24. R (B 1) —Q Kt 1, R—B 8 ch ; 25. R×R

Position after White's 23rd move.

(if 25. B×R ?, Q—B 8 ch and mates next move), Q×R ; 26. Q—R 6 and White has a strong attack.

II.—23. ....P—B 5 ; 24. Q×P, R—B 1 ; 25. Q—K 3, R×Kt ; 26. Q×R, Q×B ; 27. Q—R 5 ch, K—Q 1 ; 28. Q—B 7 !, Q—R 3 ; 29. R—K Kt 1 and White should win.

24. Kt—Kt 5

This move only results in the improvement of Black's position, Black's Rook being better placed for the defence on K Kt 2 than on K Kt 1.

A little better was 24. R×P at once, although in this case Black's position would have been preferable after 24. ....Q—K 5.

24. ......   R—Kt 2
25. R×P   P—R 3 !
26. Kt—B 3

The Knight is compelled to retreat, for if 26. R—B 1, P—B 5 ! ; 27. R×Q (or 27. Q×P, P×Kt), P×Q ; 28. R×R ch, Kt×R, and White has three pieces *en prise*.

26. ......   P—B 5 !

The initial move of the decisive attack. White cannot capture this Pawn because of 27. Q×P, Q—Q 6 !,

followed by 28. ....R—K B 2, and Black wins.

27. Q—K 2   Q—K 5 !
28. Q—Q 1

If 28. R—K 1, Q×Q ; 29. R×Q, B—Kt 4 ; 30. R—K 1, B—Q 6 followed by 31. ....B—K 5, and Black has a winning position.

28. ......   Kt—B 3

Position after White's 29th move.

29. R—K 1

The game could not be saved, *e.g.:*

I.—29. R—R 4, Kt×K P, etc.

II.—29. R—R 3, Kt×Q P ; 30. R—K 1, Kt×Kt ! ; 31. R×Q, P×R ; 32. R×Kt, P×R ; 33. B×P, R—Kt 5 ; 34. B—Kt 3 (or 34. Q—Q 2, R—Q Kt 1 !), R (Kt 5)—Q B 5, and Black wins.

29. ......   Kt×R !

This Queen-sacrifice is the logical sequel to the preceding moves. It enables Black's Q B at last to take an active part in the attack against the opposing King.

30. R×Q   P×R
31. Kt—R 4   P—K 6 !

The point ! White's Knight will now be hopelessly pinned by Black's Q B on the long diagonal, after which the gain of this piece will be merely a question of time.

32.	Q—R 5 ch	K—B 1
33.	P×P	P×P
34.	B×P	

Or 34. Q—B 3 ch, K—Kt 1 ; 35. Q×P, B—B 3 ch ; 36. Kt—B 3, R—B 1, and wins.

34.	......	B—B 3 ch
35.	Kt—B 3	K—Kt 1

Still simpler was 35. R—Q Kt 1 ! ; 36. P—R 4, R—Q Kt 6. However, the text-move is quite sufficient to win.

36.	Q—R 3 !	B—Q 4
37.	B×P	R—Kt 3
38.	Q—R 5	B—K 5 !
39.	B—Kt 5	R—B 1
40.	K—Kt 1	R×Kt
41.	Q—Kt 4	Kt—Kt 4 !
42.	P—R 4	

Obviously 42. Q×B would lead to mate in three moves.

42.	......	Kt—B 6
43.	K—R 2	R—B 7 ch
44.	K—R 3	B—B 4

White resigns.

INDEX OF OPENINGS

*Note:—The Numbers in heavy type denote
the games in which Alekhin had White.*

INDEX OF NAMES

*Note:—The Numbers in heavy type denote
the games in which Alekhin had White.*

MY BEST GAMES
OF CHESS
1924-1937

ALEXANDER ALEKHINE

BIOGRAPHICAL NOTE

Alexander Alekhine was born in Moscow on the 1st November, 1892, and, as a chess player, he attained at the age of sixteen the title of Master, and in 1914 that of Grand Master. After taking his Law degree in 1914 he entered the Russian Foreign Office, but at the Revolution he emigrated to France where he later obtained the degree of Docteur en Droit of Paris University.

He has won many International Tournaments, and, moreover, has established three world records for Blindfold Chess. He won the World Title from Capablanca in 1927, successfully defended it against Bogoljubow in 1929 and 1937, lost it by one point against Dr. Euwe in 1935 and won it back from him by six points in 1937.

MEMOIR OF ALEKHINE
By J. DU MONT

IN RECORDING the life of Alexander Alekhine, the annalist has the difficult task of remaining objective, of avoiding being carried away by his genius, by the glory of his achievements, or being led astray by a feeling of commiseration for the tragedy of his life.

Born of a wealthy and notable family in Czarist Russia, he enjoyed as a child and a youth all the advantages which this implies He made use of his opportunities and made good progress in his early studies of the law. In his spare time he developed his marked talent for chess and was a recognised master at the age of 16.

Until the first world war broke out there was no cloud in his sky. He was then, at the age of 22, playing in and winning an important tournament at Mannheim. Then the storm burst and, together with other foreign masters, he was interned by the Germans. He managed to escape to Switzerland and returned home, via Siberia, to join the Russian Army. He was twice wounded and twice decorated. Then the second blow fell ! The Russian Revolution broke out and, as a member of the aristocracy, he had little hope of coming out unscathed. In fact, he and his family lost their all and he was lucky to escape with his life. It is said that chess saved him from the worst. Be that as it may, he had, for the next few years, to teach chess in schools and universities.

In 1921 he was allowed to take part in a tournament in Triberg, but he did not return to Russia and made his way to Paris. Here, starting life anew, he became a chess professional and began his long list of triumphs by taking part in all important tournaments, his great ambition being to establish his fame so securely that a match with Capablanca would have to follow.

In spite of the very exacting nature of these exertions, he managed, in his stride as it were, to renew his legal studies and to become a Doctor-at-Law of the French Faculty, a tribute indeed to his energy and his immense capacity for work.

By 1927 he had so established his superiority over all other contenders that his claim to be the rightful challenger for the world title could no longer be denied. How he won that match in 1927 is a matter of history. Thus he had built up for himself, by his own exertions, a new era of prosperity. In the years following upon his accession to the chess throne he conscientiously carried on his work, taking part in almost all masters' tournaments, and in these he even improved on all his previous achievements. He developed incidentally his gift for blindfold play, continually increasing the number of opponents he took on simultaneously until he reached the staggering number of thirty-two. In point of numbers this has been exceeded since ; in point of strength of the opposition and quality of the play it has never been equalled.

There is little doubt that these exhibitions undermine the stamina of the protagonists and cannot be good. In Russia, to-day the chess country *par excellence*, blindfold exhibitions are forbidden by law. These tremendous exertions left their mark on a highly sensitive temperament already shaken by the vicissitudes he had to fight against in early life, and periodically Dr. Alekhine gave way to drink, a circumstance not unprecedented in the life of many a genius.

Thus he was hardly at his best when he met Dr. Euwe for the Championship in 1935. Dr. Euwe, playing magnificent chess, won by a small margin. With a readiness unheard of in championship chess Dr. Euwe immediately agreed to a return match. This took place two years later. In the meantime Dr. Alekhine had had the strength of mind to give up entirely both drinking and smoking and he relentlessly carried out his determination to make himself fit. He won the match in decisive fashion and thus we had the unique spectacle of a Champion magnanimously granting his defeated opponent a return match almost at once and of the ex-Champion regaining his throne.

Nevertheless, there had been some falling off in Dr. Alekhine's powers, and several masters of the younger generation had legitimate claims to a match for the Championship. This aroused the Champion's natural combativeness and he accepted in 1939 the challenge of undoubtedly the strongest of the younger contenders, M. Botvinnik. This would probably have been the finest match ever played, for it is certain that Dr. Alekhine would not have come unprepared or unfit.

All the preliminaries had been arranged and settled, and the match was to be played in Russia, when the second World War broke out. Dr. Alekhine was at the time in Buenos Aires taking part in the international team match, where he captained the French players. He refused to allow his team to play the German team and returned to France by the first available boat to join the French Army. After the collapse of France he intended going to America for a return match with Capablanca ; he went as far as Lisbon. Here he waited in vain for the permit that was to enable him to leave Europe. Whether the reason was that permits were impossible to get immediately after "Pearl Harbour" or that Capablanca, after working hard for a return match, had lost interest, is difficult to say.

It was about that time that news reached Dr. Alekhine that his wife was in France in the hands of the Germans. He tried to get permission to join her. The German authorities, realising the

Champion's propaganda value, gave this permission on condition
that he wrote two articles on Chess for the German *Pariser Zeitung*.
It is a fact that he was able to return to France and that two articles
appeared in the German-controlled press over his name.

These articles were received by all sections of the chess world
with the greatest indignation. They were in fact a violent anti-
Jewish and pro-Nazi diatribe. They were at the same time so
utterly senseless that no unprejudiced person could believe in Dr.
Alekhine's authorship. When years later he saw these articles he
declared most solemnly that not a single word was from his pen.

In the meantime he and his wife were directed to take up residence
in Prague from where, for the next two years, he attended various
tournaments at Vienna, Munich and Salzburg, etc. His detractors
claim that he was a willing tool in the hands of the Germans and
had a prosperous time in their territory. This does not tally with
the description given by the Portuguese Champion, Francisco Lupi,
when he first met Dr. Alekhine after his return to Spain. Instead of
the fine physical specimen of a man, such as he expected to meet,
he found "a tall, very thin man waiting for me, whose words and
gestures were those of an automaton. . . . It was Alekhine."

The effect of the condemnation by fellow chess players on a man
who always had thrived on popularity can well be imagined. In
addition, for the second time in his life, he had lost all he had. His
fine home in France had been, as he put it, scientifically ransacked by
the invader. Neither Spain nor Portugal could afford him the living
to which he was accustomed or in fact, any living at all. The chances
in France were even worse at the time.

And so we see him in 1945-6 living in a Lisbon boarding house,
with his material circumstances gradually getting worse, suffering in
addition from severe heart trouble. His only hope was England ;
the British chess world, be it said to its honour, was not prepared to
condemn a man unheard. Indeed the first ray of light came when
he was invited to take part in the London Tournament of 1946.
The Champion's distress was overwhelming when the invitation was
cancelled because of the objections of the Dutch and American
Federations. Some of the masters had threatened to withdraw their
entries !

It was about this time that Dr. Alekhine decided to return to
France and to defend himself before the French Chess Federation.
He applied for a visa, but the Spanish frontier had been closed and
the visa never reached him.

Dr. Alekhine was still living in Lisbon and his affairs were at the
lowest ebb when a telegram arrived from Mr. Derbyshire, the President
of the British Chess Federation, transmitting a challenge to a match

by the Russian champion, M. Botvinnik, on the terms that had been agreed in 1939. The Moscow Chess Club was providing 10,000 dollars for the match, which was to take place in England subject to the British Chess Federation's approval. Dr. Alekhine was to receive two-thirds of the amount.

This sudden change of fortune proved too much for the sick man and resulted in a heart attack. As soon as he recovered he accepted the challenge and started his preparations for the match. In the last letter to reach this country the Champion asked whether it would be possible to get a visa to England from where he would more easily reach France. He also enquired whether a practice match with Dr. Tartakower could be arranged.

Then came weeks of weary waiting until the meeting of the British Chess Federation had taken place at which it was to be decided whether the Federation would agree to sponsor the match. This meeting took place on March 23rd in the afternoon, and by a unanimous vote the Federation gave their agreement.

The same night Dr. Alekhine breathed his last. . . .

Alekhine's chess career can be divided into four periods. During the first, which ended with the advent of the first world war, his opportunities of playing in master-tournaments were infrequent. He entered the Military School at St. Petersburg in 1909 at the age of 17 (he was born in 1892) and could not take part in tournaments more than, on an average, once a year. His early development was in consequence comparatively slow, though even so he succeeded in gaining the first prize on three occasions.

Practically nothing was heard of Alekhine between the years 1914-1921, which covered the world war and the Russian Revolution, though he won the Russian Championship at Moscow in 1920.

The second period of his chess career began with his return to Western Europe in 1921, when, circumstances leaving him no choice, he devoted himself entirely to Chess. During the following six years he played in many great tournaments and his dazzling sequence of brilliant victories were the talk of the chess world. It is during this time that he scored perhaps the most astonishing of his many successes —he became a Doctor-at-Law of the French Faculty.

The match with Capablanca gave him the world's title and was the culmination of the second period. It can be said that he had reached the zenith of his powers, perhaps the zenith to which human endeavour can attain.

The third period of his career, which started with his winning the Championship, lasted until the advent of the second world war. Between 1927 and 1936 his successes in tournaments were unequalled by any master at any time in the history of Chess. In particular at

San Remo 1930 and Bled 1931, though many of the greatest masters of the day took part, he left the field so far behind that he was at that time indisputably in a class by himself.

The first signs of retrogression were his lost match to Euwe in 1935 and his comparative failure at Nottingham, a very strong Tournament in which he gained only the sixth prize, with Botvinnik and Capablanca equal first, by far his worst result for twenty-four years. Although he regained the Championship from Dr. Euwe in 1937, having seemingly regained his powers to the full, in the AVRO Tournament of 1938, younger players, in Keres, Fine and Botvinnik, were ahead of him. Whether he could have re-established himself in the match with Botvinnik which had been agreed in 1939 is an open question which no one can answer with any degree of certainty.

The fourth period of Dr. Alekhine's chess career is a tragedy, as was his life during that period. He still won tournaments in Germany and occupied territory during the war and after that in Spain and Portugal, but the opposition was comparatively weak on the whole and made no call on his combative instinct. The quality of his play showed a marked falling off, as can be expected, apart from other considerations, when the opposition is not of the first order. Whether the match with Botvinnik, finally arranged on the day of Dr. Alekhine's death, would have heralded for the Champion a fifth and glorious period in his career is doubtful, but I feel certain that with Dr. Alekhine's wonderful powers of recuperation and his iron determination, it would have been the match of the century.

Dr. Alekhine's achievements, tabulated for the period covered by this book, are given below. His results up to 1937 have appeared in the first volume of his games. It would take too much space to refer in detail to the various tournaments in which he took part. Let it suffice to state that he played in seventy tournaments apart from five team tournaments.

In these seventy tournaments he won the first prize forty-one times, sharing the first prize on nine occasions. He won or shared the second prize fourteen times. On no occasion since 1911 did he fail to win a prize when taking part in a tournament !

Alekhine contributed few works to the literature of Chess. Three important books are available in the English language : the New York Tournament and two volumes of his own games. The value of all three lies in the annotation. For objectivity, clarity and clear-cut finality, they stand alone. The reason why he wrote so little is that he would not have been interested in writing for the average player, even if he could, and the writing of "pot-boilers," no matter how remunerative, was foreign to his nature.

As to his style of play, it was that of the true artist ; it was art for art's sake. The inventing of a method, the playing according to set principles, were not for him. His play was neither classical nor hyper-modern. It combined the best of all known styles in one harmonious whole ; technique was to him a means to an end. He was truly a great artist.

In everyday life he was a striking personality, with a fine physique and excellent manners, at home in any company. In some ways his character was curiously contradictory. Although at the chessboard or in the tournament room he had the utmost self-possession, away from the Chess atmosphere he was very shy, so that many casual acquaintances thought him supercilious, even arrogant.

Yet, after a game with one of his weaker brethren, no great master has ever been more ready to spend his time going over the game, analysing the positions, explaining his motives and freely giving encouragement and advice. He had not a few detractors, but what great man has ever been without them ?

There is, however, one serious lapse which can be held up against him—his failure to allow Capablanca a return match. There was a deep antagonism between the two men, who had once been friends. How it arose, whether suddenly or gradually, is not known, nor will it ever be decided who was in the wrong. In my opinion, whatever may have been the circumstances of the case, it was Alekhine, as the "man in possession," who should have given way, it was he who should have shown a more generous spirit. Had he done so, who knows but that, after the fall of France, when he tried to go to America, a helping hand might not have been extended to him, and the whole tragic chapter which followed might never have been written.

But whatever his faults may have been, his sad end more than atoned for them. Among lovers of Chess his name will live for ever with those of Philidor, Morphy, Lasker and Capablanca.

TOURNAMENTS

DATE		PRIZE	P.	W.	D.	L
1927	Kecskemet	1	16	8	8	–
1929	Bradley Beach	1	9	8	1	–
1930	San Remo	1	15	13	2	–
1930	Hamburg—Team Tournament ..	–	9	9	–	–
1931	Nice—Consultation Games ..	1	8	4	4	–
1931	Prague—Team Tournament ..	–	18	10	7	1
1931	Bled	1	26	15	11	–
1932	London	1	11	7	4	–
1932	Berne	1	15	11	3	1
1932	Mexico City	1 & 2 eq.	9	8	1	–
1932	Pasadena	1	11	7	3	1
1933	Folkestone—Team Tournament	–	12	8	3	1
1933	Paris	1	9	7	2	–
1933-4	Hastings	2	9	4	5	–
1934	Zurich	1	15	12	2	1
1935	Warsaw—Team Tournament ..	–	17	7	10	–
1935	Orebro	1	9	8	1	–
1936	Bad Nauheim	1 & 2 eq.	9	4	5	–
1936	Dresden	1	9	5	3	1
1936	Podebrady	2	17	8	9	–
1936	Nottingham	6	14	6	6	2
1936	Amsterdam	3	7	3	3	1
1936-7	Hastings	1	9	7	2	–
1937	Margate	3	9	6	–	3
1937	Kemeri	4 & 5 eq.	17	7	9	1
1937	German Quadrangular Tourney	2 & 3 eq.	6	3	1	2
1938	Montevideo	1	17	9	8	–
1938	Margate	1	9	6	2	1
1938	Plymouth	1 & 2 eq.	7	5	2	–
1938	AVRO	4,5 & 6 eq.	14	3	8	3
1939	Caracas	1	10	10	–	–
1939	Buenos Aires—Team Tournament	–	10	5	5	–
1939	Montevideo	1	7	7	1	–

MATCHES

		PLAYED	WON	LOST	DRAWN
1927	Capablanca	34	6	3	25
1929	Bogoljubow	25	11	5	9
1934	Bogoljubow	26	8	3	15
1935	Euwe	20	8	9	13
1937	Euwe	25	10	4	'11

The following are the results of the tournaments during the war years and after :—

1941, Munich, 2nd and 3rd with Lundin ; 1941, Cracow, 1st and 2nd with Schmidt; 1942, Salzburg, 1st; 1942, Munich, 1st; 1942, Cracow, 1st ; 1942, Prague, 1st and 2nd with Junge ; 1943, Prague, 1st ; 1943, Salzburg, 1st and 2nd with Keres ; 1944, Gijon, 1st ; 1945, Gijon, 2nd and 3rd with Medina ; 1945, Sabadell, 1st ; 1945, Almeria, 1st and 2nd with Lopez Nunez ; 1945, Melilla, 1st ; 1945, Caceres, 2nd.

In addition he played two short matches with Dr. Rey Ardid and Francisco Lupi, each of which he won by 4 wins, 1 loss, and 3 draws.

CONTENTS

PART I (1924-1927)

TOURNAMENT GAMES
AND MATCH WITH CAPABLANCA

PART II (1929-1934)

TOURNAMENT GAMES
AND MATCHES WITH BOGOLJUBOW

PART III (1934-1937)

TOURNAMENT GAMES
AND MATCHES WITH DR. EUWE

PART IV (1924-1933)

SIMULTANEOUS AND BLINDFOLD PLAY
EXHIBITION AND CONSULTATION GAMES

PART I (1924-1927)

Tournament Games and Match with Capablanca

GAME 1

KING'S INDIAN DEFENCE

New York Tournament, March, 1924.

Black : R. Reti

1. P—Q 4	Kt—K B 3
2. P—Q B 4	P—K Kt 3
3. P—K Kt 3	......

Nowadays 3. Kt—Q B 3, P—Q 4 ; 4. B—K B 4 followed by P—K 3, etc., is considered a promising line.

3.	B—Kt 2
4. B—Kt 2	Castles
5. Kt—Q B 3	P—Q 3
6. Kt—B 3	Kt—B 3

If Black has nothing better (and this seems to be the case) than to induce the advance of White's Pawn to Q 5—where, to be sure, it shortens for the time being the diagonal of the Bishop, but, on the other hand, brings considerable pressure upon Black's position— then his plan of development surely is not to be recommended.

7. P—Q 5	Kt—Kt 1
8. Castles	B—Kt 5

The exchange of this Bishop is not reasonable and merely lessens the power of resistance in Black's position. Likewise unsatisfactory would be 8. ....P—K 4 on account of 9. P×P (*e.p.*), P×P ; 10. B— Kt 5, etc., as played in my game against Sir G. Thomas in Carlsbad, 1923. On the other hand, there comes into consideration the move 8. .... P—Q R 4 in order to secure the square Q B 4 for the Knight for a while ; but in this case also White would maintain his superior position, by means of P—K R 3, B— K 3, Q—B 2, P—Q Kt 3, P—Q R 3 and, finally, P—Q Kt 4.

9. P—K R 3	......

It was important to clear the situation before the opponent completed his development.

9.	B×Kt
10. P×B	......

Much better than to recapture with the Bishop, by which process either the K's Pawn would have remained inactive a long time or, if advanced, would have restricted the action of his own pieces. After the text-move, however, he takes over the guarding of the important square K 5, and, moreover, Black must reckon with an eventual hostile action on the K's file opened hereby.

10.	P—K 3

The K's Pawn had to be exchanged, but it would have been relatively better for Black to have done so through 10. ....P—K 4. White thereupon would have had only *one* good reply (11. P×P *e.p.*), inasmuch as 11. P—K B 4, P×P ; 12. B×P, Q Kt—Q 2, etc., clearly would have been quite tolerable for Black. After the actual move, on the other hand, White has the pleasant choice between two good continuations.

11. P—B 4   ......

Even more favourable than 11. P×P, P×P; 12. R—K 1, Q—Q 2, etc.; whereupon it would have been by no means easy to profit from the weaknesses of Black's centre.

11. ......   P×P
12. P×P   ......

Now, however, Black has to make his choice between three distinct evils : (I) Weakness on Q B 2 if he should allow the Pawn position to remain intact. (II) Weakness on Q B 3 if after....P—B 4,P×P (*e.p.*) he should recapture with the Pawn and later on be forced to play .... P—Q 4. (III) And, finally, the line actually selected by him, through which he obtains an isolated Q's Pawn the protection of which, made difficult through the powerful co-operation of the hostile Bishops, will soon lead to a decisive weakening of his Q's side.

12. ......   P—B 4
13. P×P (*e.p.*)   Kt×P
14. B—K 3   Q—Q 2
15. Q—R 4   ......

A most effective square for the Queen, from which this piece will exert a troublesome pressure upon Black's Queen's wing.

15. ......   Q R—B 1
16. Q R—Q 1   ......

Both players follow out the same idea, that is, their Q Kt's Pawn must be removed beyond the reach of the hostile Bishops. Incidentally, 16. B×P would not do here, of course, on account of 16. ....R— R 1, etc.

16. ......   P—Kt 3
17. P—Kt 3   ......

This move has the additional purpose of further protecting the Queen in anticipation of the subsequent complications. How important this is will soon become apparent.

17. ......   K R—Q 1
18. R—Q 3   ......

It would have been premature to play Kt—Kt 5 at once, on account of 18. ....P—Q 4, etc. Now, however, White threatens to make this move after doubling the Rooks and therefore Black endeavours, through an exchange, to relieve the pressure exerted by the White Queen.

18. ......   Kt—K 2 ?

In this way, indeed, it cannot be done and Black immediately is at a material disadvantage. Somewhat better would have been 18. .... Kt—Q R 4 ; 19. Q—R 3, B—B 1 ; 20. K R—Q 1, etc., with a difficult game for Black, to be sure, but yet making defence possible.

19. Kt—Kt 5 !   P—Q 4

Clearly forced.

20. Kt×P   ......

This line was also made possible by White's 17th move.

20. ......   R—R 1
21. B×Kt P   Q×Q

Black has nothing better, because after 21. ....R (Q 1)—Kt 1 White would have continued simply with 22. Q×Q, Kt×Q ; 23. B—K 3, R— Kt 2; 24. B×Q P, Kt×B ; 25. R× Kt, R (R 1)×Kt; 26. B×R, R×B; 27. R (B 1)—Q 1, etc., with a decisive superiority.

22. P×Q   R—Q 2
23. Kt—Kt 5   R×P

Threatening also 24. ....R—

Kt 5 ; 25. R—Kt 3, R×R ; 26. P×R, R—Kt 2, etc.

24. Kt—B 3	R—R 3
25. R—Kt 1	R—Kt 2
26. B—B 5	R×R ch
27. Kt×R	Kt—B 3

The position is now cleared up, White having maintained his passed Pawn while Black's Queen's Pawn still remains weak.

28. Kt—B 3 !	......

The quickest method of winning. While he relinquishes the Q R's Pawn, White in return is enabled to force an entrance for his Rook into the enemy camp, whereby the decisive Pawn attack is made possible. The tame 28. P—R 3 would have permitted the opponent a more stubborn resistance after 28. ....R—R 4 ; 29. B—K 3, R—Kt 4, etc.

28.	R—R 4
29. B—K 3	Kt—Q Kt 5

After 29. ....P—Q 5 there would follow not 30. B×P, Kt×B ; 31. R×Kt, Kt—Q 4 ! etc., with drawing chances—but 30. B×Kt !, P×Kt ; 31. P—Q R 4, winning.

30. R—Q 2	P—R 3

If at once 30. ....Kt—K 5, then 31. Kt×Kt, P×Kt ; 32. R—Q 8 ch, B—B 1 ; 33. P—B 5 and wins.

31. P—Q R 4 !	......

Threatening 32. B—Kt 6 and thereby forcing Black's next move.

31.	Kt—K 5
32. Kt×Kt	P×Kt
33. R—Q 8 ch	K—R 2
34. B×P	R×P

If 34. ....P—B 4, then 35. R—Q 7 !, K—R 1 (or P×B ; 36. B—Q 4, R—Q 4 ; 37. R×B ch, K—R 1; 38. R—Q 7 disc. ch., followed by

the exchange of Rooks, and wins) ; 36. B—Q 4, B×B ; 37. R×B, P×B ; 38. R×Kt,. and wins.

Position after Black's 34th move.

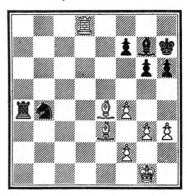

35. P—B 5 !	......

The initiation of the deciding Pawn charge. For the present 36. P×P ch, P×P ; 37. R—Q 6, etc., is threatening.

35.	R—R 3
36. P—R 4	P—R 4

Forced on account of the threat 37. P—R 5, etc.

37. P—Kt 4 !	R—R 4

Or 37. ....R P×P ; 38. P—R 5 and wins.

38. B P×P ch	B P×P
39. P×P	R×P
40. B—Kt 5 !	......

Winning at least the exchange.

40.	B—B 6
41. R—Q 7 ch	K—Kt 1
42. B×P	......

Now, after 42. ....R—R 1, White wins immediately by the advance of the R's Pawn.

Resigns.

GAME 2

IRREGULAR DEFENCE

New York Tournament, March, 1924.

Black : D. JANOWSKI

1.	P—Q 4	Kt—K B 3
2.	P—Q B 4	P—Q 3
3.	Kt—Q B 3	B—B 4 ?

This move would be reasonable if White had already developed his K's Knight, after which the control of his K 4 would temporarily remain in Black's hands. But in the actual situation the Bishop, after White's P—K 4, will have no future whatsoever. The late Janowski had certainly very fine feeling for handling the pair of Bishops—but was never the great openings connoisseur his contemporaries liked to represent him.

4.	P—K Kt 3	. . . . . .

Even 4. P—K B 3 and P—K 4 would have strategically refuted Black's Bishop's move.

4.	. . . . . .	P—B 3
5.	B—Kt 2	Q Kt—Q 2
6.	P—K 4	B—Kt 3
7.	K Kt—K 2	P—K 4
8.	P—K R 3	. . . . . .

Preparing B—K 3. From now on Black has only the choice between more or less unsatisfactory moves.

8.	. . . . . .	Q—Kt 3
9.	Castles	Castles

This supplies the opponent with an objective for a direct attack, which, owing to the unfortunate position of the Black pieces, will have catastrophic consequences. Instead, 9. ....B—K 2 ; 10. B—K 3, Q—B 2, etc., would have permitted a steadier resistance.

10.	P—Q 5 !	. . . . . .

Demolishing all Black's hopes for eventual delivery by means of .... P—Q 4. The temporary release of the square Q B 5 is, in comparison with this main motive, altogether immaterial.

10.	. . . . . .	Kt—B 4
11.	B—K 3	P×P
12.	B P×P	Q—R 3

Acceptance of the Pawn sacrifice would have led to a clearly losing position—for instance, 12. ....Q× Kt P ; 13. B×Kt, P×B ; 14. Q—R 4, Q—Kt 3 ; 15. P—B 4 !, P×P ; 16. P×P, etc. ; but the continuation in text is likewise without prospects.

13.	P—B 3	. . . . . .

Simple and decisive—Black has no longer a defence against P—Q Kt 4. If, for instance, 13. .... Q—Q 6, then, of course, 14. Q—B 1, etc.

13.	. . . . . .	K—Kt 1
14.	P—Kt 4	Kt—Q 2
15.	P—Q R 4	Q—B 5
16.	Q—Q 2	. . . . . .

Good enough ; but, considering White's tremendous positional advantage, there was no need for combining. The simple 16. R—Q Kt 1, followed by Q—Q 2 and K R—B 1, would have won without the slightest effort.

16.	. . . . . .	Q×Kt P

In such a position one may "eat" anything !

17.	B×P ch	K—R 1
18.	Q R—Kt 1	Q—R 4
19.	B—K 3	Kt—B 4
20.	R—Kt 5	Q—B 2
21.	P—R 5	K Kt—Q 2

Black has weathered the first onset more or less successfully ; but inasmuch as White can attack the hostile King with all his seven pieces, while Black's King's side is still undeveloped and his Q's Bishop has long since forgotten that it is able to move, White's win is merely a matter of time.

22. Kt—B 1   R—B 1
23. Kt—Kt 3   Kt—R 3

If 23. .... Kt × Kt, then 24. P—R 6 ! forcing 24. .... P—Kt 3 (for after 24. .... Kt × Q or R ? 25. P × P ch would have forced mate).

24. Kt—R 4   B—K 2

Black makes up his mind to give up the exchange, knowing that, if 24. .... K—Kt 1, White with 25. R—Q B 1, Q—Q 1 ; 26. R—B 6 would have proceeded to institute a decisive attack.

Position after Black's 24th move.

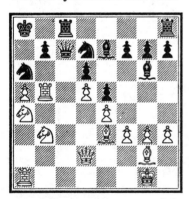

25. Kt—Kt 6 ch   ......

The crisis. After 25. .... Kt × Kt ; 26. P × Kt, Q *ad lib.*; 27. R × Kt ch would win immediately.

25. ......   K—Kt 1
26. R—Q B 1   K Kt—B 4
27. Kt × Kt   P × Kt

28. Kt × R   R × Kt
29. B—B 1   Q—Q 2
30. R—Kt 6   P—B 5

Or 30. .... B—Q 1 ; 31. R—Kt 2, still winning the Pawn.

31. R × P   R × R
32. B × R   Q × R P
33. Q—K Kt 2   ......

Technically simpler than 33. B × Kt, which would have won also.

33. ......   Q × Q ch
34. K × Q   B—Q 1
35. R—Kt 2   K—B 1
36. B × Kt   P × B
37. B—Kt 6   B—Kt 4
38. R—B 2 ch   K—Kt 2
39. P—Q 6   P—B 4.
40. P—Q 7   Resigns.

GAME 3

QUEEN'S GAMBIT DECLINED (TCHIGORIN'S DEFENCE)

Paris Tournament, February, 1925.

Black : E. COLLE

1. P—Q 4   P—Q 4
2. P—Q B 4   Kt—Q B 3
3. Kt—K B 3   B—Kt 5
4. Q—R 4   ......

A new move which I introduced here in order to avoid the usual variations deriving from 4. P × P, B × Kt, etc. I had the more reason to do so as the late Belgian Champion was a fine exponent of this particular defence and had obtained with it a number of notable successes.

4. ......   B × Kt
5. K P × B   P—K 3

After 5. .... P × P White can either play 6. B—K 3 or, even

better, sacrifice a Pawn for a big
advantage in development by continuing 6. Kt—B 3, Q×P ; 7. B—
K 3 followed by K B×P, etc.

6.	Kt—B 3	B—Kt 5
7.	P—Q R 3	.....

It is worth while to lose a *tempo*
in order to be immediately informed
as to the intentions of Black's
Bishop.

7.	......	B×Kt ch
8.	P×B	Kt—K 2
9.	R—Q Kt 1	R—Q Kt 1
10.	P×P	......

In the Baden-Baden Tournament
—which was played shortly after
this one—I played against the same
opponent 10. B—Q 3 and obtained
a more convincing positional advantage. I reproduce here that game,
because besides White's more accurate opening play it contains also a
very instructive Q's and R's ending
which probably induced Dr. Lasker
to select it as one of the few games
he included in his classical "Manual
of Chess."

This was its continuation : 10.
P×P ; 11. B×P, Castles ; 12.
Castles, Kt—Q 4 ; 13. Q—B 2, Kt
(B 3)—K 2 ; 14. B—Q 3, P—K R 3 ;
15. P—Q B 4, Kt—Q Kt 3 ; 16.
R—Q 1, Kt (Kt 3)—Q B 1 ; 17.
P—K B 4, P—Q Kt 3 ; 18. B—Kt 2,
P—Q B 3 ; 19. Q—K 2, Kt—Q 3 ;
20. Q—K 5, Kt—K 1 ; 21. P—
Q R 4, R—Kt 2 ; 22. K R—K 1, Kt—
B 3 ; 23. R (Kt 1)—Q 1, R—Q 2 ;
24. B—B 2, P—R 3 ; 25. Q—K 2 !,
Q—Kt 1 ; 26. P—Q 5 !, B P×P ;
27. B×Kt, P×B ; 28. Q—Kt 4 ch,
K—R 1 ; 29. P—B 5 !, Kt×P ; 30.
B×Kt, P×B ; 31. Q×P, Q—Q 1 ;
32. P×P, R—Q 3 ; 33. Q—B 4 !,
K—R 2 ; 34. Q—K 4 ch, K—R 1 ;
35. Q—K 3, K—Kt 2 ; 36. Q—Q 3 !,
P—Q R 4 ; 37. R—K 3, R—K Kt 1 ;
38. R—K R 3, Q—Q 2 ; 39. Q—K 3,
P—B 4 ; 40. R—Kt 3 ch, K—R 2 ;

41. R×R, K×R ; 42. Q—Kt 3 ch,
K—R 2 ; 43. Q—Q Kt 3, K—Kt 2 ;
44. P—K R 3, Q—Q 1 ; 45. Q—
Kt 3 ch, K—R 2 ; 46. Q—K 5 !,
Q—Q 2 ; 47. R—Q 3, P—B 3 ; 48.
Q—Q 4, Q—Q 1 ; 49. Q—Q B 4 !,
Q—Q 2 ; 50. R—Q 4, K—Kt 2 ; 51.
Q—Q 3, K—B 2 ; 52. P—Kt 4 !,
K—B 1 ; 53. P×P, Q—K 1 ; 54.
R—K 4, Q—R 4 ; 55. R—K Kt 4,
Q—B 2 ; 56. Q—K 3, Q—K R 2 ;
57. R—Kt 6, Black resigns.

10.	......	Q×P
11.	B—Q 3	Castles
12.	Castles	Q—Q 3 (!)

A good positional move freeing
Q 4 for the Knight and preventing
White's B—K B 4.

13.	Q—B 2	Kt—Kt 3
14.	P—K B 4	Q Kt—K 2

Preparing an action in the centre
starting with P—Q B 4.

15.	P—Kt 3	K R—Q 1
16.	R—Q 1	P—Kt 3
17.	P—Q R 4	......

This weakens the square Q Kt 4
and thus allows Black to obtain a
kind of initiative in the centre.
Correct was 17. B—Kt 2, and if 17.
....P—Q B 4, then 18. P—B 4 !,
P×P ; 19. B×P with some advan-
tage, as neither 19. ....Q×B ; 20.
B×Kt nor 19. ....Q×R P ; 20.
R—Q R 1, Q—Kt 5 ; 21. R—R 4,
Q—Q 3 ; 22. B—K 5 ! etc., would
be favourable for Black.

17.	......	Kt—Q 4 !
18.	B—Q 2	P—Q B 4
19.	P—B 5	......

Still trying to maintain a slight
pressure. The variation 19. P—
Q B 4, Kt—Kt 5 ; 20. B×Kt, P×B;
21. P—Q B 5, P×P ; 22. P×P, Q—
B 2 would have offered even less
prospect of winning.

19.	K P × P
20. B × P	P × P
21. P × P	Q Kt—K 2
22. B—Q Kt 4	Q—K B 3
23. Q B × Kt	.....

After 23. B—K R 3, Kt—Q 4 !
the pair of Bishops would be of
little use. White therefore tries to
take advantage of his passed Pawn
in conjunction with the open Q B's
file.

| 23. ...... | Q × B |
| 24. Q R—QB1 | ..... |

But the immediate 24. P—Q 5
was more consequent, for Black
could now increase his prospects of
a draw by answering 24. ....P—
Kt 4 !

24.	R—Q 4
25. B—K 4	R—Q 2
26. P—Q 5	Q—B 3
27. R—K 1 !	.....

The initial move of a rather
hidden mating conception.

| 27. ...... | R (Kt 1)—Q 1 |
| 28. Q—B 6 ! | Q—Kt 4 |

Black is right in avoiding the
exchange of Queens as both 28. ....
Q × Q ; 29. P × Q and 28..... Kt—
K 2 ; 29. Q × Q, P × Q ; 30. P—Q 6 !
would be decidedly in White's
favour. But strange as it may seem,
the square K Kt 4 for the Queen—
which looks the most natural—will
prove fatal. The right move was
28. ....Q—Q 5 after which there
would not be anything decisive for
White as yet.

| 29. B × Kt | R P × B |

As the answer shows, necessary
was 29. ....B P × B (of course not
Q × B ; 30. Q × R) ; 30. Q—K 6 ch,
R—B 2 ; 31. R—B 8, R × R ; 32.
Q × Q R ch, R—B 1 after which
White would have had the pleasant
choice between 33. R—K 8, Q—

K B 3 ; 34. R × R ch, Q × R ;
35. Q—B 6 and 33. Q—K 6 ch,
K—R 1 ; 34. P—Q 6, Q—Q 7 ; 35.
R—K 2, Q—B 8 ch ; 36. K—Kt 2,
Q—B 3 ch ; 37. K—R 3 most likely
winning in either case.

Position after Black's 29th move.

| 30. Q × R ! | ..... |

This Queen's sacrifice is only possible because Black's K Kt 4 is
occupied by the Queen, and the
King, therefore, will have no escape
after the Rook's doubling on the
8th rank.

30.	R × Q
31. R—K 8 ch	K—R 2
32. Q R—B 8	R—Q 1
33. R (K 8) × R ! Resigns.	

GAME 4

QUEEN'S GAMBIT DECLINED
(SLAV DEFENCE)

Paris Tournament, February,
1925.

Black : K. OPOCENSKY

1. P—Q 4	P—Q 4
2. P—Q B 4	P—Q B 3
3. Kt—Q B 3	.....

My second match with Dr. Euwe, in which the seemingly promising answer 3. ....P×P was refuted in a convincing manner, has proved that the text-move is at least as good as the fashionable 3. Kt—K B 3.

3.	Kt—K B 3
4. P—K 3	B—B 4
5. P×P	Kt×P

If 5. ....P×P then, of course, 6. Q—Q Kt 3 with advantage.

6. B—B 4	P—K 3
7. K Kt—K 2	......

Introduced by Rubinstein against Bogoljubow at Hastings, 1922, and creating for Black a number of difficulties because of the inactive position of his Q's Bishop and his backward development.

7.	Q Kt—Q 2
8. P—K 4	Kt×Kt
9. Kt×Kt	B—Kt 3
10. Castles	Q—R 5

After the more natural 10. .... B—Q Kt 5 White would maintain his positional advantage by playing simply 11. P—K B 3. The Queen's move prepares for castling on the Queen's side, and at the same time guarantees to the Bishop the square K R 4 in case of White P—K B 4—B 5.

11. P—Q 5 !	......

This centre action afforded an exact calculation as Black will now force the weakening move P—K Kt 3. But White had practically no other way of keeping the initiative—after 11. P—K B 3, Castles Q R Black's prospects would have been excellent.

11.	K P×P
12. P—K Kt 3	Q—B 3
13. P×P	B—Q B 4 ?

Black's first and already decisive mistake. He now loses the possibility of castling and finally succumbs because of his inability to co-ordinate the action of the Rooks. Necessary was first 13. ....Kt—K 4 and only after 14. B—K 2, B—Q B 4 ; if in that case 15. K—Kt 2 renewing the threat P—B 4, etc., then 15. ....P—K R 4 ! after which White would have been practically forced to answer 16. P—K R 4 followed by B—Kt 5, etc. The position in that case would remain full of dynamite, but by no means hopeless for the second player.

14. R—K 1 ch	K—B 1
15. P—B 4	Kt—Kt 3
16. B—Kt 3	P—K R 4
17. P—K R 4	......

From the 14th move onwards White has only one idea—to prevent the co-operation of Black's Rooks.

17.	K—Kt 1
18. P×P	P×P
19. R—Q B 1	......

After this White cannot prevent the exchange of one of his Bishops against the Knight.

19.	B—Q 5
20. Kt—K 4	B×Kt
21. R×B	P—B 4

Or 21. ....B×Kt P ; 22. R—B 5 !, Kt—Q 4 ; 23. B×Kt. P×B ; 24. R×P with a decisive advantage.

22. Q—K 2	......

Starting the final attack against Black's K B 2.

22.	P—Kt 3
23. B—Kt 5	Q—Q 3

Attacking White's K Kt 3.

24. Q—B 3	Q—B 1

Position after Black's 24th move.

25. R×B ! ......

Eliminating the only active enemy's piece and thus practically breaking down any resistance.

25. ...... P×R
26. R—B 6 ! K—R 2

After 26. ....K—Kt 2 White would have sacrificed another Rook: 27. R × Kt P ch !, K × R (or P × R ; 28. Q—Kt 7 ch followed by mate) ; 28. Q—B 6 ch, K—R 2 ; 29. B × B P, R—K Kt 1 ; 30. Q—B 5 ch, K—Kt 2 ; 31. Q—Kt 6 ch, K—R 1 ; 32. B—B 6 ch and mate at the next move.

27. B×P R—B 1
28. R × Kt P Resigns.

GAME 5

GIUOCO PIANO

Baden-Baden Tournament, May, 1925.

White : DR. S. TARRASCH

1. P—K 4 P—K 4
2. Kt—K B 3 Kt—Q B 3
3. B—B 4 B—B 4
4. P—B 3 B—Kt 3

5. P—Q 4 Q—K 2
6. Castles Kt—B 3 (!)

This move, introduced by me instead of the usual 6. ....P—Q 3, leaves White less choice because his K's Pawn is now attacked.

7. R—K 1 P—Q 3
8. P—Q R 4 P—Q R 3
9. P—K R 3 ......

A more or less necessary preparation for B—K 3.

9. ...... Castles
10. B—K Kt 5 ......

As White had no advantage to gain by provoking Black's next move he would have done better by playing 10. B—K 3 at once.

10. ...... P—K R 3
11. B—K 3 ......

If 11. B—R 4 then of course 11. .... K—R 1 followed by R—K Kt 1 and P—K Kt 4.

11. ...... Q—Q 1 !

This paradoxical move—the most difficult in the game—is very effective. The double idea is to prepare an eventual action in the middle—starting by ....P×P followed by ....P—Q 4 and, at the same time, free the K's file for the K's Rook.

12. B—Q 3 R—K 1
13. Q Kt—Q 2 B—R 2 (!)

Played in view of White's possible Kt—Q B 4.

14. Q—B 2 P×P

At the right time, as White cannot well retake with the Pawn because of 15. ....Kt—Q Kt 5.

15. Kt×P Kt—K 4
16. B—B 1 P—Q 4 !

After this Black becomes at least as strong in the centre as his opponent. The tactical justification of the move is shown by the variation 17. P—K B 4, Kt—Kt 3 ; 18. P—K 5, Kt—R 4 ! etc.∓

17. Q R—Q 1	P—B 4
18. Kt—Kt 3	Q—B 2
19. B—K B 4	......

Also after 19. P×P, Kt×P ; 20. Kt—B 4, Kt×Kt ; 21. B×Kt, Kt × B ; 22. R×Kt, R×R ; 23. P×R, Q—K 2 Black would have kept the slightly better prospects.

19.	Kt—B 6 ch !
20. Kt×Kt	Q×B
21. P×P ?	......

The decisive mistake, after which the game ends rapidly. I expected instead 21. P—K 5 and hoped after 21. ....B—B 4 ; 22. Q—Q 2, Q×Q ; 23. R×Q, Kt—K 5 ; 24. R (Q 2)—Q 1 (R×Q P ?, B—K 3) Q R—Q 1 to be able to exploit the advantage of the two Bishops.

Position after White's 21st move.

21.	B—B 4 !

An important intermediate move, after which there is not a sufficient defence. Much less convincing would be 21. ....B×P because of 22. P×B, Q×Kt ; 23. B—Kt 2, etc.

22. B—Q 3	......

Or 22. Q—Q 2, Q×P ; 23. Kt—B 1, B—B 7 ! ; 24. R×R ch, R×R ; 25. R—K 1, Kt—K 5 ; 26. Q—B 4, P—B 5 ; 27. Kt—Q 4, B×Kt ; 28. P×Kt, Q—Kt 5 ! with a winning advantage for Black.

22.	B×P

And not 22. ....B×B ; 23. Q×B, P—B 5 because of 24. Q—Q 2.

23. P×B	Q×Kt
24. R×R ch	......

After the immediate 24. B—B 1 and the following exchange of Rooks by Black he would, of course, have lost his only hope—the passed pawn. But after the text move Black forces the game by a mating attack.

24.	R×R
25. B—B 1	R—K 4
26. P—B 4	......

26. P—Q 6 would not, obviously, alter matters.

26.	R—Kt 4 ch
27. K—R 2	Kt—Kt 5 ch
28. P×Kt	R×Kt P

Threatening an unavoidable mate.

Resigns.

GAME 6

KING'S FIANCHETTO

Baden-Baden Tournament, May, 1925.

White : R. Reti

1. P—K Kt 3	P—K 4
2. Kt—K B 3	......

An experiment which Réti never repeated after the present game.

White intends to play the Alekhine's Defence with colours reversed, *i.e.*, with one *tempo* more. But the way he uses that *tempo* (P—K Kt 3) could have turned to his disadvantage (see next note).

2. ......   P—K 5
3. Kt—Q 4   P—Q 4

Black is satisfied with a free development of his pieces and about even middle game prospects. But he could obtain more by playing 3. ....P—Q B 4 !; 4. Kt—Kt 3, P— B 5 ; 5. Kt—Q 4, B—B 4 ; 6. P— Q B 3, Kt—Q B 3, thus bringing *ad absurdum* White's "development."

4. P—Q 3   P × P
5. Q × P   Kt—K B 3
6. B—Kt 2   B—Kt 5 ch

Trying at all costs to bring as rapidly as possible all pieces into action. But nowadays I would probably have thought more about the security of the dark-coloured squares of my position and therefore have avoided the following exchange of Bishops.

7. B—Q 2   B × B ch
8. Kt × B   Castles
9. P—Q B 4 ! ......

Apart from his eccentric first move, Réti plays the opening very well ; Black would not have any advantage by answering 9. ....P— Q B 4 because of 10. Kt—Kt 3 threatening both 11. Kt × P and 11. P × P.

9. ......   Kt—R 3

Comparatively the best ; but it cannot be denied that White obtains now a sort of pressure on the half-open Q B's file.

10. P × P   Kt—Q Kt 5
11. Q—B 4   Q Kt × QP

12. Q Kt—Kt 3   P—B 3
13. Castles (K R) R—K 1
14. K R—Q 1   B—Kt 5
15. R—Q 2   ......

After 15. P—K R 3 Black would have brought his Bishop to K 5 via R 4 and Kt 3.

15. ......   Q—B 1
16. Kt—Q B 5   B—R 6 !
17. B—B 3   ......

By his previous move Black had offered a Pawn, the acceptance of which would have been fatal for White, for instance : 17. B × B, Q × B ; 18. Kt × Kt P, Kt—K Kt 5 ; 19. Kt—B 3, Kt (Q 4)—K 6 ! ; 20. P × Kt, Kt × K P ; 21. Q × B P ch, K—R 1 ! ; 22. Kt—R 4, R—K B 1 and wins.

17. ......   B—Kt 5

Giving the opponent the choice between three possibilities : (1) to exchange his beloved "fianchetto" Bishop ; (2) to accept an immediate draw by repetition of moves (18. B—Kt 2, B—R 6 ; 19. B—B 3, etc.) which in such an early stage always means a moral defeat for the first player, and (3) to place the Bishop on a worse square (R 1). He finally decides to play "for the win" and thus permits Black to start a most interesting counter-attack.

18. B—Kt 2   B—R 6
19. B—B 3   B—Kt 5
20. B—R 1   ......

At last !

20. ......   P—K R 4 !

In order by the exchange of this Pawn to weaken White's K Kt 3.

21. P—Q Kt 4   P—Q R 3
22. R—Q B 1   P—R 5
23. P—R 4   P × P
24. R P × P   Q—B 2
25. P—Kt 5   ......

Consequent, but very risky to say the least. By playing 25. P—K 4, Kt—Kt 3 ; 26. Q—Kt 3, Q Kt 1—Q 2 etc. ! White could meet the immediate threats against his King, but the obstruction of the Bishop's diagonal would at the same time end his hopes on the other wing.

25. ......   R P×P
26. P×P   ......

Position after White's 26th move.

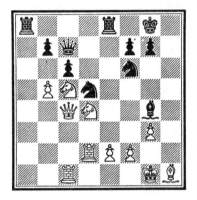

26. ......   R—K 6 !

It seems almost incredible that this spectacular move not only stops White's attack but even brings him serious trouble. And yet it is so. It is obvious enough that the Rook cannot be taken because of 27. .... Q×P ch, followed by 28. .... Kt×P and wins ; and also that White has to do something in order to parry 27. ....R×P ch !, etc.

27. Kt—B 3   ......

As the following shows, this natural move loses perforce. Also insufficient was 27. K—R 2 because of 27. ....Q R—R 6 ! ; 28. Kt (B 5)—Kt 3 (not 28. P×R, Kt×P followed by Kt—B 8 ch etc.), Q—K 4 ! ; 29. P×B P, P×B P with a powerful attack as 30. P×R would still be bad because of 30.

....Q—R 4 ch followed by 31. .... Q—R 6. The only chance of salvation was 27. B—B 3 !, B×B ; 28. P×B !, P×P ; 29. Kt×P, Q—Q R 4 ! still with advantage for Black, as 30. R×Kt ? would lose immediately after 30. ....R—K 8 ch ; 31. R×R, Q×R ch followed by 32. R—R 8.

27. ......   P×P
28. Q×P   Kt—B 6 !
29. Q×P   ......

After 29. Q—B 4 the answer 29. ....P—Q Kt 4 ! would be decisive.

29. ......   Q×Q

And not 29. ....Kt×P ch because of 30. R×Kt !, Q×Q ; 31. R×R ! with some saving chances for White.

30. Kt×Q   Kt×P ch
31. K—R 2   ......

Or 31. K—B 1, Kt×P ch ; 32. P×Kt, B×Kt ; 33. B×B, R×B ch ; 34. K—Kt 2, R (R 1)—R 6 ; 35. R—Q 8 ch, K—R 2 ; 36. R—R 1 ch, K—Kt 3 ; 37. R—R 3, R (B 6)—Q Kt 6 ! and wins.

Position after White's 31st move.

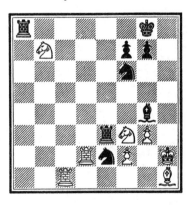

31. ......   Kt—K 5 !

The beginning of a new combination—which, however, is the absolutely logical consequence of the previous manœuvres—aiming, after a series of twelve practically forced moves, at the capture of White's exposed Knight at Q Kt 7. Black's Rook is still taboo as 32. P × R ?, Kt (K 5) × R ! would lose the exchange.

32. R—B 4 !   ......

Comparatively the best defence.

32. ......   Kt × B P

Insufficient would be 32. .... Kt × R because of 33. Kt × Kt ! or 32. ....B × Kt because of R × Kt ! etc. The situation is still very complicated.

33. B—Kt 2   B—K 3 !

One of the important links of the combination.

34. R (B 4)—B 2 ......

Here, and in the following, White, as it is easy to see, has no choice.

34. ......   Kt—Kt 5 ch
35. K—R 3   ......

Not 35. K—R 1 because of 35. .... R—R 8 ch.

35. ......   Kt—K 4 disc. ch
36. K—R 2   R × Kt !
37. R × Kt   Kt—Kt 5 ch
38. K—R 3   Kt—K 6 disc. ch
39. K—R 2   Kt × R
40. B × R   Kt—Q 5

If now 41. R—K 3 (B 2) then 41. ....Kt × B ch ; 42. R × Kt, B—Q 4 ! (the final point !) winning a piece.

Resigns.

I consider this and the game against Bogoljubow at Hastings, 1922 (cf. My Best Games 1908–23) the most brilliant tournament games of my chess career. And by a peculiar coincidence they both remained undistinguished as there were no brilliancy prizes awarded in either of these contests !

GAME 7

QUEEN'S GAMBIT DECLINED (ORTHODOX DEFENCE)

Baden-Baden Tournament, May, 1925.

Black : DR. K. TREYBAL

1. P—Q 4	P—Q 4
2. P—Q B 4	P—K 3
3. Kt—Q B 3	Kt—K B 3
4. B—Kt 5	Q Kt—Q 2
5. P—K 3	B—K 2
6. Kt—B 3	Castles
7. R—B 1	P—B 3
8. B—Q 3	P × P
9. B × B P	Kt—Q 4
10. B × B	Q × B
11. Kt—K 4	......

A very safe, but harmless move, for which I had a marked predilection during a certain period of my career, including the Capablanca Match. Now I have come to the conclusion that the old 11. Castles, although not extremely promising, still offers more fighting chances than the Knight's move.

11. ......   Q Kt—B 3

After this answer, however, Black will have difficulties in freeing his game by means of ....P—K 4, or ....P—Q B 4 and therefore White's position will soon become much preferable. Good methods in order to obtain equality are : 11. .... K Kt—B 3, and after 12. Kt—Kt 3 either 12. ....Q—Kt 5 ch (Capablanca) or even 12. ....P—K 4 (Dr. Lasker).

12. Kt—Kt 3	Q—Kt 5 ch
13. Q—Q 2	Q×Q ch
14. K×Q	R—Q 1
15. K R—Q 1	B—Q 2
16. Kt—K 5	B—K 1
17. K—K 2	K—B 1
18. P—B 4	P—K Kt 3

It is very seldom advisable in the end-game to place the Pawns on the squares of the colour of their own Bishop. A more logical plan was 18. ....Kt—Q 2, eventually followed by ....P—B 3.

19. K—B 3	Q R—B 1
20. B—Kt 3	R—B 2
21. Kt—K 2	Kt—K 2
22. P—Kt 4	K R—B 1
23. Kt—Kt 3 !	......

After this, Black's preparations for ....P—Q B 4 prove useless, as this move would now have fatal consequences after 24. P—Kt 5— for instance : I—24. ....Kt (B 3)— Q 4 ; 25. P×P, R×P ; 26. R×R, R×R ; 27. Kt—K 4, R—B 2 ; 28. Kt—Q 6, with a tremendous positional advantage for White. II—24. .... Kt—Q 2 ; 25. Kt× Kt ch, B×Kt ; 26. R×P, R×R ; 27. P×R, K—K 1 ; 28. K—B 2 and White would retain the extra Pawn.

23. ......   Kt (B 3)—Q 4

Therefore this purely passive move, which permits White's following effective Knight's manœuvre.

24. Kt—K 4   R—Q 1

After 24. ....P—K B 3 White would exchange two minor pieces for a Rook and two Pawns, thus obtaining a won position—for instance, 25 Kt—B 5 !, P×Kt ; 26. Kt×P ch, K—Kt 1 ; 27. Kt×R, P—K 5 ch (otherwise 28. P—K 4) ; 28. K×P, R×Kt ; 29. K—B 3 followed by P—K 4 ±.

25. Kt—B 5	P—Kt 3
26. Kt—R 6	R (B 2)—B 1
27. P—K 4	......

Position after White's 27th move.

27. ......   P—B 3

A desperate attempt to get some freedom for his pieces. After 27. ....Kt—B 3 (or Kt—B 2 ; 28. Kt×Kt followed by 29. P—Q 5 ±) ; 28. P—Kt 5, Kt—Q 2 ; 29. Kt— K Kt 4, K—Kt 2 ; 30. P—K R 4, etc., he would rapidly perish from asphyxia.

28. P×Kt	P×Kt
29. P—Q 6 !	......

Forcing a decisive win of material; if now 29. ....P—K 5 ch, then 30. K×P, R×P ; 31. K—K 5 !, R (B 1) —Q 1 ; 32. Kt—B 7 and wins.

29.	R×P
30. B P×P	R—Q 4

30. ....R (Q 3)—Q 1 ; 31. B× K P would be even more hopeless.

31. B×R	Kt×B
32. P—Q R 3	......

The beginning of the rather instructive technical part. First and foremost, White must force the exchange of the opponent's central Knight.

32.	P—K Kt 4
33. Kt—Kt 4	Kt—K 2
34. Kt—Q 3	Kt—Q 4
35. P—K R 4 !	P×P

If 35. ....P—K R 3, then 36. P×P, followed by Kt—B 2—K 4 (or K R 3), etc.

36. Kt—B 4	Kt×Kt
37. K×Kt	......

White's next manœuvre will be the elimination of the K R 4 Pawn and the return of the King to the centre, in order to release the Rook from the protection of the Queen's Pawn.

37.	R—Q 1
38. K—Kt 5	K—Kt 2
39. K×P	R—Q 4
40. K—Kt 5	R—Q 1
41. K—B 4	R—Q 2
42. K—K 3	R—Kt 2
43. P—Kt 4	......

The beginning of the third phase —the blockade of Black's weak spots.

43.	P—Q R 3
44. R—B 1	R—R 2
45. R—B 6	R—K 2
46. P—Q R 4	K—Kt 1
47. P—R 5	P—Kt 4
48. P—Q 5 !	......

This Pawn sacrifice, in order to permit the victorious entrance of the King into the enemy's camp, is the absolutely logical conclusion of the whole procedure.

48.	K P×P

Or, 48 ... B P×P; 49. R—Q B 8, followed by R—Q R 8, etc.

49. P—K 6	K—Kt 2
50. P—Kt 5	P—R 4

51. K—Q 4	R—Q B 2
52. K—B 5	R—B 1
53. K—Kt 6	P—Q 5
54. P—K 7 !	Resigns.

Although this game, and the next one, do not exhibit any particularly thrilling points, I have included them in this collection because they illustrate in a convincing way the methods to follow in order to exploit an advantage in space obtained in the opening stage.

GAME 8

ALEKHINE'S DEFENCE

Baden-Baden Tournament, May, 1925.

White : Sir G. A. Thomas

1. P—K 4	Kt—K B 3
2. P—Q 3	......

A very tame continuation, which does not offer prospects of any opening advantage.

2.	P—B 4
3. P—K B 4	Kt—Q B 3
4. Kt—K B 3	P—K Kt 3
5. B—K 2	B—Kt 2
6. Q Kt—Q 2 (?)	

After this unnatural-looking move White's game remains very cramped. A much lesser evil was 6. P—B 4 ceding the square Q 4 but preventing the double advance of Black's Queen's Pawn.

6.	P—Q 4
7. Castles	Castles
8. K—R 1	P—Kt 3
9. P×P	Q×P

Even better than 9. ....Kt×P, which move would permit the answer 10. Kt—K 4.

10. Q—K 1	......

The Pawn sacrifice by 10. Kt—
K. 5 would prove insufficient after
10. ....Kt × Kt ; 11. P × Kt, Q ×
K P ; 12. Kt—B 4 (or 12. B—B 3,
R—Kt 1 ; 13. Kt—B 4, Q—B 2),
Q—K 3 ! ; 13. B—B 3, Kt—Q 4,
etc.

10.	......	B—Kt 2
11.	Kt—B 4	Kt—Q 5
12.	Kt—K 3	Q—B 3
13.	B—Q 1	Kt—Q 4 !

Practically forcing the exchange
of three minor pieces, and thus
increasing by the simplest method
the positional advantage already
acquired. A similar procedure was
adopted by me in a game against
A. Evenssohn (see *My Best Games
1908–1923*).

14. K Kt × Kt   ......

The consequences of an attempt
to win a Pawn by 14. Kt (K 3) × Kt
would be sad : 14. ....Q × Kt ; 15.
Q × K P, K R—K 1 ; 16. Q—Kt 5,
Kt × Kt ; 17. B × Kt, Q × Q ; 18.
P × Q, B × B ; 19. P × B, R—K 7 ∓.

14.	......	P × Kt
15.	Kt × Kt	Q × Kt
16.	B—B 3	Q—Q 2
17.	B × B	Q × B
18.	P—B 4	......

Otherwise he would remain with
the awful weakness at Q B 2.

18.	......	P × P (*e.p.*)
19.	P × P	Q R—B 1
20.	B—Kt 2	......

Only slightly better would be 20.
B—Q 2.

| 20. | ...... | K R—Q 1 |
| 21. | R—B 3 | B—B 3 |

Releases the Queen from the
worry about K 2.

Position after Black's 21st move.

22. P—Q 4   ......

The positional capitulation after
which Black will have comparatively easy winning play, because of
the full control of the light-coloured
squares. But owing to the threat
....Q—R 3 in connection with the
doubling of Rooks on the Q's file,
White had already no real choice.

22.	....	Q—Q 4
23.	Q—K 3	Q—Q Kt 4 !
24.	Q—Q 2	R—Q 4
25.	P—K R 3	P—K 3
26.	R—K 1	Q—R 5
27.	R—R 1	P—Q Kt 4
28.	Q—Q 1	R—B 5

Also good was, of course, 28. ....
Q × Q ; but Black is not in a hurry.
The adversary will not be able to
avoid the exchange.

29.	Q—Kt 3	R—Q 3
30.	K—R 2	R—R 3
31.	K R—B 1	B—K 2
32.	K—R 1	R (B 5)—B 3 !

Intending to force White to exchange Queens after ....Q—B 5
followed by ....R—R 5 and ....
R (B 3)—R 3.

33. K R—K 1   B—R 5 !

Chasing the Rook from the K's file ; because if, for instance, 34. R—K 2, then 34. ....Q×Q ! 35. P×Q, R×R ch ; 36. B×R, R—R 3 ; 37. B—Kt 2, R—R 7 ; 38. P—Q Kt 4 (or 38. K—R 2, P—Q R 4 !), B—Kt 6 ; 39. P—Q 5, B×P (simpler than 39. ....P×P ; 40. P—Q B 4 !) etc., winning easily.

| 34. R—K B 1 | Q—B 5 |
| 35. Q×Q | ...... |

Otherwise Black would play, as mentioned, 35. ....R—R 5, etc.

35.	R×Q
36. P—R 3	B—K 2
37. K R—Kt 1	B—Q 3 !

Forcing also the K Kt's Pawn on to a dark-coloured square.

38. P—K Kt 3	K—B 1
39. K—Kt 2	K—K 2
40. K—B 2	K—Q 2
41. K—K 2	K—B 3

After having protected the Q Kt's Pawn Black threatens ....R (B 5)—R 5.

42. R—R 2	R (B 5)—R 5
43. K R—Q R 1	K—Q 4
44. K—Q 3	R (R 3)—R 4
45. B—B 1	P—Q R 3
46. B—Kt 2	P—R 4

Threatening, of course, 47. .... P—R 5.

| 47. P—R 4 | P—B 3 ! |

After this White is without defence against ....P—K 4, etc.

48. B—B 1	P—K 4
49. B P×P	P×P
50. B—Kt 2	......

Or 50. P×P. B×K P; 51. B—B 4, B×B ; 52. P×B, K—K 3 ! (the simplest), and wins.

50.	P×P
51. P×P	P—Kt 5 !
Resigns.	

The late Nimzowitsch—who was rather reluctant to comment on the games of his colleagues—distinguished this one by including it as an example in his remarkable book, *My System.*

GAME 9

IRREGULAR DEFENCE

Baden-Baden Tournament, May, 1925.

Black : F. MARSHALL

| 1. P—Q 4 | Kt—K B 3 |
| 2. P—Q B 4 | P—Q 4 |

This move is very seldom adopted in Master play and in fact cannot be recommended. It partly succeeds, however, in the present game because of the not quite accurate opening play of White.

| 3. P×P | Kt×P |
| 4. P—K 4 | ...... |

As this advance could not be prevented by Black, it should have been delayed, and only executed after the development of the King's side pieces. A good plan here was 4. P—K Kt 3 followed by B—Kt 2, reserving P—K 4 for a more favourable moment.

| 4. ...... | Kt—K B 3 |
| 5. B—Q 3 | ...... |

Also after 5. Kt—Q B 3 Black could have obtained an even game by answering 5. ....P—K 4.

5.	P—K 4 !
6. P×P	Kt—Kt 5
7. Kt—K B 3	Kt—Q B 3
8. B—K Kt 5 !	......

White realises that he cannot obtain any kind of advantage by trying to keep the extra-Pawn. If, for instance, 8. B—K B 4, then 8. ....Kt—Q Kt 5 ! ; 9. B—Kt 5 ch, B—Q 2 ; 10. B×B ch, Q×B ; 11. Q×Q ch, K×Q ; 12. Castles, Kt—B 7 ; 13. R—Q 1 ch, K—B 1 ; 14. P—K R 3 (or Kt—K Kt 5), Kt—K R 3 and White's positional advantage would not compensate the loss of the exchange.

8.	B—K 2
9. B×B	Q×B
10. Kt—B 3	Q Kt×P
11. Kt×Kt	Q×Kt

But here Black decidedly over-estimates his position. Instead of the text move which—as the following convincingly proves—only exposes his Queen to a Pawn attack, he could obtain a game with even prospects by continuing 11. .... Kt×K P ; 12. Castles, Castles ; 13. B—K 2, B—K 3, etc.

12. P—K R 3	Kt—B 3
13. Q—Q 2 !	......

It is certainly surprising to what extent the simple Queen's manœuvre — by which White strengthens the dark coloured squares of his position—improves his chances for the middle game. From now on Black will be gradually dragged into a lost position without having made a move which could be considered an actual mistake.

13.	B—Q 2
14. Q—K 3 !	......

Not only taking control of the squares Q 4 and Q B 5 but, above all, preventing Black's castling (Q R).

14.	B—B 3
15. Castles (Q R)	Castles (K R)

As Black cannot bring his King in safety on the Queen's side (if 15. ....Q—Q R 4 then 16. B—B 4 ! ±) he has practically no choice.

16. P—B 4	Q—K 3

After 16. ....Q—Q R 4 ; 17. P—K 5 Black would (as well as in the actual game) lose a Pawn by continuing 17. ....Kt—Q 4 ; 18. Kt × Kt, B×Kt ; 19. B×P ch followed by Q—Q 3 ch and Q×B.

17. P—K 5	......

With the main threat 18. P—B 5.

17.	K R—K 1
18. K R—K 1	Q R—Q 1

Better was 18. ....Kt—Q 2 after which White would have continued his attack by 19. P—K Kt 4, etc. The Rook's move permits him to obtain the win by a forced sequence of moves.

19. P—B 5	Q—K 2
20. Q—Kt 5	Kt—Q 4
21. P—B 6	Q—B 1

Position after Black's 21st move.

22. B—B 4 !	......

The action of this Bishop on the diagonal Q R 2—K Kt 8 proves immediately decisive. It is important to notice that Black does not dispose here of the intermediate move 22. ....P—K R 3 because of 23. P × P ! winning a piece.

22.	Kt × Kt
23. R × R	R × R
24. P × P !	......

Much more convincing than 24. P—K 6, R—Q 4 !

| 24. ...... | Kt × P ch |

Or 24. ....Q—K 1 ; 25. B × P ch !, K × B ; 26. R—B 1 ch, K—K 3 ; 27. R—B 6 ch, K—Q 4 ; 28. R—B 8 and wins.

| 25. K—Kt 1 ! | ...... |

And not 25. B × Kt, Q—B 4 ch.

| 25. ...... | Q—K 1 |
| 26. P—K 6 ! | ...... |

Now even stronger than 26. B × P ch.

| 26. ...... | B—K 5 ch |
| 27. K—R 1 | ...... |

Also possible was 27. R × B, R—Q 8 ch ; 28. K—B 2, Q—R 5 ch ; 29. P—Q Kt 3, Kt—Kt 5 ch ; 30. K × R, etc., but the text move is simpler.

| 27. ...... | P—K B 4 |

Despair ; as 27. ....P × P would lose after 28. B × P ch, Q × B ; 29. Q × R ch, K × P ; 30. Q—Q 4 ch, followed by 31. R × B.

28. P—K 7 disc. ch	R—Q4
29. Q—B 6 !	Q—B 2
30. P—K 8 Queen's ch followed by mate in two.	

GAME 10

QUEEN'S GAMBIT DECLINED (SLAV DEFENCE)

Semmering Tournament, April, 1926.

White : J. DAVIDSON

Brilliancy Prize

1. P—Q 4	P—Q 4
2. P—Q B 4	P—Q B 3
3. Kt—K B 3	Kt—B 3
4. P—K 3	P—K 3

The fashionable move nowadays is 4. ... B—B 4, as the so-called "Meran" system inaugurated by the text move is considered to be rather favourable for White.

| 5. Kt—B 3 | Q Kt—Q 2 |
| 6. Q—B 2 | ...... |

The natural—and best—move is 6. B—Q 3. But at that time the system mentioned was not yet elaborated in all its details.

6.	B—Q 3
7. B—Q 3	Castles
8. Castles	Q—K 2
9. P—K 4	P × B P
10. B × P	P—K 4

Thus Black has obtained a position similar to the one which Tchigorin considered as perfectly playable, but with the appreciable advantage that his Queen already occupies the natural developing square K 2, while the White Queen is not particularly well posted at Q B 2.

| 11. R—Q 1 | P × P |
| 12. Kt × P | Kt—Kt 3 ! |

Better than 12. ....Kt—K 4 ; 13. B—B 1, Kt—Kt 3 ; 14. Kt—B 5, B × Kt ; 15. P × B, Kt—K 4 ;

16. B—K Kt 5 with a good game for White.

13. B—B 1   R—Q 1

Threatening 14.... B×P ch ; 15. K×B, R×Kt ; 16. R×R, Q—K 4 ch, etc., and thus inducing White to weaken his King's position.

14. P—K R 3   B—B 2

Threatening to win a piece by 15. ....R×Kt followed by 16. ....Q—K 4.

15. B—K 3   R—K 1 !

Black's previous move attacked the Queen's Bishop at K 3, and this one forces the other Bishop to move on the third rank. As will be seen, both Bishops are now badly posted for they obstruct the action of some of the other pieces and, besides, they can be attacked by the enemy's Knights.

16. B—Q 3   Kt—R 4
17. Q Kt—K 2   P—Kt 3

Chiefly in order to prepare, by protecting the square K B 4, the move Kt—Q 2.

18. R—K 1   Kt—Q 2
19. Kt—K B 3   ......

After this retreat Black gets a definite pull. I expected here 19.... P—K B 4 with the continuation 19. K (Q 2)—B 3 ; 20. P—K 5, Kt—Q 4; 21. B—Q 2, B—Kt 3 after which, although Black's game would still remain preferable, White would not be without some fighting chances.

19. ......   B—Kt 3 !

Expecting to increase the positional advantage already obtained —after 20. B×B, R P×B—on account of the open Q R's file. In order to avoid this unpleasant variation White tries with his two next moves to complicate matters, but only succeeds in accelerating the catastrophe.

20. B—K Kt 5   Q—B 4 !

If now 21. Q×Q, Kt×Q ; 22. Kt—B 1 (forced)—then 22. .... P—B 3 ; 23. B—Q 2, Kt×B ; 24. Kt×Kt, Kt—Kt 6 ; 25. P—K 5, B—K B 4, with a winning positional advantage.

21. Kt—B 3   Kt—K 4 !

Forcing the following exchange and thus renewing the attack on the diagonal Q Kt—K R 7, which will prove decisive.

22. Kt × Kt   Q × Kt
23. B—K 3   B—B 2
24. Kt—K 2   ......

Also 24. P—K Kt 3, B×R P, etc. would have lost in the long run.

24. ......   Q—R 7 ch
25. K—B 1   ......

Position after White's 25th move.

25. ......   B×P !

This sacrificing combination is neither particularly complicated nor unusual. But its value is considerably increased by the fact that it forms the logical conclusion of the previous positional play.

26. P×B	Q×R P ch
27. K—Kt 1	B—R 7 ch
28. K—R 1	Kt—B 5 !

Doubtless the shortest way to a win.

29. Kt×Kt	......

If 29. B×Kt then 29. ....B—Kt 6 disc. ch followed by mate in two moves.

29.	B×Kt disc. ch
30. K—K Kt 1	B—R 7 ch
31. K—R 1	Q—B 6 ch !

The point of the whole combination which forces the win of the Queen for a Rook and a Bishop.

32. K×B	R—K 4
33. Q—B 5	......

The only move.

33.	R×Q
34. B×R	Q—R 4 ch
35. K—Kt 2	Q×B

The rest is merely a matter of routine. 36. R—K 3, R—K 1 ; 37. Q R—K 1, Q—K 4 ; 38. Q R —K 2, R—K 3 ; 39. P—Kt 3, R—B 3 ; 40. R—Kt 3, K—Kt 2 ; 41. B—Kt 1, R—B 5 ; 42. B—Q 3, R—R 5 ; 43. K—B 3, Q—B 5 ch ; 44. K—Kt 2, Q—B 8 ; 45. K—B 3, P—K R 4 ; 46. R—B 2, Q—Q 8 ch ; 47. K—K 3, R—R 8 ; 48. K— Q 4, P—R 5 ; 49. R—K 3, R—K 8 ; 50. R×R, Q×R ; 51. R—K 2, Q— Q R 8 ch ; 52. K—B 4, P—Q Kt 4 ch. White resigns.

GAME 11

QUEEN'S INDIAN DEFENCE

Semmering Tournament, April, 1926.

White : A. RUBINSTEIN

Brilliancy Prize

1. P—Q 4	Kt—K B 3
2. P—Q B 4	P—K 3
3. Kt—K B 3	P—Q Kt 3
4. P—K Kt 3	B—Kt 2
5. B—Kt 2	B—Kt 5 ch

This simplification is hardly advisable, as White's Queen's Bishop should develop less activity in the future than Black's King's Bishop. More promising, therefore, is 5. .... B—K 2.

6. Q Kt—Q 2	......

For reasons just mentioned 6. B—Q 2 seems to be the logical answer.

6.	Castles
7. Castles	P—Q 4

As the following shows, this is good enough to equalise. A good manœuvre was also 7. ....R—K 1 followed by ....B—K B 1.

8. P—Q R 3	B—K 2
9. P—Q Kt 4	P—B 4

The right way to keep the balance in the centre. Unsatisfactory in the positional sense would be 9. .... P—Q R 4 ; 10. P—Kt 5.

10. Kt P×P	Kt P×P
11. P×B P	......

Also 11. R—Kt 1, Q—B 1 ; 12. Q—Kt 3, B—R 3, etc., would be satisfactory for Black.

11.	B×P

12. B—Kt 2   Q Kt—Q 2
13. Kt—K 5   Kt × Kt
14. B × Kt   Kt—Kt 5 !

This diversion is by no means as harmless as it looks. White loses the game chiefly because he under-estimates its importance.

15. B—Q B 3   ......

And not 15. B—Kt 2, Q—Kt 3, etc.

15. ......   R—Kt 1

At this moment 15. ....Q—Kt 3 would have been answered by 16. P—K 3. The text move prepares an eventual advance of the Q's Pawn.

16. R—Kt 1   ......

Although this move cannot be considered a decisive mistake, it certainly facilitates the opponent's plans. Unsatisfactory would be also 16. P—K R 3, Kt × B P ! ; 17. R × Kt, Q—Kt 4 ! ; 18. Kt—B 1, B × R ch ; 19. K × B, P × B P, etc. to Black's advantage. But by continuing 16. P × P, B × Q P ! ; 17. Kt—K 4 ! (and not 17. P—K 4, Kt × B P ! ; 18. R × Kt, B × R ch ; 19. K × B, Q—Kt 3 ch ; 20. K—B 1, B—Kt 2, etc.∓), with the subsequent dislodging of the threatening Black Knight, White could still obtain an even game.

16. ......   P—Q 5 !
17. R × B (?)   ......

Rubinstein does not foresee the surprising 18th move of Black and consequently will find himself at a material disadvantage. The only possibility here was, 17. B—Kt 4, Q B × B ; 18. K × B, Q—B 2 reaching a position which would be in

Black's favour, too, but hardly in a decisive way.

17. ......   R × R
18. B × R   ......

Position after White's 18th move.

18. ......   Kt × B P !

By this pseudo sacrifice Black forces the win of at least a Pawn with an overwhelming position. Of course, ineffective would be the immediate 18. ....P × B because of 19. Kt—K 4, etc.

19. K × Kt   ......

Other moves were no better, to say the least. For instance :
I—19. Q—R 1 (19. R × Kt ? P × B and wins), P × B ; 20. Kt—Kt 3, Kt—Kt 5, disc. ch ; 21. Kt × B, Q—Q 5 ch.
II—19. B—R 5, Kt × Q ; 20. B × Q, P—Q 6 disc. ch ; 21. P—K 3, Kt × K P ! with an easy win for Black in both cases.

19. ......   P × B disc. ch
20. P—K 3   ......

Or 20. K—K 1, P × Kt ch ; 21. Q × P, Q—Kt 3, with a rapidly winning attack.

20.	......	P × Kt
21.	K—K 2	Q—Kt 1
22.	B—B 3	R—Q 1
23.	Q—Kt 1	Q—Q 3

Gaining the square Q Kt 5 for the Bishop.

24.	P—Q R 4	P—B 4
25.	R—Q 1	B—Kt 5
26.	Q—B 2	Q—B 4
27.	K—B 2	P—Q R 4
28.	B—K 2	P—Kt 4
29.	B—Q 3	P—B 5 !

If now 30. B × P ch, K—R 1; 31. Q—K 4, then 31. ....Q × P ch; 32. K—Kt 2, P—B 6 ch; 33. K—R 3, Q—K 7 ! ; 34. Q—Kt 6, P—Kt 5 ch; 35. K—R 4, B—K 2 ch; 36. K—R 5, Q × P ch, and wins.

Resigns.

GAME 12

QUEEN'S GAMBIT ACCEPTED

Semmering Tournament, April, 1926.

Black : E. GRUENFELD

1.	P—Q 4	P—Q 4
2.	P—Q B 4	P × P
3.	Kt—K B 3	B—K Kt 5

This move, recommended in the last edition of Collijn's Swedish Manual, was introduced in Master play by Bogoljubow in his game against Vukovic at the Vienna Tournament, 1922. The present game shows the danger connected with the early development of the Bishop in case of the slightest inexactitude on Black's part.

4.	Kt—K 5	B—R 4
5.	Kt—Q B 3	P—K 3 ?

Already at the 5th move Black

commits the decisive positional mistake ! Necessary was 5. .... Kt—Q 2, after which I intended to play 6. Q—R 4, P—Q B 3 ; 7. Kt × Kt, Q × Kt (not P—Q Kt 4 ; 8. Kt × Kt P, P × Kt ; 9. Q × Kt P, Q × Kt ; 10. Q × B) ; 8. Q × B P followed by P—K 4 and B—K 3 with a good game.

6.	P—K Kt 4 !	B—Kt 3
7.	P—K R 4	P—K B 3

A sad necessity !

8.	Q—R 4 ch	......

Also 8. Kt × B, P × Kt ; 9. P—K 3, etc., was good enough.

8.	......	P—B 3
9.	Kt × B	P × Kt
10.	Q × P	K—B 2
11.	P—K 4	Kt—Q 2
12.	B—K 3	Q—R 4
13.	P—Q R 3	......

It was important to prevent .... Q—Kt 5.

13.	......	R—K 1
14.	P—B 4	Kt—K 2
15.	Castles	......

Instead 15. P—K B 5, Kt—Q B 1, etc., would hardly prove more convincing than the simple text move.

15.	......	Kt—B 1
16.	P—B 5	Kt—Q 3
17.	Q—R 2 !	......

After 17. Q—Kt 3 Black could play 17. P—B 4, which move now would lose a piece because of 18. Q P × P followed by P—Q Kt 4.

17.	......	P—K Kt 4
18.	P—R 5	P—Q Kt 4

Black has no longer even more or less satisfactory moves.

Position after Black's 18th move.

19. P—K 5 !   ......

In conjunction with the next move this advance is absolutely decisive. Not quite so good would be the immediate 19. B—Q 3 because of 19. ....P—Kt 5.

19. ......   B P×P

If instead 19. ....P—Kt 5 then 20. P×Kt, P×Kt; 21. P×P ch, R×P; 22. B—Q B 4 and wins.

20. B—Q 3 !   P—K 5

Or 20. ....Kt—B 5; 21. B×Kt, P×B; 22. Q×P, etc., with an easily won game.

21. Kt×K P	Kt×Kt
22. B×Kt	Kt—B 3
23. P×P ch	R×P
24. B—Kt 6 ch !	......

Stronger than the win of the exchange by 24. B—B 5.

24.	K—K 2
25. B×Kt P	P—Kt 5
26. B—B 5	R—K 7
27. K R—K 1	......

If now 27. ....Q—Kt 4, then 28. P—R 4 !, Q—R 3; 29. B—Q 3, etc.;

and if 27. ....R×R then 28. R×R ch, K—Q 1; 29. Q—B 7 ! followed by mate.

Resigns.

GAME 13

QUEEN'S INDIAN DEFENCE

Dresden Tournament, May, 1926.

White : F. SAEMISCH

| 1. P—Q 4 | Kt—K B 3 |
| 2. Kt—K B 3 | ...... |

The opinion that 2. P—Q B 4 is a better move here, is nowadays almost unanimous. But at the time this actual game was played some of the Masters still "feared" the so-called Budapest Gambit (2. ....P—K 4 as answer to 2. P—Q B 4).

| 2. ...... | P—Q Kt 3 |
| 3. P—B 4 | ...... |

If 3. P—K Kt 3, then 3. ....B—Kt 2; 4. B—Kt 2, P—Q B 4 !

3.	B—Kt 2
4. P—K 3	P—K 3
5. B—Q 3	B—Kt 5 ch
6. B—Q 2	B×B ch
7. Kt×B	P—Q 3
8. Castles	Q Kt—Q 2
9. Q—B 2	......

White has obtained a fairly good position which he could still improve by continuing 9. Kt—Kt 5, and if 9. .... P—K R 3 then 10. K Kt —K 4, Castles; 11. P—B 4, P—Q 4 (or 11. Kt×Kt; 12. B×Kt !); 12. Kt—K 3, P—B 4; 13. Q—K 2 followed by Q R—Q 1, etc. The text move, although not actually bad, is still rather aimless and allows Black to preserve his well-posted Bishop.

9. ......   Castles

| 10. Q R—Q 1 | Q—K 2 |
| 11. Kt—Kt 5 | ..... |

Two moves too late !

| 11. ...... | P—K R 3 |
| 12. Kt—R 7 | ..... |

Or 12. K Kt—K 4, K R—Q 1, etc., analogous to the text continuation.

12.	K R—Q 1
13. Kt × Kt ch	Kt × Kt
14. Kt—K 4	P—B 4
15. Kt × Kt ch	Q × Kt
16. P × P	.....

White has succeeded in exchanging almost all the minor pieces, but he is still very far from obtaining the draw he was obviously playing for, as Black's Pawn's position is much more elastic. The exchange in text has the evident disadvantage of opening to the opponent the Q Kt's file, but on the other hand the alternative 16. B—K 4 would also be not quite satisfactory because of 16. ....P—Q 4 ! ; 17. B— B 3 (or 17. P × Q P, K P × P followed by ....P—B 5 ∓), B—R 3 ; 18. P—Q Kt 3, Q R—B 1, etc. to Black's advantage.

| 16. ...... | Kt P × P ! |

After 16. ....Q P × P Black on account of the symmetrical Pawn position could hardly have avoided a draw.

17. R—Q 2	Q R—Kt 1
18. K R—Q 1	B—B 3 !
19. P—Q Kt 3	.....

Of course not 19. B—R 7 ch, K—R 1 ; 20. R × Q P ?, R × R ; 21. R × R, R × Kt P and wins. But now White threatens both the gain of a Pawn and 19. B—K 4 which would lead to a further simplification.

Position after White's 19th move.

| 19. ...... | Q—K 4 ! |

A very important move, which not only parries the threats mentioned but also prepares a further improvement of Black's position by means of ....P—B 4. White has therefore nothing better than to offer the exchange of Queens, thus producing an ending which proves (because of the typical Pawn constellation) very instructive in spite of the apparent simplicity.

20. Q—Kt 2	Q × Q
21. R × Q	P—Q R 4
22. R (Kt 2)—Q 2	K—B 1
23. B—B 2	K—K 2

The first result of Black's middle-game strategy. The so-called weakness at Q 3 is purely illusory, and White's troubles on the Q R and Q Kt files are on the contrary very real.

24. P—B 3	P—R 5 !
25. K—B 2	P × P
26. B × P	.....

After 26. P × P Black would of course get the full control of the Q R file.

| 26. ...... | P—B 4 |

It might be useful to prevent P—K 4.

27. K—K 2	R—Kt 5
28. K—Q 3	B—R 5

The only, but effective, method to prove the weakness of White's Q R 2 and Q B 4.

29. B × B	......

Or 29. K—B 3, K R—Q Kt 1 !; 30. R—Kt 2 (R × Q P ?, R × B ch ! and wins), P—Q 4 ! etc. ±

29.	R × B
30. R—Q Kt 1	......

Costs a Pawn which in this kind of position is generally decisive. But also 30. R—Q B 1, R—R 6 ch ; 31. K—K 2, K R—Q R 1 ; 32. R (B 1)—B 2, R—Q 3 followed by K—B 3 and P—Q 4 would prove, in the long run, hopeless.

30.	R—R 6 ch
31. K—K 2	......

After 31. R—Kt 3, K R—Q R 1 Black's win would have been even simpler.

31.	R—B 6
32. P—Q R 4	R—R 6 !

Much better than 32. ....R × B P ; 33. R—R 2, after which White's passed Pawn would create some trouble for Black.

33. R—Kt 7 ch	R—Q 2
34. R(Q2)—QKt2	R × R P
35. R × R ch	K × R
36. R—Kt 7 ch	K—B 3
37. R × P	R × P
38. R—Kt 6	......

White wins the Pawn back, but this proves to be without any effect as Black's Rook will occupy the 7th rank and his King is able to support the free Q B Pawn. The rest is merely routine.

38.	K—Q 4
39. R × R P	R—B 7 ch
40. K—B 1	P—B 5
41. R—R 8	P—B 6
42. P—R 4	......

Or 42. R—Q B 8, P—K B 5 !; 43. P × P, K—Q 5 ; 44. P—K R 4, K—K 6 ; 45. K—Kt 1, K × B P ; 46. P—R 5, K—Kt 4 ; 47. P—K Kt 4, P—Q 4, etc., winning easily.

42.	R—Q 7
43. K—K 1	R × P
44. R—Q B 8	P—B 7
45. P—R 5	R—R 7
46. P—R 6	R × P
47. R × P	R—R 8 ch
48. K—Q 2	R—R 7 ch
49. K—Q 3	R × R

Resigns.

GAME 14

QUEEN'S INDIAN DEFENCE

Dresden Tournament, May, 1926.

White : A. RUBINSTEIN

Brilliancy Prize

1. P—Q 4	Kt—K B 3
2. Kt—K B 3	P—K 3
3. B—B 4	P—Q Kt 3
4. P—K R 3	......

It was certainly not necessary to prevent Black's Kt—K R 4 at this moment. The weakening of the square K Kt 3 gave me the idea of a quite unusual but, as the following proves, very effective system of development.

4.	B—Kt 2
5. Q Kt—Q 2	B—Q 3 !

After this, White has the unpleasant choice between (1) the exchange, which strengthens Black's position in the middle ; (2) 6. P—

K 3, which would spoil, after 6.
....B × P, his Pawn position ; and
(3) 6. B—Kt 5 after which Black
would secure the advantage of the
pair of Bishops by means of ....
P—K R 3.

6.	B × B	P × B
7.	P—K 3	Castles
8.	B—K 2	......

And not 8. B—Q 3 as he intends
to play Kt × Kt after Black's P—
Q 4, followed by Kt—K 5.

8.	......	P—Q 4
9.	Castles	Kt—B 3
10.	P—B 3	......

If 10. Kt—K 5 then 10. ....
Kt—K 2 followed by ....P—Q 3, etc.

10.	......	Kt—K 5 !

Black has already obtained the
initiative.

11.	Kt × Kt	P × Kt
12.	Kt—Q 2	P—B 4
13.	P—K B 4	......

Otherwise Black would play ....
Q—K Kt 4 preventing the text-
move for a long time.

13.	......	P—K Kt 4 !

Black must play most energetically before the opponent finds time
to co-ordinate the activity of his
pieces.

14.	Kt—B 4	P—Q 4
15.	Kt—K 5	Kt × Kt

Much better than 15. ....P × P ;
16. Kt × Kt ! followed by 17. R × P,
etc.

16.	Q P × Kt	......

In case of 16. B P × Kt Black

would eventually break through by
means of ....P—B 5.

16.	......	K—R 1
17.	P—Q R 4 (?)	......

White has no time for this
counter attack. His only chance of
a successful defence was 17. P—
K Kt 3 followed by 18. K—R 2,
etc. After he has missed this
opportunity Black gradually exerts
an overwhelming pressure.

17.	......	R—K Kt 1
18.	Q—Q 2	P × P !

At the right time, as White
cannot retake with the Pawn on
account of 19. ....Q—R 5 with the
double threat 20. ....Q × R P or
20. ....R × Kt P ch !

19.	R × P	Q—Kt 4
20.	B—B 1	Q—Kt 6 !

Forcing White's next King's
move and thus preparing the win
of a *tempo* at the 23rd move.

21.	K—R 1	Q—Kt 2
22.	Q—Q 4	B—R 3 !
23.	R—B 2	......

White has most obviously no
choice.

23.	......	Q—Kt 6 !

Compare the note to Black's 20th
move.

24.	R—B 2	B × B
25.	R × B	Q R—Q B 1

Still working with gains of *tempi*
as he threatens now 26. ....R—B 5.

26.	P—Q Kt 3	R—Q B 2
27.	R—K 2	Q R—K Kt 2
28.	R—B 4	......

Position after White's 28th move.

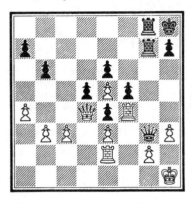

28. ......   R—Kt 3 !

After this move a highly original position is obtained, the outstanding particulars of which are the following : Black's immediate threat is 29. ....R—R 3 ; 30. Q—Q 1, Q—Kt 2 winning the King's Pawn, as 31. Q—Q 4 would be answered by 31. ....R×R P ch. If White tries to parry this by playing 29. Q—Q 1, Black still answers with 29. ....R—R 3 !, thus putting the opponent in a position of a complete Zugzwang.

As a matter of fact (1) R at K B 4 could not move because of 30. .... Q×K P. (2) R at K 2 is tied by the defence of the squares K 3 and K Kt 2. (3) The King could not move because of 30. ....R (or Q)× R P. (4) The Queen could not move either on the first rank—because of 30. ....Q—Kt 2 ! etc., nor on the Q's file—because of 30. ....R×P ch ! etc. (5) Finally in the event of 30. P—B 4 Black would win by 30. ....P—Q 5 ! etc., and in the event of 30. P—Q Kt 4— by 30. ....Q—Kt 2 ; 31. Q—Q 4, R—Q B 1 ! followed by 32. .... R—B 5.

Therefore White offers a Pawn in the hope of exchanging a pair of Rooks and thus weakening the enemy's attack.

29. Q—Kt 4   R—R 3
30. P—R 4   ......

Now absolutely forced.

30. ......   Q—Kt 2 !

Much better than the rather prosaic 30. .... R×P ch. If now 31. Q—Q 6, then 31. ....R—Kt 3 ; 32. R (B 4)—B 2, P—B 5 ! ; 33. P×P, P—K 6 ! and wins.

31. P—B 4   R—Kt 3
32. Q—Q 2   R—Kt 6 !

Threatening 33. ....R—R 6 ch ; 34. K—Kt 1, Q—Kt 6 ; and, if immediately 33. K—Kt 1, then 33. ....P—Q 5 ! ; 34. P×P, P—K 6 ! ; 35. Q—Q B 2 (Kt 2), R—R 6 followed by Q—Kt 6 and wins. White is helpless.

33. Q—K 1   R×Kt P
Resigns.

GAME 15

NIMZOWITSCH'S DEFENCE

New York Tournament, March, 1927.

Black : A. NIMZOWITSCH

1. P—Q 4   Kt—K B 3
2. P—Q B 4   P—K 3
3. Kt—Q B 3   B—Kt 5
4. Q—B 2   P—Q 3

The only fashionable move nowadays (see, for instance, my second match with Dr. Euwe) is 4. .... P—Q 4.

5. B—Kt 5   Q Kt—Q 2
6. P—K 3   P—Q Kt 3
7. B—Q 3   B—Kt 2
8. P—B 3   ......

By retaining control on his K 4 White makes it very difficult for the opponent to form a suitable plan of further development.

8.	B × Kt ch
9. Q × B	P—B 4
10. Kt—R 3 !	......

Black expected here either 10. Kt—K 2 or 10. R—Q 1, both permitting him to simplify matters by means of 10. .... Kt—Q 4 !. The move selected permits White to make an effective use of his Bishops.

| 10. ...... | P—R 3 |
| 11. B—B 4 | ...... |

And not 11. B—R 4 because of the possibility of .... P—Kt 4—Kt 5, etc.

| 11. ...... | Q—K 2 |
| 12. B—Kt 3 ! | ...... |

Black threatened 12. .... P—K 4 eventually followed by .... P—K 5.

| 12. ...... | P—K 4 ? |

This not too unnatural attempt to clear the situation in the middle is most likely already the decisive error. After the simple 12. .... Castles K R White would not have found it very easy to exploit the unmistakable weakness of the dark-coloured squares of Black's position.

| 13. P × K P | P × P |
| 14. Castles (Q R) | P—Kt 3 |

14. .... P—K 5 ; 15. B—K 2, etc. would be useless, and the immediate 14. Castles (Q R) would have been met by 15. B—B 5, P—Kt 3 ; 16. B × K P !, P × B ; 17. R × Kt followed by 18. B × Kt or 18. B × R, etc., with a decisive advantage.

| 15. B—Q B 2 | ...... |

This Bishop will prove very useful on the diagonal Q R 4—K 8.

15.	Castles (Q R)
16. B—Q R 4	K R—K 1
17. Kt—B 2	Q—K 3

Black wants to dislodge the ominous White King's Bishop, but this plan costs a lot of time which White will utilise to strengthen his pressure on the Queen's file in a decisive manner. A slightly better chance of salvation was offered by 17. .... Kt—R 4, and if 18. R—Q 2 then 18. .... Kt × B ; 19. P × Kt, R—R 1 ! ; 20. K R—Q 1, Kt—Kt 1, etc.

18. Kt—Q 3	R—K 2
19. R—Q 2	Q R—K 1
20. K R—Q 1	......

If now 21. .... Kt—R 4 then simply 22. B × Kt ch, R × B ; 23. Kt × B P and wins.

| 20. ...... | B—B 3 |
| 21. B—Q B 2 ! | ...... |

Position after White's 21st move.

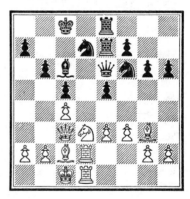

| 21. ...... | Kt—R 4 |

In this rather harmless-looking position—with only one pawn exchanged and none of White's pieces posted further than his third rank ! —Black is already completely helpless against the threats of 22. Kt × B P followed by 23. R—Q 6, or alternatively 22. P—Kt 4. If, for instance, 21. .... K—B 2 (in order to protect his Q 3), then 22. P—Q Kt 4 !, P × P ; 23. Kt × Kt P, Kt

—B 4 ; 24. Kt—Q 5 ch, B×Kt ; 25.
P×B, Q—Q 3 ; 26. P—K B 4 ! and
wins. And after the text move
Black loses the Queen and a Pawn
for a Rook and Knight, after which
the rest is merely a matter of
technique.

Although this game is one of my
happiest achievements in the
domain of the openings strategy,
it has passed almost unnoticed,
merely because of its length and
the predilection of most of the chess
journalists for short "brilliancies."
Yet it was certainly not my fault
that Nimzowitsch (whose hopes for
the second prize were more than
strongly compromised by this loss)
decided to fight a desperate struggle
to the bitter end.

22.	Kt×B P !	Kt×Kt
23.	R—Q 6	Kt×B
24.	P×Kt	Q×R
25.	R×Q	R—B 2
26.	P—Q Kt 4	Kt—Kt 2
27.	R×B	......

It is obvious that every reduction
of material will from now on be in
White's favour.

27.	......	R×R
28.	B—R 4	R (K 1)—K 3
29.	B×R	R×B
30.	Q×P	......

This particular exchange opens
new fields of action for both White's
Queen and King.

30.	......	R×P ch
31.	K—Q 2	P—K R 4
32.	P—Q R 3	......

White's next object will be to tie
up Black's Rook and Knight. He
succeeds, by bringing his Queen
into a very strong position in the
middle of the board (see 43rd move).

32.	......	R—B 2
33.	Q—K 8 ch	Kt—Q 1
34.	P—K 4	R—Q 2 ch

35.	K—K 3	R—B 2
36.	K—B 4	......

Also good was 36. K—B 2 followed by K—Kt 1—R 2 and eventually P—K B 4—B 5, etc. But
White wants his King to participate
in the final battle.

36.	......	R—B 6
37.	P—R 4	R—B 7
38.	Q—K 7	R—B 2
39.	Q—B 6	R—B 7
40.	Q—K 7	R—B 2
41.	Q—Q 6	Kt—K 3 ch
42.	K—K 5	......

Or 42. K—K 3—B 2—Kt 1, etc.,
as mentioned in the previous note.

42.	......	Kt—Q 1
43.	Q—Q 5 !	R—B 3
44.	K—B 4	......

From now on White decides to
provoke the move ....P—Q R 4
which will create a new weakness at
Black's Q Kt 3.

44.	......	Kt—K 3 ch
45.	K—K 3	R—B 6 ch
46.	K—K 2	R—B 2
47.	P—B 4	Kt—Q 1
48.	K—K 3	R—B 6 ch
49.	K—Q 4	R—B 2
50.	K—K 5 !	P—Q R 4

Now practically forced, as after
50. ....R—B 3 ; 51. P—B 5 !, etc.,
there would not be a satisfactory
move left.

51.	Q—R 8 ch	K—Q 2
52.	P—Kt 5	K—K 2

Instead 52. ....R—Kt 2 ; 53.
K—B 6, etc., would have been
perfectly useless.

53.	P—B 5 !	......

And not 53. Q—Kt 8 ? because of
53. ....Kt—K 3 ! winning the
Queen because of the mating threat
at Q B 4.

53.	P—B 3 ch
54. K—Q 4	R—Q 2 ch
55. K—K 3	P×P
56. P×P	......

After this Black's K R's Pawn is bound to fall rapidly.

56.	Kt—B 2
57. Q—B 3	Kt—K 4

This Knight's position, though good, is not a sufficient compensation for the further material loss.

58. Q×P	R—Q 6 ch
59. K—B 2	R—Q 7 ch
60. K—B 1	R—Q 5
61. Q—R 7 ch	K—Q 3

If 61. ....Kt—B 2 then 62. Q—Kt 8, followed by Q—Q Kt 8 with the win of the Q Kt Pawn.

62. Q—Q Kt 7	Kt—Q 2
63. Q—B 6 ch	K—K 2
64. Q—K 6 ch	K—Q 1
65. Q—Kt 3	R—Q Kt 5
66. Q—Q 1	K—K 2
67. Q—K 2 ch	K—Q 1
68. Q—R 2	K—K 2
69. K—K 2 !	R—K 5 ch

Or 69. ....K—Q 1 ; 70. Q—Kt 8 ch, followed by 71. P—K Kt 4, etc.

70. K—B 3	R—Q Kt 5
71. K—K 3	Kt—B 4
72. Q—Kt 8	Kt—Q 2
73. P—K Kt 4 !	......

This brings now a prompt decision.

73.	R×R P
74. P—Kt 5	P×P
75. Q×P ch	K—Q 3
76. Q—Kt 6 ch	K—B 2
77. Q—B 6 ch	K—Q 1
78. P—B 6	R—R 8
79. P—Kt 4	R—K B 8
80. P—Kt 5	R—K B 4
81. Q—R 8 ch	K—B 2
82. Q—B 6 ch	K—Q 1
83. P—Kt 6 !	......

If now 83. ....R×P then 84. P—Kt 7 and if 83. Kt×P then 84. Q—Q 6 ch followed by 85. P—Kt 7, etc.

Resigns.

GAME 16

QUEEN'S PAWN'S OPENING

New York Tournament, March, 1927.

Black : F. MARSHALL

Brilliancy Prize

1. P—Q 4	Kt—K B 3
2. P—Q B 4	P—K 3
3. Kt—K B 3	Kt—K 5

This unnatural and time-wasting move can be successfully answered in different ways. One of the simplest is 4. Q—B 2 and in the event of 4. ....P—Q 4 or 4. ....P—K B 4 ; 5. Kt—B 3, etc.

4. K Kt—Q 2	......

With the obvious idea of exchanging at K 4 and developing the other Knight at Q B 3. The present game proves rather convincingly the soundness of this scheme.

4.	B—Kt 5

A typical Marshall trap : if now 5. P—Q R 3 then 5. ....Q—B 3 ! with an immediate win !

5. Q—B 2	P—Q 4

Or 5. ....P—K B 4 ; 6. P—Q R 3 forcing the exchange of both Black's developed pieces.

6. Kt—Q B 3	P—K B 4
7. K Kt×Kt	......

After this White will easily force the opening of the central files, by means of P—K B 3 and eventually

P—K 4. And as he is better developed, this opening must secure him a substantial positional advantage.

| 7. ...... | B P × Kt |
| 8. B—B 4 | ...... |

This Bishop will protect the King's position against any sudden attack.

| 8. ...... | Castles |
| 9. P—K 3 | P—B 3 |

White was threatening, by means of 10. P—Q R 3, to force the exchange of the Bishop at Kt 5 for his Knight (10. P—Q R 3, B—Q 3 ?; 11. B × B followed by 12. B P × P, K P × P ; 13. Kt × Q P !, etc.),

| 10. B—K 2 | Kt—Q 2 |
| 11. P—Q R 3 | ...... |

I considered this as being sounder play than 11. Castles, Kt—B 3 ; 12. P—B 3, Kt—R 4 ! ; 13. P × P, Kt × B ; 14. R × Kt, R × R ; 15. P × R, P × B P, etc.

| 11. ...... | B—K 2 |

After the exchange at B 6 his dark-coloured squares would have remained helplessly weak.

| 12. Castles | B—Kt 4 |

There is hardly anything better.

| 13. P—B 3 ! | B × B |
| 14. P × B | R × P |

Instead, 14. ....P × B P ; 15. R × P, Kt—B 3 ; 16. P—B 5 ! would be a sad enough alternative because of the weakness at K 3. By the text move, in conjunction with the three following moves, Marshall tries to save his compromised game through combinative play.

| 15. P × K P | R × R ch |

| 16. R × R | P—K 4 |

Or 16. ....P × B P ; 17. B × P, Kt—Kt 3 ; 18. Q—B 2 !, etc., with a clear advantage.

| 17. Q—Q 2 ! | ...... |

The initial move of the decisive manoeuvre. If now 17. ....Q—Kt 3 then 18. P—B 5, Q—R 4 ; 19. P × Q P, K P × P ; 20. P—Q Kt 4 !, P × Kt ; 21. Q—Kt 5, Q—B 2 ; 22. P—Q 6, P—K R 3 ; 23. Q—K 7 and wins.

| 17. ...... | P—B 4 |

Trying to increase the tension at any cost, as the Pawn exchanges would have proved rapidly disastrous.

Position after Black's 17th move.

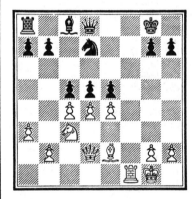

| 18. P × K P ! | ...... |

Erroneous would have been instead 18. Kt × Q P, B P × P ; 19. Q—Kt 4 because of 19. ....Kt—B 3.

| 18. ...... | P—Q 5 |
| 19. Q—B 4 ! | ...... |

This sacrifice in connection with the "quiet" 21st move is doubtless the safest and quickest method to force a victory.

Not 19. Kt—Q 5 because of 19.
.... Kt × K P followed by 20. ....
Q—Q 3 etc.

| 19. ...... | P × Kt |

Forced.

| 20. Q—B 7 ch | K—R 1 |
| 21. P × P ! | ...... |

This alone proves the correctness
of the sacrifice. Tempting, but
premature, would have been instead
21. P—K 6 because of 21. .... Kt—
B 3 ; 22. P—K 7, Q—Kt 1 ; 23.
R × Kt, B—Kt 5 ! ; 24. Q × Q ch,
K × Q ; 25. R—Q 6, R—K 1 !, etc.∓

21.	Q—Kt 1
22. Q—K 7	P—K R 3
23. B—R 5 !	......

And not 23. P—K 6, Kt—B 3 ;
24. P—K 5, Kt—R 2 !, etc.

| 23. ...... | P—Q R 4 |

If 23. .... Q × B P then of course
24. B—B 7.

24. P—K 6	P—K Kt 3
25. P × Kt	B × P
26. R—B 7	Resigns.

GAME 17

QUEEN'S GAMBIT DECLINED
(ORTHODOX DEFENCE)

Kecskemet Tournament, July,
1927.
Black : Dr. L. Asztalos.

Brilliancy Prize

1. P—Q 4	P—Q 4
2. P—Q B 4	P—K 3
3. Kt—K B 3	Kt—K B 3
4. B—Kt 5	P—K R 3

This is, rightly, considered not
satisfactory because Black's pair
of Bishops will not quite compensate for White's advantage in
space. The modern line 4. .... B—
Kt 5 ch in connection with 5. ....
P × P (forming the so-called Vienna
variation) has not yet been analysed
to its ultimate end, but offers anyhow more fighting chances than the
one chosen here.

5. B × Kt	Q × B
6. Kt—B 3	P—B 3
7. Q—Kt 3	......

The right preparation for P—K 4.

7.	Kt—Q 2
8. P—K 4	P × P
9. Kt × P	Q—B 5
10. B—Q 3	B—K 2
11. Castles	Castles
12. K R—K 1	R—Q 1
13. Q R—Q 1	Q—B 2

In consequence of the variation
selected, Black has a lot of difficulties in developing his pieces, especially the Queen's Bishop. The
Queen's retreat is practically forced,
as 13. .... Kt—B 1, for instance,
would have been answered by 14.
Q—Q B 3 with the threat of 15.
Kt—K 5,

| 14. Kt—Kt 3 | Kt—B 1 |
| 15. Q—B 3 ! | ...... |

White intends to continue with
Kt—R 5 followed by P—Q 5
which would force a fatal weakening
of Black's King's position. Black's
next manœuvre parries that danger,
but at the cost of the disorganisa-
tion of the Queen-side Pawns.

15.	P—Q R 4
16. P—Q R 3	P—R 5
17. Kt—K 5	......

After 17. Kt—R 5 the answer 17.
.... Q—R 4 would force the exchange of Queens.

| 17. ...... | Q—R 4 |

18. Q—B 1	B—Q 2
19. P—B 5 !	......

The logical reply to the advance of Black's Q R's Pawn. White threatens now to install his Knight at Q Kt 6 and thus forces the following Pawn's move which deprives the Q B 3 Pawn of its natural protection.

19.	P—Q Kt 4
20. B—K 4	Q—B 2
21. Q—B 3	......

Threatening 22. Q—K B 3, etc.

21.	B—K 1
22. Kt—K 2 !	......

The beginning of a series of manœuvres against which Black has no adequate defence. In the first place White threatens to bring his Knight via Q B 1 to Q Kt 4 and in order to prevent this Black is forced to exchange his valuable Knight, thus leaving his K R 2 defenceless.

22.	R—R 3
23. Kt—B 1	Kt—Q 2
24. Kt × Kt	R × Kt
25. Kt—Q 3	R—Q 1
26. Kt—K 5	B—B 1

Hoping to build a new defensive position by means of ....P—Kt 3 followed by ....B—Kt 2 ; but White's next move does not leave him the time to do it.

27. P—R 4 !	R (R 3)—R 1

If 27. ....P—K Kt 3 then 28. P—R 5, P—Kt 4 ; 29. P—B 4 ! with a speedy demolition of Black's last ramparts.

28. B—Kt 1	......

Threatening 29. Q—B 2, P—K Kt 3. 30. P—R 5, etc.

28.	P—R 4
29. Q—B 3	P—Kt 3
30. P—K Kt 4	P × P

31. Q × Kt P	B—Kt 2
32. B—R 2 !	......

An important move which prevents the advance of Black's K B's Pawn. Black cannot prepare this advance by playing 32.....Q—K 2, as the answer 33. Kt × Kt P ! would win immediately.

32.	P—Kt 5 !

An ingenious, but insufficient resource : if 33. P × P then 33. .... P—R 6; 34. P × P, R × R P, etc., with some counter-play.

33. B—B 4 !	P × P
34. P × P	Q—R 4
35. Q—K 4	......

Best. Premature would be 35. Kt × Kt P, R × P ! ; or 35. P—R 5, P × P; 36. Q × R P, R × P !, etc.

35.	Q—B 2
36. Q—B 4	......

Preparing the following Pawn's move, against which no defence exists.

36.	Q R—Kt 1
37. P—R 5 !	P × P
38. K—R 1	R—Kt 2
39. R—K Kt 1	Q—K 2

Position after Black's 39th move.

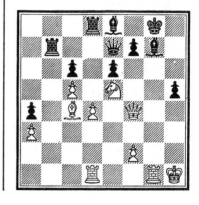

40. R × B ch !   ......

Black hoped that he had defended himself against this possibility by his last move. Yet the combination still works because of the unexpected point at the 42nd move.

40. ......   K × R
41. R—Kt 1 ch   K—R 2
42. Kt × K B P ! ! ......

Only so ! If now 42. .... Q × Kt, then 43. B—Q 3 ch, Q—Kt 3 ; 44. B × Q ch, B × B ; 45. R × B ! K × R ; 46. Q—K 4 ch, K—Kt 2 ; 47. Q—K 5 ch ! and Black, after a few further checks, would inevitably lose one of his Rooks.

Resigns.

GAME 18

CARO-KANN DEFENCE

Kecskemet Tournament, July, 1927.

Black : Dr. S. Tartakower

1. P—K 4   P—Q B 3
2. P—Q 4   P—Q 4
3. Kt—Q B 3   P × P
4. Kt × P   Kt—K B 3
5. Kt—Kt 3   ......

In the Hastings Tournament of 1936-37 I successfully tried against W. Winter the Pawn's sacrifice 5. B—Q 3, recommended by Dr. Tarrasch shortly before his death. This game continued 5. .... Q × P ; 6. Kt—K B 3, Q—Q 1 ; 7. Q—K 2, Kt × Kt (slightly premature would be here 7. .... Q Kt—Q 2 as four (!) amateurs in consultation played against me in Majorca, January, 1935—because of the unpleasant answer 8. Kt—Q 6 mate ....) 8. B × Kt, Kt—Q 2 ; 9. Castles, Kt—B 4 ; 10. R—Q 1, Q—B 2 ; 11. Kt—K 5 ! Kt × B ; 12. Q × Kt, B—K 3 ; 13. B—B 4, Q—B 1 ; 14. Kt—B 4 !

P—K Kt 4 !? ; 15. B × Kt P, R—K Kt 1 ; 16. B—K B 4, B × Kt ; 17. Q × B, Q—Kt 5 ; 18. P—K Kt 3, P—K 4 ; 19. R—K 1 (a more elegant solution was 19. Q—Kt 3 ! as 19. .... Q or P × B would have led to an immediate disaster after 20. Q × Kt P), Castles ; 21. R × K P and Black resigned after a few moves.

5. ......   P—K 4

Most probably sufficient to equalise. But in order to achieve this Black must play the next moves with care.

6. Kt—K B 3   P × P
7. Kt × P   ......

Also 7. Q × P, Q × Q ; 8. Kt × Q, B—Q B 4 ; 9. Kt Q 4—B 5, Castles ; 10. B—K 3 played by me against Capablanca in New York, 1927, does not give any serious chances of favourable complications.

7. ......   B—Q B 4

Already a rather serious loss of time. Indicated was the immediate 7. .... B—K 2 followed by castling with a satisfactory position.

8. Q—K 2 ch !   B—K 2

Or 8. .... Q—K 2 ; 9. Q × Q ch, B × Q ; 10. Kt (Q 4)—B 5 with some advantage for White.

9. B—K 3   P—B 4 (?)

This attempt to prevent White's Q R castling fails completely. A much lesser evil was 9. .... Castles ; 10. Castles, Q—R 4 ; 11. K—Kt 1, Kt—Q 4 ; 12. Q—K B 3 with no immediate danger for Black.

10. Kt (Q 4)—B 5 Castles
11. Q—B 4 !   ......

An important move which prepares with tempo (attacking Black's

Q B 4) the development of the K's Bishop.

11. ......   R—K 1

Also after the immediate 11. .... P—Q Kt 3 White would gradually obtain a winning attack by continuing 12. R—Q 1 followed by Q—K R 4, etc.

12. B—Q 3   P—Q Kt 3
13. Castles (Q R) B—R 3

It is obvious that other moves would also lead to a more or less rapid catastrophe.

Position after Black's 13th move.

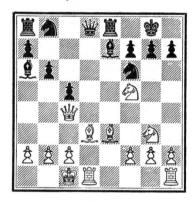

14. Kt—R 6 ch ! ......

By making this forcing combination White calculated that his opponent cannot obtain three pieces for the Queen, but—as a consequence of the weakness of his Q R 1 —K R 8 diagonal—only two ; the remainder is compulsory for Black.

14. ......   P × Kt
15. B × P ch !   Kt × B

If 15. .... K—R 1 then 16. Q × K B P followed by 17. Kt—B 5 with a mating attack.

16. Q—Kt 4 ch   K—R 1

17. R × Q   R × R

Or 17. B × Q ; 18. Q—B 3, etc.

18. Q—K 4   Kt—Q B 3
19. Q × Kt   B—K B 1
20. Kt—B 5   B—B 5
21. B × R P   B—Q 4
22. Q—B 7   Q R—B 1
23. Q—B 4   R—B 3
24. B × B   R × B
25. Q—K 5 ch   Kt—B 3
26. Kt—Q 6 !   Resigns.

GAME 19

QUEEN'S PAWN OPENING

Kecskemet Tournament, July, 1927.

White : H. KMOCH

1. P—Q 4   P—Q 4
2. Kt—K B 3   P—Q B 3
3. P—K 3   ......

After this tame move Black has no difficulty with his Queen's Bishop. More usual and better is 3. P—Q B 4, leading to the Slav Defence of the Queen's Gambit Declined.

3. ......   B—B 4
4. B—Q 3   P—K 3
5. Castles   ......

The exchange here or at the next move certainly cannot be recommended.

5. ......   Q Kt—Q 2
6. P—B 4   K Kt—B 3
7. Q—B 2   ......

It is easily comprehensible that White wants to clear the situation in the middle as soon as possible. 7. Kt—Q B 3 would have been simply answered by 7. .... B—K 2.

7. ......   B × B
8. Q × B   Kt—K 5

In order to eliminate as many light pieces as possible, because White will sooner or later obtain some more space by playing P—K 4.

9. K Kt—Q 2   Q Kt—B 3
10. Kt—Q B 3   ......

After 10. Kt×Kt, Kt×Kt; 11. P—B 3, Kt—B 3; 12. P—K 4, P×B P; 13. Q×P, Q—Kt 3; 14. Kt—Q B 3, R—Q 1; 15. R—Q 1, B—K 2 followed by ....Castles, etc., White's position would have remained rather shaky.

10. ......   Kt×K Kt
11. B×Kt   B—K 2
12. P—K 4   ......

The surplus freedom which White obtains by this move will be neutralised by the necessity for him to protect permanently his Queen's Pawn. But he hardly had another plan at his disposal as blocking attempts would fail, e.g. : 12. P—B 5, P—K 4 !; or 12. P—B 4, P—B 4 !—both rather in Black's favour.

12. ......   P×P
13. Kt×P   Castles
14. B—B 3   Q—B 2

Q Kt 3 was also a good square for the Queen.

15. Q R—Q 1   Q R—Q 1
16. R—Q 2 ?   ......

White loses this game not because of the opening, which was more or less satisfactory, but chiefly because of his altogether passive and conventional play. Here, for instance, he could quite safely play 16. P—K B 4, preventing the Black Queen from occupying that square. From now on the chances of the second player can be considered as decidedly the better ones.

16. ......   Q—B 5 !
17. Kt×Kt ch   B×Kt

18. K R—Q 1   R—Q 2
19. Q—Kt 3   ......

The exchange of Queens would doubtless increase White's drawing prospects. But Black can easily avoid it.

19. ......   Q—B 4
20. P—B 4   ......

The main object of this move seems to be the prevention of the eventual replies ....B—Kt 4 or ....P—K 4.

20. ......   K R—Q 1
21. Q—K 3   P—K R 4 !

Not only giving a loophole for the King but also blocking White's King's side (22. P—K R 3, P—R 5, etc.).

22. P—Q Kt 4   ......

This facilitates the job of Black, who will immediately eliminate the opponent's Q B 4, and thus obtain full control over his Q 4.

22. ......   P—Q Kt 4 !
23. Q—B 3   ......

This attempt to save by tactical means a strategically very sick position leads to a rapid debacle. But also after the quieter 23. P—B 5, R—Q 4 followed by ....P—K Kt 4 !, etc., the game could hardly last very long.

23. ......   P×P
24. Q×B P   Q×P
25. Q×B P   P—K 4 !

Obtaining a decisive material advantage.

26. Q—K 2   P×P
27. R—Q 3   ......

If this blockade would be possible Black would have had to face some technical difficulties. But as it is, he succeeds in forcing an immediate win by a keenly calculated combination.

Position after White's 27th move.

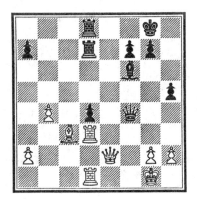

27. ......   P×B !

The chief variation of this transaction is both pretty and convincing : 28. R×R, R×R ; 29. Q—K 8 ch, K—R 2 ; 30. Q×R, Q—K 5 ! ! ; 31. Q×K B P (or Q—Q 5, Q×Q ; 32. R×Q, P—B 7 and wins, as 33. R—Q B 5 is refuted by 33. ....B—Q 5 ch), P—B 7 ; 32. Q×R P ch, K—Kt 1 and wins.

28. R×R   R×R
29. R×R   ......

Loses instantly.

29. ......   B—Q 5 ch
30. K—R 1   ......

Or, 30. R×B, Q×R ch ; 31. K—B 1, Q—B 5 ch ; 32. K—K 1, Q×Kt P etc.

30. ......   Q—Q B 8 ch

Resigns.

GAME 20

FRENCH DEFENCE

First Match-Game, Buenos Aires, September, 1927.

White : J. R. Capablanca

1. P—K 4   P—K 3
2. P—Q 4   P—Q 4
3. Kt—Q B 3   B—Kt 5
4. P×P   P×P
5. B—Q 3   Kt—Q B 3
6. Kt—K 2   K Kt—K 2
7. Castles   B—K B 4
8. B×B   ......

Other moves like 8. P—Q R 3 or 8. Kt—Kt 3 would also prove perfectly harmless. This game shows once more that, if White has any fighting ambitions, he must avoid in this variation the Pawn exchange at the 4th move.

8. ......   Kt×B
9. Q—Q 3   Q—Q 2
10. Kt—Q 1   ......

The beginning of a long series of slightly inferior moves. The natural development move, 10. B—K B 4, which Black intended to answer by 10. ....Castles Q R would have led to a more lively struggle.

10. ......   Castles K R
11. Kt—K 3   Kt×Kt
12. B×Kt   ......

White's minor pieces are now obstructing the vital K's file. This is a convincing proof of the inexactitude of his opening strategy.

12. ......   K R—K 1
13. Kt—B 4   ......

As the answer proves, the Knight has no future on this square.

Natural and good enough for a draw was 13. B—K B 4 followed by P—Q B 3, etc.

13. ......   **B—Q 3 !**

Thus Black proposes a trans-action whose results would be very satisfactory for himself. If, namely, 14. Kt×Q P, B×R P ch ; 15. K× B, Q×Kt ; 16. P—Q B 4 then 16. ....Q—R 4 ch ; 17. K—Kt 1, Q R—Q 1 ; 18. P—Q 5, R—Q 3 and White's King position would be in danger.

14. K R—K 1   ......

White continues to play super-ficially. Indicated was first 14. P—Q B 3.

14. ......   Kt—Kt 5
15. Q—Kt 3 ?   ......

After this he will be obliged at least to spoil his Pawn position in rather an ugly way. The lesser evil was 15. Q—Q 2, Q—B 4 ; 16. K R—Q B 1, P—K R 4 ! (threatening R—K 5 followed by P—K R 5) with some positional advantage for Black.

15. ......   Q—B 4
16. Q R—B 1 ?   ......

After this further mistake, the game can hardly be saved as Black now wins a Pawn, with a fairly good position. Necessary was 16. Kt—Q 3 after which Black, it is true, would have obtained a far superior end game by continuing 16. ....Kt×Kt ; 17. Q×Kt, Q× Q ; 18. P×Q, B—Kt 5 ; 19. K R—Q B 1, P—Q B 3, eventually followed by ....P—Q R 4 !, etc.

Position after White's 16th move.

16. ......   Kt×B P !
17. R × Kt   Q × Kt

This is the possibility overlooked by Capablanca at his 16th move. He expected only 17. ....B×Kt after which he would have re-estab-lished the balance by 18. R—B 5, etc.

18. P—Kt 3   ......

It is merely a matter of taste whether this or 18. Q×Q P, Q× R P ch.; 19. K—B 1, P—Q B 3, etc., is preferable.

18. ......   Q—B 4

Tempting was also 18. ....Q—B 6 ; 19. Q×Kt P, P—K R 4 ; 20. Q—Kt 5, P—R 5 ; 21. Q—K 2, Q—B 4, etc., with a good attack. But the decision to keep the material advantage obtained can certainly not be blamed.

19. Q R—K 2   P—Q Kt 3
20. Q—Kt 5   P—K R 4
21. P—K R 4   R—K 5

Threatening 22. ....R×R P !, etc.

22. B—Q 2 (!)   ......

This temporary sacrifice of a second Pawn offers comparatively the best saving chances—in case Black accepts it. Perfectly hopeless would have been 22. Q—Q 3, QR—K 1 ; 23. B—Q 2, Q—K 3, etc.

22. ...... R × Q P

This acceptance—which had to be calculated very carefully—was by no means necessary. Simple and convincing was instead 22. .... Q R—K 1, as after the exchange of the White Queen for two Rooks by 23. Q × R ch, R × R ; 24. R × R ch, K—R 2, etc. Black, because of his considerable positional advantage, would have but little difficulty in forcing the win.

23. B—B 3 R—Q 6

Also after 23. ....R—K Kt 5 (23. ....R—Q B 5 ? ; 24. R—K 5 ! etc.) ; 24. B—K 5 White would have finally won back one of his minus Pawns.

24. B—K 5 R—Q 1
25. B × B R × B

Technically simpler than the un-aesthetic 25. .... P × B ; 26. Q—B 6 !, etc.

26. R—K 5 Q—B 6

Of course not 26. ....Q—Kt 3 ; 27. R—Kt 5, etc.

27. R × R P Q × R

And here 27. ....R—K 3 would be another way of suicide (28. Q—K 8 ch !, etc.).

28. R—K 8 ch K—R 2
29. Q × R ch Q—Kt 3
30. Q—Q 1 R—K 3 !

An interesting conception. Black gives back his plus Pawn in order to combine the advance of the free Q's Pawn with a mating attack.

Much less convincing would be 30. ....P—Q 5 because of the answer 31. Q—B 3 threatening both 32. Q—R 8 and 32. P—R 5.

31. R—Q R 8 R—K 4 !

Intending to place the Queen behind the Rook and at the same time preparing the formation of the Pawn chain Q Kt 3—Q B 4—Q 5.

32. R × P P—Q B 4
33. R—Q 7 (?) ......

Shortens the agony. I expected, instead, 33. K—Kt 2, P—Q 5 ; 34. R—R 3, Q—K 3 ! ; 35. Q—B 3, P—Q B 5 followed by the decisive advance of the Q's Pawn.

33. ...... Q—K 3
34. Q—Q 3 ch P—Kt 3
35. R—Q 8 P—Q 5
36. P—R 4 ......

Despair !

36. ...... R—K 8 ch

This direct attack is convincing enough. But Black could also take immediate advantage of the exposed position of the adventurous Rook—for instance, 36. ....Q—K 2 ! ; 37. R—Q Kt 8, Q—B 2 ; 38. Q—Kt 3, R—K 3 ; 39. R—Q R 8, Q—Kt 2 and the Rook would be lost because of the threat 40. .... R—K 8 ch, etc.

37. K—Kt 2 Q—B 3 ch
38. P—B 3 R—K 6
39. Q—Q 1 Q—K 3
40. P—K Kt 4 R—K 7 ch
41. K—R 3 Q—K 6
42. Q—K R 1 Q—B 5 !

After this there is no way of preventing the next Rook move.

43. P—K R 5 R—K B 7

Resigns.

GAME 21

QUEEN'S GAMBIT DECLINED
(CAMBRIDGE SPRINGS
DEFENCE)

Eleventh Match-Game, Buenos
Aires, October, 1927.

White : J. R. CAPABLANCA

1. P—Q 4	P—Q 4
2. P—Q B 4	P—K 3
3. Kt—Q B 3	Kt—K B 3
4. B—Kt 5	Q Kt—Q 2
5. P—K 3	P—B 3
6. Kt—B 3	Q—R 4
7. Kt—Q 2	B—Kt 5
8. Q—B 2	P×P
9. B×Kt	Kt×Kt
10. Kt×P	Q—B 2
11. P—Q R 3	B—K 2
12. B—K 2	......

White does not need to hurry to
prevent ....P—Q B 4 by playing
12. P—Q Kt 4, as that advance
would be still premature because of
13. Kt—Kt 5, Q—Kt 1 ; 14. P×P,
B×P ; 15. P—Q Kt 4, B—K 2 ; 16.
Kt—R 5, etc. ±

12.	Castles
13. Castles	B—Q 2

And here also 13. ....P—Q B 4
would not have been advisable for
analogous reasons.

14. P—Q Kt 4	P—Q Kt 3

Safer would be first 14. ....K R
—Q 1 followed by ....B—K 1.
Black's plan to continue by 15.
....P—Q R 4 ; 16. P×P, P—
Q Kt 4 will be parried by the
following answer.

15. B—B 3 !   ......

If now 15. ....P—Q R 4 then
16. Kt—K 5 !, P×P ; 17. Kt—
Q Kt 5, etc., with the advantage.

15.	Q R—B 1
16. K R—Q 1	K R—Q 1
17. Q R—B 1	B—K 1
18. P—K Kt 3	......

A good positional move, the immediate object of which is to prevent the answer ....Q—B 5 in case
of P—K 4.

18.	Kt—Q 4
19. Kt—Kt 2	Q—Kt 1

More exact was the immediate
19. ....Q—Kt 2 keeping in mind
the possibility of ....Q—R 3.

20. Kt—Q 3	B—Kt 4

With the eventual threat ....Kt
×K P, etc.

21. R—Kt 1	Q—Kt 2
22. P—K 4	Kt×Kt
23. Q×Kt	Q—K 2 (?)

Disadvantageous, as his King's
Bishop will now be put temporarily
out of play.   Correct was 23. ....R
—B 2 and if 24. B—Kt 2 then
24. ....B—B 3 ; 25. P—K 5, B—
K 2 ; 26. Q R—B 1, Q—B 1, after
which Black could quietly wait for
further developments.

24. P—K R 4 !	B—R 3
25. Kt—K 5	......

Threatening 26. Kt—Kt 4

25.	P—Kt 3
26. Kt—Kt 4 (?)	......

Now it is White's turn to miss
the best move !   After 26. Kt—
B 4 !, B—Kt 2 ; 27. P—K 5, P—
K R 4 ; 28. Kt—Q 6, Black would
have nothing better than to start to
fight for a draw by sacrificing the
exchange for a Pawn ; 28. ....R×
Kt ; 29. P×R, Q×P ; 30. Q—B 4 !
etc. ±

26.	......	B—Kt 2
27.	P—K 5	P—K R 4
28.	Kt—K 3	P—Q B 4 !

Black profits by the great opportunity to free at last his Q's Bishop, correctly realising that White will be unable to take real advantage of the open Q Kt's file.

| 29. | Kt P × P | ...... |

If 29. Q P × P then 29. ....P × P; 30. R × R, Q × R ; 31. P × P, Q—B 2, etc.

| 29. | ...... | P × P |
| 30. | P—Q 5 | ...... |

This attempt to complicate matters—most unusual for Capablanca—turns decidedly to Black's advantage. An easy draw was obtainable by 30. R—Kt 7, R—Q 2 ; 31. R × R, B × R ; 32. P—Q 5 (or 32. P × P, B—K 1 ; 33. P—B 6, Q—B 2, etc.), P × P ; 33. Kt × P, Q—K 3 ; 34. Kt—B 4, B × K P, followed by a general liquidation and Bishops of different colours.

| 30. | ...... | P × P |
| 31. | Kt × P | Q—K 3 |

Of course not 31. ....Q × K P ; 32. Q × Q, B × Q ; 33. Kt—K 7 ch, etc.

Position after Black's 31st move.

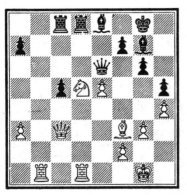

| 32. | Kt—B 6 ch(?) | ...... |

As the following shows, the exchange thus forced only facilitates Black's task, as his passed Pawn will from now on largely compensate him for the troubles connected with the appearance of a White Pawn at his K B 3. Comparatively better was 32. R—Kt 7, B × P ; 33. Q—R 5, K—Kt 2 ; 34. R × R P and Black's advantage—the pair of Bishops—would not yet have been decisive.

32.	......	B × Kt
33.	P × B	R × R ch
34.	R × R	B—B 3 !

White cannot exchange the Bishops, as in that case he would lose his only pride—the Pawn at B 6.

35.	R—K 1	Q—B 4
36.	R—K 3	P—B 5 !
37.	P—R 4	......

Realising the inferiority of his position, White begins to "swindle." If now 37. ....B × P, then 38. B—K 4, Q—Kt 5 (Q—Q 2 ; 39. R—B 3, K—R 2 ; 40. Q—K 5, etc., would even lose) ; 39. B—B 3, Q—Q 2 ; 40. R—K 7, Q—Q 6 ; 41. Q × Q, P × Q ? ; 42. R × R P etc., with a draw in view. But after the following simpler answer Black's position is even better than before, as he obtains the full control upon his Q Kt 5.

37.	......	P—R 4
38.	B—Kt 2	B × B
39.	K × B	Q—Q 4 ch
40.	K—R 2	Q—K B 4
41.	R—K B 3	Q—Q B 4
42.	R—B 4	......

After 42. R—K 3, Q—Kt 3, White would not have any useful move at his disposal (43. R—K B 3, Q—Q B 3 ! etc.).

42. ......   K—R 2

This was not necessary here : it was much more important to prevent White's next move by 42. ....Q—Kt 3. But insufficient would be the tempting 42. .... Q—Kt 5 ; 43. Q—K 3, Q×R P because of 44. R—B 5 !, Q—Kt 5 ; 45. R×R P, P×R ; 46. Q—R 6, Q—B 1 ; 47. Q—Kt 5 ch etc., with a perpetual check.

43. R—Q 4   Q—B 3 ?

A miscalculation, after which White could have saved the game. Correct was still 43. ....Q—Kt 3 ! and if 44. R—B 4 then 44. .... K—Kt 1 obtaining the same position as he could have had two moves earlier.

44. Q×R P   ......

Forced, but good enough.

44. ......   P—B 6

If instead 44. ....Q×B P then 45. R—K B 4 with the following possibilities : (a) 45. .... Q—Kt 2 ; 46. Q—Q 5 ; (b) 45. ....Q—K 3 ; 46. Q—B 3 followed by P—R 5, with no danger for White in either case.

45. Q—R 7 !   K—Kt 1

Other moves, also, cannot force the win against correct replies—for instance :

I. 45. .... Q×B P ? ; 46. R—K B 4, Q×R ; 47. P×Q, P—B 7 ; 48. Q×P ch., K—R 3, 49. P—B 5 ! etc.

II. 45. ....Q—B 2 ; 46. Q×Q followed by 47. R—Q 1, etc.

III. 45.....R—B 2 ; 46. Q—Kt 8, P—B 7 ; 47. R—Q 8, Q× B P ! ; 48. R—R 8 ch ! ! (That was the move I had overlooked when I started the

combination by playing 43. ....Q—B 3), Q×R ; 49. Q× R, etc., with salvation in all cases.

46. Q—K 7   ......

If now 46. ....P—B 7 then 47. R—Q 8 ch, R×R ; 48. Q×R ch. K—R 2 ; 49. Q—K 7, Q—K 3 ; 50. Q—B 7, etc., forcing a draw.

46. ......   Q—Kt 3

Position after Black's 46th move.

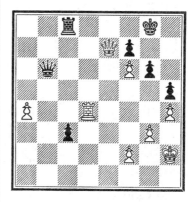

47. Q—Q 7 ?   ......

Capablanca does not take full advantage of the opportunity given to him by my 43rd move, and the game again takes its natural course. By playing 47. R—Q 7 ! he could have obtained a draw, as after 47. ....Q×P ch (if 47. ....R—K B 1 then 48. P—Q R 5, Q×R P ; 49. R—Q R 7, Q—Q 4 ; 50. R—Q 7, Q—Q R 4 and the White Rook, because of the threat Q×R ch ! would eternally persecute the Queen) ; 48. K—R 1 ! (48. K—R 3 would lose, as in the main variation the Black Queen would reach the square K 3 *with check*), Q—R 7 ; 49. R—Q 8 ch, R×R ; 50. Q×R ch, K—R 2 ; 51. Q—K B 8 and there would not be anything better than perpetual check, White's K B 6

Pawn remaining invulnerable. A most unusual escape !

| 47. ...... | Q—B 4 ! |
| 48. R—K 4 | ...... |

Now the only way to parry 48. ....P—B 7.

48.	Q × P ch
49. K—R 3	Q—B 8 ch
50. K—R 2	Q—B 7 ch
51. K—R 3	R—B 1
52. Q—B 6	......

Again the only move.

52.	Q—B 8 ch
53. K—R 2	Q—B 7 ch
54. K—R 3	Q—B 8 ch
55. K—R 2	K—R 2 !
56. Q—B 4	......

If 56. Q × B P, then 56. .... Q B 7 ch ; 57. K—R 1, R—Q 1 ; 58. Q—K 1, Q—B 6 ch ; 59. K—R 2, R—Q 8 and wins.

| 56. ...... | Q—B 7 ch |
| 57. K—R 3 | Q—Kt 8 ! |

The decisive manœuvre. As an alternative 57. ....P—B 7 would be insufficient because of 58. R—K B 4 ! followed by R—B 1.

| 58. R—K 2 | ...... |

Instead, 58. P—K Kt 4 would have led to a pretty finish : 58. ....P—B 7 !, Q × B P, R—K 1 ! !, etc.

| 58. ...... | Q—B 8 ch ? |

For the second time Black misses an easy win !

The right sequence of moves (which I actually intended by playing 57. ....Q—Kt 8 !) was 58. Q—R 8 ch ; 59. R—R 2, Q—K B 6 !, after which White could not play 60. R—Q B 2 because of 60. .... Q—B 4 ch ; and he would be helpless against the threat 60..... Q × B P, etc. (If 60. Q—K B 4, then 60. ....Q—Q 8 ! etc.).

| 59. K—R 2 | Q × P |
| 60. P—R 5 ? | ...... |

Instead of securing the draw by 60. R—Q B 2, R—K 1 ; 61. K—Kt 2 ! (threatening either 62. R × P or 62. R—K B 2) Capablanca commits another error and should now lose instantly.

| 60. ...... | R—Q 1 ? |

An immediate decision could be obtained by 60. ....Q—B 8 ! ; 61. Q—K 4, R—Q 1 or Q Kt 1. After the text move the win should become again quite a problem.

| 61. P—R 6 ? | ...... |

After 61. K—Kt 2 Black could only obtain a Queen's ending with three Pawns against two, which, with the right defence, should most probably end in a draw. Now at last, it is the end !

61.	Q—B 8 !
62. Q—K 4	R—Q 7
63. R × R	P × R
64. P—R 7	P—Q 8 Queens
65. P—R8 Queens	Q—Kt 8 ch
66. K—R 3	Q (Q8)—K B 8 ch

If now 67. Q—Kt 2 then 67. .... Q—K R 8 mate.

Resigns.

In my opinion this game has been praised too much, the whole world over. It was doubtless very exciting both for the players—who were continuously short of time—and the public. But its final part represents a true comedy of errors in which my opponent several times missed a draw and I missed about the same number of winning opportunities. In short, but for its outstanding sporting importance (it became, in fact, the crucial point of the match) I would hardly have included it in this collection.

GAME 22

QUEEN'S GAMBIT DECLINED (ORTHODOX DEFENCE)

Twenty-first Match-Game, October, 1927.

White : J. R. CAPABLANCA

1. P—Q 4	P—Q 4
2. P—Q B 4	P—K 3
3. Kt—Q B 3	Kt—K B 5
4. B—Kt 5	Q Kt—Q 2
5. P—K 3	B—K 2
6. Kt—B 3	Castles
7. R—B 1	P—Q R 3

Although with this less usual defence I obtained quite a success in this match (+1,=7—0), I consider it now as not being satisfactory because of the possible answer 8. P × P, adopted by Capablanca in the 23rd, 25th and 27th games.

8. P—Q R 3 (?) ......

This tame rejoinder will be convincingly refuted (as a winning attempt, of course) in the present game. It has since completely disappeared from the master's practice.

8.	P—R 3
9. B—R 4	P × P
10. B × P	P—Q Kt 4 !

More natural and better than 10. ....P—Q Kt 3 which, however, in the 13th, 15th, 17th, and 19th games proved sufficient for maintaining the balance of the position.

11. B—K 2	B—Kt 2
12. Castles	......

In the event of 12. P—Q Kt 4

Black would have obtained the initiative by 12. ....P—Q R 4 ! ; 13. Q—Kt 3, P × P ; 14. P × P, P—K Kt 4 ; 15. B—Kt 3, Kt—Q 4, etc.

12.	P—B 4
13. P × P	Kt × P
14. Kt—Q 4	

As White has not an atom of advantage the logical course for him was to simplify matters by means of 14. Q × Q, K R × Q ; 15. K R—Q 1, etc. Entirely wrong would be, instead of the text move, 14. B × Kt, B × B ; 15. Kt × Kt P, because of 15. ....Q × Q ; 16. K R × Q, Kt—Kt 6 ; 17. R—B 7, B × Kt ; 18. B × B, P × Kt ; 19. B × R, R × B∓.

14. ......   Q R—B 1

Preventing once and for all Kt × Kt P.

15. P—Q Kt 4   ......

Weakening, without necessity, the square Q B 4. Simpler was 15. B—B 3, Q—Kt 3 ; 16. Q—K 2, etc.

15.	Q Kt—Q 2 !
16. B—Kt 3	......

In the event of 16. B—B 3 I intended to play 16. ....Q—Kt 3 ; 17. Kt—K 4, R × R ; 18. Q × R, R—B 1, after which the White Queen would have had no good square at her disposal, for instance : (I) 19. Q—Kt 1 ? or Q 2 ?, Kt × Kt, etc., (II) 19. Q—Kt 2, P—Kt 4 ; 20. Kt × Kt ch, B × Kt∓, (III) 19. Q—Q 1 or K 1, P—Kt 4—also to Black's advantage. The text move is therefore comparatively the best.

16.	Kt—Kt 3
17. Q—Kt 3	......

In order to answer 17. ....Kt—B 5 by 18. K R—Q 1, Q—Kt 3, 19. P—Q R 4, etc.

| 17. ...... | K Kt—Q 4 |

A good move connected with the positional threat 18. ....Kt × Kt ; 19. R × Kt, B—Q 4 ; 20. Q—Kt 2, R × R ; 21. Q × R, Q—R 1, followed by R—Q B 1 with advantage. White's answer is practically forced.

18. B—B 3	R—B 5 !
19. Kt—K 4	Q—B 1
20. R × R	.....

I am inclined to consider this exchange as the decisive positional error, as from now on Black, taking advantage of the formidable position of his Knight at Q B 5, will be able gradually to concentrate all his pieces for a forcing action in the centre. White's correct move was 20. Q—Kt 1, threatening both 21. Kt—Q 6 or B—Q 6 ; if in that case 20. ....K R—Q 1, then 21. Kt—Q 2, R × R ; 22. R × R, Q—R 1 ; 23. B—B 7, and White would succeed in exchanging some further material without compromising his position.

Still, the text move can by no means be considered as an actual blunder ; and Capablanca lost this game only because he did not realise in time the dangers of his position and was, in the issue, regularly outplayed.

| 20. ...... | Kt × R |
| 21. R—B 1 | Q—R 1 ! |

Threatening 22. ....Kt × Kt P or K P, and thus forcing White to abandon control of the light-coloured squares in the middle.

| 22. Kt—B 3 | ...... |

If 22. Kt—B 5, then 22. .... B × Kt ; 23. P × B, R—B 1 ; 24. B—K 2, R × P ; 25. B × Kt, Q—Q B 1, etc., winning a Pawn.

| 22. ...... | R—B 1 |

Threatening 23. ....Kt—Q 7, etc.

23. Kt × Kt	B × Kt
24. B × B	Q × B
25. P—Q R 4	.....

The wish to reduce the Pawn material on the Q's side is natural, but White's position still remains compromised, inasmuch as his Q Kt's Pawn will become a welcome object of attack in the end game.

| 25. ...... | B—B 3 |
| 26. Kt—B 3 | ...... |

Of course not 26. R—Q 1 because of 26. ....P × P ; 27. Q × P, Kt—Kt 7 ; 28. Q × P, R—R 1 and wins.

Position after White's 26th move.

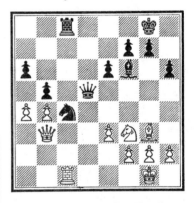

| 26. ...... | B—Kt 7 ! |

In order to play ....P—K 4 without restricting the activity of the Bishop. The tactical justification of this move is shown by the following variations :

I   27. R—Q 1, P × P ! ; 28. Q × P, Kt—Kt 3 ; 29. R × Q, Kt × Q ; 30. R—Q 1, Kt—B 6 ; 31. R—K 1, R—B 5 ; 32. B—Q 6, Kt—K 5 ; 33. B—K 7, P—B 3 ; 34. R—Kt 1, K—B 2 ; 35. K—B 1, B—B 6, etc., with an easy win in the end game.

II   27. R—Kt 1, Kt—R 6 ! ; 28. Q × B, Kt × R ; 29. Q × Kt, Q—Kt 6; 30. Q—K B 1, P × P ; 31. P—K R 3, P—R 6 and wins.

27. R—K 1	R—Q 1
28. P×P	P×P
29. P—R 3	......

This emergency exit is absolutely necessary.

| 29. ...... | P—K 4 |
| 30. R—Kt 1 | P—K 5 ! |

The beginning of the end.

| 31. Kt—Q 4 | ...... |

Or *A*. 31. Kt—K 1, Q—Q 7 ; 32. Q—B 2 (32. K—B 1, R—R 1 ; 33. R—Q 1, R—R 6 and wins), Q×Q ; 33. Kt×Q, R—Q 7 ; 34. Kt—K 1, Kt—R 6 and wins. *B*. 31. Kt—R 2, Q—Q 6 ! ; 32. R×B !, Q×Q ; 33. R×Q, R—Q 8 ch ; 34. Kt—B 1, Kt—Q 7 ; 35. R—R 3, Kt×Kt and White would be helpless.

| 31. ...... | B×Kt |
| 32. R—Q 1 | ...... |

Loses immediately. But also after 32. P×B, Q×P, etc., the game could not have lasted long.

| 32. ...... | Kt×P ! |
| Resigns. | |

This and the 34th game are, in my opinion, the most valuable of the match.

GAME 23

QUEEN'S GAMBIT DECLINED (ORTHODOX DEFENCE)

Thirty - second Match - Game, Buenos Aires, November, 1927.

Black : J. R. CAPABLANCA

1. P—Q 4	P—Q 4
2. P—Q B 4	P—K 3
3. Kt—Q B 3	Kt—K B 3
4. B—Kt 5	Q Kt—Q 2

5. P—K 3	P—B 3
6. P×P	K P×P
7. B—Q 3	B—K 2
8. K Kt—K 2	......

This Knight's development was played here for the first time. Because of White's success in the present game, it became fashionable in the following years. In my opinion it is neither better nor worse than the usual Kt—K B 3 ; only, if he elects to castle on the Queen's side White has to be particularly careful, as Black's counter-attack on this wing may easily become more dangerous than his own initiative on the King's side.

| 8. ...... | Castles |

In this kind of position ....P—K R 3 is generally played before castling, in order not to allow White to answer this Pawn's move by P—K R 4. If Black had done this, my answer would have not been 9. B—R 4, but 9. B—K B 4.

| 9. Kt—Kt 3 | Kt—K 1 |

There is hardly another way of emancipation, as 9. ....R—K 1 would have been very strongly answered by 10. Kt—B 5.

| 10. P—K R 4 | ...... |

The natural consequence of the whole opening plan.

10.	Q Kt—B 3
11. Q—B 2	B—K 3
12. Kt—B 5	B×Kt
13. B×B	Kt—Q 3
14. B—Q 3	......

Of course not 14. B×Kt, Kt×B, etc., with equality. This text move forces Black to weaken his King's position.

| 14. ...... | P—K R 3 |
| 15. B—K B 4 | ...... |

In case of 15. Castles (Q R) Black would have been able to try a counter-attack starting by 15. .... P—Q Kt 4, etc.

| 15. ...... | R—B 1 |

Black intends to start an action on the Q B's file, as soon as his opponent castles Queen's side, and hereby overlooks the combinative reply. A more logical course was 15. ....R—K 1, intending ....K Kt—K 5.

| 16. P—K Kt 4 ! | ...... |

This advance, made possible through the fact that 16. ....Kt × Kt P ? ; 17. B × Kt followed by 18. B—B 5, etc., would lose the exchange for Black, considerably strengthens White's position and leaves Black but little choice.

16.	K Kt—K 5
17. P—Kt 5	P—K R 4
18. K B × Kt	......

White decides to accept the (forced) Pawn sacrifice, although he realises that the ensuing ending will be extremely difficult to win—if possible at all—owing to the very effective position of the black Rook on the second rank. A promising alternative was 18. Q B × Kt. Kt × B ; 19. Castles (Q R) (not 19. P—Kt 6 immediately, because of 19. ....B × P with counterplay), Kt—Kt 4 ; 20. K—Kt 1, Kt × Kt ; 21. Q × Kt and, in spite of the different-coloured Bishops, Black would not have found it easy to obtain a draw.

18.	Kt × B
19. Kt × Kt	P × Kt
20. Q × K P	Q—R 4 ch
21. K—B 1	......

White cannot risk the variation 21. K—K 2, Q—Kt 4 ch ; 22. K—B 3, K R—K 1, etc.

| 21. ...... | Q—Q 4 ! |

The point of Black's counterplay : after the forced exchange of Queens the only open file will become a very important factor in his favour.

22. Q × Q	P × Q
23. K—Kt 2	R—B 7
24. K R—Q B 1	......

It is obviously of importance to eliminate one pair of Rooks. If now 24. ....R × Kt P, White would secure a strong end-game advantage by means of 25. K R—Q Kt 1 !, etc.

24.	K R—B 1
25. R × R	R × R
26. R—Q Kt 1	K—R 2

Black prepares to take advantage of the fact that the light-coloured squares of White's position are insufficiently protected. White's next moves show the only appropriate defence against this plan.

| 27. K—Kt 3 | K—Kt 3 |
| 28. P—B 3 | P—B 3 ! |

And not 28. ....K—B 4 ? because of 29. P—K 4 ch, etc. Both sides, so far, are treating the difficult end-game in the right manner.

| 29. P × P | B × P |
| 30. P—R 4 | ...... |

Preparing to relieve the Rook from the defence of the Queen's side Pawns.

| 30. ...... | K—B 4 |
| 31. P—R 5 | R—K 7 |

Black is threatening now (in the event of 32. P—Q Kt 4, for instance) 32. ....P—K Kt 4 ! ; 33. P × P, B × Kt P ; 34. B × B, K × B, after which 35. P—B 4 ch, K—B 4 ; 36. K—B 3, R—K R 7 ; 37. R—Kt 1, R—R 6 ch ; 38. R—Kt 3, R × R ch !

etc., would only lead to a drawn Pawn ending.

Position after Black's 31st move.

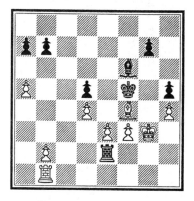

32. R—Q B 1   . . . . .

If White wants to play for a win he is compelled to give back (at least temporarily) the extra-Pawn. But a more efficient and, taking into consideration his two last moves, logical, method of doing it, was 32. P—R 6 ! After 32. . . . . P × P (32. . . . . P—Kt 3 ; 33. B— Kt 3, etc.) the answer 33. R—Q R 1! would have prevented 33. . . . . P— K Kt 4, because of 34. P × P, B × Kt P ; 35. P—K 4 ch ! etc. ; while after 33. . . . . R × Kt P ; 34. R × P, R—Kt 2 ; 35. R—R 5, etc., White's positional advantage would become decisive. After the move selected, Black will be able to put up a long and not altogether hopeless resistance.

32. . . . . . .   R × Kt P
33. R—B 5   K—K 3
34. P—K 4   B × Q P

Here, as on several future occasions in this game, Black could have played differently, but it is doubtful if it would have altered the final result. If, for instance, 34. . . . . P × K P, then 35. P—Q 5 ch, K— B 4 ; 36. P—Q 6 disc. ch, K—K 3 ;

37. P × P, R—Kt 6 ch ; 38. K—Kt 2, B × R P ; 39. R × R P, followed by 40. R—R 7 and the fight against the central passed Pawns would prove extremely difficult.

35. R × Q P   B—B 6

By playing 35. . . . . B—B 7 ch ; 36. K—R 3, R—Kt 6 ; 37. R— K 5 ch, K—B 2, he could temporarily save the Pawn, but his position after 38. B—Kt 5 ! would still look very compromised.

36. R × P   P—Q R 3

If 36. . . . . B—K 8 ch ; 37. K— R 3, R—K B 7, then 38. R—K 5 ch ! followed by 39. R—K B 5 ch, or 39. R—Q 5 ch—Q 3, etc., still keeping the plus Pawn.

37. B—B 7   B—K 8 ch

Or 37. . . . . R—Kt 4 ; 38. R— K Kt 5 ! etc.

38. K—Kt 4   R—Kt 7 ch
39. K—R 3   . . . . . .

Of course not 39. K—B 4, B— Q 7 mate !

39. . . . . . .   R—K B 7
40. K—Kt 4   R—Kt 7 ch
41. K—R 3   R—K B 7
42. P—B 4 !   R—B 6 ch
43. K—Kt 2   . . . . . .

Another method of suicide occurred here : 43. K—Kt 4, R— Kt 6 mate.

43. . . . . . .   R—B 7 ch
44. K—R 3   R—B 6 ch
45. K—Kt 2   R—B 7 ch
46. K—Kt 1   R—B 7
47. B—Kt 6   R—B 5

This facilitates White's task, as it enables his King to give effective support to the central Pawns. Better was 47. . . . . B—Kt 6, after which White would have tried to

obtain the victory by means of 48.
R—K 5 ch (K—Q 3 ; 49. R—K Kt 5
or K—B 2 ; 49. P—R 5 ! etc.).

Position after Black's 47th move.

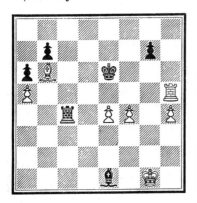

48. K—Kt 2 !   ......

By this move White obtains at
last a clearly won position. It is
obvious that after 48.   ....R×
K P ? ; 49. K—B 3 Black would
immediately lose.

48.	......	P—Kt 3
49.	R—K 5 ch	K—Q 2
50.	P—R 5 !	P×P
51.	K—B 3	P—R 5

51. ....R—B 6 ch ; 52. K—K 2,
B—Kt 6 ; 53. B—K 3, P—R 5 ; 54.
R—R 5, etc., would not help any
better.

52.	R—R 5	R—B 6 ch
53.	K—Kt 4	R—B 5
54.	K—B 5 !	......

Apparently falling into the trap,
but in reality selecting the surest
and quickest way to make use of
the passed Pawns.

| 54. | ...... | B×P |
| 55. | R—R 7 ch | ...... |

Of course not 55. B×B, R—B 4
ch ; 56. K—Kt 4 ? because of 56.

....R×R followed by 57. ....P—
R 6 winning.

55.	......	K—B 3
56.	B×B	R—B 4 ch
57.	K—K 6 !	R×B
58.	P—B 5	R—R 6
59.	P—B 6	R—K B 6
60.	P—B 7	P—Kt 4
61.	R—R 5 !	......

The neat final point of this
colourful ending.

61.	......	P—R 6
62.	R—K B 5	R×R
63.	P×R	......

If now 63. ....P—R 7 ; 64. P—
B 8 queen's, P—R 8 queen's, then
65. Q—R 8 ch, etc., wins.

Resigns.

GAME 24

QUEEN'S GAMBIT DECLINED

Thirty-fourth—and last—Match-
Game, Buenos Aires, November,
1927.

Black : J. R. CAPABLANCA

1.	P—Q 4	P—Q 4
2.	P—Q B 4	P—K 3
3.	Kt—Q B 3	Kt—K B 3
4.	B—K Kt 5	Q Kt—Q 2
5.	P—K 3	P—B 3
6.	P—Q R 3	......

This quiet move, whose main
object is to avoid the Cambridge-
Springs Defence, should hardly
promise White more than a comfortable equality. I selected it here
merely in order to come out of the
book variations as rapidly as
possible.

6.	......	B—K 2
7.	Kt—B 3	Castles
8.	B—Q 3	P×P

A sound alternative was 8. ....
P—K R 3 ; 9. B—R 4, P—B 4,
etc.

9. B × B P	Kt—Q 4
10. B × B	Q × B

Also possible was 10. ....Kt ×
Kt.

11. Kt—K 4	K Kt—B 3
12. Kt—Kt 3	P—B 4

12. ....P—Q Kt 3, followed
by ....B—Kt 2—as played by
Maroczy against me at San Remo
in 1930—is worth consideration.
The text manœuvre has the slight
drawback of not yet solving the
problem of the development of the
Queen's Bishop.

13. Castles	Kt—Kt 3
14. B—R 2	P × P
15. Kt × P	P—Kt 3

In order to be able to answer
P—K 4 by ....P—K 4 without
ceding the square K B 4 to the
White Knights.

16. R—B 1	......

Threatening   eventually   Kt—
Q Kt 5.

16.	B—Q 2
17. Q—K 2	Q R—B 1
18. P—K 4	P—K 4
19. Kt—B 3	K—Kt 2

Black should here exchange both
Rooks, as after 19. ....R × R ; 20.
R × B, R—B 1 ; 21. R × R ch,
Kt × R, the move 22. Kt—Kt 5
could have been sufficiently met by
22. ....B—K 1, etc. The text
move, and especially the next one,
brings his position suddenly into
danger.

20. P—R 3	P—K R 3 ?

Position after Black's 20th move.

21. Q—Q 2 !	......

This harmless-looking move is in
reality very hard to meet. White's
main threat is 22. Q—R 5, and if
Black should try to parry this by
the counter-attack, 21. ....B—B 3
(or Kt 4), then an unexpected diversion on the King's side would make
a rapid end : 22. Kt—R 4 !, Kt ×
P (or 22. ....B × P ; 23. Q—K 3 !
or 22. ....B—Q 2 ; 23. Q—R 5,
etc.) ; 23. Kt (R 4)—B 5 ch, P × Kt ;
24. Kt × P ch, K—B 3 ; 25. Q ×
R P ch, K × Kt ; 26. P—Kt 4, mate !
The only move which offers some
prospects of a successful defence is
that suggested by Dr. Lasker, 21.
....Kt—R 5 ! In that case, White
would simply continue to strengthen
his position—for instance, by means
of 22. K R—Q 1.

21.	B—K 3 ?

The position has proved too difficult for Black ; he now loses a Pawn
and, after a desperate struggle, the
game and the match. The following
sharp combinations, as well as the
subsequent Queen-and-Rook ending,
are both exciting and instructive.

22. B × B	Q × B
23. Q—R 5	Kt—B 5

Or 23. ....Q—Kt 6 ; 24. Q×
K P, Kt—B 5 ; 25. Q—Q 4, etc. ±

24.	Q × R P	Kt × Kt P
25.	R × R	R × R
26.	Q × P	Kt—B 5
27.	Q—Kt 4	R—Q R 1
28.	R—R 1	Q—B 3 !

Threatening to blockade the
Q R's Pawn by 29. ....R—R 5, and
also (at least apparently) to win the
King's Pawn. But White's two
next moves put the situation in the
true light.

29.	P—Q R 4 !	Kt × P
30.	Kt × P	......

Thus avoiding the pitfall 30.
Kt × Kt, Q × Kt ; 31. R—Q B 1,
R—Q B 1 ; 32. Kt × P (?), Kt—K 6!;
33. Q × Q, R × R ch ; 34. K—R 2,
Kt—B 8 ch, followed by Kt—Kt 6
disc. ch, and Kt × Q, after which
Black could even win.

30.	......	Q—Q 3 !

In the circumstances comparatively the best, as both pairs of
Knights will now soon disappear
from the board.

31.	Q × Kt	Q × Kt
32.	R—K 1	Kt—Q 3
33.	Q—Q B 1 !	Q—B 3
34.	Kt—K 4	Kt × Kt
35.	R × Kt	......

The winning procedure which
follows is a rather elaborate one,
and consists in combining the
threats connected with the passed
Pawn and an attack against the
somewhat exposed Black King.
First and foremost, White will succeed in controlling the important
diagonal, Q R 1—K R 8.

35.	......	R—Q Kt 1
36.	R—K 2	R—Q R 1
37.	R—R 2	R—R 4
38.	Q—B 7 !	Q—R 3

Obviously, the only way to prevent the advance of the passed
Pawn.

39.	Q—B 3 ch	K—R 2
40.	R—Q 2	.....

With the deadly threat 41. R—
Q 8,

40.	......	Q—Kt 3
41.	R—Q 7	.....

The sealed move. Black's next
manœuvres offer the only chance,
if not to save the game, at least to
permit a longer resistance.

41.	......	Q—Kt 8 ch
42.	K—R 2	Q—Kt 1 ch
43.	P—Kt 3	R—K B 4
44.	Q—Q 4	.....

Threatening 45. P—R 5 ! followed by R—Q 8.

44.	......	Q—K 1
45.	R—Q 5	R—B 6

The Queen's ending would be, of
course, tantamount to resignation.

46.	P—R 4	.....

White does not need to prevent
the Black Queen's following manœuvre, which finally leads to an
easily won Rook's ending for him.

46.	......	Q—K R 1
47.	Q—Kt 6 !	......

At this moment the exchange
would be premature, as it would
allow Black to bring his Rook
behind the passed Pawn.

47.	......	Q—R 8
48.	K—Kt 2	R—B 3

If 48. ....R—R 6 White wins as
follows : 49. R—Q 7, K—Kt 1 (or
K—Kt 2 ; 50. Q—K 6 ! or Q—R 7 ;
50. Q—K B 6, etc.) ; 50. Q—Q 8 ch,

K—Kt 2 ; 51. Q—K 7, Q—R 7 ;
52. Q—K 5 ch, K—R 2 ; 53. Q—
K B 6, etc.

49. Q—Q 4   ......

Now the right moment to exchange has come, as it is the *White*
Rook that will get behind the
passed Pawn.

49.	Q × Q
50. R × Q	K—Kt 2

Instead 50. ....R—R 3 would
have immediately lost after 51. K—
B 3, followed by K—K 4—Q 5, etc.

51. P—Q R 5	R—R 3
52. R—Q 5	R—K B 3
53. R—Q 4	R—R 3
54. R—R 4	K—B 3
55. K—B 3	K—K 4
56. K—K 3	P—R 4
57. K—Q 3	K—Q 4
58. K—B 3	K—B 4
59. R—R 2	K—Kt 4
60. K—Kt 3	......

White makes use of every opportunity, by repetition of moves, to
gain time with the clock, so as to
avoid a slip just before the capture
of the title.

60.	K—B 4
61. K—B 3	K—Kt 4
62. K—Q 4	......

If now 62. ....K—Kt 5, then
63. R—R 1 ! etc.

62.	R—Q 3 ch
63. K—K 5	R—K 3 ch
64. K—B 4	K—R 3

65. K—Kt 5	R—K 4 ch
66. K—R 6	R—K B 4
67. P—B 4	......

The simplest method to force the
capitulation was 67. K—Kt 7, R—
B 6 ; 68. K—Kt 8, R—B 3 ; 69.
K—B 8 !, R—B 6 (or R—B 4 ; 70.
P—B 4) ; 70. K—Kt 7, R—B 4 ;
71. P—B 4, etc.

67.	R—B 4 !
68. R—R 3	R—B 2
69. K—Kt 7	R—Q 2
70. P—B 5	......

Another inexact move. A more
direct way was first 70. K—B 6,
and only after 70. ....R—B 2 ; 71.
P—B 5, P × P ; 72. K × P, R—B 4
ch ; 73. K—B 6, R—B 2 ; 74. R—
K B 3, K × P ; 75. R—B 5 ch, and
wins ;

70.	P × P
71. K—R 6	P—B 5
72. P × P	R—Q 4
73. K—Kt 7	R—K B 4
74. R—R 4	K—Kt 4
75. R—K 4 !	K—R 3
76. K—R 6	R × R P

Or 76. ....K—Kt 2 ; 77. R—K 5,
R × P ; 78. K—Kt 5 !, R—B 8 ;
79. K × P, P—B 4 ; 80. K—Kt 5,
P—B 5 ; 81. R—K B 5, P—B 6 ;
82. K—Kt 4 and wins.

77. R—K 5	R—R 8
78. K × P	R—K Kt 8
79. R—Kt 5	R—K R 8
80. R—K B 5	K—Kt 3
81. R × P	K—B 3
82. R—K 7	Resigns.

PART II (1929-1934)

Tournament Games and Matches with Bogoljubow

GAME 25

QUEEN'S GAMBIT ACCEPTED

Bradley-Beach Tournament, June 1929.

Black : H. STEINER

Brilliancy Prize

1. P—Q 4	P—Q 4
2. P—Q B 4	P × P
3. Kt—K B 3	Kt—K B 3
4. P—K 3	P—K 3
5. B × P	P—B 4
6. Castles	P—Q R 3
7. Q—K 2	Q Kt—Q 2

If 7. .... Kt—B 3, the best answer according to the latest practice (Euwe-Alekhine, fifth match-game, 1937, and Alekhine-Böök, Margate, 1938) would still be 8. Kt—B 3 !

8. Kt—B 3	Q—B 2

If Black did not want to risk the "fianchetto" development which, in fact, is hardly recommendable (for instance, 8. ....P—Q Kt 4 ; 9. B—Kt 3, B—Kt 2 ; 10. R—Q 1, B—K 2 ; 11. P—K 4 !, P—Kt 5 ; 12. P—K 5, P × Kt ; 13. P × Kt, etc. ±, as in the game Alekhine-Letelier, Montevideo, 1938) he should simply play 8. ....B—K 2 ; for the square Q B 2 for the Queen, in case of the following Q's Pawn advance, will prove a very unfortunate one.

9. P—Q 5 !	P × P
10. B × P	......

One of Black's troubles from now on will consist in the fact that in case of the exchange of this Bishop, White would always recapture *with tempo.*

10.	B—Q 3
11. P—K 4	Castles
12. B—Kt 5	Kt—Kt 5

In order to develop his Q's side pieces Black is forced to lose time with this Knight, and, moreover, facilitate the dangerous advance of White's K B's Pawn.

13. P—K R 3	K Kt—K4
14. Kt—K R 4 !	......

In view of Black's cramped position the right policy is to avoid exchanges. Besides, Black is now forced to prevent the move Kt—B 5, and consequently has even less choice than before.

14.	Kt—Q Kt 3
15. P—B 4	Kt—B 3
16. P—B 5 !	......

A paradoxical, but most effective, continuation of the attack, by which White "sacrifices" the central square K 5. The "natural" advance 16. P—K 5 instead would have left White—strange as it may seem—after 16. ....B—K 2 with but an insignificant positional advantage.

16.	Kt—K 4
17. Q—R 5	R—K 1

Parrying the threat 18. P—B 6 which now would be met by 18. .... P—K Kt 3 ; 19. Q—R 6, B—B 1.

54

18. R—B 4   B—K 2

This will be refuted by a pretty combination, but, as Black still could not take the powerful Bishop —after 18. . . . . Kt × B ? follows 19. Kt × Kt, Q—B 3 ; 20. Kt—B 6 ch !, P × Kt ; 21. B × P, etc.—there was no longer a sufficient defence.

Position after Black's 18th move.

19. P—B 6 !   . . . . . .

Because of Black's last move White is enabled to effect this advance *in spite of the possible defence* 19. . . . . P—Kt 3 ; 20. Q—R 6, B—B 1—and this because of the following combination : 19. . . . . . . P—Kt 3 ; 20. Kt × P ! !, P × Kt (or A) ; 21. B × P ch !, K × B ; 22, P × B disc. ch, K—K 3 (or K—Kt 1 ; 23. R—B 8 ch, R × R ; 24. P × R = Q ch, K × Q ; 25. Q—R 8 ch, K—B 2 , 26. Q—R 7 ch, winning the Queen) ; 23. R—B 6 ch, K × P (or K—Q 2 ; 24. R—Q 1 ch, etc.) ; 24. Q—R 7 ch, K—Q 1 ; 25. R—Q 6, mate.

(A) 20. . . . . Kt × Kt ; 21. B × P ch !, K × B ; 22. Q × P ch, K—K 3 ; 23. Q × Kt and wins. After the following retreat which permits the opening of the K B's file, the game is also practically over.

19. . . . . . .   B—B 1

20. P × P   B × P
21. Q R—K B 1   B—K 3
22. Kt—B 5   . . . . . .

Threatening also R—R 4, etc.

22. . . . . . .   B × B
23. Kt × K B !   Kt—Kt 3
24. Kt × R   R × Kt
25. Kt × B   Resigns.

GAME 26

QUEEN'S GAMBIT DECLINED (SLAV DEFENCE)

First Match-Game, Wiesbaden, September, 1929.

Black : E. BOGOLJUBOW

1. P—Q 4   P—Q 4
2. P—Q B 4   P—Q B 3
3. Kt—K B 3   Kt—K B 3
4. Kt—B 3   P × P
5. P—Q R 4   P—K 3

It has been my peculiar luck that this illogical move (instead of the natural 5. . . . . B—K B 4) has been adopted against me, with a disastrous effect, no less than four times, namely (besides the present game) by Bogoljubow again (Nottingham, 1936), by Dr. Euwe (19th Match-Game, 1935), and by the late German master, Helling, in Dresden, 1936.

6. P—K 4   B—Kt 5
7. P—K 5   Kt—Q 4

In the three other games mentioned the reply was 7. . . . . Kt—K 5, which is at least as bad as the text move.

8. B—Q 2   B × Kt

If, instead, 8. . . . . P—Q Kt 4, then 9. Kt—K 4, B—K 2 ; 10. P—

Q Kt 3 !, etc., winning back the Pawn with decidedly the better position.

9.	P × B	P—Q Kt 4
10.	Kt—Kt 5 !	......

An important move with many objects, one of which, and not the least important, is to prevent Black's 10. Castles, because of the answer 11. Q—Kt 1 ! followed by 12. P × P, etc. ±

10.	......	P—B 3

Prevents the manœuvre Kt—K 4 —Q 6 ch, but at the cost of a serious compromising of the central position.

11.	P × B P	Kt × P

Or 11. Q × P ; 12. P × P, P × P ; 13. Kt—K 4, Q—K 2 ; 14. B— Kt 5, followed by Q—R 5 ch, etc. ±

12.	B—K 2	P—Q R 3

12. ....Castles ; 13. P × P, P— K R 3 (if 13. ....P × P then 14. B—B 3, Kt—Q 4 ; 15. Q—Kt 1, etc.) ; 14. P—Kt 6 !, Q × P ; 15. Kt—B 3, etc., would prove in the long run positionally hopeless.

13.	B—B 3 !	......

With the threat 14. P × P, etc., which is by no means easy to parry. If, for instance, 13. ....Kt—Q 4, then 14. Q—Kt 1 !, P—Kt 3 ; 15. Kt × R P, R × Kt ; 16. Q × P ch, R—B 2 ; 17. B—R 5 followed by 18. Q—Kt 8 ch and wins. Or 13. ....R—Q R 2 ; 14. B—K B 4, R— Kt 2 ; 15. P × P, R P × P ; 16. R— R 8, etc., also with a winning attack.

13.	......	P—K R 3

Already mere desperation.

14.	B—R 5 ch	Kt × B
15.	Q × Kt ch	K—Q 2
16.	Kt—B 7	Q—K 1
17.	Q—Kt 6	R—Kt 1
18.	B—B 4	B—Kt 2

Or 18. ....R—B 1 ; 19. Kt— K 5 ch, K—Q 1 ; 20. Q—K 4, etc.

19.	B—Kt 3	K—K 2
20.	B—Q 6 ch	......

A bit of cat-and-mouse play.

20.	......	K—Q 2
21.	Castles K R	P—B 4
22.	P × B P	B—Q 4
23.	P × P	P × P
24.	R × R	B × R
25.	R—R 1	Kt—B 3

Position after Black's 25th move.

26.	Kt—K 5 ch !	......

If now 26. ....Kt × Kt ; 27. R—R 7 ch, K—B 3, then 28. Q—K 4 mate.

Resigns.

GAME 27

QUEEN'S GAMBIT DECLINED
(SLAV DEFENCE)

Fifth Match-Game, Wiesbaden, September, 1929.

Black : E. BOGOLJUBOW

1. P—Q 4	P—Q 4
2. P—Q B 4	P—Q B 3
3. Kt—K B 3	Kt—K B 3
4. Kt—B 3	P × P
5. P—Q R 4	B—B 4
6. Kt—K 5	P—K 3

A simple and good move ; but by making it here (and in the third match game, in which I adopted the less logical answer 7. P—K B 3), Bogoljubow, as the following shows, did not fully understand its real value.

| 7. B—Kt 5 | B—K 2 |

Decidedly too passive : the right continuation is 7. ....B—Kt 5 (introduced by me in a consultation game, played against Bogoljubow and Dr. Seitz immediately after the match) ; 8. P—K B 3, P—K R 3 ! (as in my eleventh match game against Dr. Euwe, Groningen, 1937) obtaining at least an even game.

| 8. P—B 3 | P—K R 3 |
| 9. P—K 4 ! | ...... |

This move, which by the position of Black's King's Bishop at Kt 5 would have been answered by 9. ....P×B ; 10. P×B, P—Q Kt 4 ! ; 11. P×K P, P×K P ; 12. Q—B 2, Castles ! etc.∓, in the actual position practically shuts out the opponent's Queen's Bishop for the rest of the game.

| 9. ...... | B—R 2 |

Or 9. ....P×B ; 10. P×B, P×

P ; 11. B×P, Castles ; 12. P—R 4 ! etc. to White's advantage.

10. B—K 3	Q Kt—Q 2
11. Kt×Q B P	Castles
12. B—K 2	P—B 4

The following exchanges are decidedly in White's favour as they do not eliminate the main defect of Black's position—the awkward situation of his Queen's Bishop.

13. P×P	B×B P
14. B×B	Kt×B
15. P—Q Kt 4	Kt—R 3

Also unsatisfactory was 15. .... Q×Q ch ; 16. R×Q, Kt×R P ; 17. Kt×Kt, P—Q Kt 4 ; 18. Kt (B 4)—Kt 6 !, R P×Kt ; 19. B×Kt P, etc. ±

| 16. Q×Q | K R×Q |
| 17. Kt—R 2 ! | ...... |

The only way to keep the positional advantage, as 17. P—Q Kt 5 would cede the important square Q B 5, and 17. R—Q Kt 1 would have permitted a promising counterattack starting by 17. ....Kt—Q 4 !

| 17. ...... | Kt—Kt 1 |

White threatened 18. Kt—R 5, R—Q Kt 1 ; 19. Kt×Kt P, etc.

| 18. K—B 2 | Kt—B 3 |
| 19. K R—Q 1 | Kt—Q 5 |

Instead, 19. ....R×R ; 20. R× R, R—Q 1, would have been rapidly fatal : 21. P—Kt 5, R×R ; 22. B×R, Kt—Q 1 ; 23. Kt—Q 6, followed by 24. Kt—Kt 4 and 25. Kt—B 8 ! etc.

| 20. Q R—B 1 | K—B 1 |

The first step towards the emancipation of the Bishop at R 2 by means of B—Kt 1, Kt—K 1, P—

B 3, etc. But this plan will obviously take a long time, which
White will use for a decisive
strengthening of the pressure on the
Q's side. From now on the game
develops in a perfectly logical
manner.

| 21. B—B 1 | Kt—K 1 |
| 22. Kt—B 3 | ...... |

A strong alternative here was 22.
Kt—R 5 ; for instance :
I. 22. .... Q R—Kt 1 ; 23. Kt—
B 3, P—Q Kt 3 ; 24. R×Kt !,
R×R ; 25. Kt—B 6, Q R—Q 1 ;
26. K—K 3, R (Q 5)—Q 3 ; 27.
Kt×R, R×Kt ; 28. Kt—Kt 5.
II. 22. ....P—Q Kt 3 ; 23. Kt—
Kt 7, R—Q 2 ; 24. B—Kt 5 !,
R×Kt ; 25. R×Kt, with a tre-
mendous positional advantage in
both cases.

| 22. ...... | P—B 3 |
| 23. Kt—R 5 | Q R—Kt 1 |

This natural-looking answer gives
White the opportunity for the
following combination, which wins
a Pawn per force. Better was 23.
....P—Q Kt 3 ; 24. Kt—Kt 7, R—
Q 2 ; 25. B—Kt 5, R×Kt ; 26. R×
Kt, R—B 2 ; 27. Kt—K 2, R×R ;
28. Kt×R, R—B 1 ; 29. Kt—Q 3,
etc. ; with some possibilities of
defence in spite of the indisputable
advantage of White.

Position after Black's 23rd move.

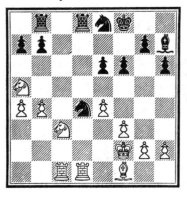

| 24. Kt—Kt 5 ! | ...... |

Eliminating the enemy's central
Knight just at the right moment :
if Black could have found time for
a further consolidation by means of
....P—K 4 there would be a very
little left of White's pressure on the
Q's side.

| 24. ...... | Kt×Kt |

Obviously forced.

| 25. R×R | R×R |
| 26. Kt×P ! | R—Q Kt 1 |

Or 26. ....R—Q 7 ch ; 27. K—
K 3, Kt (Kt 4)—Q 3 ; 28. K×R,
Kt×Kt ; 29. R—B 8, followed by
30. R—R 8 and R×Q R P, etc.,
winning.

| 27. Kt—B 5 | K—K 2 |

Because of the threat 28. Kt—Q 7
ch the Knight had still to keep
quiet. The following end-game,
with an extra-Pawn and a far better
position, is actually a walk-over for
White.

| 28. P×Kt ! | ...... |

Much more effective than 28. B×
Kt, because now Black's Q R Pawn
becomes extremely weak.

28.	Kt—Q 3
29. R—R 1	Kt—B 1
30. B—B 4	B—Kt 1

After 30. .... P—K 4 White
would win immediately by 31.
B—K 6, etc.

| 31. P—B 4 | B—B 2 |
| 32. P—K 5 | ...... |

All Black's pieces will be gradually stalemated, and the White
King will soon be in a position to
pay a significant visit to the adversary's Knight in its very residence.

32.	P×P
33. P×P	R—Kt 3
34. K—K 3	B—K 1
35. R—R 5	B—Q 2
36. K—Q 4	B—K 1

Black has nothing left but patiently to wait for the execution.

37. P—K R 4	B—Q 2
38. B—K 2	R—Kt 1
39. Kt×B	K×Kt
40. B—B 3 !	......

Preventing the manœuvre .... R—Kt 2—B 2 which would allow Black to prolong the agony.

40.	R—Kt 3
41. K—B 5	R—Kt 1
42. P—R 5	K—Q 1
43. B—B 6	K—K 2
44. R—R 3	K—K 2
45. B—K 4	K—K 2
46. K—B 6 !	......

Now the Knight must perish.

46.	K—Q 1
47. R—Q 3 ch	K—K 2
48. K—B 7	Resigns.

GAME 28

QUEEN'S INDIAN DEFENCE

Eighth Match-Game, Wiesbaden, September, 1929.

White : E. BOGOLJUBOW

| 1. P—Q 4 | Kt—K B 3 |
| 2. P—Q B 4 | P—Q Kt 3 |

Although this system of development is by no means easy to refute, it can hardly be considered absolutely correct as it allows White in such an early stage of the game to get full control upon the central squares ; and the fact that Black can attack the Pawn's centre by means of ....P—Q B 4 should not offer him full compensation for the lack of space he will have to suffer from after the next 10-15 moves. Undoubtedly sounder is therefore 2. ....P—K 3.

3. Kt—Q B 3	B—Kt 2
4. P—K B 3	P—Q 4
5. P×P	Kt×P
6. P—K 4	Kt×Kt
7. P×Kt	......

White's position looks now rather promising ; but he spoils it in a very few moves by adopting a totally wrong middle game plan.

| 7. ...... | P—K 3 |
| 8. B—Kt 5 ch | ...... |

Neither better nor worse than the immediate 8. B—Q 3, as Black's ....P—Q R 3 will not prove weakening to his position in the course of the game.

8.	Kt—Q 2
9. Kt—K 2	B—K 2
10. Castles	P—Q R 3
11. B—Q 3	P—Q B 4
12. B—Kt 2 ?	......

A really bad move which shows an entire misconception of the needs of the present situation. White had instead the choice between at least two good Bishop moves— 12. B—K 3, and 12. B—K B 4. Also 12. P—Q R 4 (in order to fix Black's slight weakness at Q Kt 3) came into consideration. From now on Black gradually gets the initiative.

| 12. ...... | Q—B 2 |
| 13. P—K B 4 | ...... |

This allows Black to win a couple of *tempi* by attacking the insufficiently protected central Pawns. A lesser evil was 13. P—K 5, temporarily restricting the field of activity of Black's Knight.

| 13. ...... | Kt—B 3 |
| 14. Kt—Kt 3 | P—K R 4 ! |

By his last aimless moves White has provoked an immediate King's attack.

15. Q—K 2	P—R 5
16. Kt—R 1	Kt—R 4
17. Q—Kt 4	......

In spite of his previous indifferent play White probably could still have held the game if he had recognised his mistake at the 12th move and had removed his Bishop to Q B 1. The seemingly more aggressive move here made by him instead, in reality relieves Black from the worry about his Q's R Pawn, and thus permits him to castle Q's side with an overpowering position.

| 17. ...... | Castles (Q R) |
| 18. Q R—K 1 | ...... |

If 18. P—B 5 then 18. .... Kt—B 3 (19. Q×Kt P ?, R—R 2), followed by 19. .... P—K 4 with advantage.

| 18. ...... | K—Kt 1 |
| 19. P—B 5 | ...... |

This attempt to blockade the centre proves unsuccessful as Black can secure strong diagonals for both his Bishops. But the game already was strategically lost.

| 19. ...... | P—K 4 |
| 20. P—Q 5 | P—B 5 ! |

Securing the future of the K's Bishop.

| 21. B—B 2 | B—B 4 ch |

| 22. Kt—B 2 | P—K Kt 3 ! |

And after this the Q's Bishop will also develop a deadly activity on the diagonal Q B 1—K R 6.

| 23. P×P | Q R—Kt 1 |
| 24. B—B 1 | ...... |

A much too belated sign of remorse !

| 24. ...... | B—Q B 1 |
| 25. Q—B 3 | R×P |

Position after Black's 25th move.

| 26. K—R 1 | ...... |

White is anxious to save his Queen (which Black threatened to win by 26. .... B—K Kt 5) and overlooks the following mating combination. However, his position was hopeless anyhow—if, for instance, 26. B—K 3, then 26. .... B×B ; 27. R×B, Kt—B 5 ; 28. P—Kt 3, P×P ; 29. P×P, P—B 4 followed by 30. .... Q—K R 2 and mate.

26.	Kt—Kt 6 ch !
27. P×Kt	P×P disc. ch.
28. Kt—R 3	B×Kt
29. P×B	R×P ch
30. K—Kt 2	R—R 7 mate

GAME 29

KING'S INDIAN DEFENCE

Seventeenth Match-Game, Berlin, October, 1929.

Black : E. BOGOLJUBOW.

1. P—Q 4	Kt—K B 3
2. P—Q B 4	P—K Kt 3
3. P—B 3	P—Q 4

Although this system is not quite sound, it is by no means as easy to meet as it looks at first sight, because White's central position may eventually become weak. Care is therefore required from the first player.

4. P × P	Kt × P
5. P—K 4	Kt—Kt 3
6. Kt—B 3	B—Kt 2
7. B—K 3	Kt—B 3 ?

But Black, also, must make the correct opening moves, which he does not on this occasion. Necessary was 7. ....Castles, as played by Bogoljubow against me in Bled, 1931. The right answer for White would have been in that case 8. P—K B 4 !

The text-move is most likely already a decisive positional error.

8. P—Q 5	Kt—K 4
9. B—Q 4	P—K B 3

Practically forced, as after 9. ....Castles ; 10. P—B 4, Kt—Q 2 ; 11. B × B followed by 12. Q—Q 4 ch, Castles (Q R), P—K R 4, etc., White would have obtained a winning King's attack.

10. P—B 4 (?)	......

This is sufficient in order to keep some opening advantage—but much more unpleasant for Black would have been first 10. P—Q R 4 ! as in that case he would not have had the possibility of playing ....

P—K 4 which in the actual game somewhat relieved his cramped position.

10.	Kt—B 2
11. P—Q R 4	P—K 4

Otherwise the "hole" at his K 3 would rapidly prove fatal.

12. P × P (*e.p.*)	B × P
13. P—R 5	Kt—Q 2
14. P—R 6	......

By an analogous manœuvre on the K's side I obtained a winning position in the decisive game against Rubinstein in The Hague, 1921. In the present position it is certainly not so forcible, but still strong enough.

14.	P—Kt 3
15. B—Kt 5	......

Threatening 16. B—B 6 followed by 17. Kt—Kt 5, etc.

15.	Q—K 2

In order to answer 16. B—B 6 by 16. ....Castles (Q R).

16. K Kt—K 2	P—Q B 4
17. B—B 2	Castles (Q R)

In making this risky move Bogoljubow probably already planned the sacrifice at K 4 which, doubtless, gave him some fighting chances. He can hardly be blamed for that decision, inasmuch as the alternative 17. ....Castles (K R); 18. Kt—Q 5, B × Kt (or 18. ....Q—Q 3; 19. K Kt—B 3, etc.±); 19. Q × B, K R—Q 1 ; 20. Castles (Q R), Kt—B 1 ; 21. Q—Kt 7, etc., would have left him but very few chances of salvation.

18. Q—R 4	P—B 4
19. P—K 5	......

At this moment the move 19. B—B 4 would not have led to anything particular after 19. ....Kt—Kt 1 ;

20. B×B ch, Q×B ; 21. Kt—Kt 5, Kt—B 3 (or R—Q 2), etc.

19. ......   P—Kt 4

Forcing White to show his hand, as after 20. P—K Kt 3, P×P ; 21. P×P the sacrifice 20 ....Kt (Q 2) × P ! etc., would have been more than disagreeable.

20. B—B 4 !   Q Kt× P !

A passive resistance commencing by 20. ....Kt—Kt 1 would soon prove hopeless after 21. B×B ch, Q×B ; 22. Castles K R with the strong threat 23. P—Q Kt 4, etc. But now White will be obliged to play very exactly in order to keep an advantage.

21. B×B ch   Q×B
22. P×Kt   Kt×P
23. Castles   Q—B 5 !

The point of the sacrifice : after 24. Q×Q, Kt×Q ; 25. Kt—Kt 5, K—Kt 1, etc., Black hopes to get some further material for his piece, after which the end game would have offered him not too bad prospects ; and if 24. Q—B 2, then Q—Q 6 with about the same result. White's following move, therefore, came quite unexpectedly for him.

Position after Black's 23rd move.

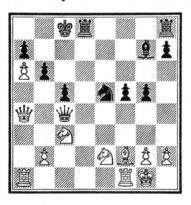

24. P—Q Kt 4 !   ......

White sacrifices another Pawn— thus re-establishing the equilibrium of forces—only in order to avoid the exchange of Queens. If now 24. ....P×P, then 25. Kt—Kt 5 !, Q×Kt (K 2) ; 26. K R—K 1, Q— Q 7 ; 27. Kt×R P ch, K—Kt 1 ; 28. Kt—B 6 ch ! etc., winning.

24. ......   Q×Kt P
25. Q—B 2   Kt—Q 6

The only defence against the double threat 26. R—Q R 4 and 26. Q×B P ch.

26. K R—Kt 1   Q—B 5
27. R—R 4   Q—K 3

If instead 27. ....Q—B 2 then 28. B—Q 4 !, P×B (or B×B ch ; 29. Kt×B, R×Kt ; 30. R×R, P×R ; 31. Q×Kt, P×Kt ; 32. Q× Q B P ch and wins) ; 29. Kt—Q 5 disc. ch !, Kt—B 4 ; 30. Kt×P ch !, P×Kt ; 31. R×Kt P followed by 32. P—R 7 and wins.

28. Kt—Kt 5   K—Kt 1

A longer resistance was possible after 28. ....Kt×B ; 29. K×Kt (and not 29. Kt×R P ch, K—Kt 1 ; 30. Q×B P ?, R—Q 8 ch ! etc.), K—Kt 1 ; but by continuing 30. Kt—Kt 3, K R—B 1 ; 31. R— R 3 ! (followed by 32. R—K 3 or Q 3, etc.)—White would still increase his pressure in a decisive manner.

29. Kt (K 2)—Q 4 !   Q—K 5

Or 29. ....B×Kt ; 30. B×B, R×B ; 31. R×R, Q—K 6 ch ; 32. K—B 1 and the Rook is taboo because of a mate in two in case of its capture.

30. Kt—Q B 3   Q—K 1
31. Q×Kt   P×Kt
32. B×P   Q—K 3
33. Q—B 3 !   Q—B 2

34. B × Kt P   ......

If now 34. ....P × B; 35. R × P ch, K—B 1, then 36. Q—B 6 ch, Q—B 2; 37. R—Kt 8 ch !, K × R; 38. P—R 7 ch, and mate in two.

Resigns.

GAME 30

RUY LOPEZ

Twenty - second Match - Game, Amsterdam, November, 1929.

White : E. BOGOLJUBOW.

1. P—K 4	P—K 4
2. Kt—K B 3	Kt—Q B 3
3. B—Kt 5	P—Q R 3
4. B—R 4	P—Q 3
5. P—B 3	......

The fashionable move here— especially after Keres' win against me in Margate, 1937—is 5. P— Q B 4. But for how long ? Black seems to be able to obtain quite a satisfactory position by continuing 5. ....B—Q 2; 6. Kt—B 3, Kt— B 3 ; 7. P—Q 4, Kt × Q P ; 8. B × B ch, Q × B ; 9. Kt × Kt, P × Kt ; 10. Q × P, B—K 2 followed by .... Castles etc.

5.	B—Q 2
6. P—Q 4	P—K Kt 3
7. B—K Kt 5	......

As the following shows, White has no means of exploiting the diagonal Q Kt 3—K Kt 8, and, on the other hand, K B 2 will prove a suitable square for Black's King's Knight. It looks as though after 5. P—Q B 3 White's opening advantage is bound to vanish within a few moves and that, therefore, the usual 5. B × Kt ch followed by 6. P—Q 4 offers him more fighting chances.

7.	P—B 3
8. B—K 3	Kt—R 3
9. Castles	B—Kt 2
10. P—K R 3	......

In order to prevent .... Kt—K Kt 5 in case of Q Kt—Q 2.

10.	Kt—B 2
11. Q Kt—Q 2	Castles
12. P × P	......

White—rightly—recognises that a further maintaining of the tension in the centre would be rather to Black's advantage and aims at simplification. The problem of the defence has been solved in this game in quite a satisfactory way.

| 12. ...... | Q P × P |

Also 12. ....B P × P—in the hope of exploiting the K B's file—could be played. White would in that case probably try to bring a Knight to Q 5 after the moves 13. B—Kt 3, P—K R 3 ; 14. P—Q R 4, followed by Kt—B 4, B—Q 2, Kt—K 3, etc. I preferred the text-move because of the tempting possibility of attacking shortly White's central position by means of .... P—K B 4.

13. B—B 5   ......

In order to provoke the move ....P—Q Kt 3, which slightly weakens Black's Queen's side position.

13.	R—K 1
14. B—Kt 3	P—Q Kt 3
15. B—K 3	Q—K 2
16. Q—K 2	......

Or 16. B—Q 5, Q R—Q 1 ; 17. Q—K 2, Kt—Kt 1 followed by .... B—K 3, etc.

| 16. ...... | Q Kt—Q 1 |
| 17. B—Q 5 | ...... |

Still playing for simplification which Black cannot well avoid as 17. ....P—Q B 3 would lose a Pawn after 18. B × Kt ch following by 19. B × Kt P.

| 17. ..... | B—B 3 |
| 18. P—B 4 ? | ..... |

But this is certainly not in accordance with the requirements of the position, as the Pawn at Q 5 after ....P—K B 4 will become very weak. Necessary was 18. B × B, Kt × B ; 19. K R—Q 1, etc., with only a slight advantage for Black because of the possibility (after a due preparation) of the K B's Pawn's advance.

| 18. ..... | B × B |
| 19. B P × B | ..... |

Even worse would be 19. K P × B, P—K B 4, etc.

| 19. ..... | P—K B 4 |
| 20. Kt—B 4 | Kt—Kt 2 |

Black is by no means in a hurry to play ....P—B 5 as the combined threat of this advance and an eventual ....P × K P will limit White's choice of moves much more than any direct action.

| 21. Q R—B 1 | Q R—Q 1 ! |

Deliberately permitting the following transaction which only apparently relieves White from his troubles in the centre. Instead, 21. ....K R—Q 1 would have left the Queen unprotected and thus have allowed the counter-action 22. P × P, P × P ; 23. B—Q 4 ! (R × P, 24. K R—K 1, P—K 5 ; 25. B × B, K × B ; 26. Kt—K 3 ! ±) etc.

22. P—Q 6	Q Kt × P
23. Kt × Kt	R × Kt
24. Q × P	Q—Q 2 !

An important intermediate move

securing with *tempo* (the threat ....P—K B 5) the control of the open file.

| 25. R—B 2 | P—B 4 |
| 26. P—Q R 4 | P—K B 5 ! |

Now the time has come, as the following advance of the K Kt's Pawn will be connected with the formidable threat 28. ....P—Kt 5 ; 29. P × P, Q × Kt P, etc., with a mating attack.

| 27. B—Q 2 | P—K Kt 4 |
| 28. Q—Kt 5 | ..... |

Although practically forced, this move actually brings but little help, as, after the Queen's exchange proposed here, Black not only obtains a far superior end game, but also—a very rare case considering the reduced material—a direct attack against the enemy's King.

| 28. ..... | Q × Q |
| 29. P × Q | R—Q 6 ! |

Freeing the important square Q 3 for the Knight.

| 30. R—R 1 | Kt—Q 3 |
| 31. R—R 6 | R—Kt 1 |

If now 32. Kt × Kt P, then simply 32. ....B—B 3 ; 33. Kt—B 3, Kt × K P, etc., with a sufficient positional advantage. And if 32. R—B 3, then 32. ....P—B 5 ! ; 33. R × R, P × R ; 34. R—R 3, Kt × K P ; 35. R × P, R—R 1 ! ; 36. R—R 3, R—Q 1, etc., winning.

| 32. B—B 3 | ..... |

As inoperative as the rest.

32.	Kt × K P
33. B × P	B × B
34. Kt × B	R—Q 8 ch
35. K—R 2	.....

Position after White's 35th move.

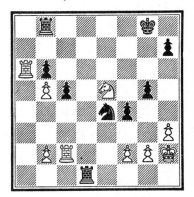

35. ......   Kt—Q 7 !

This sudden stroke—threatening mate in three by 36. ....Kt—B 8 ch, etc.—should have won at least the exchange. But Bogoljubow, as so often, prefers suicide to a long agony.

36. P—K R 4   R—K 1 !
37. Kt—B 3   ......

Or 37. Kt—Kt 4, R (K 1)—K 8 ; 38. K—R 3, R—R 8 ch ; 39. Kt—R 2, P—K R 4 ! ; 40. P × P, Kt—B 8 followed by mate.

37. ......   Kt × Kt ch
38. P × Kt   R (K 1)—K 8
39. K—R 3   P—R 4 !
Resigns.

GAME 31

RUY LOPEZ

San Remo Tournament, January, 1930.

White : F. D. YATES

1. P—K 4   P—K 4
2. Kt—K B 3   Kt—Q B 3
3. B—Kt 5   P—Q R 3
4. B—R 4   P—Q 3
5. Kt—Q B 3   ......

An unusual way to fight against the Steinitz Defence delayed.

White's idea was probably to play P—Q B 3 after having brought the Q's Knight to Q 5 ; but in the meantime Black succeeds in exchanging the "Spanish" Bishop, and thus obtains the advantage of the pair of Bishops with a more elastic Pawn skeleton.

5. ......   B—Q 2
6. P—Q 3   ......

Logical—but more promising was still 6. B × Kt followed by 7. P—Q 4.

6. ......   P—K Kt 3
7. Kt—Q 5   P—Q Kt 4 !

Necessary because if White could have succeeded in fulfilling his plan (8. P—Q B 3) he would have in fact obtained a superiority in space.

8. B—Kt 3   Kt—R 4
9. B—Kt 5 !   ......

The weakening of the diagonal Q R 2—K Kt 8, thus provoked, could eventually become of some importance—especially if White should decide to retain the corresponding Bishop.

9. ......   P—K B 3
10. B—Q 2   P—B 3

Necessary, as after the immediate 10. ....Kt × B White, after 11. R P × Kt, would have threatened 12. B—R 5, etc. with advantage.

11. Kt—K 3 (?)   ......

Comparatively better was 11. B × Kt, Q × B ch ; 12. Kt—B 3, after which Black would be compelled, before undertaking any action in the centre, to finish his development by means of ....Kt—R 3—B 2, followed by ....B—Kt 2 and Castles. After the text-move his task in increasing his advantage in space will be, on the contrary, a comparatively easy one.

11. ......   Kt × B

| 12. R P×Kt | Kt—R 3 |
| 13. P—Q Kt 4 | ..... |

The real trouble for White consists in the fact that he has no secure squares for his Knights, and, on the other hand, if he tries to open the position the Black Bishops will become over-powerful.

| 13. ...... | P—K B 4 |

If White's previous move had been 13. P—Q 4, this answer would prove even more effective.

| 14. Q—K 2 | Kt—B 2 |
| 15. Kt—B 1 | Q—K 2 |

Quiet positional play : Black is in no particular hurry to play .... P—B 5 as White has nothing else to do but try to stabilise the situation in the centre—even at the cost of a few *tempi*.

16. Kt—Kt 3	P—B 5
17. Kt—B 1	P—Kt 4
18. B—B 3	P—K R 4 !

Planning 19. ....P—R 5 and only after 20. P—K R 3 — P—Kt 5 ; 21. P×P, B×P followed by ..... Kt—Kt 4, P—R 6, etc. In order to prevent this pinning, White decides to weaken his dark-coloured squares by playing P—K B 3.

19. Kt (B 3)—Q 2	B—Kt 5
20. P—B 3	B—K 3
21. P—Q 4	......

If 21. Kt—Q Kt 3 Black would not have exchanged his valuable Q's Bishop for the Knight, but would have played 21..... P—Q B 4 followed by ....Kt—Q 1—B 3— Q 5.

| 21. ...... | B—Kt 2 |
| 22. Q—Q 3 | ...... |

The "combination" 22. P—Q 5, P×P ; 23. R×P, R×R ; 24. Q×P

ch, Q—Q 2 ; 25. Q×R, P—Q 5, etc. would lose a piece.

| 22. ...... | P×P |
| 23. B×P | Kt—K 4 |

The occupation of this powerful central square signifies the strategical decision.

| 24. Q—K 2 | Castles (K R) |

As the position from now on will become still more open, the co-operation of the Rooks will be vital.

| 25. P—R 3 | P—B 4 ! |

The beginning of the decisive action.

| 26. B—B 3 | ...... |

Instead 26. P×P, P×P ; 27. B× Kt, B×B, etc., would be perfectly hopeless.

26.	P×P
27. B×P	Kt—B 3
28. B—B 3	B×B

The advantage is already so definite that the combined action of the two Bishops is no longer needed.

| 29. P×B | ...... |

Position after White's 29th move.

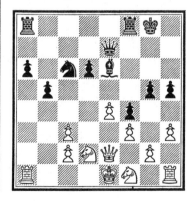

29. ......   Q—B 3

This move cannot actually be severely criticised as it wins a Pawn and allows Black after a few moves to simplify matters, and to obtain a technically rather easily won endgame. Still, Black did not need to give his opponent, even temporarily, the square White's K 4 for the Knight. Logical was therefore 29. ....Q—K Kt 2! (30. P—K 5, P—Q 4! etc.) after which all the tenacity of Yates would not have succeeded in prolonging the game much longer. I did not play my Queen to K Kt 2 in order to prevent the possibility of 30. Q—Q 3, Kt—Kt 5; 31. Q×Q P attacking the Bishop; but 31. ....Kt× B P ch; 32. K—Q 1, Kt×R (or even 32. ....R—B 3) would in that case be decidedly favourable for Black. White's play from now on is an example of a patient and ingenious defence in a theoretically lost position.

30. P—K 5 !   Kt×P
31. Kt—K 4   Q—K 2
32. Kt (B 1)—Q 2 B—B 5
33. Kt×B   Kt×Kt

Threatening 34. ....P—Q 4 as well as 34. ....Kt—K 6. One would think that the game can last only a couple of moves more.

34. R—Q 1 !   ......

Threatening 35. R—Q 5.

34. ......   Q—K 4
35. Q—Q 3 !   ......

Again preventing 35. ....Kt—K 6 because of 36. Q×Q P etc. Besides, White threatens now 36. Q—Q 5 ch, etc.

35. ......   R—B 4
36. Castles !   ......

Thus White definitely saves himself from a debacle in the middle-game, as—strange as it may seem—Black would hardly obtain a sufficient advantage by playing 36. .... Kt—K 6. The continuation would be 37. Kt×Q P !, R—Q 1 (or R—B 3; 38. K R—K 1, R—Q 1); 38. K R—K 1, R—B 3; 39. Q—K 4 ! (the point of the defence) after which 39. ....Q×B P would be a mistake because of 40. Kt×Kt P ! etc.; and also 39. ....Q×Q; 40. Kt×Q, R×R; 41. Kt×R ch, K—B 2; 42. R×R, Kt×R; 43. Kt—K 4 would not be yet quite convincing (43. ....P—Q R 4; 44. Kt—Q 6 ch or 43. ....K—K 3; 44. Kt—B 5 ch). Black's next move is therefore the simplest method of obtaining a winning end-game advantage.

36. ......   P—Q 4 !

Not only the extra-pawn is given back, but even the passed Q R's Pawn will be sacrificed in order to establish the Rook on the 7th rank. The following ending is sharp and full of tactical points.

37. Q×P ch   ......

There is, obviously, no choice left.

37. ......   Q×Q
38. R×Q   R×R
39. Kt—B 6 ch   K—B 2
40. Kt×R   R—Q 1

Instead 40. ....P—R 4; 41. Kt—B 7, R—Q Kt 1; 42. R—Q Kt 1, etc., would not have been convincing.

41. Kt—Kt 4   R—Q 7 !
42. R—R 1   ......

The main variation I expected was 42. Kt×R P, Kt—K 6; 43. R—Kt 1, R×Kt P ch; 44. K—R 1, R×B P; 45. R×P, P—Kt 5 !; 46. R P×P, P×P; 47. P×P, P—B 6 and wins.

42.	. . . . . .	P—Q R 4
43.	Kt—B 6	R × B P
44.	Kt × P	Kt—K 6
45.	R—Kt 1	R × P ch
46.	K—R 1	R—Kt 6

Not as simple as it looks would be instead 46. . . . . P—Kt 5 because of 47. R P × P, P × P; 48. Kt—B 6 !, etc.

47.	Kt—B 6 !	R × P ch
48.	K—Kt 1	R—Kt 6 ch
49.	K—R 2	K—B 3
50.	Kt—Q 4	P—K Kt 5 !

This exactly-timed advance in fact saves the Q Kt's Pawn because of the strong threats it involves.

| 51. | P × P | Kt × P ch |
| 52. | K—R 1 | P—B 6 |

Threatening mate in two, and thus forcing the rejoinder.

53.	R—K B 1	R—R 6 ch
54.	K—Kt 1	P—B 7 ch
55.	K—Kt 2	R × P
56.	R—K R 1	. . . . . .

Yates is still fighting ! Instead 56. Kt × P would lose rapidly after 56. . . . . R—Kt 6 ; 57. Kt—Q 4, R—Q 6 ; 58. Kt—B 2, R—Q 7 etc.

| 56. | . . . . . . | R—Q 6 ! |
| 57. | Kt—K 2 | . . . . . . |

Or 57. Kt × P, R—Q 7 ; 58. R—R 3, R—Q 8, etc.

| 57. | . . . . . . | R—Q 7 |
| 58. | Kt—Kt 3 | R—Kt 7 ! |

Starting the final combination. 58. . . . . Kt—R 7 at once would be of course wrong because of 59. Kt—K 4 ch.

| 59. | Kt × P ch | K—K 4 |
| 60. | Kt—Kt 3 | Kt—R 7 ! |

An elegant stroke by which Black

forces the exchange of Knights and keeps his two extra Pawns.

61.	Kt—B 1	Kt × Kt
62.	R—R 5 ch	K—Q 5
63.	K × Kt	P—Kt 5
64.	R—R 8	R—B 7
65.	R—Q Kt 8	K—B 6
66.	R—Kt 7	P—Kt 6
Resigns.		

GAME 32

FRENCH DEFENCE

San Remo Tournament, January, 1930.

Black : A. NIMZOWITSCH

1.	P—K 4	P—K 3
2.	P—Q 4	P—Q 4
3.	Kt—Q B 3	B—Kt 5
4.	P—K 5	P—Q B 4
5.	B—Q 2	. . . . . .

This rather tame move in connection with the following Knight's manœuvre should not cause Black much trouble. More promising—perhaps only because less explored—seems 5. Q—Kt 4 or even 5. P × P.

5.	. . . . . .	Kt—K 2
6.	Kt—Kt 5	B × B ch
7.	Q × B	Castles
8.	P—Q B 3	P—Q Kt 3

The wish to solve the Queen's Bishop's problem as rapidly as possible is, by the second player in the French Defence, quite legitimate, —but in this particular position the attempt will prove a failure *as Black cannot succeed in exchanging that piece against White's King's Bishop.* Good—and natural enough —was, instead of this, 8. . . . . Kt— B 4 ! (preventing Kt—Q 6) as played with success by the same Nimzowitsch against Dr. Lasker in Zurich, 1934.

9. P—K B 4   B—R 3

Trying to force White's P—Q R 4 in order to play afterwards Kt—Q B 3—R 4, etc. But, as will be seen, the second part of this plan cannot be executed.

10. Kt—B 3   Q—Q 2
11. P—Q R 4   Q Kt—Q B 3
12. P—Q Kt 4 !   ......

Strangely enough, this more or less conventional move (by which White prevents ....Kt—R 4 and at the same time forces a clearing of the situation in the centre) created at the time a kind of small sensation ; the late Dr. Tarrasch, for instance, called it in his comments "highly original." To my mind more surprising than the move is the fact that a player of Nimzowitsch' class, when adopting the plan started by 8. ....P—Kt 3, did not take this possibility into serious consideration.

12. ......   P × Kt P

Comparatively better than 12. ....P—B 5, after which White would not have much technical difficulty in exploiting, in a decisive manner, his advantage in space on the King's side.

13. P × P   B—Kt 2
14. Kt—Q 6   P—B 4 ?

The decisive strategical error in an already compromised situation. In view of the threatening advance of White's Q R's Pawn the only chance of obtaining some more space lay in 14. ....P—Q R 4 ; 15. B—Kt 5 (better than 15. P—Kt 5, Kt—Kt 5), P × P ; 16. Castles, after which the initiative of White—who would have to spend some time in regaining the Q Kt's Pawn—would not develop so rapidly. By moving his K B's Pawn, Nimzowitsch was obviously afraid of an attack against

his King—and that was the one thing in the present game he did not have to worry about !

15. P—R 5 !   ......

As 15. ....P × P ; 16. P—Kt 5 ! followed by 17. R × P, etc., is now obviously bad for Black, this advance secures for the white Bishop the most important square Q Kt 5.

15. ......   Kt—B 1

The elimination of the terrible Knight at Q 6—which under other circumstances would signify the beginning of a complete emancipation—does not in fact bring Black any relief.

16. Kt × B   Q × Kt
17. P—R 6   Q—K B 2

To his misfortune 17. ....Q—K 2 does not work, because of 18. B—Kt 5 !, Kt × Kt P ? ; 18. R—Kt 1, etc.

18. B—Kt 5   ......

From now on Black may play what he likes—he will be unable to protect sufficiently his squares Q B 3 and Q B 2. The following hopeless tie-up is only the unavoidable consequence of that organic evil.

18. ......   Kt (B 1)—K 2
19. Castles (K R) P—R 3

Although Kt—Kt 5 was not yet a threat it could become one in the near future. Besides, the immediate 19. ....R—Q B 1 would not change the situation a bit : Black loses not because of lack of time, but because of lack of space.

20. K R—B 1   K R—B 1
21. R—B 2   ......

If now 21. ....Kt—Q 1 then simply 22. R (R 1)—Q B 1, R × R ;

23. R×R, R—Q B 1; 24. R×R, Kt×R; 25. Q—B 3 followed by Q—B 7, and wins.

| 21. ...... | Q—K 1 |
| 22. Q R—B 1 | ...... |

This and the next move are not the most exact ones, as the winning formation : Q B 1, R 5—Q B 2 and B 3, was to be reached in three moves instead of five, as occurred in the actual game : 22. R—R 3 ! followed by Q R—B 3 and Q—B 1.

22.	Q R—Kt 1
23. Q—K 3	R—B 2
24. R—B 3 !	......

From now on, White wins in the shortest number of moves.

| 24. ...... | Q—Q 2 |

In order to give the King the possibility of protecting the Rook at Q B 2—a desperate idea in a desperate position !

| 25. R (B 1)—B 2 | K—B 1 |
| 26. Q—B 1 | R (Kt 1)—B 1 |

Position after Black's 26th move.

27. B—R 4 ! ......

The last link of the positional attack started by 15. P—Q R 5.

In order to save the piece threatened by 28. P—Q Kt 5 Black must sacrifice the Q Kt's Pawn. After this he succeeds in protecting the important squares with the King, but must still resign as a consequence of a complete *Zugzwang.* An instructive finish !

27.	P—Q Kt 4
28. B×P	K—K 1
29. B—R 4	K—Q 1
30. P—R 4 !	......

After a couple of irrelevant Pawn moves Black will be obliged to play Q—K 1 after which P—Q Kt 5 wins immediately.

Resigns.

GAME 33

NIMZOWITSCH'S DEFENCE

San Remo Tournament, January, 1930.

White : DR. M. VIDMAR

1. P—Q 4	Kt—K B 3
2. P—Q B 4	P—K 3
3. Kt—Q B 3	B—Kt 5
4. Q—B 2	P—Q 4
5. P—Q R 3	B×Kt ch
6. Q×B	Kt—K 5
7. Q—B 2	Kt—Q B 3

According to the actual views of the theory, 7. ....P—Q B 4 ; 8. P×B P, Kt—Q B 3, etc., is sufficient for equalising. The text-move —in connection with the following pawn-sacrifice—was introduced by me in the present game, and was considered, for quite a long time, a kind of refutation of 5. P—Q R 3. Only recently have a few tournament games and subsequent analysis cast doubt on the efficiency of Black's counter-play. As the idea occurred to me only during this game and as I have never tested it

since, I would not be at all surprised if a further, detailed analysis
will definitely prove its insufficiency.

8. P—K 3   . . . . . .

After 8. Kt—B 3, P—K 4 ; 9.
P × P, B—B 4 ; 10. Q—Kt 3, Kt—
R 4 ; 11. Q—R 4 ch, P—B 3 ; 12.
P × P, Q × P, etc., Black should
obtain a good positional compensa-
tion for the minus pawn.

8. . . . . . .   P—K 4
9. P—B 3 ?   . . . . . .

Very harmless, to say the least ;
White should have entered into the
main variation starting with 9. P ×
Q P, which would have brought
him, after a rather venturesome
King's trip, it is true, two minor
pieces for a Rook, and a safe enough
position. The play might be : 9.
. . . . Q × P ; 10. B—B 4, Q—R 4 ch;
11. P—Kt 4 !, Kt × Kt P ; 12. Q ×
Kt, Kt—B 7 doub. ch, ; 13. K—K 2,
Q—K 8 ch ; 14. K—B 3, Kt × R ;
15. B—Kt 2, B—K 3 ! (Fine's
move) ; 16. P—Q 5, Castles (Q side) ;
17. P × B, P × P ; 18. K—Kt 3 !
after which the few threats Black
would still possess would hardly
compensate for his material loss.
After the text-move, Black gets an
advantage in development without
having sacrificed anything in exchange.

9. . . . . . .   Kt—B 3

A premature attack would be 9.
. . . . Q—R 5 ch ; 10. P—Kt 3, Kt ×
Kt P ; 11. Q—B 2, Kt—B 4 ; 12.
P × Q P, etc. ±

10. P × Q P   Q × P
11. B—B 4   . . . . . .

This gain of a *tempo* is not enough
compensation for all the time
wasted previously.

11. . . . . . .   Q—Q 3

12. P × P   Kt × P
13. B—Q 2   . . . . .

Not satisfied with the results of
the opening play, White begins to
set little traps, which, however, will
prove quite ineffective. Comparatively better than this artificial
development was 13. Kt—K 2
followed by O—O.

13. . . . . . .   Castles !

Rightly ignoring White's combination.

14. B—Kt 4   . . . . . .

Also, 14. R—Q 1, Q—Q Kt 3, etc.,
would be in Black's favour.

14. . . . . . .   P—B 4
15. R—Q 1   . . . . . .

Of course not 15. Q B × P, Q × B;
16. B × P ch, R × B ; 17. Q × Q,
Kt—Q 6 ch, etc. But also the
intermediate move in the text, on
which White obviously relied, is of
little help.

15. . . . . . .   Q—B 3 !

The point of Black's active
defence : if now 16. Q B × P, then
16. . . . . Kt × B ; 17. Q × Kt (or 17.
B × R, K × B, etc.), P—Q Kt 3, etc.,
winning a piece. White must therefore remove his Bishop.

16. B—Q 2   B—B 4 ! ?

From now on Black's trouble will
be that he will have too many
promising continuations at his disposal, and therefore it will be
extremely difficult to decide each
time which is actually the best. As
the game goes, he succeeds in winning, by interesting tactical play,
first a Pawn and finally the exchange—but White still preserves,
almost to the end, excellent drawing
chances ! Consequently, something

must have been out of order in Black's method of exploiting his considerable positional advantage. Most likely, the rational way consisted not in trying to profit by the insufficient protection of White's King's Pawn, but in increasing two already existing advantages : (1) the Pawn majority on the Queen's side, and, especially, (2) the weakness of the light coloured squares in White's camp. Therefore, the tempting Bishop-move should have been replaced by the simple variation, 16. ....Kt × B ; 17. Q × Kt, B—K 3 ; 18. Q—B 2, Q—Kt 4 ! etc.∓, after which White would hardly succeed in bringing his King into safety.

18. Q—B 2, Q—Kt 4 ! etc.∓, after which White would hardly succeed in bringing his King into safety.

17. Q × B	Kt × B
18. B—B 1	K R—K 1

By no means convincing was here 18. ....Q R—Q 1 ; 19. R × R, R × R ; 20. Kt—K 2, Kt—Q 4 ; 21. Q—Q 3 ! threatening 22. P— K 4, etc.

19. K—B 2   R—K 3

Planning the following intermezzo, which wins a pawn perforce.

20. Kt—R 3 !   ......

Comparatively better than 20. Kt—K 2, since the Knight can eventually be useful at K Kt 5. After the unlucky opening, Dr. Vidmar defends his compromised position with extreme care and determination.

20.	Kt—K 5 ch !
21. K—K 1	......

Of course, the Knight was taboo because of 21. ....R—B 3.

21.	K Kt—Q 3
22. Q—Q 3 !	......

If 22. Q—Q 5, Black would

naturally have avoided exchange of Queens with 22. ....Q—Kt 4.

Position after White's 22nd move.

22. ......   Kt × K P !

The point of the previous moves of Black, whose aim is *not* to exchange the two Rooks for the Queen, but simply to win back the Bishop, remaining with an extra Pawn. However, as White will now be able to force the exchange of Queens, the fight is by no means near its end.

23. B × Kt	P—B 5 !
24. Q—Q 5	......

Otherwise Black plays 24. .... Kt—K B 4.

24.	R × B ch
25. K—B 2	Q × Q

After this, Black will have almost no choice for the next 10-12 moves, when an extremely difficult ending of R+2 Ps v. Kt+3 Ps will be reached. Possibly a somewhat more promising alternative was, therefore, 25. ....R—K 3 ; 26. Q × Q (else Black will avoid this exchange) P × Q ; 27. K R—K 1, R × R ; 28. K × R, Kt—B 4 ! eventually followed by ....Kt—K 6. But at this stage it was not at all easy to decide which line would leave White less drawing chances.

26. R × Q   R—Q 6

This was, of course, planned on the previous move. After 26. .... R—K 3 ; 27. K R—Q 1, etc., White would easily obtain a draw.

27. R × R	P × R
28. R—Q 1	Kt—B 5
29. R × P	Kt × Kt P
30. R—Kt 3	Kt—B 5
31. R × P	Kt × P
32. Kt—Kt 5	......

At last White succeeds in justifying the move 20. Kt—R 3. Obviously enough, Black has no time for protecting his K B P, since, after 32. ....P—K B 3, the manœuvre Kt—K 6—B 7 would immediately force a draw.

32.	P—Q R 4
33. Kt × B P	P—R 5

33. ....Kt—B 5 would be useless, because of 34. R—B 7.

34. Kt—Q 6	Kt—B 7
35. R—Kt 2	......

Otherwise the passed Pawn goes through.

35.	P—R 6 !
36. R × Kt	P—R 7
37. R × P ?	......

It is difficult to explain why White takes the Pawn at once instead of playing 37. R—B 1, P=Q ; 38. R × Q, etc., which would give him the option of playing the King to Kt 3 (as in the actual game) or making another move. Actually, after 38. ....R × R ; 39. P—Kt 4 ! Black's win, if possible at all, would be even more remote than in the line selected.

37. ......   R × R ch

38. K—Kt 3   K—B 1

Black's plan evidently consists in gradually restricting the activity of both White's pieces and in trying to create Pawn-weaknesses in the enemy's structure. Whether this can be carried out against an impeccable defence is another question. Not having seen an end-game like this in the literature devoted to that branch of chess, I confess I was rather expecting my opponent to succeed in finding an impregnable defensive position for both his Knight and King.

Position after Black's 38th move.

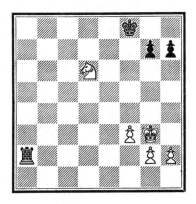

39. P—R 4   ......

It is difficult to suggest exactly what White's manœuvres must be in order to prevent the gradual advance of Black's King, but one positional consideration is beyond dispute : *White's Pawns should not be touched without necessity or without real prospects of being exchanged.* Although the move in the text can hardly be considered a decisive mistake, it certainly helps the execution of the first part of Black's plan, for from now on the White King will have to take care not only of K Kt 2 but also, eventually, of K R 4.

| 39. ...... | K—K 2 |
| 40. Kt—K 4 | P—R 3 |

Necessary, in order to permit the King's advance.

41. Kt—B 2	K—K 3
42. Kt—Q 3	K—B 4
43. Kt—B 4	R—R 5
44. Kt—Q 3	R—Q B 5
45. Kt—B 2	R—B 3
46. Kt—R 3	K—K 4

Black now threatens to bring his King to K B 8, for instance : 47. Kt—B 4, K—Q 5 ; 48. K—B 2, R—B 7 ch ; 49. K—Kt 3, K—K 6 ; 50. Kt—Q 5 ch, K—K 7 ; 51. Kt—B 4 ch, K—B 8 ; after this, the next step would be to secure square K B 7 for the King by using *zugzwang* and even that would not yet be the end of the winning procedure !   One may therefore imagine how welcome was White's next Pawn-move, which afforded me a number of new attacking possibilities.

| 47. P—R 5 ? | ...... |

Depriving Black of square K Kt 3 —but, as will be seen, the control of K Kt 4 was far more important.

47.	R—B 7
48. Kt—B 4	R—Q 7 !
49. Kt—R 3	......

Already he has no choice.

49.	K—Q 5
50. Kt—B 4	K—K 6
51. Kt—K 6	......

Impatience or despair ? If the latter, it was already justified, because the retreat 51. Kt—R 3 would mean sure defeat : 51. .... R—Q R 7 ! ; 52. Kt—B 4, R—R 4 ; winning, to begin with, the adventurous R P.

| 51. ...... | R—Q 4 |

The beginning of the end, since 52. K—R 4 no longer helps because of ....R—K 4 ! ; 53. Kt×P, R—

K Kt 4 followed by R × Kt P, etc.

| 52. P—B 4 | R—K B 4 ! |

The K B P is much more important than the K R P, which, anyhow, is bound to be captured sooner or later.

| 53. K—Kt 4 | R—B 3 ! |

Preventing White from protecting the B P by 53. P—Kt 3, which would be played against 53. .... K—K 5.

| 54. P—B 5 | R—B 2 |

Not the shortest way, which was : 54. ....K—K 5 ; 55. Kt×P, R—B 2 ; 56. Kt—K 6 (or Kt—K 8, K—K 4 !), R×P ; 57. P—K Kt 3, R—K 4 ; 58. Kt—B 4, R—Kt 4 ch ; 59. K—R 4, K—B 6 and wins.

| 55. P—Kt 3 | ...... |

Hastening the end.   After 55. Kt—Q 8 !, R—B 3 ; 56. Kt—K 6, Black would have adopted the variation given above starting with 55. ....K—K 5 !

55.	K—K 5
56. Kt—B 5 ch	K—Q 5 !
57. Kt—Kt 3 ch	K—K 4
Resigns.	

My games with Dr. Vidmar have generally been full of life and struggle.

GAME 34

QUEEN'S GAMBIT DECLINED

San Remo Tournament, January, 1930.

Black : G. MAROCZY

1. P—Q 4	P—Q 4
2. P—Q B 4	P—K 3
3. Kt—Q B 3	Kt—K B 3
4. B—Kt 5	B—K 2
5. P—K 3	Q Kt—Q 2
6. Kt—B 3	Castles
7. R—B 1	P—B 3

The recent praxis seems to show that the intermediate move 7. .... P—K R 3 gives Black more opportunities of solving the centre-problem in a satisfactory way than this old-fashioned so-called "Capablanca's freeing manœuvre" (although it had already been played, for instance, by Mason in Hanover, in 1902).

8.	B—Q 3	P × P
9.	B × B P	Kt—Q 4
10.	B × B	Q × B
11.	Kt—K 4	P—Q Kt 3

An attempt to solve immediately the problem of the Q's Bishop. Although it is rewarded in the present game by a partial success (at least in the opening stage) it can hardly be recommended, as White could play the following moves more energetically. Instead, Dr. Lasker's idea 11. ....K Kt—B 3 ; 12. Kt—Kt 3, P—K 4 ! (*see* Game No. 70) seems to be sufficient for equalising.

12.	Castles	B—Kt 2
13.	Kt—Kt 3	P—Q B 4
14.	P—K 4	......

An interesting alternative here was 14. B—Kt 5 in order to answer 14. ....P × P ? by 15. P—K 4 ! followed by R—B 7. Black would have in that case to deal with the usual troubles caused in this variation by an insufficiently prepared advance of the Q B Pawn.

14.	......	K Kt—B 3
15.	R—K 1	......

White's previous move would have found its logical justification if he had continued here with 15. P—Q 5 ; for instance, 15. .... P × P, 16. P × P, Q—Q 3 ; 17. Kt—B 5, Q—B 5 ; 18. Kt—K 7 ch, K—R 1 ; 19. B—Kt 5 ! after which the Queen's Pawn would remain an important factor in White's favour.

By the selected quiet continuation (due chiefly to the fact that having started the tournament by five straight wins I did not want, in the sixth round, to take any chances), White still keeps a slight positional advantage—but against an end-game specialist like Maroczy White's winning prospects become rather problematical.

15.	......	P × P
16.	B—Kt 5 !	......

If instead 16. P—K 5, then 16. ....Kt—Kt 5 ! ; 17. Q × P, B × Kt ; 18. P × B, K Kt × P ! ; 19. R × Kt, Kt × R ; 20. Q × Kt, Q R—B 1, etc., to Black's advantage.

16.	......	K R—B 1
17.	Q × P	R—B 4
18.	B × Kt	Kt × B
19.	P—Q Kt 4	R × R
20.	R × R	R—Q B 1
21.	R × R ch	B × R
22.	Q—B 3	......

The position is not quite as dead a draw as one may think at the first glance. For the moment, for instance, Black will have to lose time in order to parry White's threats on the Q B's file.

22.	......	Q—Q 1
23.	Kt—Q 4	B—Kt 2
24.	P—B 3	......

One of White's advantages consists in the fact that Black's Bishop, owing to the general Pawn structure, has but very poor prospects.

24.	......	Kt—B 3

In order to be able to oppose the Queen at B 2—doubtless the right scheme.

25.	Kt—B 1	......

This Knight had obviously nothing more to do at K Kt 3.

| 25. ...... | Kt—K 1 |
| 26. Kt—K 3 | P—Q R 3 |

Maroczy seems not to be in a mood to play the purely passive end-game which he could obtain by the—otherwise logical—26. .... Q—B 2 ; 27. Q×Q, Kt×Q ; 28. Kt—B 4, Kt—K 1 ! White's advantage in space in this variation would be evident, but as the direct threat 29. Kt—Kt 5 could be sufficiently parried by 29. .... B—R 3 the draw-conclusion would be still probable. After the move made, Black on the other hand will hardly be able to offer the exchange of Queens because of the weakness of his Q Kt 3.

| 27. P—Q R 4 ! | ...... |

The intended P—R 5 will fulfil a double object : (i) fix Black's weakness at Q R 3 ; (ii) secure the strong Q B 5 square for a Knight.

| 27. ...... | P—K R 3 |
| 28. P—R 3 | ...... |

Not in order to give the King a— here unnecessary—loophole, but simply planning to move that piece, eventually, to the centre, and therefore putting the K R's Pawn on a protected square.

| 28. ...... | P—K R 4 ? |

Black's 26th move, although not very logical (avoiding the exchange of Queens and creating a weakness on the Q's side), was hardly sufficient to compromise the situation seriously. But this peculiar Pawn's move—the significance of which will not be explained by Black's further play—by creating a new (although, one must admit, for the moment hardly perceptible) weak spot at Black's K Kt 4, procures White unmistakable winning chances.

| 29. P—R 5 | P×P |

| 30. P×P | Q—Q 3 |
| 31. Kt—Kt 3 | B—B 3 |

The desire to bring the Bishop on to a more active square (Q Kt 4) is reasonable ; but White seizes at once the opportunity to bring his central Pawns forward, and thus limits the action of the hostile Knight.

32. P—K 5 !	Q—B 2
33. Kt—B 5	B—Kt 4
34. P—K B 4	......

The slight weakening of the light-coloured squares occasioned by this advance does not matter any longer, as the Bishop is already pinned to the Q R's Pawn.

| 34. ...... | Q—Q 1 |
| 35. P—B 5 | ...... |

The only winning possibility for White consists in combining the pressure on the Q's side with direct threats against the Black King.

35.	P×P
36. Kt×B P	Q—Kt 4
37. Kt—Q 4 !	......

An important tactical detail (37. .... Q×K P ; 38. Kt×B, etc.).

| 37. ...... | Kt—B 2 |
| 38. Kt—B 3 | ...... |

From now on Black will realise that he erred by playing .... B— K R 4.

| 38. ...... | Q—B 5 |
| 39. K—B 2 | ...... |

Thus showing that he is already willing to exchange Queens. As a matter of fact the end-game after 39. .... Kt—Q 4 ; 40. Q—Q 4, Q×Q ; 41. Kt×Q, B—B 5 ; 42. Kt—B 5 ! followed by Kt—Q 6 would be extremely critical, if not hopeless, for Black.

39. ......   Q—B 4
40. Q—Q 2   K—R 2

Instead, 40. ....Kt—K 3; 41. Kt—Kt 7! followed by Kt—Q 6+ would have enabled him to resist longer. The following winning procedure is instructive.

Position after Black's 40th move.

41. Kt—K 4!   ......

If now 41. ....Kt—K 1 then 42. Kt—Kt 3, Q—Kt 3; 43. Q—Q 8, etc., with gradual strangulation. Black prefers, therefore, to sacrifice a Pawn in order to get rid of at least one of the tedious Knights.

41. ......   Kt—K 3
42. Kt—Q 6   Q—Kt 8

If 42. .... Q—Kt 3 White wins by 43. Kt × B, P × Kt; 44. P—R 6, since 44. ....Kt—B 4 does not work because of 45. Kt—Kt 5 ch, Q × Kt; 46. Q × Q, Kt—K 5 ch; 47. K—K 3, Kt × Q; 48. P—R 7.

43. Kt × P   B—B 3
44. Kt (B 7)—Kt 5 ch   Kt × Kt
45. Kt × Kt ch   K—Kt 3
46. P—R 4   ......

Thus White has taken the maximum of advantage from the weakness of Black's K Kt 4!

46. ......   K—B 4

The threat was 47. Q—Q 6 ch, K—B 4; 48. Q—K 6 ch, K—B 5; 49. P—Kt 3 mate.

47. P—K 6   Q—Kt 4
48. Q—B 2 ch   ......

The object of the following checks is to prevent *with tempo* Black's ....Q—Q B 4 ch and thus make possible the further advance of the passed Pawn.

48. ......   K—K 4
49. Q—B 3 ch   K—Q 3
50. Q—Kt 3 ch   K—Q 4
51. Q—B 3 ch   K—K 4
52. Q—K 3 ch   K—B 3

Or 52. ....K—Q 3; 53. Q—B 4 ch! etc.

53. Q—Q B 3 ch   K—Kt 3
54. P—K 7   Q—K B 4 ch
55. K—K 3   ......

The King is here—for once—even safer than on the wing (55. K—Kt 1, Q—Kt 8 ch, etc.).

55. ......   B—K 1
56. Q—Q 4   B—Kt 4
57. Q—Q 6 ch   Q—B 3
58. Kt—K 4!   Resigns.

GAME 35

DUTCH DEFENCE

San Remo Tournament, January, 1930.

Black : Dr. S. Tartakower

1. P—Q 4   P—K 3
2. P—Q B 4   P—K B 4
3. P—K Kt 3   Kt—K B 3
4. B—Kt 2   B—Kt 5 ch
5. Kt—Q 2   Kt—K 5

Black is aiming to exchange the pieces he has just developed—a doubtful strategy, to say the least. More in the spirit of the opening chosen would be 5. ....Castles; 6. P—Q R 3, B—K 2, etc.

6. P—Q R 3	Kt × Kt
7. B × Kt	B × B ch
8. Q × B	Castles
9. Kt—R 3	......

Chiefly in order to enforce the control of Q 5 in case Black selects the development ....P—Q 3 and ....P—K 4.

9.	P—Q 4

After this the dark squares of Black's position may sooner or later become very weak; and White, in order to exploit that weakness, decides to free the centre from Pawns as rapidly as possible. Although it was very difficult to foresee at this moment that Black, after the transaction projected, would have at his disposal adequate defence against the many threats, a slower policy—like 10. R—Q B 1 (instead of 10. P × P), P—B 3; 11. Castles, Q—K 2; 12. Q—K 3! followed by Kt—B 4, etc.—would have been more appropriate in order to take advantage of Black's manœuvre of the 5th-7th moves.

10. P × P	P × P
11. Kt—B 4	P—B 3
12. Castles (KR)	Q—K 2
13. P—Q Kt 4!	......

The real object of this move—besides a "minority" attack which by means of the continuation P—Q R 4 was also quite possible—is to open for the Queen the way to Q R 2. The following will prove the importance of that diversion.

13.	P—Q R 3
14. P—B 3	......

All in accordance with the plan inaugurated by his 10th move. But Black, by keeping a cool head, succeeds in emerging from the skirmish without much damage.

14.	Kt—Q 2
15. P—K 4	B P × P
16. B P × P	P × P
17. Q—R 2 ch	.....

Sadly enough, the tempting 17. B × P does not work—for instance, 17. ....Q × B; 18. Q R—K 1, Q—B 4; 19. Q—R 2 ch (or 19. Kt—K 6, Q—Kt 3; 20. Kt × R, Kt × Kt, etc. ∓), R—B 2!; 20. R—K 8 ch (or K 7), Kt—B 1— and Black escapes.

17.	K—R 1
18. Kt—K 6	......

Unconvincing is 18. Q—K 6, R—K 1! etc.

18.	R × R ch
19. R × R	Kt—B 3
20. Kt—Kt 5	P—K R 3
21. Q—B 7!	......

This strong move, which forces the exchange of Queens because of the threat 22. R × Kt!, etc., had to be foreseen when the centre-action was started; otherwise Black would have obtained even the better game.

21.	Q × Q
22. Kt × Q ch	K—R 2
23. Kt—Q 6	......

This menacing Knight position secures White the recapture of the sacrificed Pawn; but on the other hand, Black should, in the meantime, find the opportunity to finish his development and obtain equality.

23.	B—K 3?

Obviously over-estimating the value of the central Pawn. The right way was 23. ....P—Q R 4!; 24. Kt × K P (if 24. P—Kt 5 then simply 24. ....P × P), P × P; 25.

Kt × Kt ch (or 25. P × P, Kt—Q 4),
P × Kt ; 26. P × P, K—Kt 2 with a
probable draw in view.

24. Kt × Kt P   B—Q 4
25. R—K 1 !   ......

Otherwise Black, in many cases,
could play ....P—K 6.

25. ......   R—R 2
26. Kt—B 5   P—Q R 4

Giving White a passed Pawn ;
but the Rook, naturally, cannot
always remain pinned to the Q R
Pawn.

27. P × P   R × P
28. P—Q R 4   R—R 1

With the object of occupying the
Q Kt's file, or (as actually happens)
of diminishing somewhat White's
pressure against the K's Pawn.

29. R—R 1   R—R 4
30. R—R 3 !   ......

Still with the object of preventing
....P—K 6.

30. ......   K—Kt 3

Black hopes to have just time to
execute the important manœuvre
Kt—K 1—Q 3, but is prevented
from this by what Dr. Tartakower
himself calls " the combinative
wonder."

31. P—K R 3   K—B 4
32. K—B 2   Kt—K 1

Everything according to the preconceived plan. Instead, 32. ....
P—R 4 would have prevented the
following surprise, but after 33. K—
K 3, etc., the tying of all Black
pieces would in any case have led
to material loss.

Position after Black's 32nd move.

33. B × P ch !   ......

At first sight, having in view the
(very poor) transaction 33. ....
B × B ; 34. Kt × B, K × Kt ; 35. R—
K 3 ch, K × P ; 36. R × Kt, R × P,
etc. ; but in reality forcing a technically rather easily won Rook end-
game with an extra Pawn.

33. ......   B × B
34. P—Kt 4 ch   ......

The simple but very unkind point:
34. ....K—B 5 ; 35. Kt—K 6 mate !

34. ......   K—B 3
35. Kt × B ch   K—K 3
36. K—K 3   Kt—Q 3
37. K—Q 3   Kt × Kt
38. K × Kt   P—R 4

Black realises that "quiet" play
would not leave him any chances—
for instance, 38. ....K—Q 3 ; 39.
K—Q 3, K—Q 4 ; 40. R—R 1, P—
B 4 ; 41. P × P, K × P ; 42. K—B 3,
etc.—cf. my last match-game with
Capablanca. He tries, therefore, to
create attacking objects on the
King's side, but only hastens the
end by accepting the following
Pawn sacrifice.

39. P—Kt 5 !   R × P

After 39. ....K—Q 3 ; 40. P—
R 4 his situation would be even
worse than before.

40.	P—R 5	R—Q Kt 4
41.	P—R 6	R—Kt 1
42.	P—R 7	R—Q R 1
43.	P—R 4 !	P—Kt 4
44.	P × P	P—R 5
45.	R—R 6	K—B 2
46.	K—B 4	P—R 6
47.	K—Kt 3	K—Kt 3
48.	P—Q 5 !	K × P
49.	P × P	K—B 4
50.	P—B 7	Resigns.

GAME 36

QUEEN'S INDIAN DEFENCE

San Remo Tournament, January,
1930.

White : K. AHUES

1.	P—Q 4	Kt—K B 3
2.	Kt—K B 3	P—Q Kt 3
3.	P—K 3	B—Kt 2
4.	Q Kt—Q 2	......

This system of development has
been favoured by Rubinstein and
the late Belgian Champion, Colle.
It is not particularly aggressive but
not without sting—especially if
White succeeds in time in opening
for his Q's Bishop a suitable
diagonal.

4.	......	P—B 4
5.	B—Q 3	P—K 3
6.	P—B 3	B—K 2
7.	Q—K 2	......

White is over-cautious. More in
the spirit of the variation selected
would have been 7. P—K 4, and
only after 7. ....P—Q 3 ; 8. Q—
K 2, as after the move made Black
succeeds by the following original
answer in preventing the advance
of the King's Pawn.

7.	......	Kt—Q 4 !

With by no means hidden inten-
tions : if P—K 4, then ....Kt—
B 5 ; if P—Q B 4, then ....Kt—
Kt 5, etc. !

8.	P × P	......

With this exchange White starts
an elaborate manœuvre the ultimate object of which is to bring
the Q's Bishop on the diagonal
Q R 1—K R 8. As a matter of
fact there is hardly a more promising line to be recommended for
him.

8.	......	P × P
9.	Kt—B 1	......

He does not play this Knight to
Q B 4 as he intends to dislodge
Black's central Knight by P—Q B 4.

9.	......	Q—B 2
10.	Kt—Kt 3	Kt—Q B 3
11.	B—Q 2	P—K Kt 4 !

A bold idea, connected in one
variation with the offer of a Pawn
and based on the following general
considerations : Black possesses on
the King's side an elastic Pawn
mass, not obstructed by his own
pieces ; the natural thing for him
to do is therefore to try to gain
space by gradually advancing these
Pawns. But which Pawn shall he
start with ? The move 11. ....P—
K R 4 would be met by 12. P—
K R 4 ! stopping any further action
on that side ; on the other hand 11.
....P—B 4 would also have been
premature as it would allow White
to open the position by 12. P—K 4,
P × P ; 13. Q × P ! etc. There remains the text move, which, by
the way, is more effective than the
preparatory 11. ....Castles, permitting White to answer 12. P—
Q R 3 ! followed by P—Q B 4, etc.

12.	P—B 4	K Kt—Kt 5
13.	B—B 3	......

One must admit that White plays at least logically—the diagonal Q R 1—K R 8 is for the time being his only counter-chance.

13.	. . . . . .	Kt × B ch
14.	Q × Kt	Kt—Kt 5
15.	Q—K 2	. . . . .

The main variation considered by Black when playing 11. . . . . P—K Kt 4 was 15. Q—Kt 1, P—B 3 ; 16. Kt × P (or 16. P—Q R 3, Kt—B 3 ; 17. Kt × P, Kt—K 4 ! ∓), B × Kt P ; 17. R—K Kt 1, B—Kt 2 ; 18. Kt × R P, Castles !, etc., with a more than sufficient positional compensation for the material sacrificed.

15.	. . . . . .	R—K Kt 1
16.	P—Q R 3	Kt—B 3
17.	Kt—Q 2	Kt—K 4
18.	Q—R 5	. . . .

White, obviously not satisfied with his position, is looking for complications. Of course Black's chances would also have remained superior (chiefly because of the possibilities offered by the pair of Bishops) after the quiet 18. P—B 3.

| 18. | . . . . . . | Castles |

Even more forcible would have been 18. . . . . . . B × P ; 19. R—K Kt 1, B—B 3 ; 20. Q × R P, Castles, etc. ∓. After the text-move White decides to renounce—at the cost of two *tempi* !—making that compromising transaction.

19. Castles (KR)   P—B 4

Threatening 20. . . . . P—Kt 5.

20. Q—K 2   P—K R 4 !

No reason to give the opponent even one moment's relief !

21. Kt × R P   . . . . . .

White is forced to take this Pawn, as otherwise its advance would be too painful.

21. . . . . . .   R—Kt 3

Threatening 22. . . . . R—K R 3 followed by Q R—R 1, etc., with a deadly effect.

22. P—B 4   . . . . . .

The exchange thus proposed will bring the Knight into an excellent defensive position—but, unfortunately for White, only for a very short time. However, as White did not have even a shade of counter-play, his King's position was in the long run indefensible anyhow.

22.	. . . . . .	P × P
23.	Kt × P	R—R 3
24.	P—R 3	R—Kt 1

With the strong threat 25. . . . . Kt—Kt 3, etc.

| 25. | B × Kt | Q × B |
| 26. | Kt—B 3 | Q—Kt 2 |

Position after Black's 26th move.

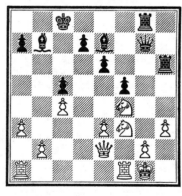

27. Q R—Q 1   . . . . . .

After this Black wins the Pawn back and at the same time demolishes the last fortifications protecting the enemy's King. But also the protection of the K R's Pawn by 27. K—R 1 would have led to an untenable position after 27. ....B—Q 3 ; 28. Q—K B 2, Q—Kt 5 ! (threatening 29. K B × Kt ; 30. P×B, R×R P ch ! etc.) ; 29. K—Kt 1, R×P ! ; 30. Kt×R, Q×Kt (R 6), etc.

27.	......	P—K 4 !
28.	Kt—Q 5	R×P
29.	Q—Q 2	B×Kt
30.	P×B	P—K 5
31.	P—Q 6	P×Kt
32.	R×P	R×R
33.	P×B	Q×K P
	Resigns.	

GAME 37

NIMZOWITSCH'S DEFENCE

San Remo Tournament, January, 1930.

Black : H. Kmoch

1.	P—Q 4	Kt—K B 3
2.	P—Q B 4	P—K 3
3.	Kt—Q B 3	B—Kt 5
4.	B—Q 2	......

One of the most harmless answers to Black's 3rd move. Also the present game shows that Black, by making even the simplest moves, can obtain a middle-game with even prospects.

4.	......	Castles
5.	P—K 3	P—Q 4
6.	Kt—B 3	P—B 4
7.	P—Q R 3	......

Again a passive move. In playing the opening of this game I was decidedly not in my happiest mood ! First 7. Q—B 2, and only after 7. .... Kt—B 3 ; 8. P—Q R 3, B×Kt ; 9. B×B, etc., which leads to a more colourful position.

| 7. | ...... | B×Kt |
| 8. | B×B | Kt—K 5 |

Perfectly logical as a further simplification, is here only in favour of the second player.

| 9. | R—B 1 | ...... |

Even now 9. Q—B 2 was more promising.

9.	......	Kt×B
10.	R×Kt	P×Q P
11.	K P×P	Kt—B 3 !

Black does not hurry with 11. ....P×P, since after 12. P—B 5 he would be able to start a successful battle in the centre by answering 12. ....P—K 4 !

| 12. | B—K 2 | P×P |
| 13. | B×P | ...... |

It is not difficult to see that the opening play has resulted rather in Black's favour, as White's isolated Pawn is decidedly not an ornament to his position and, on the other hand, the advantage in space which he still possesses has for the moment not much importance, because of the absence of vulnerable spots in the enemy's position. White's only chance, therefore, is to try to create a King's side attack —and the reader will see how difficult this task proved to be against the author of *Die Kunst der Verteidigung.*

13.	......	Q—B 3
14.	Castles	R—Q 1
15.	R—Q 3	B—Q 2
16.	R—K 1	......

In spite of his scarcely brilliant prospects White still decides to play for a win, and does not try therefore to exchange the isolated Pawn. Otherwise he would have played here 16. Q—Q 2, preparing P—Q 5, which move at this moment was

not good because of the answer 16.
....Kt—R 4 !

| 16. ...... | B—K 1 |
| 17. Q—Q 2 | Kt—K 2 |

Now Black becomes ambitious also and prevents for a while P—Q 5.

| 18. Kt—Kt 5 ! | Kt—Q 4 |

But not 18. .... Kt—B 4 because 19. Kt × K P !, P × Kt ; 20. R × P and wins.

| 19. R—K B 3 | Q—K 2 |
| 20. R—K Kt 3 | ...... |

White is anxious to provoke a weakening Pawn-move on Black's King's side, and therefore protects the Knight in order to be able to play Q—Q 3.

| 20. ...... | P—K R 3 |
| 21. Kt—B 3 | ...... |

It was difficult to decide which Knight's retreat was best. I finally rejected 21. Kt—K 4 because of the possible answer 21. ....Q—R 5 ; however, also in that case White, after 22. P—K R 3 ! Q—B 5 ; 23. Q—K 2, etc., would have kept fairly good attacking chances.

| 21. ...... | Q—B 3 |
| 22. R—K 4 | ...... |

Defending Q 4 and K B 4 and threatening eventually K R—K Kt 4. But Black's next Knight's man-œuvre again protects everything.

22.	Kt—K 2
23. Kt—K 5	Kt—B 4
24. R—Q 3	......

A mistake would have been 24. R—K B 3 because of 24. ....B—B 3 ; Kt × B, P × Kt, etc. ∓

| 24. ...... | Q R—B 1 |

| 25. P—R 3 ! | ...... |

White profits by the fact that the opponent does not threaten anything of importance to secure an escape for his King. The follow-ing part of the game will clearly show the significance of this quiet preparatory move.

| 25. ...... | Kt—Q 3 ? |

Seizing the first opportunity for a further simplification which, how-ever, will this time prove perfectly welcome to White. As a matter of fact the Knight at this stage was too important a defensive piece to be eliminated. Instead, 25. .... B—B 3 ! offered—temporarily at least—a quite sufficient defence ; for instance, 26. Kt × B, P × Kt (not R × Kt because of 27. P—Q 5 !) or 26. R—K 1, B—Q 4, etc. =

| 26. R—B 4 | Kt × B |
| 27. Kt × Kt | Q—Kt 4 |

This move has been generally criticized as time-wasting, but also after 27. ....Q—K 2 ; 28. Kt—K 5 White would obtain the better fighting chances. If in that case 28. ....P—B 3 then 29. Kt—Kt 4 threatening eventually sacrifices at K B 6 or K R 6.   Speaking in general, the Black King is from now on quite insufficiently protected.

| 28. R—K Kt 3 | Q—Q 4 |
| 29. Kt—K 3 | Q—B 3 |

Exchange of Queens would be here, of course, paradise for him !

| 30. K—R 2 | ...... |

The pleasant consequence of White's 25th move.

| 30. ...... | Q—B 8 |

Hoping for 31. Q—R 5, Q—B 2, etc. But White selects the right square for his Queen.

31. Q—Kt 4 !   Q—B 2

Position after Black's 31st move.

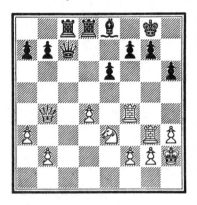

32. P—Q 5 !   ......

Such an effective advance of the would-be weakling must certainly have pleased the greatest friend of the isolated Queen's Pawns, the late Dr. Tarrasch ! It is obvious enough that in case of .... P × P (here or on the next move) the answer Q—Q 4 would have led to a rapid debacle for Black. But also by the defence selected he will be forced to give up at least the exchange.

32. ......   P—Q R 4
33. Q—K 4   ......

Of course not 33. Q—Q 4, P—K 4.

33. ......   R—Q 3 !
34. Q—K 5   P—K Kt 3
35. Q—R 5 !   ......

Instead the tempting 35. R—B 4 would have led to nothing after 35. .... R—B 3 ! and also 35. Kt—Kt 4 would have brought after 35. .... P × P, etc., *only* the exchange for a Pawn.

35. ......   R × P

Instead of resigning. I should have preferred 35. .... K—R 2, 36. Kt—Kt 4 ! !, P × Q; 37. Kt—B 6 ch. followed by mate.

36. Kt × R   P × Kt
37. Q × R P   Resigns.

GAME 38

NIMZOWITSCH'S DEFENCE

Hamburg Team Tournament, July, 1930.

White : G. Stahlberg

Brilliancy Prize

1. P—Q 4   Kt—K B 3
2. P—Q B 4   P—K 3
3. Kt—Q B 3   B—Kt 5
4. Q—Kt 3   P—B 4
5. P × P   Kt—B 3
6. Kt—B 3   Kt—K 5
7. B—Q 2   Kt × Q B P

This move became a fashion after the game Bogoljubow-Nimzowitsch, in the San Remo Tournament, brilliantly won by Black. It is doubtless more logical than the former 7. .... Kt × B ; 8. Kt × Kt after which White by castling Q side will soon obtain a strong pressure on the open file.

8. Q—B 2   P—B 4
9. P—Q R 3   ......

Thus White obtains—at least temporarily—the pair of Bishops. Strangely enough, Bogoljubow, in the game above-mentioned, delayed this move until it became actually a mistake and by making it at that moment gave his opponent the game out of hand ! It came about this way : 9. P—K 3, Castles ; 10. B—K 2, P—Q Kt 3 ; 11. Castles (Q R), P—Q R 4 ! ; 12. P—Q R 3, P—R 5 ! ! etc. ∓.

9.	......	B × Kt
10.	B × B	Castles
11.	P—Q Kt 4	Kt—K 5
12.	P—K 3	P—Q Kt 3
13.	B—Q 3	......

He could play also 13. B—Kt 2 but would not have obtained by doing this any real advantage : for instance, 13. ....B—Kt 2 ; 14. B—Q 3, Q—K 2 ! and 15. B × Kt, P × B ; 16. Q × P would turn to Black's advantage after 16. ....Kt × Kt P ; 17. Q × B, Kt—Q 6 ch, etc.

13.	......	Kt × B
14.	Q × Kt	B—Kt 2
15.	Castles (K R)	Kt—K 2

It certainly looks risky to leave the central dark squares without adequate defence—but I estimated that something had to be done in order to prevent White increasing his pressure in the middle by means of P—Q B 5.

16.	B—K 2	......

Threatening to bring a Rook and the Queen on the open file with unpleasant consequences for Black.

16.	......	Q—K 1
17.	K R—Q 1	Q R—Q 1

Not yet 17. ....P—B 5 because of 18. P × P, R × P ; 19. Q—Q 2, etc.

18.	P—Q R 4	......

The serious defect of this otherwise strategically justified advance is that it takes decidedly too much time and thus permits Black to build the ensuing instructive attack. Undoubtedly better was therefore 18. Q—K 5 with the strong threat 19. Q—B 7. The game would have continued in that case 18. ....P—B 5 !; 19. Q—B 7 ! (and not 19. P × P, Kt—Kt 3 ; 20. Q—B 7, Kt × P∓), B × Kt ; 20. B × B, P × P ; 21. P × P, Kt—B 4 with the double

tendency 21. ....Kt × K P and 21. ....Kt—R 5. Although White would not find time in this variation to exploit the weakness of Black's Queen's side he would still have been perfectly able to protect his King—and this was for the moment the most important problem !

18.	......	P—B 5 !

From now on, and until the end, all Black's moves are very exactly timed. It is hardly possible to replace any one of them by a better one.

19.	P—R 5	P × K P
20.	Q × K P	Kt—B 4
21.	Q—B 3	P—Q 3 !

A simple but very effective defence against White's R—Q R 7.

22.	P × P	P × P
23.	Kt—K 1	......

If 23. R—R 7, then of course 23. ....R—Q 2, threatening to win a piece by 24. ....B × Kt, etc.

23.	......	P—K 4

Securing the square Q 5 for the Knight. As may be noticed, the weakness of the dark squares has been, without apparent effort, transformed into strength.

24.	R—R 7	......

Hoping to complicate matters after 24. ....R—Q 2 ; 25. P—B 5 with the threat 26. B—Kt 5. But Black has at his disposal an important intermediate move.

24.	......	Kt—Q 5 !
25.	Q—K 3	R—Q 2

Threatening 26. ....B—B 6, etc.

26.	R—R 2	R (Q 2)—KB 2
27.	P—B 3	......

One would suppose that this Pawn, besides being protected by its neighbour, and easily supported by 3—4 Pieces, cannot possibly form a welcome object for Black's attack. And yet White's K B 3 will be captured, almost inevitably. It was certainly the unusualness of Black's winning stratagem which induced the judges to award to this game the Brilliancy Prize.

27.	......	R—B 5
28.	B—Q 3	Q—R 4

Threatening 29. ....P—K 5 !, etc.

29.	B—B 1	Q—Kt 4 !

With the main threat 30. .... R × B P ! forcing the win of the Queen.

White's answer is forced.

30.	R—K B 2	......

Position after White's 30th move.

30.	......	P—K R 3 !

A terrible move in its simplicity. Black threatens 31. ....R × P ! ; 32. Q × Q, R × R, etc., and in case of 31. Q—Q 2 (comparatively the best) he would play 31. ....B × P ; 32. Kt × B, Kt × Kt ch ; 33. R × Kt,

R × R ; 34. Q × Q, R × B ch ; 35. R × R, R × R ch ; 36. K × R, P × Q ; 37. K—K 2, K—B 2 ; 38. K—B 3, K—K 3 ; 39. K—K 4, P—Q Kt 4 !, etc., with a won Pawn end-game. White's next move practically does not change anything.

31.	K—R 1	R × B P !

With the same point as mentioned above.

Resigns.

GAME 39

QUEEN'S INDIAN DEFENCE

Prague Team Tournament, July, 1931.

Black : E. ANDERSEN

1.	P—Q 4	Kt—K B 3
2.	P—Q B 4	P—Q Kt 3

I have tried this fianchetto development (before ....P—K 3) on several occasions at the beginning of my professional career in the early twenties—and also played it with success in a match-game in 1929 against Bogoljubow (*cf.* No. 28). Its disadvantage consists in allowing White considerable freedom in the centre ; its merit in forcing the opponent to select a definite opening plan possibly earlier than he would like to.

3.	Kt—Q B 3	B—Kt 2
4.	Q—B 2	......

About 4. P—K B 3 see the game above-mentioned.

4.	......	P—K 3 ?

But this is not in accordance with 2. ....P—Q Kt 3. The only logical continuation consists in 4. ....P—Q 4 ; 5. P × P, Kt × P ; 6.

Kt—B 3 (in case of 6. P—K 4 Black can play 6. ....Kt×Kt ; 7. P× Kt, P—K 4), P—K 3 ; 7. P—K 4, Kt×Kt ; 8. P×Kt, B—K 2 followed by ....Kt—Q 2 and, eventually, ... P—Q B 4, etc., with fighting chances.

5. P—K 4	B—Kt 5
6. P—B 3 !	......

Avoiding the doubling of Pawns on the Q B's file. Black has now not the slightest compensation for White's predominance in the centre.

6.	Castles
7. B—Q 3	......

Threatening 8. P—K 5, etc.

7.	P—K R 3
8. Kt—K 2	P—Q 4

Something had to be undertaken in order to increase the activity of the minor pieces—and the way selected is probably not worse than any other ; at least Black will now have, for a short time, the illusion of a "counter-attack" starting by ....P—Q B 4.

9. B P×P	P×P
10. P—K 5	K Kt—Q 2
11. Castles	P—Q B 4

If instead 11. ....B—K 2, then 12. Kt—B 4±.

12. P—Q R 3	B×Kt

After 12. ....B—R 4 the Pawn-sacrifice 13. P—Q Kt 4 ! P×Kt P ; 14. Kt—Kt 5, etc., would bring Black into a hopeless position.

13. P×B	Kt—Q B 3
14. B—K 3	......

Also the combination starting by 14. P—K 6 in connection with Kt—K B 4, etc., was strong enough ; but the simple concentration of the

forces by keeping the Pawn-structure in the centre intact brings a more rapid decision.

14.	P×P
15. P×P	R—B 1
16. Q—Q 2 !	......

As Black's answer was obvious, this move must be considered as the beginning of the final combination. Another, purely positional, and much slower, method of keeping some advantage consisted in 16. Q—Kt 1, Kt—R 4 ; 17. P—B 4, Kt—B 5 ; 18. B—B 1, etc.

16.	Kt—R 4

Intending, if nothing special happens, to force the exchange of one of White's Bishops by 17. ....Kt—B 5.

Position after Black's 16th move.

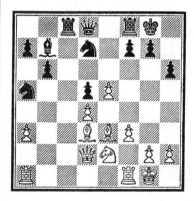

17. B×P !	......

Of course the offer cannot be accepted : this is by far the easiest part of the combination. But the complications issuing from the best defence, actually selected by Black, demanded a thorough examination.

17.	Kt—Kt 6
18. Q—B 4	R—B 3 !

If instead 18. ....Kt×R, then
19. Q—Kt 3, P—Kt 3 ; 20. B×P,
K—R 1 ; 21. B—B 5, R—Kt 1 ;
22. Q—R 3, and wins.

19. B—K Kt 5   P—B 3

White was also threatening 20.
Q—R 4.

20. P×P   Kt×R

His last chance, which will be
annihilated by the following intermediate check.

21. B—R 7 ch !   K—R 1

The alternative was 21. ....
K×B ; 22. Q—R 4 ch, K—Kt 3
(or K—Kt 1 ; 23. P—B 7 ch) ; 23.
Kt—B 4 ch, K—B 4 ; 24. P—Kt 4
mate.

22. Q—R 4 !   Kt×P
23. Kt—B 4   ......

If now 23. ....P—K Kt 3, then
24. Q—R 6 ! with debacle.

                              Resigns.

GAME 40

QUEEN'S GAMBIT DECLINED
(SLAV DEFENCE)

Prague Team Tournament, July,
1931.

Black : H. WEENINK

1. P—Q 4   P—Q 4
2. P—Q B 4   P—Q B 3
3. Kt—K B 3   Kt—K B 3
4. P—K 3   B—B 4

As my first championship match
with Dr. Euwe has proved, this
move happens to be sufficient for
equality, and therefore White does
better by playing 4. Kt—Q B 3
instead of 4. P—K 3.

5. P×P   B×Kt ?

But the exchange of the Bishop
just developed is completely out of
place.   Strangely enough, it has
been warmly recommended by the
great openings specialist, Dr. Tarrasch, although its defects (the
cession of the centre and of the
pair of Bishops to White) are obvious at a first glance. Good enough
is, instead, the simple 5. ....P×P ;
6. Q—Kt 3, Q—B 2, etc.

6. R×B   Q×P
7. P—Q R 3   ......

Also tempting was the Pawn
sacrifice 7. Q—B 2, Q×R P (or
P—K 3 ; 8. P—Q Kt 4 !) ; 8. B—
B 4, Q—R 4 ch ; 9. B—Q 2, Q—
B 2 ; 10. P—K 4, etc. But why
take chances when the simple continuation assures an unquestionable
positional advantage ?

7. ......   P—K 3
8. Q—B 2   B—K 2

A mistake would be 8. ....P—
B 4 because of 9. P—Q Kt 4 ! etc.

9. B—Q 3   P—K R 3

The immediate 9. ....Castles
would be refuted by 10. P—K 4
followed by P—K 5.

10. P—K 4   Q—Q 1
11. Castles   Q Kt—Q 2
12. P—Q Kt 4 ! ......

Not only preventing for a long
time ....P—Q B 4, but also preparing the following further development of the Queen's Rook.

12. ......   Castles
13. Q—K 2   R—K 1

In order to have the defence ....
Kt—B 1 in case White should play
14. P—K 5 followed by Q—K 4.

14. R—Kt 3 !   ......

Although this Rook will not move
until the end of the game, it will
play an important part in the
following attack. But the text-
move has also another purpose—
to free the square Q Kt 1 for the
Bishop.

14. ......   Q—B 2
15. B—Kt 1   Kt—R 2

This induces White to clear, at
last, the situation in the centre, as
from now on there will be no time
to install a black Knight at Q 4.
But also the demonstration on the
Queen's side by means of 15. ....
P—Q R 4 would end in White's
favour : 16. Q—B 2 (threatening
P—K 5), Kt—B 1 ; 17. P—Kt 5,
etc. ±

16. P—K 5   P—K B 4

Black prefers to execute this
sooner or later unavoidable advance
immediately, because after 16. ....
Kt (R 2)—B 1, for instance, it
could be prevented by 17. P—
K Kt 4 ! The following exchange
gives his pieces some more freedom
—at least temporarily ; but on the
other hand K 3, and also the other
light-coloured squares of his position, remain weaker than ever.

17. P × P (e.p.)   B × P
18. Q—K 4   ......

By this and the two following
moves the Queen will be brought
without loss of time into a very
strong attacking position.

18. ......   Kt (R 2)—B 1
19. Q—Kt 4   ......

Threatening, of course, 20. B × P.

19. ......   K—R 1
20. Q—R 5   Kt—R 2

White was threatening now 21.
B × P !, P × B ; 22. Q × P ch, K—
Kt 1 ; 23. Kt—Kt 5 etc., with a
speedy win.

21. R—K 1   ......

Bringing the only inactive piece
into play and preventing at the
same time 21. ....P—K 4 because
of the possible answer 22. B—
K B 4 !

21. ......   Q R—Q 1

There is not much use in such a
"development"—however, the position was hopeless, anyhow.

Position after Black's 21st move.

22. P—Kt 4 !   ......

This little Pawn threatens by its
further advance to set on fire the
black King's residence—and cannot
possibly be stopped from that dark
design.

22. ......   Q—Q 3

Hoping to parry 23. P—K Kt 5
by 23. ....Q—Q 4. But White has
in reserve an intermediate move.

23. B—Kt 6 !   R—K B 1
24. P—K Kt 5   B × Q P

There is no choice.

25. P×P   Kt (Q 2)—B 3

White threatened mate in three moves.

26. P×P ch   K×P
27. Q—R 6 ch   K—R 1

Or 27. ....K—Kt 1 ; 28. Kt×B, Q×Kt ; 29. R—K Kt 3, and wins.

28. Kt×B   Q×Kt
29. B—Kt 2 !   ......

If now 29. ....Q—Q 2 (the only possible defence), then 30. R—Q 3 !, Q—Kt 2 ; 31. B×Kt ! followed by mate in three moves.

Resigns.

GAME 41

RETI'S OPENING

Prague Team Tournament, July, 1931.

Black : E. STEINER

1. Kt—K B 3   Kt—K B 3
2. P—B 4   P—B 4
3. P—Q 4   ......

Somewhat premature. As White does not have to worry about the answer 3. ....P—Q 4 in case of 3. Kt—Q B 3 (because of 4. P×P, Kt×P ; 5. P—K 4, Kt—Kt 5 ; 6. B—B 4±), he should select that move in order to be able to answer 3. ....Kt—B 3 by 4. P—Q 4 and 3. ....P—K 3 by 4. P—K 4.

3. ......   P×P
4. Kt×P   P—K 3
5. P—Q R 3   ......

I did not like after 5. Kt—B 3 the possibility of 5. ....B—Kt 5 ;

6. Q—Kt 3, B—B 4—and decided simply not to allow the unpleasant Bishop move. But even playing with White one cannot afford to lose such an important *tempo* in the opening stage without the risk of giving the opponent the initiative. Therefore—although the move P—Q R 3 proved in the actual game to be a distinct success —I must most emphatically recommend the reader *not to make it,* but to try instead, for instance, 5. Kt—Q B 3, B—Kt 5 ; 6. B—Q 2.

5. ......   Kt—K 5

To an eccentricity Black answers by another, bigger one, which allows White again to take the lead in the fight for the central squares. Correct was the natural 5. ....P—Q 4, and if 6. P×P, then 6. .... B—B 4 ! ; 7. Kt—Kt 3, B—Kt 3, followed by ....P×P and .... Castles with a splendid development.

6. P—K 3   P—B 4
7. Kt—Q 2   Kt—K B 3
8. P—Q Kt 3   B—K 2
9. B—Kt 2   Castles
10. B—Q 3   ......

In spite of the delaying 5th move White has already acquired an appreciable advantage in development. It becomes evident that something was not in order with 5. ....Kt—K 5.

10. ......   Kt—B 3
11. Castles   Kt—K 4

A complicated manœuvre in order to prevent White from playing P—K 4—which would occur, for instance, after 11. ....P—Q Kt 3 ; 12. Kt×Kt, P×Kt ; 13. Q—K 2, P—B 4 ; 14. P—K 4, etc. ±.

12. B—B 2   Kt—Kt 3

Hoping to get counter-chances in

case of 13. P—K 4, P×P; 14. Q Kt×P, P—Q 4; 15. Kt×Kt ch, B×Kt, etc. But White is in the fortunate position of being able to increase his pressure without opening prematurely the central files.

13. P—B 4 !   Kt—Kt 5

After 13. ....P—Kt 3 the advance 14. P—K 4 would become much more effective than previously—for instance 14. ....P×P; 15. Q Kt×P, B—Kt 2; 16. Kt—K Kt 5, etc. ±

14. Q—K 2   Q—B 2
15. P—K R 3   Kt—R 3

Black has succeeded in prohibiting P—K 4—but at what price ! Both his Knights are out of play and his Queen's side is still undeveloped. No wonder that White will have plenty of time to gain more and more space and gradually bring the opponent to despair. The reader may compare this game with some other specimens of entanglement-policy in this collection—as, for instance, those against Nimzowitsch and Yates (San Remo), Mikenas (Folkestone), Winter (Nottingham). In all of them the losers became victims of their passivity and lack of a definite plan in the opening stages.

16. P—K Kt 4   P—Kt 3
17. P—Kt 5   Kt—B 2
18. Q Kt—B 3   B—Kt 2
19. P—K R 4   B—B 4

An attempt to create complications in case of the immediate 20. P—R 5, which would be answered by. 20. ....Kt×B P ! ; 21. P×Kt, Q×P, etc.∓. But White does not need to hurry !

20. Q—R 2 !   Q R—K 1
21. P—R 5   Kt—K 2
22. Q R—K 1   ......

Preparing Kt—Kt 5 followed by P—Q Kt 4 :

22. ......   Kt—B 3

If 22. ....P—Q R 3 then 23..P—Q Kt 4, B×Kt; 24. B×B, Q×Q B P; 25. B×Q Kt P, etc. ±

23. Kt—Kt 5   Q—Q 1
24. P—Kt 4   B—K 2
25. Q—Q 2 !   ......

All of a sudden Black's K Kt 2 has become deadly weak—a not unusual phenomenon in overcramped positions !

Position after White's 25th move.

25. ......   B×K Kt P

This kind of desperate sacrifice must be met as a rule with the greatest care as it *may* contain more poison than appears at first. In view of the threat 26. Q—B 3, Black, as a matter of fact, had practically no choice : 25. ....P—Q 3 ; 26. Kt (Kt 5)—Q 4, Kt×Kt ; 27. Kt×Kt, Q—Q 2 ; 28. Q—B 3 would be, if possible, even more welcome for White.

26. P×B   Kt×K Kt P
27. Q—Kt 2 !   ......

The most convincing refutation of the "offer."

27.	Kt × Kt ch
28. R × Kt	R—K 2
29. Kt—Q 6	B—R 1
30. P—K 4	......

Putting an end to all kinds of "swindles" on the diagonal K R 1—Q R 8.

30.	Q—Kt 1
31. R—Kt 3	P—K 4
32. Kt × B P	R × Kt
33. P × R	Kt—Q 5
34. B—K 4	Kt × P
35. B × B	Kt × R
36. B—Q 5 ch	Resigns.

GAME 42

QUEEN'S GAMBIT DECLINED (SLAV DEFENCE)

Bled Tournament, August, 1931.

Black : J. STOLTZ

1. P—Q 4	P—Q 4
2. P—Q B 4	P—Q B 3
3. Kt—K B 3	Kt—K B 3
4. Kt—B 3	P × P
5. P—Q R 4	B—B 4
6. Kt—K R 4	......

The main objection which can be made against this move is that White wastes time in order to exchange a piece he has already developed. However, the idea (of Dr. Krause) of eliminating at all costs the ominous black Queen's Bishop is not as anti-positional as generally thought, and, at least, has not been refuted in the few games where it was tried.

6.	P—K 3

Natural and good enough. White, it is true, will enjoy a pair of Bishops, but as long as Black is able to control the central squares he should not have much to fear. Less satisfactory for him, on the contrary, would be 6. ....B—B 1 (as played for instance by Dr. Euwe in the 15th game of our 1935 Match). In that case White (besides, of course, the draw-opportunity 7. Kt—B 3) would have the choice between 7. P—K 3, P—K 4 ; 8. B × P (of course not 8. P × P ?, Q × Q ch ; 9. Kt × Q, B—Kt 5 ch∓ played—to my sorrow—in the game mentioned), P × P ; 9. P × P, with slightly the better prospects—or 7. P—K 4, P—K 4 ; 8. B × P ! P × P ; 9. P—K 5, etc., leading to complicated situations like those of the 6th game of the 1937 Match. Anyhow, an interesting field for investigation.

7. Kt × B	P × Kt
8. P—K 3	Q Kt—Q 2
9. B × P	Kt—Kt 3

The Knight has little to do here —but something had to be done to prevent 10. Q—Kt 3.

10. B—Kt 3	B—Q 3
11. Q—B 3	Q—Q 2

Black will lose this game chiefly because from now on he decides to avoid the "weakening" move .... P—K Kt 3 and tries to protect his K B 4-Pawn by artificial methods. As a matter of fact there was not much to say against 11. ....P—K Kt 3, as 12. P—K 4 ? would have been refuted by 12. ....Kt × K P ; 13. Kt × Kt, Q—K 2 !—and 12. P—Q R 5 answered by 12. ....Kt (Kt. 3)—Q 4 ; 13. Kt × Kt, Kt × Kt, etc.

12. P—R 3 !	......

Threatening 13. B—B 2, P—K Kt 3 ; 14. P—K Kt 4, etc.±. Black's next move parries the danger.

12. ......   Kt—B 1
13. P—R 5   ......

Playing simultaneously on both sides of the board—my favourite strategy. The threat is now 14. P—R 6, P—Q Kt 3 ; 15. P—Q 5 ! etc.

13. ......   Kt—K 2
14. B—Q 2   ......

Instead, White could at once try 14. P—K Kt 4, but to do so would be to miss the developing Bishop's move which he makes now. Besides, it was not without importance to prepare against certain eventualities the possibility of castling on the Queen's side.

14. ......   R—Q Kt 1

This plausible move—made in order to weaken the effect of the possible advance P—Q R 6—will prove an important, if not decisive, loss of time. The only possibility of offering a serious resistance consisted in 14. ....P—K R 4 !

Position after Black's 14th move.

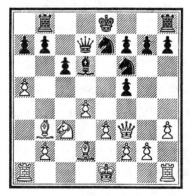

15. P—K Kt 4 ! ......

Through this transaction White at least obtains the extremely important square K 4.

15. ......   P—Q Kt 4

According to his aggressive style, Stoltz tries to solve the difficult problem in a purely tactical way—with the result that his Queen's side soon becomes lamentably weak. Also 15. ....P × P ; 16. P × P, Q × P ; 17. Q × Q, Kt × Q ; 18. R—K Kt 1, P—K B 4 ; 19. P—K B 3, Kt—B 3 (after 19. ....Kt—R 7 ; 20. K—K 2, etc., the Knight would not come out alive) ; 20. R × P, etc., would have been quite unsatisfactory for Black ; but the quiet 15. ....Castles (to which White's best answer would be 16. R—K Kt 1) would still leave him some possibilities of defence.

16. P × P   ......

17. P—Kt 5 would be answered by 16. ....P—Kt 5 ! by which Black would have obtained the central squares for his Knights.

16. ......   Q × P
17. Q × Q   Kt × Q
18. B—B 2 !   ......

White will succeed in exploiting the Queen's side weakness before the opponent finds time to concentrate his forces for the defence. The following part of the game is convincing and easy to understand.

18. ......   Kt—R 5
19. K—K 2   Castles
20. Kt—K 4   Kt × Kt
21. B × Kt   P—Q B 4

The exchange of this Pawn brings him but a slight relief as the fatal weakness of the Queen's side squares still remains.

22. P × P   B × P
23. Q R—Q B 1   B—Q 3

Or 23. ....Q R—B 1 ; 24. P—R 6 threatening 25. B—Kt 7 followed by 26. B—R 5, etc.

24. R—B 6	Q R—Q 1
25. R—R 6	K R—K 1
26. B—B 6	R—K 2

For the moment everything is more or less in order as 27. B × P, R—Kt 2, etc., would not be convincing. But White's following move—by which the lack of co-ordination of Black's pieces is underlined in a most drastic way—brings the fight to a rapid end.

27. R—Q 1 !	Kt—B 4

The Bishop did not have any suitable square of retreat. If for instance 27. . . . . B—Kt 1, then 28. B—Kt 4, R × R ; 29. B × R ! and wins.

28. B—Kt 4	P—K Kt 3
29. B—B 5 !	. . . . . .

Threatening to confiscate the Q R's as well as the Q Kt's Pawn. Black, in his despair, sacrifices the exchange.

29.	B × B
30. R × R ch	K—Kt 2
31. R—Q 5 !	. . . . . .

Faulty would be 31. R—Q 7 or 31. B × P because of 31. . . . . Kt—Q 5 ch, etc.

31.	B—Q 5
32. R—Q 7	. . . . . .

Now, after the square Q 4 has been taken by the Bishop, this move is strong.

32.	R—K 4
33. K—Q 3	B × Kt P
34. R (R 6) × P	R—B 4
35. R × P ch	K—R 3
36. R × P ch	K—Kt 4
37. R (Q R 7)—K B 7 !	. . . . . .

With the most unpleasant threat 38. P—B 4 ch, etc.

Resigns.

GAME 43

FRENCH DEFENCE

Bled Tournament, September, 1931.

Black : A. NIMZOWITSCH

1. P—K 4	P—K 3
2. P—Q 4	P—Q 4
3. Kt—Q B 3	B—Kt 5
4. Kt—K 2	. . . . . .

This move, which is quite satisfactory in the MacCutcheon Variation (1. P—K 4, P—K 3 ; 2. P—Q 4, P—Q 4 ; 3. Kt—Q B 3, Kt—K B 3 ; 4. B—K Kt 5, B—Kt 5 ; 5. *Kt— K 2*), is perfectly harmless at this moment. I selected it, however, in the present game because I knew that already on one occasion (against Sir G. Thomas in Marienbad, 1925) Nimzowitsch had shown an exaggerated voracity (6. . . . . P—K B 4) without having been duly punished for it.

4.	P × P
5. P—Q R 3	B × Kt ch

Also 5. . . . . B—K 2 is good enough for equality.

6. Kt × Kt	P—K B 4

Played against all the principles of a sound opening strategy, as the dark-coloured squares of Black's position will become very weak, especially because of the exchange of his King's Bishop. The correct reply which secures Black at least an even game is 6. . . . . Kt—Q B 3 ! and if 7. B—Q Kt 5 then 7. . . . . Kt—K 2 followed by Castles, etc.

7. P—B 3	. . . . . .

The sacrifice of the second Pawn is tempting, most probably correct —and yet unnecessary, as White could obtain an excellent game without taking any chances, by playing first 7. B—K B 4, and if 7. ....Kt—K B 3 then 8. P—K B 3, P×P; 9. Q×P, after which 9. ....Q×P would be refuted by 10. Kt—Q Kt 5.

7. ......   P×P
8. Q×P   Q×P

Contrary to the opinion of the theorists, this move is as good—or as bad—as 8. ....Q—R 5 ch; 9. P—K Kt 3, Q×Q P: in that case White would play 10. Kt—Kt 5 and Black would not have had—as in the actual game—the defence .... Q—R 5 ch, P—K Kt 3; Q—K 2, etc.

9. Q—K Kt 3 ! ......

A by no means obvious continuation of the attack. White's main threats are 10. Kt—Q Kt 5 (.... Q—K 5 ch; 11. B—K 2) and 10. B—K B 4, or K 3.

9. ......   Kt—K B 3

This bold move is Black's comparatively best chance. Insufficient would be 9. ....Kt—K 2 because of 10. B—K 3 !, Q—B 3; 11. Castles (Q R), etc. ±

10. Q×Kt P   Q—K 4 ch ?

Inconsequent and therefore fatal. Black—in order to keep a fighting game—should give up also the Q B's Pawn, as after 10. ....R—K Kt 1; 11. Q×B P, Kt—Q B 3 there would not be a win for White by means of 12. Kt—Kt 5, because of 12. ....Q—R 5 ch !; 13. P—K Kt 3, Q—K 5 ch; 14. K—B 2, Q×B P ch, followed by ....Kt—K 5, etc. The check in the text allows White to win a development *tempo*—and time in such a tense position *is* a decisive factor.

11. B—K 2   R—Kt 1
12. Q—R 6   R—Kt 3

13. Q—R 4   ......

White does not need to protect his K Kt's Pawn by 13. Q—R 3, as after 13. ....R×Kt P the answer 14. B—K B 4 would have been decisive.

13. ......   B—Q 2
14. B—K Kt 5   B—B 3
15. Castles (Q R) B×P

Under normal circumstances this capture should be considered as another mistake, but as—owing to White's tremendous advance in development — Black's game is hopeless (if, for instance, 15. Q Kt—Q 2 then also 16. K R—K 1 followed by a move with the K's Bishop) his morbid appetite cannot spoil anything more.

16. K R—K 1   B—K 5
17. B—R 5   Kt×B
18. R—Q 8 ch   K—B 2
19. Q×Kt   ......

Final Position.

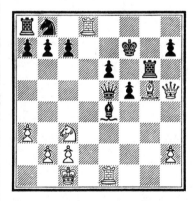

Nimzowitsch quite rightly resigned here, as there are no more decent moves for Black—even 19. ....K—Kt 2 would lose the Queen after 20. Kt×B, P×Kt; 21. B—R 6 ch, etc. ! This was, I believe, the shortest defeat in his career.

GAME 44

QUEEN'S GAMBIT DECLINED
(LASKER'S DEFENCE)

Bled Tournament, September, 1931.

Black : DR. M. VIDMAR

1.	P—Q 4	P—Q 4
2.	Kt—K B 3	Kt—K B 3
3.	P—B 4	P—B 3
4.	Kt—B 3	P—K 3

This is not exact, since in the orthodox defence the move .... P—Q B 3 is not always of use. Until now (summer, 1939) no clear way has been found for White to gain an advantage after 4. .... P×P.

5. B—Kt 5   ......

Also, 5. P—K 3 is thought to be good for White.

5.	......	B—K 2
6.	P—K 3	Castles
7.	Q—B 2	Kt—K 5
8.	B×B	......

Has anybody ever tried in this kind of position P—K R 4 ? The move might be taken into consideration.

8.	......	Q×B
9.	B—Q 3	Kt×Kt

After 9. .... P—K B 4 ; 10. Kt—K 5, Kt—Q 2 ; 11. Castles, the exchanges in the centre should profit White, since he would have a minor piece more in play than the opponent.

10. P×Kt   ......

In this particular case, more promising than 10. Q×B, because Black will be forced to lose a *tempo* for the protection of his K R P.

10. ......   K—R 1

As the sequence will prove, this is only a temporary defence (11. B×R P ?, P—K Kt 3), and that permits White, from now on, to build up his plan of attack. Less binding was, anyhow, 10. .... P—K R 3.

11. P×P !   ......

Both logical and psychological chess. The object of this exchange is, first and foremost, to prevent Black's obtaining, by means of .... P×P followed by .... P—Q B 4 and .... P—Q Kt 3, the diagonal Q R 1—K R 8 for his Bishop ; but, independently of this consideration, White was entitled to suppose that, *after having avoided weakening his K Kt 3 by not playing .... P K R 3, Black would now profit by this and try to bring his Bishop to K Kt 3 via Kt 5 and R 4.* By provoking this last manœuvre, White rightly considered that the opening of files on the King's side—ensuing from the eventual capture of Black's K R P—could only be favourable to the better developed party.

11.	......	K P×P
12.	Castles	B—Kt 5

If 12. .... Kt—Q 2, White would have started a promising play in the middle with 13. Q R—K 1, Kt—B 3 ; 14. Kt—K 5 followed by P—K B 4, etc. The text-move is the start of an adventure.

13.	Kt—K 5	B—R 4
14.	B×P !	......

This Bishop will now be in no more danger than his black colleague.

14.	......	P—K Kt 3
15.	P—K Kt 4	B×P

Thus Black, for the time, avoids material loss—but his horse still remains in the stable and White's defensive moves serve at the same time for attacking purposes.

16. Kt×B	Q—Kt 4
17. P—K R 3	K×B
18. P—K B 4	Q—R 5
19. K—R 2	Kt—Q 2

At last.

20. Q R—Kt 1 !   ......

Provoking the answer, which weakens Black's Q B P. How important this detail is will appear half-a-dozen moves later on.

20.	P—Kt 3
21. R—Kt 1	Kt—B 3
22. Kt—K 5	......

Threatening 23. Kt×Kt P, the K B P, and also the Q B P.

22. ......   Kt—K 5

Not only parrying all the threats (23. Kt×Q B P, R—Q B 1) but also intending to simplify by 23. ....Q—B 7 ch.

23. Q R—K B 1   K—Kt 2

Black's possible threats on the K R-file are insignificant in comparison with White's attack along the K B and K Kt-files.

24. R—K Kt 4   Q—R 3

Position after Black's 24th move.

25. P—B 5 !   ......

The tactical justification of this energetic advance is based on two variations—that played in the actual game, and the other starting with 25. ....P—K Kt 4. In that case I intended *not* to exchange two Rooks for the Queen by continuing with 26. P—B 6 ch, Kt×P ; 27. R×P ch, Q×R ; 28. R—K Kt 1, Q×R ch ; 29. K×R, Kt—K 5 (which also would be good but, still, not quite decisive)—but to sacrifice the exchange : 26. R×Kt !, P×R ; 27. P—B 6 ch, K—R 1 (or Kt 1) ; 28. Q×P, etc., with a winning positional advantage. Dr. Vidmar selected, therefore, the by far more promising line of resistance.

25. ......   Q×P !

This finally loses *only* the exchange for a Pawn and leads to a difficult end-game. It is easy to see that, apart from 25. ....P— K Kt 4, there was nothing else to do.

26. Q—K Kt 2   Q—Q 7

Or, 26. ....P—K Kt 4 ; 27. P— B 6 ch, K—R 2 ; 28. R—R 4 ch !, K—Kt 1 ; 29. Kt× Q B P, etc., with even more tragical consequences.

27. P—B 6 ch	K—Kt 1
28. Kt×Q B P	......

The deserved reward for the well-timed 20th move.

28.	Q×Q ch
29. K×Q	K R—K 1

There was no other reasonable defence against the threatened mate in two.

30. Kt—K 7 ch   R×Kt

And now 30. ....K—B 1 would have been victoriously answered by

31. Kt×P (not 31. R—R 4 ?, Kt×
K B P) threatening both 31. R—
R 4 and 31. Kt—B 7.

31. P×R   R—K 1

Again forced, since 31. ....Kt×
P would lose rapidly after 32. R—
B 1 followed by R—B 7 or even-
tually R—B 6.

32. P—B 4 !   ......

Without this possibility, whereby
White secures a passed Pawn, the
win would be still rather doubtful.

32. ......   R×P
33. P×P   Kt—B 6
34. P—Q 6   R—Q 2
35. R—B 1   Kt—Kt 4

If 35.......Kt×R P, White, in
order to force the win, would select
the following sharp continuation :
36. R—B 8 ch, K—Kt 2 ; 37. P—
Q 5 ! (threatening to win the
Knight), P—R 4 ; 38. R—B 7,
R×P ; 39. R—K B 4, R—K B 3
(otherwise White gets a mating
attack) ; 40. K—B 3, Kt—Kt 5 ;
41. R×R, K×R ; 42. K—K 4—
and in spite of the level material
Black would lose, as his two Queen-
side Pawns would have but a short
life.

36. R—K Kt 5 ! Kt×P (Q 3)

After 36. ....Kt×P (Q 5) the
win would be technically easier :
37. R—Q 5, Kt—B 4 ; 38. R—B 7 !,
R×P (or R—Q 1 ; 39. P—Q 7) ; 39.
R×R, Kt×R ; 40. R×R P, etc.

37. R—Q 5 !   ......

From now on, the purely technical part of the end-game begins.
Through combined play of his two
Rooks and King, White must make
the utmost of the pinning of the
hostile Knight.

37. ......   K—B 1
38. R—K 1 !   ......

The black King must not be
allowed to approach the centre
before all White's units are brought
to the most effective squares.

38. ......   R—Q 1
39. K—B 3   R—Q 2

It is obvious enough that the
exchange of Rooks, after 39. ....
Kt—Kt 2, would not make any
serious resistance possible.

40. K—B 4   K—Kt 2
41. R—K 8 !   ......

A further restriction of Black's
moving capacities.

41. ......   K—B 3
42. P—K R 4   K—Kt 2
43. P—R 4   K—B 3
44. R—Q B 8 !   ......

Intending to substitute for the
vertical pinning an even more
effective horizontal one.

44. ......   K—K 3
45. R—K 5 ch   K—B 3
46. R—B 6   R—Q 1
47. P—Q R 5 !   P—Q Kt 4

Black must lose a Pawn and
prefers to do it this way, since, after
47. ....P×P ; 48. R×P, R—Q 2 ;
49. R (B 6)—R 6, etc., White would
also force the exchange of Rooks.

48. R×P   K—K 3
49. R—K 5 ch   K—B 3
50. R—R 6   R—Q 2
51. K—Kt 4   R—Q 1
52. K—B 3 !   ......

A little finesse : it is more advantageous for White to make the
advance P—R 5 at the moment
when the Black Rook is at Q 1,
because then he will capture the
Q R P, having the other Rook at K 5.

52.	R—Q 2
53. K—B 4	R—Q 1
54. P—R 5	P × P
55. R × K R P	R—Q 2
56. R—K 5	R—Q 1
57. R × P	. . . . . .

Now White takes this Pawn without permitting the reply ....Kt—B 4, which would have been possible before the exchange of the K Kt P.

57.	Kt—B 5
58. R—R 6 ch	K—Kt 2
59. R—Kt 5 ch	K—B 1
60. K—K 4	. . . . . .

The rest is easy.

60.	K—K 2
61. R—Q B 5	Kt—Q 3 ch
62. K—Q 3	K—K 3
63. R (B 5)—B 6	K—Q 4
64. R × Kt ch	R × R
65. R × R ch	K × R
66. P—R 6	Resigns.

APPENDIX TO THE GAME ALEKHINE-
VIDMAR (44)

Two Rooks v. Rook and Knight

End-games with two Rooks against Rook and Knight are comparatively uncommon, and the manuals devoted to the end-game —even the most up-to-date, such as the recent edition of E. Rabinovitsch's excellent work—do not give any convincing examples. The materially stronger party should win in the majority of cases, but not without serious technical difficulties.

According to the general opinion, I succeeded, against Vidmar, in finding the shortest and most instructive winning method, and I owe, in a great part, this achievement to a practical lesson that I received in the beginning of my career (in St. Petersburg, 1914) from the great end-game artist, Dr. Lasker. That lesson cost me a full point, for I happened to be the man with the Knight! Dr. Lasker, to the general surprise, demonstrated that even with one Pawn on each side (and *not* a passed Pawn) the stronger party is able to force the decisive exchange of Rooks.

Since the game with Dr. Vidmar I have had the opportunity of playing the same kind of ending twice, and both times the winning procedure had the same characteristics: (1) Restriction of the Knight by binding and, eventually, pinning it. (2) Gradual undermining of the strong points, which, as a rule, happen to be in the middle. (3) Threats to exchange Rooks, which always means a step forward— especially if the Knight-party does not possess passed pawns. Other tactics, such as centralization of the King, freeing of Pawns, etc., are, of course, common with those of all types of end-games.

I have not fully commented on the two following games for this collection, because, although they are interesting, I do not count either among my best achievements. Kashdan, to his bad luck and without knowing it, repeated, up to the 15th move, a variation known as lost for Black since the Carlsbad Tournament, 1929 ; and against Dr. Bernstein, instead of winning the exchange, I could have forced the gain of a full piece and, consequently, his resignation. Nevertheless, I believe both these end-games—in connexion with the previous one—may be of use to the student.

With *Kashdan (Black), Pasadena,* 1932, the characteristic end-game began after the moves : 1. P—Q 4, Kt—K B 3 ; 2. P—Q B 4, P—K 3 ; 3. Kt—Q B 3, P—Q 4 ; 4. B—Kt 5, Q Kt—Q 2 ; 5. P × P, P × P ; 6. P—K 3, P—B 3 ; 7. B—Q 3, B—

K 2 ; 8. Q—B 2, O—O ; 9. K Kt—
K 2, R—K 1 ; 10. O—O—O, Kt—
K 5 ? (the same mistake was made
by Spielmann against Nimzowitsch,
Kissingen, 1928, and by Sir G. A.
Thomas against Spielmann, Carls-
bad, 1929); 11. B×Kt, P×B; 12.
P—K R 4 !, P—K B 4 ; 13. Q—
Kt 3 ch, K—R 1 ; 14. Kt—B 4,
Kt—B 3 ; 15. P—R 5, P—K R 3 ; 16
Q—B 7 !, Kt—Kt 1 ; 17. Kt—Kt 6
ch, K—R 2 ; 18. Kt×B, R×Kt
(forced) ; 19. B×R, Q×B ; 20. Q×
Q, Kt×Q ; 21. P—Q 5 !, B—Q 2 ;
22. P×P, B×P ; 23. R—Q 6, R—
Q B 1 ; 24. K R—Q 1, Kt—Kt 1 ;
25. R—Q 8, R—B 2 ; 26. R—K B 8,
Kt—B 3 ; 27. R (Q 1)—Q 8, Kt×P ;
28. R×P, Kt—B 3 ; 29. K—Q 2,
K—Kt 3 ; 30. R—B 5, R—K B 2 ;
31. R—Q 6, K—R 2 ; 32. R—
K B 5, K—Kt 3 ; 33. R—Q R 5,
P—R 3 ; 34. Kt—Q 5, B×Kt ;
35. Q R×B, K—R 2—when the
following position was reached :—

Position after Black's 35th move.

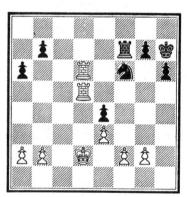

36. R—K B 5   ......

The combined vertical and horizontal pinning is similar to what
happened in the Vidmar-game.

36.	K—Kt 3
37. R—Q B 5	K—R 2
38. K—K 2	......

In order to parry the move ....
Kt—Kt 5, by P—B 3. If Black
should now remain passive, White
would advance his Pawn to Q Kt 6,
after the exchange at Kt 5, and then
play R—Q B 7.

38.	P—K Kt 4
39. P—Q Kt 4	K—Kt 2
40. P—R 4	Kt—Kt 5

The only possible attempt.

41. P—B 3	P×P ch
42. P×P	Kt—R 7
43. P—B 4 !	P×P
44. P×P	Kt—Kt 5

The old story ! 44. ....R×P
would be fatal since 45. R—B 7 ch,
etc., would force the exchange of
Rooks.

45. K—B 3	Kt—B 3
46. P—Kt 5	Kt—Q 2
47. R (B 5)—Q 5	Kt—B 3
48. R—K B 5 !	......

Again the pinning as a method
for gaining an important *tempo*.

48.	K—Kt 3
49. R—B 5	P×P
50. R×P	......

Here even more effective than
50. P×P.

50.	R—B 2
51. R (Kt 5)—Kt 6	R—B 2
52. P—R 5	K—Kt 2
53. R—Kt 5	R—B 2
54. R (Q 6)—Kt 6	R—B 6 ch
55. K—K 2	R—B 5
56. R×P ch	K—Kt 3
57. P—B 5 ch	K—Kt 4
58. P—R 6	R—Q R 5
59. P—R 7	Kt—K 5
60. K—K 3 !	......

If now 60. ....Kt—Q 3, then
61. P—B 6 disc. ch !, Kt×R ; 62.
P—B 7, etc.

                    Resigns.

Against Dr. Bernstein the task was even more difficult because his Knight was strongly posted at Q 4, protected by a Pawn. The previous moves, before the end-game position under discussion was reached, were : *Black, Dr. O. Bernstein, Zurich, 1934.* 1. P—Q 4, P—Q 4 ; 2. P—Q B 4, P —K 3 ; 3. Kt—Q B 3, Kt—K B 3 ; 4. B—Kt 5, B—K 2 ; 5. P—K 3, P—K R 3 ; 6. B—B 4, P—B 3 ; 7. Kt—B 3, Q Kt—Q 2 ; 8. P×P, Kt×P ; 9. B—Kt 3, Q—R 4 ; 10. Q—Kt 3, O—O ; 11. B—K 2, Q Kt —B 3 ; 12. Kt—Q 2 !, P—B 4 ; 13. Kt—B 4, Q—Q 1 ; 14. P×P, B×P ; 15. B—B 3 !, P—Q Kt 3 ; 16. O—O, Q—K 2 ; 17. Kt—Q Kt 5, P—Q R 3; 18. Q Kt—Q 6, B—Q 2 ; 19. P— K 4 !, P—Q Kt 4 ; 20. P×Kt, P×Kt ; 21. Kt×Q B P, Kt×P ; 22. K R—K 1, Q—Q 1 ; 23. Q R— Q 1, Q—B 1 ; 24. R—Q B 1 !, R— R 2 ? (a mistake in an already very compromised position) ; 25. Kt— Q 6, Q—B 3 ; 26. Kt—K 4, R— Kt 2 ; 27. R×B ? (instead, 27. Q— Q 1 !, R—Kt 4 ; 28. P—Kt 4, etc. would have won immediately), R×Q ; 28. R×Q, R×B ; 29. R— Q 6, R×B ; 30. R P×R, B—Kt 4 ; 31. Kt—B 5, R—B 1 ; 32. R—Q B 1, P—Kt 4 ; 33. Kt—Kt 3, R—Kt 1 ; 34. Kt—Q 4, K—Kt 2 ; 35. Kt×B, P×Kt.

Position after Black's 35th move.

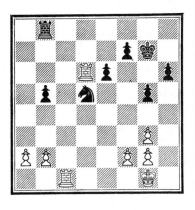

White's first object is to prevent Black's King from approaching the centre, which is achieved by the move :—

36. R—B 5 !   ......

—which, for the moment, also ties up the black Rook.   But after the answer

36. ......   P—Q Kt 5

White must also parry the threat 37. .....—R—Q R 1 by playing

37. R—R 6   ......

and now everything is ready for the centralization of the King, which will permit the exploitation of the Queen's side advantage.

37. ......   Kt—B 3

An attempt to stop the normal course of events by means of tactical threats.

38. K—B 1   Kt—K 5
39. R—B 7   K—Kt 3
40. K—K 2   R—Kt 4
41. K—K 3   ......

This dissolves the counter-attack started with Black's 37th move. If now, 41. ....R—K 4 ?, then 42. P—B 4, etc.

41. ......   Kt—B 3
42. R—B 4   ......

Preventing also 42. ....Kt— Kt 5 ch.

42. ......   P—R 4
43. P—B 3   K—B 4

Now this King's advance has not much importance as his White colleague is also in the centre.

44. K—Q 3   Kt—Q 4
45. R—R 7   P—B 3

46. R—K 4   . . . . .

Making room for the King.

46. . . . . . .   R—Kt 3
47. P—K Kt 4 ch ! . . . . . .

The beginning of the decisive part of this end-game. In order to have a free hand on the Queen's side, White must eliminate any danger on the other wing and the text-move answers that purpose, since it puts an end to Black's possible threat . . . . P—R 5 ; P × P, P × P followed by . . . . Kt—B 5, etc.

47. . . . . . .   K—Kt 3
48. P × P ch   K × P
49. P—K Kt 3   K—Kt 3
50. K—B 4   P—B 4

Something must be done against the threat 51. K—B 5.

51. R—K 2   K—B 3
52. K—B 5   . . . . . .

Intending R—Q 7—Q 6, etc.

52. . . . . . .   R—Kt 1
53. R—R 6   R—K 1
54. R—Q 6 !   . . . . . .

Threatening 55. R (K 2) × P ch, R × R ; 56. K × Kt, etc., and thus forcing at last the Knight to leave the central square.

54. . . . . . .   P—B 5
55. P × P   Kt × P
56. R (K 2)—Q 2 . . . . . .

Forcing the exchange of Rooks —or the win of the Q Kt P.

56. . . . . . .   R—Q R 1
57. P—Kt 3   K—K 4
58. R—Q 8   R—R 2
59. K × P   Kt—Q 4 ch
60. K—B 5   R—B 2 ch
61. K—Kt 5   R—B 6
62. R—K 2 ch   K—B 5

63. R—B 8 ch   K—Kt 6
64. R—K 5 !   . . . . .

But not 69. R × P ? since . . . . Kt—B 2 ch and Black will take two Rooks for one.

64. . . . . . .   Kt—B 5
65. R × P ch   K × P
66. R—K 5   R—K 6
67. R × Kt ch !   Resigns.

I believe that these three examples taken as a whole represent a rather important contribution to the chapter Two Rooks against Rook and Knight (with Pawns).

GAME 45

QUEEN'S GAMBIT DECLINED
(TARRASCH'S DEFENCE)

Bled Tournament, August, 1931.

White : V. PIRC

1. P—Q 4   P—Q 4
2. P—Q B 4   P—K 3
3. Kt—Q B 3   P—Q B 4
4. P × Q P   B P × P

This interesting Pawn-offer (instead of the usual 4. . . . . K P × P) has been analysed by some German amateurs, and introduced in international practice—if I am not mistaken—by Dr. Tartakower. As subsequent investigations have proved, Black, in spite of the superiority of his development, should not be able, against adequate defence, to prevent the opponent emerging from the opening with an extra-pawn and a safe position.

5. Q—R 4 ch   . . . . . .

Better than 5. Q × Q P, Kt—Q B 3.

5. . . . . . .   B—Q 2

An error would be here 5. ....
Q—Q 2 because of 6. Kt—Q Kt 5!±

6. Q×Q P   P×P
7. Q×Q P   Kt—Q B 3

Black could also play 7..... Kt—
K B 3 after which 8. Q×Kt P,
Kt—Q B 3, etc., would have been
decidedly too risky for White ; but
8. Q—Q 1 followed by P—K 3, etc.,
would have led to the same variations as could easily occur after
the move in text.

8. B—Kt 5   ......

On account of White's backward
development it would be safer for
him to use this Bishop for defensive
purposes on the Queen's side, and
to play instead 8. P—K 3 (....Kt—
B 3 ; 9. Q—Q 1). However, the
text-move cannot be considered as
an actual mistake.

8. ......   Kt—B 3
9. Q—Q 2   P—K R 3

This rather harmless attempt to
create (in case of the natural answer
10. B—R 4) new threats in connection with .....B—Q Kt 5, followed
by ....P—K Kt 4 and ....Kt—
K 5, has unexpected and pleasant
consequences.

10. B×Kt   ......

This certainly gives Black more
attacking chances than the retreat
mentioned, but would not have
proved too bad if White had taken
full advantage of the square Q 5
which he gains by this exchange.

10. ......   Q×B
11. P—K 3   Castles
12. Castles ?   ......

The decisive error, permitting
Black to regain the gambit-pawn

with a persisting pressure. Necessary was 12. Kt—Q 5 ! and if
12. ....Q—Kt 3 (best) then 13.
Kt—K 2 followed by K Kt—K B 4
or Q B 3 with possibilities of defence. Black has now the opportunity to carry on a King's attack
in the "good old style."

12. ......   B—K Kt 5
13. Kt—Q 5   ......

Too late !

13. ......   R×Kt !
14. Q×R   ......

Position after White's 14th move.

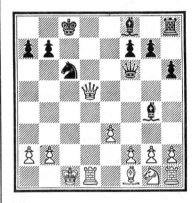

14. ......   B—Q R 6 !

After 14. ....B×R ; 15. Q×B,
Q×B P ; 16. Q—Kt 4 ch, P—B 4 ;
17. Q—K 2, Q×Q followed by ....
B—Q B 4, Black would probably
have won after a long end-game.
The move chosen by him shows the
decision, plainly justified under the
circumstances, to find a winning
solution in the middle-game.

15. Q—Kt 3   ......

There is nothing better ; if, for
instance, I. 15. P×B, then 15. ....
Q—B 6 ch ; 16. K—Kt 1, R—Q 1 ! ;

17. Q×R ch, Kt×Q with the double threat 18. ....B×R and 18. ....B—B 4 ch. II. 15. R—Q 2, then 15. ....B×P ch ! ; 16. R×B, Q—B 6 ch ; 17. K—Kt 1 (or 17. R—B 2, Q—R 8 ch followed by ....R—Q 1), Q—K 8 ch ; 18. K—B 2, R—Q 1 and wins.

15.	......	B×R
16.	Q×K B	Q×B P
17.	Q—Q 3	B—Kt 5 !

And not 17. ....R—Q 1 because of 18. Kt—R 3 !, Q—B 3 ; 19. Q—Q B 3, etc., with chances of salvation.

| 18. | Kt—B 3 | B×Kt |

Also here 18. ....R—Q 1 would have been out of place because of 19. Q—K 2, etc.

19.	Q—B 5 ch	K—Kt 1
20.	Q×B	Q—K 8 ch
21.	K—B 2	......

If he had given up the Pawn the agony would not have lasted long : 21. Q—Q 1, Q×P ch ; 22. Q—Q 2, Q—K 3 ! ; 23. K—Kt 1, R—Q 1 ; 24. Q—B 4 ch, K—R 1, etc., with quite a few deadly threats.

21.	......	R—Q B 1
22.	Q—Kt 3 ch	Kt—K 4
		disc. ch. !
23.	K—Kt 3	Q—Q 8 ch
24.	K—R 3	R—B 4 !

Quick death is now unavoidable —for instance A. 25. P—Q Kt 4, R—B 6 ch ; 26. K—Kt 2, Q—B 8 mate.   B. 25. P—Q Kt 3, R—R 4 ch ; 26. K—Kt 4, Q—Q 7 mate ; and the prettiest.   C. 25. K—Kt 4, Q—Q 7 ch ! 26. K×R, P—Kt 3 ch; 27. K—Kt 5, Q—R 4 mate.

Resigns.

GAME 46

QUEEN'S GAMBIT ACCEPTED

Bled Tournament, August, 1931.

Black : S. FLOHR

1.	P—Q 4	P—Q 4
2.	P—Q B 4	P×P
3.	Kt—K B 3	Kt—K B 3
4.	P—K 3	P—K 3
5.	B×P	P—B 4
6.	Castles	Kt—B 3
7.	Q—K 2	P—Q R 3
8.	R—Q 1	......

Peculiarly enough, this move—which does not contain any real threat and is therefore at this particular moment, to say the least, inexact—was almost unanimously adopted at the time the actual game was played. After Euwe's win against me, in the 5th Match-game, 1937, and my win against Böök at Margate, 1938, "theory" will probably recognise the natural development move 8. Kt—B 3 ! as the best.

| 8. | ...... | P—Q Kt 4 |
| 9. | P×P | ...... |

The positional refutation of 9. P—Q 5 ! ? consists in 9. ....P×P ; 10. B×Q P, Kt×B ; 11. P—K 4, Q—K 2 ! 12. R×Kt, B—K 3, etc.∓.

9.	......	Q—B 2
10.	B—Q 3	B×P
11.	P—Q R 4	......

Hoping to disorganise Black's position on the Queen's side, and succeeding in doing so because of the following inferior rejoinder.

| 11. | ...... | P—Kt 5 ? |

After this a number of squares on this sector will remain insufficiently protected and, what is more,

Black will remain without any hope of a counter-attack as White's position is practically without weaknesses. A quite different situation would have been produced by the right answer 11. ....P×P! which would give Black, as a compensation for the weak Q R's Pawn, a counter - attack against White's Q Kt's Pawn.

12. Q Kt—Q 2   Castles

Slightly better, although not entirely satisfactory, was 12. .... Kt—Q R 4, as played, for instance, by Flohr in a Match-game against Dr. Euwe in 1932.

13. Kt—Kt 3   B—K 2
14. P—K 4   Kt—Q 2

The possibility of 15. P—K 5 in connection with Q—K 4 was certainly unpleasant.

15. B—K 3   Kt (Q 2)—K 4

The intended exchange of Knights does not bring relief as it does not help to solve the important problem of the co-ordination of Black's Rooks. Slightly preferable was therefore 15. ....B—Kt 2; 16. Q R—B 1, Q—Kt 1.

16. Kt×Kt   Kt×Kt
17. Q R—B 1   Q—Kt 1
18. B—B 5 !   ......

From now on every exchange will facilitate the exploitation of the organic Pawn's weaknesses created by Black's 11th move.

18. ......   B×B
19. Kt×B   Q—Kt 3
20. Q—R 5 !   Kt—Q 2

As the Knight was the only active piece of Black's, it would have been advisable not

to remove it unless necessary. By playing 20. ....P—B 3 he could offer some more resistance, although White's advantage after 21. B—B 1, R—Q 1 ; 22. R—Q 4 ! followed by Q—Q 1, etc., would still remain considerable.

21. B—K 2   P—Kt 3

In order to open, without loss of time, a "hole" for the King ; but, as the following shows, this move weakens the King's side, *especially as White is by no means in a hurry to exchange Queens.* Black should rather take the Knight immediately.

22. Q—Kt 5   Kt×Kt
23. R×Kt   P—Q R 4

One of White's positional threats was also 24. P—Q R 5.

24. P—R 4   ......

The punishment for 21. ....P—Kt 3.

24. ......   B—R 3
25. B—B 3 !   ......

White's Bishop is here stronger than Black's. White threatens now everywhere and everything (26. P—R 5 ; 26. R×R P ; 26. R—Q 7, etc.).

25. ......   P—B 3
26. Q—K 3   ......

And from now on he begins to speculate on the unprotected position of the enemy's Queen !

26. ......   Q R—Q 1
27. R×R   R×R

Or 27. ....Q×R ; 28. P—K 5, P—B 4 ; 29. R—B 6, B—B 1 ; 30. Q—B 5, etc., with a winning position.

Position after Black's 27th move.

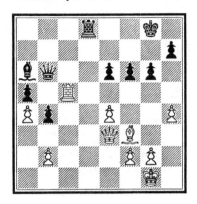

28. P—K 5 !   . . . . . .

Forcing either the win of a Pawn by an overwhelming position after 28. . . . . P × P ; 29. Q × P (even stronger is perhaps first 29. P— R 5 !), or the catastrophe which occurs in the actual game.

The immediate 28. R—B 8 was not convincing because of 28. . . . . Q—Q 3.

28. . . . . . .   P—B 4
29. R—B 8 !   . . . . . .

Winning at least a Rook.

Resigns.

GAME 47

RUY LOPEZ

Bled Tournament, September, 1931.

White : G. Stoltz

1. P—K 4	P—K 4
2. Kt—K B 3	Kt—Q B 3
3. B—Kt 5	P—Q R 3
4. B—R 4	P—Q 3
5. P—Q 4	P—Q Kt 4
6. B—Kt 3	Kt × P

7. Kt × Kt	P × Kt
8. B—Q 5	. . . . . .

If the unusual 5th move of White has a point at all, it can be only the Pawn-offer 8. P—Q B 3, after which acceptance Black would have some difficulties of development. The Bishop-move in the text in connection with the ensuing exchange finally gives Black, on the contrary, an advantage in space.

8.	R—Kt 1
9. B—B 6 ch	. . . . . .

White is obviously in a hurry to "simplify" matters. If he was told that this is the easiest way to obtain a draw, he was certainly ill-advised.

9.	B—Q 2
10. B × B ch	Q × B
11. Q × P	Kt—B 3
12. Kt—B 3	. . . . . .

12. Q—R 7 does not lead to anything after 12. . . . . Q—B 1.

12.	B—K 2
13. Castles	Castles
14. B—Q 2	. . . . . .

This Bishop has no good squares of development. In a training-game with clocks played in Paris, 1933, Dr. Bernstein tried against me 14. B—Kt 5, but after 14. . . . . P—Kt 5 ; 15. Kt—Q 5 (15. Kt— K 2, Kt × K P loses a Pawn), Kt × Kt, had to resign as 16. Q × Kt would have been answered by 16. . . . . R—Kt 4.

14.	K R—K 1
15. Q—Q 3	P—Kt 5
16. Kt—K 2	. . . . . .

Inconsequent, as he had here more reasons than before to pursue his policy of exchanges. After 16. Kt—Q 5, Kt × Kt ; 17. Q (or P) × P, Q—Kt 4, etc., Black would have only a slightly more comfortable end-game, which by right play by White could, however, eventually end in a draw. After the text-move White's task will become much more complicated.

16.	Q—B 3
17. P—K B 3	.....

In the event of 17. Kt—Kt 3 the answer 18. .... Kt—Kt 5—followed by .... Kt—K 4 or .... B—B 3— would be strong. The Pawn's move, however, weakens the dark-coloured squares (especially K 3) and thus gives to Black's initiative a concrete object.

17.	P—Q 4 !
18. P × P	.....

Otherwise he would lose this Pawn with practically no compensation.

18.	Kt × P
19. Q R—K 1	B—B 3
20. P—Q B 4	.....

Also 20. P—Q B 3, which was slightly preferable, would not prove quite satisfactory after 20. .... Q—B 4 ch ; 21. Kt—Q 4, K R—Q 1, etc.∓

20.	Q—B 4 ch
21. R—B 2	Kt—K 6
22. P—Q Kt 3	Q R—Q 1
23. B × Kt	R × B
24. Q—B 2	.....

As is easy to see, the last 3-4 moves were practically forced. Black has not only obtained the full control of the board, but is even in a position to obtain a material advantage. The final part of the fight does not lack, however, some sort of piquancy.

24.	B—R 5 !
25. P—Kt 3	R × B P
26. R—K B 1	B—Kt 4
27. K—Kt 2	R × R ch

28. R × R	Q—B 3 ch
29. K—R 3	.....

Forced, because of Black's threats 30. .... R—Q 7 or 30. .... B—K 6.

29.	B—K 6
30. R—B 1	.....

Position after White's 30th move.

30.	R—Q 4 !

Not yet decisive was 30. .... R—Q 3 (or Q 7) because of 31. Q—K B 5 with counter-attack ; but after the text-move the co-operation of the Rook will leave White without defence.

31. Kt—B 4	Q—Q 2 ch
32. P—Kt 4	R—Q 5
33. Q—K Kt 2	.....

He still succeeds in finding defensive moves—but it obviously cannot long go that way.

33.	P—Q B 3
34. Kt—R 5	B—Kt 4 !

After this there is no remedy against 35. .... P—K Kt 3, etc.

35. Q—K 2	P—K Kt 3
36. Kt—Kt 3	P—K R 4
37. Kt—K 4	Q × P ch !

Only *apparently* allowing White to reach a Rook-ending with only one Pawn less : in reality it will be only Black who will keep a Rook.

38. Q×Q	P×Q ch
39. K×P	R×Kt ch
40. K×B	K—Kt 2

Black's next move would be now 41. ....P—K B 3 ch ! followed by 42. ....R—K 4 ch, winning the Rook. Therefore—

Resigns.

GAME 48

QUEEN'S GAMBIT DECLINED (ORTHODOX DEFENCE)

Bled Tournament, September, 1931.

Black : G. MAROCZY

1. P—Q 4	P—Q 4
2. P—Q B 4	P—K 3
3. Kt—Q B 3	Kt—K B 3
4. B—Kt 5	B—K 2
5. P—K 3	Q Kt—Q 2
6. Kt—B 3	Castles
7. R—B 1	P—K R 3
8. B—R 4	P—B 3
9. B—Q 3	P—Q R 3

The fashionable continuation, by which in fact Black has but little to fear is 9. ....P×P ; 10. B×P, P—Q Kt 4 ; 11. B—Q 3, P—Q R 3 and if 12. P—Q R 4 (12. P—K 4 ?, Kt×K P∓ : Euwe-Alekhine, 28th game, 1935), then simply 12. .... P×P.

10. Castles	P×P
11. B×P	P—B 4

It is rather risky to delay the development of the Queen's side. Instead, 11. ....P—Q Kt 4, fol-

lowed by ....B—Kt 2 and .... P—Q B 4 was still a fairly good alternative.

12. P—Q R 4 !   ......

This move, in connection with the following isolation of the central Pawn, gives the game its character. After 12. B—Q 3 or 12. Q—K 2, P—Q Kt 4, etc., it would develop on conventional lines—and probably end by an honourable draw.

12. ......   Q—R 4

Maroczy from now on plays very enterprising chess, combining defensive moves with counter-attacks against White's weaknesses at Q R 4 and Q 4.

13. Q—K 2   P×P !

At the right moment as 14. Kt×P, Kt—K 4 ; 15. B—Q Kt 3, Kt—Kt 3 ; 16. B—K Kt 3, P—K 4 etc., would be in Black's favour.

14. P×P	Kt—Kt 3
15. B—Q 3 !	......

Practically leaving the Q R's Pawn to its fate. For the moment, it is true, it cannot well be taken because of 16. Kt—K 4 ! with a very strong attack ; but it remains weak almost until the—dramatic—end.

15.	B—Q 2
16. Kt—K 5	......

Threatening 17. B×Kt followed by 18. Q—K 4, etc.

16.	K R—Q 1
17. P—B 4	......

White had decided already, by 12. P—Q R 4, to conduct the whole game in a fortissimo style. Although the result justified this method, I am by no means sure that it was the most logical way to exploit the—unquestionable—advantage in space. Here, for instance, the simple move 17. Q—B 3 was to be seriously taken into consideration as (1) 17. ....Kt×P would still be answered by 18. Kt—K 4 !± (2) 17. ....B×P would be obviously unsatisfactory because of 18. Q×Kt P, and (3) after 17. .... B—B 3 ; 18. Kt×B, P×B ; 19. K R—Q 1, etc., Black's Pawn weaknesses would be at least as vulnerable as White's.

17. ......   B—K 1
18. Kt—Kt 4   ......

The logical consequence of the previous move. White offers the Queen's Pawn, as its defence by 18. K R—Q 1 or 18. B—B 2 would permit Black to parry the important threats by means of Q (or K) Kt—Q 4.

18. ......   R×P

Black, on the other hand, has nothing better than to accept the offer, as by other moves White's attack would remain—with even material—at least as strong as in the actual game.

19. B×Kt   B×B
20. Kt×B ch   P×Kt
21. Kt—K 4   ......

Black's King's position is now dangerously compromised, especially as he cannot well protect the *square* P—K B 3 (if 21. Kt—Q 2, then 22. P—K B 5 ! with a strong attack).

21. ......   Q R—Q 1 ?

But he could—and should—save the *Pawn* K B 3 by playing 21. .... P—K B 4, to which White would reply 22. Kt—B 6 ch, K—B 1 (or

K—Kt 2 ; 23. Kt—R 5 ch followed by P—Q Kt 3) ; 23. P—Q Kt 3 ! and try afterwards to exploit the weakness of the opponent's dark-coloured squares—with an uncertain result.   The counter-attack initiated by the text-move will be refuted chiefly because White will succeed in protecting his Bishop *indirectly*, without any loss of time.

22. Kt×B P ch   K—B 1
23. Kt—R 7 ch !   ......

Perhaps Maroczy had underestimated this check. If now 23. ....K—Kt 1, then 24. Q—Kt 4 ch, K—R 1 ; 25. Q—R 4 !, R×B ; 26. Q×P and wins.

23. ......   K—K 2
24. P—B 5 !   ......

The first indirect defence : if 24. ....R×B ? then 25. P—B 6 ch followed by 26. Q×R ch, etc.

24. ......   R(Q 1)—Q 3

But after this everything seems to be again in order, as the King has got a comfortable escape at Q 1. The following reply, which was by no means easy to find, however, turns the tables :—

Position after Black's 24th move.

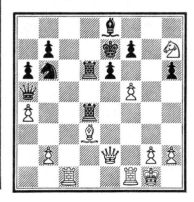

25. P—Q Kt 4 ! ! ......

A surprising solution of the attacking problem, the idea of which is as follows : White *succeeds* either (in case of 25. ....R × P) *by playing* 26. Q—R 5 ! *without permitting the strong answer* 26. .... Q—Q 7 ! *or (as in the actual game) by entering with the Queen into Black's position via K 5.*

25. ......   Q × Kt P

An interesting finish would have occurred after 25. ....R × P—26. Q—R 5 !, P—K 4 ! ; 27. P—B 6 ch, K—Q 1 ; 28. Q × R P !, R × B ; 29. Q—B 8, R—Q 2; 30. R—Q B 5, Q × P ; 31. R × P and wins.

26. Q—K 5 !   ......

Threatening 27. Q—B 6 ch, K— Q 2 ; 28. Kt—B 8, mate.

26. ......   Kt—Q 2

Protects both critical squares and —apparently—at last wins the Bishop.

27. Q—R 8 !   R × B

Losing one move earlier than he should. The best reply 27. .... Q—Kt 3 would have forced White to disclose the last point of the combination started by his 25th move—28. P—Q R 5 ! (the triumph of the neglected Pawn !) with two variations : (a) 28. ....Q × P ; 29. R—B 8, or (b) 28. ....Q—R 2 ; 29. P—B 6 ch, etc., as in the actual game.

28. P—B 6 ch !   ......

If 28. .... Kt × P, then 29. Q × Kt ch and 30. Kt—B 8 mate ; if 28. ....K—Q 1, then 29. Q × B ch ! and 30. R—B 8 mate.

Resigns.

GAME 49

CARO-KANN DEFENCE

London Tournament, February, 1932.

Black : W. WINTER

1. P—K 4	P—Q B 3
2. P—Q 4	P—Q 4
3. P × P	P × P
4. P—Q B 4	......

One of the best ways to meet the Caro-Kann. Nowadays it is slightly out of fashion, in my opinion without much reason and probably only temporarily.

4.	Kt—K B 3
5. Kt—Q B 3	Kt—B 3
6. Kt—B 3	......

If 6. B—Kt 5 (Botwinnik's move), then 6. ....P—K 3 ; 7. Kt—B 3, B—K 2, etc., with a slightly cramped but solid enough defensive game.

6.	B—Kt 5
7. P × P	K Kt × P
8. B—Q Kt 5	Q—R 4

Introduced by me in a game against Nimzowitsch (Bled, 1931), in which my opponent, after 9. Q— Kt 3 !, B × Kt ; 10. P × B, Kt × Kt made the curious miscalculation 11. B × Kt ch, P × B ; 12. Q—Kt 7 ? —and after 12. ....Kt—Q 4 disc. ch ; 13. B—Q 2, Q—Kt 3 ! ; 14. Q × R ch, K—Q 2 ; 15. Castles, Kt— B 2, was forced to give up a piece by 16. B—R 5, making further resistance practically hopeless. However, the Queen's move is—as the present game shows—decidedly too risky. The correct line is 8. .... R—B 1 ; 9. P—K R 3, B × Kt ; 10. Q × B, P—K 3, etc., with about even prospects.

9. Q—Kt 3 !	B × Kt

| 10. P×B | Kt×Kt |
| 11. P×Kt | P—K 3 |

Black has obtained, it is true, the better Pawn position, but as the following efficient Pawn sacrifice of White will show, his King's position is by no means safe. The next part of the game is highly instructive, as White's attack needed, in order to succeed, a particularly exact calculation.

| 12. P—Q 5 ! | ...... |

It is necessary to sacrifice the Pawn at once, as after 12. Castles, R—Q 1 Black would obtain a satisfactory position.

| 12. ...... | P×P |
| 13. Castles | Castles |

The only move. After 13. .... B—K 2 ; 14. R—K 1, the pin on the King's file would be deadly.

| 14. B×Kt | P×B |
| 15. R—Kt 1 | Q—B 2 |

Or 15. .... K—Q 2; 16. P—Q B4!, etc., with a tremendous attack.

| 16. Q—R 4 | R—Q 2 |
| 17. B—Q 2 ! | ...... |

A difficult move, much more effective than 17. B—K B 4 or K 3. In spite of his accurate defence Black will be unable to prevent a gradual further demolition of his King's residence.

| 17. ...... | B—B 4 |
| 18. P—Q B 4 | K—Q 1 |

Again comparatively the best, as 18. ....B—Kt 3 would fail because of 19. P—B 5 !, B×P ; 20. Q—R 6 ch, K—Q 1 ; 21. B—R 5, B—Kt 3 ; 22. R×B, etc.

| 19. B—R 5 | B—Kt 3 |
| 20. B×B | P×B |

| 21. Q—R 8 ch ! | ...... |

The objects of this rather profound Queen's manœuvre are the following :—

(1) If White plays at once 21. P×P, Black can answer 21. .... R×P ; 22. K R—Q 1, K—K 2 ! ; 23. R×R, P×R ; 24. R—K 1 ch, K—B 3 ; 25. Q—R 4 ch, K—Kt 3, and White would have no more than perpetual check. Therefore he has to prevent the Black King escaping via K 2.

(2) In some important variations a White Rook has to be posted at Q R 4—so the Queen frees that square in view of that eventuality.

21.	Q—B 1
22. Q—R 3	Q—Kt 1
23. P×P	P×P

After 23. ....R×P ; 24. K R—Q 1, R—K 1 ; 25. R×R ch, P×R ; 26. R—Q 1, Q or R—K 4 ; 27. P—B 4 Black would have no adequate defence.

Position after Black's 23rd move.

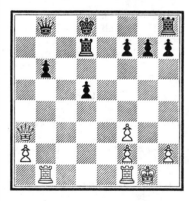

| 24. R—Kt 4 ! | ...... |

The winning move, as Black has no time to play 24. ....R—K 1 on account of 24. R—Q R 4, etc.

| 24. ...... | Q—Q 3 |

25. R—K 1 !   R—B 2

Or 25. ....R—K 2 ; 26. R—Q 1,
etc., with a winning attack.

26. Q—Kt 3   R—K 1
27. R—Q 1   R—K 4

Obviously, Black cannot protect
both his Pawns.

28. R × Kt P   R—B 3
29. R × R   R—Kt 4 ch

Forced (29. ....Q × R ; 30. Q—
Kt 8 ch, etc.).

30. K—R 1   Q × R
31. R—K 1 !   ......

Initiating the final attack.

31. ......   Q—B 3
32. Q—Kt 8 ch   K—Q 2
33. P—B 4   R—Kt 3

I expected here 33. ....R—R 4 ;
34. Q—K 8 ch, K—Q 3 ; 35. R—
Q B 1 !, R × P ch ; 36. K—Kt 1 !
forcing the win.

34. Q—K 8 ch   K—B 2
35. R—B 1 ch   K—Kt 3
36. R—Kt 1 ch   K—B 4
37. Q—Kt 5 ch   Resigns.

GAME 50

QUEEN'S INDIAN DEFENCE

London Tournament, February,
1932.

White : MISS VERA MENCHIK

1. P—Q 4   Kt—K B 3
2. P—Q B 4   P—K 3
3. Kt—K B 3   P—Q Kt 3
4. P—K 3   ......

A tame developing system but by
no means a bad one. Black has
thereby no opening difficulties, providing he does not over-estimate his
position, and realises that although
he has sufficient forces to *control*
White's K 4, he is not yet developed
enough for *occupying* it.

4. ......   B—Kt 2
5. B—Q 3   B—Kt 5 ch
6. B—Q 2   B × B ch
7. Q Kt × B   ......

This Knight is not very happily
placed at Q 2. More promising
would be, therefore, 7. Q × B, followed by Kt—B 3.

7. ......   P—Q 3
8. Castles   Q Kt—Q 2
9. Q—B 2   Q—K 2
10. K R—Q 1   Castles (K R)
11. Kt—K 4   P—K Kt 3

A good move, the object of which
is, as the continuation shows, to
avoid exchange of the Q's Bishop.
It is to Black's interest to keep as
many pieces as possible on the
board, his Pawn position being
much more elastic than his
opponent's.

12. R—Q 2   Kt × Kt
13. B × Kt   P—Q B 3 !
14. Q—R 4   ......

Probably hoping to provoke the
answer 14. ....P—Q Kt 4 which
move would be advantageously
answered by 15. Q—Kt 3 !

14. ......   K R—B 1
15. B—Q 3   P—Q B 4
16. Q—Q 1   ......

None of the White pieces has
a suitable square. But it will still
be some time before Black will
be able to obtain a serious initiative.

16. ......   Kt—B 3
17. P × P   Kt P × P

The right way to recapture, as

the backward Queen's Pawn is very easy to protect in this kind of position.

18. Q—K 2	Kt—R 4
19. Q R—Q 1	R—B 1 !

Preparing the advance of the K B's and the K's Pawns.

20. P—K 4	Kt—B 5
21. Q—K 3	P—K 4
22. B—B 1	Q R—Q 1

Up to this point Black's tactics have been irreproachable, but here 22. ....K R—Q's, followed by Kt —K 3—Q 5 would be more convincing as it would prevent White's next attempt.

23. P—Q Kt 4 !   ......

An interesting Pawn sacrifice in a difficult position. If now 23. .... P × P ; 24. Q × R P, R—R 1 ; 25. Q—Kt 6, B × P, then 26. Q × Q P, Q × Q ; 27. R × Q, B × Kt ; 28. P × B, R × R P ; 29. R—Kt 6, with good drawing chances for White.

23.	Kt—K 3
24. R—Kt 2	B—R 1
25. P × P	Kt × P
26. Kt—Q 2	P—B 4
27. P × P	P × P

With the opening of the K Kt's file, Black gets at last the basis for a powerful King's attack.

28. P—B 3	Q—K Kt 2

Threatening 29. ....P—B 5, followed by .... P—K 5.

29. R (Q 1)—Kt 1	K—R 1
30. Kt—Kt 3	Kt—K 3
31. R—Q 2	Kt—Kt 4
32. K—R 1	R—K Kt 1
33. R—K B 2	......

The only defence against 33. .... Kt × B P,

33.	Q R—K 1 !
34. R—Q 1	R—K 3

Position after Black's 34th move.

35. P—B 4	......

Desperation, as Black was threatening 35. ....R—R 3 followed by 36. ....R × P ch ; 37. ....Q—R 3 ch ; 38. ....Kt—R 6 ch, etc. And after 35. P—Q B 5, P—Q 4, etc., he would win by the simple advance of his centre Pawns.

35.	P × P
36. Q—Q 4	R—K 4 !
37. P—B 5	P × P
38. Kt × P	Kt—R 6
39. R—Kt 2	P—B 6 !
40. P—Kt 3	P—B 7 disc. ch

This is the longest Bishop's check I ever gave in my life !

Resigns.

GAME 51

RUY LOPEZ

London Tournament, February, 1932.

Black : G. KOLTANOWSKI

Brilliancy Prize

1. P—K 4	P—K 4
2. Kt—K B 3	Kt—Q B 3
3. B—Kt 5	P—Q R 3

4. B—R 4	P—Q 3
5. B×Kt ch	P×B
6. P—Q 4	P×P

The usual defensive scheme is here 6. ....P—K B 3, followed by Kt—K 2—Kt 3, etc. But Black in this game obviously wants a free diagonal for his K's Bishop.

7. Kt×P	B—Q 2
8. Castles	P—Kt 3
9. Kt—Q B 3	......

White has nothing better than this calm development of forces—in the hope that the slight weakness of the dark-coloured squares in Black's camp sooner or later will give him real chances.

9.	B—Kt 2
10. R—K 1	Kt—K 2
11. B—B 4	Castles
12. Q—Q 2	P—Q B 4
13. Kt—Kt 3	......

Not 13. Kt—B 3 because of 13. ....B—Kt 5. But 13. K Kt—K 2 came seriously into consideration.

13.	Kt—B 3
14. B—R 6	B—K 3
15. B×B	K×B
16. Kt—Q 5	P—B 3
17. Q R—Q 1	R—Q Kt 1
18. Q—B 3	Q—B 1
19. P—Q R 3	R—B 2
20. P—R 3 !	......

This and the following moves were by no means easy to find as, in preparing the decisive combination, I had to keep in mind at the same time the possibility of the simplifying variation beginning by ....B×Kt.

| 20. ...... | Q—Kt 2 |
| 21. R—K 3 | Q—Kt 4 |

As the sequel shows, Black should here play 21. ....B×Kt—but after 22. P×B, Kt—Q 5 ; 23. Kt×Kt,

P×Kt ; 24. R×P, Q×Kt P ; 25. Q—Q 2, White would still keep a real, if not easily realisable, positional advantage.

Position after Black's 21st move.

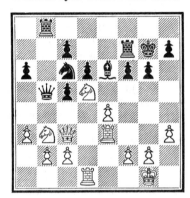

22. Kt×P (B 7) ! ......

As a rule, so-called "positional" sacrifices are considered more difficult, and therefore more praiseworthy, than those which are based exclusively on an exact calculation of tactical possibilities. The present position offers, I believe, an exception, as the multitude and complexity of the variations following the Knight's sacrifice demanded much more intensive mental work than any general evaluation of mutual possibilities.

| 22. ...... | R×Kt |
| 23. R×P | B—B 5 |

Black had several other answers, but all of them would finally lose, as shown below : (I.) 23. ....B×Kt ? ; 24. Q×P ch, followed by 25. R×B, etc. (II.) 23. .... Kt—Q 5 ?; 24. Kt×Kt, etc. (III.) 23. .... Q—B 5 ; 24. Kt×B P ! etc. (IV.) 23. ....Kt—Q 1 ; 24. R—K B 3, R—K B 2 ; 25. Kt×B P, etc. (V.) 23. ....B—B 2 ; 24. R×B P !, Kt—Q 5 ; 25. Kt×Kt, P×Kt ; 26. Q×R, K×R ; 27. R—B 3 ch, etc.

(VI.) 23. ....R—K 1 ; 24. Kt×P,
Kt—Q 1 ; 25. P—Q Kt 4, Kt—B 2 ;
26. R×B, etc.   (VII.) 23. ....K—
B 2 ; 24. R—B 3, K—K2 ; 25. P—
Q R 4, Q—Kt 3 (best) ; 26. R×B ch,
K×R ; 27. Kt×B P ch, K—Q 3 (or
K—B 2 ; 28. Q×B P ch, K—Kt 1 ;
29. Kt—K 6 ! etc.) ; 28. Q×P ch,
K×Kt ; 29. R—B 3 ch, K—Kt 5 ;
30. Q—Q 6 ch and wins.

24. P—Q R 4 !	Q×P
25. Kt×P	Q—Kt 4
26. Q×P ch	K—Kt 1
27. Kt—Q 7 !	R—Q 1

Or 27. ....R—K 1 ; 28. Q—
Q B 3 and wins.

28. R—K B 3	Q—Kt 5
29. P—B 3	Q—Kt 4
30. Kt—K 5 !	R (Q 1)—Q B 1
31. Kt×Kt	

If now 31. ....R×Kt, then 32.
R—Q 8 ch winning.

Resigns.

GAME 52

BUDAPEST DEFENCE

London Tournament, February,
1932.

Black : DR. S. TARTAKOWER

1. P—Q 4	Kt—K B 3
2. P—Q B 4	P—K 4
3. P×P	Kt—K 5

Less usual, but not better than
3. ....Kt—Kt 5 against which
move I have had (excepting
the Gilg-game, Semmering, 1926)
rather pleasant experiences, too.
Here, for instance, two typical short
"Budapest" stories.

I. *Black*, E. Rabinowitsch, Baden-
Baden, 1925. 1. P—Q 4, Kt—
K B 3 ; 2. P—Q B 4, P—K 4 ; 3.
P×P, Kt—Kt 5 ; 4. P—K 4, Kt×
K P ; 5. P—K B 4, Kt—Kt 3 ; 6.
Kt—K B 3, B—Q B 4 ; 7. P—
K B 5 !, Kt—R 5 ; 8. Kt—Kt 5 !,
Q—K 2 ; 9. Q—Kt 4, P—K B 3 ;

10. Q—R 5 ch !, P—K Kt 3 ; 11.
Q×Kt, P×Kt ; 12. B×P, Q—B 2 ;
13. B—K 2, Castles ; 14. R—K B 1,
Kt—B 3 ; 15. Kt—B 3, Kt—Q 5 ;
16. P×P, Q×Kt P ; 17. R×R ch,
B×R ; 18. B—R 5, Q—Q Kt 3 ;
19. Castles (Q R), B—Kt 2 ; 20.
R—K B 1, Kt—K 3 ; 21. B—B 7
ch, K—R 1 ; 22. B×Kt, P×B ; 23.
B—R 6 ! Resigns.

II. *Black :* Dr. Seitz, Hastings,
1925-1926. 1. P—Q 4, Kt—K B 3 ;
2. P—Q B 4, P—K 4 ; 3. P×P, Kt
—Kt 5 ; 4. P—K 4, Kt×K P ; 5.
P—K B 4, Kt (K 4)—Q B 3 ; 6.
B—K 3, B—Kt 5 ch ; 7. Kt—Q B 3,
Q—K 2 ; 8. B—Q 3, P—K B 4 ; 9.
Q—R 5 ch, P—K Kt 3 ; 10. Q—B 3,
B×Kt ch ; 11. P×B, P×K P ; 12.
B×K P, Castles ; 13. B—Q 5 ch !,
K—R 1 ; 14. Kt—R 3, P—Q 3 ; 15.
Castles (K R), B×Kt ; 16. Q×B,
Q—Q 2; 17. P—K B 5 !, P×P ;
18. Q R—Q Kt 1 !, P—B 5 ; 19. B×
B P, Q×Q; 20. B—K 5 ch. Resigns.

| 4. Kt—Q 2 | Kt—B 4 |

If 4. ....B—Kt 5, then 5. Kt—
B 3 followed by P—Q R 3, in order
to obtain the advantage of the two
Bishops.

5. K Kt—B 3	Kt—B 3
6. P—K Kt 3	Q—K 2
7. B—Kt 2	P—K Kt 3
8. Q Kt—Kt 1 !	......

This at first sight surprising move
is in reality perfectly logical. After
Black has clearly shown his intention to develop the King's Bishop at
K Kt 2, White has no longer to
reckon with any action on the
diagonal K 1—Q R 5. There is no
reason, therefore, for delay in placing his Knight on the dominating
square Q 5.

8.	Kt×P
9. Castles	Kt×Kt ch
10. P×Kt	B—Kt 2
11. R—K 1	Kt—K 3
12. Kt—B 3	Castles
13. Kt—Q 5	Q—Q 1
14. P—B 4	P—Q B 3

He has willy-nilly to dislodge the White Knight—thus creating a dangerous weakness at Q 3—because after the immediate 14. .... P—Q 3 the temporary sacrifice 15. P—K B 5, etc., would be too dangerous for him.

15.	Kt—B 3	P—Q 3
16.	B—K 3	Q—B 2
17.	R—Q B 1	B—Q 2
18.	Q—Q 2	Q R—Q 1
19.	K R—Q 1	B—B 1
20.	Kt—K 4	Kt—B 4

This will be finally refuted by the combination starting with White's 24th move—but owing to the weakness mentioned above Black's position was already very difficult. Unsatisfactory would be, for instance, 20. ....P—Q 4 ; 21. P×P, R×P ; 22. Kt—B 6 ch, followed by 23. B×R, etc., winning the exchange ; or 20. ....P—Q B 4 ; 21. P—K B 5 !, P×P ; 22. Kt—Q B 3, Kt—Q 5 ; 23. Kt—Q 5, Q—Kt 1 ; 24. B—Kt 5, etc. ± ; and after the comparatively safest 20. ....P—Q Kt 3, White could also easily increase his advantage in space by continuing 21. P—Q Kt 4, etc.,

21.	Kt×Q P !	Kt—R 5
22.	P—Q B 5	Kt×Kt P
23.	R—K 1	......

Position after White's 23rd move.

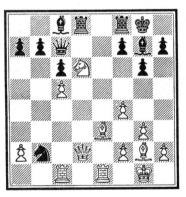

23.	......	P—Q Kt 4

This rejoinder—the logical consequence of the three previous moves—will prove insufficient ; but Black did not have any saving course : for instance, 23. ....B—K 3 ; 24. B—Q 4 ! or 23. ....B—B 4 ; 24. P—Kt 4 !, B×P ; 25. B—Q 4, in each case with a decisive advantage for White.

24.	P×P (e.p.) !	......

A surprising but not very complicated combination. The only difficulty consisted in the necessity of foreseeing this possibility several moves before, when making the capture 21. Kt×Q P.

24.	......	Q×Kt
25.	Q×Q	R×Q
26.	P×P	B—Kt 2
27.	B—B 5	R (Q 3)—Q 1
28.	B×R	K×B
29.	B×P	B×B
30.	R×B	R—R 1

The last moves of Black were practically forced and, his position being absolutely hopeless, he prefers a quick end. If, instead of this, 30. ....B—Q 5, then 31. R—Q 6, also winning immediately.

31.	R—Kt 6	R×P
32.	R—Kt 8 mate	

GAME 53

CARO-KANN DEFENCE

Berne Tournament, July, 1932.

Black : SULTAN KHAN

1.	P—K 4	P—Q B 3
2.	P—Q 4	P—Q 4
3.	P×P	P×P
4.	P—Q B 4	Kt—K B 3
5.	Kt—Q B 3	Kt—B 3
6.	Kt—B 3	B—Kt 5

7. P×P   K Kt×P
8. B—Q Kt 5   P—Q R 3

About 8. ....Q—R 4 see the game against Winter (No. 49). The point of the text-move is a positional Pawn-offer, by no means easy to refute over the board.

9. B×Kt ch   P×B
10. Q—R 4 !   Kt×Kt

The logical consequence of his 8th move, as 10. ....B—Q 2 ; 11. Kt—K 5, etc., would be obviously to White's advantage.

11. Q×P ch   B—Q 2
12. Q×Kt   R—B 1
13. Q—K 3   B—Kt 4

It becomes evident that Black is not without compensation for the minus Pawn : White's Q's Pawn is isolated and—what is more important—he will be forced, in order to be able to castle, to weaken by the following moves his Q's side.

14. P—Q R 4   B—B 5
15. P—Q Kt 3   B—Q 4
16. Castles   Q—Kt 3
17. B—Q 2 !   ......

A poor strategy would be to protect the Knight Pawn by 17. R—Q Kt 1, after which Black would have found time to finish his development by 17. ....P—K 3, B—Q 3 (K 2) and Castles.

17. ......   P—K 3

If, instead, 17. ....Q×Kt P, then 18, K R—B 1 ! .:..R×R ch ; 19. R×R, Q×Q ; 20. P×Q, P—K 3 (or B×Kt ; 21. P×B, K—Q 2 ; 22. B—R 5, etc.) ; 21. R—Q B 7 followed by R—R 7±.

18. K R—B 1   R—Q Kt 1

Comparatively better than the exchange.

19. Kt—K 5   P—B 3

Probably under-estimating the strength of the reply ; but also 19. ....B—K 2 was not satisfactory : for instance, 20. Kt—B 4, Q×Kt P; 21. Q×Q, R×Q ; 22. Kt—Q 6 ch ! etc. ±

20. Kt—B 6 !   ......

The object of this Knight manœuvre is to make a definite end to Black's attacks against the Q Kt's Pawn.

20. ......   R—R 1

The only move, as 20. ....R—B 1 would be inferior because of 21. Kt—Kt 4 !

21. Kt—R 5   ......

Intending eventually 22. R—B 6 ! etc.

21. ......   K—B 2

This King's position in an early stage of the game is more familiar to Sultan Khan than to European or American players, as in Indian Chess castling is effected in three movements: (1) K—K 2, Q 2 or B 2; (2) a Rook move from its original square ; (3) a Knight's move, with the King back on the first rank and on the side of the Rook's movement —this provided the King has not been under check in the meantime. Returning to the present game, one must admit that Black, owing to the threat above mentioned, did not have, in reality, anything better than the King's move.

22. Kt—B 4   Q—Kt 2
23. Q—Kt 3   B—K 2
24. P—R 5   ......

The initial move of the decisive scheme : the establishment of the Knight at Q Kt 6 will permit White to take full advantage of the Q B's file.

24.	Q R—Q 1
25. Kt—Kt 6	B—B 3
26. R—B 4 !	......

This had to be exactly calculated, because of the possible answer 21. ....P—K 4, in which case White had decided to give back the extra Pawn, in order to obtain a strong direct attack. The continuation would be 27. Q R—Q B 1 !, R×P ; 28. R×B, R×B ; 29. Q—Kt 4 !, K R—Q 1 ; 30. Q—K 6 ch, K—B 1 ; 31. P—K R 3, R—Q 8 ch ; 32. R×R, R×R ch ; 33. K—R 2, etc. ±

26.	K R—K 1
27. Q R—Q B 1	B—Kt 4
28. R—B 7	Q—K 5

Position after Black's 28th move.

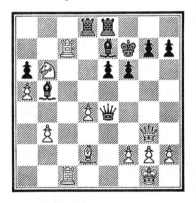

29. P—Q 5 !   ......

Instead of the simple 29. B—B 3 —which in the long run would probably also prove sufficient—White decides to force the game by a sharply calculated combination. If Black had tried now his best practical chance by 29. .... P×P the following variation would have occurred : 30. R—K 1, B—K 7 ; 31. Kt—R 4 ! (one of the important links of White's com-

bination), P—Q 5 ; 32. Kt—B 5, Q—B 7 ; 33. R×B, Q—Q 8 ch ; 34. R—K 1, Q×B ; 35. K—B 1! and Black would be defenceless against the many threats. The remaining moves would probably be 35. .... K—Kt 1 ; 36. Kt—K 6, P—K Kt 3 ; 37. Kt×R, Q×R ch ; 38. K×R, B—Q 3 disc. ch. ; 39. K—Q 2, B× Q ; 40. R P×B, R×Kt ; 41. R— B 6, R—Q 4 ; 42. P—Q Kt 4, after which Black would have to resign.

29. ......   K—Kt 1

Leads to an even more rapid debacle because of White's 31st move.

30. R—K 1	Q—B 4
31. B—Kt 4 !	R—Q 2

As useless as anything else.

32. R×R	B×R
33. B×B	P×P

Or 33. ....R×B ; 34. Q—Q 6 and wins.

34. Q—Q 6   Resigns.

GAME 54

RUY LOPEZ

Berne Tournament, July, 1932.

Black : H. Grob

1. P—K 4	P—K 4
2. Kt—K B 3	Kt—Q B 3
3. B—Kt 5	P—Q R 3
4. B—R 4	Kt—B 3
5. Castles	P—Q 3
6. P—B 3	......

Also good is here 6. B×Kt ch, P×B ; 7. P—Q 4, Kt×P ; 8. Q— K 2, P—K B 4 ; 9. Q Kt—Q 2, Kt×Kt ; 10. Kt×Kt ! and White will regain the Pawn with advantage ; for instance, 10. ....P—K 5 ;

11. P—K B 3, P—Q 4 ; 12. P×P,
Q P×P ; 13. Kt×P !, etc. ±

6.	B—Kt 5
7. P—Q 4	P—Q Kt 4
8. B—Kt 3	B—K 2
9. B—K 3	......

Instead, the wing-demonstration
9. P—Q R 4 was quite in order.
The continuation selected leads to
a very complicated game in the
centre.

9.	Castles
10. Q Kt—Q 2	P—Q 4 !

At this moment I felt that I had
been "lured" into a variation prepared beforehand by my opponent.
This is what happened : A few years
before the Berne Tournament—to be
exact in 1925—I gave in Basle a
time - handicap exhibition, with
clocks, against 10 first-class amateurs, where the following game,
*identical with the present one until
the 10th move of White inclusive*, was
played and published (because of
the instructive attack and the
pretty finish) in the Swiss Press as
well as in one of my German books :
Black : K. Meck. 10. ....Kt—
Q R 4 ; 11. B—B 2, P—Q B 4 ; 12.
P—K R 3, B×Kt ; 13. Q×B, Kt—
Q 2 ; 14. Q R—Q 1, Q—Q B 2 ; 15.
B—Kt 1, Q R—Q 1 ; 16. Q—Kt 3,
K R—K 1 ; 17. P—K B 4, Kt—
Q B 3 ; 18. B P×P, P×P ; 19. P—
Q 5, Kt—Q R 4 ; 20. Kt—B 3, Kt—
B 5 ; 21. B—R 6, P—Kt 3 ; 22. R—
B 2, B—B 1 ; 23. Q—R 4, B—K 2 ;
24. Kt—Kt 5 !, Kt—Q 3 ; 25. Q R—
K B 1, B×Kt ; 26. B×B, R—Q B 1 ;
27. R×P !, Kt×R ; 28. R×Kt,
P—K R 4 ; 29. R—K B 3, R—
K B 1 ; 30. R—Kt 3, R—B 2 ; 31.
B—K 7, K—R 2 ; 32. B—Q 3, P—
B 5 ; 33. B—K 2, Q—Kt 3 ch ; 34.
K—R 2, Kt—B 3 ; 35. P—Q 6,
R×B ; 36. Q×Kt !, R—K Kt 2 ;
37. B×R P, R (B 1)—K Kt 1 ; 38.

Q—R 4 !, P—Kt 4 ; 39. B—Kt 6
double ch, followed by mate in two.
It is certainly to the credit of the
talented Swiss master to have found
the exact spot where his country-
man went wrong, and to have
substituted for the harmless 10. ....
Kt—Q R 4 the promising central
action in the text ; and it can be considered as his bad luck that the
whole variation (as the present game
seems to prove) is still not quite
satisfactory in spite of the improvement. Anyhow, I had quite a few
minutes of anxiety before discovering the way which finally assured
me the advantage.

11. P×Q P	P×P
12. P×P	K Kt×P

White has now to solve a double
problem : to free his K's Knight
from the unpleasant pin, and at the
same time to undertake necessary
measures in order to meet effectively the threatening advance of
Black's K B's Pawn.

13. Q—Kt 1 !   ......

This is the hidden solution :
White intends to protect his Q's
Bishop through a counter-attack
against Black's central Knight.

13. ......   P—B 4

Not only an attack, but also a
defence against the possibility of
Q—K 4.

14. P—Q R 3 !   ......

Freeing the square Q R 2 (1) for
the Bishop in case of 14. ....Kt—
Q R 4 (2) for the Queen—if played
as in the actual game.

14.	K—R 1
15. Q—R 2	......

Position after White's 15th move.

15. ......   K Kt—Kt 5 ! ?

Black continues to speculate, but will soon be forced to recognise that he has been outplayed in the battle for the central squares. Also after 15. ....Kt—Kt 3 ; 16. B—K 6 ! followed by P—Q 5, etc., White would easily have obtained the best of it.

16. P × Kt   Kt × Kt P
17. Q—Kt 1   P—B 5

The material equilibrium will be thus re-established, but not for long, as White's Knight at K 5 will exert a tremendous pressure.

18. Kt—K 5   B—K B 4

Or 18. ....B—R 4 ; 19. Q—K 4 ! P × B ; 20. P × P, B—B 3 ; 21. R—B 5 ! etc., with an overwhelming position.

19. Q—Q 1   P × B
20. P × P   Kt—Q 4
21. Kt—B 6 !   ......

The simplest, as it wins two minor pieces for a Rook by avoiding the middle-game complications. Not convincing would have been instead 21. R × B, R × R ; 22. P—K 4, because of 22. ....R × Kt, etc.—

but 21. Q—R 5, P—K Kt 3 (not 21. ....Kt × P ? ; 22. R × B and wins) ; 22. Kt × Kt P ch, B × Kt ; 23. Q × Kt, etc., was an equally pleasant alternative.

21. ......   Kt × K P
22. Kt × Q   Kt × Q
23. Kt—B 6   B—Kt 4
24. K R × Kt !   ......

Instead, 24. Q R × Kt would—strangely enough—permit Black a convincing escape by means of 24. ....B—K 6 ch ! 25. K—R 1 ; B × Kt ; 26. R × B, B—K 5 !, etc.

24. ......   B—K 6 ch
25. K—R 1   B—Kt 5
26. Kt—B 1   ......

Of course not 26. Kt—B 3, R × Kt ! etc.

26. ......   B × R
27. R × B   B—B 5
28. B—Q 5 !   ......

This Bishop's manœuvre prevents ....Q R—K 1—K 7.

28. ......   Q R—K 1
29. B—B 3   R—B 3
30. K—Kt 1   P—Kt 3

Obviously a loss of time if one compares this with the next move ; but in this position a *tempo* more or less cannot have any influence on the final outcome. If, for instance, 30. ....P—K Kt 4, then 31. P—K R 3, B—K 6 ch ; 32. Kt × B, R × Kt ; 33. P—Q 5, R—Kt 6 ; 34. R—Q 2 with an easy technical job for White.

31. R—R 1   P—Kt 4
32. P—K R 3   B—K 6 ch
33. Kt × B   ......

Of course not 33. K—R 1, P—K Kt 5 ! etc.

33. ......   R × Kt

34. R × P	R—Kt 6
35. B—Q 5 !	......

The beginning of a successful mating attack.

35.	R × P
36. R—R 8 ch	K—Kt 2
37. R—Kt 8 ch	K—R 3
38. Kt—K 5	K—R 4
39. R—Kt 7	K—R 5
40. K—R 2	P—R 3
41. B—B 3	R—Q 7
42. R—Kt 6 !	P—K Kt 5

Obviously forgetting to resign.

43. R × Kt P ch	K—R 4
44. R—Kt 3 disc. ch	K—R 5
45. Kt—Kt 6 ch	R × Kt
46. R × R	P—Kt 5
47. R—Kt 4 ch	K—R 4
48. K—Kt 3	R—Q 6
49. R—Kt 7 disc. ch	R × B ch
50. K × R	Resigns.

GAME 55

COLLE'S SYSTEM

Berne Tournament, July, 1932.

Black : S. FLOHR

1. P—Q 4	P—Q 4
2. Kt—K B 3	Kt—K B 3
3. P—K 3	......

This quiet move—the idea of which is to postpone the fight for the centre until White has brought his King into safety — procured the regretted Belgian champion a long series of brilliant victories. Its objective value had been already put in question by the variation 3. ....B—K B 4 ; 4. B—Q 3, P—K 3 ! introduced by me at San Remo, 1930, against the same player and adopted since, for instance, by Dr. Euwe against me in a match game, 1935. The defence chosen

here by Flohr allows White to fulfil his plan of development.

3.	P—K 3
4. B—Q 3	P—B 4
5. P—B 3	Kt—B 3
6. Q Kt—Q 2	Q—B 2
7. Castles	B—K 2
8. Q—K 2	Castles
9. P—K 4	......

As I found out afterwards, this rather natural move had not been tried before. By adopting the usual 9. P × P, B × P ; 10. P—K 4, I would have been put in the not altogether pleasant position of having to fight against another innovation of mine (game against Gilg, Kecskemet, 1927)—namely, 10.....B—Q 3!; 11. R—K 1, Kt—Kt 5 ! etc., with about even prospects.

9.	P × K P

Unsatisfactory would be 9. .... P × Q P because of 10. P—K 5 !, Kt—Q 2 (or Kt—K R 4 ; 11. Kt— Q Kt 3 threatening P—K Kt 4) ; 11. P × P, Kt—Q Kt 5 ; 12. B— Kt 5 !, P—Q R 3 ; 13. B—R 4±.

10. Kt × P	P × P
11. Kt × P	......

Not 11. P × P, as it is in White's interest to exchange the maximum of pieces able to attack his isolated Pawn.

11.	Q Kt × Kt
12. P × Kt	Kt × Kt

Instead 12. ....Kt—Q 4 ; 13. Q—B 3 ! etc., would have led to a more complicated middle-game position. However, the text-move should have been sufficient for equality.

13. B × Kt	P—B 4

But from now on Flohr decidedly over-estimates his position, which he very seldom does. After the simple 12. ....B—Q 2 ; 13. Q—B 3, B—Q B 3, the natural outcome would have been a draw.

14. B—B 3   B—B 3

This move and the next one are the logical consequences of the unfortunate attempt to exploit the "weakness" at Q 4. Comparatively better was still 14. ....B—Q 2.

15. R—Q 1   R—Q 1
16. B—K 3   P—B 5 ?

Suicidal. But also after the comparatively better 16. ....P—K Kt 4 ; 17. P—K R 3, Q—Kt 2 ; 18. Q R—B 1, it would soon become evident that White's Q's Pawn could be captured only at the price of a further decisive compromising of Black's position.

17. Q R—B 1   Q—Q 3
18. B—Q 2   B×P

This Pawn is poisoned, as the answer shows. But also 18. ....R—Q Kt 1 ; 19. P—Q R 3 ! threatening 20. B—Kt 4, etc., was already practically hopeless.

19. B—R 5 !   R—Q 2

If the Rook leaves the Q's file, then 20. Q—B 4 ! wins immediately.

Position after Black's 19th move.

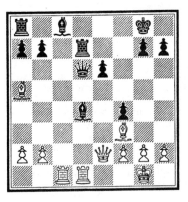

20. R×B !   ......

The convincing refutation of Black's ultra-materialistic tendencies in this game.

20. ......   Q×R
21. Q×P ch   R—B 2

After 21. ....K—B 1 ; 22. R—K 1, P—K Kt 3 ; 23. B—B 3 Black would lose the Queen.

22. R×B ch   R×R
23. Q×Q R ch   R—B 1
24. Q×P   R—K 1
25. P—K R 3   ......

But not 25. B—B 3 ? because of 25. ....Q×B !

25. ......   Q—B 4
26. B—B 3   Q—K 2
27. B—Q 5 ch   K—R 1
28. Q×Q   Resigns.

GAME 56

RUY LOPEZ

Pasadena Tournament, August, 1932.

Black : H. STEINER

1. P—K 4   P—K 4
2. Kt—K B 3   Kt—Q B 3
3. B—Kt 5   P—Q R 3
4. B—R 4   Kt—B 3
5. Castles   B—B 4

Having been for a period rather partial towards this move (cf. "My Best Games" 1908–1923), I must, to my regret, now admit that it is not quite sufficient against accurate play. And as 5. ....P—Q 3 has been recently also somewhat discredited, Black has been practically brought back to the old choice between the speculative 5. ....Kt×P and the cautious 5. ....B—K 2.

6. P—B 3	Kt × P
7. P—Q 4	B—R 2
8. Q—K 2	.....

I decided to follow here the line of play adopted against me by Yates at Hastings, 1922; although White obtained in that game only a draw I hoped to find over the board some better moves than those made by Yates—but there actually happened to be none. Much better than the Queen's move is 8. R—K 1 (which is also more logical, as it brings a new piece into action), and if 8. ....P—B 4, then 9. Q Kt—Q 2, Castles ; 10. Kt × Kt, P × Kt ; 11. B—K Kt 5, followed by 12. R × P with a clear advantage.

8.	P—K B 4
9. P × P	Castles
10. B—Kt 3 ch	K—R 1
11. Q Kt—Q 2	Q—K 1

An interesting idea à la Marshall : Black sacrifices 1—2 Pawns for a rapid development, after which White's position will, for. a while, look somewhat critical. However, the attempt can, and will, be refuted ; much to be preferred was therefore (as happened in the Hastings game mentioned) 11. .... P—Q 4 ; 12. P × P (*e.p.*) Kt × Q P ; 13. Kt—B 4, P—B 5 ! ; 14. Q Kt— K 5 (or 14. Kt × Kt, P × Kt ! ; 15. R—Q 1, B—K Kt 5), Kt × Kt ; 15. Kt × Kt, Q—Kt 4, etc., with fairly good prospects for Black.

12. Kt × Kt	P × Kt
13. Q × K P	P—Q 4 !

The point of the first sacrifice— Black will develop his Q's Bishop with tempo.

14. B × P	.....

Better than 14. Q × Q P, B—Kt 5; 15. Kt—Kt 5, Kt × P, etc., with unpleasant threats.

14.	B—B 4
15. Q—K R 4	Kt × P
16. B × Kt P !	.....

The only way to meet successfully Black's attack against K B 2. Unsatisfactory would be, instead, 16. Kt × Kt, Q × Kt ; 17. B × Kt P, because of 17. ....B—Q 6 ! ; 18. B × R, B × B P ch ! ; 19. K—R 1, Q—K 1 ! (stronger than 19. .... B × R ; 20. Q—K 4 !), etc., with a strong pressure of Black.

16.	R—Q Kt 1
17. Kt × Kt	R × B

If now 17. ....Q × Kt, then 18. B × R P ! parrying Black's main threat ....B—Q 6. This was the point of White's 16th move.

18. R—K 1 !	.....

Black has no means of profiting by this momentary weakening of White's K B 2.

18.	R—Kt 4
19. Kt—B 3	Q—B 1
20. P—B 4	R—Kt 2
21. P—Q Kt 3	.....

In connection with the next move a much more rapid solution than the passive 21. P—K R 3.

21.	B—Kt 5
22. B—R 3 !	.....

Practically forcing the reply which makes an end to Black's hopes on his diagonal Q R 2— K Kt 8.

22.	P—B 4

Of course not 22. ....R—B 3 because of 23. Q × B.

23. Kt—K 5	.....

From now on White has an easy job.

| 23. ...... | B—B 4 |
| 24. P—K Kt 4 ! | ...... |

In order to force the Black Bishop to abandon the defence of White's K Kt 6.

| 24. ...... | P—K Kt 4 |

Despair.

| 25. B—Kt 2 | ...... |

A spectacular move (25. ....P × Q ; 26. Kt—B 7 double ch, K—Kt 1; 27. Kt—R 6 mate)—but the simpler 25. Q—R 5 was also good enough. Not so convincing, on the contrary, would have been 25. Q × Kt P, R—Kt 2 ; 26. B—Kt 2, K—Kt 1 ! etc.

| 25. ...... | K—Kt 1 |

Hoping after 26. Q × Kt P ch, R—Kt 2, etc., to enter the last variation mentioned.

| 26. Q—R 5 ! | B—K 3 |

Position after Black's 26th move.

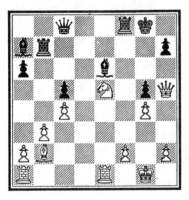

| 27. Kt—Q 7 ! | ...... |

A kind of "pendant" to the final move of the Borochow-game (No. 117). In case of 27.....Q × Kt, White forces the win like this : 28. Q × Kt P ch, K—B 2 ; 29. Q—B 6 ch,

K—Kt 1 ; 30. Q—R 8 ch !, K—B 2 ; 31. Q × R P ch, K—K 1 ; 32. Q—Kt 6 ch, K—K 2 ; 33. Q R—Q 1 !, Q—B 3 ; 34. Q—Kt 5 ch, K—B 2 ; 35. Q—B 6 ch and mate in two.

Resigns.

GAME 57

KING'S FIANCHETTO

Folkestone Team Tournament, July, 1933.

Black : V. MIKENAS

| 1. P—K 4 | P—K Kt 3 |

This move is rightly considered as inferior, as it concedes White the full control of the central squares. It is, however, not quite easy for the first player to transform this advantage in space into a decisive one.

2. P—Q 4	B—Kt 2
3. Kt—Q B 3	P—Q 3
4. Kt—B 3	Kt—Q 2
5. B—Q B 4	P—K 3

By choosing this Pawn-structure, Black, strategically, prevents in this stage of the game a further advance of White's central Pawns, as both P—K 5, P—Q 4 or P—Q 5, P—K 4, would allow the second player to obtain later an initiative in the centre by means of ....P—Q B 4 or ....P—K B 4. White's strategy in the next stage of the game will consist, therefore, in restricting more and more—by leaving the central position intact—the already limited field of action of the enemy's pieces.

| 6. Castles | Kt—K 2 |
| 7. P—Q R 4 ! | ...... |

A very important move in this kind of position, worthy to be noticed by the student. Its aim is either to prevent the fianchetto of Black's Queen's Bishop (P—Q Kt 3, P—Q R 5±) or induce Black to weaken — by answering ....P—Q R 4—his Q Kt 4.

7.	Castles
8. B—K 3	P—K R 3

Preventing 9. Q—Q 2, followed by B—K R 6, which would eliminate the only more or less active Black piece.

9. Q—Q 2	K—R 2
10. P—K R 3	......

In order not to count any more with the possibility ....Kt—K B 3 and if P—K 5, then ....Kt—Kt 5, etc.

10.	P—Q B 3

This, obviously, weakens his square Q 3—a circumstance which, however, should not have had a decisive character. Besides, it is already extremely difficult to indicate a suitable plan of further development for Black.

11. B—B 4	P—Q 4

Also unsatisfactory was 11. .... P—K 4 ; 12. P×P, P×P (in case of retaking with pieces on K 4, Black would, after the exchange of Queens, finally lose his K B's Pawn). 13. B—K 3±. But by playing 11. ....Kt—Kt 3 ; 12. B—Q 3, P—Q R 4, Black could obtain a comparatively steadier position than after the compromising Pawn move in the text.

12. B—Q 3	P—Q R 3 ?

Black does not realise that his square Q 3 has to be protected at all costs. From now on, the dominating position of White's Q's Bishop will alone prove sufficient to decide the battle. Necessary was,

therefore, 12. ....Kt—B 3 (—K 1) with a playable game, although White would still find it easy to increase his pressure—for instance, by means of 13. P—R 5, etc.

13. B—Q 6	P—K B 4

Or 13. ....Kt—B 3 ; 14. P—K 5, Kt—K 1 ; 15. B—R 3, followed by P—K R 4, etc., with an easy King's attack.

14. P—K 5	R—K Kt 1

Position after Black's 14th move.

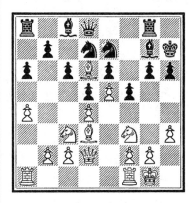

15. P—K R 4	......

White's overwhelming positional advantage allows him quietly to select the method he prefers for entering the enemy's not too well protected fortress. Besides the textmove, which inaugurates an irresistible plan (*status quo* on the King's side ; opening of a file on the other wing), he could also start a King's attack with the spectacular coup 15. Q—Kt 5, which, however, would not give any immediate results after the right answer 15. ....B—B 1, and if 16. Kt—K 2 (or 16. Q—R 4, P—Kt 4 ; 17. Q—R 5, Kt—K Kt 3) then 16. .... R—Kt 2 with at least a temporarily sufficient defence.

15. ......   P—Kt 3 !

Preparing ....Kt—B 1, which here would be a mistake, because of 16. Q—Kt 5 ! etc. But from now on this Queen's move can be met by ....R—R 2 !

16. Kt—K 2   Kt—B 1
17. P—Q R 5   ......

Before breaking in, White weakens to a maximum the dark-coloured squares of Black's position ; the final section of the game will illustrate the usefulness of this procedure.

17. ......   P—Q Kt 4
18. P—K Kt 3 !   ......

In connection with the next two moves, a prophylactic manœuvre, by which White prevents once for all any serious attempt by Black to obtain an attack against his King.

18. ......   R—R 1
19. K—Kt 2   K—Kt 1
20. R—R 1   K—B 2

The King is no better here than at K R 2. But as Black is not yet in a mood to resign he has willy-nilly to move something . . .

21. Kt—B 4   R—K Kt 1
22. P—Kt 3   ......

After this, White's strategical scheme becomes quite obvious—there is no more defence against P—Q B 4 in connection with the opening of the Q Kt's or Q B's file.

22. ......   Kt—R 2
23. P—B 4   B—Q 2
24. Q R—Q B 1   B—K B 1
25. B—K 2 !   ......

Freeing the square Q 3 for the Knight, and at the same time preventing the advance of Black's K Kt's Pawn—for instance, 25.

....P—K Kt 4 ? ; 26. R P × P, Kt × P ; 27. Kt × Kt ch, P × Kt (or R × Kt ; 28. Kt—R 3 followed by B—R 5 ch and wins) ; 28. B—R 5 ch, K—Kt 2 ; 29. Kt × K P ch, B × Kt ; 30. Q × Kt P ch, followed by mate.

25. ......   Kt—B 1
26. P × Q P   ......

It does not happen often that a game is strategically decided much before the first capture, which here signifies not the beginning, but practically the end of the fight.

26. ......   B P × P

Or 26. ....Kt × B ; 27. P × P ch, B × P ; 28. Kt × B, K × Kt ; 29. R × P and wins.

27. B × B   . . ...

The Bishop has done more than his duty and can now quietly disappear.

27. ......   Kt × B
28. R—B 5   Kt—Q R 2
29. Kt—Q 3   K—Kt 2

As a consequence of White's 18th-20th moves, the rejoinder ....P—Kt 4 would obviously be entirely in his favour.

30. K R—Q B 1   R—B 1
31. R × R   B × R
32. Q—B 3   ......

All the dark squares in Black's camp are as many open wounds. No wonder that he decides to try the following desperate diversion.

32. ......   K—R 2
33. Q—B 5   R—Kt 2
34. Q—Kt 6 !   ......

All very simple, but with deadly effect. The Knight, after having been brought to Q B 5, will undertake the execution.

34.	Q—K 2
35. Kt—B 5	P—K Kt 4

At last ! But as the following convincingly proves, this attempt is now perfectly harmless.

36. P × P	P × P
37. Kt—K 1 !	......

In order to meet 37. ....P—B 5 by 38. B—Kt 4 ! and 37. .... P—Kt 5 by 38. Kt—Q 3 followed by Kt—B 4.

37.	Kt—Kt 3
38. Kt (K 1)—Q 3	P—B 5
39. R—R 1 ch	K—Kt 1
40. B—Kt 4	P × P
41. P × P	......

The agglomeration of forces on the K Kt's file is rather picturesque. Instead of the following "sacrifice," Black could as well resign.

41.	Kt—R 5 ch
42. P × Kt	P × P
43. Kt—B 2	R—B 2
44. Kt × K P	K—R 2
45. Q—Q 6	Resigns.

A strangulation game à la Rubinstein or Dr. Tarrasch of the early days.

GAME 58

RUY LOPEZ

Folkestone Team Tournament, July, 1933.

White : L. STEINER

1. P—K 4	P—K 4
2. Kt—K B 3	Kt—Q B 3
3. B—Kt 5	P—Q R 3
4. B—R 4	P—Q 3
5. P—B 3	B—Q 2
6. P—Q 4	Kt—K B 3
7. Q—K 2	B—K 2
8. Castles	Castles

Threatening now 9. .... Kt × Q P.

9. B—Kt 3	Q—K 1

Right or wrong, this move is my invention, one of the ideas of which is to exert a frontal pressure on the K's file after ....B—Q 1. Before it gets called by the name of a particularly hospitable city or of a particularly generous patron of chess (as happened, for instance, with the "Kecskemet" move ....B—K 1) I suggest calling it the "Timbuktu" variation. At least this will be the author's choice.

10. Q Kt—Q 2	K—R 1 !

Black does not play yet 10. .... B—Q 1, as there is still a hope of utilising this piece in a more active way. With the move in the text he prepares eventually ....Kt—K Kt 1, followed by ....B—K B 3 or ....P—K B 3, etc.

11. P × P	......

Not 11. Kt—B 4, because of 11. ....P × P ; 12. P × P, P—Q 4, etc. But comparatively better is the simplifying variation 11. R—K 1, aiming at Kt—B 1—Kt 3, etc.

11.	P × P
12. Kt—B 4	B—Q B 4
13. P—Q R 4	......

Interesting enough, this normallooking move creates—as will be shown in the course of the game—a slight weakness at Q Kt 3. Preferable was 13. B—B 2 (threatening to gain space by means of 14. P—Q Kt 4, etc.), P—Q R 4 ; 14. B—K 3, etc., with about even prospects.

13.	P—Q R 4

Prophylactic. White's B—B 2 must not be accompanied by the expansion threat P—Q Kt 4 !

14. B—Kt 5   ......

A rather superficial developing move. Instead, 14. B—K 3 was still preferable.

14. ......   Kt—K R 4 !

With this energetic reply (instead of the tame 14. ....Kt—K Kt 1, probably expected by White), Black obtains a solid initiative. White's comparatively best reply was now 15. K Kt × P, after which an end-game would be reached with better prospects for Black :—15. ....Kt × Kt ; 16. Q × Kt (not 16. Kt × Kt because of 16. ....Q × Kt followed by 17. ....P—K B 3, with the win of a piece), Kt × Kt ; 17. B × Kt—and now *not* 17. ....Q × K P (as suggested by the annotators), but 17. ....P—K B 3 ! ; 18. Q × Q, K R × Q ; 19. B—K 3, B × B ; 20. P × B, R × P—with unpleasantness for White ; if, for instance, 21. B—Q 5, then R × K P ; 22. B × Kt P, R—Q Kt 1 ; 23. K R—Q 1, B—K 1 etc., with a clear advantage.

In view of these rather sad prospects it is not altogether surprising that Steiner chose a risky counter-demonstration, the consequences of which were by no means easy to calculate.

15. Kt—K R 4   Kt—B 5
16. Q—B 3   ......

If 16. B × Kt, P × B ; 17. Q—R 5, Black would have had the good reply 17. ....P—K B 4 !

16. ......   P—B 3 !

This is the move which probably was underestimated by White ; after the following forced exchange, the Knight at R 4 will be exposed to attacks and the domination by Black of his K 4 will soon prove decisive.

17. B × Kt   P × B
18. Kt—B 5   P—K Kt 3 !

Wins an important *tempo* in comparison with the immediate 18. ....P—K Kt 4.

19. Kt—R 6   P—K Kt 4
20. P—K Kt 4   ......

Black threatened 20. ....Q—Kt 3 ; 21. Kt—Kt 4, P—R 4 and also—as it happens in the game—20. ....B—K 3, etc.

20. ......   B—K 3

Planning 21. ....B × Kt ; 22. B × B, Kt—K 4 ; 23. Q—K 2, P—B 6.

21. Kt—Q 2   Kt—K 4
22. Q—R 3   Q R—Q 1
23. B × B   ......

If this Bishop could have been protected by the Q R's Pawn (compare the note to the 13th move of White), White would still have temporary defence in 23. Q R—Q 1. But now this move would simply be answered by 23. ....R × Kt, etc.

23. ......   Q × B
24. Kt—Kt 1   ......

If 24. Q R—Q 1, then 24. ....R—Q 6, followed by 25. ....K R—Q 1 would win a piece.

24. ......   R—Q 6
25. Q—R 5   ......

Position after White's 25th move.

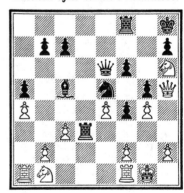

It is almost unbelievable that a position like this could occur in a modern master-game after 25 moves of a Ruy Lopez !

26. ......   Kt—B 6 ch

If now 27. K—R 1, then 27. .... Q × K P ; 28. Kt—B 7 ch, R × Kt ; 29. Q × R, Kt—R 5 disc. ch ; 30. P—K B 3 ; 31. Q × P ch, followed by mate in two.
Resigns.

GAME 59

QUEEN'S GAMBIT DECLINED
(ORTHODOX DEFENCE)

Paris, October, 1933.

Black : J. ZUKIERMAN

1. P—Q 4	P—Q 4
2. P—Q B 4	P—K 3
3. Kt—Q B 3	Kt—K B 3
4. B—Kt 5	B—K 2
5. P—K 3	Q Kt—Q 2

Nowadays (1939) 5. ....P— K R 3 is the fashion.

| 6. Kt—B 3 | Castles |
| 7. R—B 1 | P—Q Kt 3 |

This old-fashioned fianchetto defence cannot be considered quite satisfactory as Black will not be able to avoid some Pawn weaknesses in the centre.

| 8. P × P | P × P |
| 9. B—Kt 5 | ...... |

The most logical way to exploit the slight weakness of Black's Queen's side. Instead, a "play for the attack" by posting this Bishop on the diagonal Q Kt 1—K R 7, would be quite out of place as Black's King position is for the moment perfectly safe.

9.	B—Kt 2
10. Castles	P—Q R 3
11. B—Q R 4	P—B 4 ?

This at first sight logical move finds here a decisive refutation. But also after the more cautious 11. ....R—B 1 and 12. B—Kt 3 ! etc., Black's position would remain unsatisfactory.

12. K B × Kt !   ......

Much more exact than 12. P × P, Kt × P, etc., with a playable game for Black, as it happened in a game Capablanca-Teichmann in 1913. If now 12. ....Q × B, then 13. P × P, P × P ; 14. Kt—Q R 4 ! with a decisive position advantage.

12.	Kt × B
13. B × B	Q × B
14. P × P	Q × B P

In order not to lose a Pawn immediately, Black is forced to expose his Queen dangerously—and this circumstance, added to the most unfortunate position of his Bishop, will enable White to discover without much difficulty the winning procedure.

15. Kt—Q 4   ......

Threatening 16. Q Kt—Kt 5, followed by 17. R—B 7, etc.

| 15. ...... | Q R—B 1 |
| 16. Kt—B 5 | K—R 1 ! |

A defence against the threat 17. Kt × Q P and at the same time a pitfall : namely, if 17. Kt × Kt P— hoping to win a Pawn after 17. .... K × Kt ; 18. Q—Kt 4 ch, etc.— then, 17. ....P—Q 5 ! ; 18. P × P, Q—K Kt 4, or 18. Q × P, Q × Q ; 19. P × Q, R—K Kt 1, etc., to Black's advantage.

17. Kt—K 2 !   ......

In order to force the exchange of Queens at Q 4 without alteration of the Pawn constellation. It is noteworthy how helpless Black's position will be in the following end-game !

17.	......	Q—Kt 5
18.	Q—Q 4	Q × Q
19.	Kt (K 2) × Q	R × R

Or 19. ....Kt—B 4 ; 20. Kt—Q 6, R—Q Kt 1 ; 21. P—Q Kt 4, etc. ±

| 20. | R × R | Kt—B 4 |

Instead 20. ....R—B 1 ? ; 21. R × R ch followed by 22. Kt—Q 6 would have lost a piece immediately.

| 21. | Kt—Q 6 | B—R 1 |

Again forced, as can easily be seen.

| 22. | P—Q Kt 4 | Kt—Q 6 |
| 23. | R—B 7 | ...... |

Of course not 23. Kt × B P ch, K—Kt 1, etc. ∓

| 23. | ...... | K—Kt 1 |

Position after Black's 23rd move.

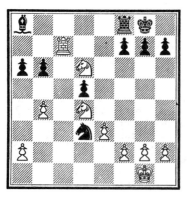

| 24. Kt—B 8 ! | ...... |

After 24. P—Q R 3, Black could easily have saved his Bishop by playing 24. ....Kt—K 4 followed by ....Kt—B 5 after which a long resistance would be possible. With the text-move, White starts an attack against the unfortunate Bishop which is obviously unable to escape from its fate.

| 24. | ...... | Kt × Kt P |
| 25. | Kt × P | ...... |

Threatening 25. R—R 7, etc.

| 25. | ...... | R—Kt 1 |
| 26. | Kt—Q 7 | ...... |

But not 26. R—R 7, B—Kt 2 ; 27. Kt—Q 7, R—Q B 1 followed by 28. ....B—B 3 saving the piece.

26.	......	R—Q 1
27.	P—Q R 3	Kt—Q 6
28.	R—R 7	R—Q B 1
29.	K—B 1	......

After this 30'. Kt—Kt 6 etc., is unavoidable.

Resigns.

GAME 60

RUY LOPEZ

Paris Tournament, October, 1933.

White : E. ZNOSKO-BOROVSKY

1.	P—K 4	P—K 4
2.	Kt—K B 3	Kt—Q B 3
3.	B—Kt 5	P—Q R 3
4.	B—R 4	Kt—B 3
5.	Castles	P—Q 3

Safer is first 5. ....B—K 2, as after the text-move White, according to the latest investigation, can obtain an advantage by continuing 6. B × Kt ch, P × B ; 7. P—Q 4, Kt × K P ; 8. R—K 1, P—

K B 4 ; 9. P × P, P—Q 4 ; 10. Kt—
Q 4, P—B 4 ; 11. Kt—K 2 followed
by Kt—K B 4, etc.

6.	P—Q B 3	B—Q 2
7.	R—K 1	B—K 2
8.	P—Q 4	Castles
9.	Q Kt—Q 2	B—K 1

This original move (the idea of
which is to keep the central position
intact by means of ....Kt—Q 2
and utilise—after P—K B 3—the
Q's Bishop on diagonal K 1—K R 4)
was introduced by me (after the
moves 9. ....K—R 1 ; 10. P—
K R 3) in my game against L.
Steiner in Kecskemet, 1927.

Afterwards it was baptised (not
by me) the Kecskemet Variation.
This denomination is illogical, inasmuch as ....B—K 1 is the key-
move not of a "variation" but of a
system !

The present game presents some
theoretical interest as it shows that
White, even if he is playing only for
a draw, cannot obtain an absolute
equality by liquidating the tension
in the centre after the move in text.

10.	B × Kt	B × B
11.	P × P	P × P
12.	Kt × P	B × P
13.	Kt × B	Q × Q !

A mistake would be 13. .... Kt ×
Kt, because of 14. Kt—Q 7 ! etc.

14. Kt × Kt ch   ......

After 14. R × Q, Kt × Kt, there
would be still enough material left
for complicating the fight.   After
the exchange of the Knights White
expect to reach a "dead draw"
position (14. ....B × Kt ; 15. R ×
Q, B × Kt ; 16. B—K 3, etc.).
But . . .

14. ......   P × Kt !

The only way—and an absolutely
safe one—to play "for the win."

15. R × Q   P × Kt

Position after Black's 15th move.

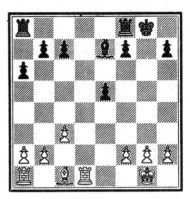

The end-game position thus
reached is by no means as easy to
conduct—especially for the first
player—as it looks.   Black's plan
of campaign—which will prove a
complete success—is divided into
the following parts :—

(1) Exchange of one pair of
    rooks.
(2) Bringing the King to K 3
    where he will be protected
    from a frontal attack by the
    King's Pawn and be used to
    prevent the entrance of the
    remaining White Rook at
    Black's Q 2.
(3) By operating with the Rook
    on the open K Kt's file and
    advancing the K R's Pawn,
    force the opening of the
    K R's file.
(4) After this the White King—
    and eventually also the
    Bishop—will be kept busy
    in order to prevent the
    intrusion of the Black Rook
    at White's K R 1 or 2.
(5) In the meantime Black, by
    advancing his Q R's and
    Q Kt's Pawns will sooner or
    later succeed in opening one
    file on the Queen's side. And
(6) as at that moment the White
    King will still be on the

other wing, the first player will not dispose of sufficient forces to prevent the final intrusion of the enemy's Rook on his first or second rank.

Granted that if White had, from the beginning, realised that there actually existed a danger of losing this end-game, he probably would by extremely careful defence have saved it. But as it happened, Black played with a definite plan, and White only with the conviction that the game must be a draw. And the result was a very instructive series of typical stratagems much more useful for inexperienced players than the so-called "brilliancies."

16. B—R 6   . . . . . .

Certainly not an error but a proof that White has not grasped as yet the spirit of the position. Otherwise he would not have been anxious to "force" the exchange of one pair of Rooks which, as mentioned, is quite welcome to the opponent.

16. . . . . . .   K R—Q 1
17. K—B 1   . . . . . .

A more aggressive line starting by 17. P—K Kt 4 would perhaps be advisable. But Black would also in this case maintain opportunities for complicating matters after 17. . . . .P—K B 3, followed by K—B 2 —K 3, etc.

17. . . . . . .   P—K B 4
18. R × R ch   R × R
19. P—K Kt 3   . . . . . .

19. . . . .P—B 5 was a serious threat.

19. . . . . . .   K—B 2
20. B—K 3   P—K R 4
21. K—K 2   K—K 3
22. R—Q 1   R—K Kt 1 !

If now 23. P—K R 4, then 23. . . . .R—Kt 5 with the strong threat 24. P—B 5. White is therefore practically forced to allow the opening of the K R file.

23. P—K B 3   P—R 5
24. B—B 2   P × P
25. P × P   R—K R 1
26. B—Kt 1   B—Q 3
27. K—B 1   . . . . . .

In order to meet 27. . . . .P—K 5 by 28. P × P, P × P ; 29. K—Kt 2, etc.

27. . . . . . .   R—K Kt 1
28. B—B 2   P—Q Kt 4 !

Now Black shows his cards. In the event of White leaving his Pawn position on the Queen's side intact, the attacking plan would be . . . . P—Q B 4—B 5 followed by P—Q R 4 and P—Q Kt 5 ; his next Pawn move shortens the procedure.

29. P—Q Kt 3 ?   P—R 4
30. K—Kt 2   P—R 5
31. R—Q 2   . . . . . .

In case of 31. P—Q Kt 4, the intention was 31. . . . .R—Q B 1 ; 32. B—B 5, R—Q R 1 ! followed by R—R 3,—Q B 3, etc.∓

31. . . . . . .   P × P
32. P × P   R—Q R 1

Thus Black has reached the position he aimed at when starting this end-game. His positional advantage from now on will prove sufficient for the victory, especially as he always can succeed in forcing the advance of his King by pinning the White Rook through the defence of one of the weak Pawns.

33. P—Q B 4   . . . . . .

Practically the only attempt, as 33. P—Q Kt 4, for instance, would

prove immediately fatal after 33.
....R—R 8 ; 34. R—Q 3, R—R 6,
etc.

33. ......   R—R 6 !

The winning course.

34. P—B 5	B—K 2
35. R—Kt 2	P—Kt 5
36. P—Kt 4	......

One of the last resources: he tries
to create a passed Pawn which *may*
become a force in case of the exchange of the Bishops. But Black
does not need to hurry with that
exchange.

36.	P—B 5
37. K—B 1	R—R 8 ch
38. K—K 2	R—Q B 8

With the main object 39. ....
R—B 6 definitely pinning all
enemy's pieces. White's next
Rook's expedition is therefore
merely desperation.

39. R—R 2	R—B 6
40. R—R 7	K—Q 2
41. R—Kt 7	R × Kt P
42. R—Kt 8	R—Kt 7 ch
43. K—B 1	P—Kt 6
44. K—Kt 1	K—B 3
45. K—B 1	K—Q 4

Of course not 45. .... B × P ? ;
46. B × B, K × B ; 47. P—K Kt 5,
etc., with drawing chances. But a
slightly quicker procedure was 45.
....P—K 5 ! ; 46. P × P, P—B 6,
etc.

46. R—Kt 7	P—K 5 !
47. P × P ch	K × P
48. R × B P	K—B 6
49. R × B	R × B ch
50. K—K 1	P—Kt 7
51. R—Q Kt 7	R—Q B 7
52. P—B 6 !	......

A nice final joke : 52. ....R—
B 8 ch ; 53. K—Q 2, P—Kt 8
(Queens) ; 54. R × Q, R × R ; 55.

P—B 7, etc. But Black had exactly
calculated that his other passed
Pawn would force the win !

52.	K—Kt 6 !
53. P—B 7	P—B 6
54. K—Q 1	R × P
55. R × P	P—B 7
Resigns.	

GAME 61

QUEEN'S GAMBIT DECLINED
(SLAV DEFENCE)

Second Match - Game, Baden-
Baden, April, 1934.

Black : E. BOGOLJUBOW

1. P—Q 4	Kt—K B 3
2. P—Q B 4	P—Q B 3
3. Kt—Q B 3	P—Q 4
4. P—K 3	P—K 3
5. B—Q 3	Q Kt—Q 2
6. Kt—B 3	P × P
7. B × B P	P—Q Kt 4
8. B—Q 3	P—Q R 3
9. Castles	......

Nowadays the leading masters
consider that 9. P—K 4, P—B 4 ;
10. P—K 5, P × Q P ; 11. Kt × Kt P,
Kt × K P ; 12. Kt × Kt, P × Kt ; 13.
Q—B 3 !, etc., is decidedly advantageous for White. But in 1934 the
13th move of White in this variation
had not yet been sufficiently considered and the Meran variations
shares stood pretty high. Therefore
the quiet move in text.

| 9. ...... | P—B 4 |
| 10. P—Q R 4 | ...... |

10. Q—K 2 played experimen-
tally instead of this in the games
Sämisch-Capablanca (Moscow,1925)
and Dr. Vidmar-Bogoljubow (Bled,
1931) brought to the first players—
at least in the opening stages—only
disappointment.

10.	P—Kt 5
11. Kt—K 4	B—Kt 2
12. Q Kt—Q 2	......

After his tame 9th move White has hardly any other way to complicate matters without disadvantage than this attempt to blockade the opponent's Q's side.

12.	B—K 2

Black does not need to prevent the opponent's next move as he is sufficiently developed to start almost immediately a counter-action in the centre.

13. P—R 5	Castles
14. Kt—B 4	Q—B 2
15. Q—K 2	Kt—Kt 5

Black has obtained a fairly good position, but from now on begins to over-estimate his chances. Instead of the adventurous text-move, which finally leads to the win of a Pawn but allows the intrusion of the White Knight at Kt 6, with a powerful effect, he would have done better to simplify matters—for instance, by means of 15. .... B—K 5.

16. P—K 4 !	......

A surprise for Black who most likely expected only the half-suicidal 16. P—K Kt 3....

16.	P × P
17. P—K R 3	K Kt—K 4

To 17. ....K Kt—B 3 White would have answered 18. B—Kt 5, Kt—B 4 ; 19. Kt—Kt 6, Q R—Q 1 ; 20. Q R—B 1, Q—Kt 1 (these moves are recommended by Bogoljubow in the match book as the best ones for Black) and now not 21. P—K 5 ? (Bogoljubow) but 21. B × Kt !, P × B ; 22. R—B 4, P—K 4 ; 23. Kt—K R 4, etc., with an ample positional compensation for the minus Pawn.

18. K Kt × Kt	Kt × Kt
19. B—B 4	B—Q 3
20. B × Kt	B × B
21. Kt—Kt 6	......

The point of the sacrificial combination initiated by the 16th move. From now on the Knight will paralyse the whole Black's Queen's side.

21.	R—R 2

In case of 21. ....Q R—Q 1 White would not have taken the Q R's Pawn at once, but would have first prevented the eventual advance of the Q's Pawn by playing 21. K R—Q 1 ! with a distinct positional advantage.

22. Q R—B 1	Q—Q 3

Or 22. ....Q—Q 1 ; 23. Q—Q 2 !, B—Q 3 ; 24. P—B 4, etc. ±

23. R—B 4	P—B 4 ?

The opening of the K's file leads, owing to Black's multiple Pawn weaknesses, to a rapid catastrophe. But also the quieter 23. ....B—B 5 recommended by Bogoljubow is not satisfactory, as after 24. K R —Q 1, P—K 4 ; 25. Q—K 1, etc., White would have regained the Pawn, still maintaining a strong pressure.

24. P × P	P × P
25. K R—K 1 !	......

The threat to change Queens at K 6 with an easily-won end-game now makes Black desperate, and he tries to elaborate a complicated attacking combination, which, however, is bound to fail because of the uselessness of his Q's Rook.

25.	Q—Kt 3
26. P—B 3	......

Position after White's 26th move.

26. ......   R—K 1

In the event of Bishop's moves Bogoljubow gives the following variations :

I. 26. ....B—Kt 6 ; 27. Q—K 6 ch, K—R 1 ; 28. Q × Q, P × Q ; 29. R—K 6, R—Q 1 ; 30. R × K Kt P, P—B 5 ; 31. R—K 6.

II. 26. ....B—B 5 ; 27. R × Q P, Q—Kt 6 ; 28. B—B 4 ch, K—R 1 ; 29. Q—K 7—with a win for White in both eventualities.

27. P—B 4   Q—Kt 6
28. P × B   R × P
29. R—B 8 ch ! ......

The refutation.

29. ......   K—B 2
30. Q—R 5 ch   ......

The alternative 30. R—B 7 ch was not quite as elegant, but slightly more rapid ; for instance, 30. .... K—Kt 3 ; 31. R × Kt P ch ! or 30. ....K—Kt 1 ; 31. B—B 4 ch, K—R 1 ; 32. R—B 8 ch, followed by 33. Q × R, etc.

30. ......   P—K Kt 3
31. Q × R P ch K—B 3
32. R—B 8 ch   K—Kt 4
33. P—R 4 ch   K—B 5
34. Q—R 6 ch   P—Kt 4

35. R × P ch ! R × R
36. Q—Q 6 ch   K—Kt 5
37. B × R ch and mate in three.

GAME 62

QUEEN'S GAMBIT DECLINED (SLAV DEFENCE)

Fourth Match-Game, Villingen, April, 1934.

Black : E. BOGOLJUBOW

1. P—Q 4   P—Q 4
2. P—Q B 4   P—Q B 3
3. Kt—Q B 3   Kt—B 3
4. P—K 3   P—K 3
5. B—Q 3   Q Kt—Q 2
6. P—B 4   ......

Not a happy opening idea, as it enables Black to undertake quickly a successful action in the centre. Still, as the game actually developed, White had at one moment the opportunity to equalise without much difficulty.

6. ......   P × P

This, in connection with the next four moves, is a natural and good method of development.

7. B × B P   P—Q Kt 4
8. B—Q 3   B—Kt 2
9. Kt—B 3   P—Q R 3
10. P—Q R 4   ......

The idea of advancing this Pawn to Q R 5—analogous to the previous game—is, in this position, much too elaborate. The logical course was 10. Castles, P—Q B 4 ; 11. P—B 5, etc.

10. ......   P—Kt 5
11. Kt—K 2   P—B 4
12. Castles   B—K 2
13. P—R 5 ?   ......

And even now 13. P—B 5, P×P ;
14. B×P, Castles ; 15. Kt—Kt 3
would have led to a colourful game
with chances for both sides. After
the move made, White can only
hope, by careful play, to equalise.

13. ......   Castles
14. Kt—Kt 3   P—Kt 3 !

It was now vital to prevent 15.
P—B 5.

15. Q—K 2   P×P
16. P×P   ......

The isolation of the central Pawn
is certainly a bold decision, but—as
the course of the game shows—
more apt to equalise the chances
than the alternative 16. Kt×P,
Kt—B 4, etc.

16. ......   Kt—Kt 1

Threatening to win a Pawn with
impunity by 17. ....Kt—B 3.

17. Kt—K 5 !   ......

If 17. P—B 5 !? Black would
hardly accept the piece sacrifice, as
after 17. ....K P×P ; 18. B×B P,
P×B ; 19. Kt×P White's threats
would become too strong ; but by
answering 17. ....B×Kt ; 18.
Q×B, Q×P ch ; 19. K—R 1,
Q Kt—Q 2 with the threat 20. ....
Kt—K 4 Black would obtain the
upper hand. After the text-move
he would, on the contrary, get in
great trouble by playing 17. ....
Q×Q P ch ; 18. B—K 3 followed by
19. Kt—Q B 4 or K R—Q 1, etc.±

17. ......   Kt—B 3 !

Doubtless the right answer,
which definitely annihilates White's
attacking hopes. The following exchange is practically forced.

18. Kt×Kt   B×Kt
19. B—B 4 ?   ......

But this is decidedly too optimistic, as after Black's simple defensive next move White will have no
compensation for the permanent
weakness of his central position.
Good enough for a draw was 19.
B×R P—which was, by the way,
the only logical consequence of the
previous Knight's manœuvre. If
in that case 19. ....R×B ; 20.
Q×R, Q×P ch ; 21. K—R 1,
Q—Q 4, then 22. Q—K 2, B—Kt 4 ;
23. Q—B 3, B×R ; 24. Q×Q,
Kt×Q ; 25. Kt×B ; and White,
to say the least, has certainly
nothing to fear. Bogoljubow in
the match-book indicates two other
moves, which, in my belief, are
equally harmless. They are (a)
19. ....R—R 2, which can be
answered by 20. R—Q 1, Q—R 1 ;
21. B—Kt 5 ; (b) 19. ....Kt—Kt 5,
after which White would even
obtain a sort of counter-attack by
means of 20. Q×Kt, R×B (or
Q×P ch ; 21. K—R 1, R×B ; 22.
Q—K 2, followed by 23. B—K 3,
etc.) ; 21. P—B 5 ! etc.

19. ......   B—Kt 2
20. B—K 3   Q—Q 3

Dr. Lasker, in his excellent booklet about this match, claims (in my
opinion quite correctly) that Black
has already a strategically won position ; besides he also tries to prove
that *a forced win* could be obtained
here by means of 20. ....Kt—Q 4,
and gives with that line of play
variations going as far as the 35th
move ! But, strangely enough, in
doing so he does not take in consideration the simple move that I
would certainly have made in
answer to 20. ....Kt—Q 4. This
move is 21. Kt—K 4, eventually
followed by Kt—B 5, etc. And it
is more than probable that Bogoljubow did not select the otherwise
natural 20. .... Kt—Q 4 because
he did not want to permit the
unhappily placed White Knight to
take an active part in the battle.

21. Q R—Q 1	K R—K 1
22. P—Kt 3	.....

As both White's Q's Bishop and Knight have no future, he wants at least to strengthen the position of his other Bishop; moreover, the text-move, as will be seen, facilitates the protection of the Q R's Pawn.

22.	B—K B 1
23. R—Q 3	.....

Owing to his numerous weaknesses White is reduced to a complete passivity. Luckily for him, Black does not prove to be equal to the situation either strategically or tactically.

23.	Q—B 2
24. Q—R 2	B—Q 3
25. B—Q 2	Q—B 3

The pressure against White's K Kt 2 is extremely painful for the first player—and would become even more so if Black had not deliberately removed his Queen from this dominating position (see 29th move)....

26. B—K 1	Q R—Q 1
27. R—Q 2	B—K 2

A strange move. Why not the obvious 27. ....B—Kt 1 followed by 28. ....B—R 2 ?

28. Q—Kt 2	R—Q 2
29. R—Q B 2	.....

"A tactical mistake," says Dr. Lasker. But in this desperate position I would be curious to see the move which by subsequent analysis would not appear a "tactical mistake" ! In other words, White was lost whatever he played.

29.	Q—Q 3 ?

As White was not threatening anything there was no reason to delay matters. 29. ....Kt—Kt 5 ! would have won at least a Pawn by a still dominating position.

This game—more than any other —proves how useless from the sporting point of view was the arrangement of this second match, and at the same time explains my indifferent play on a number of occasions. I felt sure that Bogoljubow was no longer able to take advantage of the opportunities my play might present to him, and— very unfortunately for the general artistic value of the present match— the score 7 to 1 in my favour after the 22nd game, fully justified my sanguine outlook.

30. Kt—K 2	.....

At last the poor Knight begins to contribute to the defence; but White's prospects still remain pretty dark.

30.	Kt—Q 4
31. Q—B 1	B—Q 1
32. B—Kt 3	Q—K 2

Bogoljubow claims—and probably he is right—that 32. ....Q— B 3 would have led to favourable complications for Black; but also the simple 32. ....P—K B 4 was good enough. On the other hand, the Queen's manœuvre, inaugurated by the text-move, only leads to the exchange of Queens and thus relieves White from the worry about his K Kt 2. An unhappy strategy !

33. R—R 2	Q—B 3
34. Q—Q 2	Q—B 4
35. B—Q 3	Q—B 3
36. B—B 4	B—K 2
37. Q—Q 3	R—K B 1
38. B—K 1	Q—B 4
39. Q—Q 2	Q—K 5

At last deciding to simplify matters, and thus implicitly admitting that in the last 20 moves absolutely nothing has been achieved.

40. B—Q 3	Q—K 6 ch
41. B—B 2	Q×Q
42. R×Q	.....

The position thus reached is naturally still in Black's favour. But to win, it would require the end-game art of a Lasker or a Capablanca of the old days, even considering the fact that the game was adjourned here. But if the game is not easy to win for Black it is difficult to imagine how he can lose it.

42.	R—Q B 1
43. B—B 4	K—Kt 2
44. P—K Kt 3	......

The possibility of this defensive move is the result of the disappearance of the Queens, as before that a further weakening of the diagonal K R 1—Q R 8 would have proved rapidly fatal.

44.	R (B 1)—Q 1
45. R—B 1	P—K R 3

The beginning of a dangerous plot—against his own position. Instead 45. ....Kt—B 6 ! would still keep the positional advantage.

46. B—Q 3	P—B 4
47. R (Q 2)—B 2	P—Kt 4 ?

As the surprising answer shows, this advance leads at best only to equality. But 47. ....K—B 2, suggested afterwards by Bogoljubow, would not prove effective, as White could in that case play, for instance, 48. K—B 1 eventually followed by Kt—Kt 1—B 3—K 5, etc.

48. P—Kt 4 !   ......

Black could not well accept the Pawn's sacrifice thus offered—for instance 48. ....P×Kt P ; 49. P—B 5 !, K—B 2 ; 50. P×P ch, K×P ; 51. Kt—Kt 3 followed by 52. R—K 1 ch, etc.± But he could—and should—play 48. ....P×B P ; 49. P× B P, K—B 2, etc., with about a balanced position.

48. ......   Kt×B P ?

This exchange of his best-posted piece against the cripple at K R 2 definitely spoils Black's position. It is interesting to observe from now on the joyous revival of all White's pieces, which for hours were hardly able to move.

49. Kt×Kt	P×Kt
50. P×P	P—K 4

In the vain hope that White will be satisfied with Bishops of different colours after 51. P×P followed by 52. P—B 6 ch, etc.

51. R—K 1 !   P×P

Not foreseeing the following pretty combination. His only chance of salvation was 51. .... B—K B 3, which White would have answered by 52. R—B 4 !, P×P ; 53. R×Kt P, etc., with much the better prospects.

Position after Black's 51st move.

52. R × B ch !　　......

The unexpected point of this at first sight harmless transaction is the inevitable promotion of the K B's Pawn. As it is easy to see, Black has from now on an absolutely fixed line of play.

| 52. ...... | R × R |
| 53. B—R 4 | K—B 2 |

Otherwise 54. P—B 6 ch.

54. B × R	K × B
55. R—B 7 ch	R—Q 2
56. P—B 6 ch	K—K 1
57. B—Kt 6 ch !	......

More exact than 57. P—B 7 ch, R × P ; 58. B—Kt 6, B—Q 4, etc.

57.	K—Q 1
58. P—B 7	K × R
59. P—B 8 = Q	P—B 6
60. Q × Kt P	R—Q 3
61. B—Q 3	Resigns.

GAME 63

BENONI'S DEFENCE

Ninth Match-Game, Pforzheim, April, 1934.

White : E. BOGOLJUBOW

1. P—Q 4　　P—Q B 4

I consider the choice of this move (which in consequence of my success in the actual game became for a time a sort of fashion) as one of my chess sins. Because if a champion, being human, cannot sometimes help adopting inferior opening moves, he must at least avoid those which he himself considers as not quite satisfactory.

2. P—Q 5	P—K 4
3. P—K 4	P—Q 3
4. P—K B 4	......

This decidedly premature rejoinder can only be explained by the fact that Bogoljubow had again missed a win in the previous game, and was particularly anxious to make a better show in this one. A natural and good line is, instead, 4. Kt—Q B 3 and in case of 4. .... P—Q R 3 ; 5. P—Q R 4 followed by Kt—K B 3—Q 2—Q B 4, etc., which would secure to White the initiative for a long time.

| 4. ...... | P × P |
| 5. B × P | Q—R 5 ch |

It was hardly worth while to provoke the weakening move P—K Kt 3 at the cost of a development *tempo*. The simple 5. .... Kt—K 2 followed by .... Kt—Kt 3, etc., would keep the control on K 4, with a fairly good game.

6. P—Kt 3　　......

The Pawn's sacrifice 6. B—Kt 3 would not be correct because 6. .... Q × P ch; 7. B—K 2, B—K B 4, etc.

| 6. ...... | Q—K 2 |
| 7. Kt—Q B 3 ? | ...... |

It was essential to prevent Black's following move by 7. Kt—K B 3! after which 7. .... Q × P ch, 8. K—B 2, etc., would be too risky ; Black would play instead 7. .... B—Kt 5 ; 8. Kt—Q B 3, P—Q R 3, followed by .... Q Kt—Q 2, etc., with about even chances.

7. ......　　P—K Kt 4 !

The strong position of his K's Bishop on the long diagonal secures Black, from now on, an easy, pleasant game.

8. B—K 3	Kt—Q 2
9. Kt—B 3	P—K R 3
10. Q—Q 2	......

Aimless would have been instead
10. Kt—Kt 5, K—Q 1 ! etc.

10.	K Kt—B 3
11. Castles (Q R)	Kt—Kt 5
12. B—K 2	......

Also 12. B—R 3—recommended
by Bogoljubow—Kt × B ; 13. Q ×
Kt, B—Kt 2, etc., would not have
relieved White of his troubles.

| 12. ...... | B—Kt 2 |
| 13. K R—B 1 | Kt × B |

It was certainly tempting to add
the advantage of the two Bishops
to that already acquired. But as
the Knight at Kt 5 was well posted
and White's Q's Bishop for the time
being was harmless, the immediate
13. ....P—Q R 3 was possibly
even more consequent.

14. Q × Kt	P—R 3
15. Kt—K Kt 1	P—Kt 4
16. Q R—K 1	B—Kt 2
17. Kt—Q 1	......

This Knight must be brought to
K B 5—the only strong point of
White's position.

| 17. ...... | Castles (Q R) |
| 18. B—Kt 4 | ...... |

As the Bishop has not many
prospects its exchange against the
dangerous black Knight can hardly
be criticised.

18.	K—Kt 1
19. B × Kt	R × B
20. Q—Q 2	......

Again the natural consequence of
the manœuvre started by his 17th
move.

| 20. ...... | P—K Kt 5 ! |

Immobilising White's King's
Knight and thus securing the important square K 4 for the Queen.

21. Kt—K 3	Q—K 4
22. P—B 3	P—K R 4
23. Kt—B 5	B—K B 3

Position after Black's 23rd move.

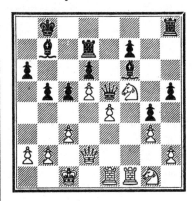

| 24. Q—B 4 ? | ...... |

The exchange of Queens transforms a difficult, but by no means
hopeless, position (White could,
for instance, try 24. K—Kt 1
as a preparation for 25. Kt—R 4)
into a lost one.

It is interesting that Bogoljubow
is rather prone to make this
mistake ; for instance, in the 11th
game of the same match, in
the position reached after Black's
34th move, namely :—

White (Bogoljubow) : *K* : K Kt 1,
Q : Q B 4, *RR* : Q 1 and Q 3,
Kt : K Kt 3, *PP* : Q R 4, K 3, K B 2,
K B 4, and K R 4. *Black* (Dr.
Alekhine) : *K* : K R 1, *Q* : K B 3,
RR : Q Kt 7 and K B 1, *B* : Q B 4,
PP : Q R 4, Q 3, K B 4, K Kt 3
and K R 4—instead of trying a
counter-attack, with an uncertain
result, by means of 35. Q—Q R 6,
he preferred to exchange Queens :
35. Q—Q B 3 ?, Q × Q ; 36. R × Q,
R—Q R 7 ; 37. R—B 4, R—Q Kt 1
—and had to resign after a few
more desperate moves.

About the same thing, if not in
quite such typical form, occurred in
the 5th and 22nd games of our first

match (see Part II). But also—strangely enough—my other match opponent, Dr. Euwe, has the same peculiar tendency to exchange Queens at inappropriate moments : compare, for instance, the 7th and 24th games of the 1935 match, the second match game and especially the third exhibition game of 1937.

I am mentioning these coincidences by no means in order to put undue blame on my opponents, but merely to remind the average amateur how particularly difficult the question of an opportune Queen's exchange is, and how much attention this question deserves. If even the leading exponents of our game are often inclined to fail rightly to appreciate their end-game chances, what, really, is to be expected from the "di minores" ?

| 24. ...... | Q × Q |
| 25. P × Q | R (Q 2)—Q 1 ! |

Threatening to dislodge the Knight at K B 5, which position has been weakened through the obstruction of the K B's file by a Pawn. Besides his other advantages Black has now also got the Pawn majority on the opposite wing to the White King. The game is strategically over.

| 26. P—B 4 | ...... |

This attempt to find another safe square (Q B 4) for the Knight will be refuted by Black's 27th move. But otherwise 26. ....B—B 1, etc., would rapidly prove fatal for White.

26.	P × P
27. Kt—K 3	P—B 6 !
28. P—Kt 3	B—Q 5
29. Kt—B 4	P—B 4 !

Bringing at last the second Bishop into activity, after which White might as well resign.

| 30. P—K 5 | P × P |

31. P × P	B × Q P
32. R × P	Q R—K B 1
33. R × R ch	R × R
34. P—K 6	R—K 1
35. P—K 7	Q B × Kt
36. P × B	B × Kt
37. R × B	R × P
38. P—K R 3	P × P
39. K—B 2	P—R 7
40. R—Kt 1 ch	R—Kt 2
41. R—K R 1	R—Kt 7 ch
42. K × P	R × P
43. K—Q 3	K—B 2
44. K—K 4	K—B 3
45. K—B 5	P—R 4
46. K—Kt 5	P—Q R 5
Resigns.	

GAME 64

RUY LOPEZ

Sixteenth Match-Game, Bayreuth, May, 1934.

Black : E. BOGOLJUBOW

1. P—K 4	P—K 4
2. Kt—K B 3	Kt—Q B 3
3. B—Kt 5	P—Q R 3
4. B—R 4	Kt—B 3
5. B × Kt	Q P × B

I believe Bogoljubow is right in stating that 5. ....Kt P × B is an even more convincing answer to the rather artificial fifth move of White. As a matter of fact, I chose in this game the exchange variation of the Lopez chiefly because, although playing with the White pieces, I did not cherish any particular ambitions ; as a consequence of the match arrangements I had spent the whole previous night in travelling by car from Munich to Bayreuth and felt hardly fit for intensive mental work.

| 6. Kt—Q B 3 | B—Q 3 |
| 7. P—Q 3 | P—B 4 |

8. P—K R 3	B—K 3
9. B—K 3	P—K R 3
10. P—Q R 4 !	......

If immediately 10. Kt—Q 2, then 10. ....P—Q Kt 4 ; 11. P—Q R 4, P—Q B 3, etc. But now White "threatens" to obtain an absolutely safe position by means of Kt—Q 2—B 4, etc.

10.	P—B 5 (?)

By opening the position in the centre at this particular moment Black only increases the activity of the opponent's pieces. A reasonable manœuvre, instead, would be 10. ....Kt—Q 2 followed by ....Kt—Kt 1—Q B 3, etc.

11. P—Q 4	P×P

If 11. ....B—Q Kt 5, then 12. P—Q 5.±

12. B×Q P	B—Q Kt 5
13. Castles	P—B 3 (?)

A strange move which weakens his Q Kt 3 without any necessity. He should, instead, castle and would probably obtain a draw after 14. P—K 5, B×Kt ; 15. B×B, Kt—Q 4 ; 16. Q—Q 2, etc.

14. P—K 5	Kt—Q 4

Now practically forced, as 14. ....B×Kt ; 15. P×Kt !, B×B ; 16. Kt×B, Q×P ; 17. Kt×B, P×Kt ; 18. Q—R 5 ch ! followed by 19. Q—Q B 5, etc., would have been decidedly to White's advantage.

15. Kt—K 4	Kt—B 5

A lesser evil was 15 ....Castles.

16. B—B 5 !	......

The logical exploitation of the weak dark-coloured squares of Black's position.

16.	B×B
17. Q×Q ch	R×Q
18. Kt×B	P—Q Kt 3 ?

A miscalculation. Necessary was 18. ....R—Q Kt 1, although after 19. Kt×B, Kt×Kt (P×Kt is not better) ; 20. P—R 5 ! (threatening both 21. R—R 4 and 21. Kt—Q 2, etc.) his position would remain anything but pleasant.

19. Kt—Kt 7 ?	......

Black's R's Pawn was by no means poisoned and its capture would prove rapidly decisive. For instance, 19. Kt×R P, B—B 1 ; 20. Kt—B 7 ch, K—Q 2 ; 21. Kt—R 8 (this is the move I overlooked in my calculations), Kt—Q 4 ; 22. P—R 5 (also 22. K R—Q 1 is good enough), P×P ; 23. R×P, B—Kt 2; 24. R—R 7, R—Q Kt 1 ; 25. R—K 1 !, P—Q B 4; 26. P—K 6 ch, and Black would obviously not succeed in capturing the adventurous Knight. After the timid text-move Black temporarily recovers.

19.	R—Q 2
20. Kt—Q 6 ch	K—K 2
21. Kt—Q 4	B—Q 4
22. P—K Kt 3 !	......

The value of this bold move—by making which White, after having missed the win at his 19th move, played only for a draw—has been completely misapprehended by the critics—Bogoljubow, Nimzowitsch, Dr. Lasker and others. They all claim that White, without any necessity, is taking chances and should now get into difficulties. In reality (a) *the defences of the K Kt's Pawn would prove unsatisfactory* as (I) 22. P—K B 3 would be answered by 22. ....P—K Kt 3 ! threatening both 23. ....P—Q B 4 and 23. ....P—K B 3 ; (II) after 22. Kt (Q 6)—B 5 ch, K—B 1 Black would again threaten 23. ....P—Q B 4, etc. ; (III) in the event of 22.

Kt (Q 4)—B 5 ch, Black would be perfectly entitled to play 22. .... K—K 3 ! ; 23. Kt × Kt P ch, K × K P and if 24. Kt (Q 6)—K 8 then simply 24. .... Kt × Kt P ! etc., with advantage. (b) *After the acceptance of the sacrifice by the opponent, White, even by an adequate defence, would have no trouble in obtaining a draw.*

22. ......   Kt × R P ch
23. K—R 2   Kt—Kt 4
24. P—B 4   Kt—K 5
25. Kt (Q 6)—B 5 ch   K—Q 1 ?

Playing for a counter-attack and obviously not taking into consideration the interesting 27th move of White. Necessary was 25. .... K—B 1, which would be answered by 26. Kt—K 3, K—Kt 1 ; 27. P—B 5, K—R 2 ; 28. P—K 6, etc., with an ample compensation for the minus Pawn.

26. Kt × Kt P   P—B 3
27. Q R—Q 1 !   ......

The *tempo* thus gained (27. .... R × Kt ? ; 28. Kt—K 6 ch) secures White a net, if not yet a decisive, advantage.

27. ......   K—B 1
28. Kt (Q 4)—K B 5   P × P

The alternative 28. .... R—K Kt 1 would also have left White with the better end-game chances : for instance, 29. Kt—R 5, P × P ; 30. P × P, R—K 1 ; 31. Kt—B 6 !, Kt × Kt ; 32. P × Kt, R—K 7 ch ; 33. K—R 3, and now either (A.) 33. .... B—K 3 ; 34. P—K Kt 4, B × Kt ; 35. P × B, or (B.) 33. .... B—Kt 7 ch ; 34. K—Kt 4, B × R ; 35. R × R, K × R ; 36. P—B 7, R—K 1 ; 37. P × R (Q) ch, K × Q ; 38. P—Q B 3 ! followed by Kt × R P, etc.— both to White's advantage.

29. P × P   R—Kt 1 ?

After the previous exchange this move is already a decisive mistake, instead of which 29. .... Kt—Kt 4 ; 30. R × B !, R × R (better than P × R ; 31. P—K 6 ±) ; 31. Kt—K 7 ch, K—Q 2 ; 32. Kt × R, P × Kt ; 33. R—B 6, R—K Kt 1, etc., still offered chances of salvation.

Position after Black's 29th move.

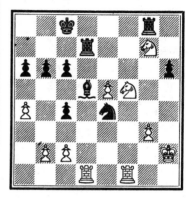

30. P—K 6 !   ......

This short, sharp combination with a promotional point is a true pendant to the final attack of the fourth game.

30. ......   R (Q 2) × Kt
31. Kt × R   R × Kt
32. R × B   ......

The Bishop must be eliminated as he protects Black's K B 2.

32. ......   P × R
33. R—B 8 ch   K—B 2
34. R—B 7 ch   K—Q 3

A sad necessity, as after 34. .... R × R ; 35. P × R, this Pawn could not be stopped.

35. R × R   K × P
36. R—Kt 6 ch   K—K 4
37. K—Kt 2   ......

The black Pawns will not run away !

37.	......	P—Q Kt 4
38.	P—R 5	P—Q 5
39.	R × Q R P	P—Kt 5
40.	K—B 3	P—B 6
41.	P × P	Kt P × P
42.	R—K 6 ch !	K × R
43.	K × Kt	Resigns.

GAME 65

QUEEN'S GAMBIT ACCEPTED

Seventeenth Match-Game, Kissingen, May, 1934.

White : E. BOGOLJUBOW

1.	P—Q 4	P—Q 4
2.	P—Q B 4	P × P
3.	Kt—K B 3	Kt—K B 3
4.	Kt—Q B 3	......

Unusual, but playable. The logical course is, however, the immediate regain of the Gambit Pawn (4. P—K 3 followed by 5. B × P).

| 4. | ...... | P—Q R 3 |
| 5. | P—K 4 ? | ...... |

But this is merely an adventure, which could be selected only by a player who had already but little to lose (the state of the match was at that moment 5 to 1 in my favour). Necessary was 5. P—Q R 4 followed by 6. P—K 3, etc.

| 5. | ...... | P—Q Kt 4 |

Of course ! As Black has no really weak spots the following attacking moves of White are easy to meet.

6.	P—K 5	Kt—Q 4
7.	Kt—Kt 5	P—K 3
8.	Q—B 3	......

Also 8. Q—R 5, Q—K 2, etc., would prove harmless.

8.	......	Q—Q 2
9.	Kt × Kt	P × Kt
10.	P—Q R 3	......

It is most certainly unpleasant to be compelled to make such defensive moves while in material disadvantage ; but the threat 10. ....B—Q Kt 5 ch was too strong.

| 10. | ...... | Kt—B 3 |
| 11. | B—K 3 | Kt—Q 1 |

As the following shows, this relieves the Queens of the defence of the Queen's Pawn.

| 12. | B—K 2 | Q—B 4 ! |

Because if 13. Q × P ? then 13. ....B—Kt 2 wins the Queen.

| 13. | Q—Kt 3 | P—R 3 |
| 14. | Kt—R 3 | ...... |

Or 14. Kt—B 3, Q—Kt 5, etc.

| 14. | ...... | P—Q B 3 |

Prepares the following successful escapade.

| 15. | P—B 4 | Q—B 7 ! |
| 16. | Q—B 2 | ...... |

Apparently defending everything, as both 16. ....Q × Kt P ; 17. Castles, or 16. ....P—B 6 ; 17. P—Q Kt 4 !, etc., would be dangerous for Black. But there is a big surprise coming.

Position after White's 16th move.

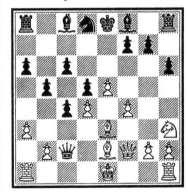

16. ......   B × P !

It becomes more and more difficult to find original combinations
in chess, especially in the earlier
stages of the game.   This, I think,
is one of them : although the
Bishop's move *has* been made in
analogous positions (for instance,
with White's Pawn at Q R 2 and
his Bishop at Q B 1) it has not, to
my knowledge, ever before been
combined with the idea of a Rook's
capture after R × B, Q × Kt P, etc.

17. Castles   ......

There is no choice, as 17. R × B,
Q × Kt P, 18. R—R 5, Q—Kt 5 ch ;
19. B—Q 2, P—B 6, etc., would
lose rapidly.

17. ......   B × P
18. Q R—K 1   B—B 4

The idea of posting this Bishop at
K 5 and of castling (Q's side) afterwards is doubtless good enough.
But with Black's overwhelming
material advantage (three Pawns !)
he had every reason to simplify
matters : 18. .... B × Kt ; 19. P × B,
Kt—K 3, and if 20. P—B 5, Kt—
Kt 4, etc., would probably settle
matters even more quickly.

19. P—Kt 4   B—K 5
20. P—B 5   Kt—Kt 2
21. Kt—B 4   ......

If 21. Q—R 4—in order to prevent Black's next move—the
answer 21. .... P—B 4 ! would be
very strong.

21. ......   Castles (Q R) !
22. Q—Kt 3   P—Kt 4

One of the easiest methods, as
White's activity on the K B's file
will be rapidly paralysed by the
still threatening (and unavoidable)
counter-attack .... P—Q B 4.

23. P × P (*e.p.*)   P × P
24. B—Q 1   Q—B 6
25. Kt—K 6   Q R—K 1
26. R—B 6   R—K 2
27. Q R—B 1   K R—K 1
28. Kt—B 4   ......

After 28. Kt—B 5, Kt × Kt ; 29.
R × P ch, K—Kt 2 ; 30. R × Kt,
the Queen's sacrifice 30. .... Q ×
Q P !, etc., would make an end.

28. ......   Kt—Q 1
29. Q—B 2   ......

Or 29. Kt × Kt P, B × Kt ; 30.
R × B,   P—B 4 !, etc., winning
easily.

29. ......   Q—R 6
30. B—B 3   B × B
31. Q × B   P—Kt 4
32. Kt—K 2   R—K 3
33. R—B 5   Q—Q 6
34. P—R 4   R—Kt 3
35. P—R 5   R—K 3
36. Q—B 2   P—B 4 !

At last !

37. R—B 3   Q—B 7
38. Q—K 1   Kt—B 3
39. R (B 1)—B 2   Q—K 5
40. Kt—Kt 3   Q × Kt P
41. K—Kt 2   B × Q P
Resigns.

GAME 66

QUEEN'S GAMBIT ACCEPTED
(IN FACT)

Twenty-fifth Match-Game, Berlin,
June, 1934.

White : E. BOGOLJUBOW

1. P—Q 4   P—Q 4
2. P—Q B 4   P—Q B 3
3. Kt—K B 3   P × P

An unusual line of play (instead
of 3. .... Kt—K B 3) which is

certainly not refuted in the present game.

4. P—K 3	B—Kt 5
5. B×P	P—K 3
6. Kt—B 3	.....

Bogoljubow thinks that he could here get some end-game advantage by continuing 6. Q—Kt 3, Q—Kt 3 ; 7. Kt—K 5 ; yet after 7. ....B—B 4 ; 8. Kt—Q B 3, Kt—B 3 ; 9. P—K B 3, K Kt—Q 2 !, etc., there would not have been much to expect for White.

6.	Kt—Q 2
7. P—K R 3	B—R 4
8. P—Q R 3	.....

Very slow. But as Black does not plan any action in the centre such preventive moves cannot be criticised.

8.	K Kt—B 3
9. P—K 4	B—K 2
10. Castles	Castles
11. B—B 4	P—Q R 4

As White is, for the time being, stronger in the centre, Black undertakes a diversion on the Q's wing. Its result will be the exchange of a couple of pieces which will gradually relieve his somewhat cramped position.

12. B—Q R 2	Q—Kt 3
13. P—K Kt 4	B—Kt 3
14. Q—K 2	Q—R 3 !
15. Q—K 3	.....

The exchange of Queens would obviously deprive him of any serious winning hopes.

15.	P—Kt 4
16. Kt—K 5	Kt×Kt

Also possible was 16. ....P—Kt 5 ; 17. Kt×B, R P×Kt ; 18. Kt—K 2, P—B 4—but I was not particularly enthusiastic about the

variation 19. P—K 5, Kt—Q 4 ; 20. B×Kt, P×B ; 21. B—Kt 3 followed by P—B 4, etc. ; and, besides, I believed in the future of my temporarily encaged Q's Bishop.

17. B×Kt	P—Kt 5
18. B×Kt	B×B
19. Kt—K 2	.....

After this, Black definitely gets the initiative, which he will keep until the very end. But also after 19. Kt—R 4 (recommended by Nimzowitsch and Bogoljubow), P×P ; 20. P×P, P—K 4 ! ; 21. P—Q 5, B—K 2, etc., his prospects would remain satisfactory.

19.	P×P
20. P×P	P—B 4
21. Q R—B 1	P×P
22. Kt×P	B×Kt !

The exchange of the active K's Bishop looks at first sight surprising, but in reality offers the greatest possibilities of exploiting the weak spots of White's position both in the centre and on the King's wing.

23. Q×B	K R—Q 1
24. Q—B 4 !	Q—Kt 2

The interesting variation 24. .... Q×Q ; 25. R×Q, R—Q 6 ; 26. P—B 4 !, R×Q R P ; 27. R—K B 2, R×R P ; 28. P—B 5, R—Kt 6 ch ; 29. K—R 2, R×Kt P ; 30. P×B, R×Kt P, etc., would have brought Black 4 Pawns for the piece, but no real winning chances.

25. P—B 3	P—R 4

Without having a "hole" for his King Black cannot dream of launching a serious offensive. At the same time this Pawn move is the first step for the emancipation of the prisoner at K Kt 3.

26. Q—K 2	R—Q 5
27. Q—K 3	.....

Dr. Lasker suggests instead of this, 27. K R—Q 1, which, however, after the exchange of Rooks, would lead to about the same position as the one we reached after the 33rd move.

27. ......   R—Q 2

After 27. ....Q R—Q 1, White would have forced the exchange of Queens by playing 28. B—Q 5, Q—Kt 7 ; 29. R—Q Kt 1, etc.

28. P × P   ......

White hopes to obtain some counter-attack on the Q B's file and in order to win a *tempo* for doubling the Rooks, gives some fresh air to the poor Bishop. Bogoljubow indicates as a better line 28. K R—Q 1, Q R—Q 1 ; 29. R × R, R × R ; 30. B—B 4—but after 30. ....P—Q R 5 ! followed by ....P—K R 5 the dark-coloured squares of his position would still remain very weak.

28. ......   B × R P
29. R—B 5   B—Kt 3
30. K R—B 1   Q R—Q 1 !
31. B—B 4   ......

He cannot take the R's Pawn because of 31. ....Q—Kt 7 ! with an immediate win.

31. ......   R—Q 8 ch
32. B—B 1   R × R
33. R × R   P—R 5 !

In spite of the fact that this Pawn cannot, for the present at least, be supported by the Bishop, it is by no means weak, as Black will be perfectly able to protect it by counter-attacks.

34. R—B 4   R—Q 8
35. R—Kt 4   ......

Not 35. R × P because of 35. .... R × B ch followed by 36. ....Q—Kt 4 ch.

35. ......   Q—B 2

Threatening mate in three by 35. ....Q—Kt 6 ch, etc.

36. P—B 4   Q—Q 1 !
37. Q—B 2   ......

37. R × P would be refuted by 37. ....R × B ch and 38. ....Q—Q 8 ch. The end is approaching.

Position after White's 37th move.

37. ......   P—B 4 !

The resurrection of the Bishop, which will not only rescue the Q R's Pawn but also contribute to an effective exploitation of White's disorganised King's position.

38. P—K 5   B—K 1
39. R—Kt 6   Q—B 1
40. R—Q 6   ......

Or 40. K—R 2, Q—B 6 ! and wins.

40. ......   R—B 8
41. Q—Q 4   ......

There is no defence left. If for instance 41. K—R 2, then 41. .... R—B 7 ; 42. R—Q 2, R × R ; 43. Q × R, Q—B 4 ! winning a Pawn and the game.

41. ......   K—R 2

In order to answer 42. R—Q 8 by 42. ....Q—R 3 ! etc.

42. K—B 2   Q—B 7 ch
43. Q—Q 2   ......

Or 43. B—K 2, B—Kt 4 ; 44. Q—Q 2, B×B ! ; 45. Q×B, Q—B 4 ch., etc., winning.

43. ......   Q—B 4 ch

44. Q—K 3   ......

If 44. Q—Q 4 then 44. ....Q× R P after which White could also quietly resign.

44. ......   R×B ch
Resigns.

This game practically finished the Match, as it gave me 15 points to my opponent's 10.

PART III. (1934-1937)

TOURNAMENT GAMES AND MATCHES WITH DR. EUWE

GAME 67

QUEEN'S PAWN OPENING

Zurich Tournament, July, 1934.

Black :
MARQUIS S. ROSELLI DEL TURCO

1. P—Q 4	P—Q 4
2. Kt—K B 3	Kt—K B 3
3. P—K 3	P—K 3

Not a mistake, of course, but 3. ....B—B 4 ; 4. B—Q 3, P—K 3 ! would solve without disadvantage the otherwise rather tiresome problem of the Queen's Bishop's development.

4. B—Q 3	P—B 4
5. P—Q Kt 3	......

An old—and rather harmless—method of mobilisation instead of which the modern Colle's System starting by 5. P—Q B 3 offers more attacking possibilities. It succeeds here, however, because Black answers it by an unjustified clearing of the situation in the middle.

5.	P×P ?

Oddly enough, this exchange—which opens for White the central file without compensation (as there is nothing for Black to do with the Q B's file)—is not made infrequently even by very experienced players. The course of the present game illustrates the faultiness of this strategy in a typical way.

6. P×P	B—Q 3
7. Castles	Castles

8. B—Kt 2	Kt—B 3
9. P—Q R 3	......

More exact than immediately 9. Q Kt—Q 2, as after 9. ....Q—B 2 ! Black would threaten both 10. ....Kt—Q Kt 5 and 10. ....P—K 4.

9.	P—Q Kt 3
10. Q Kt—Q 2	B—Kt 2
11. Q—K 2	Q—B 2
12. Kt—K 5	Kt—K 2
13. P—K B 4	Q R—B 1
14. Q R—B 1	......

In order to add to the already existing advantages (greater space in the centre and chances on the King's side) another trump—the dynamization of the Q B's Pawn. However, the general situation after the erroneous exchange at the 5th move is so favourable for White that a King's attack could be carried through *even without using that trump*. A characteristic example of such an attack is my game (given below) with Asgeirson (Black) from the Folkestone Team Tournament, 1933, which, with a slight inversion of moves, soon reached the same type of position as the present game: 1. P—Q 4, Kt—K B 3 ; 2. Kt—K B 3, P—K 3 ; 3. P—K 3, P—B 4 ; 4. B—Q 3, Kt—B 3 ; 5. P—Q R 3, P×P ? ; 6. P×P, P—Q 4 ; 7. Castles, B—Q 2 ; 8. P—Q Kt 3, B—Q 3 ; 9. R—K 1, R—Q B 1 ; 10. B—Kt 2, Castles ; 11. Kt—K 5, B—Kt 1 ; 12. Kt—Q 2, P—K Kt 3 ; 13. Q—B 3, Kt—K R 4 ; 14. Q—K 3, Kt—Kt 2 ; 15. Q—R 6, Kt—K 2 ; 16. P—K Kt 4 !, K—R 1 ; 17. Q Kt—B 3, Kt—Kt 1 ; 18. Q—R 3, B—K 1 ; 19. B—Q B 1,

B—Q 3 ; 20. Kt—Kt 5, P—K R 4 ;
21. P × P, Kt × P (or 21. . . . .P × P ;
22. Kt—R 7 !, winning the exchange) ; 22. Kt (Kt 5) × P ch !,
B × Kt ; 23. B × P, B × B ; 24. Kt ×
B ch, K—Kt 2 ; 25. Kt × R, Q × Kt;
26. Q—Kt 4 ch ! Resigns.

14. . . . . . .   P—Kt 3

This, in connection with the two
next moves, does not prove sufficient to meet the threatening advance of White's K Kt's Pawn. But
equally an attempt by Black to post
his Knight at K 5 would not
succeed—for instance, 14. . . . .Q—
Kt 1 ; 15. R—B 2 !, Q—R 1 ; 16.
R—K 1, followed by P—K Kt 4,
etc. ±.

15. P—K Kt 4   P—K R 4
16. P—R 3   K—Kt 2

As will be seen, this only facilitates the advance of White's Q B's
Pawn.

17. P—B 4   Q—Q 1

Position after Black's 17th move.

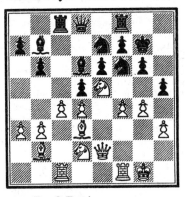

18. P—Q B 5 !   . . . . . .

This is the strategical decision, as
White forces herewith a protected
passed Pawn on the Q's side without
weakening his pressure on the other
wing. Black, obviously, cannot
now play 18. . . . .P × B P ; 19. P ×
B P, B × P ch because of 20. R × B !

followed by 21. P—Kt 5, etc.,
winning.

18. . . . . . .   B × Kt
19. B P × B   Kt—Q 2
20. P—Kt 4   R P × P
21. R P × P   R—K R 1

The occupation of this file is
without importance, as the light
pieces cannot co-operate.

22. Kt—B 3   P × P
23. Kt P × P   Kt—Q B 3
24. Q—K 3 !   . . . . . .

Threatening 25. Kt—Kt 5.

24. . . . . . .   Q—K 2
25. K—Kt 2   . . . . . .

Threatening now 25. R—K R 1 !
followed by Q R—B 1 and B—B 1,
etc., and thus inducing Black to
take desperate action in the centre.

25. . . . . . .   P—B 4
26. P × P ch (*e.p.*) Kt × P
27. Q—Kt 5   R—R 3
28. R—K R 1   Q R—K R 1
29. R × R   R × R
30. R—K 1 !   . . . . . .

Even stronger than 30. R—K R 1
which would win only a Pawn.

30. . . . . . .   Kt—Q 1
31. Kt—K 5   Kt—Kt 1

Or 31. . . . .Kt—B 2 ; 32. Kt × Kt
followed by 33. Q—K 5, etc., with
an easy win.

32. B—B 1 !   . . . . . .

One of the points of 30. R—K 1.

32. . . . . . .   Q—K 1
33. R—B 1   B—B 3
34. R—B 6 !   Kt × R
35. Q × R ch   K—Kt 1
36. B—Kt 5   . . . . . .

Wins about two light pieces.

Resigns.

GAME 68

RUY LOPEZ

Zurich Tournament, July, 1934.

Black : H. JOHNER

1. P—K 4	P—K 4
2. Kt—K B 3	Kt—Q B 3
3. B—Kt 5	P—Q R 3
4. B—R 4	Kt—B 3
5. Castles	P—Q 3

This permits White to start an immediate action in the centre without being obliged to protect first the K P by R—K 1 or Q—K 2, which would be the case after 5. ....B—K 2.

6. P—B 3	B—Q 2
7. P—Q 4	B—K 2
8. P—Q 5	......

This blockade manœuvre was introduced by Bogoljubow in a Match-game against me (Rotterdam 1929). Its peculiarity is to lead generally to slow positional battles of heavy calibre.

8.	Kt—Q Kt 1
9. B—B 2	B—Kt 5

Keres tried against me in the Team Tournament at Warsaw 1935 a more aggressive line of play involving the renunciation of castling and starting with 9. ....P—K R 3. The continuation, 10. P—B 4, Q—B 1 ; 11. Kt—K 1, P—K Kt 4 ; 12. Kt—Q B 3, Kt—R 4 ; 13. Kt—K 2 ! (of course not 13. Q × Kt, B—Kt 5), Kt—B 5 ; 14. Kt—Kt 3, P—Q B 3 ; 15. Kt—B 5, P × P ; 16. B × Kt, Kt P × B ; 17. B P × P, B × Kt ; 18. P × B—proved, however, favourable to the first player who, by taking advantage of the open Q B file, succeeded in forcing resignation by the 37th move. For ....P—Q R 4 ! in conjunction with Kt—

Q R 3—Q B 4, see my consultation game against Kashdan (No. 119).

10. P—B 4	Q Kt—Q 2
11. P—K R 3 !	......

In the above-mentioned game, Bogoljubow played here 11. Kt—B 3, and after 11. ....Kt—B 1; 12. P—K R 3 ?—this is now out of place since the Bishop can simply remove to Q 2—was Black able to start a King's attack by the pawn-sacrifice, ...P—K Kt 4 ! and to obtain soon a won position.

11.	B—R 4
12. Kt—B 3	Castles
13. P—K Kt 4	B—Kt 3
14. Q—K 2	......

Preparing for Kt—K R 4, which, played immediately, would have been met by 14. ....B × P, etc.

14.	Kt—K 1
15. B—Q 2	P—K R 3

The seemingly more aggressive 15. ....P—K R 4 would be favourably answered by the manœuvre Kt—Q 1—K 3—K B 5.

16. K—Kt 2	B—R 2
17. R—R 1	P—K Kt 4 !

By constructing this pawn-barricade, Black at least eliminates the immediate danger that threatens his King.

18. P—K R 4	P—K B 3
19. Kt—Q 1	R—B 2
20. Kt—K 3	......

This Knight must be exchanged at K B 5 before Black finds time to bring a Knight to his K B 5 via K Kt 3.

20.	Kt—B 1
21. Kt—B 5	B × Kt
22. Kt P × B	R—R 2

One must admit that Black defends his position logically. He now succeeds in still bringing a Knight to K B 5 by another route (K Kt 2 —K R 4), but it's his bad luck that his other pieces are too poorly placed to permit a really effective resistance !

23. Q R—K Kt 1	Kt—Kt 2
24. K—B 1	Q—K 1
25. Kt—R 2	Kt—R 4
26. Kt—Kt 4	Kt—B 5
27. Q—B 3 !	......

Threatening B × Kt, K P × B ; 29. Q × P !, Kt P × Q ; 30. Kt × R P doub. ch. followed by mate.

| 27. ...... | K—Kt 2 ! |

The only parry ; for 27. ....K— R 1 would soon lose after 28. Kt × R P !, R × Kt ; 29. P × P, etc.

28. P × P	R P × P
29. R × R ch	Kt × R
30. R—R 1	K—R 1
31. R—R 6	Q—B 2
32. B—Q 1	R—K Kt 1
33. Q—Q Kt 3 !	......

As all Black's pieces are more or less engaged on the King's side, the Queen undertakes a little promenade on the other wing—not for sight-seeing, but in order to grab anything insufficiently protected. This material win, by no means accidental, is the logical consequence of a persistent initiative, which prevented Black from protecting at the same time all his vulnerable spots.

| 33. ...... | P—Kt 3 |
| 34. Q—R 4 | B—B 1 |

If 34. ....P—R 4, then 35. Q— Q 7, etc., winning rapidly.

35. Q × P	B × R
36. Kt × B	Q—Kt 2
37. Kt × R	K × Kt

38. Q—B 8 ch	Kt—B 1
39. B × Kt	K P × B
40. Q—K 8	......

After gaining a material advantage, the attack, as so often, vanishes, and White must now be particularly careful against a possible counter-attack ; for instance, Black's strong threat was 40. .... Q—K 2 and ....Q—K 4.

40.	P—Kt 5 !
41. Q—R 5	P—B 6
42. B—R 4	Kt—R 2
43. B—B 2	......

The necessary preparation for the surprising assault in the middle.

| 43. ...... | Kt—B 1 |

If 43. ....Kt—Kt 4, White would win through 44. Q × P, Q— R 3 ; 45. K—Kt 1 !—for instance, I. 45. ....K—B 1 ; 46. B—Q 1, Kt—R 6 ch ; 47. K—B 1, Q—Q 7 ; 48. Q × B P. II. 45. ....Q—Kt 2; 46. Q—Kt 3 with an easy technical work in both cases.

Position after Black's 43rd move.

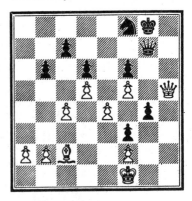

| 44. P—K 5 ! ! | ...... |

The sealed move at the adjournment, which transforms a complicated technical problem into a sharp, short, winning procedure.

44. ......   Q P×P

Or 44. ....B P×P; 45. P—B 6 !,
Q×P; 46. Q×P ch followed by 47.
B—K 4, etc., with no more fight
left.

45. P—Q 6 !   P—B 4

After 45. ....P×P, the third
point, 46. P—B 5 ! threatening 47.
B—Kt 3 ch, etc., would successfully
finish the work.

46. B—K 4   Q—Q 2
47. Q—R 6 !   ......

More exact than 47. Q×P ch.

Resigns.

GAME 69

BENONI'S DEFENCE

Zurich Tournament, July, 1934.

White : F. GYGLI

1. P—Q 4   P—Q B 4
2. P—Q 5   P—K 4
3. P—K 4   P—Q 3
4. P—K Kt 3   ......

An elaborate method of development which does not cause Black
much trouble. White should, in
my opinion, try this opening to
combine the two following strategical ideas : (1) Occupation of the
square Q B 4 by a Knight and the
strengthening of that position, and
(2) preparation of the advance P—
K B 4 *which has, however, to be
executed only as an immediate reaction to Black's P—K B 4.* In the
latter case the opening of the position in the middle should always
end to the advantage of the party
who has already a superiority in
space.

4. ......   P—B 4

5. Kt—Q B 3   Kt—K B 3
6. B—Kt 2   B—K 2

Also the immediate 6. ....P—
Q Kt 4 (7. Kt×P, Kt×P, etc.)
came into consideration. As Black
does not take advantage of that
possibility, White would have done
better to prevent it now by playing
7. P—Q R 4.

7. K Kt—K 2   P—Q Kt 4 !

The tactical consequences of this,
positionally, quite justified advance
had to be carefully examined, as
the following proves.

8. P×P   P—Kt 5
9. Kt—K 4   B×P
10. Kt×B P   ......

A tempting, but unsatisfactory,
transaction, as it only helps the
deployment of Black's forces. Still,
a tame alternative would only
underline the inefficiency of the
first opening moves.

10. ......   P×Kt
11. P—Q 6   P—K 5 !

And not 11. ....B—K 5 ; 12.
B×B, Kt×B ; 13. Q—Q 5±.

12. P×B   Q×Q ch
13. K×Q   K×P
14. B—K 3   Q Kt—Q 2

The middle-game without Queens,
resulting from the exchanges in the
centre, is in Black's favour—chiefly
because of the uncomfortable position of White's King, preventing
the combined action of the Rooks.

15. P—K R 3   P—K R 4
16. P—R 3   P—R 4
17. P×P   R P×P
18. K—Q 2   K—B 2 !

An important move, whose object
is to prevent the capture of the

Q B's Pawn *with check* in case of ....Kt—K 4.

19. Kt—B 4 ?   ......

This proves an important, if not decisive, loss of time, and was obviously based on a tactical miscalculation. By playing 19. P—Q Kt 3 White would still keep a playable—although inferior—game.

| 19. ...... | P—K Kt 4 |
| 20. Kt—K 2 | ...... |

White probably intended to play 20. R × R, R × R ; 21. Kt × R P—and found out now that this would have led to a hopeless position after 21. ....Kt × Kt ; 22. P—Kt 4, Kt—B 5 ; 23. B × Kt, P × B ; 24. P × B, P—B 6 ; 25. B—B 1, K—B 3, etc. But what will happen after the retreat in the text is not very much better for him either.

| 20. ...... | Kt—K 4 ! |

With the threats ....Kt—B 5 ch and ....Kt—B 6 ch, both of which cannot be parried.

| 21. R × R | R × R |
| 22. R—Q 1 | Kt—B 6 ch |

Even more convincing than 22. ....Kt—B 5 ch ; 23. K—K 1, Kt × Kt P; 24. R—Kt 1, etc.

| 23. B × Kt | P × B |
| 24. Kt—B 1 | P—B 5 ! |

Puts the White Knight in a stalemate position in which it will remain until the very end.

| 25. K—K 1 | P—Kt 5 |

There is no hurry to take the Q B's Pawn as White's answer is compulsory : if 26. P × P ? then 26. ....P × P followed by 27. ....R—K R 1 and ....Kt—K 5 with a mating attack.

| 26. P—R 4 | B × P |
| 27. R—Q 4 | ...... |

Position after White's 27th move.

| 27. ...... | P—B 6 ! |

Forcing a powerful passed Pawn and, at the same time, finishing the encircling of the enemy's King. White cannot play now 28. R × Kt P because of 28. ....R—Q 1 ; 29. B—Q 4, R × B ! ; 30. R × R, P × P and wins.

28. P × P	P × P
29. R—K B 4	K—K 3
30. R—Q B 4	Kt—Q 4
31. B—Kt 5	K—Q 3
32. B—R 6	......

White has still fewer and fewer moves at his disposal.

32.	R—K 1 ch
33. K—B 1	B—Q 8 !
34. R—Q 4	B—K 7 ch
35. K—K 1	......

Or 35. K—Kt 1, B—Kt 4 ! followed by ....R—K 8 ch, B—B 8, B—Kt 7 and R—R 8 mate.

35.	K—B 3
36. B—Kt 5	B—B 5 disc ch
37. K—Q 1	K—B 4 !

Capturing the Rook, in the very middle of the board !

38.	R × Kt ch	K × R
39.	K—B 2	R—K 7 ch !
40.	K × P	R × P

Resigns.

GAME 70

QUEEN'S GAMBIT DECLINED
(ORTHODOX DEFENCE)

Zurich Tournament, July, 1934.

Black : DR. EM. LASKER

1.	P—Q 4	P—Q 4
2.	P—Q B 4	P—K 3
3.	Kt—Q B 3	Kt—K B 3
4.	Kt—B 3	B—K 2
5.	B—Kt 5	Q Kt—Q 2
6.	P—K 3	Castles
7.	R—B 1	P—B 3
8.	B—Q 3	P × P

As mentioned elsewhere, this exchange gives Black more defensive resources if preceded by ....P—K R 3 ; B—R 4.

9.	B × P	Kt—Q 4
10.	B × B	Q × B
11.	Kt—K 4	......

This move, "my patent," is as good as the more usual 11. Castles, but probably not better. In both cases White usually gets an advantage in space and has not to worry about a possible loss.

| 11. | ...... | K Kt—B 3 |
| 12. | Kt—Kt 3 | P—K 4 |

An interesting attempt by Lasker to solve swiftly the problem of the Queen's Bishop. Capablanca regularly played here in our Match-games 12. ....Q—Kt 5 ch, and, after the exchange of Queens, suc-

ceeded in drawing, but not without difficulties.

| 13. | Castles | P × P |
| 14. | Kt—B 5 | ...... |

This sharp-looking move is in reality less aggressive than the straightforward 14. P × P, which, on account of the open K's file, would cause Black real development trouble—for instance, 14. ....Kt—Kt 3 ; 15. R—K 1, Q—Q 3 ; 16. B—Kt 3, and, if 16. ....B—Kt 5, then 17. P—K R 3, B × Kt ; 18. Q × B, etc., offering the Queen's Pawn for a strong attack. After the text move, White will be practically forced to take at Q 4 with a piece and to allow, as a consequence, an unwelcome simplification.

| 14. | ...... | Q—Q 1 |
| 15. | K Kt × P | ...... |

If 15. Q (or P) × P, then .... Kt—Kt 3.

15.	......	Kt—K 4
16.	B—Kt 3	B × Kt
17.	Kt × Kt	Q—Kt 3 ?

Underestimating, or overlooking, the answer, which gives White a strong and hardly resistible attack. The right move, sufficient for equality, is 17. ....P—K Kt 3, played by Flohr against Euwe at Nottingham, 1936. Neither 18. Q—Q 6 (R—K 1 !), nor 18. Kt—Q 6 (Q—K 2) would then prove successful.

| 18. | Q—Q 6 ! | Q Kt—Q 2 |

Also 18. ....Kt—Kt 3 ; 19. Kt—R 6 ch, P × Kt ; 20. Q × Kt, Q—Q 1 ; 21. Q—Q B 3, would be bad enough.

19.	K R—Q 1	Q R—Q 1
20.	Q—Kt 3	P—Kt 3
21.	Q—Kt 5 !	......

With the main threat 22. R—Q 6, Black has already no real defence,

21.	......	K—R 1
22.	Kt—Q 6	K—Kt 2
23.	P—K 4 !	......

Not only in order to use this Pawn as an attacking factor, but also, as will be seen, to free the third rank for the Rooks.

| 23. | ...... | Kt—Kt 1 |
| 24. | R—Q 3 | P—B 3 |

24. ....P—K R 3 would have led to a pendant-variation, viz., 25. Kt—B 5 ch, K—R 2 ; 26. Kt × R P !, P—B 3 ; 27. Kt—B 5 !, P × Q ; 28. R—R 3 ch and mate follows.

25. Kt—B 5 ch   K—R 1

Position after Black's 25th move.

26. Q × P !

The spectacular final coup of an attack that could hardly have been conducted in a more effective manner after Black's superficial 17th move.   [Resigns]

GAME 71

QUEEN'S GAMBIT DECLINED (ORTHODOX DEFENCE)

Orebro Tournament, May, 1935.

Black : E. LUNDIN

| 1. | P—Q 4 | P—Q 4 |
| 2. | P—Q B 4 | P—K 3 |

3.	Kt—Q B 3	Kt—K B 3
4.	B—Kt 5	Q Kt—Q 2
5.	Kt—B 3	P—B 3
6.	P—K 4	......

This old move—a radical method of avoiding the Cambridge Springs' Defence—has been adopted by me twice with success in the 1929 Match against Bogoljubow and also on a few occasions later. Its advantage is to gain at once some space in the centre, its defect—to allow early exchanges of minor pieces, which facilitates the mobilisation of Black's pieces.

| 6. | ...... | P × K P |
| 7. | Kt × P | B—K 2 |

Besides this simple developing move, Black has at his disposal at least three other continuations, each involving a different plan of development :
I. 7. ....Q—Kt 3. This counter-attack aims at an immediate material win at the cost of time and, eventually, space—a dangerous and to my mind, unchessy idea, which, however, in this particular case is by no means easy to refute.   In the eleventh match-game against Bogoljubow, I adopted the ultra-cautious 8. Kt × Kt ch, P × Kt ; 9. B—B 1— and soon obtained a winning attack, but only because my opponent, with his typical over-estimation of his resources, replied with 9. .... P—K 4 ? instead of 9. ....Q—B 2, thus opening the position before having finished development. The continuation was : 10. B—Q 3, P × P ; 11. Castles, B—K 2 ; 12. R—K 1, Kt—B 1 ; 13. Kt—R 4 !, B—K 3 ; 14. Kt—B 5, B—Kt 5 ; 15. Kt—Kt 7 ch, K—Q 2 ; 16. R— K 4 !, R—K Kt 1—after which White could have made a rapid end by playing 17. Kt—B 5 ! with the threat R × P ch, etc.
Also successful, but not quite convincing, was another attempt of mine against Colle at Bled, 1931,

where I played—after 7. ....Q— Kt 3 ; 8. B—Q 3. My opponent decided to accept the pawn-offer, but did it in not the most secure way : instead of 8. ....Kt × Kt ; 9. B × Kt, Q—Kt 5 ch !—introduced with success by Dr. Euwe in a consultation-game against Flohr— he played immediately 8. ....Q × Kt P, allowing White to bring his King into safety. The attack that developed afterwards—on the basis, first of a space advantage and, later, of the two Bishops supremacy— was both typical and instructive. The game went on as follows : 9. Castles, Kt × Kt ; 10. B × Kt, Kt— B 3 ; 11. B—Q 3, Q—Kt 3 ; 12. R—K 1, B—K 2 13. Q—B 2, P— K R 3 ; 14. B—Q 2, P—B 4 ; 15. B—B 3, P × P ; 16. Kt × P, Castles ; 17. Kt—B 5 !, Q—Q 1 ; 18. Kt × B ch, Q × Kt ; 19. Q R—Kt 1, R—Q 1; 20. R—K 3, P—Q Kt 3 ; 21. Q— K 2 !, B—Kt 2 ; 22. R—Kt 3, Kt— K 1 ; 23. R—K 1, K—B 1 ; 24. Q—Kt 2, P—B 3 ; 25. B—Kt 4, Kt—Q 3 ; 26. K R—K 3, K—B 2; 27. P—B 4 !, Q—Q 2 ; 28. Q—K 2, R—K 1 ; 29. Q—R 5 ch, K—Kt 1 ; 30. Q—Kt 6, P—B 4 ; 31. B × Kt, Q × B ; 32. B × P, Q × P ; 33. Q—R 7 ch, K—B 1 ; 34. B—Kt 6, Q—Q 5 ; 35. B × R, R × R ; 36. K—R 1, Q—B 3 ; 37. Q—R 8 ch, K—B 2 ; 38. Q × R ch ! Resigns.

As neither attempt can be considered satisfactory from the theoretical point of view, White must, after 7. ....Q—Kt 3, complete his development in a way that will not permit an unwelcome reduction of the fighting units. With this idea, I would recommend a continuation that has been tried but once by Marshall against Tchigorin in Hannover, 1902, and completely forgotten since, viz. : 8. P—B 5 !, Q × Kt P—and only now 9. B—Q 3 followed by 10. Castles, with ample positional compensation for the Pawn.

II. 7. ....*B—Kt* 5 *ch*, with the object of exploiting the temporary weakness of the diagonal K 1— Q R 5 and, at the same time, of preparing a break-through in the centre by ....P—K 4. The idea is, however, too artificial and too time-wasting to become a success. The following game, played by me in the Warsaw Team Tournament, 1935, illustrates in a drastic way White's possibilities in this variation : Black, Silbermann (Roumania). 8. Kt—B 3, Q—R 4 ; 9. B—Q 2, Q—B 2 ; 10. B—Q 3, P— K 4 ; 11. P × P, Kt × P ; 12. Q—K 2, Kt—Q 2 ; 13. Castles (K R), Castles; 14. Kt—Q 5 (a rather original combination by which White finally wins the exchange for a Pawn), P × Kt ; 15. B × B, Kt × B ; 16. Q × Kt, P × P ; 17. Q—K 3 !, Q—Kt 3 (if ....R—Q 1, then 18. Q—K 7 with a winning position) ; 18. B × R, Q × Q ; 19. P × Q (the following end-game is harder to win than one would think, especially as Black defends himself with great determination), K × B ; 20. Q R— Q 1, K—K 2 ; 21. R—Q 5, P—B 3 ; 22. K R—Q 1, P—Q Kt 3 ; 23. R— Q 6, Kt—B 4 ; 24. R—Q 8, B— Kt 2 ; 25. R × R, B × R ; 26. Kt— Q 4, B—K 5 ; 27. R—Q B 1, B— Q 4 ; 28. Kt—B 5 ch, K—K 3 ; 29. Kt × P ch, K—K 4 ; 30. Kt—R 5 !, B—B 2 ; 31. Kt—B 4, Kt—K 5 ; 32. P—Q R 3, P—Kt 4 ; 33. R— Q 1, Kt—B 4 ; 34. R—Q 8, P— Q R 3 ; 35. K—B 2, Kt—R 5 ; 36. R—Q 7, B—Kt 3 ; 37. R—Q 5 ch, K—K 5 ; 38. R—Q 2, B—B 4 ; 39. P—R 3, P—B 6 (this tempting advance is met by a mating threat, which decides the game at once. Compare with the same end-game stratagem in the games against Tartakover from San Remo and the 24th of the 2nd match with Euwe) ; 40. R—Q 4 ch, K—K 4 ; 41. K—B 3 !, Kt—K 3 ; 42. P × P, B—Q 2 ; 43. Kt—Q 3 ch, K—B 4 ; 44. R—Q 6. Resigns.

III. 7. ....*P—K R* 3 !, practically forcing the exchange of White's Q's Bishop. Although, after

8. B×Kt, Kt×Kt ; 9. Kt—B 3, P—Q Kt 3 followed by .... B—Kt 2 etc., White would still enjoy more freedom, at least temporarily, Black's chances for the future, because of the two Bishops, would be quite satisfactory, and that is why I have recently given up the otherwise playable 6. P—K 4.

| 8. Kt—B 3 | Castles |
| 9. Q—B 2 | ...... |

This move in connection with Castles (Q R) had, I believe, never been made before my 1929 Match with Bogoljubow. On a previous occasion, Gilg played against Spielmann 9. B—Q 3 and Castles (K side), after which Black can easily equalise with .... P—B 4.

| 9. ...... | P—K 4 ! |

A new and interesting attempt to liberate the Q's Bishop, and which forces White to play very carefully in order to maintain advantage in space. Decidedly too passive is, instead, 9. .... P—Q Kt 3 ; 10. Castles, as, for instance, my two following games rather convincingly show :

I.   Black, Bogoljubow ; 19th Match Game, 1929. 10. .... B—Kt 2 ; 11. P—K R 4, Q—B 2 ; 12. B—Q 3, K R—K 1 ; 13. K—Kt 1, Kt—B 1 ; 14. B×Kt !, B×B ; 15. Kt—K 4, P—B 4 ; 16. Kt×B ch, P×Kt ; 17. Q—Q 2, Kt—Kt 3 ; 18. P—R 5, Kt—B 5 ; 19. R—R 4, B×Kt ; 20. P×B, P—K 4 ; 21. P—Q 5, Q—Q 3 ; 22. P—R 6 !, K—R 1 ; 23. Q—B 2, Kt×B ; 24. Q×Kt, R—K Kt 1 ; 25. P—B 4 !, R—Kt 3 ; 26. Q—B 5, P—R 3 ; 27. R—K 1, P×P ; 28. R×P ! (by giving up the K R P White gets the full control of the central file and, gradually, an irresistible King's attack), R×P ; 29. R (B 4)—K 4, R—K Kt 1 ; 30. R—K 7, R—K B 1 ; 31. P—R 4 !, R—R 5 ; 32. R—K 8, R×R ; 33. R×R ch, K—Kt 2 ;

34. Q—B 8, K—R 3 ; 35. R—Kt 8 !, Q—K 2 ; 36. K—R 2, P—Kt 4 ; 37. R—Kt 3 !, P—B 4 ; 38. Q× K B P, P—B 3 ; 39. R—K 3, Q—K B 2. Here I played 40. R—K 6 and eventually won in 77 moves ; but 40. Q—K 6 ! would have forced an almost immediate resignation.

II.   Black, J. Vasquez, Mexico City Tournament, Sept., 1932. 10. .... P—B 4 ; 11. P—K R 4, Q—B 2 ; 12. P—Q 5, P×P ; 13. P×P, P—Q R 3 ; 14. B—Q 3, P—R 3 ; 15. B—R 7 ch, K—R 1 ; 16. Kt—K 4 !, B—Q 3 ; 17. B—B 5, Kt×Kt ; 18. Q×Kt, Kt—K 4 ; 19. Kt×Kt, B×Kt ; 20. P—Q 6 !, B×Q P ; 21. Q×R, B×B ; 22. Q—B 3, B—Kt 3 ; 23. P—R 5, B—R 2 ; 24. B×P !, B—K 4 ; 25. B—Kt 5, P—B 4 ; 26. P—R 6, P—K B 5 ; 27. Q—Q 5 !, P—B 6 ; 28. P×P ch, Q×P ; 29. R×B ch !, K×R ; 30. R—R 1 ch, K—Kt 3 ; 31. B—R 6, B—B 5 ch ; 32. B×B, R×B ; 33. P×P, Q—Q 5 ; 34. Q—Kt 8 ch, K—B 3 ; 35. R—R 6 ch, K—K 2 ; 36. R—K 6 ch. Resigns.

| 10. Castles | ...... |

The acceptance of the offer would be favourable to Black, for instance: 10. P×P, Kt—Kt 5 ; 11. B—B 4, B—B 4 ; 12. Kt—K 4, B—Kt 5 ch, or, 10. Kt×P, Kt×Kt ; 11. P×Kt, Kt—Q 2 ; 12. B×B, Q×B ; 13. P—B 4, P—B 3, etc.—in both cases with enough compensation for the Pawn.

10.	P×P
11. Kt×P	Q—R 4
12. P—K R 4	......

As the reader may see from the games above, this move is an important link in the plan inaugurated by 9. Q—B 2.

| 12. ...... | Kt—B 4 |
| 13. K—Kt 1 | R—Q 1 |

If 13. .... B—K 3, White would not exchange this Bishop at once,

but first finish his development as in the actual game—B—K 2—B 3, etc.

14. B—K 2	Q—B 2
15. B—B 3 !	......

Judiciously resisting the temptation to dislodge the Knight by 15. P—Q Kt 4, since, after 15. .... Kt—K 3 ; 16. P—R 3, P—B 4 !, Black would obtain a counter-attack he cannot count upon after the positional text-move.

15.	P—Q R 4
16. K R—K 1	......

At this particular moment the Rook is more useful in the centre, especially as the King's attack is very slow to develop owing to Black's well-timed preventative manœuvres.

16.	P—K Kt 3

Almost necessary if he wants to dislodge White's central Knight by ....Kt—K 3. Besides, the move also involves the direct threat 17. ....R × Kt, followed by 17. .... B—K B 4.

17. P—K Kt 4	Kt—K 3
18. Kt × Kt	B × Kt
19. P—R 5 !	......

Threatening 20. P × P, R P × P ; 21. R × B ! etc., and not worrying about the Q B P, since 19. .... B × P is met by 20. R × B !, Q × R ; 21. Kt—K 4, R × R ch ; 22. Q × R, etc., with a winning advantage.

19.	R × R ch
20. Kt × R	Kt—K 1

In order to prevent the sacrifice of the exchange at his K 3.

21. B—R 6	B—B 3
22. P × P	R P × P

Position after Black's 22nd move.

23. Kt—B 3 !	......

I count this Pawn sacrifice amongst my most difficult combinations, since it was extremely hard to calculate that the little material left in the main variation would prove sufficient to increase the pressure in a definite way. And a win *was* necessary, for both my opponent and myself had 7½ out of 8 and this was the last round !

23.	B × B P

Otherwise, after 24. Kt—K 4, White would have an easy attacking game.

24. Kt—K 4	Q—K 4

This counter-attack will be refuted by White's next two moves. The main variation mentioned arises from 24. ....B—Q 4, and its real difficulty lay in finding, after 25. Kt × B ch, Kt × Kt ; 26. Q—B 3, Q—Q 3 ; 27. B × B, P × B, the two quiet moves 28. *R—K R 1*, Q—K 3 (if ....P—Q 5, then 29. Q—K R 3, etc.) ; 29. *P—K B 3 !*, with the chief threat Q—Q 2—K R 2, after which the open K R-file would sooner or later triumph.

25. P—Kt 5 !	......

The Bishop thus attacked cannot be moved because of 26. Kt—B 6 ch.

25. ......   Q—Kt 4

This was obviously the point of the previous move : the piece is temporarily saved, but Black now loses because of the weakness of his K Kt 2.

26. Kt×B ch	Kt×Kt
27. Q—B 3 !	R—K 1
28. R—Q B 1	......

And not 28. P×Kt, Q—B 4 ch ; 29. K—R 1, R×R ch followed by 30. ....Q×B.

28.	Q—B 4 ch
29. K—R 1	K—R 2
30. Q×B	Resigns.

GAME 72

QUEEN'S GAMBIT DECLINED (SLAV DEFENCE)

First Match-game, Amsterdam, October, 1935.

Black : DR. M. EUWE

1. P—Q 4	P—Q 4
2. P—Q B 4	P—Q B 3
3. Kt—K B 3	Kt—K B 3
4. Kt—B 3	P×P
5. P—Q R 4	B—K B 4
6. Kt—K 5	......

It has been proved in our second match that this aggressive move, which has been fashionable for about ten years, is decidedly less promising than the natural 6. P—K 3. Black's best answer to the text-move is, however, not 6. .... Q Kt—Q 2 but 6. ....P—K 3, and, if 7. B—Kt 5, B—Kt 5 ; 8. P—K B 3, then 8. ....P—K R 3 ! etc. (11th Match-game, 1937).

6.	Q Kt—Q 2
7. Kt×Q B P	Q—B 2
8. P—K Kt 3	P—K 4
9. P×P	Kt×P
10. B—K B 4	K Kt—Q 2
11. B—Kt 2	B—K 3

Black does not need to cede to the white Queen the square Q B 2 ; but—as the first Match-game, 1937, convincingly showed—even by the best continuation, 11. ....P—K B 3 ; 12. Castles, R—Q 1 ; 13. Q—B 1, B—K 3 White obtains a clear positional advantage by continuing 14. Kt—K 4 !

| 12. Kt×Kt | Kt×Kt |
| 13. Castles | B—K 2 |

Black tries in the following to avoid the weakening of his K 3 through ....P—K B 3 and gradually gets into great difficulty because of the insufficient protection of his Knight.

14. Q—B 2   ......

Threatening either Kt—Q 5 or Kt—Kt 5—Q 4, etc. Black can hardly succeed in keeping his pair of Bishops much longer.

14. ......   R—Q 1

Also 14. ....Q—R 4 ; 15. Kt—Kt 5 ! etc., would be advantageous for White.

| 15. K R—Q 1 | Castles |
| 16. Kt—Kt 5 | R×R ch |

If immediately 16. ....Q—R 4, then 17. R×R, R×R ; 18. B×Kt, P×Kt ; 19. B×Q Kt P, R—Q 7 ; 20. Q—B 6, etc. ±.

| 17. R×R | Q—R 4 |
| 18. Kt—Q 4 | B—B 1 |

Position after Black's 18th move.

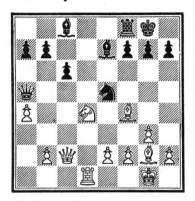

19. P—Q Kt 4 !   ......

The spectacular beginning of a "minority" attack whose immediate result will be the obtaining of the extremely important square Q 5. The tactical justification of the text-move is shown by the following variation : 19. ....B×P ; 20. Kt—Kt 3, Q—B 2 ; 21. Q—K 4, B—B 6 (or B—Q 3 ; 22. Q—Q 4 and wins) ; 22. R—Q B 1, B—Kt 7 (or P—K B 4 ; 23. Q—B 2, etc.) ; 23. R—B 2, P—K B 4 ; 24. Q—Kt 4 ! etc., with a winning position.

19.	Q—B 2
20. P—Kt 5	P—B 4
21. Kt—B 5	P—K B 3

After this the weakness of the light-coloured squares will soon prove fatal. But also after 21. ....B—K B 3 ; 22. Kt—Q 6, R—Q 1 ; 23. Kt—B 4 !, etc., the realisation of White's positional advantage would have been merely a matter of time.

22. Kt—K 3	B—K 3
23. B—Q 5 !	......

Even more effective than 23. Kt —Q 5.

23.	B×B
24. R×B	Q—R 4

There is no longer a defence left. If, for instance, 24. ....R—Q 1, then simply 25. B×Kt, P×B ; 26. Q—B 5, etc., winning easily.

25. Kt—B 5	Q—K 8 ch
26. K—Kt 2	B—Q 1
27. B×Kt	P×B
28. R—Q 7 !	......

Finishing the game by a mating attack.

28.	B—B 3
29. Kt—R 6 ch.	K—R 1
30. Q×B P	......

If now 30. ....R—K 1 then 31. Q—Q 5 !, P×Kt ; 32. Q—B 7, B—K 2 ; 33. R×B followed by mate.

Resigns.

GAME 73

FRENCH DEFENCE

Third Match-Game, Amsterdam, October, 1935.

Black : Dr. M. Euwe

1. P—K 4	P—K 3
2. P—Q 4	P—Q 4
3. Kt—Q B 3	B—Kt 5
4. P—Q R 3	......

This seldom-played move is certainly better than its reputation and has not been even nearly refuted either by the actual game or by the subsequent analysis. Less recommendable is, in spite of its practical success, another attempt made by me in the ninth game of the same match, which continuation was : 4. Q—Kt 4 (too risky because of the yet unsettled situation on the Q's side), Kt—B 3 ; 5. Q×Kt P, R—Kt 1 ; 6. Q—R 6, R—Kt 3 ; 7. Q—K 3, Kt×P ? (by playing 7. ....P—B 4 ! Black would have obtained a sound initiative) ; 8. B—Q 3 !, P—K B 4 ; 9. Kt—K 2,

P—B 4 ; 10. B×Kt, B P×B ; 11. Q—R 3 !, Kt—B 3 ; 12. Q×R P, Q—B 3 ; 13. Kt—B 4 !, P×P ; 14. Kt×R, P×Kt ; 15. P—Q Kt 3, Kt—K 2 ; 16. Kt×Kt, B×Kt ; 17. P—K R 4, Q—B 2 ; 18. Q—R 8 ch, Q—B 1 ; 19. Q×Q ch, K×Q ; 20. B—Kt 5, P—K 4 ; 21. P—K B 3 !, P×P ; 22. P×P ? (After 22. B×B ch, K×B ; 23. P×P, etc., White would have but little trouble to force the win ; the less exact text-move leads to an interesting end-game with Bishops of different colours), B—Q R 6 ! ; 23. P—B 4 !, B—K B 4 ; 24. P×P, B×P ; 25. Castles ch, K—Kt 1 ; 26. Q R—B 1 !, B×R ; 27. R×B, B—B 4 ; 28. R×P, R—Q B 1 ; 29. R—B 3, R—B 1 ; 30. B—B 6, B—K 5 ; 31. R—Kt 3 ch, K—B 2 ; 32. P—R 5 !, R—B 1 ; 33. R—Kt 7 ch, K—K 3 ; 34. P—R 6 !, P—Q 5 ; 35. P—R 7, R—B 8 ch ; 36. K—B 2, R—B 7 ch; 37. K—Kt 3, B×P ; 38. R×B, R×P ; 39. K—B 4, P—Kt 4 ; 40. K—K 4, R—K 7 ch ; 41. K×P, Resigns.

4.	......	B×Kt ch
5.	P×B	P×P
6.	Q—Kt 4	Kt—K B 3

A safer alternative was 6. .... K—B 1 ; 7. Q×P at K 4, Q Kt—Q 2 followed by Q Kt—B 3, etc. After the text-move the dark-coloured squares of Black's position become decidedly weak.

7.	Q×Kt P	R—Kt 1
8.	Q—R 6	P—B 4
9.	Kt—K 2	Q Kt—Q 2

In order to relieve the Queen from the protection of the other Knight. If 9. .... Kt—B 3 White's simplest answer would be 10. P×P !, but also 10. B—Kt 5 as played by Romanovski against Botvinnik in the half-final of the Soviet Championship, 1938, would be sufficient for equalising, for White lost that game only because he was outclassed in the later stages.

| 10. | Kt—Kt 3 | R—Kt 3 ? |

After this loss of time Black's game becomes very difficult. Comparatively better was to play for further complications by 10. .... Q—R 4, although White's prospects would remain more favourable even in that case after 11. B—Q 2, Q—R 5 ; 12. P×P ! etc.

| 11. | Q—K 3 | Kt—Q 4 |

He must already look for a compensation for his Pawn at K 5 which is now bound to be lost.

| 12. | Q×P | Kt×P |
| 13. | Q—Q 3 | Kt—Q 4 |

Also 13. .... P×P ; 14. Q×P, Q—B 3 ; 15. Q×Q, Kt×Q ; 16. B—Q 3, R—Kt 2 ; 17. B—Q 2, etc. would not be satisfactory. As a matter of fact Black's game after his inconsiderate tenth move was hardly to be saved.

14.	B—K 2	Q—B 3
15.	P—Q B 3	P×P
16.	P×P	Kt (Q 2)—Kt 3

The exchange of Black's best posted piece by 16. .... Kt—B 5 ; 17. B×Kt, Q×B ; 18. Castles (K R) etc., would only have made matters easier for White.

Position after Black's 16th move.

17. B—R 5 !   ......

This Bishop-manœuvre, consisting of four consecutive moves, forces a practically decisive weakening of Black's Pawn position. The following play on both wings is very instructive and, I believe, typical of my style.

| 17. ...... | R—Kt 2 |
| 18. B—B 3 | ...... |

Threatening 19. Kt—R 5.

18.	Q—Kt 3
19. B—K 4 !	P—B 4
20. B—B 3	K—B 1
21. P—Q R 4 !	......

The diagonal Q R 3—K B 8 is here the best field of activity for the Bishop.

21.	R—Q B 2
22. Castles (K R)	B—Q 2
23. B—R 3 ch	K—Kt 1
24. P—R 5	R—B 6

This leads to the loss of a Pawn without any improvement of Black's position ; but also the apparently better move 24. .... Kt—B 5 would not have saved the day. The continuation would be 25. B—B 5 ! (stronger than 25. Kt × P, K—R 1 ! etc.), Kt—K 4 ; 26. P × Kt, R × B ; 27. K R—B 1, Q R —Q B 1 ; 28. R × R, R × R ; 29. Q—Q 4 ! winning at least the Q R P by an overwhelming position. The remaining part is—in spite of Black's desperate efforts to 'swindle' —easy enough.

25. Q—Kt 1 !	Kt—R 5
26. B × Kt	P × B
27. Q × Kt P	Q—Q B 3
28. P—R 6 !	......

If now 28. .... Q × Q ; 29. P × Q, R—Kt 1, then 30. K R—Kt 1, Kt— Kt 3 ; 31. B—Kt 4 followed by R × R P and wins.

28.	Kt—Kt 3
29. B—B 5	P—B 5
30. Kt—B 5 !	......

More exact than 30. Kt—K 2 which would also be sufficient.

30.	K—R 1
31. Kt—K 7	Q—K 3
32. B × Kt	B—B 3

Mere desperation.

| 33. Kt × B | R—K Kt 1 |

Threatening perpetual check by 34. .... R × Kt P ch, etc.

| 34. Kt—K 5 ! | R—Kt 2 |
| 35. Q—Kt 8 ch ? | ...... |

As in so many games of that unfortunate match, I played, after the decision was practically reached, too rapidly—without, however, in this particular case, affecting the ultimate result. Instead, 35. B × R P ! would force Black to resign immediately.

35.	R—B 1
36. Kt—Kt 6 ch	R × Kt
37. Q × B P	Q × B
38. Q—K 5 ch	R—Kt 2
39. Q × P	R—Q 1
40. Q—K 5	Q × Q P
41. Q × Q	Resigns.

GAME 74

KING'S INDIAN DEFENCE

Fourth Match-Game, The Hague, October, 1935.

White : DR. M. EUWE

1. P—Q 4	Kt—K B 3
2. P—Q B 4	P—K Kt 3
3. Kt—Q B 3	P—Q 4
4. Q—Kt 3	......

The praxis of the last two to three years has proved that this Queen's move is less effective than 4. B—B 4, B—Kt 2 ; 5. P—K 3, Castles ; 6. Q—Kt 3, P—B 3 ; 7. Kt—B 3 etc., with an unquestionable advantage in space.

| 4. ...... | P×P |
| 5. Q×B P | B—Kt 2 |

Also playable is 5. ....B—K 3 ; 6. Q—Kt 5 ch, Kt—B 3 ; 7. Kt—B 3, but now *not* 7. ....R—Q Kt 1 (as in the second match game, 1935) but 7. ....Kt—Q 4 ! etc., with fairly good counter-chances.

| 6. B—B 4 | P—B 3 |
| 7. R—Q 1 ? | ...... |

An artificial and unnecessary move, instead of which 7. Kt—B 3, Castles ; 8. P—K 4, etc., was indicated. Black can now obtain at least an even game.

| 7. ...... | Q—R 4 |

Threatening 8. ....B—K 3.

| 8. B—Q 2 | P—Q Kt 4 ? |

There are some moves of mine in the first Euwe match which I actually simply cannot understand. Neither before nor since have I played such decidedly unsound Chess, especially in the openings ! Here, for instance, the spoiling of the Pawn-skeleton on the Queen's side cannot even be excused by the lack of other promising continuations; for the simple 8. ....Q—Kt 3 ; 9. B—B 1, B—B 4 followed by .... Castles would have secured Black a distinct advantage in development. I am adding, however, the present game to this collection in spite of the poor opening strategy of both sides—because of the particularly interesting tactical complications of the well-played middle-game.

| 9. Q—Kt 3 | P—Kt 5 |

Has the advantage of being at least consistent ; Black prevents P—K 4 —but at what a price !

| 10. Kt—R 4 | Kt—R 3 |
| 11. P—K 3 | B—K 3 |

Black could also play immediately 11. ....Castles (K R) since 12. B×Kt, B×B ; 13. Q×Kt P, Q—Q 4 or 13. B×P, Q—Q Kt 4, etc., would be in his favour. But he would not like in that case the answer 12. B—Q B 4.

| 12. Q—B 2 | Castles (K R) |
| 13. P—Q Kt 3 | ...... |

If instead 13. Q×B P then 13. ....Kt—B 2 with the threats 14. ....B—Q 2 or 14. ....B×R P.

| 13. ...... | Q R—Kt 1 |
| 14. B—Q 3 | ...... |

Because of his slightly belated development White decides not to take the Q B's Pawn—and rightly so ; after 14. Q×B P, B—B 1 ! the open Q B's file would become a dangerous weapon in Black's hands —for instance, 15. Kt—B 3, B—Kt 2 ; 16. Q—B 2, K R—B 1 ; 17. Q—Kt 1, Kt—K 5, eventually followed by ....Kt—B 6, etc.

| 14. ...... | K R—B 1 |
| 15. Kt—K 2 | ...... |

Obviously underestimating the value of the following Pawn offer; otherwise he would have continued with 15. B×Kt, Q×B ; 16. Kt—B 5, Q—Kt 4 ; 17. Kt—K B 3 ! (but not 17. Kt×B, P×Kt followed by ....P—K 4, etc., with a good game for Black), Kt—Q 2 ; 18. R—Q B 1, etc., with the better end-game prospects. This possibility clearly proves the unsoundness of Black's 8th and 10th moves.

15. ......   **P—B 4 !**

An absolutely correct combination which would have given—against White's best defence—easy equality. But as a matter of fact my opponent, fortunately for me, underestimated the danger.

16. B × Kt   Q × B
17. Kt × P   Q—Kt 4
18. Kt—B 4 ?   ......

Permitting Black to open the centre and thus put the opponent's house in flames. The correct defence consisted in 18. P—K 4 !, Kt—Q 2 ; 19. B—K 3, B × Q P ; 20. Kt × B, Q × Kt ; 21. Q × Q, Kt × Q, etc., with a probable draw as a result.

18. ......   **B—Kt 5 !**
19. P—B 3   ......

If 19. R—Q B 1 the answer 19. ....P—K 4 would also have been strong.

19. ......   **P—K 4 !**
20. Kt (B 4)—Q 3 ......

Equally unsatisfactory was 20 P × B, P × Kt, etc. ∓

Position after White's 20th move.

20. ......   **P × P !**

A pretty and exactly calculated

piece offer, which White is practically forced to accept, since both 21. P × P, Kt—Q 4 ! and 21. P—K 4, Kt—Q 2 would have left him even fewer chances of salvation.

21. P × B   P × P
22. B × K P   ......

A comparatively more difficult variation for Black was 22. B × Kt P, Kt—Q 4 ; 23. P—Q R 3, P—Q R 4 ; 24. Q—B 4 !, P × B ! ; 25. Q × Kt, P × P ; 26. R—K B 1 (or 26. P—Kt 4, B—B 6 ch followed by ....B × P), P—R 7 ! ; 27. R × B P, B—B 6 ch ; 28. K any, R × Kt and wins.

22. ......   Kt × P
23. B—B 4   ......

Anything else was equally unsatisfactory—for instance : I. 23. B—Kt 1, B—B 6 ch ; 24. K—B 1, R—Kt 3, etc. II. 23. B—B 2, B—B 6 ch ; 24. K—B 1, R—B 3 ! ; 25. K—Kt 1, Kt × B ; 26. Q × Kt, R—Q 1, etc., with a winning position.

23. ......   B—B 6 ch
24. R—Q 2   ......

Obviously forced.

24. ......   R × Kt !
25. Kt × R   ......

If 25. B × R then 25. ....Q—K 1 ch ! wins immediately.

25. ......   Q × Kt

Black has at last enough from all the complications and selects the clearest variation, which secures him a slight material advantage (Queen and Pawn against two Rooks) by persisting attack. A shorter way to victory was, however, 25. ....R—K 1 ch ! with the following main variation : 26. Kt—K 4, P—B 4 ; 27. K—Q 1, R × Kt ; 28. R—Q 8 ch, K—B 2 ; 29. B—

Kt 5, P—B 5 ! ; 30. K—B 1, R—
K 7 ; 31. Q—Q 3, Q × B ! and wins.

26. B × R	Q—K 2 ch
27. K—Q 1	Kt—K 6 ch
28. K—B 1	Kt × Q
29. R × Kt	P—K R 4 !

A necessary preparation for
B—Kt 2.

30. R—Q 1	B—Kt 2
31. P—K R 3	P—R 4

Black's chief trumps—which by
right use must guarantee the win—
are (1) the permanent insecurity of
White's King ; (2) the unprotected
position of the Bishop, whose efforts
to find a safe square are bound to
fail. The game remains lively and
instructive until the very end.

32. B—B 4	Q—K 5
33. B—B 7	Q—K 6 ch
34. K—Kt 1	P—Q R 5 !

By this break-up, which could not
in the long run be prevented, Black
wins perforce at least the exchange.

35. P × P	P—Kt 6
36. P × P	Q × P ch
37. K—B 1	B—R 3 ch
38. K R—Q 2	Q × Q R P
39. B—K 5	......

Instead, 39. K—Q 1 would have
slightly prolonged the game, as
Black would be compelled first to
force the white King back on the
Q's side by means of 39. .... B × R ;
40. K × B, Q—K 5 ! ; 41. K—B 1,
Q—K 8 ch, etc.—and only after
that decide the game on the other
wing through a gradual advance of
his Pawns supported by the King.

39.	K—R 2
40. B—B 3	Q—Kt 4 !

Preventing 41. K—Q 1.

41. B—Q 4	......

White no longer has satisfactory
moves left. If, for instance, 41.
B—R 1, then 41. ....Q—B 8 ch,
followed by ....B—Kt 2 ch, etc.

41.	Q—K 7 !
42. P—Kt 4	Q—K 8 ch
43. K—Kt 2	B × R
44. R—B 8	B—B 8 ch !

Resigns.

GAME 75

FRENCH DEFENCE

Seventh Match-Game, Utrecht,
October, 1935.

Black : Dr. M. Euwe

1. P—K 4	P—K 3
2. P—Q 4	P—Q 4
3. Kt—Q B 3	B—Kt 5
4. Kt—K 2	P × P
5. P—Q R 3	B—K 2

Even more convincing is 5. ....
B × Kt ch ; 6. Kt × B, Kt—Q B 3
with at least an even game.
This possibility practically refutes
White's fourth move.

6. Kt × P	Kt—Q B 3

Also here the Knight's move is
good enough. In the fifth game of
this match I tried here 7. B—K 3
(if 7. P—Q B 3 then 7. ....
P—K 4), but did not obtain after
7. ....Kt—B 3 ; 8. K Kt—B 3,
Castles (threatening already Kt ×
Kt followed by P—K B 4) more
than equality. Therefore I decided
to try in the present game the
following paradoxical-looking Pawn
move, the obvious idea being to
combine the fianchetto development
of the King's Bishop with a possible
Pawn attack on the King's side.

7. P—K Kt 4 !?	P—Q Kt 3

This is not even an attempt at a
refutation and White soon obtains
the kind of position he was aiming

at. True enough, the most natural answer 7. ....P—K 4 would also not be convincing, because of 8. P—Q 5, Kt—Q 5 ; 9. K Kt—Q B 3 (but not 9. Kt×Kt, Q×Q P !∓)— and if 9. ....P—K B 4 then 10. P×P, B×P ; 11. B—K 3, etc., with fair fighting chances for White ; but 7. ....Kt—K B 3 ! ; 8. Kt×Kt ch, B×Kt ; 9. B—K 3, Q—Q 4, etc., would have secured for Black a comfortable development of all his forces and thus prove the inefficiency of White's seventh move.

8.	B—Kt 2	B—Kt 2
9.	P—Q B 3	Kt—B 3
10.	K Kt—Kt 3	Castles ?

Even if it could be proved that Black can find an adequate defence against the following King's attack, the text-move should still be condemned as bringing Black's game into danger without any profit or necessity. After the simple 10. ....Q—Q 2 followed by .... Castles (Q R) White would remain with an unimportant advantage in space but without any real attacking prospects.

| 11. | P—K Kt 5 | Kt×Kt |
| 12. | Kt×Kt | K—R 1 |

Preparing for ....P—K B 4 which White prevents by his following strong move.

13. Q—R 5 !   ......

If now 13. ....P—K B 4 then of course 14. P—Kt 6 with deadly effect.

13. ......   Q—K 1

Threatening again ....P—K B 4 but allowing the following promising combination. Safer was, anyhow, 13. ....Kt—Q R 4, as the variation 14. P—Kt 4, Kt—Kt 6 ; 15. Kt—B 6, P×Kt ; 16. B×B,

P—K B 4 ! etc., would not be dangerous for Black. In that case White would improve his pressure by finishing his development—14. B —R B 4 eventually followed by Castles (Q R), etc. ±

Position after Black's 13th move.

14. Kt—B 6 !   ......

A correct Pawn-offer securing White a strong and most likely irresistible offensive.

14. ......   B×Kt

The alternative was 14. ....P× Kt ; 15. P×P, Kt—R 4 (if 15. .... B×P ? then 16. B—K 4 followed by mate) ; 16. P×B, Q×P ; 17. B×B, Kt×B ; 18. B—Kt 5, P— K B 3 ; 19. B—R 6, R—K Kt 1 ; 20. Castles (Q R), Kt—Q 3 ; 21. K R—K 1, etc., with a clear advantage for White.

| 15. | P×B | P×P |
| 16. | Q—R 4 | Q—Q 1 |

Forced, since 16. ....Q—K 2 would lose a piece after 17. B—K 4 ! etc.

17. B—B 4 !   ......

This continuation of the attack— which point consists in the Bishop's retreat on the next move—was by no means easy to find. Black's comparatively best chance was now to give back his extra-Pawn by playing 17. ....P—K B 4—although after 18. Q×Q, Q R×Q; 19. B×P, R—Q 2; 20. B—B 4, Kt—R 4; 21. R—K Kt 1! etc., White's end-game advantage would be quite evident.

| 17. ...... | P—K 4 |
| 18. B—Kt 3 ! | P—B 4 |

There is hardly anything better now. If, for instance, 18. ....P×P then 19. Castles (Q R) !, etc., with an easy attacking play.

| 19. P×P | ...... |

Also here 19. Castles (Q R) was strong. But the simple recuperation of the material sacrificed is, considering White's powerful attacking possibilities, convincing enough.

| 19. ...... | R—K Kt 1 |
| 20. B—B 3 ? | ...... |

But this inexact move permits Black to inaugurate a saving counter-attack. Practically decisive was instead 20. Q—R 3 ! after which 20. ....Q—Q 6 would have been refuted by 21. B—R 4 ! and 20. .... R—Kt 5 by 21. Castles ! threatening P—K B 3 with a win of material by persisting attack.

| 20. ...... | Q—Q 6 ! |

An ingenious resource; but, as the following shows, Black, in adopting it, did not actually realise how many interesting possibilities it opened to him.

| 21. B—K 2 | ...... |

White has nothing better, since 21. B×Kt ? would be fatal, because of 21. ....B—R 3 !: 22. Q—R 5, R—Kt 5 ! etc.

Position after White's 21st move.

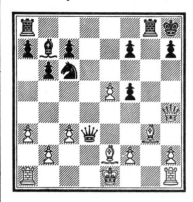

| 21. ...... | Q—K 5 ? |

Leading to a lost end-game. From an objective point of view it is certainly a pity that Black avoids the fantastical complications deriving from 21. ....Q—B 7 !—a move which by right continuation would have secured him a draw. Here follows the main variation as well as some minor possibilities :

22. *Q—B* 6 *ch, R—Kt* 2 ; 23. *R— K Kt* 1 *!* (a) *Q×P* ; 24. *P—K* 6 *! !, Q×R ch* ; 25. *B—Q* 1, *Kt—Q* 5 *! !*; (b) 26. *Q×R ch ! (c) K×Q* ; 27. *B—R* 4 *ch, K—R* 3 *! (d)* 28. *B— Kt* 5 *ch, K any* ; 29. *B—R* 4 *ch, etc. Draw by perpetual check.*

(a) Not good is the plausible 23. P—K 6 because of 23. ....R—K 1!; 24. K R—Kt 1 !, B—R 3 ! ! (.... R×P ; 25. B—K 5 ! and wins) ; 25. B×B, R×P ch ; 26. B—K 5, Q— K 5 ch ; 27. K—B 1, Q×B, etc., with advantage for Black.

(b) But not 25. ....R—Q 1 nor 25. ....Q—Kt 8 because of the answer 26. B—Q 6 ! ! with a win for White.

(c) There are no winning chances for White by the continuation 26. Q×Kt, P—K B 3 !; 27. Q×B P, B—B 6 ; 28. K—Q 2, Q—R 7 ch ; 29. B—B 2, B—K 5 etc.

(d) Instead 27. ....K—B 1 loses : 28. P—K 7 ch, K—K 1 ; 29.

R—Kt 8 ch, K- -Q 2 ; 30. R—Q 8 ch and wins.

| 22. Q × Q | P × Q |
| 23. B—R 4 ! | ...... |

The winning move, probably overlooked by Black when he played 21. .... Q—K 5. After 23. Castles (Q R) he would have obtained excellent drawing chances by continuing 23. .... R × B ! ; 24. R P × R, Kt × P etc.

23.	P—K R 3
24. Castles	Q R—K 1
25. B—B 6 ch	K—R 2
26. P—K B 4 !	P × P e.p.
27. B × P	......

Of course much stronger than winning the exchange for a Pawn by 27. B—Q 3 ch, etc. The White Bishops are now dominating the board and Black is unable to prevent the intrusion of the hostile Rook on his second rank.

| 27. ...... | Kt—R 4 |

The exchange of Bishops, which possibly would have saved the battle in the early middle game, does not bring any relief at this stage.

| 28. B × B | Kt × B |
| 29. R—Q 7 | ...... |

The beginning of the execution.

29.	Kt—B 4
30. R × P ch	K—Kt 3
31. R × P	Kt—Q 6 ch
32. K—Kt 1	......

Also the simple 32. K—B 2 was good enough.

32.	K—B 4
33. R—Q 1	Kt × K P
34. R—B 1 ch	K—K 5
35. R × P	Kt—B 5

Or 35. .... Kt—B 6 ; 36. R—R 4 ch, K—K 6 ; 37. B—Q 4 ch, etc. Black's game is quite hopeless.

36. R—Q 7	K—K 6
37. R—K 1 ch	K—B 6
38. R × R	R × R
39. R—Q 4	Kt—K 6
40. R—K R 4	Kt—B 4
41. R—Q Kt 4	Resigns

GAME 76

VIENNA OPENING

Twenty-seventh Match - Game, The Hague, December, 1935.

Black : DR. M. EUWE

1. P—K 4	P—K 4
2. Kt—Q B 3	Kt—K B 3
3. B—B 4	Kt × P
4. Q—R 5	Kt—Q 3
5. B—Kt 3	......

Instead, 5. Q × K P ch, Q—K 2, etc., leads to a perfectly even game. Being compelled to play for a win at any price, I decided to allow my opponent to make the offer of an exchange which for about 30 years has been known to give him excellent attacking chances. It is : 5. .... Kt—Q B 3 (!) ; 6. Kt—Kt 5. P—K Kt 3 ; 7. Q—B 3, P—B 4 ; 8, Q—Q 5, Q—B 3 ; 9. Kt × B P ch, K—Q 1 ; 10. Kt × R, P—Kt 3 (or Q Kt 4) followed by .... B—Q Kt 2 after which White would have to suffer—for a while, at least. It is, however, psychologically easy to understand that with two points ahead Euwe did not want to take such chances.

| 5. ...... | B—K 2 |
| 6. Kt—B 3 | Kt—B 3 |

Instead, 6. .... Castles would be slightly premature because of the possibility 7. P—K R 4.

7. Kt × P   Kt × Kt ?

An instructive opening mistake. Black underestimated the potential power of the opponent's K's Bishops which could be eliminated after 7. ....Castles ; 8. Kt—Q 5, Kt—Q 5 !; 9. Castles, Kt × B ; 10. R P × Kt, Kt—K 1, etc., with about even prospects. After the text-move White succeeds in preventing for rather a long time the normal development of Black's Q's side and maintains a gradually increasing pressure.

8. Q × Kt   Castles
9. Kt—Q 5 !   ......

It was important to prevent 9. ....B—K B 3.

9. ......   R—K 1
10. Castles   B—B 1
11. Q—B 4   P—Q B 3

As Black will not succeed in playing ....P—Q 4, this move does not make matters easier for him. Worth considering was, instead, 11. ....P—Q Kt 3, since 12. Kt × B P (Q × Kt ? ; 13. B × B P ch±) would be erroneous because of 12. .... R—K 5 !

12. Kt—K 3   Q—R 4
13. P—Q 4   ......

Chiefly in order to prevent 13. ....Q—K 4. That Black has temporarily the control upon his K 5 is comparatively unimportant.

13. ......   Q—R 4

Of course not 13. ....R—K 5 because of 14. B × B P, etc.

14. P—Q B 3   Kt—K 5

If 14. ....Kt—Kt 4, then 15. P—Q R 4, B—Q 3 ; 16. Q × B P ch, Q × Q ; 17. B × Q ch followed by P × Kt, etc., to White's advantage.

Position after Black's 14th move.

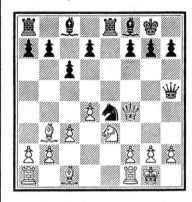

15. P—B 3 !   ......

By this important intermediate move White practically forces the isolation of Black's Q P and thus obtains an appreciable end-game advantage.

15. ......   Kt—Kt 4

There is nothing better. If, for instance, 15. ....B—Q 3, then 16. Q × B P ch ! etc., finally winning a Pawn, and if 15. ....Kt—B 3 then 16. Kt—Kt 4 ! etc., also with a strong advantage.

16. P—Q 5 !   ......

Threatening, of course, 17. P— K R 4.

16. ......   P × P
17. Kt × P   Kt—K 3
18. Q—Kt 4   ......

The seemingly more energetic 18. Q—Kt 3, Q—Kt 3 ; 19. P—K B 4 would, in fact, not be so clear because of 19. ....B—B 4 ch ; 20. K—R 1, Q × Q ; 21. P × Q, R— Q Kt 1 ; 22. P—B 5, Kt—B 1, etc.

18. ......   Q—Kt 3
19. B—K 3   P—Kt 3
20. Q R—Q 1   B—Kt 2

21. Q × Q	. . . . .

After all White's forces have been mobilised there is time for transforming the battle into an end-game in which Black's Pawn weaknesses will become even more apparent than they are at the moment.

21.	R P × Q
22. K R—K 1	Q R—B 1
23. K—B 2	B—B 4

What else ? If, for instance, 23. . . . . Kt—B 4, then 24. B—B 2 followed by the doubling of Rooks against Black's weakness at Q 2.

24. B × B	B × Kt

If 24. . . . . P × B then 25. Kt—K 3 followed by Kt—Q B 4—Q 6, etc., with a big advantage. But 24. . . . . R × B would possibly have allowed a more stubborn resistance.

25. B × B	Kt × B
26. R × R ch	R × R
27. P—Q Kt 4 !	. . . . . .

The point of the previous exchanges. White—rightly—considers that in the following Rook endgame his Pawn majority on the Q's side, *supported by the King and strengthened by the fact that the enemy's King is completely out of play*, will become decisive. Black, obviously, cannot avoid the exchange of minor pieces as 27. . . . . Kt—R 5 ; 28. B—Kt 3 followed by R × Q P, etc., would be hopeless.

27.	Kt—K 3
28. B × Kt	Q P × B
29. R—Q 7	. . . . . .

After 29. P—Q B 4, R—Q B 1 ; 30. R—Q B 1, K—B 1, etc., White's advantage would not be decisive.

29.	R—Q B 1
30. R × R P	R × P
31. R—R 8 ch	K—R 2

Position after Black's 31st move.

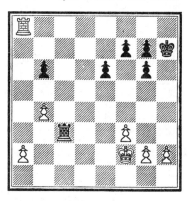

32. P—Q R 4 ?	. . . . . .

This rather obvious mistake in a technically won position has not —to my knowledge—been noticed by any of the eminent critics who have devoted many pages to the analysis of the possibilities offered by this end-game. The main disadvantage of the text-move is that it leaves the squares Q R 3 and Q Kt 3 free for the Black Rook, which therefore from now on can be dislodged from the third rank only at cost of valuable time. Correct— and simple enough—was 32. *K— K 2 !* after which the black Rook would be (1) either dragged into a purely passive position—as in the actual game—after 33. K—Q 2, etc.; (2) or forced to undertake immediately the counter-attack 32. . . . . R—B 7 ch with the result 33. K— Q 3, R × Kt P ; 34. K—B 4 !—and one would not need to count *tempi* in order to realise that White's passed Pawns, supported, if necessary, by the King, will be by far the quickest. The fact that I missed this simple win after having deserved it by the previous difficult positional play, proves once more the poor form I was in in 1935. In the second match I—fortunately—took advantage of such opportunities regularly and without hesitation (compare, for instance, the analogous King's man-œuvre connected with the offer of the whole Q's side in the second game, 1937, No. 97) !

32. ......   R—Kt 6

Hopeless would be 32. ....R—B 7 ch because of 33. K—K 3 fol-lowed by the King's march to the Q's side ; but after 32. ....P—K 4 ! (certainly a difficult move to find in a practical game) there would not be—according to several Soviet Masters, supported by Dr. Lasker—any forced win for White.   Even if so (some of their variations are by no means convincing), this would only prove that White's previous move was an even bigger omission than it actually seemed to be ; but for the general appreciation of the *character* of the Rook ending reached after Black's 28th move all that analysing has no importance whatsoever.

33. P—Kt 5   P—K Kt 4
34. K—K 2   ......

Because of Black's loss of time at his 32nd move this King's trip will be successful even now.

34. ......   P—K 4
35. K—Q 2   P—B 3
36. K—B 2   R—Kt 5
37. K—B 3   R—Q 5

Black has succeeded in prevent-ing the formation of *two* passed Pawns, but, to his bad luck, *one* Pawn, supported by the King, is amply sufficient !

38. R—R 6   K—Kt 3
39. R × P   R × P
40. R—R 6   R—Q 5
41. P—Q Kt 6 Resigns

GAME 77

QUEEN'S GAMBIT ACCEPTED

Bad Nauheim Tournament, May, 1936.

White : K. AHUES

1. P—Q 4   P—Q 4
2. P—Q B 4   P × P
3. Kt—K B 3   P—Q R 3

This move, in connection with the next, was introduced by me in the third game of the 1934 Match with Bogoljubow.   Even if it can be convincingly proved (which has not been done) that the Bishop's de-velopment at K Kt 5 is not good for Black, the text-move will still be used by those who prefer to avoid the variations starting with White's Q—R 4 ch.

4. P—Q R 4   ......

White has no reason for prevent-ing ....P—Q Kt 4, since the varia-tion 4. P—K 3, P—Q Kt 4 ; 5. P—Q R 4, B—Kt 2 ; 6. P × P, P × P ; 7. R × R, B × R ; 8. P—Q Kt 3, etc., is to his advantage.   The text-move, besides losing time, weakens also White's Q Kt 4 and, therefore, has to be decidedly condemned.   The two following positional fights may give an idea as to Black's possi-bilities after 4. P—K 3, B—Kt 5. The character of the ensuing con-flict depends on whether White leaves the pawn-structure intact in the centre (as in I), or tries to solve the centre-problem in a dynamic way (as in II).

I. *White :* E. Zinner (*Podebrad,* 1936). 4. *P—K 3, B—Kt 5 ; 5. B × P, P—K 3 ; 6. P—K R 3— B—R 4 ; 7. Q—Kt 3, R—R 2 (or ....B × Kt ; 8. P × B, P—Q Kt 4) ; 8. P—Q R 4, Kt—Q B 3 ; 9. B—Q 2, Kt—B 3 ; 10. B—B 3, Kt—Q 4 ; 11. Q Kt—Q 2, Kt × B ; 12. P × Kt, Kt—R 4 ; 13. Q—R 2, Kt × B ; 14.*

Q×Kt, B—Q 3 ; 15. R—Q Kt 1, O—O ; 16. O—O, B—Kt 3 ; 17. R—Kt 2, P—Q B 3 ; 18. Q—Kt 3, P—Kt 4 ; 19. P—B 4, R—Kt 2 ; 20. R—R 1, R—Kt 1 ; 21. K R—R 2, B—B 2 ; 22. Q—Q 1, B—Q 6 ! ; 23. B P×P, B P×P ; 24. Kt—K 1, B—Kt 3 ; 25. Q—K 2, Q—Q 3 ; 26. Q Kt—B 3, P—Kt 5 ! ; 27. Kt—Q 3, B—K 5 ; 28. Kt—B 5, B—Q 4 ; 29. Kt—Kt 3, K R—B 1 ; 30. R—R 1, P—Q R 4 ; 31. R—Q B 1, B—Kt 3 ; 32. Q R—B 2, R×R ; 33. Q×R, Q—Q 2 ! ; 34. P—K 4, B×Kt ; 35. Q×B, R—Q B 1 ; 36. R—B 4, R×R ; 37. Q×R, P—R 3 ; 38. P—Q 5, Q×R P ; 39. Q—B 8 ch, K—R 2 ; 40. Q—Kt 7, B—Q 1 ! ; 41. Q×B P, Q—R 8 ch ; 42. K—R 2, Q—B 3 ; 43. Q—Q 7, P—Kt 6 ; 44. P—R 4, P—Kt 7 ; 45. Q—Kt 5, P×P ; 46. Resigns.

II.   *White : Axelsson (Orebro, 1935).* (The six first moves as in the previous game.) 7. O—O, Kt—K B 3 ; 8. Kt—B 3, Kt—B 3 ; 9. B—K 2, B—Q 3 ; 10. P—Q Kt 3 (better than P—Q R 3 played in an analogous position by Bogoljubow in the game mentioned above), O—O ; 11. B—Kt 2, Q—K 2 ; 12. *P—K 4*, B×Kt ; 13. B×B, Q R—Q 1 ; 14. Kt—K 2, B—B 4 ; 15. R—B 1, B—Kt 3 ; 16. Q—B 2, P—K 4 ; 17. P—Q 5, Kt—Q Kt 5 ; 18. B—R 3 !, P—Q R 4 ; 19. Q—B 4, Kt—K 1 ; 20. K R—Q 1, Q—R 5 ! ; 21. B×Kt, Q×P ch ; 22. K—R 1, P×B ; 23. Q×Kt P, Kt—Q 3 ; 24. P—Q R 4, R—R 1 ; 25. R—K B 1, Q—R 5 ; 26. Q—Q 2, P—Kt 3 ! ; 27. P—Kt 3, Q—K 2 ; 28. Kt—B 3, P—K B 4 ; 29. P×P, P×P ; 30. Q R—K 1, Q—Kt 2 ; 31. P—Q Kt 4, P—K 5 ; 32. B—Q 1, Kt—B 5 ; 33. Q—B 1, Kt—K 4 ; 34. B—K 2, P—B 3 ! ; 35. P×P, P×P ; 36. R—Q 1, K—R 1 ; 37. P—R 5, R—K Kt 1 ; 38. Q—B 4, B—B 2 ; 39. Q—B 2, Kt—Q 6 ! ; 40. Resigns.

4. ......   Kt—K B 3
5. P—K 3   B—Kt 5

6. B×P   P—K 3
7. Kt—B 3   Kt—B 3

As one may see from the prefixed games, this Knight's development belongs to the system inaugurated by ....B—K Kt 5. In this particular position it is more appropriate than ever, Black having at his disposal, if needed, the square Q Kt 5.

8. B—K 2   B—Kt 5
9. Castles   Castles
10. Kt—Q 2   ......

White is over-anxious to simplify and allows, to his disadvantage, the following advance of Black's K P. The quieter 10. B—Q 2 would probably leave him more equalising chances.

10. ......   B×B
11. Kt×B   P—K 4 !

As the opening of the central files through P×K P would be here, or on the following moves, obviously to the benefit of the better developed party, White will practically be compelled to allow a further advance of this Pawn, after which the activity of his Bishop will be limited to a minimum.

12. Kt—K B 3   R—K 1
13. B—Q 2   B—Q 3

The exchange of the opponent's poorest piece would be, of course, a grave strategical error.

14. Kt—Kt 3   P—K 5
15. Kt—K 1   B×Kt !

After this exchange, the immobilised Pawn mass on the King's side will be unable to prevent in the long run the attacking formation ....Kt—K Kt 5 and ....Q—K B 4 (or K R 4). The little counter-demonstration that White will now undertake on the open Q B-file can be parried without effort or loss of time.

16. R P × B   Kt—K 2

The full control upon Black's Q 4 is the key of the situation.

17. P—Q Kt 4   Q—Q 2
18. Kt—B 2   Q Kt—Q 4
19. Kt—R 3   P—Q Kt 4 !

Confining the mobility of the hostile Knight.

20. P × P   P × P
21. Q—K 2   P—B 3

This Pawn could eventually become weak—had not Black already prepared a plan for an irresistible mating attack !

22. Kt—Q B 2   Q—B 4

White cannot even answer this move by P—K B 3—his Knight being unprotected—and he has nothing better than to prepare a desperate King's flight.

23. K R—Q B 1 P—R 3

A useful precaution—especially as White has left such small choice of moves.

24. R—R 5   Q R—B 1
25. Kt—R 1   ......

The Knight dreams of at last reaching a more suitable square (Q B 5), but it is much, much too late !

25. ......   Kt—Kt 5

With the strong threat 26. .... Q—R 4

26. K—B 1   ......

Position after White's 26th move.

26. ......   R—K 3 !

A similar stratagem to that in the Dresden game against Bogoljubow (No. 79) : Black gives up a useless unit in order to gain the K B P and thus denude the enemy's King.

27. R × Kt P   R—K B 3
28. Q R—B 5   Kt × B P
29. K—K 1   ......

Or, 29. K—Kt 1, Kt—Kt 5 followed by ....Q—R 4 and mate.

29. ......   Kt—Q 6 ch
30. K—Q 1   Q—B 8 ch
31. B—K 1   R—B 7 !

Expecting 32. Q × Q, after which I would have the pleasant choice between the Knight-mate at Q Kt 7 and K 6.

White resigns.

GAME 78

QUEEN'S GAMBIT DECLINED
(CAMBRIDGE SPRINGS
DEFENCE)

Bad Nauheim Tournament, May,
1936.

Black : E. BOGOLJUBOW

1.	P—Q 4	P—Q 4
2.	P—Q B 4	P—K 3
3.	Kt—Q B 3	Kt—K B 3
4.	B—Kt 5	Q Kt—Q 2
5.	P—K 3	P—B 3
6.	Kt—B 3	Q—R 4
7.	Kt—Q 2	......

The most logical reply to Black's
6th move, for it reduces his possibilities on the diagonal Q R 4—K 8
to a minimum.

7.	......	B—Kt 5
8.	Q—B 2	P × P

Obtaining the pair of Bishops,
which, however, is hardly sufficient
compensation for the abandonment
of the centre. The older 8. ....
Castles together with ....Kt—K 5
is comparatively more promising.

9.	B × Kt	Kt × B
10.	Kt × P	Q—B 2
11.	P—K Kt 3	Castles

Useless would be 11. ....P—B 4,
because of 12. B—Kt 2, after which
12. ....P × P would be met by 13.
Q—R 4 ch.

12.	B—Kt 2	B—Q 2

Here, also, 12. ....P—B 4, would
have led to nothing after 13. Castles,
P × P ; 14. Kt—Kt 5, etc. But,
after the text-move, White has to
count upon the possible advance of
the Q B P, which explains his next
two moves.

13.	P—Q R 3	B—K 2
14.	P—Q Kt 4	Kt—Q 4
15.	Castles (K side)	......

15. Kt—K 4 also came into consideration, but I estimated that
White's advantage after the exchange of Knights would be convincing enough and that there was
not, therefore, any necessity for
trying to complicate matters by
avoiding it.

15.	......	Kt × Kt
16.	Q × Kt	K R—Q 1
17.	Q R—B 1	......

The right utilisation of the pair
of Rooks on the half-open files often
presents a very difficult problem.
Here, for instance, it was obvious
enough that *one* Rook has to be
posted on the Q B-file in order to
make the realisation of ....P—
Q B 4 even more difficult, but
where develop the other—at Q Kt 1
or Q 1 ? As the reader will see, I did
not select here the most effective method, thus permitting my
opponent to obtain, at one moment,
a fairly even game. The correct
scheme was K R—Q B 1 and Q R—
Kt 1.

17.	......	B—K 1
18.	K R—Q 1	Q R—B 1
19.	Kt—R 5	......

Trying, through the threat P—
Q Kt 5, to provoke Black's next
move. But far more important was
still 19. R—Kt 1 !, P—Q Kt 3 ; 20.
K R—Q B 1, preventing the freeing
....P—Q B 4.

19.	......	P—Q R 3
20.	Kt—B 4	P—Q Kt 3 !
21.	R—Q Kt 1	......

Too late !

21.	......	B—B 3

Black still prepares for ....P—

Q B 4, not realising that he could—and should—play it immediately. As White would not profit either from I. 22. Kt × Kt P ! ?, P × Kt P !; 23. Q × Q, R × Q ; 24. P × P, R—Q Kt 1 ; 25. Kt—R 8, R—R 2, or from II. 22. Kt P × P, P × P ; 23. R—Kt 7, P × P ; 24. R × P, R × R ; 25. R × Q, R—Q 8 ch, followed by R × R∓, he would have had nothing better than 22. Kt P × P, P × P ; 23. P—Q 5 !, P × P ; 24. B × P, B—Q R 5 ; 25. R—Q 3, B—K B 3 ; 26. Q—Q 2, B—Q Kt 4, etc., with a draw in prospect owing to the unavoidable "different coloured" Bishops. Now White succeeds in taking full advantage of his opportunity.

22. K R—Q B 1 ......

Protects the Knight once more in order to make possible, after 22. ....P—B 4 ?, the manœuvre 23. Kt P × P, P × P ; 24. R—Kt 7, etc.

22. ......   Q—R 2
23. Q—B 2 !   ......

Definitely preventing ....P—Q B 4 and threatening to advance the Q R P in order to gain the square Q Kt 6 for the Knight.

23. ......   R—B 2
24. P—Q R 4   B—K 2

Or 24. ....P—B 4 ; 25. P—R 5 !, etc.

25. P—R 5   P × P
26. P × P   P—Q B 4

Now this move has no more effect, since the White pieces have in the meantime taken possession of the commanding spots. It is instructive to observe how little the famous "two Bishops" have to say here, if chiefly because of a previous inexact handling of the heavy pieces.

27. Kt—Kt 6   B—Q Kt 4
28. P—Q 5   P × P

29. B × P !   ......

Much stronger than 29. Kt × P, for the Bishop will be very useful at B 4 for blocking the passed Pawn.

29. ......   B—B 1
30. R—Q 1   R—Q 3
31. B—B 4   ......

At the same time, White gets control of the open file, his powerful Knight preventing the free manœuvring of Black's Queen and Rook. The second player deservedly pays the penalty for his short-sighted 21st move.

31. ......   R × R ch
32. R × R   Q—Kt 1
33. Q—Q 3   Q—K 1
34. Q—Q 8   ......

From now on simplicity is trump !

34. ......   R—K 2
35. Q × Q   B × Q

After 35. ....R × Q, there would have been a short, sharp win : 36. B × B, P × B ; 37. P—R 6, P—B 5 ; 38. P—R 7, P—B 6 ; 39. R—Q 7 !, B—B 4 ; 40. P—R 8 = Q R × Q ; 41. Kt × R followed by 42. R—Q 8 ch and 43. R—Q B 8.

36. R—Q 8   B—B 3

Position after Black's 36th move.

37. B × P ......

This first material win is absolutely decisive, since Black cannot even try to obtain compensation by 37. ....R—R 2 because of 38. Kt—B 8 ! etc. In spite of White's inexactitude on the 17th and 19th moves, the game is a fairly good illustration of the Cambridge Springs Defence with White's 7. Kt—Q 2.

37.	P—Kt 3
38. B—B 4	R—Kt 2
39. K—B 1	K—Kt 2
40. K—K 2	B—K 2
41. R—Q B 8	B—Kt 7
42. P—B 3	P—R 4
43. P—K 4	B—R 6
44. R—K 8	B—K B 1
45. P—R 6	R—B 2
46. P—K 5 !	......

Preventing ....B—Q 3 and threatening now 47. R—Q Kt 8 followed by R—Kt 7 etc.

46.	B—Q 2
47. Kt × B	R × Kt
48. R—Kt 8	Resigns.

GAME 79

THREE KNIGHTS' GAME

Dresden Tournament, May, 1936.

Black: E. BOGOLJUBOW

1. P—K 4	P—K 4
2. Kt—K B 3	Kt—Q B 3
3. Kt—B 3	P—K Kt 3

Playing at his best Bogoljubow would hardly have selected such an obviously inferior defence—since he knows very well how to play the Four Knights' game with Black (see, for instance, his game against Maroczy, London, 1922).

4. P—Q 4	P × P
5. Kt—Q 5 !	B—Kt 2
6. B—K Kt 5	Q Kt—K 2

This unnatural looking move is already the only one, since after 5. ....P—B 3 ; 6. B—K B 4, P—Q 3, the diagonal K Kt 1—Q R 7 would become fatally weak.

7. P—K 5 ......

White has the choice between this only seemingly more aggressive move—which in fact is leading to a favourable end-game—and the simple 7. Kt × P, with excellent middle-game prospects after 7. ....P— Q B 3 ; 8. Kt × Kt, Kt × Kt ; 9. Q— Q 2 followed by Castles (Q R), etc. Possibly this way was the more logical one.

7. ......   **P—K R 3 !**

Otherwise 8. Kt—B 6 ch. would be too strong.

8. B × Kt ......

The sacrifice of a pawn by B— B 6, B × B ; 9. Kt × B ch, Kt × Kt ; 10. P × Kt, Kt—Kt 1 followed by ....Q × P would not have paid.

8.	Kt × B
9. Q × P	Kt × Kt
10. Q × Kt	......

White's advantage in space begins to become alarming, so Black must try to exchange Queens as quickly as possible in order to avoid an unanswerable King's attack.

10. ......   **P—Q B 3**

If 10. ....P—Q 3 then 11. Castles, B—K 3 ; 12. Q—Kt 5 ch ! etc. ±

11. Q—Q 6	B—B 1
12. Q—Q 4	Q—Kt 3
13. Castles !	......

By offering his K B P, White wins an important developing *tempo*. Black rightly refuses this offer, for, after 13. ....B—B 4 ; 14. Q—B 3, B×P ; 15. Kt—Q 4 !, his position would have rapidly gone to pieces.

13.	Q×Q
14. Kt×Q	......

An interesting and difficult moment. White decides not to prevent the opening of the centre followed by the emancipation of the Bishop, for he is entitled to expect appreciable profits from the two central files dominated by his Rooks. The consequences of the alternative 14. R×Q, B—Kt 2 ; 15. R—K 4, P—Q Kt 4, followed by ....B—Kt 2 and .... Castles (Q R) were, to say the least, not evident, especially as it would be Black who would have the initiative for opening the position.

14.	P—Q 4

Almost forced, because White, in addition to all the other unpleasantnesses, threatened P—B 4—B 5.

15. P×P *e.p.*	B×P
16. B—B 4	Castles
17. K R—K 1	......

The White pieces are beautifully placed while Black's Q B is still looking for a suitable square. Its next sally is the best proof of the difficulties he has to deal with.

17.	B—K Kt 5
18. P—K B 3	B—B 1
19. P—K Kt 3	......

Holding the square K B 4 and now threatening 20. Kt×P.

19.	B—Q B 4
20. Kt—Kt 3	......

The beginning of an interesting Knight's manœuvre for the strengthening of the pressure against Black's K B 2. Also good was 20. P—K Kt 4 followed by P—K R 4-5, etc.

20.	B—Kt 3
21. Kt—Q 2	......

If 21. R—K 7, then 21. ....K—Kt 2 and eventually ....K—B 3.

21.	B—R 6
22. Kt—K 4	B—R 4

In order to save the Q Kt P by ....P—Q Kt 4.

23. P—B 3	Q R—Q 1
24. Kt—Q 6	......

If 24. R×R the answer would not be 24. ....R×R ; 25. Kt—B 2 ! followed by 26. R—K 7 ± but 24. ....B×R ; 25. Kt—Q 6, P—Q Kt 4 ; 26. B—Kt 3, B—B 3, etc. =

24. ...:...	P—Q Kt 4
25. B—Kt 3	R—Q 2

Protects for the time being all the vulnerable points. Speaking in general, one must admit that, after his extravagant opening, Bogoljubow has defended his position most carefully and still preserves fighting chances.

26. Kt—K 8	......

A sound alternative was 26. Kt—K 4, R×R ch ; 27. R×R, although Black would still have a temporary defence by 27. ....K—Kt 2, etc. The text manœuvre is linked with a temporary sacrifice of a Pawn and leads, with the best defence, at least to the capture of Black's K B P.

26.	R×R ch
27. K×R	B—Kt 7

This counter thrust is Black's best chance. After, for instance,

27. ....B—Q 1, White would increase the pressure without much trouble by 28. Kt—Q 6, B—K B 3 ; 29. K—K 2, etc.

28. Kt—B 6 ch .....

White realises that the Black King will be at least no better at R 1 than at K Kt 1, and therefore takes the opportunity of gaining time on the clock. If Black, on his 29th move, had played .... K— Kt 1, I intended to continue as in the actual game, 30. K—B 2, B × K B P; 31. Kt—Q 6, leading to variations examined further on.

28.	K—Kt 2
29. Kt—K 8 ch	K—R 1
30. K—B 2 !	B × K B P
31. Kt—Q 6	B—Q 4 ?

After Black's stubborn defence so far, this misappreciation of the position seems incredible, as by the further exchange, White obtains : (1) The elimination of Black's pair of Bishops ; (2) The Pawn majority on the Queen's side ; (3) The central square Q 4 for his Knight ; (4) Play against Black's isolated Q P ; (5) The possibility of penetrating with his Rook via K 7 or K 8. Any one of these considerations taken separately should have deterred Bogoljubow from selecting the text-move, and, in fact, he could have set his opponent a by no means easy task by playing 31. .... K—Kt 2. My intention was to continue with 32. R—K 7, and, if 32. .... B—Kt 3 (best), then 33. B × B P, B—B 4 ; 34. B—Kt 3 dis. ch, K—R 1 ; 35. Kt—B 7 ch, K—Kt 2 (but not .... K—R 2 ; 36. Kt—Kt 5 ch, followed by mate) ; 36. R—Kt 7 !, B— K 5 ch ; 37. K—Q 1, K—B 3 ; 38. Kt × R P, R—Q 1 ch ; 39. K—K 2, and Black would not have found sufficient compensation for the minus Pawn. Still, it would have been some kind of a fight, whereas what now happens merely reminds one of precisely executed butcher's work !

32. B × B	P × B
33. Kt × P	B—Kt 3
34. K—Q 3	K—Kt 2
35. P—Q Kt 4	.....

White's game now plays itself.

35.	R—Q 1
36. P—Q R 4	P—R 3
37. Kt—Q 4	R—Q 3
38. R—K 8	P—K R 4

If, instead, ... R—K B 3, White would first play P—R 5.

| 39. R—Q R 8 | R—K B 3 |

A desperate trap. Needless to say anything else would be equally hopeless.

Position after Black's 39th move.

40. R × P ! .....

White walks into the trap and proves that this is the quickest way to win !

40.	B × Kt
41. R × R	B × R
42. P—R 5	.....

The extra Bishop is unable to stop the two passed Pawns. If, for instance, 42. ....B—Q 1, then simply 43. K—Q 4, followed by K×Q P, K—B 6, etc.

42. ......   B—K 4
43. P—Kt 5 !   P—R 5

Or ....B—B 2 ; 44. P—Kt 6, B—Q 1 ; 45. K—Q 4, etc.

44. P—R 6   ......

Settles the matter, for 44. .... P×P would be answered by 45. P×P, and if 44. ....B×P then 45. P—R 7.

Resigns.

GAME 80

RUY LOPEZ

Podebrad Tournament, June, 1936.

Black : E. ELISKASES

1. P—K 4   P—K 4
2. Kt—K B 3   Kt—Q B 3
3. B—Kt 5   P—Q R 3
4. B—R 4   Kt—B 3
5. Castles   B—K 2
6. R—K 1   P—Q Kt 4
7. B—Kt 3   P—Q 3
8. P—B 3   Kt—Q R 4
9. B—B 2   P—B 4
10. P—Q 3   ......

More usual is 10. P—Q 4, which enables White—if he wants to—to blockade the position in the centre by P—Q 5 in order to start a not very promising attack on the King's side. The text-move aims at first finishing development on the Q's side and to play P—Q 4 only afterwards—when, or if, it appears opportune.

10. ......   Kt—B 3
11. Q Kt—Q 2   Castles

12. Kt—B 1   R—K 1

A quite acceptable plan—if it had been conceived for defensive purposes only. Another plausible way to finish development without much inconvenience was 12. ....B—K 3 ; 13. Kt—K 3, P—R 3 followed by ....Q—B 2 and ....Q R—Q 1.

13. Kt—K 3   P—Q 4 ?

A typical mistake : Black is in a hurry to "punish" White for having delayed P—Q 4, and himself starts an operation in the centre—but, as will be promptly shown, at a very unfortunate moment. Logical was 13. ....B—B 1, especially as 14. Kt—Q 5 was not then to be feared : 14. ....Kt×Kt ; 15. P×Kt, Kt— K 2 ; 16. P—Q 4, K P×P ; 17. P×P, P—B 5 !, etc. The chances in that case would be about even.

14. P×P   Kt×P
15. Kt×Kt   Q×Kt
16. P—Q 4 !   ......

The refutation : White opens the position in the centre at a moment when the opponent has not yet finished his development and thus succeeds in taking full advantage of the various insufficiently protected points (Kt at Q B 3 the first) in Black's camp.

16. ......   K P×P
17. B—K 4   Q—Q 2

Or, 17. ....Q—Q 3 ; 18. B—B 4.

18. P×P   B—B 3

Otherwise the further advance of the centre Pawn would prove overwhelming — for instance, 18. ....B—Kt 2 ; 19. P—Q 5, Kt—Q 1; 20. Kt—K 5, Q—Q 3 ; 21. B—B 4, etc., with all positional trumps in the hand.

Position after Black's 18th move.

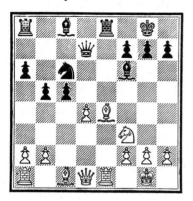

19. B—Kt 5 ! ......

The main idea of this move is shown by the following short variation :—19. ....B×P ; 20. B—B 5 !, R×R ch ; 21. Q×R, Q—Q 3 ; 22. Q—K-8 ch, Q—B 1 ; 23. B×P ch and wins the Queen ; and since 19. ....B×B ; 20. Kt×B, P—K Kt 3 ; 21. P×P etc. would have led to a hopelessly lost end-game, Black, *nolens volens*, must try the following sacrifice of the exchange.

19.	R×B !
20. R×R	B×P
21. Kt×B	Kt×Kt

If Black could have found time to finish the development of his Queen's side, White's slight material gain would have been very difficult to exploit. White, therefore, must act with extreme energy.

22. Q—R 5 ! ......

The point of this rather difficult attacking move may be seen from the continuation : 22. ....B—Kt 2; 23. R—R 4 !, P—K R 3 ; 24. B× R P, Kt—B 4 ; 25. B×P ! and Black would be mated in two if 25. .... K×B.

| 22. ...... | B—Kt 2 |

Also 22. ....Q—B 3 ; 23. Q R—K 1, B—K 3 ; 24. R—R 4, B—B 4 ; 25. B—K 7 ! would not prove sufficient.

| 23. R—R 4 | Q—B 4 |

Since 23. ....P—K R 3 loses at once (*cf.* above note), Black has no choice.

| 24. B—K 3 ! | ...... |

Another surprising point of the attacking manœuvre : White forces the exchange of Queens and at the same time dislodges the Knight from its strong central post. After the "normal" moves, 24. .... Q×Q ; 25. R×Q, Kt—B 7 ; 26. R—Q 1 !, Kt×B ; 27. P×Kt, P—B 5 ; 28. R—Q B 5 followed by 29. R—Q 7, the end-game would be quite easily won. Black's next mistake, therefore, only shortens the agony.

| 24. ...... | R—Q 1 ? |
| 25. R×Kt | Resigns. |

GAME 81

SICILIAN DEFENCE

Podebrad Tournament, June, 1936.

Black : P. Frydman

1. P—K 4	P—Q B 4
2. Kt—K B 3	Kt—Q B 3
3. P—Q 4	P×P
4. Kt×P	Kt—B 3
5. Kt—Q B 3	P—Q 3
6. B—K Kt 5	......

The idea of this move is to eliminate the possibility of .... P—K Kt 3 and ....B—Kt 2 (The Dragon Variation), and it practically forces Black to adopt the so-called Scheveningen Variation, one of the characteristics of which is the ex-posed—although quite defensible—Queen's Pawn on the open file. White would be mistaken, however, if he thought that from now on he could count on a serious opening advantage ; for my part, in spite of a 100% success with the text-move, I am very far from that illusion.

| 6. ...... | P—K 3 |
| 7. Kt—Kt 3 | ...... |

This harmless removal, typical of many variations in the Sicilian, contains—as, amongst others, the present game shows—more venom than one would suppose. For 7. B—Q Kt 5 see my game against Foltys at Margate (No. 92).

| 7. ...... | B—K 2 |
| 8. Q—Q 2 | ...... |

This attempt to enforce the pressure against Q 6 should be met by 8. ....P—K R 3 ! and—only after 9. B—R 4—Castles, with the threat 10. ....Kt × K P etc., equalising easily. White should, therefore, play 9. B—K 3 (instead of B—R 4), but Black, anyhow, would not for the time being have to worry about his Queen's Pawn.

| 8. ...... | Castles ? |

Strangely enough, this so plausible answer is already a decisive mistake, for from now on Black will only have the choice between different evils.

| 9. Castles | ...... |

Threatening 10. B × Kt, B × B (P × B would permit a winning King's attack starting with 11. Q—R 6) ; 11. Q × P, etc. Black has therefore no time either for the preventative ....P—Q R 3 or for the simplifying ....P—K R 3.

| 9. ...... | Kt—Q R 4 |

Hoping, after 10. B × Kt, Kt × Kt ch ; 11. R P × Kt, B × B ; 12. Q × Q P, to obtain a counter-attack through 12. ....Q—R 4 etc.; but White's strong next move stops this plan.

| 10. K—Kt 1 ! | Kt × Kt |
| 11. R P × Kt | ...... |

The point of the 10th move is that Black can no longer play 11. ....Q—R 4 because of 12. Kt—Q 5, and, likewise, 11. ....Q—Kt 3 would have led to a rapid debacle after 12. B × Kt, B × B ; 13. Q × Q P, Q × B P ; 14. P—K 5, B—Kt 4 ; 15. P—R 4 !, B—B 5 ; 16. B—Kt 5 ! threatening 17. Q × R ch ! with mate in two. His next move is therefore the only way, if not to save the day, at least to prolong the fight.

11.	Kt—K 1
12. B × B	Q × B
13. Kt—Kt 5	B—Q 2

Expecting, not without reason, that White's doubled Pawns will cause him some technical trouble in finding the winning procedure.

14. Kt × Q P	Kt × Kt
15. Q × Kt	Q × Q
16. R × Q	B—B 3
17. P—K B 3	K R—Q 1
18. R × R ch	R × R
19. B—Q 3	......

The ensuing end-game is highly instructive. In the first place, White intends to take full advantage in the trumps he already possesses :· the open Q R-file and especially the dominating spot Q R 5.

| 19. ...... | P—K 4 |

Gaining some space in the centre and intending eventually to use the Rook on the third rank.

| 20. K—B 1 | K—B 1 |

21. K—Q 2	K—K 2
22. R—R 1	P—Q R 3
23. K—K 3	R—Q 3
24. R—R 5 !	......

Just at the right moment, as the obligation to protect the King's Pawn will prevent Black from undertaking the intended diversion with the Rook.

24.	P—B 3
25. P—Q Kt 4	K—Q 2
26. P—K Kt 3 !	......

Of course, 26. P—Kt 5, P×P ; 27. B×P would be premature because of 27. ....R—Q 8 etc. The advance in the centre, started by the text-move, will force the Black Rook to leave the open file.

26.	P—K Kt 4
27. P—K B 4	Kt P×P ch
28. P×P	R—K 3

After 28. ....P×P ch ; 29. K×P followed by R—R 5 etc., White's work would be easier.

29. P—B 5 !	R—K 2

If 29. ....R—Q 3, then 30. R—R 1—K Kt 1, etc., and the White Rook would have an easy play on the King's side. Now, on the other hand, the doubled Pawn can at last be dissolved.

30. P—Kt 5 !	P×P
31. B×P	R—Kt 2
32. B×B ch	K×B
33. R—R 8	R—Kt 7

This counter attempt is Black's only chance, since 33. ....R—K B 2 ; 34. R—K 8 followed by R—K 6 ch would be fatal.

34. R—B 8	R×R P
35. R×P ch	K—B 4

With the menace 36. ....R—R 6 ch followed by .... K—Q 5.

Position after Black's 30th move.

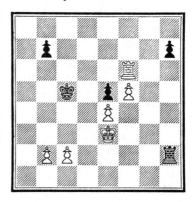

36. P—Kt 4 ! ch ......

The first link in the final combination ; White gains the square Q 6 for his Rook.

36. ...... K—B 5 !

If 36. ....K×P, then 37. R—K 6 etc., wins easily.

37. R—Q 6 ......

Threatening 38. R—Q 5, which, however, Black tries to prevent in an ingenious manner.

37.	R—R 6 ch
38. K—K 2	R—R 5
39. K—B 3	P—R 4 !

Still making efforts—which are in fact crowned with a kind of " moral " success—to complicate matters. By making this move, Black suggests that White cannot win by playing the natural 40. R—Q 5—and the opponent believes him !

40. R—K 6 ......

This can hardly be called an error since it wins perforce and is coupled with another pretty point. But with 40. R—Q 5 ! White could prove to his opponent that his trap ....was not a trap at all. The continuation would be : 40. .... R—B 5 ch ; 41. K—K 3, R × B P ; 42. P × R, K × R ; 43. P—B 4 ch, K—Q 3 ; 44. P—Kt 5, P—Kt 3 (or P—R 5 ; 45. K—B 3, etc.) ; 45. P—B 6, K—K 3 ; 46. P—B 5 and wins. The idea behind that Pawn end-game is that while Black's passed Pawns are separated by only two files and can therefore be stopped by the hostile King, White is able to obtain passed Pawns at a distance of three files from each other. This example is worthy of notice.

40. ......   R—B 5 ch

If 40. ....K—Q 5, then 41. P—B 3 ch (a second, deviating offer) followed by 42. R × P, etc.

41. K—K 3   P—R 5
42. R × P   P—R 6 !

Very neat—but White's material advantage assures him a safe defence against tactical tricks of this kind.

43. R—Q 5   R—R 5
44. R—Q 4 ch ! K—B 6
45. R—Q 1   P—R 7
46. R—K R 1   R—R 6 ch
47. K—B 4   R—R 5 ch
48. K—K 5   K—Q 7
49. P—B 6   K—K 6
50. K—Q 6 !   R × P
51. R × P   R—Q 5 ch
52. K—K 6   Resigns.

GAME 82

QUEEN'S GAMBIT DECLINED (ORTHODOX DEFENCE)

Podebrad Tournament, June, 1936.

Black : J. FOLTYS

1. P—Q 4   P—Q 4
2. P—Q B 4 P—K 3

3. Kt—Q B 3 Kt—K B 3
4. B—Kt 5   B—K 2
5. P—K 3   Q Kt—Q 2
6. Kt—B 3   Castles
7. Q—B 2   ......

This fashionable move—which, for reasons unknown, was disdained for about a quarter of a century—allows Black to start a counter-attack in the centre through 7. ....P—Q B 4 ; but, as this action cannot be supported by Rooks, the resulting opening of files should turn to White's advantage. Therefore, in my opinion, one should consider, instead of 7. .... P—Q B 4, the following system : 7. ....P—B 3 ; 8. P—Q R 3 (preventing ....Kt—K 5), P—K R 3 ; 9. B—R 4, Kt—K 1 ; 10. B × B (or 10. B—Kt 3, Kt—Q 3), Q × B, followed by ....Kt—Q 3, etc.

7. ......   P—B 4
8. R—Q 1   ......

As Black's reply proves sufficient to equalise, better would have been, as I played in two match games in Buenos Ayres—8. P × Q P, Kt × P ; 9. B × B, Q × B ; 10. Kt × Kt, P × Kt ; 11. P × P, followed by B—K 2 and Castles, with a secured slight end-game advantage.

8. ......   Q—R 4
9. B—Q 3   P—K R 3
10. B—R 4   Kt—Kt 3

A good move, which forces White to clear the situation in the centre before he has castled.

11. P × Q P   B P × P

Although not directly bad, this intermediate move certainly cannot be recommended, for it permits White to complicate matters without taking many chances. Incisive and good enough for equalising

was 11. ....Q Kt × P, threatening
12. ....Kt—Q Kt 5 or eventually
....P × Q P etc.

12. P—Q 6 ! ......

This should not bring much—
but, still, it was a relief for White
to be able to leave the routine,
"theoretical" path and force the
opponent to find the best answer by
himself !

12. ...... **B × P**

Better than 12. ....P × Kt ; 13.
P × B, P × P ch ; 14. R—Q 2, R—
K 1 ; 15. B × Kt, P × B ; 16. Q × P,
etc. ±

13. B × Kt **P × B ?**

But this weakening of the King's
side was certainly unnecessary.
After 13. ....P × Kt ; 14. B × B P,
B—Kt 5 ! ; 15. B × B, Q × B ch ;
16. Q—Q 2, etc., the positional
advantage left to White would be
negligible.

14. Kt × P **B—Kt 5**

The Bishop's position at Q 3 was
not safe and, besides, the following
exchange will give Black some kind
of compensation for the disorganised left wing.

15. Castles **B × Kt**
16. P × B **B—Q 2**
17. P—Q B 4 ! ......

This Pawn is about as weak here
as at B 3—but now, at least, it
makes the important square Q 5
inaccessible to the Black Knight.

17. ...... **B—R 5**
18. Kt—Kt 3 **Q—Kt 5**
19. Q—K 2 ! ......

Both an attacking and a defensive
move. If now 19. ....B × Kt, then
first 20. R—Kt 1.

19. ...... **K R—B 1**
20. R—Kt 1 **Kt × P**

This looks very dangerous and,
in fact, proves fatal. But, as the
Black King has been abandoned to
his fate by all his troops, it is, in
truth, already too late to prevent a
direct assault by passive tactics. If,
for instance, 20. ....B × Kt, then
21. R × B, Q—K 2 (or, ...Q—B 1 ;
22. Q—B 3, etc.) ; 22. Q—Kt 4 ch,
K—B 1 ; 23. Q—R 4, K—Kt 2 ; 24.
P—B 4 with an easy attack.

21. Kt—Q 4 **Q—B 4**

When taking the Pawn on the
previous move, Black probably calculated that he would have a saving
defence should White make the
natural move 22. R × P. Actually,
the position of the second player
would have been precarious enough
even so, especially in view of
White's threat 23. Kt × K P, which
would win promptly, for instance,
after 22. ....R—B 2, or 22. ....
Kt—Q 3, or 22. ....B—K 1. Also
22. ....Kt—K 4 would lose rapidly
after 23. Q—R 5, Q—B 1 ; 24. P—
B 4, Kt × B ; 25. Kt × K P etc.—
but 22. ....Q—Q 4, in order to
answer 23. Kt × K P ? by 23. ....
Q × Kt and 23. R—Kt 4 by ....
Kt—Kt 3, etc., would still prolong
the battle. The following combination by White is, therefore, the most
convincing way to force a decisive
advantage.

Position after Black's 21st move.

22. Kt × P !	......

Leads finally "only" to the win of a Pawn—but, by the weakening of Black's King's position, *permits White to force favourable exchanges*, which will prove amply sufficient.

22.	P × Kt
23. Q—Kt 4 ch	K—R 1

After 23. ....K—B 1, death would be quicker : 24. R × P, Q—K Kt 4 ; 25. Q × K P, Kt—K 4 ; 26. P—B 4 !, etc.

24. R × P	......

Threatening mates at K Kt 7 and K R 7.

24.	R—B 2
25. R × R	Q × R
26. B × Kt	P—K 4
27. Q—R 4	Q—K Kt 2
28. B—Q 5	......

As Black's King is now adequately protected, White rightly decides to simplify matters.

28.	R—Q 1
29. Q × B	R × B
30. Q—B 6 !	......

It was important to prevent Black's doubling the pieces on the central file.

30.	Q—K B 2
31. P—K R 3	......

In order to make also the Rook active.

31.	K—Kt 2
32. R—Kt 1	R—Q 2
33. P—Q R 4 !	......

This Pawn now threatens to come as far as R 6, after which R—Kt 7 would be decisive. Black is therefore practically forced to offer the exchange of Queens.

33.	R—B 2
34. Q—Kt 5	Q—Q 2
35. Q × Q ch	R × Q
36. R—Kt 5 !	......

The following end-game will be easily won, and chiefly because of the dominating position of the Rook.

36.	K—Kt 3
37. P—Kt 4	P—K R 4
38. K—Kt 2	P × P
39. P × P	R—Q 3
40. R—R 5	P—R 3
41. K—Kt 3	R—B 3
42. P—B 4 !	P × P ch
43. P × P	R—Kt 3
44. R—Q B 5 !	......

The Rook will prove even more effective on the 7th rank than on the 5th. If now 44. ....R—Kt 5 then simply 45. R—B 6, R × R P ; 46. P—Kt 5 and wins.

44.	K—Kt 2
45. R—B 7 ch	K—R 3
46. R—R 7	R—Kt 6 ch
47. K—R 4	R—Kt 5

Or 47. ....R—Kt 3 ; 48. P—R 5, R—B 3 ; 49. R—K B 7 !, K—Kt 3 ; 50. R—Q Kt 7 followed by 51. R—Kt 6 and wins.

48. R × P	Resigns.

For if 48. ....R × P then 49. R × P ch ! etc.

GAME 83

QUEEN'S INDIAN DEFENCE

Podebrad Tournament, June, 1936.

White : MISS V. MENCHIK

1. P—Q 4	Kt—K B 3
2. Kt—K B 3	P—Q Kt 4

At such early stages it is a sound principle not to give the opponent an objective, such as this : the enterprise may succeed, as it does here, but only if the adversary continues to develop the pieces without trying to avail oneself of the unusual situation. Instead of the fianchetto-development as selected by the Ladies' World Champion, a good method would have been, for instance, 3. B—B 4, B—Kt 2 ; 4. P—K 3, P—Q R 3 ; 5. P—Q R 4, P—Kt 5 ; 6. P—B 4, and, whether Black takes *en passant* or not, his position remains slightly inferior.

3. P—K Kt 3	B—Kt 2
4. B—Kt 2	P—K 3
5. Castles	B—K 2
6. Q Kt—Q 2	......

Owing to her pointless mobilization-plan, White has obtained no advantage from the opening. The text-move, which prepares for the exchange of Black's exposed Q Kt P is not worse than 6. P—Q R 4 (....P—Q R 3, etc.) and is certainly better than 6. P—Kt 3 (....P—Kt 5 ! etc.).

| 6. ...... | Q—B 1 ! |

Protecting the Bishop in order to answer 7. R—K 1 by 7. ....Kt —K 5 ! ; and after 7. P—B 4, the Queen will obviously find a large field of action on the Queen's side.

7. P—B 4	P × P
8. Kt × P	Castles
9. P—Kt 3	......

As so often in the Queen's Indian Defence, White cannot find a suitable square for the Queen's Bishop. Comparatively better than the text-move which weakens the Q's side, is 9. Kt—K 5, in order to clear as soon as possible the situation on the diagonal K R 1—Q R 8.

| 9. ...... | P—Q R 4 ! |

Not only preventing once for all Kt—Q R 5 (which on the previous move would be met by ....B—Q 4), but also threatening eventually ....P—R 5.

10. P—Q R 3 ?   ......

A decisive strategical error in an already delicate position. White should profit from the fact that the threat mentioned was not of an immediate character by proposing exchange of Bishops with 10. B—Q R 3. After 10. ....B × B ; 11. Kt × B, Kt—B 3 followed eventually by ....Kt—Q Kt 5, Black's position, although superior, would not be anything like so easy to improve decisively as after the text-move, which creates an incurable weakness on Q Kt 3.

10.	B—Q 4
11. Q—B 2	Q—Kt 2
12. B—Kt 2	......

White has only the choice between a few evils; for instance, after 12. B—Q 2, Kt—B 3, Black would already threaten 13. ....Kt × P.

12.	Kt—B 3
13. Kt—K 1	Q R—Kt 1
14. B × B	......

The only way that temporarily saves the Pawn.

| 14. ...... | P × B ! |

Much stronger than 17. ....Kt × B—the point is Black's next move.

| 15. Kt—Q 2 | ...... |

Position after White's 15th move.

| 15. ...... | Kt—K 5 ! |

Thus Black becomes master of the central sector. The Q Kt P is not lost immediately but cannot long escape its fate. This purely positional battle is, in my opinion, noteworthy chiefly because of the methods adopted by Black in order to exploit his opening advantage : these methods, unusual at first sight, were in fact quite simple.

| 16. K Kt—B 3 | ...... |

If 16. Kt × Kt, then, of course, 16. ....Q × P ! etc., winning material.

| 16. ...... | P—B 4 |
| 17. K R—Kt 1 | Q—Kt 4 ! |

If now 18. P—K 3 (which was comparatively the best), then 18. ....Q—K 7 ; 19. R—K B 1, P—Kt 4 ! ; 20. Q R—K 1, Q—Kt 4 ; 21. Kt × Kt, Q P × Kt ; 22. Kt—Q 2, P—Q 4 ; 23. R—B 1, R—Kt 3 and White would be finally executed on the King's flank ; but Miss Menchik prefers to succumb in open fight.

| 18. Kt × Kt | B P × Kt |
| 19. Kt—K 5 | Kt × Kt |

Simplest. 19. ....Q × Kt P would probably have won also, but after 20. Q—B 1, more resistance would have been possible than in the endgame forced by the text-manœuvre.

| 20. P × Kt | Q—B 4 ! |

Rough, but extremely sound.

21. Q × Q	B × Q
22. P—K 3	R × Kt P
23. B—Q 4	B × B
24. P × B	K R—B 6 !

Wins perforce a second Pawn.

25. R × R	R × R
26. R—Q B 1	P—B 3
27. P—K 6	P × P

28. R × P	K—B 2
29. R—B 7 ch	K—B 3
30. P—Kt 4	P—R 3
31. P—K R 4	R × P
Resigns.	

GAME 84

FRENCH DEFENCE

Nottingham Tournament, August, 1936.

Black : DR. M. EUWE

1. P—K 4	P—K 3
2. P—Q 4	P—Q 4
3. P—K 5	......

I adopted this favourite move of Nimzowitsch's for the first time in my career only because I thought that Dr. Euwe, after his failure in the games of the 1935 Match (continued by 3. Kt—Q B 3, B—Kt 5), had in the meantime made a particularly careful study of that line of play. Although the result of the opening-play in the present game was rather in my favour, I shall hardly repeat an experiment permitting Black to assume from the very beginning a kind of initiative and to obtain (at the cost of his Pawn configuration, it is true) a free development of his pieces.

| 3. ...... | P—Q B 4 |
| 4. Kt—K B 3 | ...... |

In the last years of his activity Nimzowitsch preferred the peculiar move 4. Q—Kt 4, thus showing the clear design to exploit immediately the advantage of space obtained on the K's side. The idea has, however, some inconveniences, as, for instance, the following short game, in which I had to fight against it in the Montevideo Tournament, 1938 (White : J. Canepa), shows in a characteristic way : 4. ....Kt— Q B 3 ; 5. Kt—K B 3, K Kt—K 2 (if this move was not played before, this would only be a further proof of the short-sightedness of Lady Theory ; because the development-problem of this Knight, *being here the most elaborate one,* must be solved on the very first opportunity) ; 6. P—B 3, Kt—B 4 ; 7. B—Q 3, P × P ! ; 8. Castles, B—Q 2; 9. R—K 1, P × P ; 10. Kt × P, P—K Kt 3 ; 11. B—K Kt 5, B—K 2 ; 12. Q—B·4, Q Kt—Q 5 ! ; 13. B—B 6, Kt × Kt ch ; 14. P × Kt, R—K Kt 1 ; 15. K—R 1, B—Q B 3 ; 16. B × Kt, Kt P × B ; 17. B × B, Q × B ; 18. Kt—K 2, P—Q 5 ! ; 19. Kt × P, Q—Q Kt 5 ! ; 20. R—K Kt 1, R × R ch ; 21. R × R, Castles ; 22. R—Q 1, Q × Kt P ; 23. R—Q 2, R × Kt ! ; 24. R × R, Q × B P ; Resigns.

| 4. | . . . . . . | Kt—Q B 3 |
| 5. | B—Q 3 | . . . . . . |

The central Pawn is sacrificed only temporarily, but its recovery will cost White some valuable time. The whole plan can, therefore, hardly lead to more than a balanced position.

| 5. | . . . . . . | P × P |
| 6. | Castles | P—B 3 |

If 6. ....Q—Kt 3 White could transform the game into a regular gambit by 7. P—B 3, P × P ; 8. Kt × P, etc., with some chances of success.

7. B—Q Kt 5   . . . . . .

There is nothing better than to re-establish equilibrium in material; if, for instance, 7. B—K B 4, then 7. ....P—K Kt 4 followed by .... P—Kt 5.

7.	. . . . . .	B—Q 2
8.	B × Kt	P × B
9.	Q × P	P × P
10.	Q × K P	. . . . . .

It was by no means easy to decide which move is better—this or 10. Kt × P. My actual choice was determined by the consideration that in retaking with the Knight I would in most variations be practically obliged to exchange Black's "bad" Q's Bishop at Q 2; while I already hoped here to be able to chase his dark-coloured colleague successfully.

| 10. | . . . . . . | Kt—B 3 |
| 11. | B—B 4 | . . . . . . |

Preventing ....Q—Kt 1 and preparing the protection of the K B P by B—Kt 3.

11.	. . . . . .	B—B 4
12.	Kt—B 3	Castles
13.	B—Kt 3	. . . . . .

White's slight advantage (the control of his K 5) is extremely difficult to exploit—especially as Black still possesses the pair of Bishops and two open files for his Rooks. In the following section of the game, however, neither player takes the maximum advantage of his opportunities.

13. . . . . . .   Q—K 2

Here, for instance, 13. ....Q—K 1, in order to be able to answer 14. Q Kt—R 4 by 14.....B—K 2—was decidedly more promising.

14. P—Q R 3 (?) . . . . . .

White should without lingering attack the K's Bishop by 14. Kt—Q R 4, for instance, 14. .... B—Kt 3 (14. ....B—Kt 5 ; 15. P—Q R 3, B—R 4 ; 16. P—Kt 4, B—Q 1 ; 17. Kt—B 5, etc., would be decidedly too artificial) ; 15. Kt × B, P × Kt ; 16. Q—B 7 ! ± The text-move allows Black to "save" his Bishop.

14. . . . . . .   P—Q R 4

15. K R—K 1   . . . . .

I did not occupy this open file with the other Rook, in view of the possible answer 15. . . . . B—B 1, which, however, would not be dangerous : 15. Q R—K 1, B—B 1; 16. R—Q 1 ! followed by K R—K 1, etc. ±

15. . . . . . .   R—R 2 ?

Comparatively better was 15. . . . . B—Kt 3 in order to answer 16. Kt—Q R 4 by . . . . B—Q 1.

16. Kt—Q R 4   R—Kt 2

A mistake would be 16. . . . . Kt—K 5 because of 17. Kt × B, Kt × Kt (Q × Kt ; 18. R × Kt) ; 18. Q—Q 6 ! and wins.

17. Q—B 3   . . . . . .

Even this rather risky and complicated manœuvre finally turns to White's advantage ; but still more convincing was the simple 17. Kt × B, Q × Kt ; 18. R—K 2 followed by the exploitation of the dark-coloured squares.

17. . . . . . .   B—R 2
18. Q × R P   . . . . . .

Because of Black's counter-attack against K B 2 this win of material will have only temporary character.

18. . . . . . .   Kt—K 5
19. Q—R 6 !   . . . . . .

But for his intermediate move White would even have the worst of it, as Black threatened eventually . . . . R—Q R 1, etc.

19. . . . . . .   B—K 1
20. P—Q Kt 4   . . . . .

Preparing the following counter-

sacrifice which makes an end of Black's immediate threats.

20. . . . . . .   P—K Kt 4 ?

This move has been generally blamed, and with reason, since Black will soon have to regret the compromising of his King's position. But most of the critics were mistaken in believing that instead 20. . . . . P—K 4 would be not only satisfactory but even advantageous for Black. In that case I intended to sacrifice the exchange, thus obtaining fair winning prospects— for instance, 21. R × Kt !, P × R ; 22. Q—B 4 ch, B—B 2 ; 23. Q × K P, B—Q 4 ; 24. Q × K P, B × Kt ; 25. Q × Q, R × Q ; 26. P × B, R × P ; 27. K—Kt 2, R—K B 1 ; 28. P— Q B 4, B—Q 5 ; 29. R—Q 1, etc. ± Black's comparatively best counter-chance was therefore 20. . . . . B— R 4 ; 21. Kt—B 5 ! (but not 21. Q × B P, B—K 1 ! ; 22. Q—R 6, B—Kt 4 ; 23. Q—R 5, Q—K 1, etc. ∓), B × Kt ; 22. P × B, B × Kt ; 23. P × B, R × P ; 24. Q × B P, Kt × Q B P, etc., still with fighting possibilities. It must be admitted, however, that even after the inferior text-move the second player will keep for rather a long time some practical saving chances, which he will try to exploit with the energy of despair.

21. Kt—B 5 !   . . . . . .

According to programme and very efficient, as Black's strongest Bishop will now disappear.

21. . . . . . .   B × Kt

Not 21. . . . . Kt × Kt ; 22. P × Kt, B × P because of 22. R × P ! etc.

22. P × B   Kt × Q B P
23. Q—K 2   Kt—K 5
24. Q—K 3   . . . . . .

White's superiority has now

become evident. His Pawns are much more soundly placed ; he still has the control of K 5, typical in this variation ; and, last but not least, he has a rather menacing Q R P.

| 24. | ...... | B—Kt 3 |

Even against the somewhat better 24. ....P—B 4 White would maintain his advantage by simply advancing his passed Pawn. But the exchange of two minor pieces, possible after the text-move, facilitates his task considerably.

25.	Kt—K 5 !	P—B 4
26.	Kt × B	P × Kt
27.	P—K B 3	Kt × B
28.	P × Kt	K—B 2
29.	P—Q R 4 !	......

In order to exploit Black's weaknesses in the centre and on the K-side, White makes first a demonstration on the other wing, forcing the opponent to leave some vulnerable spots uncovered.

| 29. | ...... | R—Q R 1 |
| 30. | K—B 2 | ...... |

With the sudden threat of a mating attack starting with R—R 1.

| 30. | ...... | R—Kt 7 |
| 31. | R—K 2 | P—B 5 |

Under the circumstances the best, although not quite sufficient. As a matter of fact no human being could hope to protect at the same time : (1) The Q R-file ; (2) the K R-file ; (3) the Q B P ; (4) the K P ; (5) the K Kt P ; and (6) the square K 4. It is really a little too much !

| 32. | R—R 1 | K—Kt 1 |

Position after Black's 32nd move.

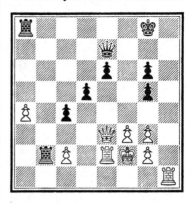

| 33. | Q—K 5 ! | ...... |

From now on both players produce —unlike the first part of the game —really first-class Chess. Particularly interesting is the method adopted by Dr. Euwe to avoid a rapid debacle and the chances he succeeds in finding in spite of the unavoidable loss of two Pawns.

33.	......	Q—R 2 ch
34.	K—B 1	R—Kt 8 ch
35.	R—K 1	R × R ch
36.	K × R	Q—K Kt 2 !

Of course the only move, after which White, if he wants to play for a win, will have to proceed with exceptional care.

| 37. | Q × K P ch | K—B 1 |
| 38. | Q × Q P ! | ...... |

Instead 38. Q—Q 6 ch, Q—K 2 ch, etc., would only lead to a draw. But now the white King seems to be in even greater danger than the black one.

| 38. | ...... | Q—B 6 ch |

The alternative was 38. ....R—K ch ; 39. K—Q 2 ! (not 39. K—B 2, Q—R 2 ch ; 40. K—B 1, K—Kt 2 ! threatening Q—K 6), Q—

B 3 ; 40. R—R 7 ! after which 40.
....R—Q 1 would lose at once
because of 41. R—R 8 ch, etc.

39. K—B 2 !   R—K 1

Hopeless would be 39. ....Q×
Q×B P ch ; 40. K—Kt 1, Q—
Kt 8 ch ; 41. K—R 2, Q—Kt 1 ;
42. Q×B P, etc.

40. P—Kt 4 !   . . . . . .

Checks at Q 6 and then Q 7
would be useless. The Queen is
best placed in the centre.

40.	. . . . . .	Q—K 6 ch
41.	K—Kt 3	Q—B 5 ch
42.	K—R 3	R—K 2

If 42. ....K—Kt 2, then 43.
Q—Q 7 ch.

43. Q—Q B 5 !   . . . . . .

The right move. After 43. P—
Kt 3, Q—K 6 ! the win would be
doubtful.

| 43. | . . . . . . | Q—B 3 |
| 44. | P—Kt 3 | . . . . . . |

Not 44. R—K 1, Q—R 1 ch ; 45.
K—Kt 5, Q—R 5 mate !

44. . . . . . .   Q—R 1 ch

If 44. ....Q×P then 45. R—K 1
wins.

45.	K—Kt 2	Q—B 6
46.	R—R 7	Q×Q B P ch
47.	K—R 3	Q—K 7
48.	R×R	Q×R
49.	Q×B P	. . . . . .

In the following difficult Queen
end-game Black's drawing chances
are based mainly on the fact that
the White King cannot well be
brought into safety. If, however,
White's Pawn at K Kt 4 were at
K B 2 Black's game would be ripe
for resignation.   But not only that :
by mere chance Black can even,
in certain circumstances (for
instance, if White's passed Pawn
is brought as far as R 7) speculate
on a stalemate by playing his King
to K R 3. No wonder that the
game lasts over thirty moves more,
and, but for the inexactitude of
Black on the 61st move, would
probably have lasted even longer !

49.	. . . . . .	Q—K 8
50.	Q—B 5 ch	K—B 2
51.	K—Kt 2	Q—Q R 8
52.	Q—Q B 2	K—B 3
53.	Q—Kt 3	K—K 4 ?

We were both very short of time,
which explains the text-move and
the inadequate reply.   The King
should, of course, return to K Kt 2.

54. K—B 2 ?   . . . . . .

The last move before time control, instead of which 54. Q—Kt 8
ch, K—Q 4 (or K—K 3 ; 55. Q—
K 8 ch) ; 55. Q—Kt 8 ch—winning
both K Kt's Pawns for the Q R P—
would finish the game rapidly.

54.	. . . . . .	K—B 3
55.	Q—Kt 6 ch	K—Kt 2
56.	Q—Kt 4	. . . . . .

The game was adjourned here for
the second time, and White starts
on the serious final task.   His plan
is (1) to play as soon as possible
P—R 5 ; (2) after that to eliminate
once for all any possibility of stalemate combinations by playing P—
B 4.

56.	. . . . . .	Q—R 8
57.	Q—K 1	Q—R 7 ch
58.	K—K 3	K—R 2
59.	P—R 5	Q—R 7
60.	Q—Q 2	Q—R 8
61.	K—K 2	K—R 3

The best chance of a long resistance consisted in 61. ....Q—R 8.

After the text-move White gets in P—B 4 in the most favourable circumstances, leaving him no difficulties for his final King's trip which makes his passed Pawn irresistible.

62. P—B 4 !	P×P
63. P×P	Q—R 5
64. K—B 2 !	......

In order to play P—Kt 5 at the moment when Black cannot answer with .... K—R 4.

64.	K—R 2
65. P—Kt 5	Q—R 6
66. Q—Q 7 ch	K—R 1
67. Q—B 8 ch	K—R 2
68. Q—B 7 ch	......

Thus the Queen protects both R P and B P, and the King is ready for the final walk.

68.	K—R 1
69. K—K 2	Q—R 7 ch
70. K—K 3	Q—Kt 6 ch
71. K—Q 4	Q—Kt 5 ch
72. K—Q 5	Q—Kt 4 ch
73. K—Q 4	......

The third adjournment. White could also play 73. K—K 6, and after 73. ....Q—B 4 ch ; 74. K—K 7, Q—B 1 ch ! ; 75. K—Q 7. But he did not need it.

73.	Q—R 3
74. Q—Kt 6	Q—B 1
75. Q—Q 6 !	......

The simplest scheme.

75.	Q—B 7
76. P—R 6	Q—Q 7 ch
77. K—K 5	Q—B 6 ch
78. K—K 6	Q—B 1 ch
79. K—K 7	K—R 2
80. Q—Q 7 !	Q—B 6
81. K—K 6 dis. ch	

At last forcing the exchange of Queens.

Resigns.

GAME 85

FRENCH DEFENCE (IN EFFECT)

Nottingham Tournament, August, 1936.

White : W. WINTER

1. P—Q 4	P—K 3
2. P—K 4	P—Q 4
3. P×P	......

This move is generally adopted to show that White is only playing for a draw. But, as a matter of fact, Black will at least have not fewer opportunities for complicating, if he wants to do so, than in most of the other variations of the French.

3.	P×P
4. B—Q 3	Kt—Q B 3
5. Kt—K 2	B—Q 3
6. P—Q B 3	......

Giving Black the welcome chance of taking the initiative. The alternative, however, 6. Q Kt—B 3, Kt—Kt 5 would lead either to the exchange of White's K's Bishop or to its removal to ineffective squares after 7. B—Kt 5 ch, P—B 3.

| 6. ...... | Q—R 5 ! |

It was important to prevent 7. B—K B 4.

| 7. Kt—Q 2 | B—K Kt 5 ! |

A correct offer of a Pawn. After 8. Q—Kt 3, Castles ; 9. Q×Q P, Kt—B 3, followed by ....K R—K 1, Black would have an overwhelming advantage in development.

| 8. Q—B 2 | Castles |
| 9. Kt—B 1 | ...... |

If 9. B—B 5 ch then simply 9. .... K—Kt 1.

| 9. ...... | P—K Kt 3 |

Preparing for the exchange of White's "good" Bishop (Q 3) after which the light-coloured squares of his position will become somewhat weak.

10. B—K 3   K Kt—K 2
11. Castles   B—K B 4
12. Q Kt—Kt 3   B × B
13. Q × B   P—K R 3

To secure the position of his Queen, which might become uncomfortable after White's Q—Q 2.

14. P—K B 4 ?   ......

This move, weakening without compensation important squares on the K-file, may be considered the decisive strategical mistake. Comparatively better was 14. Kt—Kt 1, followed by Kt—B 1, with a rather cramped but still defensible position.

14. ......   Q—Kt 5

Black aims—and with success—at keeping his K B 4 under control. How important this is will be evident in the second half of the game.

15. P—K R 3   Q—Q 2
16. K R—B 1   P—K R 4 !

If now 17. P—B 5, then 17. .... P—R 5 ; 18. P—B 6, Kt—K Kt 1 ; 19. Kt—R 1, R—K 1 and the white K B's Pawn would fall.

17. Kt—Kt 1   P—R 5
18. Q Kt—K 2   Kt—B 4
19. Kt—B 3   P—B 3

All White's minor pieces will henceforth suffer from an obvious lack of space, and he will therefore be unable to prevent an increasing pressure on his K-file.

20. Kt—R 2   Q R—K 1
21. B—Q 2   R—K 3
22. Kt—Kt 4   K R—K 1

23. Q R—K 1   K R—K 2
24. K—Q 1   Q—K 1
25. Q—B 3   ......

In order to move the Kt from K 2 which was at present impossible because of 25. ....R × R ch followed by ....B × P.

25. ......   Kt—R 4 !

By this manœuvre Black quickly obtains decisive material superiority. White cannot now play 26. Q × P because of 26. ....R × Kt ; 27. R × R, R × R ; 28. Q × Q Kt, Kt—Kt 6 ; 29. R—B 3, Q—K 5 ! and wins.

26. P—Q Kt 3   ......

Position after White's 26th move.

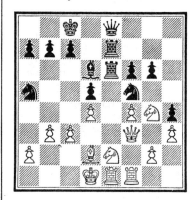

26. ......   Kt—B 5 !

A forceful finish. If 27. P × Kt, then 27. ....Q—R 5 ch ; 28. K—B 1, B—R 6 ch ; 29. K—Kt 1, R—Kt 3 ch ; 30. K—R 1, Q—B 7 and mates in two.

27. B—B 1   Kt(B5)—K6ch
28. B × Kt   Kt × B ch
29. Kt × Kt   R × Kt
30. Q—B 2   Q—Kt 4 !

Threatening 31. ....Q—Q 6 ch ;

32. K—B 1, B—R 6 mate. White is thus forced to give up a Pawn.

31.	Kt—B 1	R×B P
32.	R×R	B×R
33.	Q—K 1	K—Q 2

If Q×R, now or next move, Black replies with Q×R ch followed by Q×B P or Kt P and wins.

34.	P—B 5	R—K 6 !
35.	Q—B 2	P—Kt 4
36.	R—K 1	R—K 5
37.	R×R	......

This exchange, giving Black a strong passed Pawn, shortens matters. But White was helpless in any case.

| 37. | ...... | P×R |
| 38. | K—Q 2 | B—Q 3 |

Threatening 39. ....P—K 6 ch !

| 39. | K—B 2 | B—B 5 |
| | Resigns. | |

GAME 86

QUEEN'S INDIAN DEFENCE

Nottingham Tournament, August, 1936.

Black : C. H. O'D. ALEXANDER

Brilliancy Prize

1.	P—Q 4	Kt—K B 3
2.	P—Q B 4	P—K 3
3.	Kt—K B 3	B—Kt 5 ch
4.	Q Kt—Q 2	......

The usual move is 4. B—Q 2 in order, after the exchange of Bishops, to develop the Knight on the more natural square Q B 3. By avoiding the exchange White tries to complicate matters without actually taking too many chances.

4.	......	P—Q Kt 3
5.	P—K Kt 3	B—Kt 2
6.	B—Kt 2	Castles
7.	Castles	B×Q Kt ?

Instead of this exchange, which yields White the advantage of the pair of Bishops without necessity, Black could play either 7. ....P—Q 4 (Rubinstein–Alekhine, Semmering, 1926) or even 7.....B—K 2 followed by ....P—Q 3, ...Q Kt—Q 2, etc. In both cases he would have better equalising prospects than in the actual game.

| 8. | Q×B | ...... |

The correct recapture, as the Q's Bishop is wanted on the long diagonal.

8.	......	P—Q 3
9.	P—Kt 3	Q Kt—Q 2
10.	B—Kt 2	R—Kt 1

Black shows his hand decidedly too early. The obvious object of the text-move is to play Kt—K 5, followed by ....P—K B 4, for which purpose the Bishop must be protected, to avoid the possible answer Kt—Kt 5. But the same idea could have been combined with a mobilisation of forces, by 10. .... Q—K 2 ; 11. ....Q R—Q 1 and eventually B—R 1.

| 11. | Q R—Q 1 ! | ...... |

An interesting and effective method of meeting Black's plan. The white Q's Bishop is to play in the following development a most important and practically decisive part.

| 11. | ...... | Kt—K 5 |

If 11. ....Q—K 2, then 12. Q—K 3 (Kt—K 5 ; 13. P—Q 5).

| 12. | Q—K 3 | P—K B 4 |
| 13. | P—Q 5 ! | ...... |

This Pawn will only apparently be weak as White can easily protect it by counter-attacks.

13. ......   P×P

13. ....P—K 4 instead would lose a Pawn by 14. Kt—K R 4 ! etc.

14. P×P   Q Kt—B 3
15. Kt—R 4   Q—Q 2

If 15. ....Q Kt×P then 16. R× Kt !, B×R ; 17. Q—Q 4 wins a piece.

16. B—K R 3   ......

Again preventing ....Q Kt×P, this time because of 17. Q×Kt.

16. ......   P—Kt 3
17. P—B 3   Kt—B 4
18. Q—Kt 5   ......

Threatening not only 19. B×Kt, but also 19. B (or Kt)×P ; and if 18. ....Kt×Q P, then 19. Kt× Kt P and wins. Black's reply is therefore forced.

18. ......   Q—Kt 2
19. P—Q Kt 4   Kt (B 4)—Q 2

Equally hopeless would be 19. ....Kt—R 5 ; 20. B—R 1, etc.

20. P—K 4 !   ......

The initial move of the decisive sacrificial combination.

20. ......   Kt×K P

Black clearly based his last hopes on this ingenious stroke. If now 21. B×Q, Kt×Q ; 22. B×R, then 22. ....Kt×B ch ; 23. K—Kt 2, R×B ; 24. K×Kt, Kt—B 3 followed by Kt×P with good fighting chances.

21. Q—B 1 !   ......

Much more effective than 21. P× Kt, Q×B ; 22. P×P, Q—B 3, etc., yielding White only a possible win after a laborious end-game.

21. ......   Kt (K 5)—B 3

Position after Black's 21st move.

22. B×P !   ......

The surprising sequel of 20. P— K 4. After 22. ....P×B ; 23. Kt× P Black would either lose his Queen or be mated (23. ....Q—R 1 ; 24. Kt—R 6 ch, K—Kt 2 ; 25. Q—Kt 5 mate).

22. ......   K—R 1
23. B—K 6   ......

At last the Q P is definitely safe.

23. ......   B—R 3
24. K R—K 1   Kt—K 4
25. P—B 4 !   ......

The simplest way to force resignation.

25. ......   Kt—Q 6
26. R×Kt   B×R
27. P—Kt 4   ......

There is no remedy against P— K Kt 5.

                   Resigns.

GAME 87

QUEEN'S GAMBIT DECLINED (SLAV DEFENCE)

Nottingham Tournament, August, 1936.

Black : E. BOGOLJUBOW

1. P—Q 4	P—Q 4
2. P—Q B 4	P—Q B 3
3. Kt—K B 3	Kt—K B 3
4. Kt—B 3	P×P
5. P—Q R 4	P—K 3 ?

This was the third time within a year that I had the pleasure of meeting the indifferent text-move —and of taking advantage of it. Much better is, of course, 5. ....B—B 4.

6. P—K 4	B—Kt 5

Comparatively better, although not quite sufficient for equalising, is 6. ....P—B 4.

7. P—K 5	......

Very promising is also 7. Q—B 2, P—Q Kt 4 ; 8. B—K 2, and 9. Castles with a more than sufficient positional compensation for the Pawn.

7.	Kt—K 5

For 7. ....Kt—Q 4 see Game No. 26.

8. Q—B 2	Q—Q 4
9. B—K 2	P—Q B 4

The game with Helling, Dresden 1936, continued as follows : 9. ....Castles ; 10. Castles, Kt×Kt ; 11. P×Kt, B—K 2 ; 12. Kt—Q 2, P—Q B 4 ; 13. B×P, Q—Q 1 ; 14. Q—K 4, P×P ; 15. P×P, B—Q 2 ; 16. B—Q 3, P—K Kt 3 ; 17. B—R 3, B—Q B 3 ; 18. Q—Kt 4, R—K 1 ; 19. Kt—B 4, P—K R 4 ; 20. Q—B 4, B—K Kt 4 ; 21. Q—Kt 3, B—K R 5 ; 22. Q—K 3, Q—Q 4 ; 23. P—K B 3, B—Q 1 ; 24. Kt—Q 6, R—K 2 ; 25. B—Q B 5 !—and Black, whose Queen is imprisoned in quite a spectacular way, resigned after a very few moves.

10. Castles	Kt×Kt
11. P×Kt	P×P
12. Kt×P	......

The 19th Euwe Match-game 1935 continued as follows : 12. P×P, P—B 6 ; 13. B—Q 2 !, Q—R 4 ; 14. B×P !, B×B ; 15. R—R 3, Kt—B 3 (if B—Q 2 then 16. R×B, B×P ; 17. B—Kt 5 ch !! and wins) ; 16. R×B, B—Q 2 ; 17. R—Q Kt 1, Castles ; 18. R—B 5, Q—Q 1 ; 19. R×P, B—B 1 ; 20. R—Kt 1, Kt×P ; 21. Kt×Kt, Q×Kt ; 22. B—B 3 and with the exchange up White had a technically easy win.

By recapturing here with the Knight, I wanted to satisfy myself whether it is stronger than the line adopted by me previously. As this game proves, White also wins back the Pawn sacrificed, while keeping excellent attacking chances ; the question which of the two moves gives him the greater advantage is, therefore, rather academic.

12.	B—B 4
13. Kt—B 3 !	Kt—Q 2
14. R—Q 1	Q—B 3
15. B×P	Castles

The King must fly, because after 15. ....B×P ch ; 16. Q×B and 17. B—R 3 Black would rapidly succumb.

16. Kt—Kt 5   . . . . . .

Forcing the weakening of Black's King-side position.

16. . . . . . .   P—K Kt 3
17. B—Kt 5   Q—B 2
18. Kt—K 4   B—K 2

Of course not 18. . . . . Kt × P because of 19. Kt × B followed by B—R 3, etc.

19. P—K B 4   . . . . . .

This is not the strongest continuation of the attack. The right idea of exploiting Black's cramped position consisted in forcing the exchange of his K's Bishop by means of 19. B—K R 6, R—Q 1 ; 20. P—K B 4, followed by B—K Kt 5, etc., after which the weakness of the dark coloured squares would rapidly become fatal to the second player. The text-move was based on a slight over-estimation of White's attacking possibilities in the position which actually occurred after Black's 21st move.

19. . . . . . .   Kt—B 4
20. Kt—B 6 ch   . . . . . .

Under the circumstances more promising than 20. Kt—Q 6, which however, was quite playable.

20. . . . . . .   B × Kt
21. P × B   B—Q 2
22. B—K 3 ?   . . . . . .

I made this move instantly, having calculated the whole variation on the 19th move. Instead 22. B—R 3 !, R—Q 1 ; 23. R—Q 4, etc., would maintain the advantage of space without any offers.

22. . . . . . .   B × B
23. P × B   Kt—Q 2 !
24. P—Kt 3   . . . . . .

Comparatively best as 24. B—Q 4, Q × K B P ; 25. R—K B 1, Q—Kt 4 would give Black in addition to his material gain some attacking prospects (. . . . P—K 4).

24. . . . . . .   Kt × P
25. B—Q 4   . . . . . .

Realising that 25. R × R , P—planned already a few moves before—would be answered not by 25. . . . . R × R ; 26. P—Kt 6, etc. ±, but by 25. . . . . Kt—Q 4 ! ; 26. R × R, Kt × B ; 27. R × R ch, K × R ; 28. Q—Q 3, Kt × R ; 29. Q × Kt, Q—B 4 ch, etc, with a better Queen-ending for Black. After the text-move White obtains sufficient compensation for the Pawn, because of his powerful Bishop—but that is about all. By the following moves Black could force simplification which most probably would lead to a draw.

25. . . . . . .   Kt—Q 2
26. Q—B 2   P—Kt 3
27. R—K 1   . . . . . .

Preventing 27. . . . . P—B 3 followed by . . . . P—K 4.

27. . . . . . .   Q—B 5
28. Q R—Kt 1   Q R—B 1
29. Q—K 3   K R—K 1
30. Q—B 3   P—B 3

Black begins to play with fire. Here, or even at the next move, he should offer the exchange of Queens by . . . . Q—Q 4, since he would still be able to protect his backward Q R P. The variation 30. . . . . Q—Q 4 ; 31. Q × Q, P × Q ; 32. R × R ch, R × R ; 33. R—R 1, R—R 1 should, as mentioned, probably result in a peaceful draw. After the text-move and the next one White succeeds in building up a formidable K.-side attack.

31. R—Kt 4	Q—B 2 ?
32. R—Kt 2 !	......

Now Black's K P becomes weak.

32.	R—K 2
33. Q R—K 2	K—B 2
34. P—Kt 4	Q R—K 1
35. P—Kt 5 !	......

With a hidden purpose which Black entirely overlooks.

35.	P × P

His only chance of salvation was 35. ....P—B 4 when White would still have excellent winning prospects by continuing P—R 4—R 5, etc.

Position after Black's 35th move.

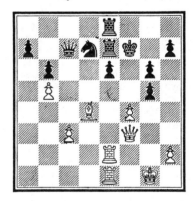

36. P—B 5 ! !	......

A problem-like move which forces the win in all variations. Besides the continuation in the text, the following possibilities came into consideration :

I. 36. ....*K P × P* ; 37. Q—Q 5 ch, K—B 1 ; 38. B—Kt 7 ch ! and wins.

II. 36. ....*Kt P × P* ; 37. Q—R 5 ch, K—B 1 ; 38. Q—R 6 ch, K—Kt 1 ; 39. Q × Kt P ch and wins.

III. 36. ....*P—K 4* ; 37. Q—Q 5 ch, K—B 1 ; 38. Q—B 6 !, Q × Q ;

39. P × Q, P × B ; 40. R × R, R × R ; 41. R × R, K × R ; 42. P—B 7 and wins.

36.	Q—K B 5

Neither better nor worse than the variations just given.

37. P × K P ch	R × P
38. Q—Q 5	......

Another winning line was 38. Q—R 3, Q—R 5 ; 39. R—B 1 ch, K—Kt 1 ; 40. R × R ! and wins.

38.	Kt—B 3

White threatened also 39. R—K B 1, etc.

39. B × Kt	Q—Kt 5 ch
40. R—Kt 2	Q—B 4
41. B—K 5	......

But not 41. Q—B 4 ?, Q—B 4 ch and Black would win !

41.	K—Kt 1
42. R—K B 2	Q—Kt 5 ch
43. K—R 1	P—K R 4
44. R—K Kt 1	Q—K R 5
45. R—B 6	K—R 2
46. R × R	R × R
47. Q—Q 7 ch	Resigns.

GAME 88

CATALAN OPENING

Nottingham Tournament, August, 1936.

White : Dr. S. Tartakower

Quality Prize

1. P—Q 4	Kt—K B 3
2. P—K Kt 3	P—Q B 4

Intending, if 3. P—Q 5, to play a King's Fianchetto. But a sounder answer to White's unusual second move is 2. ....P—Q 4.

3. Kt—K B 3   P—Q 4
4. B—Kt 2   .....

Giving Black the predominance in the centre.   A safer line was 4. P—Q B 3 entering into the Schlechter Variation of the Slav Defence with a *tempo* more.

4. ......   P×P
5. Castles   B—Kt 5

And not 5. ....Kt—B 3 ; 6. Kt×P, P—K 4 ; 7. Kt×Kt, P× Kt ; 8. P—Q B 4, etc., with superior fighting chances for White.

6. Kt×P ?   ......

This is completely in accordance with Black's wishes.   Instead 6. Kt—K 5 ! would have kept the balance of the position, since after 6. ....B—R 4 ; 7. Q×P the win of a Pawn by 7. ....B×K P would prove decidedly too risky after 8. R—K 1, B—R 4 (or R 3) ; 9. P— Q B 4, etc. ±

6. ......   P—K 4
7. Kt—K B 3 Kt—B 3
8. P—K R 3   B—K B 4

Even more exact was 8. ....B— Q 2 (but not 8. ....B—K 3 ; 9. Kt—Kt 5) after which 9. P—B 4 could be simply answered by 9. .... P×P.∓ But the text-move is, after all, also good enough.

9. P—B 4 !   P—Q 5
10. Q—Kt 3   Q—B 2 (?)

But after this White gets the opportunity of equalising chances. The more natural 10. ....Q—Q 2 (not ....Q—B 1 because of 11. Kt×K P ! followed by 12. B× Kt P±) would also be the best ; if

11. P—K 3, then 11. ....B—K 2 ; 12. P×P, P×P followed by .... Castles (K R) etc., with a clear advantage.

11. P—K 3   B—K 2

Black must now get his King into safety as rapidly as possible.

12. P×P   P×P
13. B—B 4   ......

This most important win of a *tempo* is a direct consequence of Black's inaccurate 10th move.

13. ......   Q—B 1
14. R—Q 1   Castles

Fortunately for Black he need not trouble about his centre Pawn, for he will find compensation in the capture of White's K R P. If now 15. P—Kt 4, then B—K 5 ! ; 16. Q Kt—Q 2, B—Kt 3, etc., with a complicated but not disadvantageous middle-game position.

15. Kt×P   B×P
16. Kt×Kt   P×Kt
17. B×B ?   ......

Here, and later, White makes a few indifferent moves, which rapidly spoil his, at present, defensible position.   It was obviously inadvisable to bring the black Queen through this exchange to a strong attacking post.   He should first and foremost finish his development with 17. Kt —B 3.

17. ......   Q×B
18. Q—K B 3 Kt—Kt 5
19. Kt—B 3   ......

Again underestimating Black's attacking chances.   Better was 19. Kt—Q 2 and if 19. ....P—K B 4 then 20. Kt—B 1.

19. ......   P—K B 4 !

With the powerful threat 20. ....
B—B 4, at present premature on
account of 20. Kt—K 4. From now
on Black's conduct of the King's
attack is irreproachable and explains the distinction given to this
interesting game.

20. Q—Kt 2   Q—R 4
21. R—K 1   ......

Equally unsatisfactory was 21.
B—Q 6, B × B ; 22. R × B, P—B 5,
etc. ∓

21. ......   B—B 4
22. Kt—Q 1   P—Kt 4
23. B—K 5   ......

23. B—K 3, B × B ; 24. Kt × B,
Kt—K 4 followed by P—B 5 would
give Black an equally easy attack.

23. ......   Q R—Q 1

After this there is no defence
against ....R × Kt, etc.

24. B—B 3   R × Kt !

Not only winning a Pawn, but
completely demolishing the remains
of White's fortress.

25. Q R × R   B × P ch
26. K—B 1   B × R

Tempting, but less convincing
was 26. ....B—K 6 because of the
answer 27. K—K 2 !

27. R × B   P—B 5
28. P × P   ......

The desperate resource 28. R—
K 7 would prove insufficient on
account of 28. ....Kt—K 6 ch ;
29. K—Kt 1, Q—Q 8 ch ; 30. K—
R 2, P × P ch, etc.

28. ......   R × P ch
29. K—Kt 1   ......

Position after White's 29th move.

29. ......   Kt—R 7 !

The deadly stroke. If 30. Q ×
Kt, then 30. ....R—Kt 5 ch ; 31.
K—R 1, R—R 5, etc. White chooses
another method of giving up his
Queen, but he is soon persuaded
that further resistance is quite
hopeless.

30. R—K 3   R—B 8 ch
31. Q × R   Kt × Q
32. K × Kt   Q—B 2 ch
33. K—Kt 2   Q × P
34. R—K 7   Q—Q 4 ch
35. K—R 3   P—K R 4
Resigns.

GAME 89

QUEEN'S GAMBIT DECLINED (ORTHODOX DEFENCE)

Hastings Tournament, December,
1936.

Black : Dr. M. Vidmar

1. P—Q 4   P—Q 4
2. P—Q B 4   P—K 3
3. Kt—Q B 3   Kt—K B 3
4. B—Kt 5   Q Kt—Q 2
5. P—K 3   B—K 2
6. Kt—B 3   Castles
7. R—B 1   P—B 3

8. Q—B 2   ......

Nowadays this Rubinstein move is considered rather harmless because of the reply 8. ....Kt— K 5 ! ; but as Dr. Vidmar had had an unpleasant experience with that move (in a quite analogous position) in our game at Bled (see No. 44), he decided to adopt the older and more complicated defensive method.

8. ......   P—Q R 3
9. P × P   ......

Seldom played at this particular moment, but quite in accordance with modern tendencies : against the most natural answer 9. .... K P × P, White plans a minority attack on the Queen's side.

9. ......   Kt × P

And after this the position will bear the characteristics of the so-called Capablanca Defence, but with the important difference, in White's favour, that Black has difficulties in freeing his game with ....P— K 4.

10. B × B   Q × B
11. B—B 4   ......

Of course not 11. B—Q 3 because of ....Kt—Kt 5; but 11. P—Q R 3 also came into consideration.

11. ......   Kt × Kt
12. Q × Kt   P—Q B 4

As 12. .... R—K 1 (aiming at ....P—K 4) would be efficiently answered by 13. R—Q 1 !, Black decides to start operations on the Queen's wing. After the text-move he threatens, of course, 13. .... P—Q Kt 4, etc., with a quite satisfactory game.

13. P × P   ......

A move difficult in its simplicity : White temporarily sacrifices space in order to regain it with some additional advantages. Not quite so convincing would be 13. B—K 2, P × P ; 14. Kt × P, Kt—K B 3 or 14. Q × P, P—K 4, etc., with more chances for Black to equalise than in the actual game.

13. ......   Q × P

As Black intends to avoid the exchange of Queens, more logical was 13. ....Kt × P ; 14. B—K 2, Kt—K 5 ; 15. Q—Q 4, Kt—B 3 ; 16. Castles, etc., with only a slight superiority for White.

14. B—Kt 3 !   P—Q Kt 3

Certainly the end-game after 14. ....Q × Q ; 15. R × Q would have offered but slight chances of salvation because of the possible intrusion of the White Rook on to the 7th rank and the position of his King in the middle ; but now the Black Queen will be pursued until White obtains material advantage.

15. Q—Q 2   Q—K R 4

15. ....Q—K 2 ; 16. R—B 7, etc., was even less satisfactory.

Position after Black's 15th move.

16. B—Q 1 !   ......

This modest-looking retreat practically decides the game. White not only threatens 17. R × B followed by 18. Q × Kt—which at this moment would be wrong because of ....K R—Q 1 ; Q—K 7, R—B 8 ch ; K—K 2, Q—Kt 4 ch and mate next move—but he also eventually intends to dislodge the Black Queen by means of 18. Kt—Q 4 and to occupy after that the long diagonal by B—K B 3, etc., with deadly effect.   Black is therefore forced to the following time-wasting Knight's tour, which, as a direct consequence, will lead to the loss of a Pawn.

| 16. ...... | Kt—B 4 |
| 17. P—Q Kt 4 ! | ...... |

But not 17. Kt—Q 4, because of 17. ....Q—Kt 3, threatening 18. ....Kt—Q 6 ch.

| 17. ...... | Kt—K 5 |
| 18. Q—Q 4 | B—Kt 2 |

Dr. Vidmar tries, as he usually does in compromised positions, to complicate matters. If White takes the Pawn immediately, Black might get some sort of counter-attack after (18. Q × Q Kt P), B—Q 4 ; 19. P—Q R 3, Q—Kt 3 ! (20. Castles ? Kt—Q 7) etc.   But a twenty-five years' old experience with the Yugo-Slavian Grand-Master (see, for instance, my game with him at Carlsbad, 1911, in *My Best Games, 1908-1923*) had taught me to be extra careful after having strategically outplayed him.   In fact, my next simple move left him with no hopes of further "swindles."

19. Castles   P—Q Kt 4

Instead, 19. ....B—Q 4 would be hopeless : 20. Kt—Q 2, Q—Kt 3 ; 21. B—B 2, P—B 4 ; 22. Kt × Kt, P × Kt ; 23. P—B 3 ! etc.

| 20. Kt—K 5 | Q—R 3 |
| 21. Kt—B 6 | ...... |

Forcing the following exchange, after which the Bishop will prove much more powerful than the Knight in both the middle- and end-game.

21.	B × Kt
22. R × B	Kt—B 3
23. B—B 3	......

This is the type of position I aimed at when playing 16. B—Q 1 ! It becomes quite obvious that the decentralised black Queen is unable to co-operate in the protection of the menaced Queen's flank.

| 23. ...... | Q R—Q 1 |
| 24. R—Q 6 | ...... |

White is in the agreeable position of being able to use the simplest methods—a reward of the adoption of the right strategical plan.

24.	R × R
25. Q × R	Q—R 5
26. P—Q R 3	......

Black's Pawn is now bound to fall, and, in order to prevent further damage, he has to permit the exchange of Queens.   The ensuing end-game, though theoretically won for White, still remains highly instructive, especially as Dr. Vidmar defends it with extreme care and resourcefulness.

26.	Q—Q B 5
27. Q × R P	Kt—Q 4
28. P—Q R 4 !	Kt—B 2

After 28. .... Q × Kt P ; 29. B × Kt, P × B ; 30. Q × P, etc., White would win rapidly.

29. Q—B 6	Q × Q
30. B × Q	P × P
31. R—R 1	R—Kt 1
32. R × P	K—B 1

33. P—Kt 4   . . . . .

The following winning plan is easy to explain, but technically rather hard to execute. White profits by the fact that the Black pieces are busy on the Queen's side with the passed Pawn *to create*—by gradual advance or eventual exchanges of Pawns—*permanently vulnerable points in the centre and on the King's side of Black's camp;* and only after this preliminary work is achieved can the final assault begin.

33. . . . . . .   K—K 2
34. P—Q Kt 5 !   . . . . . .

Obviously the last opportunity to secure a steady position for this Pawn.

34. . . . . . .   P—K 4

Of course not 34. . . . . Kt × P ? ; 35. R—Q Kt 4.

35. P—B 4 !   . . . . . .

Black is faced with two evils: either to give up control of White's Q 4 or, as in the game, to allow the isolation of his K P.

35. . . . . . .   P—B 3
36. P × P   P × P
37. R—R 2   . . . . . .

Frustrating 37. . . . . K—Q 3 because of 38. R—Q 2 ch, etc.

37. . . . . . .   R—Kt 3
38. R—Q Kt 2   P—R 3
39. K—B 2   K—K 3
40. K—B 3   Kt—Q 4
41. P—R 4   . . . . . .

The exchange of minor pieces, here or on the 42nd and 43rd moves, would naturally have considerably increased Black's drawing chances.

41. . . . . . .   Kt—K 2
42. B—K 4   Kt—Q 4
43. R—Kt 3   K—Q 3

44. P—Kt 5 !   . . . . . .

Prevents . . . . Kt—B 3 and diminishes the mobility of Black's K Kt P. The end-game crisis approaches.

44. . . . . . .   P × P
45. P × P   K—K 3
46. B—Q 3   . . . . . .

The Rook will gradually recover its freedom of movement.

46. . . . . . .   K—Q 3
47. R—R 3   Kt—B 2
48. R—R 7   R—Kt 1
49. K—K 4   . . . . . .

Threatening 50. K—B 5 and this practically forces the following weakening Pawn-move.

49. . . . . . .   P—Kt 3
50. R—R 3 !   . . . . . .

The time has come to dislodge the King from Q 3.

50. . . . . . .   R—Kt 3
51. B—B 4   R—Kt 1
52. R—Q 3 ch   K—B 4

Position after Black's 52nd move.

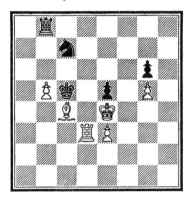

53. R—Q 7 !   . . . . . .

After about twenty preparatory

moves, the Rook enters into the enemy's formation with decisive effect. Black's following desperate fight is as good as useless, for he will no longer be able to offer the exchange of minor pieces without losing both his remaining Pawns.

53.	Kt—K 1
54. B—B 7	Kt—Q 3 ch
55. K × P	R—Kt 3
56. P—K 4	.....

Of course, not 56. B × P ?—.... Kt—B 5 ch ; 57. K—B 5, Kt × P ch, etc.

56.	Kt × Kt P

This Pawn is now of no importance, for the fight is to be decided on the other side. The rest is agony.

57. R—Q 5 ch !	K—Kt 5
58. R—Q 8	Kt—R 2
59. R—Q 6	Kt—B 3 ch
60. K—Q 5	Kt—K 2 ch
61. K—K 6	Kt—B 3
62. K—B 6	K—B 4
63. R—Q 5 ch	K—Kt 5
64. P—K 5 !	K—B 5
65. R—Q 1 dis ch	K—B 4
66. R—B 1 ch	K—Q 5
67. P—K 6	K—K 6
68. B × P	Kt—Q 5
69. B—B 7	Kt—K 7
70. R—K 1	K—B 7
71. R × Kt ch	Resigns.

GAME 90

RUY LOPEZ

Hastings Tournament, January, 1937.

Black : R. FINE

1. P—K 4	P—K 4
2. Kt—K B 3	Kt—Q B 3
3. B—Kt 5	P—Q R 3
4. B—R 4	Kt—B 3
5. Castles	B—K 2

6. R—K 1	P—Q Kt 4
7. B—Kt 3	P—Q 3
8. P—B 3	Kt—Q R 4
9. B—B 2	P—B 4
10. P—Q 4	Q—B 2
11. Q Kt—Q 2	Castles

So far everything is conventional, but here the generally adopted move is 11. ....Kt—B 3, trying to force White to a decision in the centre. The most promising continuation for White is then, 12. P—Q R 4, R—Kt 1 ; 13. P × Kt P, P × Kt P ; 14. P × B P, Q P × P ; 15. Kt—B 1 followed by Kt—K 3, etc.

12. Kt—B 1	B—Kt 5

The continuation of this game proves convincingly that the early exchange of this Bishop gives White promising attacking opportunities on the King's side—but a fully satisfactory plan is not easy to find. The comparatively most logical method seems 12. ....B—Q 2 followed by ....K R—B 1 and ....B—K B 1.

13. Kt—K 3 !	.....

The most forcible reply, which does not even oblige White to sacrifice anything on the next moves if he does not want to.

13.	B × Kt
14. Q × B !	.....

After the simple 14. P × B, White would have the pair of Bishops and some attacking chances on the basis of the open K Kt-file ; but the text-move, by which he preserves his Pawn-structure intact, is more precise and stronger.

14.	B P × P
15. Kt—B 5 ?	.....

But this risky offer—mainly explained by my being a half-point behind Fine and having to win at all costs in order to be first—cannot be recommended objectively, although after it White keeps the initiative for a quite long time. The right move was 15. P × P ! since, after 15. ....P × P ; 16. Kt—B 5, Q × B ; 17. Kt × B ch, K—R 1 ; 18. Kt—B 5 ! (threatening 19. Kt × Kt P !, K × Kt ; 20. B—R 6 ch, etc.), White would have obtained a decisive advantage. Also 15. ....Kt—Q B 3 (the answer I actually expected to 15. P × P) ; 16. P—Q 5 !, Kt—Q 5 ; 17. Q—Q 1, Kt × B ; 18. Kt × Kt (threatening 19. Kt—Kt 4, etc.), P—Q R 4 ; 19. B—Q 2 followed by R—Q B 1, etc., would have been in White's favour. The following few defensive moves of Fine's are not only good but the only ones.

15. ......   P × P
16. Q × P !   K R—B 1 !

Protecting the Knight at R 4 by an attack against White's King's Bishop.

17. Q—K Kt 3   B—B 1
18. B—Q 3   ......

If, instead, 18. B—Kt 5, then simply 18. ....Q × B ; 19. B × Kt, P—K Kt 3, etc.

18. ......   Kt—B 3
19. B—Kt 5   Kt—K 1
20. Q R—B 1 (?)   ......

As an eventual exchange of Rooks would be entirely to Black's advantage, there was no need for White to play his Rook on to the open file. Indicated was at once 20. Q R—Q 1 (see 24th move) followed by P—Q R 3 and B—Kt 1—R 2, etc. The extra *tempo* would probably have been of great importance. From now on, on the contrary, Black has a comparatively easy defensive play.

20. ......   Q—Kt 2

21. P—Q R 3   ......

The manoeuvre intended here, B—Kt 1—R 2—Q 5 induces Black to start a counter demonstration on the Queen's side, and, in order to do so, he must first force the exchange of the White Knight.

21. ......   P—K Kt 3
22. Kt—R 6 ch   B × Kt
23. B × B   ......

Black's dark squares are somewhat weak now—but his Knight at K 1 is a stout defender.

23. ......   Kt—Q 5
24. Q R—Q 1   P—Kt 5
25. P—B 4 !   ......

The opening of this file offers fair equalising prospects—but with right answers hardly more.

25. ......   P × B P

The defence of K 4 by 25. .... P—K B 3 would be advantageously met by 26. P—B 5 ! etc.

26. Q × P   P × P
27. P × P   R—B 6 !

An ingenious drawing combination : if, namely, 28. P—K 5, then 28. ....R × B ! ; 29. R × R, Kt—K 7 ch ; 30. R × Kt, Q—Kt 8 ch ; 31. K—B 2, Q × R ; 32. P—K 6 !, Q—B 4 ; 33. Q × Q, P × Q ; 34. P—K 7, P—B 3 ; 35. K—K 3 ! and the presence of White's King on the Queen's side would eliminate the danger of his losing. But as a draw meant as much as a loss to me, I did not even take this variation into serious consideration.

28. Q—B 2   Kt—K 3 ?

From now on, Fine's resistance begins gradually to weaken. The game has not developed quite according to his expectations (i.e.—the frustrated chance of simplifying by means of 28. ....R×B, etc.). After the natural 28. .... Kt—Q B 3 ; 29. B—Q B 1 !, Kt—K 4 ; 30. B—B 1 (Kt—Kt 5 ; 31. Q—Q 4), he would have slight winning chances, although the White Bishops would have *almost* counterbalanced the not over-important extra Pawn.

29. P—Q R 4   .....

This insignificant-looking Pawn will henceforth support White's threats in a very efficient way.

29. ......   Q R—B 1

Again out of place, since it will immediately become evident that his Q R P needs more protection. The other Rook should have returned to B 1.

30. R—K B 1   ......

Threatening 31. B × R P, etc.

30. ......   K R—B 2
31. R—Kt 1   Q—B 3
32. P—R 5 !   ......

Incredible but true—White has suddenly obtained a strong pressure on the Queen's side. A rather confusing result of Black's manœuvres on that sector of the board !

32. ......   Kt—B 4 ?

The evolutions of this Knight have been decidedly unlucky, and after this last one there will be no salvation. Comparatively best was 32. ....R—R 1, after which White would have increased his positional advantage with 33. Q R—B 1 followed by 34. B—Q B 4, etc. ±

33. B—Q B 4   .....

If now 33. ....Kt × P, then 34. B × P ch, K—R 1 ; 35. Q—Q 4 ch and wins. Black's answer is therefore forced.

33. ......   Q—Q 2

Position after Black's 33rd move.

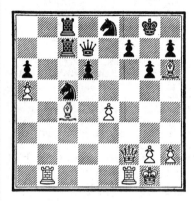

34. Q—R 2 !   .....

It is odd how sometimes exactly the same attacking ideas repeat themselves within a short period of time ! One may compare the textmove, for instance, with 37. Q—Q 2 in my game against Tylor (No. 91) where the transposition of a vertical attack by the Queen into a diagonal one brought an equally rapid decision.

34. ......   Kt × P

Or 34. ....Kt—K 3 ; 35. B × Kt etc.

35. R × P   Q × R
36. B × Q ch   R × B
37. Q—K 6 !   Resigns.

An interesting fight—but certainly influenced by the exceptional importance of the result.

GAME 91

RUY LOPEZ

Margate Tournament, April, 1937.

Black : T. H. TYLOR

1. P—K 4	P—K 4
2. Kt—K B 3	Kt—Q B 3
3. B—Kt 5	P—Q R 3
4. B—R 4	Kt—B 3
5. Castles	B—K 2
6. Q—K 2	Castles ?

A rather common error : White does not threaten anything at this moment (for instance, 7. B×Kt, Q P×B ; 8. Kt×P, Q—Q 5 ; 9. Kt—K B 3, Q×K P, etc., equalising easily) so Black thinks he has time to castle—and forgets that precisely after this move White can win a Pawn, the Bishop at K 2 being no longer protected by the King ! The correct move is, of course, 6. ....P—Q 3.

7. P—B 3 ?   ......

An exaggerated faith in the knowledge of my opponents was always the vulnerable point of my opening play ; for instance, at San Remo, 1930, I did not take a Pawn on the tenth move which my opponent, Rubinstein, left *en prise* in an even more obvious way than in this game ! It is quite obvious that 7. B×Kt, Q P×B ; 8. Kt×K P could and should have been played, since 8. ....Q—Q 5 ; 9. Kt—K B 3. Q× K P ? costs a piece after 10. Q×Q followed by 11. R—K 1. The slight advantage in development that Black would have obtained after, for instance, 8. ....R—K 1 ; 9. P—Q 3, B—Q B 4 ; 10. Kt—B 3, B—K Kt 5, would by no means compensate for the material loss. After the tame text-move well known positions will be reached.

7. ......   P—Q 3

8. P—Q 4	B—Q 2
9. P—Q 5	Kt—Kt 1
10. B—B 2	Kt—K 1

The manœuvre 10. ....P—Q R 4 followed by Kt—R 3—B 4, played by me in a consultation game against Kashdan (see No. 119), proved quite successful. But also the text-move, aiming at a rapid counter-attack in the centre, can hardly be criticised.

11. P—B 4   P—K B 4

But here he should prepare for this advance by 11. ....P—K Kt 3 followed eventually by ....Kt—Kt 2, in order not to give up completely the control upon White's K 4. From now on White obtains a clear positional advantage, which he exploits in an impeccable manner until an advanced stage of the middle-game.

12. P×P	B×P
13. B×B	R×B
14. Kt—Q B 3	Kt—Q 2
15. Kt—K 4	Kt—B 1 !

Tylor henceforth defends his difficult position extremely well until the fateful 32nd move. White would gain no advantage by playing now 16. P—K Kt 4, R—B 2 ; 17. K Kt —Kt 5, B×Kt ; 18. Kt×B, R— K 2 ; or 18. B×B, Q—Q 2, etc.

16. B—K 3	Kt—Kt 3
17. P—K Kt 3	P—R 3

In order to be able to move the King's Knight or the Queen without allowing White's Kt—Kt 5.

18. K Kt—Q 2   ......

Threatening 19. Q—Kt 4.

18.	K—R 2
19. Q—Q 3	Q—Q 2

Preparing an eventual demon-stration on the King's side starting with ....R—R 4 and Q—R 6. White has therefore no time for the logical advance P—Q Kt 4, P—Q B 5, etc.

20. P—B 4   ......

White rightly calculated that hereby he will gain the square K 6 for his Knight and that the possible sortie of the black Queen against his King will not much improve the opponent's chances.

20. ......   K—R 1

White's threat was 21. P×P, Kt×P ; 22. Kt—Kt 5 ch, etc.

21. Kt—K B 3!   ......

An important intermediate move that permits the relaxation of the tension in the centre without ceding the important square K 5 to the black Knight.

21. ......   P×P
22. Kt—Q 4   R—B 2

Quite useless would be 22. .... Kt—R 4 ; 23. Q—B 2, etc.

23. B×P (?)   ......

A slight strategical error that prevents White from taking full advantage of his strong position. The two following important con-siderations spoke in favour of re-taking with the Pawn : (1) As Black's position is somewhat cramped, White should avoid any further exchange. (2) The white Bishop was particularly useful for the protection of the dark-coloured squares. As a matter of fact, the whole next section (up to the 32nd move) is influenced by the potential power of the black Bishop, liberated from his chief antagonist.

23. ......   Kt×B
24. P×Kt   ......

It was difficult to decide whether it was advisable to provoke the exchange of one pair of Rooks by 24. R×Kt : Black's Rook at K B 2 has appreciable defensive power—but, on the other hand, the pros-pects of play with both Rooks on the open files were also tempting.

24. ......   Q—Kt 5 ch
25. K—R 1 !   ......

White had already calculated this Pawn-offer when playing 20. P—B 4. Of course the simple 25. Q—Kt 3 was also playable and would secure a comfortable end-game.

25. ......   Kt—B 3 !

Quite rightly refusing the Danä-ian Gift, since 25. ....R×P ; 26. R×R, Q×R ; 27. R—K B 1 would have catastrophic consequences for Black : I. 27. ....Q—K 4 ; 28. R—B 5. II. 27. ....Q—R 5 ; 28. Kt—B 5. III. 27. ....Q—Kt 5 ; 28. R—B 7 !, Q—R 5 ; 29. Kt—K B 3 —with an easy win in all cases.

26. Kt—K B 2   ......

An artificial - looking retreat, which, in fact, should have led only to an equal game. Appropriate was 26. Q R—K 1 or immediately 26. Kt—K 6 ; in the latter case the following curious variation would be possible : 26. ....Q—K B 4 ; 27. Q R—K 1, P—B 3 ; 28. R—K Kt 1 !, P×P ; 29. Kt×Q P !, Q×Q ; 30. Kt×R ch and mate next move.

26. ......   Q—R 4

White's previous move would have proved strong only after 26. ....Q×B P ; 27. Kt—K 6, Q—R 5 ; 28. Kt—R 3 ! threatening Kt—B 4 —Kt 6 etc. ±.

27. R—K Kt 1   .....

Now 27. Kt—K 6 is ineffective because of the simple 27. ....P—B 3 etc.

27. ......   Kt—Q 2 !

Again a very good manœuvre, which practically forces the desirable exchange of Knights.

28. Kt—K 6   Kt—B 4
29. Q—K 3   .....

Instead, 29. Q—K Kt 3 would prevent the immediate exchange at K 6 but, on the other hand, would permit 29. ....B—K B 3.

29. ......   Kt × Kt
30. P × Kt   .....

White's still existing advantage in space is herewith compensated for by the attack that this Pawn can be subjected to, while its neighbour at K B 4 will need permanent defence. The chances are now about even.

30. ......   R—B 3
31. Q R—K 1   Q R—K B 1

This Rook was needed for a guard to his K Kt P and should have been moved to K Kt 1 at once. Still, the text-move does not spoil anything yet.

32. Q—K Kt 3   P—K Kt 4 ?

An error, but an excusable one, for the following tactical attack by White was indeed very difficult to foresee. Correct was 32. ....R—K Kt 1 ; 33. R—K 4, Q—K B 4 ; 34. Q—K 3 followed by Kt—Q 3, etc., with an open fight going on.

33. Kt—R 3   .....

Although there is no direct threat in this move (34. P × P ?, R—B 6, etc.), Black's game now becomes most troublesome : he even can no longer dream of a successful attack against White's K P.

33. ......   R—B 4

34. Q—Kt 2 !   .....

A fine preparatory move to the ensuing Rooks' manœuvre, against which Black will be unable to find an adequate defence.

34. ......   P—B 3
35. R—K 3 !   .....

Only after this move does White begin to threaten. Black must now find something against 36. Kt × P !, B × Kt ; 37. R—R 3 ! followed by 38. P × B, etc.

35. ......   K—Kt 2 !

A paradoxical-looking, but, for the moment, sufficient defence.

36. R—K Kt 3   .....

Taken separately, this move—as most of its immediate predecessors —looks rather harmless. In fact, after 37. P × P, P × P ; 38. Kt × P, B × Kt ; 39. R × B ch, R × R ; 40. Q × R ch, Q × Q ; 41. R × Q ch, K—B 3, etc., the game would end in a draw ; and only the next quiet move gives to the whole attacking scheme its real significance.

36. ......   P—Q 4
37. Q—Q 2 !   B—Q 3

After 37. ....B—B 4 ; 38. R—K 1 (simplest), White's win would be easy.

Position after Black's 37th move.

38. Kt×P !   . . . . . .

The immediate object of this pseudo-sacrifice is quite obvious—Black cannot take the Knight without losing his Queen ; but the consequences of Black's rejoinder were misleading, as often happens when there are several possibilities from discovered checks.

38. . . . . . .   B×P !
39. Q—B 3 ch !   . . . . . .

The first point—White delays the "discovery" and rejects the tempting 39. P—K 7 which would prove a pure hallucination after 39. . . . . B×Q ; 40. Kt—K 6 d. ch, K—R 1 ! etc.

39. . . . . . .   R (1)—B 3

If 39. . . . . B—K 4, then 40. Kt—B 3 dis. ch, etc.

40. Kt—K 4 d. ch ! B×R
41. R×B ch   K—R 1

Or 41. . . . . K—B 1 ; 42. Q—Kt 4 ch ! and mate in a few moves.

42. Q×R ch !   . . . . . .

The final point, reminiscent of some compositions by Greco and Stamma.

42. . . . . . .   R×Q
43. R—Kt 8 ch !   . . . . . .

After 43. . . . . K×R ; 44. Kt×R ch, K—B 1 ; 45. Kt×Q, P×P ; 46. K—Kt 2, White would not even need his extra Knight to stop the Pawn on the Queen's side ; therefore—

Resigns.

GAME 92

SICILIAN DEFENCE

Margate Tournament, April, 1937.

Black : J. FOLTYS

1. P—K 4   P—Q B 4

---

2. Kt—K B 3   Kt—Q B 3

If one wants to play the "Dragon" Variation (the flank development of the King's Bishop), one had better start by 2. . . . . P—Q 3 since White will not then have an opportunity of playing B—K Kt 5 before . . . . P—K Kt 3—for instance, 3. P—Q 4, P×P ; 4. Kt×P, Kt—K B 3 ; 5. Kt—Q B 3, P—K Kt 3, etc. Still, if no improvement can be found for Black in the variation of my Nottingham game against Botvinnik (6. B—K 2, B—Kt 2 ; 7.·B—K 3, Kt—B 3 ; 8. Kt—Kt 3, B—K 3 ; 9. P—B 4, Castles ; 10. P—K Kt 4, P—Q 4 ! ; 11. P—B 5, B—B 1 ; 12. P×Q P, Kt—Kt 5 ; 13. P—Q 6 !, Q×P ; 14. B—B 5, Q—B 5 ! ; 15. R—K B 1, Q×R P ! ; 16. B×Kt, Kt×P ; 17. B×Kt, Q—Kt 6 ch ; 18. R—B 2, Q—Kt 8 ch, etc. — drawn) — it hardly seems tempting for him to adopt that line of play—providing, of course, he plays for a win.

3. P—Q 4   P×P
4. Kt×P   Kt—B 3
5. Kt—Q B 3   P—Q 3

Inadvisable is here 5. . . . . P—K Kt 3, because of 6. Kt×Kt followed by P—K 5.

6. B--K Kt 5   P—K 3

Black can also delay this move by playing, for instance, 6. . . . . B—Q 2, since 7. B×Kt, Kt P×B, etc., would have both advantages and disadvantages—but this delay would be useless for . . . . P—K 3 is still unavoidable. My game with Silva-Rocha (Black) (Montevideo, March, 1938) continued as follows : 6. . . . . B—Q 2 ; 7. B—K 2, P—Q R 3 ; 8. Castles, P—K 3 (What else ?) ; 9. Kt—Kt 3, P—Q Kt 4 ; 10. P—Q R 3, Kt—R 4 ; 11. Kt× Kt, Q×Kt ; 12. Q—Q 4 !, B—K 2 ; 13. K R—Q 1, Q—B 2 ; 14. P—Q R 4 !, P—Kt 5 ; 15. B×Kt, P×B ;

16. Q × Kt P with a decisive advantage for White.

7. B—Kt 5   . . . . .

In order to induce Black to put his Queen's Bishop at Q 2 and thus eliminate the possibility of a fianchetto-development. This system is at least as worth considering as 7. Kt—Kt 3 in conjunction with Q—Q 2 (see my game against P. Frydman, No. 81).

7. . . . . . .   B—Q 2
8. Castles   P—K R 3
9. B—K R 4   . . . . .

The present game shows that this seemingly logical retreat is not without danger. Since the main object of 6. B—K Kt 5—the prevention of the "Dragon" Variation —has been achieved, 9. B—K 3 was good enough.

9. . . . . . .   P—Q R 3
10. B—K 2   B—K 2
11. Kt—Kt 3   . . . . .

Trying to exploit the weakness at Q 6 in a similar manner as in the Frydman game ; but the Czechoslovakian master, having played in Podebrad, knew that game also and had profited by its lesson.

11. . . . . . .   Q—B 2
12. P—B 4   . . . . .

Further pressure against the Q P would prove ineffective—for instance, 12. Q—Q 2, Q R—Q 1 ! (not Castles ; 13. Q R—Q 1, Kt × K P ; 14. Kt × Kt, B × B ; 15. Q × Q P, etc. ±) ; 13. Q R—Q 1 ; B—B 1, etc., with a solid position. Therefore White decides to prepare a King's attack, counting chiefly on 12. . . . . Castles ; 13. Q—K 1 !, P—Q Kt 4 ; 14. B—K B 3 and eventually P— K Kt 4±. But Black's next move gives the battle quite another aspect.

12. . . . . . .   P—K Kt 4 !

Bold and effective, for Black secures herewith, and one may say until the end of the game, the powerful central square K 4 for his Knight. It is interesting to note that this move—solely because Black actually lost—has been completely misjudged by the critics. For instance, one of the most famous modern annotators writes the following : "This move has chiefly a psychological value, because, as it is known that Alekhine does not like defensive positions, there was but little chance that he would choose the variation 13. P × P, P × P ; 14. B × P, P—Q 4 !; 15. P—K R 3, etc." I confess that I did not accept the Pawn-offer quite independently of a would-be distaste for defensive play, but because *I actually do not like to be mated*—and this unpleasantness would most likely occur after 15. . . . . R × R P ! etc. . . . An ungrateful thing, these excursions into another master's psychology !

13. B—Kt 3 !   . . . . .

The only way to keep the balance of position, for White now obtains some pressure on the K B-file in compensation for Black's strong square for his Knight.

13. . . . . . .   P × P
14. R × P   Kt—K 4
15. Q—K B 1   Kt—R 2
16. R—B 2 !   . . . . .

Threatening 17. B × Kt followed by R × P, and thus as good as forcing . . . . Castles, after which the presence of his King will prevent Black from increasing his initiative on that side.

16. . . . . . .   Castles (K R)
17. B—R 5   P—B 3

Also almost forced, but not too disadvantageous, since in exchange for the weakening of K 3 Black has added strength for his Knight's position.

18. B—B 4   K—Kt 2
19. Q R—K 1   ......

Dreaming of seriously bothering the black King after 20. R—K 3 and R—Kt 3 ch; but the opponent prevents this in a simple and effective manner.

19. ......   Q—B 5 !

Threatening to exchange Queens, thus obtaining a good end-game because of his well-protected centre. Safest for White would be to repeat moves by 20. B—K 2, Q—B 2 ; 21. B—R 5, etc., but he prefers to risk the ensuing complicated middle-game, relying less on the strength of his position than on his greater experience.

20. Q R—K 2   B—K 1
21. B × B   Q R × B
22. Q—B 1   Kt—Kt 4
23. P—K R 3   K—R 2
24. K—R 1   R—K Kt 1

Black's King is now completely safe, the open K Kt-file is a factor in his favour, and even on the Queen's side he has some prospects of initiative owing to the Q B-file. Foltys has so far conducted the game very well and certainly should not have lost by right play.

25. Q—K 3   R—Kt 2
26. Kt—Q 4   Q R—K Kt 1 ?

But this little carelessness permits White to obtain a serious initiative. Black obviously only saw that P—Q Kt 3 was not a direct menace—for the Queen would protect the K P from Q B 1—and underestimated the importance of 28. Kt—R 4 ! If he had played

instead 26. ....P—Kt 4 !, the chances would have remained about even.

27. P—Q Kt 3   Q—B 1

Otherwise 28. B × Kt (Kt 4) and 29. Kt × P.

28. Kt—R 4 !   ......

With the strong threat 29. B × Kt (Kt 4) followed by 30. Kt—Kt 6 and 31. Kt × P.

28. ......   B—Q 1
29. P—B 4   ......

Now White has succeeded in gaining considerable space in the centre and threatens to improve his position further by 30. R—B 2 followed by P—B 5, etc. Black's next move facilitates the realisation of that plan.

29. ......   Q—Q 2
30. P—B 5 !   ......

If now 30. ....P × P, then 31. Kt × B P, Q—K 2 ; 32. B × Kt (Kt 4) followed by 33. Kt × K P or 33. B × R P etc.

30. ......   P—Q 4
31. B × Kt (Kt 4) R × B

Position after Black's 31st move.

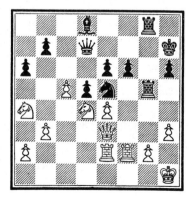

32. P—B 6 !   ......

Permitting the Knights to enter menacingly into the enemy's fortress. Besides its actual strategical value, the whole manœuvre has also a strong psychological (since "psychology" seems to be the fashion in Chess nowadays) effect : baffled by the complete change of situation, Black undoubtedly does not offer the most effective resistance in the very last stages.

32.	P × P
33. Kt—B 5	Q—Q 3
34. Q Kt × K P	R—Kt 6

Permitting the following transaction, after which the white Knights, "doubled" in an original manner on the 6th rank, will speedily make any further resistance useless. Also after the better 34. ....K R—Kt 3 (35. P × P, P × P ; 36. Kt × B, R × Kt ; 37. R—B 2, R—K 1 ; 38. Q—B 4, etc.), White would win owing to the numerous weaknesses in the opponent's position.

35. Q × P ch !   ......

It is much less this Pawn that is of importance than the possibility of an intrusion of the second Knight.

35.	K × Q
36. Kt—B 5 ch	K—R 2
37. Kt × Q	Kt—Q 6
38. R—K B 1	P × P

The loss of a second Pawn is unavoidable.

39. Kt × P	K R—Kt 3
40. Kt × B	Resigns.

GAME 93

ALEKHINE'S DEFENCE

Kemeri Tournament, June, 1937.

Black : S. RESHEVSKY

1. P—K 4	Kt—K B 3
2. P—K 5	Kt—Q 4
3. Kt—K B 3	P—Q 3
4. P—Q 4	B—Kt 5
5. P—B 4	......

There is no hurry to dislodge the Knight. The immediate 5. B—K 2 allows White, if ....P × P, to retake with the Knight without being forced to sacrifice a Pawn.

5.	Kt—Kt 3
6. B—K 2	P × P
7. Kt × P	......

This was my intention when adopting 5. P—B 4 ; but—although actually White will obtain *some* compensation for the Pawn sacrifice —it was hardly advisable to make a considerable effort in order to obtain most likely only equality. In the 29th game of my first match with Dr. Euwe I played here 7. P—B 5 and obtained an opening advantage, but only because my opponent after 7. ....P—K 5 ; 8. P × Kt, P × Kt ; 9. B × P, B × B ; 10. Q × B instead of 10. ....Kt—Q B 3 ! selected the tame move 10. .... R P × P.

7.	B × B
8. Q × B	Q × P
9. Castles	......

Permitting the exchange of the central Knight and thus facilitating Black's defence. More to the point was 9. Kt—R 3 !, Q Kt—Q 2 ; 10. Kt—B 3, or 9. ....P—K 3 ; 10. Kt—B 2 preserving in both cases three minor pieces for attacking purposes.

| 9. ...... | Q Kt—Q 2 |
| 10. Kt × Kt | ...... |

The sacrifice of the Q B P by 10.
Kt—B 3 would be aimless.

| 10. ...... | Kt × Kt ? |

Strangely enough, Reshevsky
decided to make this inferior move
after a particularly close examination of the situation. One would
think that 10. .... Q × Kt could be
automatically selected because of
the general consideration that otherwise the exposed Queen in the
centre will permit White to win
further *tempi* and thus obtain a
real compensation for the Pawn.
If Black had retaken with the
Queen my intention was to continue with 11. P—Q R 4 !, Q—B 3
(not Q Kt × R P ; 12. Q—B 3 !);
12. Kt—R 3, P—K 3 ; 13. P—R 5,
Kt—Q 2 ; 14. Kt—Kt 5 after which
Black's defensive problem would
still remain by no means an easy
one. The text-move brings his
game in danger and only the
greatest circumspection saves him
from a rapid debacle.

| 11. Kt—Q B 3 | P—Q B 3 |

The threat 12. Kt—Kt 5 was too
strong.

12. B—K 3	Q—K 4
13. Q R—Q 1	P—K 3
14. Q—B 3 !	......

An important move which practically forces Black to return his
extra-Pawn since his King had to
be removed from the centre under
all circumstances. Insufficient would
be, for instance, 14. .... B—Q 3 ;
15. P—K Kt 3 or 14. .... B—K 2 ;
15. R × Kt ! followed by 16. Q ×
K B P or 14. .... Kt—B 3 ; 15.
Kt—Q Kt 5 ! etc., with a winning
attack.

| 14. ...... | Castles ! |

| 15. B × R P | ...... |

A grave error would be instead
15. Q × K B P because of 15. ....
B—Q 3 followed by .... R—K B 1
winning ; but now White, after having equalised forces, maintains a
clear positional advantage, Black's
King's position being anything but
safe.

| 15. ...... | Q—R 4 |
| 16. B—Q 4 | ...... |

Prevents 16. .... Kt—K 4.

| 16. ...... | Q—K B 4 |

Trying to make the best of it.
The end-game after the exchange
of Queens certainly looks bad
enough, but is not *quite* hopeless.

| 17. Q—Kt 3 | ...... |

An ex-champion's decision . . .
Before 1935—and now—I would
doubtless have adopted the simple
line starting by 17. Q × Q which
would secure me virtually an
extra-Pawn on the Queen's side
and eliminate any shadow of
danger. But during the whole
period preceding the return match
I simply could not rely on my
patience and nerves—which certainly would have been required for
winning the end-game in question.

17.	P—K 4
18. B—K 3	B—Kt 5
19. Kt—R 4	......

White's best attacking chance,
since from this square the Knight
will "observe" both Q Kt 6 and
Q B 5. But Black's next manœuvre gives his King—at least temporarily—sufficient protection and,
in fact, nearly equalises the chances.

| 19. ...... | B—R 4 ! |
| 20. P—B 4 ! | ...... |

Otherwise Black would even have obtained the initiative after 20. .... B—B 2 and ....P—K 5.

20. ......   B—B 2
21. P—Q Kt 3   ......

It was important to prevent Black from playing ....Q—B 7 *with tempo*.

21. ......   P—B 3
22. P × P   Q—K 3

Of course not 22. ....Q × P ; 23. B—B 4 and wins.

23. P—K R 3 !   ......

A good positional move which, however, is neither particularly deep nor difficult to find. Its main object is to prevent the possibility ....Q—K Kt 5 after 23. ....Kt × P ; 24. Kt—B 5, and also in some other variations the protection of White's K Kt 4 was essential. I was not a little surprised to read all the compliments addressed by the critics to the modest text-move, and also to be questioned—in all seriousness—after the game was over, whether by 23. P—K R 3 I already planned to play my Queen to K R 2 on the 33rd move . . .

23. ......   K R—Kt 1

At this particular moment the K Kt P was not yet in danger—but after the exchange of one pair of Rooks on the Q's file it eventually could be taken.

24. B—Q 4   ......

With the clear purpose of lessening the tension in the centre by 25. Q—K 3 or Q B 3.

24. ......   Kt × K P

This looks rather promising, as

25. Kt—B 5 can be met by 25. .... Q—K 2 and 25. Kt—Kt 6 ch, K—Kt 1 ; 26. Q—Q B 3 ?—by 26. .... P—Q B 4, etc.—with advantage ; but a slight transposition of moves entirely changes the situation in White's favour. Comparatively better was therefore 24. ....P × P ; 25. Q—K 3, P—K 5 ; 26. P—B 5, Q R—K 1 after which Black's passed Pawn would in some way counter-balance White's threats on the Q's side.

25. Q—Q B 3 !   ......

Threatening both 26. Kt—B 5 and 26. Kt—Kt 6 ch. Black's reply is practically forced, since after 25. ....K—Kt 1 ; 26. Kt—B 5, Q—Q 3 ; 27. Q—Kt 4 ! etc., White's threats would prove stronger.

25. ......   Kt—Q 2
26. P—B 5 !   ......

This Pawn will fulfil in the following part of the game several functions of the Bishop, which from now on will merely supervise the development of events.

26. ......   K R—K 1
27. P—Q Kt 4 !   ......

A Pawn-offer, the idea of which is (27. ....Q × Q R P) 28. R—R 1, Q—K 3 (or Q—Q 4 ; 29. K R—Q 1) ; 29. P—Q Kt 5 ! threatening 30. Kt—Kt 6 ch, etc., with a very strong attack.

27. ......   Kt—Kt 1

Also after this retreat White obtains a won game—but not so much because of his direct attack as through the fact that after the following forced exchange his Bishop will become considerably stronger than the black Knight. A satisfactory defence was, however, not visible. Black's decisive—

although by no means obvious—error was most likely 24. . . . . Kt × P.

28. Kt—Kt 6 ch   B × Kt
29. P × B   Q × Q R P

After his counter-chances on the diagonal Q Kt 1—K R 7 have vanished, Black rightly estimates that his only slight chance of salvation consists in extreme recklessness. As a matter of fact I confess that at this moment I even did not consider the possibility of the capture in the text. . . .

30. Q—K Kt 3 ! . . . . . .

More exact than 30. R—Q R 1, Q—Q 4.

30. . . . . . .   R—Q 2

Or 30. . . . . Q—B 2 ; 31. R—R 1 !, R × B ; 32. R—R 8, R—K 4 ; 33. Q × R and wins.

31. B—B 5   . . . . . .

Good enough, but 31. B × P ! was simpler : if 31. . . . . P × B then 32. R × R, K × R ; 33. Q—B 7 ch, K—K 3 ; 34. R—K 1 ch and wins.

31. . . . . . .   Q—B 2
32. R—R 1   Q—Kt 3
33. Q—R 2 !   . . . . . .

After this Black can no longer prevent the unwelcome Rook's visit to Q R 8.

33. . . . . . .   R—K 4

Or I. 33. . . . . Q—Kt 4 ; 34. R—R 8, Q—K 4 ; 35. B—B 2 !, Q × Q ch ; 36. K × Q and after B—Kt 3 Black would lose the exchange with a hopeless position. II. 33. . . . . Kt—R 3 ; 34. P—Kt 5 !, Q—Kt 4 ; 35. K R—B 1 ! and wins.

34. R—R 8   R—Q 7

Black overlooks the main threat. But after a defensive move like 34. . . . . Q—K 1 White would also have won very rapidly by 35. Q—Kt 3 followed by 36. Q—Q R 3, etc.

Position after Black's 34th move.

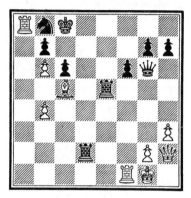

35. R × Kt ch !   K × R
36. Q × R ch ! and mate in three moves

Although in all objectivity I had to blame my 17th move (which by the way is accompanied in the Tournament Book by an !) I must admit that the final attack of this game gave me (and I hope will give the readers) much more pleasure than a scientifically correct, but purely technical exploitation of a Pawn majority on the Queen's side would do. After all, Chess is *not only* knowledge and logic !

GAME 94

QUEEN'S GAMBIT ACCEPTED

Kemeri Tournament, June, 1937.

Black : R. FINE

1. P—Q 4   P—Q 4
2. P—Q B 4   P × P
3. Kt—K B 3   Kt—K B 3

4. Q—R 4 ch   ......

This Queen's manœuvre is more effective here than in the Catalan system (after P—K Kt 3) since White may in some variations wish to develop his Bishop on the diagonal K B 1—Q R 6. But also after the more usual 4. P—K 3 White's prospects are actually considered by far the more promising, and this fact is due not to a particular variation, but to the modern method of treating, with the white pieces, the Queen's Gambit Accepted : to advance the centre Pawns at the first opportunity, eventually at a cost of heavy sacrifices. Characteristic in that order of ideas are the games Reshevsky–Vidmar (Nottingham, 1936), Euwe–Alekhine (Fifth Match-game, 1937), and, even earlier, Opocensky–Rubinstein (Marienbad, 1925). In my own recent practice the following two examples, illustrating this new tendency of White, are, I believe, noteworthy :

I. Black : R. Letelier, Montevideo, 1938. 4. P—K 3, P—K 3 ; 5. B×P, P—Q B 4 ; 6. Castles, P—Q R 3 ; 7. Q—K 2, P—Q Kt 4 ; 8. B—Q Kt 3, B—Q Kt 2 ; 9. *Kt—Q B 3, Q Kt—Q 2* ; 10. R—Q 1, B—K 2 ; 11. P—K 4 !, P—Q Kt 5 ; 12. P—K 5, P×Kt ; 13. P×Kt, Kt×P ; 14. B—R 4 ch, K—B 1 ; 15. Q P×P, Q—R 4 ; 16. P—B 6, Q×B ; 17. P×B, R—Q Kt 1 ; 18. P×P, R×P ; 19. Kt—K 5, Q—K 5 ; 20. Q×P, R—B 2 ; 21. B—R 3 !, P—Kt 3 ; 22. B×B ch, R×B ; 23. Q—Q 6, K—Kt 2 ; 24. Q×R, Q×Kt ; 25. Q—Kt 4, Resigns.

II. Black : E. Böök, Margate, 1938. 4. P—K 3, P—K 3 ; 5. B×P, P—Q B 4 ; 6. Castles, *Kt—Q B 3* ; 7. Q—K 2, P—Q R 3 ; 8. *Kt—Q B 3*, P—Q Kt 4 ; 9. B—Kt 3, P—Kt 5 (in the Euwe–Alekhine game above mentioned the continuation was 9. ....B—K 2 ; 10. P×P, B×P ; 11. P—K 4 ! etc., to White's advantage) ; 10. *P—Q 5!*, Kt—Q R 4 ; 11. B—R 4 ch, B—Q 2 ; 12. P×P, P×

P ; 13. R—Q 1 !, P×Kt ; 14. R× B !, Kt×R ; 15. Kt—K 5, R—R 2 ; 16. P×P, K—K 2 ; 17. P—K 4 !, Kt—K B 3 ; 18. B—K Kt 5, Q—B 2 ; 19. B—B 4, Q—Kt 3 ; 20. R—Q 1, P—Kt 3 (or Q—Kt 2 ; 21. Q—K 3 !, K—Q 1 ; 22. Q—Q 3 ch, K—B 1 ; 23. R—Kt 1, Q×P ; 24. Kt—B 7 ! ! and wins) ; 21. B—K Kt 5, B—Kt 2 ; 22. Kt—Q 7 !, R×Kt ; 23. R×R ch, K—B 1 ; 24. B×Kt, B×B ; 25. P—K 5 !, Resigns.

4. ......   Q—Q 2

As the white Queen will not be particularly dangerous on Q B 4 there is no reason to make such an effort to force her exchange. A sound line is, instead, 4. ....P—B 3 ; 5. Q×P at B 4, B—K B 4, etc.

5. Q×B P   Q—B 3
6. Kt—R 3   ......

There is but little difference between this move and 6. Q Kt—Q 2 since Black has nothing better, in order to justify this previous manœuvre, than to exchange Queens in both cases.

6. ......   Q×Q
7. Kt×Q   P—K 3
8. P—Q R 3   ......

It was very important to prevent ....B—Kt 5 ch.

8. ......   P—B 4 ?

A dogmatic move after which White succeeds in obtaining clear positional advantage. In his haste to counter-attack in the centre, Black for a moment forgets the importance of his Q 3. A bold, but by no means antipositional scheme was instead 8. ....P—Q R 4 (preventing P—Q Kt 4), and if 9. B—K B 4 then P—Q Kt 4 followed by ....B—Q 3. At least White would not in that case obtain so easily the advantage of the pair of Bishops.

9. B—K B 4   Kt—B 3

Slightly better was 9. ....Q Kt—Q 2 ; 10. Kt—Q 6 ch, B×Kt ; 11. B×B, Kt—K 5 ; 12. B—B 7, P—Q Kt 3, followed by ....B—Kt 2, etc. ; but the weakness of the dark-coloured squares would remain in any case.

10. P×P	B×P
11. P—Q Kt 4	B—K 2
12. P—Kt 5	Kt—Q Kt 1
13. Kt—Q 6 ch	B×Kt
14. B×B	Kt—K 5
15. B—B 7 !	......

This Bishop is practically White's only winning chance at this stage, and he must play extremely carefully in order to prevent its exchange. Inadvisable would be instead 15. B—Kt 4, P—Q R 4 ! ; 16. P×P *e.p.*, Kt×R P, etc. ; or 15. B—K B 4, P—K B 3 ! followed by P—K 4, etc., with about equal prospects in both cases.

15.	Kt—Q 2
16. Kt—Q 4 !	......

Again an important move, the idea of which is to build up the Pawn chain K 4, K B 3, K Kt 2. It was not quite easy to find, mainly because the two alternatives 16. P—K 3 and 16. P—K Kt 3 also offered some interesting possibilities.

16.	Kt—Kt 3
17. P—K B 3	Kt—Q 4
18. B—R 5	Kt(K5)—B 3

Another important variation was 18. ....Kt—Q 3 ; 19. P—K 4 (not 19. Kt—B 2, Kt—B 5, etc.), Kt—K 6 ; 20. B—Kt 4 !, P—K 4 ; 21. B×Kt, P×Kt ; 22. B—Q 3 !, Kt×Kt P ch ; 23. K—B 2, Kt—K 6 ; 24. B—K 5, etc.±.

19. Kt—B 2 !   ......

The actual point of the manœuvre inaugurated by 16. Kt—Q 4 : Black's Knight is prevented from intruding at K 6 and will be forced to play from now on a purely passive role. The chasing of the Bishop by the two Knights has thus proved a complete failure.

19.	B—Q 2
20. P—K 4	R—Q B 1

Also this intermediate move is perfectly harmless, as the white King at Q 2 cannot be seriously bothered by the half-lamed black forces.

21. K—Q 2 !	Kt—Kt 3
22. Kt—K 3	Castles

All Black's moves after 18. .... Kt—B 3 are virtually forced.

23. P—Q R 4 !   ......

Much stronger than the conventional 23. B—Q 3 which would permit the freeing manœuvre .... Kt—Q R 5—Q B 4, etc.

23.	K R—Q 1
24. B—Q 3	P—K 4

After this weakening of the squares Q 4 and K B 4 the game can hardly be saved. The only slight chance consisted in 24. .... B—K 1 eventually followed by .... K Kt—Q 2. White's tactics in that case would have remained about the same—exchange of one pair of Rooks, removal of the R 5 Bishop and dislodging of the black Knight from Q Kt 3.

25. K R—Q B 1	B—K 3
26. R×R	R×R
27. B—Kt 4	......

Preventing also the approach of Black's King to the centre and threatening eventually B—Q 6.

27. ......   Kt—K 1
28. P—R 5   Kt—Q 2
29. Kt—Q 5 !   ......

This had to be exactly calculated since the passed Pawn resulting from the exchange will be slightly exposed. Because of the formidable threat 30. Kt—K 7 ch Black must now take the Knight.

29. ......   B × Kt
30. P × B   Kt—B 4

The "little combination" thus started finds a convincing refutation in White's 32nd move. But what could he actually do ? The recommendation of the Tournament Book, 30. ....P—K Kt 3 would in the long run be perfectly hopeless after 31. P—Q 6, P—B 4 ; 32. B—Kt 1 !, K—Kt 2 ; 33. B—R 2, K—B 3 (or Kt (K 1)—B 3 ; 34. R—K 1); 34. B—Q 5, etc.

31. B—B 5 !   R—Q 1

Or 31. ....Kt—Kt 6 ch ; 32. K—Q 3, Kt—B 8 ch ; 33. K—K 3, R—B 5 ; 34. P—Q 6 and wins.

Position after Black's 31st move.

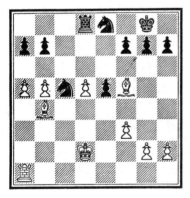

32. K—B 3 !   ......

This pretty move eliminates both threats 32. ....Kt—Kt 6 ch and

32. ....R × P ch, the last one because of the answer 33. K—B 4 ! winning a piece. White's overwhelming advantage in space now decides the battle in a few moves.

32. ......   P—Q Kt 3

Or 32. ....Kt—Q 2 ; 33. B—K 7 and wins.

33. P × P   P × P
34. B × Kt !   ......

The Bishop has done in this game more than his duty and may now retire, for the passed Q Kt's Pawn can be only stopped at a heavy loss.

34. ......   P × B
35. P—Kt 6   Kt—Q 3
36. B—Q 7 !   R × B

Instead of resigning.

37. R—R 8 ch and mate in two.

This game is probably my best purely positional achievement of the last few years.

GAME 95

QUEEN'S GAMBIT DECLINED
(ORTHODOX DEFENCE)

Quadrangular Tournament, Bad Nauheim, July, 1937.

Black : E. BOGOLJUBOW

1. P—Q 4	P—Q 4
2. P—Q B 4	P—K 3
3. Kt—Q B 3	Kt—K B 3
4. B—Kt 5	B—K 2
5. Kt—B 3	P—K R 3
6. B—R 4	Castles
7. P—K 3	P—Q Kt 3

In conjunction with ....P—K R 3, this flank development has been rather often and successfully adopted by Dr. Tartakower. The first player has several plausible ways of meeting it, not one being an actually convincing refutation. In the present game, I decided to allow Black to fulfil his plan of mobilisation or—to be more exact— the first part of it consisting in .... B—Kt 2, ...Q Kt—Q 2, ... P—Q B 4—and to try to take advantage only from one detail of the position, namely, the fact that the black Queen is deprived of the diagonal Q 1—R 4 and will not easily find a suitable square. The course of the game will show to what extent the idea proved successful. It lacks tactical points, is emotionless—but by no means dull —and is of use to the student.

| 8. R—B 1 | B—Kt 2 |
| 9. B—K 2 | ...... |

Inducing Black to win a *tempo* by the following Pawn exchange.

9.	P×P
10. B×P	P—B 4
11. Castles	Q Kt—Q 2

If 11. ....Kt—B 3, then 12. P× P, Q×Q ; 13. K R×Q and Black would get into trouble because of the possible entry of the Rook on to the seventh rank.

| 12. Q—K 2 | Kt—K 5 |

I suppose many masters would have made this move, since, by forcing the exchange of two minor pieces, it frees Black's game and, in particular, provides a safe spot for the Queen. Yet it is questionable whether the more complicated 12. ....P—R 3 ; 13. K R—Q 1, P— Q Kt 4 would not have offered more equalising prospects. After the exchange of Black's Queen's Bishop, the light-coloured squares on the Q-side become suddenly weak.

| 13. Kt×Kt | B×B |

Or 13. ....B×Kt ; 14. B— K Kt 3 ! etc.±

| 14. Kt—B 3 ! | ...... |

This simple retreat is more effective than 15. Kt—Q 6, B×Kt ; 16. Q×B, B—K 2, etc., forcing White to waste more time—or 15. B—Q 3, B—K B 3, after which Black would avoid the exchange of his Q B.

| 14. ...... | B—K B 3 |
| 15. K R—Q 1 | Q—K 2 |

At last the inter-communication between the Rooks is established, but now comes the actual point of White's last manœuvres.

16. B—R 6	Q R—Kt 1
17. B×B	R×B
18. Kt—K 4 !	......

In order to obtain full control along the Q B-file, White allows the isolation of his Q P, which, as the continuation will clearly show, is by no means weak.

| 18. ...... | P×P |
| 19. P×P | ...... |

Instead, 19. Kt×P, B×Kt ; 20. R×B, Kt—B 3, etc., would be just good enough for a comfortable draw.

| 19. ...... | R—Q 1 |

His position has become difficult. By playing 19. ....Kt—Kt 1 ; 20. Kt—K 5 !, etc., he could at least temporarily avoid the compromising of the Pawn skeleton on the King's side—but a further suitable plan of defence would be as difficult to find as after the move selected.

| 20. Q—R 6 ! | Kt—Kt 1 |

After 20. ....K R—Kt 1 ; 21. R—B 8 ch would be strong—and 20. ....Kt—B 1 ; 21. Kt×B ch, etc., would leave square Q B 3 defenceless.

21. Kt×B ch   P×Kt
22. Q—K 2   . . . . .

White has now two important trumps—the open file and Black's weak King's side. By rational exploitation this will suffice.

22. . . . . . .   Q R—Q 2
23. R—Q 3   R—Q 4
24. K R—B 3   . . . . .

As the weak Pawn requires only one protector, the Rooks can—and must—be used for exerting strong pressure on the Q B-file.

24. . . . . . .   K—R 2
25. P—K R 3   P—Q R 4

Weakens the Q Kt P—but otherwise the Q R P would need lasting defence. Already Black has only a choice between evils.

26. P—Q R 3   . . . . . .

As the opponent has no useful moves at his disposal, White can quietly correct the small defects in his Pawn structure.

26. . . . . . .   R—Kt 1
27. R—B 7   Kt—Q 2
28. R (1)—B 6   Q—B 1
29. Q—B 2 ch !   . . . . . .

More exact than 29. R—B 8, Q—Kt 2 ! ; 30. Q—B 2 ch, after which Black would have the answer 30. . . . . Q—Kt 3.

29. . . . . . .   P—B 4

Otherwise 30. R—B 8 would be even more effective.

30. R—B 8   Q—K 2
31. R × R   . . . . .

The black Rook had to be ex-

changed, for it prevented the possible activity of the Queen on the King's side.

31. . . . . . .   K × R
32. Q—B 1   K—Kt 2
33. Q—K B 4   . . . . .

Threatening 34. Q—Kt 3 ch, followed by R—B 8 ch.

33. . . . . . .   Q—Q 1
34. P—Q R 4 !   . . . . .

Preventing for once and for all . . . . R—Kt 4 and putting Black into a kind of *zugzwang* position.

34. . . . . . .   P—Q Kt 4

This natural-looking answer loses rapidly. Comparatively the best was 34. . . . . K—R 2, after which White finally forces the issue by playing the Queen over to the Queen's side—Q—B 1—Q B 4— Q R 6.

35. Q—Kt 3 ch   K—B 1

Position after Black's 35th move.

36. R—Q 6 !   . . . . . .

This wins at least a Pawn by

practically forcing the exchange of Queens. The resulting end-game will not present much difficulty, since there will be still more weaknesses to take advantage of—for instance, Black's K R 3.

| 36. ...... | Q—R 1 |

Equally hopeless would be 36. ....P×P, e.g. 37. R×R, P×R ; 38. Q—Q 6 ch, Q—K 2 ; 39. Q×P etc.

37.	P×P	Q—Kt 2
38.	R×R	Q×R
39.	P—Kt 6 !	Q—B 3
40.	Q—B 7	Q×Q
41.	P×Q	Kt—Kt 3
42.	Kt—K 5	K—K 2
43.	Kt—B 4	......

After this the passed Q Kt P will force the presence of at least one black piece on the Queen's side and the white King will in the meantime become master of the other side of the board.

43.	......	Kt—B 1
44.	Kt×P	K—Q 2
45.	K—R 2	K×P
46.	K—Kt 3	K—Q 3
47.	K—R 4	K—Q 4
48.	K—R 5	K×P
49.	K×P	P—K 4
50.	K—Kt 5	P—B 5
51.	P—R 4	P—B 3 ch

A last "try" which White meets in the simplest manner.

| 52. | K×P | P—K 5 |
| 53. | Kt—Kt 3 ch ! | K—Q 4 |

Or 53. ....K—Q 6 (B 5) ; 54. Kt—B 5 (Q 2) ch, followed by 55. Kt×K P and P—R 5, winning.

54.	P—R 5	P—K 6
55.	P×P	P×P
56.	Kt—B 1	Resigns.

GAME 96

RUY LOPEZ

Quadrangular Tournament, Bad Nauheim, July, 1937.

Black : F. Saemisch

1.	P—K 4	P—K 4
2.	Kt—K B 3	Kt—Q B 3
3.	B—Kt 5	P—Q R 3
4.	B—R 4	Kt—B 3
5.	Castles	B—K 2
6.	Q—K 2	P—Q Kt 4
7.	B—Kt 3	P—Q 3
8.	P—B 3	Castles

A safer course is 8. ....Kt— Q R 4 ; 9. B—B 2, P—B 4, etc., similar to the variation starting with 6. R—K 1.

| 9. | P—Q R 4 ! | B—Kt 5 |

This is comparatively better than 9. ....P—Kt 5 ; 10. P—R 5, or 9. ....R—Q Kt 1 ; 10. P×P, P×P ; 11. P—Q 4, etc.±—but, still, has the disadvantage of bringing the Bishop out of play if White, as in the actual game, does not accept the Pawn offer.

| 10. | P—K R 3 | ...... |

More usual is R—Q 1 followed by P—Q 4. The text-move is the beginning of a quite different plan, which aims at limiting the activity of Black's Q B to a minimum. Inadvisable would be, instead, 10. P×P, P×P ; 11. R×R, Q×R ; 12. Q×P, Kt—R 2 !, after which Black would regain the Pawn with a good position.

| 10. | ...... | B—R 4 |
| 11. | P—Kt 4 | ...... |

The main objections against this advance in this type of position are generally : (1) A possibility of the Knight's sacrifice at K Kt 4. (2)

A disturbance of White's Pawn structure by means of ....P—K R 4. As neither of these eventualities is to be feared here (for instance, 11. ....Kt×Kt P ; 12. P×Kt, B×P ; 13. Q—K 3—or 11. ....B—Kt 3 ; 12. P—Q 3, P—K R 4 ; 13. Kt—R 4±)—there was no reason for postponing the imprisonment of the Bishop.

11.	B—Kt 3
12. P—Q 3	Kt—Q R 4
13. B—B 2	Kt—Q 2 ?

The full value of the system adopted by White could only be estimated if Black had built up the classical defensive position by playing 13. ....P—Q B 4 followed by ....Q—B 2. The inconsequential text-move—probably dictated by an exaggerated fear of White's Kt—K R 4—leaves 'White a free hand both in the centre and on the Queen's side. The first victim of this strategy will be the Queen's Knight, which will be at once removed to a purely passive square and become in the following part of the game merely an object for White's combinative play.

14. P—Q Kt 4	Kt—Kt 2
15. Kt—R 3	P—Q B 3
16. B—Kt 3	Kt—Kt 3

White threatened eventually P—Q B 4, which would force Black to exchange his Q Kt P, thus weakening still further the general situation on the Queen's side. The move in the text, which prevents that danger at the cost of a *tempo*, is therefore not to be blamed.

| 17. P—R 5 | Kt—Q 2 |
| 18. B—K 3 | ...... |

In making this last preparative move to the intended Pawn advance on the Queen's side, White had to take into account the counter-attack 18. ....P—Q 4 ! ? ; 19. P×

P, P—Q B 4, which he intended to meet by 20. P—Q 6 !, B×P (Q 3) ; 21. B—Q 5, or 20. ....Kt×P ; 21. P×P, etc. ; in both cases with advantage.

| 18. ...... | K—R 1 |

Sooner or later compulsory in order to bring the Queen's Bishop to life.

| 19. P—B 4 ! | ...... |

As will be seen, White's following tactics are based on the weakness of the Knight at Q Kt 2.

| 19. ...... | Kt—B 3 |

Initiating an ingenious, although not quite sufficient, counter-attack. Indeed, he already had desperately little choice.

| 20. P × P | R P × P |

Position after Black's 20th move.

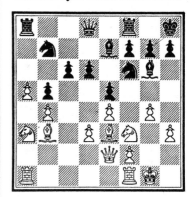

| 21. Kt × Kt P ! | ...... |

A purely positional offer or, better say, exchanging combination, which in the main variation would develop as follows : 21. ....P×Kt ; 22. P—R 6, Q—Q 2 ; 23. P×Kt, Q×P ; 24. P—Kt 5 !, R×R ; 25. R×R, Kt—Q 2 (otherwise 26. R—R 7 wins); 26. Kt—R 4, R—R 1; 27. R—R 5, and Black would finally perish principally because of his helpless Q's Bishop. No wonder, therefore, that Sämisch prefers to carry on with the exploitation of White's slightly exposed King's wing and to win an important tempo by leaving the hostile Knight *en prise.*

21.	Q—Q 2 !
22. P—R 6	Kt—Q 1
23. Kt—B 3	Kt × Kt P !

The interesting point of Black's active defence, which, however, proves comparatively harmless, since White can simply continue his "work" on the other side.

| 24. P—Kt 5 ! | ...... |

Instead, 24. P × Kt, Q × P ch ; 25. K—R 1, B—R 4 ! etc., would have assured Black of at least a draw. But now matters become very difficult for him because of the formidable threat P—Q Kt 6 and the possibility of B—Q 5 in case of ....P × P.

| 24. ...... | Kt × B |
| 25. P × Kt | ...... |

After this forced exchange, the King's position is again quite safe.

| 25. ...... | P × P |
| 26. B—Q 5 | Kt—K 3 |

To give up a Pawn by 26. .... Kt—B 3 ; 27. Kt × Kt P would certainly not be a better alternative, while 26. ....R—R 2 ; 27. K R—Kt 1, Q—B 1 ; 28. Kt × Kt P, R × P; 29. Kt—R 7 ! would have lost the exchange just the same.

27. B × R	R × B
28. Q—Q Kt 2	Kt—B 2
29. K—Kt 2	P—B 3

The exchange of the Q Kt P

against White's Q R P—here or on the next move—would mean certain death after rather long agony.

| 30. Q—Kt 3 ! | ...... |

Taking control of Q 5 and preventing at the same time ....B—K B 2.

30.	B—K 1
31. P—R 7	P—Kt 3
32. R—R 5	K—Kt 2
33. K R—Q R 1	B—B 2
34. Kt—Q 5 !	......

Otherwise Black would obtain some counter chances after .... P—Q 4 ; but now he is almost forced to exchange at Q 5, since 34. ....Q—Q B 3 would be answered by 35. Kt × B and 34. ....B—Q 1 by 35. Kt—Kt 6 !, Q—B 3 ; 36. Kt × R ! etc.

34.	Kt × Kt
35. P × Kt	B—K 1
36. P—K 4	P—K B 4

These last anæmic efforts will be rapidly stopped by an energetic final combination.

| 37. R—R 6 | P—Kt 4 |
| 38. Q—B 3 ! | P—K Kt 5 |

This would at last look like something but for the following drastic stroke.

Position after Black's 38th move.

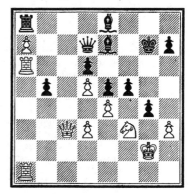

39. Kt × P !   . . . . . .

The Knights have certainly performed their best in this fight : the first one contributed in smashing to pieces Black's Queen side and his colleague can die happy after cleaving open the way to the heart of the enemy's fortress. The rest is easy.

39.	P × Kt
40. Q × P ch	K—Kt 1
41. P—Q 6 !	. . . . . .

Threatening also 42. Q—Q 5 ch.

41.	Q—B 1
42. P × B	Q—B 7 ch
43. K—R 1	Q—B 7
44. Q × B P	Resigns.

GAME 97

QUEEN'S GAMBIT DECLINED
(SLAV DEFENCE)

Second Match-Game, Rotterdam, October, 1937.

Black : DR. M. EUWE

1. P—Q 4	P—Q 4
2. P—Q B 4	P—Q B 3
3. Kt—K B 3	Kt—B 3
4. Kt—B 3	P × P
5. P—Q R 4	B—B 4
6. Kt—K 5	. . . . . .

The discovery that the text-move is not sufficient to secure White an opening advantage was one of the assets of the present match.

6. . . . . . .   P—K 3

Played twice by Bogoljubow against me in the 1929 Match. As the experiment did not succeed (he only managed to draw one game with great difficulty and lost the other) the move 6. ....P—K 3

disappeared from master practice. But, as was proved especially by the eleventh game of this match, it is, in fact, much safer than the fashionable Kmoch Variation (6. ....Q Kt—Q 2 in conjunction with Q—B 2 and P—K 4).

7. B—Kt 5   . . . . . .

As, after 7. P—B 3, B—Kt 5, the move 8. P—K 4 ? would provoke the absolutely sound sacrifice 8. ....Kt × P ! (first played by Chéron against Przepiorka in The Hague, 1928),White must not hurry to form a Pawn centre. Still, after the following answer, he had no better move than 8. P—B 3.

7. . . . . . .   B—Q Kt 5

Much more logical than 7. .... B—K 2 as played by Bogoljubow in our Fifth Match-game, 1929 (see No. 27).

8. Kt × Q B P   . . . . . .

Very harmless, since Black, instead of the complicated variation, actually selected, could simply play here 8. ....P—K R 3, and if 9. B—R 4 then 9. ....P—K Kt 4 ; 10. B—Kt 3, Kt—K 5 ; 11. R—B 1 (or Q—Kt 3, Kt—R 3), P—B 4, etc. with at least even prospects.

8. . . . . . .   Q—Q 4

Also a good move which leads after a short, sharp intermezzo to an equally balanced position.

9. B × Kt   . . . . . .

The alternative 9. Kt—K 3, Q—R 4 ; 10. Kt × B, Q × Kt, etc., was even less promising. And if 9. Q—Kt 3, then 9. ....Kt—R 3∓.

9. . . . . . .   Q × Kt

Better than 9. ....P × B ; 10.

Kt—K 3, Q—R 4 ; 11. Q—Kt 3
with slightly better prospects for
White.

10. Q—Q 2   ......

The only move, for 10. R—B 1 ?
would have been refuted by 10. ....
P × B ; 11. P—K 4, Q—R 7 ! etc.

10. ......   P × B

More promising was 10. ....Q—
Kt 6 ! ; 11. B × Kt P, R—K Kt 1 ;
12. B—R 6, Kt—Q 2, etc., with a
strong initiative for the Pawn.

11. P—K 4	Q—Kt 6
12. P × B	Kt—Q 2
13. P × P	P × P
14. B—K 2	Castles (Q R)
15. Castles	......

The last few moves were practically forced and the position thus
reached offers about equal attacking possibilities for both sides.

15. ......   P—K 4

This logical move—which brings
the Knight into a strong position
and opens the Queen's file to Black's
advantage—has been, in my opinion, unduly criticised. In any case,
15. ....Kt—Kt 3, which was
recommended instead, would expose
Black to dangerous threats after
16. P—R 5, Kt—R 5 ; 17. Q—K 3,
Kt × P ; 18. K R—B 1—and this
without offering him any real
winning prospects.

16. P × P	Kt × P
17. Q—B 1	B × Kt

As 18. Kt—K 4 was not really a
strong threat, this exchange should
have been postponed till a more
appropriate moment. Black should
have played 17. ....K R—Kt 1 ;
for if 18. Kt—K 4 (18. Q—K 3, Q ×
Kt P), then 18. ....Kt—B 6 ch ;
19. B × Kt, Q × B ; 20. Kt—Kt 3,

Q—Kt 5, etc., with a quite satisfactory position. After the move in
the text White obtains the better
chances because his Bishop will
prove superior to the Knight as
soon as the black piece is dislodged
from K 4.

18. P × B	K R—Kt 1
19. Q—K 3	K—Kt 1

Not absolutely necessary, since
he could indirectly protect his
Q R P by playing 19. ....Q—Q 4 ;
20. P—Kt 3, Q—Q 7 ; but after 21.
Q × Q, R × Q ; 22. K R—K 1 (Kt—
Q 6 ; 23. Q R—Q 1 !) White's end-
game chances would still be the
better.

20. P—Kt 3   ......

As this defensive move is unavoidable anyhow, it is better to
play it immediately.

20.	R—Q 2
21. Q R—Kt 1	Q—B 7
22. K R—K 1 !	......

The most subtle move of the
game ! With this, White prepares
for the important P—K B 4. The
immediate advance of that Pawn
would be refuted by 22. ....R—
Q 7 ! ; 23. K R—K 1, Kt—Q 6, etc.

22.	Q—Q 7
23. Q × Q	R × Q
24. P—K B 4	Kt—Kt 3
25. B—B 4	K R—Q 1

Or 25. ....R—Kt 2 ; 26. R—
K 8 ch, K—B 2 ; 27. K—R 1 ! with
advantage for White.

26. R—K 6 !   ......

In order to exchange one pair of
Rooks. It must be noted that
Black cannot play 26. ....R—
Q B 7 because of 27. B—R 6, P—
Kt 3 ; 28. R × Q B P.

26.	K R—Q 3
27. Q R—K 1	K—B 2
28. R × R	R × R

If 28. ....K × R then 29. B—
Kt 8 threatening both B × R P and
R—K 6 ch.

| 29. P—K R 4 | ...... |

In order to play the King to B 2
without being disturbed by the
Rook check on the second rank.

29.	K—Q 2
30. K—B 2	Kt—K 2
31. K—B 3	Kt—Q 4 ?

Allowing the white King to
attack successfully the K R P. It
is, however, more than doubtful
whether 31. ....P—K B 4 (which
was comparatively the best) would
have saved the game. White would
then play *not* 32. P—K Kt 4 because
of 32. ....P × P ch ; 33. K × P, R—
Kt 3 ch followed by 34. ....Kt—
B 4 with sufficient counter-chances
—but first 32. P—K R 5 ! and, only
after that preparation, P—Kt 4,
freeing his K B P with disastrous
effect for Black.

Position after Black's 31st move.

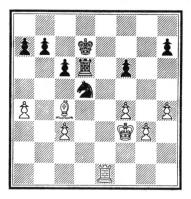

32. B—Q 3 !   ......

The decisive manœuvre forcing a

further weakening of Black's Pawn
position on the K-side. Eventual
Pawn losses on the other wing do not
matter any more because the passive position of Black's pieces
prevents him from undertaking any
serious counter-demonstration.

32.	P—K R 3
33. B—B 5 ch	K—Q 1
34. K—Kt 4 !	......

If now 34. ....Kt × Q B P then 35.
K—R 5, Kt × P ; 36. K × P, etc.,
would win easily.

| 34. ...... | Kt—K 2 |
| 35. B—Kt 1 | K—K 1 |

Or 35. ....R—Q 4 ; 36. P—B 5,
etc.

36. K—R 5	K—B 2
37. B—R 2 ch	K—B 1
38. K × P	R—Q 7

The main variation was 38. ....
Kt—B 4 ch ; 39. K—Kt 6, Kt ×
Kt P ; 40. P—B 5 followed by the
advance of the K R's Pawn.

39. B—K 6	R—Q 6
40. P—Kt 4	R × P
41. P—Kt 5	......

Even simpler than 41. R—Q 1,
Kt—Q 4. If now 41. ....P × P
then 42. B P × P, etc., winning.

Resigns.

GAME 98

QUEEN'S GAMBIT DECLINED
(SLAV DEFENCE)

Sixth Match-Game, Haarlem,
October, 1937.

Black : Dr. M. Euwe

| 1. P—Q 4 | P—Q 4 |
| 2. P—Q B 4 | P—Q B 3 |

3. Kt—Q B 3   ......

In my opinion this move gives White more chances of obtaining an opening advantage, and this for the following reasons : (1) The dangers of the continuation 3. ....., P×P *in conjunction with* 4. .... *P—K* 4 are clearly shown in the present game ; (2) the Winawer Counter-attack P—K 4 can be met in a simple and effective manner by 4. P×Q P, B P×P ; 5. *P—K* 4 *!* and if 5. ....P×K P ; 6. B—Kt 5 ch $\pm$; (3) in answer to 3. ....Kt— B 3 ; 4. P—K 3, P—K Kt 3 I suggest 5. *P—B* 3, which after 5. ....B—Kt 2 ; 6. P—K 4, P×K P ; 7. P×P, P—K 4 ! ; 8. P—Q 5, Castles ; 9. Kt—B 3 leads to a rather complicated position, still positionally favourable to White.

3. ......   P×P
4. P—K 4 !   ......

It is almost incredible that this quite natural move has not been considered by the so-called theoreticians.   White obtains now an appreciable advantage in development, no matter what Black replies.

4. ......   P—K 4

The alternative is 4. ....P— Q Kt 4 ; 5. P—Q R 4, P—K 4 (or ....P—Kt 5 ; 6. Kt—R 2, Kt— B 3 ; 7. P—K 5, Kt—Q 4 ; 8. B× P $\pm$) ; 6. P×Kt P, P×Q P ; 7. B× P!, B—Q Kt 5!; 8. R—R 4, P— Q R 4 ; 9. P×P *e.p.*, and White will emerge with a Pawn to the good.

5. B×P   ......

This sacrificial combination is certainly very tempting and, especially over the board, extremely difficult to refute ; but it is by no means the necessary consequence of White's previous move which has a value absolutely independent of the correctness of the piece sacrifice.

The *positional* exploitation of White's advantage in space consists in 5. Kt—B 3 !, P×P ; 6. Q×P, Q×Q ; 7. Kt×Q, after which Black would only get into further trouble by trying to protect the gambitpawn—for instance, 7. ....P— Q Kt 4 ; 8. P—Q R 4, P—Kt 5 ; 9. Kt—Q 1, B—R 3 ; 10. B—K 3, Kt—B 3 ; 11. P—B 3 followed by R—B 1 and B×P with a clear positional advantage.

5. ......   P×P

Fatal would be 5. ....Q×P ; 6. Q—Kt 3, Q—Q 2 ; 7. B—K Kt 5 ! with a winning attack.

6. Kt—B 3   ......

Putting before Black a most difficult practical problem . . .

6. ......   P—Q Kt 4 ?

Which he not only fails to solve but even selects a move that brings him immediately a decisive disadvantage. As a matter of fact the offer *could* be accepted since Black would have at his disposal a more effective line than the one I had analysed when proposing it. My "chief" variation was the following : 6. ....P×Kt ; 7. B×P ch, K—K 2 ; 8. Q—Kt 3, *Kt—B* 3 ; 9. P—K 5, Kt—K 5 ; 10. Castles !, Q—Kt 3 (or Kt—R 3 ; 11. Q— B 4 !, Q Kt—B 4 ; 12. B—Kt 5 ch !, Kt×B ; 13. Kt×Kt with a winning attack) ; 11. Q—B 4 !, P×P ; 12. B×P, Q×B ; 13. Q×Kt, K×B ; 14. Kt—Kt 5 ch, K—K 1 ; 15. Q— Q B 4, B—K 2 ; 16. Q—B 7 ch, K—Q 1 ; 17. Q R—Q 1 ch, B—Q 2 ; 18. Kt—K 6 ch, K—B 1 ; 19. Q×B, Q×K P ; 20. K R—K 1, Q—B 3 ; 21. R×B, Q×Q (Kt×R ; 22. Q— Q 6 winning), R×Q with a won position. But, instead of 8. .... Kt—B 3 Black could play 8. .... P×P ! ; 9. B×P, Q—Kt 3 ! ; 10. B×Kt, R×B ; 11. Q×R (or 11.

B—R 3 ch, P—B 4), *Q—Kt 5 ch* ;
12. *Kt—Q 2, Q×B*, after which his
middle game chances, in spite of
the approximate equality of forces,
should be estimated decidedly
higher than White's remaining possibilities of a direct attack. Consequently, unless an improvement
can be found in this last line of play,
White's Knight's offer will hardly
be repeated, at least in serious
practice.

7. Kt×Kt P !   ......

Dr. Euwe admits simply having
overlooked this reply. *This time*
the Knight obviously cannot be
taken because of 8. B—Q 5, etc.

7. ......   B—R 3
8. Q—Kt 3 !   ......

An important move with a triple
object : (a) to protect the King's
Bishop ; (b) to prevent the check
at Black's Q Kt 5 ; (c) to strengthen
the pressure against Black's K B 2.

8. ......   Q—K 2

If 8. ....B×Kt then 9. B×P ch,
K—Q 2 ; 10. Kt×P ! (not 10. B×
Kt ?, R×B) etc., with an easy win.

9. Castles   B×Kt
10. B×B   Kt—B 3

Of course not 10. ....P×B
because of 11. Q—Q 5.

11. B—Q B 4   Q Kt—Q 2
12. Kt×P   ......

Another winning method was 12.
P—K 5, Kt×P (if ....Kt—K 5 ;
13. Q—Kt 7) 13. Kt×Kt, Q×Kt ;
14. Q—Kt 7, R—Q Kt 1 ; 15. Q×
B P ch, K—Q 1 ; 16. Q×R P ; but
after 16. ....B—Q 3 Black would
be able to put at least as much
further resistance as after the
simple text-move.

12. ......   R—Q Kt 1
13. Q—B 2   Q—B 4

Hereafter, White, in order to win,
has only to avoid a few little traps.

14. Kt—B 5   ......

Here, for instance, 14. Kt×P
would be wrong because of 14. ....
R—B 1 !

14. ......   Kt—K 4
15. B—B 4 !   ......

And now, after the tempting 15.
Kt×P ch, K—Q 1 ! (B×Kt ? ; 16.
B×P ch) ; 16. R—Q 1 ch, K—B 2
two white pieces would be *en prise*.

15. ......   Kt—R 4

Position after Black's 15th move.

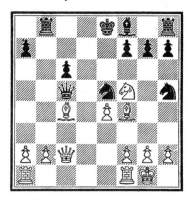

16. B×P ch !   ......

A very profitable simplification.
Less convincing would be instead
16. B×Kt, Q×B (K 4) ; 17. B—
K 2, Q—Q B 4 ; 18. Q×Q, B×Q ;
19. B×Kt, P—Kt 3, etc.

16. ......   K×B
17. Q×Q   B×Q
18. B×Kt   R—Kt 4
19. B—Q 6   ......

Threatening 20. P—Q R 4.

| 19. ...... | B—Kt 3 |
| 20. P—Q Kt 4 ! | ...... |

And now the Rook is in danger. Black cannot avoid further loss of material.

20.	R—Q 1
21. Q R—Q 1	P—B 4
22. P × P	B × P
23. R—Q 5 !	......

Winning at least the exchange.

Resigns.

GAME 99

NIMZOWITSCH DEFENCE

Eighth Match-Game, Leyden, October, 1937.

Black : Dr. M. Euwe

1. P—Q 4	Kt—K B 3
2. P—Q B 4	P—K 3
3. Kt—Q B 3	B—Kt 5
4. Q—B 2	......

I believe that this move is the most logical of the many moves possible (4. Q—Kt 3, 4. P—Q R 3, 4. B—Q 2, 4. B—Kt 5, 4. P—K 3, 4. Kt—B 3, 4. P—K Kt 3 or even 4. B—K B 4), as it achieves two important objects : it keeps control over K 4 and it prevents, temporarily at least, the doubling of the Pawns on the Queen's Bishop's file.

| 4. ...... | P—Q 4 |
| 5. P × P | ...... |

If 5. P—Q R 3, B × Kt ch ; 6. Q × B, Kt—K 5 ; 7. Q—B 2, P—Q B 4 ; 8. P × B P, Kt—Q B 3 ; 9. P—K 3, Black obtains an equal game by continuing 9. ....Q—R 4 ch ; 10. B—Q 2, Kt × B ; 11. Q × Kt, P × P ! and if 12. Q × Q, Kt × Q ; 13. R—B 1, then 13. ....P—Q Kt 4 ! ; 14. P × P *e.p.*, B—Kt 2 !

| 5. ...... | Q × P |
| 6. P—K 3 | ...... |

If 6. Kt—B 3, then, for instance, 6. ....P—B 4 ; 7. B—Q 2, B × Kt ; 8. B × B, P × P ; 9. Kt × P, P—K 4 ! (Loevenfish - Botvinnik, seventh Match-game, 1937).

6.	P—B 4
7. P—Q R 3	B × Kt ch
8. P × B	Q Kt—Q 2

There is no hurry about this Knight development. More appropriate for equalising seems to be 8. ....Castles ; 9. Kt—B 3, P—Q Kt 3 !—and if 10. B—K 2, then 10. ....P × P ; 11. B P × P, B—R 3 ! as, for instance, I played (with Black) against Grau in Montevideo, 1938.

| 9. P—B 3 | ...... |

A sound strategical scheme : White intends to meet the eventual ....P—K 4 by the counter-advance P—K 4. Still more exact would be, however, *first* 9. Kt—K 2, since then 9. ....P × P ; 10. B P × P, Kt—Kt 3 would not be satisfactory because of 11. Kt—B 3.

9.	P × P
10. B P × P	Kt—Kt 3
11. Kt—K 2	B—Q 2
12. Kt—B 4	......

Played in order to obtain a slightly superior end-game after 12. ....Q—B 3 ; 13. Q × Q, etc. If, instead, 12. Kt—B 3, then 12. ....Q—B 3 with a quite satisfactory game.

12.	Q—Q 3
13. B—Q 2	R—Q B 1
14. Q—Kt 2	K Kt—Q 4

Doubtless the best move, eliminating any immediate danger in the centre.

| 15. Kt×Kt | P×Kt |
| 16. B—Kt 4 | Q—K 3 |

If 16. ....Q—Kt 3 then 17. R—
B 1.

17. K—B 2   ......

The first move of the "Indian"
Castling (see my game with Sultan
Khan, No. 53). Actually, the King,
in this position, is quite comfortable
at K B 2.

17. ......   Kt—R 5

The first deviation from the
logical path. By far the best drawing chance consisted in 17. ....
Kt—B 5 (but not 17. ....P—B 4 ;
18. B—B 5 ! ±) ; 18. B×Kt, R×B,
thus obtaining Bishops of different
colours ; if, for instance, 19. Q R—
Q B 1, then 19. ....R×R ; 20.
R×R, B—B 3 ; 21. Q—B 3, P—
B 3 ; 22. Q—B 5, P—Q R 3 ; 23.
Q—Kt 6, Q—Q 2, with an adequate
defence.

18. Q—Q 2   P—Q Kt 3 ?

A fatal mistake, allowing White
to win by force. Necessary was 18.
....P—B 4, although White's advantage after 19. B—Q 3 followed
by R—K 1 and eventually P—K 4
would already be evident.

19. B—R 6 !   R—Q Kt 1

As the sequel shows, the threat
to imprison the Bishop by ....P—
Q Kt 4 is by no means an effective
one. But 19. ....R—B 2 ; 20.
Q R—Q B 1 would be equally
hopeless.

20. P—K 4   ......

This simple opening up of the
centre leaves Black without the
slightest saving resource.

20. ......   P—Q Kt 4

If 20. ....P—B 3, then 21. P×P,
Q×P ; 22. Q—K 2 ch !, Q—K 3 ; 23.
K R—K 1, Q×Q ch ; 24. R×Q ch,
K—Q 1 ; 25. B—K 7 ch, K—B 2 ;
26. R—B 1 ch and wins.

Position after Black's 20th move.

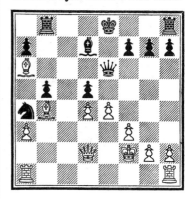

21. Q—B 4 !   ......

This powerful intermediate move
destroys Black's last hopes of
catching the opponent's K's Bishop.
If now 21. ....R—Q 1, then 22.
P×P, Q×P ; 23. K R—K 1 ch,
B—K 3 ; 24. R—K 5, Q×Q P ch ;
25. Q×Q, R×Q ; 26. B×P ch and
wins.

| 21. ...... | R—Kt 3 |
| 22. P×P | ...... |

More precise than 22. K R—K 1
which could be answered by 22.
....Kt—Kt 7 !

22.	Q×P
23. K R—K 1 ch	B—K 3
24. Q R—B 1	......

With the terrible threat 25. R—
B 8 ch.

| 24. ...... | P—B 3 |
| 25. R—B 7 ! | ...... |

More convincing than the win of
the exchange by 25. R—B 8 ch.

25.	K—Q 1
26. R × R P	.....

After this mate in a few moves is unavoidable.

Resigns.

GAME 100

CATALAN OPENING

Fourteenth Match-Game, Zwolle, November, 1937.

Black : DR. M. EUWE

1. P—Q 4	Kt—K B 3
2. P—Q B 4	P—K 3
3. P—K Kt 3	P—Q 4

The Soviet grand master, Loevenfish, played in a tournament game at Tbilisi, 1937, 3. .... B—Kt 5 ch ; 4. B—Q 2, B × B ch ; 5. Q × B, Kt—K 5 ; 6. Q—B 2, P—Q 4 ; 7. B—Kt 2, Q—K 2 ; 8. P—Q R 3, P—K B 4—and obtained a quite satisfactory position. The text-move in conjunction with the next one leads to a modern variation of the Queen's Gambit Accepted which is slightly in White's favour.

4. Kt—K B 3	.....

White need not avoid the exchange of Queens by playing 4. B—Kt 2 since after 4. .... P × P ; 5. Q—R 4 ch, Q—Q 2 ; 6. Q × B P, Q—B 3 ; 7. Q Kt—Q 2, etc., he would obtain an advantage both in space and development.

4.	P × P
5. Q—R 4 ch	Q Kt—Q 2
6. Q × Q B P	.....

There is no advantage to be obtained by delaying this capture, for instance, 6. B—Kt 2, P—Q R 3 ; 7. Kt—B 3—then 7. .... R—Q Kt 1 ! ; 8. Q × B P, P—Q Kt 4, etc., at least equalising.

6.	P—B 4

If now 6. .... P—Q R 3, then 7. Q—B 2 ! in order to answer 7. .... P—Q Kt 4 by 8. P—Q R 4. The same manœuvre would apply if Black were to play P—Q R 3 on his seventh move.

7. B—Kt 2	Kt—Kt 3

This method of playing has the disadvantage of not solving the problem of the development of the Queen's Bishop. More advisable would be first 7. .... P × P, and if 8. Kt × P, Kt—Kt 3 followed by 9. .... B—Kt 5 ch ; and if 8. Q × P, then 8. .... B—B 4, 9. Q—K R 4, B—K 2, etc., still harassing the adventurous white Queen.

8. Q—Q 3	P × P
9. Castles !	.....

In order to prevent 9. .... B—Kt 5 ch, possible, for instance, after 9. Kt × P. Black's extra-Pawn cannot be protected because of (9. .... B—B 4) ; 10. P—Q Kt 4 !

9.	B—K 2
10. Kt × P	Castles

Of course not 10. .... P—K 4 because of 11. Q—Kt 5 ch, Kt—Q 2 ; 12. Kt—B 5, etc., with clear advantage.

11. Kt—Q B 3	P—K 4

The following double exchange is rather risky for the slight disturbance of White's Pawn position on the Queen's side will be more than compensated by the advantage of the two Bishops. An interesting attempt would be 11. .... Q—Q 2 aiming both at 12. .... P—K 4 and 12. .... R—Q 1.

12. Kt—B 5	B—Kt 5
13. Q—B 2 !	B × Q Kt
14. P × B	B × Kt ?

This exchange was necessary sooner or later, it is true—but why the haste ? As Black intended to play Q—B 2 he would have been better advised to do this at once, thereby giving White not so much choice of attacking moves.

15. Q×B   Q—B 2
16. B—R 6   ......

The main object of this rather difficult move is to prevent a Knight move to Q 4, possible, for instance, after 16. B—Kt 5 ; for if *now* 16. ....K Kt—Q 4, then 17. B—K 4 !, P—Kt 3 ; 18. Q—B 3, K R—Q 1 ; 19. K R—Q 1, etc., to White's advantage.

16. ......   Q Kt—Q 2
17. Q—Kt 5 (?) ......

But by leaving his Bishop so dangerously placed, White certainly complicates matters without necessity. Simple and strong was 17. B—K 3, and if 17. ....P—K Kt 3 then 18. Q—Kt 5, etc., with a considerable positional advantage.

17. ......   Kt—K 1
18. Q R—Kt 1   ......

Also possible was 18. B—R 3— a move which I intended to play later as answer, for example, to 18. ....R—Kt 1

18. ......   Kt—B 4

The tempting 18. ....Kt—Kt 3 would have been answered by 19. P—Q R 4 !, and if 19. ....P—B 3, then 20. Q—B 5 !, P×B ; 21. P— R 5, Q—Q 2 ; 22. Q—R 5—and Black would get into serious trouble if he tried to keep the extra-piece much longer.

19. Q—Kt 4   R—Q 1

It would be hardly a wise policy to force the exchange of Queens by playing 19. ....Q—B 1 since after 20. Q×Q, R×Q ; 21. B—Kt 5, P—B 3 ; 22. B—Q 5 ch followed by 23. B—K 3 the Bishops would certainly play a vital part in the end-game.

20. B—Kt 5   R—Q 3
21. Q—Q B 4   ......

Preparing the advance of the K B P, which at this moment would have been premature—for instance, 21. P—K B 4, P—K R 3 ; 22. P×P ?, R—K Kt 3∓.

21. ......   P—Q Kt 3

White threatened also 22. B × Kt P.

22. P—B 4   R—Kt 3 !

With this and the few following strong moves Black eliminates any immediate danger.

23. Q R—Q 1   ......

Threatening 24. B—Q 8 followed by P—B 5.

23. ......   P—K 5

Preventing the above threat since 24. B—Q 8, Kt—Q 3 ! ; 25. B×Q, Kt×Q, etc., would now be to Black's advantage.

24. B—R 4 !   ......

After this well-timed retreat Black's position begins to look very precarious, since, for instance, 24. ....Kt—Q 3 ; 25. Q—Q 5, Kt— Kt 4 ; 26. R—Q B 1, R—Q 3 ; 27. Q—B 4 would be in White's favour. By the following interesting Pawn's offer Black succeeds in removing the white Queen to a less active square—but at the heavy price of a serious weakening of the position of his Knight at Q B 4.

24. ......   P—Kt 4 ! ?
25. Q—Kt 4 !   ......

The only correct answer, for 25. Q × Kt P would permit Black to place a Knight on K B 4 via Q 3 after which the threats .... Kt × B, or .... Kt—K 6 would secure him a promising initiative.

25. ......   P—Q R 4
26. Q—R 3   ......

And not 26. Q—Kt 2, or Kt 1 because of 26. .... Kt—R 5.

26. ......   P—B 4 ?

The wish to prevent P—B 5 and at the same time to secure the K's Pawn is quite understandable ; but the move has the grave inconvenience of making Black's position in the centre even more shaky than it was before. A perfectly satisfactory line was, however, hardly to be found. If, for instance, 28. .... R—Q 3 (recommended by the great theoretician, Prof. Becker, as even giving Black an advantage !) then 27. B—K 7 !, R × R (or Q × B ; 28. Q × Kt ±) ; 28. B × Kt !, R × R ch ; 29. K × B after which Black would have to suffer further material loss. Also after the comparatively better 26. .... Kt—Q 3 White would secure a definite positional advantage by the important intermediate move 27. R—Q 5 ! Black had therefore only the choice between unpleasant alternatives.

27. B—Q 8 !   ......

A most unpleasant shock : White gets his threat in first and thus prevents the harmonious co-operation of Black's forces.

27. ......   Q—R 2
28. K—R 1   R—Q R 3
29. R—Q 5   ......

The simple domination of the central file by the Rooks will soon prove decisive owing to the numerous weaknesses created by the 23.-26. Pawn moves of Black.

29. ......   Kt—K 3
30. K R—Q 1   Kt × B

If, instead, 30. .... Q—K 6, then simply 31. Q—Kt 2 and the threats would remain.

31. R × Kt   Q—K B 2
32. K R—Q 5   ......

More effective than 32. K R—Q 7, Q—B 5.

32. ......   R—Q B 3
33. R × Kt P   Q—B 5

Position after Black's 33rd move.

34. R × B P !   ......

Conclusive, as 34. .... R × R ; 35. R × Kt ch, K—B 2 ; 36. Q—K 7 ch, K—Kt 3 ; 37. B × P, etc., would be absolutely hopeless for Black.

34. ......   Q R—B 3
35. R × R   P × R
36. R—Q 4 (?)   ......

A typical "short-of-time" calculation. I was glad to find a practically forced sequence of moves that would bring me without damage over the ominous 40th move—and did not pay attention to the simple 36. Q—Kt 3, forcing an end-game with two extra-Pawns and most probably immediate resignation !

36.	Q×K P
37. Q—Kt 3 ch	K—R 1
38. R×P	Q—Q 7
39. Q—Kt 1 !	......

Technically easier than 39. P—K R 3, Kt—Q 3 with slight fighting possibilities for Black.

39.	Q×Q B P
40. Q—K 1	Q×Q ch

Or 40. ....Q—B 1 ; 41. Q×P.

41. R×Q	......

The ending is easily won, for White, besides his extra-Pawn, has a very strong Bishop against a Knight completely lacking safe squares in the centre of the board.

41.	Kt—Q 3
42. B—B 6 !	......

Immobilizing the Knight (because of the eventual threat to exchange Rooks by R—K 8) and preventing a further advance of Black's Q R P.

42.	R—Q Kt 1

Or 42. ....R—Q B 1 ; 43. B—R 4.

43. R—K 6	R—Kt 8 ch
44. K—Kt 2	R—Kt 7 ch
45. K—R 3	Kt—B 4
46. R×P	Kt—K 2
47. B—K 4	K—Kt 2
48. R—K 6	K—B 2
49. R—K R 6	R×P
50. R×P ch	K—B 3
51. R—R 6 ch	K—B 2
52. R—R 6	Resigns.

GAME 101

QUEEN'S INDIAN DEFENCE

Twenty - first Match - Game, Amsterdam, November, 1937.

White : Dr. M. Euwe

1. P—Q 4	Kt—K B 3
2. P—Q B 4	P—K 3
3. Kt—K B 3	P—Q Kt 3
4. P—K Kt 3	B—Kt 2
5. B—Kt 2	B—Kt 5 ch
6. B—Q 2	B—K 2

To the best of my knowledge this move has not been played before ; but an analogous idea in the Dutch Defence has been experimented with —first by Soviet players and subsequently by myself, mostly with satisfactory results as far as the opening was concerned. The idea of the Bishop's retreat is to take advantage of the somewhat unusual position of White's Queen's Bishop. Still, after this game I came to the conclusion that the old 5. ....B—K 2 (instead of 5. ....B—Kt 5 ch), which I adopted in the 23rd Match-game, is at least as good as the text-manœuvre.

7. Kt—B 3	Kt—K 5

Allowing White to obtain a slight advantage in space. Safer was 7. ....Castles ; 8. Castles, P—Q 4 and if 9. Kt—K 5, then Q—B 1 with an approximately even game.

8. Castles	......

He could also have played P—Q 5 at once.

8.	Castles
9. P—Q 5 !	Kt×B
10. Q×Kt	......

10. Kt×Kt also would be good, since it would have left Black with hardly anything better than 10.

....Q—B 1, parrying the threat 11.
P—Q 6 !

| 10. ...... | B—K B 3 |
| 11. Q R—Q 1 | ...... |

Wasting valuable time. After 11.
Kt—Q 4 White's game would remain definitely preferable.

| 11. ...... | P—Q 3 |
| 12. P × P | ...... |

If now 12. Kt—Q 4, then 12. ....
B × Kt followed by .... P—K 4 with
a satisfactory game for Black. The
exchange in the text also leads only
to equality as Black can easily
protect his K 3.

12.	P × P
13. Kt—Q 4	B × B
14. K × B	......

Of course not 14. Kt × P ?
because of 14. .... Q—K 2 ; 15.
Kt × R, B × Kt ; 16. P × B (Q × B,
B × R), B—Kt 2 ! remaining with
two minor pieces for the Rook.

| 14. ...... | Q—B 1 |

Intending in some variations to
make use of the square Q Kt 2—
for instance, 15. P—B 4, Kt—B 3 ! ;
16. Kt × Kt, Q—Kt 2, etc., to
Black's advantage.

15. Q—K 3	B × Kt
16. R × B	Kt—B 3
17. R—K 4	......

The beginning of an entirely mistaken plan which speedily transforms a playable position into a lost
one. A solid move was 17. R—Q 2,
but even simpler was 17. R—B 4 ;
then after the exchange of Rooks
Black's attacking chances would be
reduced to a minimum.

| 17. ...... | R—B 3 |
| 18. P—B 4 ? | ...... |

Leaving the Rook in a stalemate
position. 18. R—B 4 was still the
right move.

| 18. ...... | Q—Q 2 |
| 19. P—K Kt 4 | ...... |

Weakening the K B P and thereby
adding to all his other troubles.
Instead, 19. R—Q 1 would have
given him some chances of salvation.

| 19. ...... | Q R—K B 1 |
| 20. P—Kt 5 | ...... |

Useless, as the answer demonstrates ; but his game was already
strategically lost.

| 20. ...... | R—B 4 ! |

Black does not need to protect
his King's Pawn, since after 21.
R × P the answer 21. .... Kt—K 4
would win the exchange.

| 21. P—K R 4 | Q—B 2 |
| 22. R—B 3 | K—R 1 ! |

An important preparation for the
following advance in the centre,
instead of which the immediate 22.
.... P—Q 4 would be slightly premature because of 23. R × P, P—
Q 5 ; 24. Q—K 4, P × Kt ; 25. P ×
P !, Kt—Q 1 ; 26. R—K 7, etc.,
with some fighting chances for
White. And as 22. .... P—K 4
would also be unconvincing because
of 23. Kt—Q 5, Kt—Q 5 ; 24. Kt—
K 7 ch !, Q × Kt ; 25. R × Kt, etc.—
I decided to restrain the advance of
my central Pawns until such an advance would be absolutely decisive.

| 23. Q—Q 3 | P—Q 4 ! |

Now the time has come, since 24.
P × P, P × P ; 25. R—R 4, P—Q 5
would be quite hopeless for White.

| 24. R × P | Kt—Kt 5 ! |

Obviously stronger than 24. ....
Q×R.

25. Q—K 3   Kt—B 7

Instead, 25. ....P—Q 5 ; 26. Q—
K 4, P×·Kt ; 27. P×P, etc., would
have allowed a longer resistance.

26. Q—Q 2   Q×R
27. P×P   Q—B 2

Position after Black's 27th move.

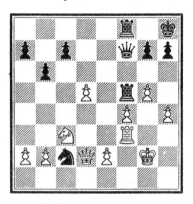

28. Q×Kt   ......

After this Black wins easily by a
direct attack. I expected, instead,
the subtler 28. K—Kt 3 (threatening
also 29. P—K 4) after which
the following striking variation
would occur : 28. ....Kt—K 8 ! ;
29. R—B 2, Kt—Kt 7 ! ; 30. P—K 3
(still fighting for the K B P), Kt ×
R P ; 31. K × Kt, P—K R 3 !, etc.,
with decisive threats.

28. ......   R × B P
29. Q—Q 3   Q—R 4
30. R × R   R × R
31. Q—R 3   R—Kt 5 ch
32. K—B 2   P—K R 3 !

If now 33. P×P, then 33. ....
Q—B 4 ch, after which' a Rook's
check would win the Queen.

Resigns.

GAME 102

RETI'S OPENING

Twenty - second Match - Game,
Delft, November, 1937.

Black : Dr. M. Euwe

1. Kt—K B 3   P—Q 4
2. P—B 4   P—Q 5
3. P—K 3   ......

After 3. P—Q Kt 4 Black could
play 3. ....P—K B 3 followed by
....P—K 4 with good prospects.
The move selected prevents this
possibility, since after 3. ....P—
Q B 4 ; 4. P—Q Kt 4, P—B 3,
White can play—*not* 5. P × B P, P—
K 4 ! with about even chances—but
5. *P × Q P, P × P ; 6. P—B 5 !* (this
last move, which appears very effective, was discovered by myself
when preparing for the match)—
after which the weakness of the
diagonal K Kt 1—Q R 7 would
cause Black considerable trouble.
If 6. ....P—K 4, then 7. B—B 4 ;
if 6. ....Q—Q 4, then 7. Q—B 2± ;
if 6. ....P—Q R 4, then 7. Q—
R 4 ch, B—Q 2 ; 8. P—Kt 5, P—
K 4; 9. B—B 4 and Black cannot
play 9. ....B × B P because of 10.
B × Kt followed by 11. Q—B 4.
In other words, the consequences of
3. ....P—Q B 4 seem to be decidedly in White's favour.

3. ......   Kt—Q B 3

On the contrary, after this move
White will find it very difficult (if
indeed possible) to obtain any
opening advantage.

4. P × P   Kt × P
5. Kt × Kt   Q × Kt
6. Kt—B 3   Kt—B 3

Even simpler is immediately 6.
....P—K 4, but as Black could
effect that advance by his next

move, the text-continuation does not yet spoil anything.

7. P—Q 3   ......

Useless would be 7. Kt—Kt 5, Q—Kt 3 ; 8. P—Q 4, P—K 4 ! ; 9. P—B 5, Q—B 3 ; 10. Kt—B 3, P—Q R 3.

7. ......   P—B 3 ?

A serious loss of time, instead of which 7. ....P—K 4 was quite sufficient. If then 8. B—K 3, simply 8. ....Q—Q 1 ; 9. P—Q 4, Kt—Kt 5 ; or if 9. B—K 2, then 9. .... P—B 4 (or even, more solid, 9. .... B—K 2)—with an approximately equal game.

8. B—K 3   Q—Q 2

With the intention of developing the Bishops on the long diagonals. But White's advantage in space becomes evident in a very few moves.

9. P—Q 4   P—K Kt 3
10. B—K 2   B—Kt 2

Threatening .... Kt—Kt 5 which would have been useless immediately because of 11. B—B 4, followed by P—K R 3.

11. P—K R 3   Castles
12. Castles   P—Kt 3
13. B—B 3   B—Kt 2
14. P—Q R 4 !   ......

In order to make a break in the centre more effective White tries first to weaken Black's Q Kt 3. The sequel will prove the soundness of this scheme.

14. ......   Q R—Q 1

In connexion with his eighteenth move this looks like a loss of time, but in reality it is almost a sad necessity since after P—Q R 5

Black will have to deal with the threat P—R 6 ; while, on the other hand, after the exchange on his Q Kt 3 he will be obliged to offer the exchange of at least one pair of Rooks.

15. P—R 5   Q—B 2

This and the next move are necessary in order to give sufficient protection to the weak square Q Kt 3.

16. Q—Kt 3   Kt—Q 2
17. P × P   P × P
18. R—R 7   R—R 1

White's main threat was 19. P—Q 5.

19. K R—R 1   P—K 3

Otherwise the imminent P—Q 5 would be even more unpleasant than it proved to be in the actual game.

20. R × R   B × R

This move has been unduly criticised. After 20. ....R × R ; 21. R × R ch, B × R ; 22. Q—R 3, B—Kt 2 ; 23. P—Q Kt 4, White would have to face a technically easier problem than in the actual game.

21. P—Q 5 !   ......

By no means an easy decision to make, as I was fully aware that the resulting exchanges would cede to Black important squares in the centre. Still, it was necessary to undertake something definite at this particular moment since (1) White has no means of improving the excellent position of his pieces ; (2) Black, on the contrary, could eventually try to form an attack against the Queen's Pawn, starting by R—Q 1 ; and (3) this is the only possibility of taking advantage of the weakness of Black's Q Kt 3, created by the advance of White's Q R P.

21.	B P × P
22. P × P	Kt—B 4

The tactical justification of the move 21. P—Q 5 resides in the variation 22. ....B × Kt ; 23. P—Q 6 !, Q × P ; 24. Q × B, B × B ; 25. B—R 6 ! winning the exchange. And if 22. ....Kt—K 4, then 23. B—K 4 still threatening P—Q 6.

23. Q—B 4	......

If 23. B × Kt, Q × B ; 24. P × P, then 24. ....B × B ; 25. P × P ch, R × P ; 26. P × B, B × Kt ; 27. R—R 7, Q—Kt 4 ch with perpetual check.

23.	P × P
24. B × P	B × B
25. Kt × B	Q—K 4

Black selects the most aggressive line, which is certainly more promising than the purely passive 25. ....Q—Kt 2 ; 26. R—Kt 1, Kt—Q 2 ; 27. Q—Kt 5 ! with a clear advantage in space for White.

26. R—Kt 1	Kt—R 5 !

An ingenious way of keeping the sick Pawn, at least temporarily. The next moves up both sides had to be most exactly calculated.

27. P—Q Kt 3	Kt—Kt 7
28. Q—B 6	P—Q Kt 4 !

The point of the previous Knight's manœuvre as this Pawn cannot be taken because of the answer 29. ....R—Q 1.

29. B—B 4 !	Q—K 3

After this, White, as the succeeding moves show, can take the Pawn. The only adequate defence consisted in 29. ....Q—K 7 ! which

would be answered by 30. R—K B 1 ! still leaving Black with the following weak spots : (a) the Q Kt P ; (b) the square K B 3 ; (c) last but not least, the insecure position of the Knight at Kt 7.

Position after Black's 29th move.

30. Q × P !	......

This seemingly very risky capture secures White a material advantage which he will succeed in keeping until the end.   If now 30. ....R—Q 1, then 31. R—Q B 1 !, R × Kt ; 32. Q—Kt 8 ch (this is why 29. B—B 4 was necessary), B—B 1 ; 33. B—R 6, Q—Q 3 (or Q—K 2 ; 34. R—B 8) ; 34. Q × Q, R × Q ; 35. R—B 8 and wins.

30.	Q—K 5
31. R—Q B 1	Kt—Q 6

Or 31. ....R—Q 1 ; 32. B—Kt 5 with variations similar to those mentioned above.

32. Q—B 4 !	......

Again the only move, but amply sufficient to maintain the advantage.

32.	Q—K 7

A grave mistake would be 32.

....B—Q 5 because of 33. Kt—B 6 ch.

33. R—B 1   Kt × B

Black has practically no choice, for 33. ....R—K 1 (threatening 34. ....Q × R ch) would be easily met by 34. B—K 3.

34. Q × Kt   ......

And not 34. Kt × Kt, Q × Q ; 35. P × Q, R—B 1 ; 36. R—B 1, B—R 3 etc.—with a probable draw.

34. ......   Q—Kt 4
35. Q—B 3 !   ......

White has still to be careful. Here, for instance, the more "natural" move 35. Q—B 4 would lead to a speedy draw after 35. .... R—Kt 1.

35. ......   R—Kt 1
36. R—Kt 1   Q—R 3
37. R—Q 1   ......

This attempt to repeat moves, due to a slight shortage of time, leads to extremely interesting complications. After the simple 37. P—Q Kt 4 White would not have much trouble in taking advantage from the possession of a passed Pawn. A plausible variation would be, for instance, 37. ....Q—B 5 ; 38. Kt—K 7 ch, K—B 1 ; 39. Kt—B 6, R—Kt 3 ; 40. P—Kt 5 !, R × P; 41. Q—R 3 ch and wins.

37. ......   Q—R 6
38. R—Kt 1   Q—R 7
39. Q—Q 3   B—Q 5

This counter-attack only compromises Black's King's position. But it is difficult to suggest a satisfactory line of play, for White is threatening simply to advance his passed Pawn.

40. R—K B 1   Q—Kt 7

The alternative 40. ....Q—R 2 would also be unsatisfactory because of 41. P—Q Kt 4, etc.

41. Kt—K 7 ch !   ......

This sealed move initiates the final attack which, after a dozen moves, leads practically by force to the win of the Queen for two pieces.

41. ......   K—B 1

The only move. Hopeless would be 41. ....K—Kt 2 ; 42. Kt—B 5 ch !, P × Kt ; 43. Q—Kt 3 ch and Q × R—or 41. ....K—R 1 ; 42. Kt—B 6, B × P ch ; 43. R × B, Q—B 8 ch ; 44. K—R 2, Q × Kt ; 45. R × P, etc.

42. Kt—B 6   B × P ch
43. K—R 2 !   ......

The idea of this Pawn sacrifice (instead of 43. R × B, Q—B 8 ch ; 44. Q—B 1, Q × Kt ; 45. R × P ch, K—Kt 1 ; 46. R—B 3 with very problematical winning chances) will become apparent only after the 48th move. The ensuing Knight manœuvre is very spectacular.

43. ......   R—K 1

If 43. ....R—Kt 2, then 44. Q—K B 3, B—Kt 3 (or B—B 4 ; 45. Q—Q 5) ; 45. Kt—Q 8 ! winning at least the exchange.

44. Q—K B 3   R—K 7

Again the only move, as is also the following. But had the White King gone to R 1 on the 43rd move, then 44. ....R—K 8 would have saved Black.

45. Kt—Q 4 !   R—Q 7
46. Kt—K 6 ch   K—K 2
47. Kt—B 4   ......

Threatening 48. Kt—Q 3.

47. ......   Q—Q 5

Or 47. .... Q—B 7 ; 48. R—Q R 1 and the exposed King would succumb to the combined attack of the three White pieces.

Position after Black's 47th move.

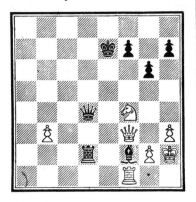

48. K—R 1 !   ......

Only this "quiet" move, which had to be calculated a long time before, justifies the attack started by 43. K—R 2. White now threatens 49. Kt—K 2, and if Black tries to prevent this by 48. .... B—R 5 he loses as follows : 49. Q—Kt 7 ch, Q—Q 2 ; 50. Q—Kt 4 ch, K—K 1 ; 51. Kt—K 6 ! (stronger than 51. Kt×P, R P×Kt ; 52. Q×B, R—Q 8 !, etc.), B—K 2 ; 52. Q—Kt 8 ch, B—Q 1 ; 53. Kt×B, Q×Kt ; 54. Q—K 5 ch, Q—K 2 ; 55. Q—R 8 ch, K—Q 2 ; 56. Q×P, R—K B 7 ; 57. R—Q 1 ch, K—B 2 ; 58. Q—R 8 etc.

48. ......   R—R 7

Or 48. .... P—R 4 ; 49. Kt—K 2, R—Q 8, etc., which would not greatly differ from the line of play actually adopted.

49. Kt—K 2   R—R 8
50. Q—Kt 7 ch   ......

Of course not 50. Kt×Q ?, R×R ch followed by .... B—Kt 8 ch winning back the Queen.

50. ......   K—B 3 ?

The game was lost, anyhow, but 50. .... K—B 1 would have prolonged the battle—for instance, 51. Kt×Q, R×R ch ; 52. K—R 2, B—Kt 8 ch ; 53. K—Kt 3, B—B 7 ch ; 54. K—B 3, B×Kt dis. ch ; 55. K—K 4, B—B 3, or 55. K—K 2, R—B 7 ch ; 56. K—K 1, K—Kt 2 ! In this variation White, in order to force resignation, would have been obliged to use his reserve trump—the passed Queen's Knight's Pawn.

51. Kt×Q   R×R ch
52. K—R 2   B—Kt 8 ch
53. K—Kt 3   B—B 7 ch
54. K—B 3   B×Kt dis. ch.
55. K—K 4   R—Q 8

Now forced, as White threatened 56. Q—R 6 ch.

56. Q—Q 5 (?)   ......

There was really no need to bother about calculating the (won) Pawn end-game after 56. .... R—K 8 ch ; 57. K×B, R—Q 8 ch ; 58. K—B 5, R×Q ch ; 59. K×R, K—K 2 ; 60. K—B 6, etc., as the simple 56. Q—B 6 ch followed by 57. Q—B 2 won immediately ! This is the only (fortunately negligible) omission I committed in this unusually difficult game.

56. ......   K—K 2
57. P—K Kt 4   P—R 4

Despair.

58. P×P   P—B 4 ch
59. K—B 3   R—Q 6 ch
60. K—K 2   R—K 6 ch
61. K—Q 2   R—K 5
62. P×P   Resigns,

GAME 103

QUEEN'S GAMBIT DECLINED
(SEMI-TARRASCH'S DEFENCE)

Twenty - fourth Match - Game,
Rotterdam, December, 1937.

Black : DR. M. EUWE

1. Kt—K B 3	P—Q 4
2. P—Q B 4	P—K 3

For 2. ....P—Q 5 see Game
No. 102.

3. P—Q 4	Kt—K B 3
4. Kt—Q B 3	P—B 4
5. P×Q P	Kt×P
6. P—K Kt 3	......

A harmless deviation from the
usual 6. P—K 4. In both cases
Black has very little trouble in
developing his pieces.

6.	P×P

Also good enough is 6. ....Kt—
Q B 3 ; 7. B—Kt 2, Kt×P ; 8.
Kt×Q Kt, Kt×Kt ; 9. P×Kt, P×
Kt ; 10. Q×P, Q×Q ; 11. P×Q,
B—Q 3 ; 12. P—Q R 4, K—K 2
with equality, as played in the last
of the exhibition games arranged
after the Match.

7. Kt×Kt	Q×Kt
8. Q×P	Q×Q
9. Kt×Q	B—Kt 5 ch

There is nothing to be said
against this check and the following
exchange.

10. B—Q 2	B×B ch
11. K×B	K—K 2 ?

But the neglect to develop the
Queen's side pieces will from now
on be the cause of all the trouble.
Indicated was 11. ....B—Q 2 ; 12.
B—Kt 2, Kt—B 3 ; 13. Kt×Kt,
B×Kt ; 14. B×B, P×B ; 15. Q R—
Q B 1, Castles ch ; 16. K—K 3, K—
B 2 with an easily defensible Rook
end-game.

12. B—Kt 2	R—Q 1
13. K—K 3	Kt—R 3

Practically forced, as his Q B 2
needed protection. But the Knight
at Q R 3 will be not only out of
play but also, as the sequel will
show, dangerously exposed. The
next part of the game, which ends
with the win of a Pawn for White,
is easy to understand but still
rather instructive.

14. Q R—Q B 1	R—Q Kt 1
15. P—Q R 3	......

Useless would be 15. Kt—Kt 5
because of 15. ....B—Q 2 (16.
Kt×R P ?, R—Q R 1).

15.	B—Q 2

Threatening now 16. ....P—K 4
which White prevents by his next
move.

16. P—K B 4	P—K B 3

This move has been criticized, in
my opinion, without much reason,
since in the long run Black would
not be able to avoid material loss
anyhow. If, for instance, 16. ....
B—K 1, then 17. P—Q Kt 4, R—
Q 2 ; 18. Kt—Kt 5, R—Q R 1 ; 19.
R—B 3 followed by 20. K R—Q B 1
and 21. R—B 8 or 21. Kt—B 7.
As it happens in the actual game
Black, in spite of his Pawn minus,
will still keep some drawing chances.

Position after Black's 16th move.

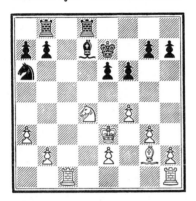

17. B—K 4 !   ......

A typical "centralization" which the late Nimzowitsch would certainly have enjoyed. White not only attacks the K R P, but threatens in some variations B—Q 3 and (what is still more important) prevents 17. ....P—K 4 because of 18. P×P, P×P ; 19. Kt—B 3, winning a Pawn.

17. ......   B—K 1

Preventing 18. B×R P, as the answer 18. ....P—K Kt 3 with the threats (a) B—B 2 followed by .... R—K R 1, or (b) ....Q R—Q B 1 followed by ....Kt—B 2, would give Black sufficient resources. But with his next two moves White succeeds in taking advantage of the weakness of Black's K 3.

18. P—Q Kt 4 !   R—Q 2
19. P—B 5 !   Kt—B 2

Comparatively better than 19. ....P—K 4 ; 20. Kt—K 6, or 19. ....P×P ; 20. B×B P, R—Q 4 ; 21. B×R P, etc.—in both cases with considerable advantage for White.

20. P×P   Kt×P
21. Kt×Kt   K×Kt
22. B×R P   ......

Thus White has obtained a material plus, but his positional advantage has in the meantime almost vanished, and Black will even succeed in obtaining some pressure on the King's file.

22. ......   P—B 4
23. R—B 5 !   ......

Preparing the exchange of Bishops at Q 5.

23. ......   P—K Kt 3
24. B—Kt 8 ch   K—B 3
25. K R—Q B 1   R—K 2 ch
26. K—B 2   B—B 3
27. B—Q 5   Q R—K 1
28. R—K 1 !   ......

By far the best, as 28. K R—B 2, B—R 5 ; 29. R—Q 2, P—Kt 3 ; 30. R—B 3, R—Q 1, etc., would lead to an unpleasant pin.

28. ......   B×B
29. R×B   P—K Kt 4
30. R—Q 6 ch   K—K 4 ?

After this desperate advance the game speedily becomes hopeless. The natural course was 30. .... K—B 2 ; 31. P—K R 4, P×P ; 32. P×P, R—K R 1 ; 33. R—Q 4 and White would still have some technical difficulties in order to force the win.

31. K R—Q 1   P—Kt 5

Equally hopeless would be 31. ....R—K 3 ; 32. R—Q 7, R (K 1) —K 2 ; 33. P—K R 4, etc.

32. K R—Q 5 ch   K—K 5
33. R—Q 4 ch   K—K 4
34. K—K 3   ......

Also possible was 34. P—K 4, which would lead to the win of a second Pawn, but still permit Black a longer resistance than in the actual game—for instance (34. P— K 4) R—Q B 1 ! ; 35. R (Q 6)—

Q 5 ch, K—K 3 ; 36. P × P ch, K—
B 3, etc. The way selected is
simple enough.

34. ......   R—K 3

Or 34. ....P—B 5 ch ; 35. K—
Q 3 ! still threatening mate.

35. R (Q 4)—Q 5   K—B 3
            ch   dis. ch.
36. K—B 4   K—Kt 3
37. R × R ch   R × R
38. R—K 5   R—Q R 3

If 38. ....R—K B 3, then 39.
P—K 4, P × P disc. ch ; 40. K ×
Kt P, R—B 7 ; 41. P—K R 4,
winning rapidly.

39. R × P   R × P
40. R—Q Kt 5 ! ......

The immediate 40. K × P would
probably win too—but the text-
manœuvre is more exact.

40. ......   P—Kt 3
41. K × P   ......

If now 41. ....R—K 6, then 42.
R—Kt 5 ch, K—R 3 ; 43. P—Kt 5 !
(the point of the 40th move), R × P ;
44. P—K R 4, after which there
would be no fighting chances for
Black.

Resigns.

GAME 104

NIMZOWITSCH DEFENCE

Twenty-fifth and last Match-
Game, The Hague, December, 1937.

White : Dr. M. Euwe

1. P—Q 4   Kt—K B 3
2. P—Q B 4   P—K 3
3. Kt—Q B 3   B—Kt 5
4. P—K 3   Castles
5. Kt—K 2   ......

This is one of the less fortunate

inventions of the great openings
artist, Rubinstein. Its weak point
is that the Knight will not have
much future either on K B 4 or on
K Kt 3 and that Black, by making
the simplest moves, will obtain a
slight advantage in development.
Preferable is therefore first 5. B—
Q 3, and if 5. ....P—Q Kt 3 then
6. Kt—K 2 (or even 6. Q—B 3) ;
or if 5. ....P—Q 4, then 6. Kt—
B 3, etc., with fairly good prospects.

5. ......   P—Q 4
6. P—Q R 3   B—K 2
7. P × P   ......

Since White intended to play
Kt—Kt 3 he would have done
better to delay this exchange. In
fact, after 7. Kt—Kt 3, P—Q B 4 ;
8. P × B P, B × P ; 9. P—Q Kt 4,
the move 9. ....P—Q 5 would have
been wrong because of 10. Q Kt—
K 4, and if 10. ....B—Kt 3 then
11. P—B 5 etc. Consequently,
Black would have been obliged to
modify his plan of development.

7. ......   P × P
8. Kt—Kt 3   ......

Rubinstein used to play here 8.
Kt—B 4—obviously in order to
prevent Black's next move, after
which the second player experiences
no more difficulty in the opening.

8. ......   P—Q B 4
9. P × P   ......

Preparing for the mistake at the
next move. As Black's ....P—
B 5 was not to be feared, White's
logical course was 9. B—Q 3, Kt—
B 3 ; 10. P × P, B × P ; 11. Castles,
etc.

9. ......   B × P
10. P—Q Kt 4 ? ......

Obviously not foreseeing the
answer, otherwise he would have
played 10. B—Q 3.

10. ......   P—Q 5 !

The point of this interesting move is that White cannot well answer it by 11. Kt—Q R 4 because of 11. ....P×P! ; 12. Q×Q (Kt or P× B ?, P×P ch ; 13. K—K 2, B— Kt 5 ch and wins), P×P ch ; 13. K—K 2, B—K Kt 5 ch ! forcing the King to move on to the Queen's file after which the Queen will be taken with check, thus saving the King's Bishop.   And as 11. Q Kt—K 4, Kt×Kt ; 12. Kt×Kt, B—Kt 3, etc. would also have been advantageous for Black, White's next move is comparatively the best.

11. P×B   P×Kt
12. Q—B 2   ......

White is decidedly in too optimistic a mood and underestimates Black's threats. Otherwise he would have tried to simplify matters by 12. Q×Q, R×Q ; 13. Kt—K 2, Kt —K 5 ; 14. P—B 3, Kt×P ; 15. Kt×P, Kt—B 3 after which, however, Black, owing to his Pawn majority on the Queen's side and better development, would still hold a slight advantage.

12. ......   Q—R 4
13. R—Q Kt 1   ......

Now 13. Kt—K 2 would not be sufficient because of 13. ....Kt— Q 4 ; 14. P—K 4, Kt—Kt 5 ! etc., winning the exchange.

13. ......   B—Q 2 !

The threat 14. ....B—R 5 is now difficult to meet. If, for instance, 14. B—B 4, B—R 5 ; 15. B—Kt 3, then 15. ....B—Kt 4, etc. ; and if 14. R—Kt 4 (which has been suggested by many annotators) then 14. ....Kt—R 3 ! ; 15. B× Kt, Q×B ; 16. P—K 4, K R— K 1 and White can neither castle nor take the ominous B P because of ....Kt—Q 4. White's decision to give up the exchange for a Pawn in order to finish at last the development of his pieces, therefore appears comparatively the wisest.

14. R—Kt 3   B—R 5
15. Q×P   Q—Q 1 !

The point of the thirteenth move. In spite of his material advantage, it will be by no means easy for Black to force the victory. The next part of the game is chiefly instructive from the tactical point of view.

16. B—B 4   Kt—R 3 !

Instead of 16. ....B×R ; 17. Q×B, Kt—R 3 ; 18. Q×P, Kt× P ; 19. Q—Kt 5 etc., which would have allowed White to preserve the two Bishops.

17. B×Kt   P×B

And not 17. ....B×R ; 18. B— Q 3 ! etc., with comparatively more counter-chances than in the actual game.

18. Castles   B×R
19. Q×B   R—Kt 1

The Q Kt-file will soon become a very important factor. After the more obvious 19. ....Q—Q 4, White, by playing 20. Q×Q, Kt× Q ; 21. P—K 4, etc., would still have some chances of saving the end-game.

20. Q—B 2   Q—Q 4
21. P—K 4   Q—Kt 6
22. Q—K 2   ......

Now, on the contrary, the endgame after 22. Q×Q, R×Q would be quite hopeless because of the weakness of White's Q R P.

22. ......   Q—Kt 4 !
23. Q—K B 3   ......

Comparatively better than 23. Q—K 3, Kt—Q 2. If White wants to avoid the exchange of Queens he must forget about his Q B P.

23. ......   Q×P
24. Kt—B 5 ?   ......

But here 24. B—K B 4, in order
to prevent the following pin, offered
a slightly better fighting chance.
The right answer for Black would
be 24. ....Q R—K 1, and if 25.
P—K 5 (R—B 1, Q—Q Kt 4 ! ; 26.
B—Q 6, R—B 1 etc.) then 25. ....
Kt—Q 2 ; 26. Kt—K 4, Q—B 7 ;
27. R—B 1, Q—Kt 7, etc., keeping
the material advantage.

24.	R—Kt 8
25. Q—B 4	......

Or 25. Q—K Kt 3, Kt—R 4 ; 26.
Q—Kt 5, K—R 1 !, etc., with an
easy defence. But now he threatens
to win the Queen by playing 26.
Q—Kt 5.

25.	Kt × P

One might suppose that after the
capture of this important Pawn the
fight would be very soon over. But
White succeeds in finding new
attacking moves again and again.

26. P—K R 4	R—K 1

Not convincing enough would be
26. ....Kt × P because of 27. K—
R 2 !

27. R—K 1	Q—B 6
28. R—Q 1	......

Threatening 29. Q × Kt.

Position after White's 28th move.

28.	Kt—Q 7 !

This spectacular move forces a
further, most welcome, simplification, after which there will be
practically no more fight left.

29. R × Kt	R × B ch

But not 29. ....Q × B ch ; 30.
K—R 2, R—Kt 7 ? because of 31.
Q—K 5 ! with a win for White !

30. K—R 2	Q—B 2
31. R—Q 6	R—B 4
32. P—K Kt 3 !	......

A very ingenious idea worthy of
a better fate. If Black executes his
threat (32. ....R × Kt) he will be
obliged after 33. R—K 6 ! ! to give
up his Queen for two Rooks (33.
....P × R ; 34. Q × Q, R × P ch ; 35.
K—R 3, P—K 4)—after which
White would be able to put up a
stubborn resistance.

32.	R—K B 1 !

But this simple answer puts an
end to the last hopes of salvation.
What follows is agony.

33. P—K Kt 4	......

Instead 33. Kt × P, K × Kt ; 34.
Q—B 6 ch, K—Kt 1 ; 35. R—Q 4,
P—K R 4 etc., would not work.

33.	P—B 3
34. K—R 3	P—K R 4

The beginning of the counter-
attack.

35. Q—Q 2	P × P ch
36. K × P	Q—B 2
37. P—R 5	......

Position after White's 37th move.

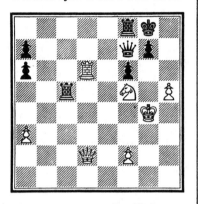

37. ......   R × Kt !

At last the most hated Knight of the match can be eliminated with decisive effect, and Black, in addition to the two extra Pawns, quickly obtains a mating attack. It was an exciting struggle !

38. K × R	Q × P ch
39. K—B 4	Q—R 5 ch
40. K—B 3	.....

If 40. K—B 5, then mate in four : 40. ....P—Kt 3 ch ; 41. K—K 6 (41. K × P, Q—R 2 mate), Q—K 5 ch ; 42. K—Q 7, Q—Kt 2 ch ; 43. K—K 6, Q—K B 2 mate.

40.	Q—R 6 ch
41. K—K 4	.....

Or 41. K—B 4, R—K 1 with the deadly threat of 42. ....P—Kt 4 mate.

41.	R—K 1 ch
42. K—Q 5	Q—Kt 6 ch
43. K—Q 4	Q × P
Resigns	

PART IV (1924-1933)

SIMULTANEOUS AND BLINDFOLD PLAY: EXHIBITION AND CONSULTATION GAMES

GAME 105

QUEEN'S GAMBIT DECLINED (SEMI-TARRASCH DEFENCE)

Played in a simultaneous exhibition in New York, January, 1924.

Black : A. KUSSMAN

1. P—Q 4	P—Q 4
2. Kt—K B 3	Kt—K B 3
3. P—B 4	P—K 3
4. Kt—B 3	P—B 4
5. B P×P	K P×P ?

Nowadays, "theory" considers—and rightly so for once—5. .... Kt × P as the only correct reply. But when this game was played, even masters did not realise the danger of the text-move; for instance, Dr. Vidmar played it against me in the London Tournament, 1922.

6. B—Kt 5 ! ......

Much more effective here than 6. P—K Kt 3, which in the regular Tarrasch Defence (with the Black Queen's Knight at Q B 3 and the King's Knight undeveloped) would be the most promising line.

6.	B—K 3
7. B×Kt	Q×B
8. P—K 4 !	P×K P
9. B—Kt 5 ch	B—Q 2

Or 9. ....Kt—Q 2; 10. Kt× K P, Q—K Kt 3; 11. B×Kt ch, B×B; 12. Castles, etc., with advantage.

10. Kt×P	Q—Q Kt 3
11. B×B ch	Kt×B
12. Castles	P×P

Facilitating White's attack. A lesser evil would be to allow the unpleasant P—Q 5.

13. Kt×P R—Q 1

After White's next move Black's Q 3 will need further protection.

| 14. Kt—K B 5 ! | Kt—K 4 |
| 15. Q—K 2 | P—Kt 3 |

Permitting an elegant finish ; but the position was, of course, lost.

Position after Black's 15th move.

16. Q—Kt 5 ch ! Kt—Q 2

The Queen could not be taken because of 17. Kt—B 6 mate.

17. K R—K 1 ......

Threatening mate again.

17.	B—Kt 5 Q
18. Kt—B 6 double ch	K—B 1
19. Kt × Kt ch	R × Kt
20. Q—K 5 !	

Threatening this time three different mates. That is too much !

Resigns.

GAME 106

CENTRE GAMBIT

Blindfold Record Exhibition on 26 Boards. New York, May, 1924.

Black : S. FREEMAN

1. P—K 4	P—K 4
2. P—Q 4	P × P
3. P—Q B 3	P—Q 4

Doubtless the best defence, permitting Black to obtain an even game.

| 4. K P × P | Q × P |

But here 4. ....Kt—K B 3 is even better.

5. P × P	B—Kt 5 ch
6. Kt—Q B 3	Kt—Q B 3
7. Kt—K B 3	Kt—K B 3
8. B—K 2	Castles
9. Castles	B × Kt

So far Black has made the right moves, but this exchange is wrong as it strengthens White's centre. Correct was 9. ....Q—Q R 4.

| 10. P × B | P—Q Kt 3 |

This, also, is not good, because the White Pawns will now advance with a win of both time and space. Better was 10. ....B—K Kt 5.

| 11. P—B 4 | Q—Q 1 |

| 12. P—Q 5 | Kt—K 2 |
| 13. Kt—Q 4 | ...... |

Preventing an effective development of the Black Bishop on the diagonal K R 3—Q B 8.

| 13. ...... | B—Kt 2 |
| 14. B—Kt 2 | ...... |

Simpler was 14. B—B 3 or 14. B—Kt 5. Still, the idea of sacrificing the central Pawn in order to increase the advantage in development was rather tempting.

14.	P—B 3
15. B—K B 3 !	P × P
16. K R—K 1	R—K 1

Instead 16. ....Q—Q 2 ; 17. Kt—Kt 5 ! was certainly not better.

| 17. Q—Q 2 | R—Kt 1 |
| 18. Q—Kt 5 | ...... |

Threatening 19. Kt—K 6 !

| 18. ...... | Kt—Kt 3 |
| 19. Kt—B 5 | ...... |

After this the attack can hardly be parried. White's next threat is the simple 20. P × P.

| 19. ...... | R × R ch |
| 20. R × R | P × P |

If 20. ....P—K R 3 then 21. Q—Kt 3, threatening both 22. B × Kt or 22. Kt—K 7 ch, etc.

| 21. B × B | R × B |
| 22. B × Kt | Q × B |

Or 22. ....P × B ; 23. Q—R 6, Q—K B 1 ; 24. R—K 8, followed by mate.

Position after Black's 23rd move.

White announces mate in four moves : 23. R—K 8 ch, Kt—B 1 ; 24. Kt—R 6 ch, Q × Kt ; 25. R × Kt ch, K × R ; 26. Q—Q 8 mate.

GAME 107

ALEKHINE'S DEFENCE

Blindfold Record Exhibition on 28 Boards, Paris, February, 1925.

Black : P. POTEMKIN

1. P—K 4	Kt—K B 3
2. Kt—Q B 3	P—Q 4
3. P × P	Kt × P
4. B—B 4	Kt—Kt 3

White's treatment of the opening was by no means a refutation of the defence adopted by Black. Besides the move in text the second player could also answer simply 4. .... Kt × Kt with excellent prospects ; if in that case 5. Q—B 3, then 5. ....P—K 3 ; 6. Q × Kt, Kt—B 3 ; 7. Kt—B 3, Q—B 3 ! ; 8. Q × Q, P × Q ; 9. P—Q 4, R—K Kt 1, followed by B—Q 2 and Castles, etc.

5. B—Kt 3	P—Q B 4
6. P—Q 3	Kt—B 3
7. Kt—B 3	Kt—R 4

Black over-estimates the value of his pair of Bishops. Indicated was 7. ....P—K 3 followed by B—K 2 and Castles with a fairly good game.

| 8. Kt—K 5 ! | Kt × B |

If 8. ....P—K 3 then 9. Q—K B 3 with advantage.

| 9. R P × Kt | Kt—Q 2 |

Slightly better was 9. ....B—K 3 followed by P—K Kt 3, etc.

| 10. Kt—B 4 ! | Kt—Kt 3 |

Equally unsatisfactory would be 10. ....P—K 3 ; 11. Kt—Kt 5 (threatening 12. B—B 4) or 10. ....P—K 4 ; 11. Q—K 2 ! But by playing 10. ....P—K Kt 3 ; 11. Q—K 2 (threatening mate) B—K Kt 2 ; 12. B—B 4, P—Q R 3 ; 13. Kt—Q 5, K—B 1 Black would still keep some chances of consolidating his position.

| 11. B—B 4 | Kt—Q 4 |

Instead 11. ....P—Q R 3 ; 12. Castles, P—K 3 would parry the immediate threats, but the position would still remain compromised. After the move made there will be practically no salvation for Black.

| 12. Kt × Kt | Q × Kt |
| 13. Castles | ...... |

Threatening now 14. Kt—Kt 6.

13.	P—Q Kt 4
14. Kt—K 3	Q—B 3
15. P—Q 4 !	P—K 3

If instead 15. ....B—Kt 2 then simply 15. R—K 1

| 16. P—Q 5 | P × P |
| 17. Kt × P | ...... |

Also 17. Q × P was extremely effective.

| 17. ...... | B—Q 3 |
| 18. R—K 1 ch | ...... |

And not 18. Kt—B 6 ch, K—K 2 !

| 18. ...... | B—K 3 |
| 19. B × B | ...... |

Simpler than the perhaps even more precise 19. Q—B 3 ! R—Q B 1; 20. R × R P, etc.

| 19. ...... | Q × B |

Position after Black's 19th move.

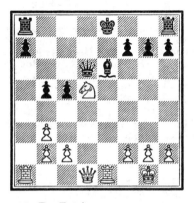

| 20. R—R 6 ! | ...... |

The combination initiated by this move wins more quickly than the prosaic 20. Kt—B 6 ch, K—K 2 ; 21. Q × Q ch, K × Q ; 22. Kt—K 4 ch with a win of a Pawn and a long end game to follow.

| 20. ...... | Q—Q 1 |

Also after 20. ....Q—Q 2 the answer 21. K R × B ch would have won easily : for instance, 21. .... P × R ; 22. R × P ch, K—Q 1 ; 23. R—K 7, Q—Q 3 ; 24. Q—Q 2, P—Q R 4 ; 25. R × Kt P, P—K R 3 ; 26. R—Kt 6 !, Q—Q 2 ; 27. Q— B 4, etc.

| 21. K R × B ch | P × R |
| 22. R × P ch | K—B 2 |

| 23. R—K 7 ch | Q × R |

Or 23. ....K—Kt 1 ; 24. Q—Kt 4 winning immediately.

24. Kt × Q	K × Kt
25. Q—K 2 ch	K—B 2
26. Q—R 5 ch	......

A little finesse : White not only wins a Pawn but also forces the King to remain in the centre.

26.	K—B 3
27. Q × B P	K R—Q 1
28. P—K Kt 4 !	......

Threatening 29. Q—K B 5 ch and thus winning a third Pawn.

Resigns.

GAME 108

KING'S INDIAN DEFENCE

Blindfold exhibition in London, January, 1926.

Black : N. SCHWARTZ

1. P—Q 4	Kt—K B 3
2. P—Q B 4	P—K Kt 3
3. P—K Kt 3	B—Kt 2
4. B—Kt 2	Castles
5. Kt—Q B 3	P—Q 3

If instead 5. ....P—B 3 then 6. P—Q 5.

| 6. Kt—K B 3 | Kt—Q B 3 |
| 7. P—Q 5 | Kt—Q R 4 |

This Knight's position will become the cause of trouble. But 7. ....Kt—Kt 1 is also not satisfactory, as was shown by my games against Sir G. Thomas in Carlsbad, 1923 (*My Best Games of Chess 1908–23*) and against Reti, New York, 1924 (No. 1 in this collection).

| 8. Q—Q 3 | P—Kt 3 |

Intending to bring the Knight as quickly as possible to Q B 4. Slightly better still was first 8. ....P—K 4, as the answer 9. P—Q Kt 4 would not be effective because of 9. .... P—K 5, etc.

9. Kt—Q 4	Kt—Kt 2
10. Kt—Q B 6	Q—Q 2
11. Castles	P—Q R 4
12. P—Kt 3	......

The routine method of dislodging the Knight from Q B 4.

12.	Kt—B 4
13. Q—B 2	B—Kt 2
14. P—K R 3 ..	......

Preventing Black's manœuvre Kt —K Kt 5—K 4.

| 14. ...... | Q R—K 1 |

Neither this move nor the next exchange was advisable. He should instead by 14. ....K Kt—K 5 ; 15. B—Kt 2, Kt × Kt, etc., try to facilitate the defence by eliminating some material.

15. P—R 3	B × Kt
16. P × B	Q—B 1
17. P—Q Kt 4	P × P
18. P × P	Kt—R3

After this the Knight will be buried alive. But also 18. .... QKt—K5 ; 19. Kt—Q Kt 5 ! was anything but pleasant.

| 19. R—R 4 ! | Kt—Q Kt 1 |

Otherwise White would force this retreat by 20. Q—R 2.

20. P—Kt 5	P—R 3
21. R—R 7	P—K 4
22. K—R 2	......

In order not to have to reckon with the answer ....Kt—R 4 in case of P—K B 4.

22.	K—R 2
23. P—K B 4	R—K 2
24. P × P	R × P
25. B—B 4	R (K 4)—K 1

After 25. R—R4 ; 26. Kt—Q 5, Kt × Kt ; 27. P × Kt, the Rook would be finally trapped.

26. Kt—Q 5	Kt × Kt
27. B × Kt	Q—Q 1
28. P—R 4	Q—K 2
29. P—K 3	K—R 1
30. K—Kt 2	......

Preventing 30. ....P—K Kt 4 by the eventual threat (after 31. P × P, P × P) R—K R 1 ch.

30.	P—B 4
31. R—K 1	K—R 2
32. P—K 4	B—K 4
33. P × P	P × P

Position after Black's 33rd move.

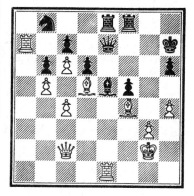

| 34. P—B 5 ! | ...... |

The beginning of a ten-move combination (of which the point is 43. B—K 6 !) forcing the win of a piece.

34.	Kt P × P
35. P—Kt 6	R—B 1
36. Q—B 3 !	K R—K 1

It is obvious enough that 36..... B × Q ; 37. R × Q ch, etc., would be hopeless.

| 37. B × B | P × B |
| 38. Q × K P ! | ...... |

Without this possibility the previous moves would be aimless.

38.	Q × Q
39. R × Q	R × R
40. R × P ch	R × R
41. P × R	R—K 1
42. P × Kt = Q	R × Q
43. B—K 6 !	......

Decisive.

43.	K—Kt 3
44. P—B 7	R—K B 1
45. P—B 8 = Q	R × Q
46. B × R	P—B 5
47. B—R 6	P—B 6
48. B—Q 3	K—B 3
49. K—B 3	K—K 4
50. K—K 3	P—R 4
51. B—B 2	K—B 3
52. K—B 4	K—Kt 2
53. K × P	K—R 3

Still hoping that the " blind " opponent will stalemate him by 54. K—B 5....

| 54. K—B 4 ! | Black resigns |

I consider this game to be one of my best achievements in blindfold chess.

GAME 109

NIMZOWITSCH'S DEFENCE

Second Exhibition Game, Amsterdam, December, 1926.

White : DR. M. EUWE

1. P—Q 4	Kt—K B 3
2. P—Q B 4	P—K 3
3. Kt—Q B 3	B—Kt 5
4. Kt—K B 3	P—Q Kt 3
5. P—K Kt 3	......

In the second exhibition game,

played after our match in 1937, Dr. Euwe played 5. B—K Kt 5, but after the right answer (5. ....P—K R 3 and 6. B × Kt, B × Kt ch ; 7. P × B, Q × B, etc.), had to play very exactly in order to avoid being at a disadvantage. But also the fianchetto development in text is perfectly harmless.

5.	B—Kt 2
6. B—Kt 2	Castles
7. Castles	B × Kt
8. P × B	P—Q 3 (?)

After this, White profits by the fact that Black's Queen's Bishop is unprotected, and forces an advantageous transaction in the centre. Had Black made the right move (8. ....Q—B 1), he would have come out of the opening stage with the rather better prospects.

| 9. P—Q 5 ! | P × P |

Although this Pawn cannot be kept, it is nevertheless better to start an open middle-game fight than to allow, after 9. ....P—K 4, the formation 10. Kt—R 4, followed by P—K 4, P—K B 4, etc. ±

| 10. Kt—R 4 | Kt—K 5 |

After 10. ....P—B 3 ; 11. P × P, Kt × P ; 12. P—Q B 4, Kt—Kt 5 ; 13. P—Q R 3, Kt—R 3 ; 14. B—Kt 2, etc., White would dominate the board.

| 11. P × P | R—K 1 |

If 11. ....Kt × Q B P, then 12. Q—Q 3, Kt—R 5 ; 13. B—K 4 !, P—K R 3 ; 14. Q—Q 4, Kt—B 4 ; 15. Kt—B 5, P—K B 3 ; 16. B—Q B 2, etc., with a decisive positional advantage.

| 12. B—Kt 2 | ...... |

I don't agree here with Dr. Euwe, who in the Dutch booklet devoted to these games rather severely criticises his 12th and 13th moves. In any case, the Pawn sacrifice suggested by him instead of the text-move is anything but convincing ; then after 12. Q—Q 3, Kt—B 4 ; 13. Q—B 2, P—Q Kt 4 ; 14. P—Q B 4, Black would have an adequate defence by continuing 14. ....P×P ; 15. B—Kt 2, Q Kt— Q 2 ; 16. Kt—B 5, Kt—B 3, etc.

12. ......   P—Q Kt 4

As 12. ....Q—B 3 (or—K Kt 4) would be inferior, because of the answer 13. Q—R 4, Black has practically no other way to prevent P—Q B 4.

13. P—Q R 4   ......

A natural and good move. After 13. Q—Q 4, recommended by Dr. Euwe, Black would have the choice between (a) the sacrifice of a Pawn, in order to keep control over White's Q B 4 ; 13. ....P—Q B 4 ; 14. P×P (e.p.), Kt×P; 15. Q—Q 3, Kt—K 4 ; 16. Q×Kt P, Q—Kt 3 ! ; 17. P—Q R 4, B—B 3, etc. (b) the exchange of Queens, which would offer fair defensive possibilities : 13. ....Q—B 3 ; 14. P— B 3, Q×Q ; 15. P×Q, Kt—Q 7 ; 16. R—B 2, Kt—B 5 ; 17. P—K 4, Kt—Q 2, etc.

13. ......   Q—Kt 4 !

Rightly deciding to eliminate White's Pawn at the cost of a further delay in the development of the Queen's side.

14. P×P   Q×Q P
15. Q—R 4 ?   ......

But here White over-estimates his chances. He should, instead, by exchanging Queens, force a favourable end-game which, however, would have been far from

hopeless for Black. For instance, 15. Q×Q, B×Q ; 16. R—R 4 !, Kt—K B 3 ; 17. P—K 3, B×B ; 18. K×B, Q Kt—Q 2 ; 19. K R— R 1, K R—Kt 1 ; 20. P—Q B 4, R— Kt 2 ; 21. B—Q 4, Kt—Kt 3 ; 22. R—Kt 4, K Kt—Q 2 ; 23. Kt—B 5 (at last !), P—K Kt 3 ; 24. Kt—K 7 ch, K—B 1 ; 25. Kt—B 6, Kt—B 4, etc., with sufficient defence. And if 15. P—Q B 4 (instead of 15. Q×Q) Black would not have taken the poisoned Pawn, but would simply have answered 15. ....Q× Q, followed by 16. ....P—Q R 3 ! with an easy defence. After the text-move, which contains only a rather obvious trap, White's advantage instantly vanishes.

15. ......   Kt—Q 2

Of course not 15. ....Q—Q 7 ? because of 16. P—Kt 6, B—B 3 ; 17. P—Kt 7 ! and wins.

16. P—Q B 4   Q—Q 7
17. Q—R 2   ......

Under the circumstances comparatively the best.

17. ......   P—Q R 3 !

Forcing a further simplification. Inferior would be 17. ....Q×K P, because of 18. Kt—B 5, P—K B 3 ; 19. Kt×Kt P !, etc.

18. B—B 1   ......

Ineffective would be the Pawn's sacrifice 18. P — Kt 6, for instance, 18. ....Kt×Q Kt P ; 19. Kt—B 5, Q—Kt 4 ! ; 20. Kt× Kt P, R—K 2 ; 21. B—K R 3, B—B 1, followed by P—K B 3, etc.∓.

18. ......   Q×Q
19. R×Q   P×P
20. R—Kt 2   ......

Slightly better than 20. R×R, B×R ; 21. P×P, Kt—B 6, etc.

| 20. ...... | Q R—Kt 1 |
| 21. P×P ? | ...... |

After this, Black succeeds in emerging from the complications with a Pawn to the good. After 21. B×Kt, R×B ; 22. P×P, B—Q 4 !, etc., he would have remained only with a positional advantage.

| 21. ...... | Kt—B 6 |
| 22. B—B 6 | ...... |

Now the only way to try to keep the balance of the position.

Position after White's 22nd move.

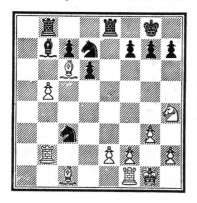

| 22. ...... | R×P ! |

An unpleasant surprise for White, justified by the variation 23. B×Kt, R×R ; 24. B×R, Kt—K 7 mate !

| 23. R—Kt 3 | ...... |

Hardly preferable would be 23. B—Q 2, Kt—R 5 ; 24. R—R 2, Kt (Q 2)—B 4, etc.

23.	B×B
24. R×Kt	B×P
25. R×P	Kt—K 4

Not the most effective way to profit by the material advantage. By 25. ....P—K R 3 !, Black could

prevent both 26. Kt—B 5 (because of 26. ....R—K 4, etc.) and 26. B—B 4 (because of 26. ....P—K Kt 4)—thus leaving White with practically no efficient answer.

| 26. Kt—B 5 ? | ...... |

The complications introduced by this move decidedly end in Black's favour. Necessary was 26. B—B 4 with the possible continuation 26. ....P—K R 3 ; 27. B×Kt, R×B ; 28. R—Kt 1, R (Kt 1)—K 1 ; 29. Kt—B 3, R—Q 4, after which Black should win—but only after a long end-game.

| 26. ...... | Kt—B 6 ch |
| 27. K—Kt 2 | ...... |

Or 27. K—R 1, R—K 4, etc.

| 27. ...... | Kt—K 8 ch ! |
| 28. K—R 3 | R—K 4 |

This would also have been the answer to 28. K—Kt 1.

| 29. R—R 1 | ...... |

He could resist longer—but without any real hope—by giving up the exchange immediately : 29. R×Kt, R×R ; 30. Kt×Q P, etc.

29.	Kt—Q 6
30. Kt—K 7 ch	K—B 1
31. B—R 3	......

The last convulsions !

31.	Kt×P ch
32. K—Kt 2	Kt×R
33. B×P	R—K 3
34. B—B 5	......

Or 34. Kt—B 6 disc. ch, R×B ; 35. Kt×R, R—Q 8, etc.∓.

34.	R—K 1 !
35. Kt—B 5 disc. ch.	K—Kt 1
36. Kt—K 7 ch	......

If 36. Kt—Q 6, then 36. ....B—
Q 6 ! ; 37. K×Kt, R—K 8 ch ; 38.
K—Kt 2, R (K 1)—K 7 ch ; 39. K—
R 3, P—R 3 ; 40. R×B P, R—
Q B 7 ; 41. B—B 2, R—K 3 and
wins.

36.	......	K—R 1
37.	K×Kt	B—Q 6
38.	K—Kt 2	P—R 3
39.	K—B 3	K—R 2
40.	P—R 4	P—R 4

Resigns.

GAME 110

KING'S INDIAN DEFENCE

Third Exhibition Game, played
in Amsterdam, December, 1926.

Black : Dr. M. Euwe

1.	P—Q 4	Kt—K B 3
2.	P—Q B 4	P—K Kt 3
3.	Kt—Q B 3	B—Kt 2

At the period when this game was
played the Gruenfeld variation was
somewhat out of fashion. Nowadays
thanks to Botwinnink, Flohr, Keres
and other masters of the younger
generation it is played more often,
although without any remarkable
success.

| 4. | P—K 4 | Castles |
| 5. | B—K 3 | ...... |

If 5. P—B 4, P—Q 3 ; 6. Kt—
B 3—then 6. ....P—B 4 ! with a
good game for Black.

5.	......	P—Q 3
6.	P—B 3	P—K 4
7.	P—Q 5	......

Better is 7. K Kt—K 2, and only
after 7. ....Kt—Q B 3 (or 7. ....
B—K 3) ; 8. P—Q 5 winning tempi.
Black would in that case have
to face unpleasant development
problems.

7.	......	P—B 3
8.	Q—Q 2	P×P
9.	B P×P	Kt—K 1

Preparing the counter attack
....P—K B 4 and preventing at
the same time White's attempt to
open the K R's file (10. P—K R 4,
P—K B 4 ; 11. P—R 5, P—B 5
followed by ....P—K Kt 4, etc.).

| 10. | Castles | P—B 4 |
| 11. | K—Kt 1 | ...... |

It is obvious enough that the
King must be removed as soon as
possible from the open file.

| 11. | ...... | Kt—Q 2 (?) |

Giving White the welcome opportunity to create—without taking
many chances—interesting complications by temporarily sacrificing
some material. By continuing 11.
....P—Q R 3 ; 12. B—Q 3, P—
Q Kt 4 ; 13. K Kt—K 2, P—B 5 ;
14. B—K B 2, Kt—Q 2 followed
by ....Kt—Kt 3 Black would have
obtained a perfectly satisfactory
position.

| 12. | Kt—R 3 ! | ...... |

In order to answer both 12.
....Q Kt—B 3 or 12. ....Kt—Kt 3
by 13. Kt—K Kt 5; for instance 12.
....Kt—Kt 3 ; 13. Kt—K Kt 5, P
—B 5 ; 14. B×Kt, Q×Kt; 15. B
—B 2, B—Q 2 ; 16. R—B 1,
Kt—B 2 ; 17. P—K Kt 4 ! or 16.
....P—Q R 3 ; 17. B—Kt 6 etc.,
with excellent prospects on account
of the open Q B's file.

| 12. | ...... | P—Q R 3 |

Also if Black had prevented the
following manœuvre by 12. ....
P—B 5, White's prospects would
have remained decidedly the more
favourable.

| 13. | P×P | P×P |

14. P—K Kt 4 ! ......

The point of his 12th move, by which he obtains the most important square K 4 for his pieces.

14. ......   **P × P**

Comparatively better than 14. ....P—B 5 ; 15. B—K B 2, etc., without any counter-chances for Black.

15. Kt—Kt 5   Q Kt—B 3
16. B—Q 3   Q—K 2

In case of 16. ....P × P I should have continued the attack by 17. Q R—K B 1 ! and if 17. ....P—K R 3 then 18. Kt—K 6, B × Kt ; 19. P × B, Kt—Kt 5 ; 20. Kt—Q 5 with enough threats to frighten an elephant to death.

17. P—K B 4 ......

Both 17. Q R—K B 1 and 17. K R —K Kt 1 were also considered. But the prospects connected with the move selected (the eventual opening of the K B file or P—K B 5 followed by Kt—K 6) were extremely tempting.

17. ......   **P—K 5**

By this counter sacrifice Dr. Euwe secures the diagonal K R 1—Q R 8 for his Bishop, and at the same time diminishes the danger threatening his King by forcing the exchange of a couple of minor pieces. Still, even so, White's chances after recapturing the sacrificed Pawn remain the better ones.

18. Kt (Kt 5) × K P ......

But this is not the most energetic method. The Pawn should have been taken by the other Knight, and if in that case 18. ....Kt × Kt ; 19. B × Kt, P—K R 3, then 20. Kt—K 6± ; or 18. ....P—K R 3 ;

19. Kt—K 6, B × Kt ; 20. P × B, Q × P ; 21. Kt—Kt 3 threatening 22. P—K B 5, etc. Black would hardly have found a way to protect his numerous weaknesses sufficiently.

18. ......   **Kt × Kt**
19. Kt × Kt ......

Now forced as 19. B × Kt ? does not go because of 19. ....B × Kt.

19. ......   **B—B 4**
20. Kt—Kt3 ......

Blockading the K Kt's Pawn in order to play P—K R 3 at the first opportunity. After 20. Kt—Kt 5, Black would protect his K 3 by means of ....Kt—B 2.

20. ......   **B × B ch**
21. Q × B   Q—B 3

A refined tactical manœuvre, very much in Dr. Euwe's style ; he provokes White's R—Q 2 in order to deprive (after P—K R 3, P × P, R × P) the first rank of its natural protection. But by correct replies all this refinement would prove useless.

22. R—Q 2   Q—B 2

Because of the threat 23. Kt— R 5.

23. P—K R 3   P × P
24. R × P   Q—Kt 3
25. P—B 5 (?) ......

Only after this second inaccuracy does Black suddenly get a kind of counter-attack. Very strong here was 25. Kt—K 4 ! and in case of 25. ....Kt—K B 3 simply 26. Kt × P, Q R—Q 1 ; 27. B—B 5 etc.; and other replies would allow White to strengthen his position further by means of R—Kt 3 or R (Q 2)— R 2, etc.

25. ......   **Q—Kt 5**

26. Q R—R 2   R—B 1 !

In case of 26. ....Kt—B 3 (which seemingly protects everything) White would play 27. B—B 1! with the strong threat 28. R—R 4. The occupation of the Q B's file gives Black some new opportunities.

Position after Black's 26th move.

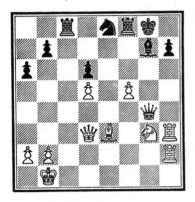

27.   P—B 6 !   ......

The main idea of this transaction is shown by the following variation : 27. .... Kt × P; 28. Kt—B 5, Q—Q B 5 ! ; 29. Kt—K 7 ch, K—B 2 ; 30. Q—B 5 !, K × Kt ; 31. Q—K 6 ch, K—Q 1 ; 32. B—Kt 6 ch, R—B 2 ; 33. R—Q B 3, Q—B 8 ch ; 34. K—B 2 and wins.

27.	R × P !
28. Q × P ch	K—B 1
29. R—R 1	......

This rather sad necessity is the direct consequence of Black's fine 21st move. But in spite of this partial success the position of the second player is still full of danger. If, for instance, 29. .... Q—Q Kt 5, then simply 30. P—Q R 3 and 30. ....R—B 8 ch ? would be refuted by 31. R × R ch. And 29. .... R—B 6 is also not satisfactory because of 30. B—R 6 ! (R × Kt ? ; 31. R × R, Q × R ; 32. Q—B 5 ch, etc.).

Consequently, Black decides to simplify matters.

29. ......   Q—Kt 3 ch

It would have been slightly better to delay this exchange by playing first 29. ....R—Q B 2, in which case White, by continuing 30. Kt—R 5 !, Q—B 4 ch ; 31. Q × Q, R × Q ; 32. Kt—B 4, etc., would maintain a strong pressure. After the text move he has a direct win.

30. Q × Q	R × Q
31. Kt—B 5 !	......

Simply threatening 32. Kt × B, etc. If now 31. ....R—Q B 2 then 32. B—Q 4 !, B × B ; 33. Kt × B and Black is without resource.

31.	B—K 4
32. R—B 3 !	Kt—B 3

Or 32. ....R—K B 3 ; 33. B—Kt 5, R—B 2 ; 34. B—K 7 ch !, R × B ; 35. Kt × Q P disc. ch and wins.

33. R—R 8 ch	R—Kt 1
34. R × R ch	K × R
35. Kt—K 7 ch	Resigns.

GAME 111

QUEEN'S INDIAN DEFENCE

Exhibition Game, New York, June, 1929.

White : F. J. MARSHALL

1. P—Q 4	Kt—K B 3
2. P—Q B 4	P—K 3
3. Kt—K B 3	B—Kt 5 ch
4. B—Q 2	Q—K 2
5. P—K 3	......

White can here obtain control on K 4 by playing 5. Q—B 2, but in that case Black would select another system : 5. ....B × B ch ; 6. Q Kt ×

B, P—Q 3 followed by . . . . P—K 4, etc.

5.	. . . . . .	P—Q Kt 3
6.	B—Q 3	B—Kt 2
7.	Q—B 2	B × B ch

In order to advance a Pawn to the centre and thus indirectly prevent White's P—K 4.

| 8. | Q Kt × B | P—B 4 |

If now 9. P—K 4, then 9. . . . . Kt—B 3∓.

9.	Castles (K R)	Kt—B 3
10.	P—Q R 3	Castles (K R)
11.	Q R—Q 1	P—Kt 3

Preventing P—Q 5, which, especially after White's last Rook move, could eventually be disagreeable.

| 12. | K R—K 1 | . . . . . . |

A refined preparation to Kt—K 4, which at this moment would not be satisfactory because of 12. . . . . Kt × Kt ; 13. B × Kt, P—Q 4 ! ; 14. P × Q P, K P × P ; 15. B × Q P, Kt × P, etc.∓

| 12. | . . . . . . | Q R—B 1 |
| 13. | Kt—K 4 | K R—Q 1 |

Technically simpler was 13. . . . . K R—K 1, since after 14. P—Q 5, P × P White himself would have been obliged to change Knights. But the move selected is at least good enough to maintain the balance of position.

| 14. | P—Q 5 | . . . . . . |

Very bold—and quite in Marshall's style : he cedes Black the Pawn majority on the Q side without getting real compensation elsewhere, since his pieces are not sufficiently co-ordinated to support an effective action in the centre. One must admit, however, that

White's position, *owing to the elasticity of Black's pawn-structure (compare the game with Miss Menchik, No. 50)*, was already slightly inferior. Black threatened—after some further preparation, such as . . . . P—Q 3—to start an action on the Q B-file by means of . . . . P × P followed by . . . . Kt—Q R 4.

| 14. | . . . . . . | P × P |
| 15. | P × P ! | Kt × Kt |

15. . . . . Kt × P would have sad consequences, e.g., 16. B—B 4, K Kt—Kt 5 ; 17. Q—B 3 !, Q × Kt ; 18. B × P ch, K—B 1 ; 19. P × Kt, etc.±

| 16. | B × Kt | Kt—R 4 |

Of course not . . . . Kt—K 4 because of 17. P—Q 6, etc.

| 17. | Kt—Q 2 | . . . . . . |

Black threatened 17. . . . . P—B 4.

| 17. | . . . . . . | P—B 5 ! |

Profiting by the fact that P—Q 6 is still not good. It becomes obvious that the transaction initiated by White's 14th move was rather favourable to his opponent.

| 18. | B—B 3 | Q—K 4 |

Threatening 19. . . . . P—B 6, etc.

| 19. | Kt—K 4 | P—Q 3 |

Black could also prevent the following Rook move by playing 19. . . . . Kt—Kt 6 after which White would have hardly anything better than 20. Q—B 3 ; but he did not think this was necessary since, owing to his advantage in space, the middle - game complications should normally end to his advantage.

| 20. | R—Q 4 | . . . . . . |

It would not be like Marshall to exchange Queens by 20. Q—B 3 in order to obtain a distinctly inferior end-game. Looking at this Rook one cannot believe that, in the prime of its existence, it intends to commit suicide soon — and yet it is so !

20. ......   P—Q Kt 4

Now threatening 21. ....Kt—Kt 6.

21. Kt—Q 2   B—R 3

In order to leave a square for the Knight in case of Q—B 3.

22. R—K 4   Q—Kt 2
23. R—K 7   ......

The road to death.

23. ......   Kt—Kt 2 !
24. Kt—K 4   ......

Probably a difficult decision—but under the circumstances the wisest course, for the alternative 24. B—Kt 4, R—B 4 ! (not .... P—B 6 ; 25. B × R, P × Kt ; 26. R—Q 1 ±) ; 25. P—K 4, Q—B 3 ; 26. R—Q 7, R × R ; 27. B × R, Q—K 2 (threatening also R × P) ; 28. B—B 6, Kt—R 4, etc., would lead to material losses without any hope of a counter-attack.

24. ......   K—B 1 !

A mistake would be 24. ....Q—B 1 ; 25. Kt—B 6 ch, K—Kt 2 because of 26. Q—B 3, etc.—to White's advantage.

25. R × Kt   B × R
26. R—Q 1   ......

Although Black is now a clear exchange ahead and his Queen's side majority is as threatening as ever, the winning problem is by no means as easy or as rapid to solve

as one would imagine. White is in a position—in case of 26. ....Q—K 4, for instance—to build a good defensive position with possibilities of a Pawn counter-attack on the King's side by means of 27. Kt—B 3, P—Q R 3 ; 28. R—Q 4, etc. Still, by that line Black with further circumspection and patience would most likely have increased his advantage in a decisive way, without having to suffer from the melodramatic complications arising from his next risky move.

26. ......   P—Q R 4 ?

Preventing 27. Kt—B 3 (because of 27. ....P—Kt 5) and looking for a quick victory. From now on, Marshall takes advantage of the hidden possibilities of his position in a really remarkable fashion, reminding one of his most glorious performances.

27. B—Kt 4 !   R—B 2

Of course not 27. ....P—K B 4 because of 28. Kt—Kt 5, but also not, for instance, 27. ....R—R 1, because of 28. P—Q R 4 ! etc.

28. Q—Q 2 !   ......

After this the situation begins to look even dangerous for Black, since the Q R P cannot be defended in a direct way.

28. ......   P—R 3 !

This is the temporary salvation, for by preventing Kt—Kt 5 Black threatens 29. ....P—B 4.

29. B—B 3   Q R—B 1

And after this 30. Q × R P can be simply answered by 30. ....Q × Kt P.

30. P—K R 4 !   ......

A new attacking idea, which Black tries to meet in an equally energetic way.

30. ......   Q—K 4

If instead, 30. ....P—K B 4, then 31. Kt—B 3, P—Kt 5 ; 32. P×P, P×P ; 33. Kt—K 2, P—B 6 ; 34. P×P, P×P ; 35. Q—B 2 followed by the promising Knight's manœuvre Q 4 (or B 4)—K 6.

31. P—R 5 !   P×P

Also after 31. ....P—Kt 4 ; 32. P—Kt 4 followed by Kt—Kt 3— B 5 or B—Kt 2 and P—B 4, Black's defence would remain difficult.

32. Kt—Kt 3   P—B 6
33. P×P   Q×B P

If 33. ....R×P, the answer would be 34. P—K 4 !

34. Q—K 2   P—Kt 5
35. P×P   P×P

At last Black has succeeded in obtaining the "winning" passed Pawn, but in the meantime the white forces have been concentrating against the hostile King, which can be defended only by the Queen, the other black pieces being, for the time, simply onlookers.

36. B—K 4 !   ......

Covering the diagonal Kt 1—R 7 and opening prospects to the Queen. In this second half of the game Marshall finds always the best moves, and it is a bit of hard luck that Black's resources prove in the end sufficient to meet his furious assault.

36. ......   Q—K 4 !

Hereafter begins a very difficult Queen's manœuvre whose object is to provoke white Pawn moves so as to enable at least one Rook to participate in a counter-attack.

37. P—B 4   Q—B 3

Otherwise White plays 38. Q×P with *tempo*.

38. Kt×P   Q—R 5 !

And not 38. ....Q—K 2 ; 39. Q—Kt 2 !, Q×B ; 40. Q—R 8 ch, K—K 2 ; 41. Q—B 6 ch, K—K 1 ; 42. Q—R 8 ch, K—Q 2 ; 43. Kt— B 6 ch, followed by 44. Q×R ch and Kt×Q.

39. P—Kt 3   ......

The weakening of the second rank will finally prove fatal—but if 39. B—B 3, the answer 39. ....Q—K 2 would now offer sufficient defence, since 40. Q—Kt 2 is met by 40. ....Q×K P ch.

39. ......   Q—R 6. !

Possible and good because 40. B—Kt 2 can be met by 40. .... B—R 3 !

40. B—B 3 !   ......

Position after White's 40th move.

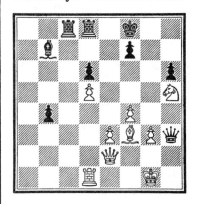

40. ......   R—B 6 !

An unexpected defence against White's two main threats—41. B—Kt 4 and 41. Q—Q Kt 2—and one that involves, in the first case, an eventual sacrifice of two exchanges : to 41. B—Kt 4 Black would reply 41. ....R×K P ! ; 42. Q×R, Q×B ; 43. R—K 1, Q×Kt ! ; 44. Q—K 7 ch, K—Kt 2 ; 45. Q×R (or 45. Q×B, Q—B 6 with a winning position) Q×Q P and wins. With his next move the then American Champion plays out a new trump, which, however, will this time prove the last.

41. Q—Q 2 !   ......

How now to meet the threat 42. Q—Q 4 without losing the passed Pawn ? My lucky star—or Marshall's unlucky one—helped me to find the right answer—but it took no less than half an hour.

41. ......   R—K 1 !

The value of this sealed rejoinder is well illustrated by comparing its consequences with the possible results of another plausible move. 41. ....B—R 3 ; 42. Q—Q 4, R—B 7 ! ; 43. Q—R 8 ch, K—K 2 ; 44. Q—B 6 ch, K—Q 2 ; (....K—K 1 ; 45. Kt—Kt 7 ch, etc.) 45. Q×B P ch, K—B 1 ; 46. Q—K 6 *ch*, Q×Q ; 47. P×Q, P—Kt 6 ; 48. B—K 4 and, to say the least, White would not lose.

42. Q—Q 4   ......

Instead 42. Q—Kt 2 would not help either, because of 42. ....B—R 3, etc.

42. ......   R—B 7
43. R—Q 2   ......

Simplification is nearly always sad for the materially weaker party, but there was no choice, as is shown by the variation 43. Q—R 8 ch, K—K 2 ; 44. Q—B 6 ch, K—Q 2 ; 45. B—Kt 4 ch !, Q×B ; 46. Q×B P ch, K—Q 1 ; 47. Q×R ch, K×Q ; 48. Kt—B 6 ch, K—K 2 ; 49. Kt×Q, P—Q Kt 6 and wins.

43. ......   R×R
44. Q×R   B—R 3 !
45. Q—K 1   ......

Practically resignation. Almost an hour's reflection persuaded Marshall that the intended 45. Q×P leads to a forced loss as follows : 45. ....Q—B 8 ch ; 46. K—R 2, Q—B 7 ch ! (but not 46. ....Q×B ; 47. Q×P ch, K—Kt 1 ; 48. Kt—B 6 ch, K—R 1 ; 49. Q×B ! and Black would not win) ; 47. K—R 3 (or B—Kt 2, B—B 8 ; 48. Q×P ch, K—Kt 1 ; 49. Kt—B 6 ch, K—R 1 and wins), B—B 1 ch ; 48. B—Kt 4, B×B ; 49. K×B, Q—K 7 ch ; 50. K—R 4, Q—R 7 ch ; 51. K—Kt 4, P—B 4 ch ! and wins.

45. ......   P—Kt 6

The passed Pawn's holiday !

46. B—Q 1   P—Kt 7
47. Q—Kt 4   ......

Leads to a similar final to the one indicated.

47. ......   Q—B 8 ch
48. K—R 2   Q—B 7 ch
49. K—R 3   B—B 1 ch
50. P—B 5   B×P ch
51. B—Kt 4   B×B
52. K×B   Q—K 7 ch
53. K—R 4   Q—R 7 ch
54. K—Kt 4   P—B 4 ch
Resigns.

In this kind of game the loser certainly deserves as much credit as the winner.

GAME 112

RETI'S OPENING

Simultaneous Exhibition of Consultation Games, New York, March, 1929.

White :
A. KEVITZ and A. PINKUS*

| 1. Kt—K B 3 | Kt—K B 3 |
| 2. P—B 4 | P—Q Kt 3 |

One of the different ways of meeting adequately White's opening play. Black intends herewith to transform the game into a typical Queen's Indian Defence.

| 3. P—K Kt 3 | B—Kt 2 |
| 4. B—Kt 2 | ..... |

Allowing Black to choose a more aggressive form of development. Instead, 4. P—Q 4, P—K 3 ; 5. B—Kt 2, etc., would lead to well-known variations.

| 4. ..... | P—K 4 |

This move has its advantages and defects, for the centre-pawn may become exposed. Still, the experiment was worth trying since not much risk is attached to it.

| 5. Kt—B 3 | B—Kt 5 |
| 6. Castles | ..... |

Decidedly too optimistic, for the doubled Pawn on the Q B-file is much more often a serious fault in the position than is generally believed and in this particular case will by no means be compensated by the pair of Bishops. Natural and good enough was 6. Q—Kt 3.

| 6. ..... | B × Kt ! |
| 7. Kt P × B | ..... |

On the same occasion the following short game was played, which shows in a drastic way the effects of exaggerated voracity in Chess : Black : I. Kashdan and H. Steiner. 1. P—Q 4, P—Q 4 ; 2. P—Q B 4, P—K 3 ; 3. Kt—Q B 3, P—Q B 3 ; 4. Kt—B 3, P × P ; 5. P—Q R 4, B—Kt 5 ; 6. P—K 3, P—Q Kt 4 ; 7. B—Q 2, Q—Kt 3 ; 8. Kt—K 5, Kt—Q 2 ; 9. P × P, Kt × Kt ; 10. P × Kt, P × P ; 11. Kt—K 4, B—K 2 ; 12. Q—Kt 4, K—B 1 ; 13. Q—B 4, P—Q R 4 ; 14. B—K 2, B—Kt 2 ; 15. Castles, P—R 4 ; 16. Kt—Kt 5, B × Kt ; 17. Q × B, R—K R 3 ; 18. P—K 4 !, P—K R 5 ; 19. R × P !, P—B 3 ; 20. P × P, Kt × P ; 21. Q × Q Kt P !, Resigns.

Even less satisfactory was 7. Q P × B. P—Q 3, etc.

| 7. ..... | P—Q 3 |

The black pawn-skeleton being on dark-coloured squares, there was obviously no need for Black to keep the King's Bishop.

| 8. P—Q 4 | P—K 5 |

Correctly calculating that the K B-file that White will be able to open now will not compensate for a new weakness thus created on the K-file.

| 9. Kt—R 4 | Castles |
| 10. P—B 3 | P × P |

Black is already in the pleasant position of being able to proceed in the simplest manner. White's trouble now is that he cannot well retake with the Pawn because of 11. ....B—R 3 ! ; 12. P—K B 4, P—B 3 followed by ....P—Q 4 with some material win. And after his next move the King's Pawn remains extremely feeble.

11. B × P	Kt—K 5
12. Q—Q 3	R—K 1
13. P—Q 5	.....

The counter-attack now starting will be very short-lived. But if White had decided to restrict the action of the black Bishop on the long diagonal, he had to do it now, since, after ....Kt—Q 2, Black obviously would not be obliged to cede square K 5.

13.	Kt—B 4
14. Q—Q 4	Q Kt—Q 2
15. B—R 5	.....

White hopes to provoke by one of the following moves the answer ....P—K Kt 3 which would eventually procure him some real chances on the K B-file ; but Black resists all temptations and quietly prepares a complete blockade.

15. ......   Kt—K 4
16. B—K B 4   Q—Q 2 !

If instead 16. ....P—Kt 3, then 17. B—B 3, P—K Kt 4 ; 18. B × Kt, P × B ; 19. Q—Kt 4, P—K R 4 ; 20. Q × R P, P × Kt ; 21. B—K 4 !, Kt × B ; 22. Q × B P ch, K—R 1 ; 23. Q—R 5 ch, K—Kt 1 ; 24. R—B 7 and White wins !

17. Kt—B 3   Kt—Kt 3
18. Kt—Q 2   Q—R 6 !
19. B × Kt   ......

The attempt to catch the aggressive Queen—19. B—R 6, P × B ; 20. B—Kt 4—would fail lamentably because of the simple 19. ....R—K 4 !

19. ......   R P × B
20. P—K 4 ·   ......

The Pawn is weaker here—if possible—than on K 2, but White had already a difficult choice.

20. ......   P—K B 3

Fixing for ever the K P and—by bringing the last Pawns on dark squares—increasing the potential range of his Bishop.

21. Q R—K 1   P—K Kt 4
22. B—K 3   R—K 2
23. K—R 1   Q R—K 1
24. B—Kt 1   B—B 1

Of course, premature would be 24. ....Kt × P ; 25. Kt × Kt, R × Kt ; 26. R × R, R × R ; 27. Q × R, Q × R ; 28. Q—K 8 ch, etc., with perpetual check. Besides, Black does not need to hurry with the liquidation at K 5 at all—*since the position must bring much more than a Pawn in the course of time.*

25. R—B 3   B—Kt 5

26. K R—K 3   ......

White has now weaknesses everywhere : (a) On the Queen's side—the doubled Pawn ; (b) in the middle—the backward King's Pawn ; (c) on the King's side—the weak light-coloured squares. As a direct consequence of this sad situation almost all White's pieces are stalemated and he has practically nothing better than to move his Bishop to and fro. No wonder that Black, instead of adopting the most evident plan—an attack with *five* pieces against the King's Pawn by means of ....Q—R 2 followed by ....B—R 4—Kt 3, which would finally force an end-game with an extra Pawn—prefers to prepare a decisive Pawn advance in the centre. The preliminary manœuvre takes, true enough, fifteen more moves, but the success of the scheme gives the game an artistic touch it would otherwise lack.

26. ......   Q—R 4

Before undertaking the long King's voyage, Black reverses the places of his Queen and Bishops in order to "observe" the central weak spot with one more piece.

27. K—Kt 2   B—R 6 ch
28. K—R 1   Q—Kt 5
29. B—B 2   P—Q R 4
30. B—Kt 1   P—Q R 5

It may be of use to prevent eventually Kt—Kt 3.

31. B—B 2   R—K 4
32. B—Kt 1   R (K 1)—K 2
33. B—B 2   K—B 2

Now it is time to bring the King to his safest spot on the board—Q R 3 !

34. B—Kt 1   K—K 1
35. B—B 2   K—Q 1
36. B—Kt 1   K—B 1

37. B—B 2	K—Kt 2
38. B—Kt 1	K—R 3
39. B—B 2	Q—R 4

The final preparations : the decisive combination demands the previous configuration of Queen and Bishop !

40. B—Kt 1	B—Kt 5
41. K—Kt 2	Q—R 6 ch
42. K—R 1	P—Kt 3

At last disclosing the winning idea.

43. B—B 2	......

Position after White's 43rd move.

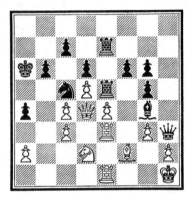

43.	P—B 4 !

The battle must be decided not by the win of a Pawn, but by direct threats against the King. If, after 44. P × P, P × P ; again 45. B—Kt 1, then 45. ....Kt—K 5 ; 46. Kt × Kt, R × Kt inevitably followed by B—B 6 ch and wins.

44. P × P	P × P
45. R × R	P × R
46. Q—K 3	......

The main variation calculated by White was 46. R × P, R × R ; 47. Q × R, B—B 6 ch ! ; 48. Kt × B, Q—B 8 ch ; 49. Kt—Kt 1, Kt—

Q 6 ! and wins. This possibility clearly proves the usefulness of the King's trip as far as Q R 8.

46.	P—K 5
47. P—Q 6 !	......

Not merely in order to make a move, but with a very definite purpose.

47.	P × P
48. B—Kt 1	......

Which is seen in the following case : 48. ....B—B 6 ch ; 49. Kt × B, P × Kt ; 50. Q × B P !, R × R ; 51. Q—R 8 mate ! But Black has at his disposal a powerful intermediate move.

48.	P—B 5 !

If now 49. P × P, then ....B—B 6 ch, etc., wins immediately.

Resigns.

GAME 113

QUEEN'S INDIAN DEFENCE

Consultation Game, Nice, May, 1931.

White: DR. ALEKHINE and Amateur

Black: G. STOLTZ and Amateur

1. P—Q 4	Kt—K B 3
2. P—Q B 4	P—K 3
3. Kt—K B 3	P—Q Kt 3
4. P—K Kt 3	B—Kt 2
5. B—Kt 2	B—K 2
6. Castles	Castles
7. P—Kt 3	......

Leading to more complicated— or at least less explored—positions than the usual 7. Kt—B 3, which, however, is also rather in White's favour, for instance : 7. ....Kt— K 5 ; 8. Q—B 2, Kt × Kt ; 9. Q × Kt,

P—Q B 4 ; 10. B—K 3, and in the case of further exchanges Black should always remain with some weak spots in the centre.

7. ......   Q—B 1

Against Dr. Euwe (23rd Match-game, 1937), I played here 7. .... P—Q 4 ; 8. Kt—K 5, P—B 4—and obtained a fighting game full of possibilities for both sides. Black's idea of exchanging only one Pawn in the centre gives White time to take advantage of the open Q B file without allowing any counter-play.

8. Kt—B 3   P—Q 4
9. P×P !   ......

At the right moment, since if 9. ....P×P the Q B can be developed with profit at K B 4.

9. ......   Kt×P
10. B—Kt 2   P—Q B 4

Positionally unavoidable — but from now on the Black Queen will "feel" (as the modern annotators say) uncomfortable *vis-a-vis* the White Rook.

11. R—B 1   ......

Threatening eventually Kt—Q R 4.

11. ......   Kt×Kt
12. B×Kt   R—Q 1

White intended 13. P×P, P×P ; leaving a weakling on the half-open file. The text-move parries this possibility, but only temporarily, and would therefore have been better replaced by 12. ....Q—Q 1.

13. Q—Q 2 !   ......

With the object, in case of 13. ....Kt—Q 2, for instance, of placing the Queen on the comfortable spot Q Kt 2 ; but Black's following

attempt to secure for his Queen the corresponding square brought me other, more aggressive ideas.

13. ......   B—Q 4
14. Q—B 4   Q—Kt 2 ?

In some way consistent—but neglect of development on the Q-side will now prove immediately fatal. After 14. ....Kt—Q 2 ; 15. P—K 4, B—Kt 2 ; 16. P—Q 5 !, P×P ; 17. P×P, B—K B 3 (not 17. ....B×P ; 18. Kt—Kt 5 winning) he would have suffered a deal longer, but would have died just the same.

15. P×P   P×P

If 15. ....B×B P, then 16. B×P ! etc.

16. P—K 4 !   B—Q B 3

Or 16. ....B×K P ; 17. Kt—Kt 5, winning.

17. Kt—K 5   B—K 1

Position after Black's 17th move.

18. Kt—Kt 4 !   ......

The peculiarity of this sudden King's attack rests in the fact that it is not facilitated by any weakening pawn-move by Black on that section of the board.

18. ......   Kt—R 3

There was hopelessly little choice left, since the "natural" answer 18. ....Kt—B 3, would have led to a disaster very like the one which actually did happen:19.B × P!,K × B; 20. Q—R 6 ch, K—Kt 1 (or .... K—R 1 ; 21. Kt—B 6 and mate on the next move) ; 21. P—K 5, P— B 3 ; 22. B—K 4 !, P—B 4 ; 23. Q × K P ch, followed by Q × P, etc., winning ; and 18. ....B—Q B 3 would allow 19. B × P, K × B ; 20. Q—R 6 ch, K—Kt 1 ; 21. R × P ! etc.

19. B × P !   Black resigns.

The principal variation is now 19. ....K × B ; 20. Q—R 6 ch, K— Kt 1 ; 21. P—K 5, B—Q B 3 ; 22. Kt—B 6 ch, B × Kt ; 23. P × B, followed by mate.

GAME 114

NIMZOWITSCH'S DEFENCE

Consultation Game, Nice, April, 1931.

White:	Black :
DR. ALEKHINE	S. FLOHR
and Amateur	and Amateur

1. P—Q 4	Kt—K B 3
2. P—Q B 4	P—K 3
3. Kt—Q B 3	B—Kt 5
4. P—Q R 3	......

Nowadays this move of Sämisch is completely out of fashion—not only because it loses a *tempo* in order to force an exchange not too unwelcome for Black, but chiefly because it occupies square Q R 3, which otherwise might be useful for the Q B.

4.	B × Kt ch
5. P × B	P—B 4

6. Q—B 2   ......

To prevent an eventual ....Kt— K 5. Black could now, by playing 6. ....P—Q 4 ; 7. P × Q P, Q × P, obtain a position known from my recent title-match as satisfactory for him ; but his text-move also does not spoil anything.

6.	Kt—B 3
7. Kt—B 3	P—Q 4
8. P—K 3	Castles
9. P × Q P	K P × P

But here he misjudges the character of the position: as the following clearly shows, the isolation of the Q P is too big a price for the Bishop's diagonal Q B 1—K R 6. By retaking with the Queen, he would obtain after 10. P—B 4, Q—Q 3 ; 11. B—Kt 2, the position of my 10th game against Euwe (Hague, Oct., 1937) which some theorists (for instance, Fine) consider even advantageous for the second player. Without going so far, one must admit that this line would afford a fighting game, with possibilities for both sides.

10. P × P !   ......

Ending any possible Black hopes of blocking with an eventual .... P—B 5.

10.	Q—R 4
11. B—Q 3	Kt—K 5

After this unnecessary effort (since White's Pawn at Q B 3 in fact cannot be taken), Black's position already becomes critical. Also 11. ....B—Kt 5 would not have sufficed to re-establish the balance, since White would permit the exchange of his Knight and simply answer 12. R—Q Kt 1 or 12. P—Q R 4 ; but 11. ....Q × B P (B 4) could and should be played.

12. Castles   ......

Of course the right move, since Black cannot play either 12. ....

Q×P (B 6), because of 13. B×Kt,
or 12. ....Kt×P (B 6), because of
13. B—Q 2.

| 12. ...... | Q×P (B 4) |
| 13. P—Q R 4 ! | ...... |

At last White has the opportunity
to correct his 4th move, and thus
eliminates the only serious defect
of his position.

13.	R—K 1
14. B—R 3	Q—R 4
15. Q R—Kt 1 !	......

If now 15. ....P—Q R 3, then 16.
P—B 4, Kt—B 3 ; 17. Kt—Kt 5
(threatening mate in two), P—
K Kt 3 ; 18. P×P, Q×Q P ; 19.
P—B 4 ! threatening B—B 4, etc.,
with a winning attack. Black's next
step must therefore be considered
a desperate attempt to alter the
normal course of the battle.

15.	Q×B P
16. B×Kt	Q×B
17. B×P ch	K—R 1

It is certainly surprising that this
move, which looks more natural
than ....K—B 1, loses rapidly
perforce, while after the better move
White would have satisfied himself
with a (very palpable, it is true)
positional advantage by playing 18.
B—B 5, etc.

Position after Black's 17th move.

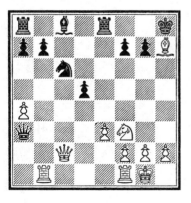

18. Kt—Kt 5 ! ....

As in the previous game against
Stoltz, the mating attack com-
mences quite spontaneously and
succeeds in a very few moves.
Flohr at the beginning of his career
was sometimes superficial in the
defence of his King's position—
compare, for instance, his well-
known defeat by Mikenas at
Folkestone. But, certainly, he has
now become one of the most cautious (if not *the* most) masters
living !

18. ......   P—K Kt 3

The consequences of this were as
easy to calculate as 18. ....R—B 1
(19. B—Kt 8 !) or 18. ....Kt—Q 1
(19. B—B 5 !). The only more or
less complicated variation is after
18. ....Q—K 2 ! which would have
led to the following finish : 19. P—
B 4 !, P—B 3 ; 20. B—Kt 8, P—
K Kt 3 ; 21. Q×P, P×Kt ; 22.
B—B 7, B—B 4 ! ; 23. Q—R 6 ch,
B—R 2 ; 24. R×P !, Q—B 1 ; 25.
Q—B 6 ch, Q—Kt 2 ; 26. Q×Q ch,
K×Q ; 27. B×R dis. ch followed
by 28. B×Kt and wins.

| 19. B×P | ...... |

Of course !

19.	P×B
20. Q×P	R—K 2
21. P—K 4 !	......

A pretty *coup de grace.* If now
21. ....P—Q 5 (there is nothing
else), then 22. R—Kt 5, B—Kt 5
(again the only move) ; 23. Q—B 6
ch, R—Kt 2 (or K—Kt 1 ; 24. Kt—
K 6 !) ; 24. R×P, Q—B 1 ; 25. R—
K B 7, etc., wins.

Resigns.

GAME 115

FRENCH DEFENCE

Simultaneous exhibition in Reyk-
javik, August, 1931.

Black : A. Asgeirsson

1.	P—K 4	P—K 3
2.	P—Q 4	P—Q 4
3.	Kt—Q B 3	Kt—K B 3
4.	B—Kt 5	B—K 2
5.	B × Kt	......

This variation has recently been favoured by the talented German master, K. Richter—but only in conjunction with 6. P—K 5 followed by 7. Q—Kt 4. The idea here was quite a different one—to maintain the tension in the centre as long as possible, finishing first the mobilisation of forces.

5.	......	B × B
6.	Kt—B 3	Castles
7.	B—Q 3	R—K 1

A loss of time; instead, 7. .... P—Q B 4 was indicated. White in that case would have hardly anything better than 8. P × B P, Q—R 4; 9. Q—Q 2, etc., with about even prospects.

8.	P—K 5	B—K 2
9.	P—K R 4 !	......

Intending, of course, to sacrifice at R 7. But is this sacrifice absolutely correct ? My opponent, the one-time champion of Iceland, hopes for the negative and starts a counter-attack. If 9. ....P—K R 3 White would have obtained also a distinct advantage by continuing 10. Kt—K 2, P—Q B 4; 11. P—Q B 3, etc.

9.	......	P—Q B 4
10.	B × R P ch	......

The soundness of this stereotyped offer is based on the possibility of White exploiting *also* the central files for attacking purposes; only the few checks on the King's side, as is easily seen, would not produce yet a decisive effect.

10.	......	K × B
11.	Kt—Kt 5 ch	K—Kt 1
12.	Q—R 5	B × Kt
13.	P × B	K—B 1

Black hoped now to come easily out of trouble after 14. Q—R 8 ch, K—K 2 ; 15. Q × P, R—Kt 1 ; 16. Q—B 6 ch, K—K 1, etc. : but White's next move showed him that the situation was much more serious than he thought.

14.	P—Kt 6 !	......

This Pawn cannot be taken since after 15. Q × P there would not be any defence against 16. R—R 8 ch, etc.

15.	......	K—K 2
16.	P × P	R—B 1
17.	Castles (Q R)	......

By no means an automatic developing move : White threatens now 18. Kt—Kt 5, which before did not go because of 17. ....Q—R 4 ch.

17.	......	P—R 3
18.	P × P	......

Threatening 19. Kt—K 4.

18.	......	Kt—Q 2

Position after Black's 18th move.

19. R×P ! !   ......

This secures the participation of all White's forces in the final attack. The main variation in case of the acceptance of this new offer is pretty : 19. P×R ; 20. Kt×P ch, K—K 3 ; 21. Kt—B 4 ch, K—K 2 ; 22. P—K 6, Kt—B 3 ; 23. Q—K 5 !, R×P ; 24. Kt—Kt 6 ch followed by mate in three moves.

19. ......   Q—R 4
20. Q—Kt 5 ch   ......

Preventing the escape of the black King to Q 1.

20. ......   K×P
21. R—R 7   R—K Kt 1
22. R—Q 4 !   ......

Not immediately 22. R×Kt ch, B×R ; 23. Kt—K 4 ? because of 23. ....Q—K 8 mate.

22. ......   Q×B P
23. R×Kt ch !   B×Kt
24. Kt—K 4   Q—Kt 5

Threatening again mate, but—

25. Kt—Q 6 ch   K—B 1
26. Q—B 6 ch !   P×Q
27. R—B 7 mate

The mating position is "pure" and, for a practical game, economical enough.

GAME 116

QUEEN'S INDIAN DEFENCE

Consultation Game played in Paris, October, 1932.

White :	*Black :*
DR. TARTAKOWER	DR. ALEKHINE
and Amateur	and Amateur

1. P—Q 4   Kt—K B 3
2. Kt—K B 3   P—Q Kt 3

3. P—K 3   B—Kt 2
4. B—Q 3   P—K 3
5. Q Kt—Q 2   P—B 4

Strategically important in order to counterbalance the now possible advance of White's King's Pawn.

6. Castles   Kt—B 3
7. P—B 4   ......

Instead of 7. P—B 3 or 7. P—Q R 3 eventually followed by P—Q Kt 3 and B—Kt 2 (Rubinstein), White adopts here a third plan, which has the slight disadvantage of a total absence of immediate threats in the centre—a circumstance that permits Black to finish quietly his development and to obtain an equal game.

7. ......   B—K 2
8. P—Q Kt 3   P×P

Also the simple 7. ....Castles followed by ....P—Q 3 was good enough. By the manœuvre in the text Black fixes White's Q P—which *may* become weak—but opens to the opponent the King's file and cedes him K 4.

9. P×P   P—Q 4
10. B—Kt 2   Kt—Q Kt 5

Less harmless than it looks at first sight : Black hopes to provoke sooner or later P—Q R 3 after which the manœuvre ....Kt—Q B 3—Q R 4 would become strong. Besides, White will have to count on the eventual ....Kt—K 5.

11. B—Kt 1   Castles
12. R—K 1   R—B 1
13. Kt—K 5   Kt—B 3 !

By no means a loss of time after his 10th move, since White's last two moves have entirely changed the situation : (1) Because of the Rook's position at K 1 Black's King's Bishop has got some prospects on Q Kt 5 ; (2) White's exposed central Knight may, under circumstances, be advantageously exchanged. Comparatively, the best for White was here still 14. P—Q R 3, which would be answered by 14. . . . . Q—B 2 followed by . . . . K R—Q 1.

14. Q Kt—B 3   . . . . . .

White seems to think that the preventative move 14. P—Q R 3 would in some way justify Black's last Knight's manœuvre and this is to punish the opponent for his "unscientific" play. But only a few moves will be needed to show whose appreciation of this position was the right one.

14. . . . . . .   B—Kt 5
15. R—K 3 ?   . . . . . .

Logical, but decidedly too risky. An about equal game could still be obtained by 15. Kt × Kt, B × Kt ; 16. R—K 3, Kt—K 5 ; 17. Kt— K 5, B—Kt 2, etc.

15. . . . . . .   Kt—K 2 !

This Knight is certainly trying to make himself useful : instead of being exchanged against a Knight it will now be posted on a very effective spot—K B 4—or else cost the life of the dangerous White's K's Bishop.

16. Kt—Kt 5   . . . . . .

Threatening the obvious sacrifice 17. B × R P ch, Kt × B ; 18. Kt × Kt, K × Kt ; 19. Q—R 5 ch followed by 20. R—K R 3—and trying at the same time to weaken the effect of Black's possible . . . . Kt—K 5.

16. . . . . . .   P—K R 3
17. Kt—R 3   . . . . . .

A sad necessity : a combination starting with 17. R—R 3 would

not work because of the simple reply 17. . . . . Kt—B 4 !

17. . . . . . .   B—Q 3

It is instructive to observe how the black pieces, after having taken advantage of the square Q Kt 5, desert it without having been forced to.

18. Q—K 2   Kt—B 4

The moment is well chosen, since the Rook cannot go back and has no safe squares on the third rank.

19. B × Kt   P × B

The pair of Bishops here are of great value because White has no permanent squares for his Knights in the centre, Black always being able to prepare and play . . . . P—K B 3.

20. R—Q B 1   R—B 2

With the main object of giving more room to the Queen.

21. P—B 3   Q—B 1
22. K R—B 3   R—K 1

Threatening simply Kt—Q 2 followed by . . . . P—B 3 and thus inducing White to simplify at positional cost.

23. P × P   Kt × P
24. R × R   B × R
25. Q—B 4   . . . . . .

Threatening eventually Kt— K B 4 ; but this threat—as a few other menaces of White in this game —is both obvious and harmless.

25. . . . . . .   Q—K 3
26. R—K 1   Q—Q 3 !

From now on the threat . . . . P— K B 3 becomes acute.

| 27. Q—R 4 | B—B 3 |
| 28. Q—R 3 | ..... |

A tame attempt to save the day by exchanging Queens. Black, of course, flatly rejects this transaction.

| 28. ...... | Kt—Kt 5 ! |
| 29. R—Q B 1 | ..... |

There was no more adequate defence against Black's next move.

Position after White's 29th move.

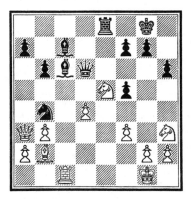

| 29. ...... | P—B 3 ! |

By making this move Black had to reckon with the following variations : I. 30. R×B, Kt×R ; 31. Q×Q, B×Q ; 32. Kt×Kt, R—K 8 ch ; 33. K—B 2, R—Q Kt 8 ; 34. B—B 3, R—Q B 8 and wins.

II. 30. Kt×B, Q×R P ch ; 31. K—B 1 (or 31. K—B 2, Kt—Q 6 ch etc.), Q—R 8 ch ; 32. Kt—Kt 1 (or 32. K—B 2, Kt—Q 6 mate), B—R 7 and wins. And also White's next desperate sacrifice permits a rapid and neat finish.

| 30. P—B 4 | P×Kt |
| 31. B P×P | R×P ! |

The prosaic 31. ....Q—K 2 ; 32. Kt—B 4, P—Q R 4, etc., would in the long run suffice, too—but the

Rook sacrifice is much more forcible.

| 32. P×R | Q—Q 7 ! |
| 33. Kt—B 2 | ..... |

As 33. R×B, Q—K 8 mate does not go, this is forced.

33.	Kt—Q 6 !
34. R—B 1	Kt×B
35. Q—K 7	Q—Q 4
36. Kt—K 4	B×P !
Resigns

GAME 117

RUY LOPEZ

Blindfold Simultaneous Exhibition in Hollywood (California), November, 1932.

Black : H. BOROCHOW

1. P—K 4	P—K 4
2. Kt—K B 3	Kt—Q B 3
3. B—Kt 5	P—Q R 3
4. B—R 4	Kt—B 3
5. Castles	Kt×P
6. P—Q 4	P—Q Kt 4
7. B—Kt 3	P—Q 4
8. Kt×K P	.....

I adopted here this old move for a particular reason : my opponent —one of the best Californian players —had defended the Ruy Lopez in exactly the same way against me in the Pasadena Masters' Tournament and reached, after the usual 8. P×P, quite a satisfactory position. Consequently, in the present blindfold game, I seized the first opportunity to leave the over-explored theoretical path. Although the text move is not the best— White's Knight having at this moment more value than Black's Knight—it is by no means a mistake.

| 8. ...... | Kt×Kt |

9. P×Kt   B—K 3

The two other playable moves
are here 9. ....B—Kt 2 and 9.
....P—Q B 3.

10. P—Q R 4   ......

This wing-diversion is too slow—
especially in view of White's insufficient development. More advisable
seems to be 10. B—K 3 followed by
P—K B 4 or Kt—Q 2.

10. ......·   Kt—B 4
11. Kt—Q 2   B—K 2

Quite right, as White does not
threaten anything.

12. Q—K 2   P—Q B 3
13. P—Q B 3   Kt × B

The exchange is the consequence
of a rather instructive misappreciation of the position. Having obtained quite a satisfactory game,
Black imagines that he can already
dictate the law. He should instead
secure his King's position by
castling, or even first play 13. ....
B—B 4, with excellent fighting
chances.

14. Kt × Kt   P × P

Of course 14. ....P—Q 5 ; 15.
Kt × P, B—B 5 ; 16. Q—B 3, B × R ;
17. Q × Q B P ch, K—B 1 ; 18. K ×
B, etc., would have been a very
bad speculation. After the text-
move, which is the logical consequence of the previous one, Black
expects 15. R × P, Q—Kt 3 ; 16.
Kt—Q 4, P—Q B 4 ; 17. Kt × B,
Q × B ; 18. P—K B 4, P—B 4, followed
by Castles (K's side), etc., with prospects of an initiative in the centre.
But the following "intermediate"
move of White shows him that the
problem to solve will be far less
easy than he imagined.

15. Kt—Q 4 !   ......

If now 15. ....Q—B 1, then 16.
P—K B 4, P—Q B 4 ; 17. Kt × B,
P × Kt ; 18. R × P, Castles ; 19. B—
K 3, etc., with positional advantage
for White. Black's answer, although
it permits the opening of the central
file, is comparatively better.

15. ......   B—Q 2
16. P—K 6   P × P
17. R × P !   ......

A second little surprise for Black;
after 17. Kt × K P, B × Kt ; 18. Q ×
B, Q—Q 2, etc., White's initiative
would vanish rapidly.

17. ......   Q—B 1

But if now 17. .....P—Q B 4, then
18. Kt × P, B × Kt ; 19. Q × B *with
an attack against the Q R's Pawn :*
and also 17. ....Castles would, as
can easily be seen, have lost
material.

18. R—K 1   K—B 2 ?

This attempt to keep all the
earthly belongings will be refuted
in a convincing manner. The only
way of resistance consisted in 18. .....
Castles ; 19. Kt × K P, B × Kt ; 20.
Q × B ch, Q × Q ; 21. R × Q, B—
B 4 ! ; 22. B—B 4, R—B 3 ; 23.
R × R, P × R, after which White, in
spite of his far superior Pawn
position, would not have found it
easy to increase his advantage in a
decisive manner.

19. Kt—B 5 !   ......

Threatening not only 20. Kt × B,
but also—in many variations—20.
Kt × Kt P !, etc. And if 19. ....
Q—K B 1 then 20. Kt—R 6 ch !,
K—K 1 (P × Kt ; 21. Q—R 5 ch,
etc.) ; 21. Kt—Kt 4, followed by
Kt—K 5, etc., with a winning
position.

19. ......   R—K 1

Also 19. ....P×Kt; 20. Q×B
ch, followed by 21. R—K 3, etc.,
would be perfectly hopeless.

20. Q—R 5 ch   K—Kt 1
21. Kt×Kt P !   R—B 1

If 21. ....K×Kt, then 22. B—
R 6 ch, followed by mate in three.

22. R—K Kt 4   K—R 1
23. R—K 3 !   P—K 4

This belated attempt to bring the
unfortunate Q's Bishop to life again
seems at first sight temporarily to
protect everything (24. Q×K P,
B—B 3, or 24. R—R 3, B—K B 4 !
etc.). But the next rejoinder brings
death.

Position after Black's 23rd move.

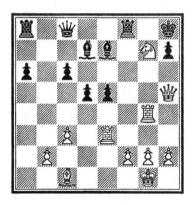

24. Kt—K 6 !   ......

Not being a problem-composer,
I am not sure whether this actually
is a "problem move." Anyhow, it
is effective enough, as 24. ....B×
Kt would have been followed by 25.
Q×R P ch, K×Q ; 26. R—R 3 ch,
B—R 5 ; 27. R×B mate.

Resigns.

GAME 118

RUY LOPEZ

Blindfold Exhibition on 15
boards, Tokyo, January, 1933.

Black : KIMURA

1. P—K 4   P—K 4
2. Kt—K B 3   Kt—Q B 3
3. B—Kt 5   P—Q R 3
4. B × Kt   Kt P × B

Although playable, this move is
seldom adopted, since 4. .....Q P ×
B gives the second player quite a
satisfactory game.

5. P—Q 4   P × P
6. Q × P   P—Q 3

More natural than 6. ....Q—B 3
tried by me against Duras in Mannheim 1914 (see, *My Best Games,*
1908–1923), which move can be
advantageously answered by 7. P—
K 5 !, Q—Kt 3 ; 8. Castles, etc.
—for the acceptance of the Pawn
sacrifice (8. ....Q×B P) would be
decidedly too dangerous for Black.

7. Castles   B—K 3
8. Kt—B 3   Kt—B 3
9. B—Kt 5   ......

The positional advantage that
White could obtain by playing here
or on the next move P—K 5, Kt—
Q 4, etc., did not look convincing
enough.

9. ......   B—K 2
10. Q—R 4   B—Q 2
11. Q R—Q 1   Castles
12. P—K 5 !   ......

Now this advance secures White
in one form or another a clear
supremacy. The main variation
I considered hereby was 12. ....
Kt—Q 4 ; 13. B × B, Q × B (or 13.
....Kt × Kt ; 14. Q—R 4 !) ; 14.

Kt × Kt, P × Kt ; 15. Q—R 3 ! etc.,
bringing Black into trouble.

12.	Kt—K 1
13. B × B	Q × B
14. P × P	P × P
15. K R—K 1	Q—Q 1

A sad necessity, since after 15.
....Q—B 3 the answer 16. Kt—
K 5 ! would be practically decisive.

16. Kt—Q 4 !   ......

If now 16. ....P—Q B 4, then
17. Kt—Q B 6, Q—B 2 ; 18. Kt—
Q 5!, Q—Kt 2; 19. K Kt—K 7 ch,
K—R 1 ; 20. Q—R 4 (threatening
R—K 4 followed by Q × P ch!)
with a strong King's attack.

16.	Q—B 2
17. R—K 7	Kt—B 3
18. Kt—B 5 !	......

The simpler 18. Q R—K 1 would
maintain the advantage without
complications, but the line selected
was tempting—and proved correct.

18. ......   Q—Q 1

The comparatively most embarrassing answer for White, whose
pieces begin to "hang." The alternative 18. ....K R—K 1 would
give him an easier job : 19. Kt—
K 4 !, Kt × Kt ; 20. Q × Kt, R × R ;
21. Q × R !, R—K 1 ; 22. Q × Q P,
Q × Q ; 23. Kt × Q, R—K 7 ; 24.
Kt—B 4, R × Q B P ; 25. Kt—K 3
and wins.

19. R × Q P   R—K 1

Seems to force the variation 20.
R × R ch, Q × R ; 21. Kt—K 3,
after which Black, by playing, for
instance, 21. ....R—Kt 1 could
still set the "blind" opponent some
problems. All the more surprising is
the following manœuvre which in
a couple of moves deprives Black
of any fighting chances.

Position after Black's 19th move.

20. Kt—K 4 !   ......

The first point of the attack
started with 18. Kt—B 5, by which
White only seemingly allows a
desirable transaction for Black.

20. ......   R × R

Forced, as 20. ....Kt × Kt ; 21.
Q R × B, etc., would be hopeless.

21. Kt × Kt ch   K—R 1

Or 21. ....K—B 1 ; 22. Kt × P
ch, K—Kt 1 ; 23. Kt—B 6 ch, K—
B 1 ; 24. Kt × R, P × Kt ; 25. Kt ×
P, Q—K 1 ; 26. Q—Q Kt 4 !, P—R
4 ; 27. Q—B 3 and wins.

22. Kt × R   Q × Kt

Expecting not without pleasure
the variation 23. Kt—K 4, B—B 4 ;
24. R—Q 4, P—Q B 4 ; 25. R—B 4,
R—Q 1, etc., with a counter attack.

23. Q—K 4 !   ......

A most disagreeable surprise for
Black : not only the mate is protected, but White himself threatens
a mate at K R 7 and thus forces the
simplification.

23. ......   Q × Q

24. Kt×Q	B—K 3
25. P—Q Kt 3	P—Kt 3

Still hoping for 26. R×P?, B—Q 4. But after White avoids this "trap" also, Black could as well quietly resign.

26. Kt—B 5	B—B 4
27. R×B P	R—K 1

I was mistaken—there *was* still a chance to give a mate on the 8th rank . . .

28. P—K B 3	R—K 7
29. R×R P	R×B P
30. Kt—K 4	B—K 3
31. P—K R 4	K—Kt 2
32. K—R 2	K—R 3
33. K—Kt 3	B—Q 2
34. P—R 4	P—B 4
35. Kt—Kt 5	R—B 6
36. R—R 7	R—Q 6
37. P—Q R 5	K—R 4
38. Kt×P	Resigns

GAME 119

RUY LOPEZ

Consultation Game, New York, September, 1933.

White :	*Black :*
I. Kashdan	Dr. Alekhine
and Amateur	and Amateur

1. P—K 4	P—K 4
2. Kt—K B 3	Kt—Q B 3
3. B—Kt 5	P—Q R 3
4. B—R 4	P—Q 3
5. P—B 3	B—Q 2
6. P—Q 4	Kt—B 3
7. Q—K 2	. . . . . .

The protection of the King's Pawn by the Queen generally brings White more inconveniences than advantages and it would have been better therefore to substitute 7.

Castles, B—K 2; 8. ....R—K 1, etc.

7.	B—K 2
8. Castles	Castles
9. P—Q 5	. . . . . .

There is hardly anything more advisable than this blocking-procedure, for Black threatens 9. .... Kt×Q P etc., and, on the other hand, 9. B—Kt 3 (or B 2) can be advantageously answered by 9. .... P×P followed by ....Kt—Q R 4 (or Q Kt 5), etc.

9.	Kt—Kt 1
10. B—B 2	P—Q R 4 !

The idea of developing the Knight at Q B 4—analogous to many variations of the Indian Defences—is both tempting and positionally justified. A good alternative would be, however, the dynamical 10..... P—Q B 3 in order to open files on the Q's side before White has finished his mobilisation.

11. P—B 4	Kt—R 3
12. Kt—B 3	Kt—B 4
13. B—K 3	P—Q Kt 3
14. P—K R 3	P—Kt 3

Aiming at....Kt—K R 4—B 5. White's following seemingly "attacking" moves are in fact played only in order to prevent that possibility.

15. B—R 6	R—K 1
16. P—K Kt 4	B—K B 1
17. B×B	. . . . . .

If 17. Q—Q 2, then 17. ....B—Kt 2 and White would eventually be forced to change in even less favourable circumstances.

17.	R×B
18. Kt—R 2	. . . . . .

The move here planned P—K B 4 which will still more weaken the dark-coloured squares of White's position, must be again considered as a kind of indirect defence against Black's threatening initiative on the K R's file. White's bad luck is that he has no more time for the otherwise indicated Pawn advance of the Q's side—P—Q Kt 3 followed by P—Q R 3, P—Q Kt 4, etc.

18. ......   Q—K 2

There is no particular hurry to play ....P—R 4 since White cannot prevent it anyhow.

19. Q—K 3   P—R 4
20. P—B 4 !   ......

A purely passive defence starting with 20. P—B 3 would prove, after 20. ....K—Kt 2 followed by ..... R—R 1, etc., practically hopeless— and the Pawn sacrifice intended by the text-move is tactically justified. The only trouble is that Black need not accept it and White's K Kt P remains weak !

20. ......   P × Kt P
21. R P × P   P × P !

After 21. ....Kt × Kt P ? ; 22. Kt × Kt, B × Kt ; 23. Q—Kt 3, B— R 4 ; 24. P—B 5 White would obtain a strong attack.

22. Q × P   K—Kt 2
23. Q R—K 1   Q R—K 1
24. K—Kt 2   ......

Probably played in view of a possible exchange of Queens in case of ....Q—K 4. But Black rightly prefers first to increase his pressure by taking advantage of the open K R's file—especially as he sees that a triple attack against his Knight at K B 3 can be successfully met by a counter-attack.

24. ......   R—K R 1
25. R—K 2   R—R 5
26. Q R—B 2   Q R—K R 1
27. K—Kt 1   ......

Now it may seem for a moment that White's pressure against Black's K B 2 and K B 3 is more effective than the counter-threats on the K R's file, but the next two moves bring the situation into its true light.

27. ......   B—K 1 !

Not only defending the K B P but also giving room to the Queen's Knight.

28. Q—Kt 5   ......

The end-game after 28. Q × Kt ch etc. would be clearly to Black's advantage because of the powerful central square K 4 for his Knight.

28. ......   K—B 1 !

In its simplicity probably the most difficult move of the game : after having protected his Queen, Black threatens now 29. ....Kt × Kt P ! etc.

29. R—Kt 2   Q Kt—Q 2

Also this retreat, which permits the following seemingly dangerous rejoinder, had to be exactly calculated.

30. Kt—Kt 5   ......

Position after White's 30th move.

| 30. ...... | Kt—K 4 ! |

The occupation of the dominating central square coincides here with the tactical decision of the game. As 31. Kt × B P would be refuted by 31. ....R × Kt !; 32. R × R, R × R ; 33. Kt × B, K Kt × Kt P ! ; 34. Q × Q ch, K × Q ; 35. B—R 4, R × P, etc., White has nothing better than to simplify and to hope for a miracle in the following end-game.

| 31. Q × K Kt | Q × Q |
| 32. R × Q | B × Kt ! |

A most important "intermediate" exchange the omission of which would leave White excellent drawing chances.

| 33. P × B | R × Kt |

In so many variations the decisive point.

| 34. R × R | R × R |
| 35. R × P ch | ...... |

The only way temporarily to avoid material loss.

35.	K × R
36. K × R	Kt × P ch
37. K—Kt 3	Kt—K 4

In spite of the even material Black has quite an easy job, for besides his passed Pawn he has an obvious supremacy (two pieces against one) on the dark-coloured squares.

38. P—Kt 3	K—B 3
39. B—Q 1	Kt—Q 6
40. K—B 3	K—K 4
41. K—K 3	Kt—B 4
42. B—B 3	P—Kt 4
43. B—R 1	Kt—Q 2

Also the immediate 43. ....P—Kt 5 was good enough.

44. B—Kt 2	Kt—B 3
45. B—B 3	P—Kt 5
46. B—K 2	.....

In case of 46. B—Kt 2 Black wins easily by 46. ....Kt—R 4 followed by ....Kt—B 5 etc.

46.	Kt × K P
47. B × P	Kt—B 3
48. B—B 3	Kt × P ch
49. K—Q 2	K—Q 5
50. P—R 3	Kt—B 6
51. B—B 6	P—R 5 !
52. K—B 2	P—Q 4
53. P × P	K—B 5 !
Resigns	

GAME 120

RUY LOPEZ

Simultaneous exhibition in Holland, October, 1933.

Black : A. MINDENO

1. P—K 4	P—K 4
2. Kt—K B 3	Kt—Q B 3
3. B—Kt 5	P—Q 3

The Steinitz Defence, which was in fashion as late as the time of the Lasker-Capablanca match, 1921, has now completely disappeared from master practice. Actually, the modern treatment with the intermediate 3. ....P—Q R 3 (the so-called Steinitz deferred) gives Black, after 4. B—R 4, P—Q 3, considerably more choice of development plans than the self-restricting text-move.

| 4. P—Q 4 | P × P |

After 4. ....B—Q 2 the most promising line for White would be 5. Kt—B 3, Kt—B 3 ; 6. B × Kt, B × B ; 7. Q—Q 3 ! etc.

| 5. Q × P | ...... |

Of course 5. Kt × P is also good. By the text-move White plans already Castles (Q R).

5.	......	B—Q 2
6.	B × Kt	B × B
7.	Kt—Q B 3	Kt—B 3
8.	B—Kt 5	B—K 2
9.	Castles (Q R)	Castles
10.	P—K R 4	......

This position has already occurred as long ago as in a tournament game of Anderssen's in Baden-Baden, 1870, in which the German champion played here 10. K R—K 1— and finally drew. In order to verify once more the value of that move I played it in Folkestone, 1933, against Anderssen's namesake, the late Danish master, E. Andersen, but although the game ended in my favour its first stage (after 10. ....Kt—Q 2 ; 11. B × B, Q × B ; 12. R—K 3, Q—B 3 ; 13. Kt—Q 5, B × Kt ; 14. P × B, Q × Q, etc. was not unsatisfactory for Black. The move in the text is sharper as Black must make some effort in order to dislodge White's Bishop from Kt 5.

10. ......   P—K R 3

Not to be condemned, because Black is not obliged to take the Bishop with the Pawn and he can do that only when it will be perfectly safe.

11. Kt—Q 5   ......

A correct and exactly calculated offer which Black should not accept. Still even more appropriate in order to maintain the tension was first 11. K—Kt 1.

11. ......   P × B ?

Although the final point of the sacrifice was very difficult to fore-see, the acceptance has to be decidedly condemned : it was obvious enough that the opening of the K R-file means here a deadly danger, and, what is more, Black had here a perfectly safe (for the moment, anyhow) defence by continuing 11. ....Kt × Kt ; 12. P × Kt, B—Q 2, etc.

12. Kt × B ch !   ......

Of course not 12. P × P, Kt × Kt ; 13. P × Kt, B × P ch, etc., with sufficient defence.

| 12. | ...... | Q × Kt |
| 13. | P × P | Kt × P |

Also after other Knight's moves the doubling of Rooks on the R's file would prove decisive. And if 13. ....Q × P, then 14. P × Kt, Q × Q ; 15. R × Q, B × Kt ; 16. P × B, K R—K 1 ; 17. R—K Kt 4 !, P—K Kt 3 ; 18. R (4)—K R 4 followed by mate.

14. R—R 5   Q—K 3

In case of the immediate 14. .... P—K B 4 White would force the win in a similar manner to the text : 15. P—Kt 6, Q—K 3 ; 16. Kt—K 5 !, Kt—B 3 (otherwise 16. Q R—R 1, etc.) ; 17. R—R 8 ch !, K × R ; 18. Q—R 4 ch, K—Kt 1 ; 19. R—R 1, etc., with an unavoidable mate.

15. Q R—K R1   P—K B 4

After this Black seems to be temporarily safe since after 16. P—Kt 6, Q × Kt P ; 17. Kt—K 5, he would obtain Rook and two minor pieces for the Queen by 17. .... Q × R ; 18. R × Q, P × Kt, etc. But a spectacular transposition of moves ruins his hopes.

Position after Black's 15th move.

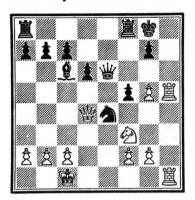

16. Kt—K 5 ! ! ......

A surprise move, whose object is to weaken the protection of Black's Q 4.

16. ......   P × Kt

As 16. ....Q × Kt ; 17. Q × Q, P × Q ; 18. P—Kt 6 loses instantly, Black has obviously no choice.

17. P—Kt 6 !   ......

The point : if now 17. ....Q × Kt P, then 18. Q—B 4 ch followed by mate in three moves. Without the preliminary 16. Kt—K 5, P × P Black would still have the defence ....P—Q 4.

Resigns.

LIST OF OPENINGS

LIST OF OPPONENTS

See separate Index of Names for Volume I
in the middle of this volume.

285

A CATALOG OF SELECTED
DOVER BOOKS
IN ALL FIELDS OF INTEREST

A CATALOG OF SELECTED DOVER
BOOKS IN ALL FIELDS OF INTEREST

CONCERNING THE SPIRITUAL IN ART, Wassily Kandinsky. Pioneering work by father of abstract art. Thoughts on color theory, nature of art. Analysis of earlier masters. 12 illustrations. 80pp. of text. 5⅜ x 8½. 23411-8

ANIMALS: 1,419 Copyright-Free Illustrations of Mammals, Birds, Fish, Insects, etc., Jim Harter (ed.). Clear wood engravings present, in extremely lifelike poses, over 1,000 species of animals. One of the most extensive pictorial sourcebooks of its kind. Captions. Index. 284pp. 9 x 12. 23766-4

CELTIC ART: The Methods of Construction, George Bain. Simple geometric techniques for making Celtic interlacements, spirals, Kells-type initials, animals, humans, etc. Over 500 illustrations. 160pp. 9 x 12. (Available in U.S. only.) 22923-8

AN ATLAS OF ANATOMY FOR ARTISTS, Fritz Schider. Most thorough reference work on art anatomy in the world. Hundreds of illustrations, including selections from works by Vesalius, Leonardo, Goya, Ingres, Michelangelo, others. 593 illustrations. 192pp. 7⅛ x 10¼. 20241-0

CELTIC HAND STROKE-BY-STROKE (Irish Half-Uncial from "The Book of Kells"): An Arthur Baker Calligraphy Manual, Arthur Baker. Complete guide to creating each letter of the alphabet in distinctive Celtic manner. Covers hand position, strokes, pens, inks, paper, more. Illustrated. 48pp. 8¼ x 11. 24336-2

EASY ORIGAMI, John Montroll. Charming collection of 32 projects (hat, cup, pelican, piano, swan, many more) specially designed for the novice origami hobbyist. Clearly illustrated easy-to-follow instructions insure that even beginning papercrafters will achieve successful results. 48pp. 8¼ x 11. 27298-2

THE COMPLETE BOOK OF BIRDHOUSE CONSTRUCTION FOR WOODWORKERS, Scott D. Campbell. Detailed instructions, illustrations, tables. Also data on bird habitat and instinct patterns. Bibliography. 3 tables. 63 illustrations in 15 figures. 48pp. 5¼ x 8½. 24407-5

BLOOMINGDALE'S ILLUSTRATED 1886 CATALOG: Fashions, Dry Goods and Housewares, Bloomingdale Brothers. Famed merchants' extremely rare catalog depicting about 1,700 products: clothing, housewares, firearms, dry goods, jewelry, more. Invaluable for dating, identifying vintage items. Also, copyright-free graphics for artists, designers. Co-published with Henry Ford Museum & Greenfield Village. 160pp. 8¼ x 11. 25780-0

HISTORIC COSTUME IN PICTURES, Braun & Schneider. Over 1,450 costumed figures in clearly detailed engravings–from dawn of civilization to end of 19th century. Captions. Many folk costumes. 256pp. 8⅜ x 11¾. 23150-X

THE WIT AND HUMOR OF OSCAR WILDE, Alvin Redman (ed.). More than 1,000 ripostes, paradoxes, wisecracks: Work is the curse of the drinking classes; I can resist everything except temptation; etc. 258pp. 5⅜ x 8½. 20602-5

SHAKESPEARE LEXICON AND QUOTATION DICTIONARY, Alexander Schmidt. Full definitions, locations, shades of meaning in every word in plays and poems. More than 50,000 exact quotations. 1,485pp. 6½ x 9¼. 2-vol. set.
Vol. 1: 22726-X
Vol. 2: 22727-8

SELECTED POEMS, Emily Dickinson. Over 100 best-known, best-loved poems by one of America's foremost poets, reprinted from authoritative early editions. No comparable edition at this price. Index of first lines. 64pp. 5³⁄₁₆ x 8¼. 26466-1

THE INSIDIOUS DR. FU-MANCHU, Sax Rohmer. The first of the popular mystery series introduces a pair of English detectives to their archnemesis, the diabolical Dr. Fu-Manchu. Flavorful atmosphere, fast-paced action, and colorful characters enliven this classic of the genre. 208pp. 5³⁄₁₆ x 8¼. 29898-1

THE MALLEUS MALEFICARUM OF KRAMER AND SPRENGER, translated by Montague Summers. Full text of most important witchhunter's "bible," used by both Catholics and Protestants. 278pp. 6⅝ x 10. 22802-9

SPANISH STORIES/CUENTOS ESPAÑOLES: A Dual-Language Book, Angel Flores (ed.). Unique format offers 13 great stories in Spanish by Cervantes, Borges, others. Faithful English translations on facing pages. 352pp. 5⅜ x 8½. 25399-6

GARDEN CITY, LONG ISLAND, IN EARLY PHOTOGRAPHS, 1869–1919, Mildred H. Smith. Handsome treasury of 118 vintage pictures, accompanied by carefully researched captions, document the Garden City Hotel fire (1899), the Vanderbilt Cup Race (1908), the first airmail flight departing from the Nassau Boulevard Aerodrome (1911), and much more. 96pp. 8⅞ x 11¾. 40669-5

OLD QUEENS, N.Y., IN EARLY PHOTOGRAPHS, Vincent F. Seyfried and William Asadorian. Over 160 rare photographs of Maspeth, Jamaica, Jackson Heights, and other areas. Vintage views of DeWitt Clinton mansion, 1939 World's Fair and more. Captions. 192pp. 8⅞ x 11. 26358-4

CAPTURED BY THE INDIANS: 15 Firsthand Accounts, 1750-1870, Frederick Drimmer. Astounding true historical accounts of grisly torture, bloody conflicts, relentless pursuits, miraculous escapes and more, by people who lived to tell the tale. 384pp. 5⅜ x 8½. 24901-8

THE WORLD'S GREAT SPEECHES (Fourth Enlarged Edition), Lewis Copeland, Lawrence W. Lamm, and Stephen J. McKenna. Nearly 300 speeches provide public speakers with a wealth of updated quotes and inspiration–from Pericles' funeral oration and William Jennings Bryan's "Cross of Gold Speech" to Malcolm X's powerful words on the Black Revolution and Earl of Spenser's tribute to his sister, Diana, Princess of Wales. 944pp. 5⅜ x 8⅜. 40903-1

THE BOOK OF THE SWORD, Sir Richard F. Burton. Great Victorian scholar/adventurer's eloquent, erudite history of the "queen of weapons"–from prehistory to early Roman Empire. Evolution and development of early swords, variations (sabre, broadsword, cutlass, scimitar, etc.), much more. 336pp. 6⅛ x 9¼.
25434-8

AUTOBIOGRAPHY: The Story of My Experiments with Truth, Mohandas K. Gandhi. Boyhood, legal studies, purification, the growth of the Satyagraha (nonviolent protest) movement. Critical, inspiring work of the man responsible for the freedom of India. 480pp. 5⅜ x 8½. (Available in U.S. only.) 24593-4

CELTIC MYTHS AND LEGENDS, T. W. Rolleston. Masterful retelling of Irish and Welsh stories and tales. Cuchulain, King Arthur, Deirdre, the Grail, many more. First paperback edition. 58 full-page illustrations. 512pp. 5⅜ x 8½. 26507-2

THE PRINCIPLES OF PSYCHOLOGY, William James. Famous long course complete, unabridged. Stream of thought, time perception, memory, experimental methods; great work decades ahead of its time. 94 figures. 1,391pp. 5⅜ x 8½. 2-vol. set. Vol. I: 20381-6 Vol. II: 20382-4

THE WORLD AS WILL AND REPRESENTATION, Arthur Schopenhauer. Definitive English translation of Schopenhauer's life work, correcting more than 1,000 errors, omissions in earlier translations. Translated by E. F. J. Payne. Total of 1,269pp. 5⅜ x 8½. 2-vol. set. Vol. 1: 21761-2 Vol. 2: 21762-0

MAGIC AND MYSTERY IN TIBET, Madame Alexandra David-Neel. Experiences among lamas, magicians, sages, sorcerers, Bonpa wizards. A true psychic discovery. 32 illustrations. 321pp. 5⅜ x 8½. (Available in U.S. only.) 22682-4

THE EGYPTIAN BOOK OF THE DEAD, E. A. Wallis Budge. Complete reproduction of Ani's papyrus, finest ever found. Full hieroglyphic text, interlinear transliteration, word-for-word translation, smooth translation. 533pp. 6½ x 9¼. 21866-X

MATHEMATICS FOR THE NONMATHEMATICIAN, Morris Kline. Detailed, college-level treatment of mathematics in cultural and historical context, with numerous exercises. Recommended Reading Lists. Tables. Numerous figures. 641pp. 5⅜ x 8½. 24823-2

PROBABILISTIC METHODS IN THE THEORY OF STRUCTURES, Isaac Elishakoff. Well-written introduction covers the elements of the theory of probability from two or more random variables, the reliability of such multivariable structures, the theory of random function, Monte Carlo methods of treating problems incapable of exact solution, and more. Examples. 502pp. 5⅜ x 8½. 40691-1

THE RIME OF THE ANCIENT MARINER, Gustave Doré, S. T. Coleridge. Doré's finest work; 34 plates capture moods, subtleties of poem. Flawless full-size reproductions printed on facing pages with authoritative text of poem. "Beautiful. Simply beautiful."–*Publisher's Weekly.* 77pp. 9¼ x 12. 22305-1

NORTH AMERICAN INDIAN DESIGNS FOR ARTISTS AND CRAFTSPEOPLE, Eva Wilson. Over 360 authentic copyright-free designs adapted from Navajo blankets, Hopi pottery, Sioux buffalo hides, more. Geometrics, symbolic figures, plant and animal motifs, etc. 128pp. 8⅜ x 11. (Not for sale in the United Kingdom.) 25341-4

SCULPTURE: Principles and Practice, Louis Slobodkin. Step-by-step approach to clay, plaster, metals, stone; classical and modern. 253 drawings, photos. 255pp. 8⅛ x 11. 22960-2

THE INFLUENCE OF SEA POWER UPON HISTORY, 1660–1783, A. T. Mahan. Influential classic of naval history and tactics still used as text in war colleges. First paperback edition. 4 maps. 24 battle plans. 640pp. 5⅜ x 8½. 25509-3

THE STORY OF THE TITANIC AS TOLD BY ITS SURVIVORS, Jack Winocour (ed.). What it was really like. Panic, despair, shocking inefficiency, and a little heroism. More thrilling than any fictional account. 26 illustrations. 320pp. 5⅜ x 8½.
20610-6

FAIRY AND FOLK TALES OF THE IRISH PEASANTRY, William Butler Yeats (ed.). Treasury of 64 tales from the twilight world of Celtic myth and legend: "The Soul Cages," "The Kildare Pooka," "King O'Toole and his Goose," many more. Introduction and Notes by W. B. Yeats. 352pp. 5⅜ x 8½.
26941-8

BUDDHIST MAHAYANA TEXTS, E. B. Cowell and others (eds.). Superb, accurate translations of basic documents in Mahayana Buddhism, highly important in history of religions. The Buddha-karita of Asvaghosha, Larger Sukhavativyuha, more. 448pp. 5⅜ x 8½.
25552-2

ONE TWO THREE . . . INFINITY: Facts and Speculations of Science, George Gamow. Great physicist's fascinating, readable overview of contemporary science: number theory, relativity, fourth dimension, entropy, genes, atomic structure, much more. 128 illustrations. Index. 352pp. 5⅜ x 8½.
25664-2

EXPERIMENTATION AND MEASUREMENT, W. J. Youden. Introductory manual explains laws of measurement in simple terms and offers tips for achieving accuracy and minimizing errors. Mathematics of measurement, use of instruments, experimenting with machines. 1994 edition. Foreword. Preface. Introduction. Epilogue. Selected Readings. Glossary. Index. Tables and figures. 128pp. 5⅜ x 8½.
40451-X

DALÍ ON MODERN ART: The Cuckolds of Antiquated Modern Art, Salvador Dalí. Influential painter skewers modern art and its practitioners. Outrageous evaluations of Picasso, Cézanne, Turner, more. 15 renderings of paintings discussed. 44 calligraphic decorations by Dalí. 96pp. 5⅜ x 8½. (Available in U.S. only.)
29220-7

ANTIQUE PLAYING CARDS: A Pictorial History, Henry René D'Allemagne. Over 900 elaborate, decorative images from rare playing cards (14th–20th centuries): Bacchus, death, dancing dogs, hunting scenes, royal coats of arms, players cheating, much more. 96pp. 9¼ x 12¼.
29265-7

MAKING FURNITURE MASTERPIECES: 30 Projects with Measured Drawings, Franklin H. Gottshall. Step-by-step instructions, illustrations for constructing handsome, useful pieces, among them a Sheraton desk, Chippendale chair, Spanish desk, Queen Anne table and a William and Mary dressing mirror. 224pp. 8⅛ x 11¼.
29338-6

THE FOSSIL BOOK: A Record of Prehistoric Life, Patricia V. Rich et al. Profusely illustrated definitive guide covers everything from single-celled organisms and dinosaurs to birds and mammals and the interplay between climate and man. Over 1,500 illustrations. 760pp. 7½ x 10⅛.
29371-8